D0069026

Utah

5th Edition

by Don & Barbara Laine

Here's what the critics say about Frommer's:

"Amazingly easy to use. Very portable, very complete."

—*Booklist*

"Detailed, accurate, and easy-to-read information for all price ranges."
—*Glamour Magazine*

"Hotel information is close to encyclopedic."

—*Des Moines Sunday Register*

"Frommer's Guides have a way of giving you a real feel for a place."
—*Knight Ridder Newspapers*

CPL

WILEY

DISCARD

Wiley Publishing, Inc.

About the Authors

Residents of New Mexico for more than 30 years, **Don** and **Barbara Laine** have traveled extensively throughout the Rocky Mountains and the Southwest. In addition to *Frommer's Utah*, they are the authors of *Frommer's Colorado*; *Frommer's Rocky Mountain National Park*; *Frommer's Zion & Bryce Canyon National Parks*. They are also the lead authors of *Frommer's National Parks of the American West*; and have contributed to *Frommer's Texas* and *Frommer's USA*. The Laines have also written *Little-Known Southwest* and *New Mexico & Arizona State Parks* (both for The Mountaineers Books).

Published by:

Wiley Publishing, Inc.

111 River St.
Hoboken, NJ 07030-5744

Copyright © 2004 Wiley Publishing, Inc., Hoboken, New Jersey. All rights reserved. No part of this publication may be reproduced, stored in a retrieval system or transmitted in any form or by any means, electronic, mechanical, photocopying, recording, scanning or otherwise, except as permitted under Sections 107 or 108 of the 1976 United States Copyright Act, without either the prior written permission of the Publisher, or authorization through payment of the appropriate per-copy fee to the Copyright Clearance Center, 222 Rosewood Drive, Danvers, MA 01923, 978/750-8400, fax 978/646-8600. Requests to the Publisher for permission should be addressed to the Legal Department, Wiley Publishing, Inc., 10475 Crosspoint Blvd., Indianapolis, IN 46256, 317/572-3447, fax 317/572-4447, E-Mail: permcoordinator@wiley.com.

Wiley and the Wiley Publishing logo are trademarks or registered trademarks of John Wiley & Sons, Inc. and/or its affiliates. Frommer's is a trademark or registered trademark of Arthur Frommer. Used under license. All other trademarks are the property of their respective owners. Wiley Publishing, Inc. is not associated with any product or vendor mentioned in this book.

ISBN 0-7645-4190-0

Editor: Liz Albertson
Production Editor: Blair J. Pottenger
Cartographer: John Decamillis
Photo Editor: Richard Fox
Production by Wiley Indianapolis Composition Services

Front cover photo: Man admiring Calf Creek Falls, Escalante National Monument
Back cover photo: Man downhill skiing, Snowbird Ski & Summer Resort

For information on our other products and services or to obtain technical support, please contact our Customer Care Department within the U.S. at 800/762-2974, outside the U.S. at 317/572-3993, or fax 317/572-4002.

Wiley also publishes its books in a variety of electronic formats. Some content that appears in print may not be available in electronic formats.

Manufactured in the United States of America

5 4 3 2 1

Contents

List of Maps

An Invitation to the Reader

In researching this book, we discovered many wonderful places—hotels, restaurants, shops, and more. We're sure you'll find others. Please tell us about them, so we can share the information with your fellow travelers in upcoming editions. If you were disappointed with a recommendation, we'd love to know that, too. Please write to:

Frommer's Utah, 5th Edition
Wiley Publishing, Inc. • 111 River St. • Hoboken, NJ 07030-5744

An Additional Note

Please be advised that travel information is subject to change at any time—and this is especially true of prices. We therefore suggest that you write or call ahead for confirmation when making your travel plans. The authors, editors, and publisher cannot be held responsible for the experiences of readers while traveling. Your safety is important to us, however, so we encourage you to stay alert and be aware of your surroundings. Keep a close eye on cameras, purses, and wallets, all favorite targets of thieves and pickpockets.

Other Great Guides for Your Trip:

Frommer's Zion & Bryce Canyon National Parks
Frommer's Grand Canyon National Park
Frommer's American Southwest
The Unofficial Guide to B&Bs and Country Inns in the Southwest
The Unofficial Guide to the Best RV and Tent Campgrounds in the Southwest & South Central Plains
Frommer's Arizona
Frommer's New Mexico

Frommer's Star Ratings, Icons & Abbreviations

Every hotel, restaurant, and attraction listing in this guide has been ranked for quality, value, service, amenities, and special features using a **star-rating system.** In country, state, and regional guides, we also rate towns and regions to help you narrow down your choices and budget your time accordingly. Hotels and restaurants are rated on a scale of zero (recommended) to three stars (exceptional). Attractions, shopping, nightlife, towns, and regions are rated according to the following scale: zero stars (recommended), one star (highly recommended), two stars (very highly recommended), and three stars (must-see).

In addition to the star-rating system, we also use **seven feature icons** that point you to the great deals, in-the-know advice and unique experiences that separate travelers from tourists. Throughout the book, look for:

Finds	Special finds—those places only insiders know about
Fun Fact	Fun facts—details that make travelers more informed and their trips more fun
Kids	Best bets for kids, and advice for the whole family
Moments	Special moments—those experiences that memories are made of
Overrated	Places or experiences not worth your time or money
Tips	Insider tips—great ways to save time and money
Value	Great values—where to get the best deals

The following **abbreviations** are used for credit cards:

AE	American Express	DISC	Discover	V	Visa
DC	Diners Club	MC	MasterCard		

Frommers.com

Now that you have the guidebook to a great trip, visit our website at **www.frommers.com** for travel information on more than 3,000 destinations. With features updated regularly, we give you instant access to the most current trip-planning information available. At Frommers.com, you'll also find the best prices on airfares, accommodations, and car rentals—and you can even book travel online through our travel booking partners. At Frommers.com, you'll also find the following:

- Online updates to our most popular guidebooks
- Vacation sweepstakes and contest giveaways
- Newsletter highlighting the hottest travel trends
- Online travel message boards with featured travel discussions

What's New in Utah

Change comes slowly to Utah—the state's mostly conservative, religious population prefers to keep things the same. But change is inevitable, even here, and a major catalyst for change was the 2002 Winter Olympics. The state of Utah lobbied and won the honor of hosting the games, and then went to work improving and creating the venues needed for the games and for all the spectators.

Thanks to the games, you'll see major improvements to the ski areas that hosted the Olympics—from Park City to Ogden. And there are other, more subtle improvements. For instance, tons of money were spent to improve roads along the Wasatch Front, including Interstate 15, and to improve parking and signage in the cities that hosted the games.

SALT LAKE CITY A building boom of hotels preceded the Olympics, and now that the crowds have gone home there is something of a surplus, so **room rates are very reasonable.** In fact, they're often considerably below the rack rates quoted in this book. Downtown Salt Lake City has a new open-air shopping mall, **The Gateway,** 90 S. 400 West (✆ 801/456-0000), which covers two city blocks and contains numerous stores, movie theaters, restaurants, and museums. The Gateway is also the location of Salt Lake City's newest attraction, **Clark Planetarium,** 110 S. 400 West (✆ 801/456-7827), a state-of-the-art facility that replaces the old Hansen Planetarium. See chapter 6 for details.

THE NORTHERN WASATCH FRONT: UTAH'S OLD WEST There's been a lot going on in Ogden, one of our favorite Utah cities. **Fort Buenaventura,** 2450 South "A" Ave. (✆ 801/399-8099), formerly a state park, is now under the management of Weber County. The new local control has made this park even better than it used to be: Among other things, the park has opened its previously limited campground to the public, and is putting in a replica Shoshone Indian camp, to be ready by summer 2004. The **George S. Eccles Dinosaur Park,** 1544 E. Park Blvd. (✆ 801/393-3466), has a new attraction, the Elizabeth Dee Shaw Stewart Museum, with hands-on exhibits of the latest dinosaur excavations. Also on Ogden's museum scene, the **Treehouse Children's Museum,** 455 23rd St. (✆ 801/394-9663), has a new but temporary home—it's former location was in a mall that was bulldozed, and its new permanent home won't be ready for several years. You saw it in Ogden during the 2002 Winter Olympics, and now you can try it yourself: The **Ice Sheet,** 4390 Harrison Blvd. (✆ 801/399-8750), now offers to teach you the fast-growing sport of curling. The Olympics also had a major effect on **Snowbasin Resort,** P.O. Box 460, Huntsville (✆ 801/620-1000), which hosted the downhill and Super G competition: Not only does the resort boast new Olympic downhill courses, but it even has a new entry road. See chapter 7 for more information.

THE SOUTHERN WASATCH FRONT: WORLD CLASS SKIING & MORE Constructed for the 2002 Winter Olympics, Park City's $100-million **Utah Olympic Park,** 3000 Bear Hollow Dr. (© 435/658-4200), has six state-of-the-art ski jumps, a 1,335-meter bobsled/luge track, a freestyle aerials training and competition hill, a ski museum, and an exhibit on the 2002 games. The facility is open year-round for tours, offers bobsled runs, and schedules camps and workshops that teach freestyle aerial and ski jumping techniques, even for amateurs. A new upscale dinner restaurant opened in Park City in 2003. **Purple Sage,** 434 Main St. (© 435/655-9505), serves what it calls American Western cuisine. For more information see chapter 8.

DINOSAURS & NATURAL WONDERS IN UTAH'S NORTHEAST CORNER Due to a major expansion project at the **Utah Field House of Natural History State Park Museum,** 495 E. Main St., Vernal (© 435/789-3799), more exhibit space and a theater should be in place by summer 2004. Near Flaming Gorge National Recreation Area, the

Red Canyon Lodge, 790 Red Canyon Rd., Dutch John (© 435/889-3759), has gone somewhat upscale, adding handsome new cabins. See chapter 9 for details.

UTAH'S DIXIE & THE COLORFUL SOUTHWEST CORNER Bad news for skiers heading to southwest Utah—**Elk Meadows Ski & Summer Resort** has closed, with no sign of reopening on the horizon. At least we still have Brian Head. See chapter 10 for information.

ZION NATIONAL PARK Construction of a new visitor center a few years back left Zion National Park with an empty building, but it's empty no more; it now houses Zion's new **Zion Human History Museum** (call park headquarters © 435/772-3256). See chapter 11.

LAKE POWELL & GLEN CANYON NATIONAL RECREATION AREA Where's all the water? Lake Powell is currently at its lowest levels in history, which is limiting boating in some sections of the lake. For current information, check with **Glen Canyon National Recreation Area** (© 928/608-6404), and in this book see chapter 14.

The Best of Utah

From its desolate red rock canyons to its soaring pine-covered peaks, Utah is spectacular. There aren't many places in the world where the forces of nature have come together with such dramatic results, creating a magnificent outdoor playground. This is also a land of cultural discovery; all the peoples who have settled here, from the ancestors of today's Pueblo Indians to Brigham Young's Mormons to mountain men and Wild West bandits, have left their distinctive mark, contributing to a wild, colorful history.

With so much to see and do, how to choose? It can be bewildering to plan your trip with so many options vying for your attention. We've made this task easier by scouring the entire state from top to bottom and choosing the very best that Utah has to offer—the places and experiences you won't want to miss.

1 The Best Utah Travel Experiences

- **Exploring Bryce Canyon National Park:** Among Utah's— and maybe the nation's—most scenic parks, Bryce Canyon is also one of the most accessible. Several trails lead down into the canyon— more like walks than hikes—so just about everyone can get to know this beautiful jewel up close. Part of the Rim Trail is even wheelchair accessible. The colorful rock formations are impressive when viewed en masse from the rim, but they become enchanting and fanciful works of art as you walk among them along the trails. See chapter 12.
- **Enjoying Capitol Reef National Park:** This tranquil park isn't as popular as Bryce or Zion, but it has a subtle beauty all its own. And it's not too demanding, either: Wander through the orchards of Fruita, hike to Cassidy Arch, stroll up the Grand Wash, or just sit under the stars roasting marshmallows over your campfire. See p. 255.
- **Houseboating on Lake Powell:** Kick back and relax while floating on the deep blue waters of Lake Powell, with towering red rocks all around and an azure sky above. This is the life—no telephone to answer, no meetings to attend, no deadlines to meet. Feeling warm? Slip over the side for a dip in the cool water. Want a little exercise? Anchor yourself at one of the canyons and hike a bit. See p. 271.

2 The Best Views

- **The Narrows, Zion National Park:** The sheer 1,000-foot-high walls are awe-inspiring and almost frightening, as they enclose you in a 20-foot-wide world of hanging gardens, waterfalls, and sculpted sandstone arches, with the Virgin River running beneath your feet. The Narrows are so narrow that you can't walk beside the river. Instead, you have to wade right through it—but the views are

Utah

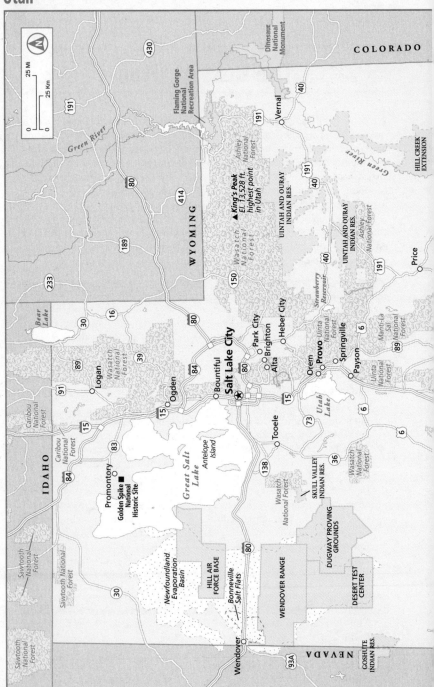

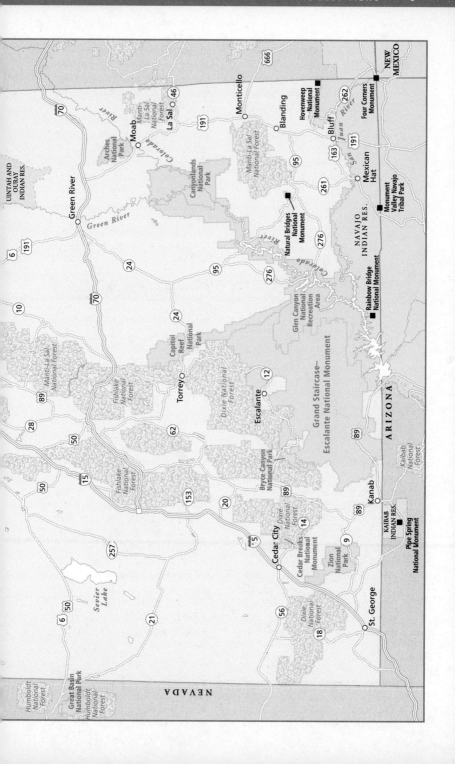

worth getting your feet wet. See p. 226.

- **Boulder Mountain Viewpoints** (between Escalante and Torrey): The panoramas from the roadside along the crest of Boulder Mountain are extraordinary. You can see majestic Capitol Reef, miles to the east, and any number of valleys and lakes nestled in between. It's like a tiny fairyland—we almost expected to see a little steam train chugging along or a horse-drawn carriage passing through. See p. 254.
- **The Queen's Garden, Bryce Canyon National Park:** Presided over by majestic Queen Victoria herself, carved in stone by Mother Nature, these thousands of colorfully striped spires present a magnificent display when viewed from the rim. From the trail below, they dazzle as the early morning sun throws them into stark relief. See p. 238.
- **Monument Valley Buttes at Sunset:** These stark sentinels of the desert are impressive at any time, but they take on a particularly dignified aura when the setting sun casts its deep colors over them, etching their profiles against a darkening sky. Although the park generally closes before sunset, you can arrange a sunset tour—it's well worth the cost. See p. 312.

3 The Best Family-Vacation Experiences

- **Camping at Cherry Hill Camping Resort** (Ogden): This fun-packed park offers something for everybody: a water park with slides, pools, and even a pirate ship, plus miniature golf, batting cages, and aeroball (it's kind of like basketball). It's like staying in a theme park—a kid's dream come true. And you're not likely to find a more immaculately groomed and well-run campground anywhere. See p. 119.
- **Taking a Ride on the Heber Valley Historic Railroad:** Take a railroad trip back in time on the "Heber Creeper," so called because of the way this historic steam train inches its way up the canyon from Provo. This once-proud passenger and freight branch line will let you experience travel the way it was in your grandparents' day. Kids of all ages, from 6 to 80, will love it. See p. 156.
- **Exploring Northeast Utah's Dinosaurland:** This is the real *Jurassic Park*—no special effects here. Stop first at Vernal's Utah Field House of Natural History State Park, where you can stroll around the Dinosaur Garden and admire the 17 life-size dinosaurs and other prehistoric creatures in a delightful garden that simulates the dinosaurs' actual habitat. Then head to Dinosaur National Monument to see and touch—yes, touch—real fossilized dinosaur bones. See p. 176.
- **Discovering Zion National Park:** The Junior Ranger Program, available at most national parks, is really extensive here, with both morning and afternoon activities all summer geared toward teaching kids about what makes this natural wonder so special. They'll have so much fun, they won't even notice they're learning something. See chapter 11.

4 The Best Scenic Drives

- **The Golden Spike Tour:** Heading out of Ogden on Old U.S. 89, you'll first pass through some fine fruit country (be sure to stop at a roadside stand). At the small town of Willard, turn west toward I-15; head north on I-15 to exit 368, and turn west on Utah 83. This will take you along the north side of the Great Salt Lake through picturesque farming communities, until you reach the turnoff to the spot where, in 1869, the last spike was driven for the transcontinental railroad, connecting East and West for the first time. If you love trains as we do, you'll thrill to both the sound of the whistle and the sight of the puffing steam as the engine chugs away and back again. See chapter 7.

- **The National Parks Tour:** From the canyons of Zion, head north along U.S. 89 through majestic forests to Red Canyon, with its walls of brilliant red rock. Then drive east on Utah 12 to Bryce

Canyon, with its fascinating amphitheaters of multicolored stone. The route from Bryce Canyon to Capitol Reef along Utah highways 12 and 24 takes in some of the most spectacular scenery in a state of unsurpassed landscapes. See chapters 11, 12, and 13.

- **Moab to Monument Valley:** This may be red rock country at its finest. From Moab, U.S. 191 south takes you past huge slabs of rock—outposts of Canyonlands National Park—through one-horse towns that have few services but enough character to make up for it. At Bluff, turn southwest on U.S. 163 and drive through more ruddy desert, past the sombrero-shaped rock for which Medicine Hat was named, and finally to the solemnity of Monument Valley. See chapters 15 and 16.

5 The Best Hiking Trails

- **Indian Trail** (Ogden): Easily accessible from downtown Ogden, this 4.2-mile trail gets you out of town quickly, into a thick forest of spruce and fir, and onto a mountainside that offers spectacular views of Ogden Canyon, including a beautiful waterfall. See p. 114.
- **Hidden Piñon Trail, Snow Canyon State Park** (St. George): This fairly easy, self-guided nature trail will reward you with breathtaking panoramic views. You'll wander among lava rock, into canyons, and over rocky flatland, along a trail lined with Mormon tea, cliffrose, prickly pear cactus, banana yucca, and other wild desert plants. See p. 198.
- **Lower Emerald Pools Trail, Zion National Park:** If green is your color, you'll love this trail—algae keeps three pools glowing a deep, rich shade of emerald. The first part of the trail, navigable by wheelchairs with assistance, leads

through a forest to the Lower Emerald Pool, with its lovely waterfall and hanging garden. The small pool just above it is so still and calm that the reflections of the towering cliffs in the water seem like a photograph lying on the ground. See p. 225.

- **Navajo Loop/Queen's Garden Trail, Bryce Canyon National Park:** To truly experience magical Bryce Canyon, you should climb down into it; this not-too-difficult trail is a good way to go. Start at Sunset Point and get the hardest part out of the way first. You'll pass Thor's Hammer and wonder why it hasn't fallen, ponder the towering skyscrapers of Wall Street, and visit with some of the park's most fanciful formations, including majestic Queen Victoria herself. See p. 238.
- **Petrified Forest Trail, Escalante State Park** (Escalante): Along this steep nature trail, you'll find

yourself walking in a stunted forest of junipers and piñons, before reaching a field strewn with colorful chunks of petrified wood.

As you progress, you'll have panoramic views of the town of Escalante and the surrounding stair-step plateaus. See p. 251.

6 The Best Mountain Biking

- **Brian Head Resort:** At 9,600 feet, there may not be a lot of oxygen, but the air is pure and clear, and the biking is great—especially when you can ride a chairlift up the mountain and bicycle down. There are trails everywhere, each with more magnificent scenery than the last. See p. 209.
- **Dave's Hollow Trail:** Situated just outside the entrance to Bryce Canyon National Park, this trail heads off into the national forest. The double track takes you through sun-dappled glades surrounded by tall ponderosa pines

and spruce trees, all the way to fishing and camping at Tropic Reservoir if you so desire. See p. 237.
- **Moab Slickrock Bike Trail:** A rite of passage for serious mountain bikers, this challenging but rewarding trail takes 4 to 5 hours to complete. Between your huffing and puffing, you'll enjoy breathtaking views of the Colorado River far below, the La Sal Mountains towering above, and the red arches of Arches National Park in the distance. See p. 281.

7 The Best Destinations for Fishing & Watersports

- **Strawberry Reservoir:** The number-one trout fishery in Utah for both cutthroat and rainbow, this gem of a lake is magnificently set among tall pines. You're really out in the woods here: The nearest town of any size is 30 miles away. So pick your spot, out in the middle of the reservoir or tucked away in a quiet nook, and cast your line for dinner—you can't beat fresh-caught trout cooked over an open fire. See p. 160.
- **Jordanelle Reservoir** (in Jordanelle Sate Park, near Park City): This boomerang-shaped reservoir offers a wide area at the dam that's perfect for speedboats, water-skiers, and personal watercraft. The southeast end of the boomerang is designated for low-speed boating. Wherever you go, you'll have the beautiful Wasatch Mountains on all sides. See p. 157.
- **The Green River through Dinosaur National Monument:**

The best way to see this spectacularly desolate country is from the river, the way explorer John Wesley Powell did in 1869. Crave excitement? Run the foaming rapids. Are peace and quiet your thing? Float mindlessly in the placid waters, leaving your troubles behind. See p. 184.
- **Lake Flaming Gorge:** Smaller and more intimate than Lake Powell, and located in a gloriously colorful setting, Lake Flaming Gorge is one of Utah's real hidden treasures. You can skim the water on skis or just doze off on the deck of a houseboat. As for the fishing, if you feel like the big ones always get away, this is the place for you—they're all big here. See p. 187.
- **Lake Powell:** This sprawling lake has what seems like zillions of finger canyons reaching off the main watercourse of the Colorado River. You could spend weeks—maybe even months—water-skiing,

swimming, fishing, exploring the myriad side canyons, and just loafing about in the sun. See p. 271.

- **The Colorado River near Moab:** Tackle the placid stretches on your own in a canoe or kayak, or sign up with one of the many outfitters and shoot the rapids. Whatever you choose, a trip down the spectacular, scenic Colorado River is an adventure you won't forget. See p. 284.

8 The Best Wildlife Watching

- **Rock Cliff, Jordanelle State Park** (near Park City): More than 160 species of birds either live here or pass through. This is an especially good place to spot eagles and other raptors who nest in the area. Boardwalks and trails throughout the riparian wetlands reduce the environmental impact of your visit, and give you a great chance to watch wetland life doing their thing. See p. 158.
- **Flaming Gorge National Recreation Area:** Take a boat trip to see bighorn sheep here. The imposing beasts are sometimes seen on Kingfisher Island and near Hideout Canyon, on the north side of the reservoir, in spring and early summer. And keep your eyes peeled for the lovely osprey and rare peregrine falcon, occasionally spotted near their nests on the high rocky spires above the lake. See p. 187.
- **Coral Pink Sand Dunes State Park** (near Kanab): If you climb the dunes early in the morning, you're sure to see the footprints of jackrabbits, kangaroo rats, and even an occasional mule deer or coyote. But the real fun comes after dark, with the late-night scorpion hunt: You can follow a park ranger out onto the dunes and, using a black light, spot the luminescent creatures as they scurry across the sand. See p. 212.
- **Escalante State Park** (Escalante): Willows and cottonwoods line the banks of the reservoir, one of the few wetland birding sites in southern Utah. This area is home to a wide variety of ducks, plus coots, grebes, herons, and swallows. You might also see eagles, osprey, American kestrels, and other raptors. Small creatures of the furry variety, including cottontail and blacktail jackrabbits, ground squirrels, and beaver, inhabit the area as well. See p. 250.

9 The Best Downhill Skiing

- **Snowbasin** (Ogden Valley): Families love Snowbasin because there's something for everyone here, no matter what your ability. The resort is particularly popular with intermediates, who love the long, easy, well-groomed cruising runs. Experts have plenty to keep them happy, too, including an abundance of untracked powder and the state's third-highest vertical drop. See p. 127.
- **Beaver Mountain** (The Northern Wasatch Front): Visiting this small, family-oriented ski area is like going home to see the folks—it's just plain comfortable. There's no glitz, no fancy anything, just lots of personal attention, plenty of snow, and great terrain with beautifully maintained trails. See p. 128.
- **Alta** (Little Cottonwood Canyon): All serious skiers make a pilgrimage to Alta at one time or another. It offers the best skiing in the state—and some of the lightest powder in the world—especially

for advanced skiers willing to hike a bit for perfect conditions. If you're not up to black-diamond level yet, don't worry: Beginners and intermediates will find plenty of cruising ground, too. And at $42 for an all-day lift ticket, Alta also happens to be one of the best skiing bargains around. See p. 138.

- **Park City and Deer Valley:** These resorts offer not only excellent powder skiing on a wide variety of terrain, but also the best shopping, nightlife, accommodations, and dining of all of Utah's ski areas—and for that matter, in all of Utah. Park City is the party town; Deer Valley is its more grown-up, sophisticated sibling. They're less than 5 minutes apart by road, so you can take advantage of the best of both. Who says you can't have everything? See p. 142 for Park City and p. 144 for Deer Valley.

10 The Best Places to Discover American Indian Culture

- **The Great Gallery in Horseshoe Canyon, Canyonlands National Park:** In a remote and hard-to-reach section of Canyonlands National Park is the Great Gallery, an 80-foot-long panel of rock art that dates back several thousand years. It's one of the biggest and best prehistoric murals you'll find anywhere. See p. 303.

- **Monument Valley Navajo Tribal Park:** For most of us, Monument Valley *is* the Old West. We've seen it dozens of times in movie theaters, on TV, and in advertisements. The Old West may be gone, but many Navajos still call this area home. A Navajo guide can give you the Navajo perspective on this majestic land and take you to areas that are not otherwise open to visitors. See p. 312.

- **Hovenweep National Monument:** This deserted valley contains some of the most striking and most isolated archaeological sites in the Four Corners area—the remains of curious sandstone towers built more than 700 years ago. These mysterious structures keep archaeologists guessing. See p. 317.

- **Mesa Verde National Park:** The largest archaeological preserve in the country is also home to the most impressive cliff dwellings in the Southwest. The sites run the gamut from simple pit houses to complex cliff dwellings, and they're all fascinating to explore. See p. 319.

11 The Best Luxury Hotels

- **The Grand America Hotel** (Salt Lake City; © **800/621-4505**): The newest luxury hotel in downtown Salt Lake City, the Grand America occupies an entire city block and offers top-notch service, amenities, and decor. The marriage of superb design and deluxe furnishings has resulted in exquisitely comfortable guest rooms and suites. See p. 78.

- **The Inn at Temple Square** (Salt Lake City; © **800/843-4668**): This quietly elegant downtown hotel offers beautifully appointed rooms, a lovely dining room, and an all-around aura of old-world graciousness. It may look formal, but it's actually quite relaxed and homey—come on in and set a spell. See p. 80.

- **Goldener Hirsch Inn** (Deer Valley; © **800/252-3373**): This place feels like a Bavarian Alps lodge, with roaring fireplaces, hand-painted furniture, windows looking out onto the ski slopes, feather-light down comforters, and the kind of personalized service you'd expect to find in a fine European hotel. See p. 150.

- **Stein Eriksen Lodge** (Deer Valley; ℂ **800/453-1302**): The Stein Eriksen is grandly elegant yet warm and welcoming, with cozy niches in the dignified lobby and lavishly comfortable suites. Attendants in the whirlpool, sauna, and fitness room are always on hand to pamper you and see to your every need, but they're so unobtrusive that you'll feel right at home—contentedly, luxuriously at home. See p. 150.

12 The Best Bed-and-Breakfasts

- **The Armstrong Mansion Bed & Breakfast** (Salt Lake City; ℂ **800/708-1333**): Housed in a four-story Queen Anne–style Victorian mansion, this elegant B&B has stained glass windows, a carved oak staircase, and replicas of the original wall stencils. Many of the 13 luxurious rooms boast whirlpool tubs. See p. 78.

- **Alaskan Inn** (Ogden; ℂ **888/707-8600**): The wilds of Alaska have arrived in Utah, with this unique and fun bed-and-breakfast, where themed rooms and cabins transport you to a land of tundra, snow-capped peaks, tall pines, polar bears, and cascading waterfalls. See p. 117.

- **Snowberry Inn Bed & Breakfast** (near Ogden; ℂ **888/334-3466**): This log B&B is lovingly decorated with antiques and collectibles, and each bedroom has its own personality. Although the house has a wide-open design with a broad front porch, it still manages to have a cozy, homelike atmosphere; guests gather in the kitchen to sip coffee and watch, or help, as breakfast is being prepared. See p. 119.

- **Hines Mansion Luxury Bed & Breakfast** (Provo; ℂ **800/428-5636**): A Victorian mansion that oozes historic ambiance, this is a wonderful place to celebrate a wedding anniversary or other romantic occasion, with complimentary sparkling cider and two-person whirlpool tubs in every room. See p. 171.

- **Seven Wives Inn Bed & Breakfast** (St. George; ℂ **800/600-3737**): This was the first B&B in Utah, and it's one of the loveliest. There are no polygamists hiding in the attic anymore (see the review), but you'll feel like you've stepped back in time. The two historic 19th-century homes are outfitted with antiques, mostly Victorian and Eastlake. We love the several decks, porches, and balconies. See p. 201.

- **Sunflower Hill Bed & Breakfast Inn** (Moab; ℂ **800/662-2786**): Loaded with country charm, this delightful B&B makes you feel like you've gone back to Grandma's, where family relics surround you during the day and handmade quilts keep you warm at night. What's more, this may be the quietest lodging in Moab, and the grassy, shady grounds are especially inviting on a hot day. See p. 288.

13 The Best Lodges

- **Red Canyon Lodge** (Flaming Gorge National Recreation Area; ℂ **435/889-3759**): This is not really a lodge at all, but rather a group of delightful cabins dating from the 1930s and remodeled in the 1990s. This complex offers a range of accommodations, from rustic to luxurious, and all have freestanding wood stoves. The forest setting, complete with private lake, is spectacular. See p. 190.

- **Bryce Canyon Lodge** (© 888/297-2757): This handsome sandstone-and-ponderosa-pine lodge is the perfect place to stay while you're visiting the national park.

The several suites are outfitted with white wicker furniture, ceiling fans, and separate sitting rooms. But our choice is the snug cabins—although small, the high ceilings give the impression of spaciousness, and the gas-burning stone fireplaces and log beams make them positively cozy. See p. 241.

14 The Best Restaurants

- **The New Yorker** (Salt Lake City; © 801/363-0166): Among our favorite Utah restaurants, the New Yorker offers superb service, a comfortable upscale decor, and a wide variety of excellently prepared American dishes. Desserts are magnificent. See p. 83.
- **Spencer's For Steaks and Chops** (Salt Lake City; © 801/238-4748): For those of us who like top-quality steaks prepared simply but perfectly, there is no place in Utah to top Spencer's. See p. 84.
- **Lamb's Restaurant** (Salt Lake City; © 801/364-7166): A delightful and sometimes innovative restaurant with reasonable prices—how can you beat that? Sit back in one of the cozy booths, relax, and enjoy a good meal while watching the who's who of Utah parade through. See p. 85.
- **Glitretind Restaurant** (Stein Eriksen Lodge, Deer Valley; © 435/649-3700): The definitive elegant restaurant of Utah, the Glitretind serves inventive, exquisitely prepared New American dishes. You'll dine in a modern, airy room with views of the spectacular Wasatch Mountains. See p. 153.

15 The Best of the Performing Arts

- **Mormon Tabernacle Choir** (Salt Lake City): Hear the glorious sounds of this world-renowned, all-volunteer choir in its home on Temple Square. When not on tour, the choir rehearses Thursday evenings and performs its weekly radio and television broadcasts Sunday mornings; both events are open to the public, free of charge. See p. 88.
- **Utah Symphony** (Salt Lake City, Park City): Who'd expect to find one of the country's top symphony orchestras in Utah? Well, here it is: an excellent ensemble that not only tours worldwide and has produced numerous recordings, but also performs each year in schools across the state. Our favorite time to enjoy this world-class orchestra is during the symphony's summer series in Park City. See p. 102.
- **Utah Shakespearean Festival** (Cedar City): To go or not to go, that is the question. If theater's your thing, go. Four of the Bard's plays, plus two by other playwrights, are presented each summer, and they're grand entertainment. See p. 207.

2

Planning a Trip to Utah

This relatively quiet, relatively unknown corner of the United States is beginning to draw nationwide, even worldwide, attention. More and more people are coming—to visit the state's majestic national parks, explore its pristine wilderness, bike its slickrock trails, ski the best powder in the world, and discover the all-around charm of its cities and towns. To some, this is America as it should be—wide-open country with plenty of room to roam, along with some of the friendliest people you'll ever meet. Of course, it isn't quite that simple, but it comes close. Don't just take it from us; find out for yourself.

Utah is an easy state to visit—you can often expect to pay less for food and lodging than you would in other parts of the country, and roads are good and generally uncrowded. But once you leave the Wasatch Front—the area around Salt Lake City, Ogden, and Provo—distances between towns are long, with few services along the way. You'll want to plan your trip carefully and make reservations as far in advance as possible for popular areas such as the national parks, and for popular times, such as ski season. The pages that follow will help you do that and more.

The presence and influence of the Mormon Church—officially known as the Church of Jesus Christ of Latter-day Saints (LDS)—makes visiting Utah a unique experience, from ordering an alcoholic beverage to visiting a historic home with two identical bedrooms, one for each wife. To learn more about modern Mormonism, as well as Utah's history in general, see the Appendix, "Utah in Depth," at the back of this book.

1 The Regions in Brief

You could take a big knife and easily cut Utah into three distinct regions: the Colorado Plateau, in the southern half of the state, where all those fantastic rock formations are; Rocky Mountain Utah, with rugged peaks, stately pines, deep blue lakes, and most of the state's residents; and the Great Basin Desert, the big middle-of-nowhere where you've always wanted to send that distant cousin you never really liked.

Because the state is so big, we've concentrated our coverage on those areas visitors tend to be most interested in, rather than trying to catalog each of the three regions from A to Z.

Truth be told, certain sections of Utah just have a whole lot of nothing. So we've organized this book by destination, based on where you'll probably want to go or where you'll base yourself while exploring outlying areas.

We start out in the **Wasatch Front.** Eighty percent of Utah's population lives in this Rocky Mountain region, the 175-mile-long north-central section of the state from Logan to Provo. **Salt Lake City** is Utah's most populous city, as well as its most cosmopolitan. It's also the international headquarters of the Church of Jesus Christ of Latter-day Saints, more commonly known as the Mormons; Temple Square is Utah's

Regions of Utah

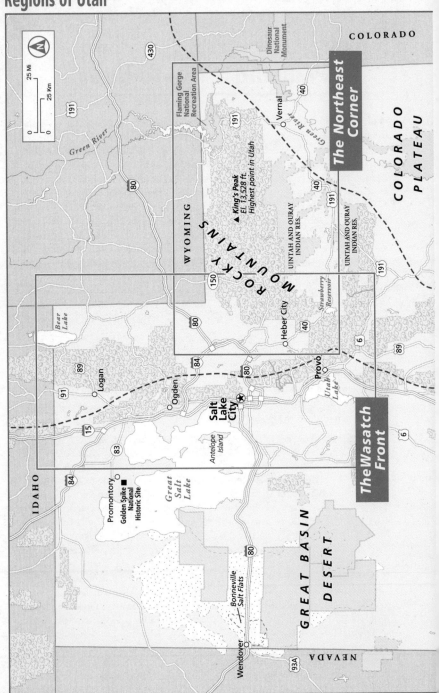

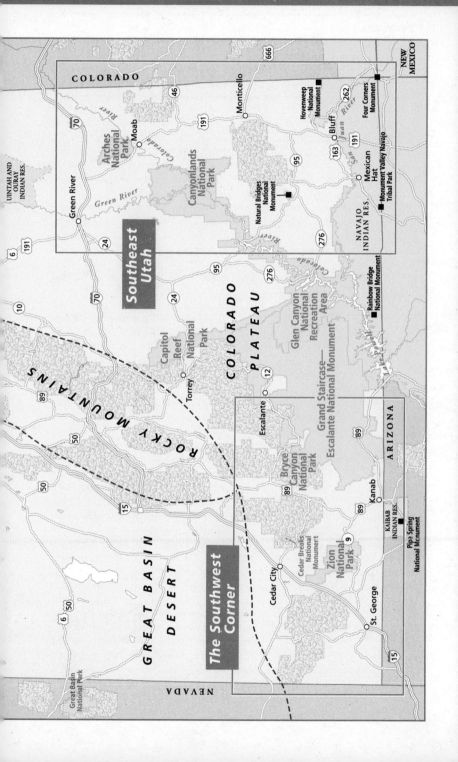

COLORADO

NEW MEXICO

UINTAH AND OURAY INDIAN RES.

Green River

Moab

Arches National Park

Green River

Green River

Colorado River

Southeast Utah

Monticello

Canyonlands National Park

Natural Bridges National Monument

Hovenweep National Monument

Bluff

Four Corners Monument

Mexican Hat

Monument Valley Navajo Tribal Park

San Juan River

NAVAJO INDIAN RES.

Colorado River

COLORADO PLATEAU

Capitol Reef National Park

Torrey

Glen Canyon National Recreation Area

Lake Powell

Rainbow Bridge National Monument

ROCKY MOUNTAINS

GREAT BASIN DESERT

Escalante

Grand Staircase—Escalante National Monument

Bryce Canyon National Park

Kanab

ARIZONA

The Southwest Corner

Cedar City

Cedar Breaks National Monument

Zion National Park

KAIBAB INDIAN RES.

Pipe Spring National Monument

St. George

Great Basin National Park

NEVADA

Impressions

TV you can make on the back lot, but for the big screen, for the real outdoor dramas, you have to do it where God put the West . . . and there is no better example of this than around Moab.
                    —John Wayne, while filming *The Comancheros* in 1961

most-visited attraction. Keep in mind, though, that Salt Lake City is still a relatively small city and not as sophisticated or glitzy as New York or Los Angeles (that may be what we like best about it). One advantage Salt Lake has over all other western cities its size, as any real-estate agent will tell you, is its location; within an hour's drive are some of the best downhill slopes in the United States. Here also is that mystery of nature, the **Great Salt Lake,** eight times saltier than any of the world's oceans.

That brings us to the rest of the Wasatch Front. We've designated the section that's roughly north of Salt Lake the **Northern Wasatch Front.** Here you'll find historic **Ogden; Logan,** Utah's northernmost town of any size; the national historic site where the Central Pacific and Union Pacific railroads met in 1869; and three ski resorts. The mountains that afford great skiing in winter also provide numerous opportunities for hiking, horseback riding, and biking in summer.

Those areas that are basically east and south of Salt Lake City we call the **Southern Wasatch Front.** This region contains beautiful **Big and Little Cottonwood Canyons,** which have some of the state's best skiing, as well as great hiking and biking in the summer; **Park City,** Utah's premier ski-resort town—and a delightful destination year-round—with a historic Main Street dominated by intriguing shops and restaurants; some fun spots just outside of Park City, including a

historic railroad, Strawberry Reservoir (a real gem of a lake), and several terrific state parks; Robert Redford's Sundance Institute; and **Provo,** a small, conservative city that's home to Brigham Young University.

The western side of Utah, beginning just west of Salt Lake City, is dominated by the vast, salty nothingness of the Great Basin Desert, which includes the pristinely white Bonneville Salt Flats, which are so flat that you can actually *see* the curvature of the earth here. The Flats are also famous for the land speed records set on them. This is not the sort of place you want to go for a picnic—it's hot, the water's undrinkable, and there's really nothing here except for **Wendover,** a little gambling town straddling the Utah-Nevada state line, which we've covered as an excursion from Salt Lake City.

Next we head to **Northeastern Utah,** with two terrific recreational areas that creep into the adjoining states: **Flaming Gorge National Recreation Area,** which wanders into Wyoming, and nearby **Dinosaur National Monument,** which extends from northeastern Utah into Colorado. Both are what we consider "Undiscovered Utah," because they're really off the beaten path and not what most people imagine when they think of the state. We love this region, however, and consider it well worth a visit.

The **Colorado Plateau,** which extends along the state's entire southern border and halfway up the east side, is where all five of Utah's national parks are located, and for good reason—it's undeniably beautiful. Ancient geologic forces, erosion, oxidation, and other natural processes have carved spectacular rock sculptures—delicate and intricate, bold and stately—and painted them in a riot of color. This is quite likely why you've come to Utah in the first place, and these chapters should help you spend your time wisely and enjoyably. Check out our chapter on **Zion National Park** for hints on how to avoid the crowds at the state's most popular national park; and see if you agree that **Bryce Canyon National Park,** with its marvelous stone sculptures (called hoodoos), is the West's best. The chapter on **Capitol Reef National Park** explains why this little-known national park is one of Utah's hidden treasures, and we direct you to some of the best ways to explore eastern Utah's beautiful red rock country in the chapter on **Moab** and **Arches and Canyonlands National Parks.**

But the Colorado Plateau isn't just national parks. Its biggest population center is in and around St. George, which you'll find described in chapter 10. This area offers historic Mormon sites; live theater, dance, and music; as well as skiing (believe it or not) and the state's best golf. If you're heading into Utah from Las Vegas, this is the first Utah town you'll see.

Utah's best destination for water sports—maybe the best in the West—is explored in chapter 14, which covers **Lake Powell and Glen Canyon National Recreation Area.** A boating vacation here is the stuff that stressed-out big-city dreams are made of.

In chapter 16, **"The Four Corners Area,"** we cover the state's southeast corner, with a few jaunts into adjacent states. Spectacular American Indian sites, such as Hovenweep National Monument, make a visit here truly worthwhile, even though you'll be driving a long way through the West's vast, empty spaces to get here.

2 Visitor Information

For advance information on the state as a whole, as well as an official state map, contact the **Utah Travel Council,** Council Hall, 300 N. State Street, Salt Lake City, UT 84114 (© **800/ 200-1160** or 801/538-1030; fax 801/ 538-1399; www.utah.com).

For information on Utah's national forests, contact the **U.S. Forest Service Regional Office,** Federal Building 324, 25th Street, Ogden, UT 84401 (© **801/625-5306;** fax 801/ 625-5127; www.fs.fed.us/r4). The best source for topographic and geological maps, as well as guidebooks and other outdoor recreation information, is the **Natural Resources Map & Bookstore,** 1594 W. North Temple, Salt Lake City, UT 84116-6100 (© **888/**

882-4627 or 801/537-3320; fax 801/ 537-3395; www.maps.state.ut.us). The Utah State Office of the **U.S. Bureau of Land Management (BLM)** is at 324 S. State St., Suite 301 (P.O. Box 45155), Salt Lake City, UT 84145-0155 (© **801/539-4001;** fax 801/539-4013; www.ut.blm.gov). For information on Utah's state parks, contact **Utah State Parks and Recreation,** 1594 W. North Temple, Suite 116 (P.O. Box 145610), Salt Lake City, UT 84114-5610 (© **800/322- 3770,** 801/538-7220, or 801/322-3770 for campground reservations; fax 801/538-7378; www.stateparks. utah.gov). You'll find additional information sources for planning your outdoor adventures in chapter 4.

Destination: Utah—Red Alert Checklist

- Some attractions (such as military installations and dams such as Flaming Gorge) have increased security. Call ahead for specifics.
- If you plan to drive through the mountains in winter, be sure to check on possible road closures first.
- If you purchased traveler's checks, have you recorded the check numbers, and stored the documentation separately from the checks?
- Did you pack your camera and an extra set of camera batteries, and purchase enough film? Don't pack your film in your checked baggage.
- Do you have a safe, accessible place to store money?
- Did you bring your ID cards that could entitle you to discounts such as AAA and AARP cards, student IDs, etc.?
- Did you bring emergency drug prescriptions and extra glasses and/or contact lenses?
- Do you have your credit card pin numbers?
- If you have an E-ticket, do you have documentation?
- Did you leave a copy of your itinerary with someone at home?

3 Money

ATMS

The easiest and best way to get cash away from home is from an ATM (automated teller machine). The **Cirrus** (© 800/424-7787; www.mastercard.com) and **PLUS** (© 800/843-7587; www.visa.com) networks span the globe; look at the back of your bank card to see which network you're on, then call or check online for ATM locations at your destination. Be sure you know your personal identification number (PIN) before you leave home and be sure to find out your daily withdrawal limit before you depart. Also keep in mind that many banks impose a fee every time a card is used at a different bank's ATM. On top of this, the bank from which you withdraw cash may charge its own fee. To compare banks' ATM fees within the U.S., use www.bankrate.com.

TRAVELER'S CHECKS

Traveler's checks are something of an anachronism from the days before the ATM made cash accessible at any time. Traveler's checks used to be the only sound alternative to traveling with dangerously large amounts of cash. They were as reliable as currency, but, unlike cash, could be replaced if lost or stolen.

These days, traveler's checks are less necessary because most cities have 24-hour ATMs that allow you to withdraw small amounts of cash as needed. However, keep in mind that you will likely be charged an ATM withdrawal fee if the bank is not your own, so if you're withdrawing money every day, you might be better off with traveler's checks—provided that you don't mind showing identification every time you want to cash one.

You can get traveler's checks at almost any bank. **American Express** offers denominations of $20, $50, $100, $500, and (for cardholders only) $1,000. You'll pay a service charge ranging from 1% to 4%. You can also get American Express traveler's checks over the phone by calling © **800/221-7282;** Amex gold and platinum cardholders who use this number are exempt from the 1% fee.

Visa offers traveler's checks at Citibank locations nationwide, as well as at several other banks. The service charge ranges between 1.5% and 2%; checks come in denominations of $20, $50, $100, $500, and $1,000. Call © **800/732-1322** for information. AAA members can obtain Visa checks without a fee at most AAA offices or by calling © **866/339-3378. MasterCard** also offers traveler's checks. Call © **800/223-9920** for a location near you.

If you choose to carry traveler's checks, be sure to keep a record of their serial numbers separate from your checks in the event that they are stolen or lost. You'll get a refund faster if you know the numbers.

U.S. dollar **traveler's checks** are accepted practically everywhere in Utah, including small towns, and can be exchanged for cash at banks and most check-issuing offices. However, be aware that smaller businesses may not be able to cash traveler's checks or even American currency in denominations over $50. You can also get cash advances on your credit card at an ATM.

CREDIT CARDS

Credit cards are a safe way to carry money, they provide a convenient record of all your expenses, and they generally offer good exchange rates. You can also withdraw cash advances from your credit cards at banks or ATMs, provided you know your PIN. If you've forgotten yours, or didn't even know you had one, call the number on the back of your credit card and ask the bank to send it to you. It usually takes 5 to 7 business days, though some banks will provide the number over the phone if you tell them your mother's maiden name or some other personal information.

For tips and telephone numbers to call if your wallet is stolen or lost, go to "Lost & Found" in the "Fast Facts: Utah" section, later in this chapter.

4 When to Go

Deciding when to visit Utah will depend on what you want to do and which sections of the state you plan to see. Generally, those traveling without children will want to avoid visiting during school vacations. In particular, stay away from ski resorts during the Christmas–New Year's holidays and avoid national parks in July and August. The best times to visit the parks and almost everything else in southern Utah are spring and fall; summers are too hot, particularly in the St. George area.

Utah has four seasons, but because of the vast range in elevations—from 2,200 to 13,528 feet—conditions vary considerably across the state. Generally, as in the other desert states, summer days are hot but nights are cool. Winters are cold and snowy, except in southwest Utah's "Dixie" (where St. George is located), where it seldom gets very cold and snow is rare. Mountain temperatures are always pleasantly cool and can be very cold at night, even in summer.

Tips Quick ID

Tie a colorful ribbon or piece of yarn around your luggage handle, or slap a distinctive sticker on the side of your bag. This makes it less likely that someone will mistakenly appropriate it. And if your luggage gets lost, it will be easier to find.

Average Monthly High/Low Temperatures (°F/°C) & Precipitation (inches)

		Jan	Feb	Mar	Apr	May	June	July	Aug	Sept	Oct	Nov	Dec
Moab	Temp. (°F)	42/19	51/25	61/33	71/42	82/50	93/58	99/65	96/63	88/53	75/41	57/30	45/21
	Temp. (°C)	6/-7	11/-4	16/1	22/6	28/10	34/14	37/18	36/17	31/12	24/5	14/-1	7/-6
	Precip. (in.)	0.6	0.5	0.7	0.9	0.7	0.4	0.5	0.8	0.7	0.9	0.7	0.7
Elev. 4,000 ft.													
Park City	Temp. (°F)	27/6	31/10	36/15	48/24	60/33	71/39	79/47	76/45	67/36	54/28	39/17	31/11
Mountains	Temp. (°C)	-3/-14	-1/-12	2/-9	9/-4	16/1	22/4	26/8	24/7	19/2	12/-2	4/-8	-1/-12
	Precip. (in.)	3.1	2.6	2.9	2.4	1.3	1.3	1.1	1.4	1.0	2.5	2.4	3.2
Elev. 8,085 ft.													
St. George	Temp. (°F)	54/27	61/32	67/37	76/44	86/52	96/61	102/68	99/66	93/57	81/45	65/34	55/27
	Temp. (°C)	12/-3	16/0	19/3	24/7	30/11	36/16	39/20	37/19	34/14	27/7	18/1	13/-3
	Precip. (in.)	1.0	0.9	1.0	0.5	0.5	0.2	0.6	0.7	0.5	0.6	0.8	0.7
Elev. 2,880 ft.													
Salt Lake	Temp. (°F)	37/20	44/27	52/30	61/37	72/45	83/53	93/62	90/60	80/50	67/39	50/29	39/22
City	Temp. (°C)	3/-7	7/-3	11/-1	16/3	22/7	28/12	34/17	32/16	27/10	19/4	10/-2	4/-6
	Precip. (in.)	1.4	1.3	1.7	2.2	1.5	1.0	0.7	0.9	0.9	1.1	1.2	1.4
Elev. 4,330 ft.													

UTAH CALENDAR OF EVENTS

January

Utah Winter Games, Salt Lake City, Park City, and other locations. Amateur athletes compete in downhill and Nordic skiing, figure skating, and hockey. Call ✆ **800/959-8824** or 801/975-4515. Ongoing through most of the month.

Sundance Film Festival, Park City. Sponsored by Robert Redford's Sundance Resort, this festival honors the best independent films with screenings and seminars. Call ✆ **801/328-3456.** Last half of January.

February

Bryce Canyon Winter Festival, Bryce. This winter celebration, with snowshoe tours, free photography clinics, and more, takes place amid the colorful rock formations of the Bryce Canyon National Park area. Call ✆ **800/468-8660.** Mid-February.

SnowShine Festival, Park City. This festival encompasses the National Free-Style Ski Jumping Championships, family ski races, snow softball, and other fun-in-the-snow events. Call ✆ **435/658-4200.** Mid-February.

March

Hostler Model Railroad Festival, Ogden. Fans of model trains gather at historic Union Station, where trains of all shapes and sizes are on display; model-train collectors can locate those hard-to-find items. Call ✆ **801/629-8446.** First week in March.

St. George Art Festival, St. George. This outside fine art festival draws artists and visitors from all over the American West. Call ✆ **435/634-5850.** Mid-March.

April

Mountain Man Rendezvous, Ogden. A gathering of mountain men at Fort Buenaventura, with black-powder shooting contests and other early-19th-century activities. Call ✆ **801/399-8099.** Early to mid-April.

Rod Benders Car Show, Moab. A grand display of vintage hot rods, plus a couple of Rod Runs, a Saturday night cruise down Main Street, and some fun contests. Call ✆ **435/259-8942.** Late April.

May

Golden Spike Reenactment, Golden Spike National Historic Site, Promontory. This reenactment commemorates the moment in 1869 when rail lines from the East and West Coasts were joined, linking the nation. A must for historic-railroad buffs. Call ℂ **435/471-2209,** ext. 18. May 10.

Great Salt Lake Birding Festival, Farmington. Birders from across the country flock to this festival, which takes place at the Davis County Fair Park, midway between Salt Lake City and Ogden. Call ℂ **801/451-3286.** May.

June

Utah's Best Dam MS 150 Bike Tour, Logan. More than 500 participants pedal 75 miles each day along Cache Valley's back roads. The money raised goes to help in the battle against multiple sclerosis. Call ℂ **801/493-0113;** www.fightmsutah.org. Mid-June.

Utah Shakespearean Festival, Cedar City. This highly respected professional theater festival produces several plays by William Shakespeare, plus a few contemporary offerings. Call ℂ **800/752-9849.** Late June through August.

Utah Arts Festival, Salt Lake City. This festival involves exhibits by artists and craftsmen, plus music and dance performances. Call ℂ **801/322-2428.** Late June.

July

Land Speed Opener, Bonneville Salt Flats, Wendover. Jet-cars and other super-fast mechanical wonders try to break speed records on the incredibly smooth salt flats, which are so flat that you can see the curvature of the earth. Call ℂ **801/785-5364.** Mid-summer through early fall.

Park City International Music Festival, The Canyons. This festival presents a spectacular series of concerts in an equally spectacular setting. Call ℂ **435/649-5309.** July to early August.

Utah Festival Opera Company, Logan. Several operas are presented in repertory each summer, from the *Mikado* to *Carmen.* Call ℂ **800/262-0074** or 435/750-0300, ext. 106. July to early August.

Utah Jazz and Blues Festival, Snowbird. Big-name musicians make this one of Utah's premier music events. Call ℂ **801/933-2110.** Late July.

Festival of the American West, Logan. A multimedia historical pageant is presented nightly; there's also a fair with traditional Old West food, music, craft demonstrations, and live entertainment, including medicine-man shows and square dancing. Call ℂ **800/225-3378** or 435/245-6050. Late July to early August.

August

Brian Head Bash, Brian Head. A weekend of bicycling tours, catered lunches on trails, prizes, and chair-lift rides for bikers, who then ride down the mountain. Call ℂ **435/677-2310.** Early August.

Railroader's Festival, Golden Spike National Historic Site. Reenactments of the Golden Spike ceremony, which united the nation by rail, plus a spike-driving contest, railroad handcar races and rides, and a buffalo-chip-throwing contest. Call ℂ **435/471-2209.** Mid-August.

Utah Belly Dance Festival, Salt Lake City. Middle Eastern dancers do their thing in Liberty Park. Call ℂ **801/486-7780;** www.kismetdance.com. Third week in August.

September

Utah State Fair, Salt Lake City. This fair has live entertainment, a horse show, a rodeo, livestock judging, arts and crafts exhibits, and typical state-fair fun. Call ✆ **801/ 581-7989.** Early September.

Mountain Man Rendezvous, Ogden. A gathering of mountain men at Fort Buenaventura, with black-powder shooting contests and other early-19th-century activities. Call ✆ **801/399-8099.** Early September.

Greek Festival, Salt Lake City. The music, dance, and food of Greece are featured, along with tours of the historic Holy Trinity Greek Orthodox Cathedral. Call ✆ **801/328-9681.** Early September.

Moab Music Festival, Moab. Live classical, jazz, bluegrass, and other types of music are presented in a beautiful red-rock amphitheater and other locations. Call ✆ **435/ 259-7003.** Mid-September.

Oktoberfest, Snowbird. This is a traditional celebration, with German music, food, and, of course, beer. Call ✆ **801/521-6040.** Six consecutive September and October weekends starting on Labor Day weekend.

October

World Senior Games, St. George. This is an extremely popular Olympics-style competition for seniors, with a variety of athletic events. Call ✆ **435/674-0550.** Mid-October.

Canyonlands Fat Tire Festival, Moab. Guided mountain-bike tours, hill climbs, and related events make up this festival. Call ✆ **435/ 259-1370.** Late October to early November.

Buffalo Roundup, Antelope Island State Park. Stop by the park and watch the annual buffalo roundup, conducted on horseback and by helicopter. Take binoculars and get a close-up view of the buffalo as they receive their annual medical exams. The event also includes a dance. Call ✆ **801/773-2941.** Late October.

November

Christmas Parade and Lighting of the Dinosaur Gardens, Vernal. Life-size replicas of dinosaurs are illuminated for Christmas. Call ✆ **435/789-6932.** Just after Thanksgiving and into December.

America's World Cup Ski Races, Park City. This event is made up of sanctioned World Cup ski races and demonstrations. Call ✆ **435/649-8111.** Late November.

Parade of Lights, Bullfrog Marina, Lake Powell. Spectators throng the area to see lights from about 50 boats reflected in the waters of Lake Powell. The ferry leads the parade, and prizes are awarded for boat decorations. A limited number of boats are available to rent and decorate; a number of privately owned boats are entered. Call ✆ **800/528-6154** or 435/684-3028. Saturday after Thanksgiving.

Ogden Christmas Parade and Christmas Village, Ogden. A parade begins the Christmas season, when the municipal park is transformed into a Christmas village, with thousands of lights, music, and animated decorations. Call ✆ **801/629-8242.** Late November through December.

Temple Square Christmas Lights, Salt Lake City. A huge, spectacular display of Christmas lights decorates Temple Square. Call ✆ **800/ 541-4955** or 801/240-1000. From the Friday after Thanksgiving to January 1.

December

Parade of Lights, Wahweap Marina, Lake Powell. The *Canyon King* paddle wheeler leads a parade of illuminated boats that seem larger than life with all their lights reflected in the waters of Lake Powell. Both spectators and participants are welcome, and prizes are awarded. Call ℂ **800/528-6154** or 520/645-2433. Early December.

Railroader's Film Festival and Winter Steam Demonstration, Golden Spike National Historic Site. This festival involves showings of classic Hollywood railroad films, plus a steam-engine demonstration. Call ℂ **435/471-2209.** Late December.

First Night Celebration, Ogden. This family party rings in the New Year with bands, storytelling, and arts and crafts, ending with a spectacular fireworks display. Call ℂ **800/255-8824** or 801/627-8288. December 31.

First Night New Year's Eve Celebration, Salt Lake City. This New Year's Eve family party brings downtown Salt Lake City alive with arts and crafts, live entertainment, storytelling, and numerous other family-oriented activities, culminating in a midnight fireworks display. Call ℂ **801/359-5118.** December 31.

5 Insurance

Check your existing insurance policies and credit-card coverage before you buy travel insurance. You may already be covered for lost luggage, cancelled tickets, or medical expenses. The cost of travel insurance varies widely, depending on the cost and length of your trip, your age, health, and the type of trip you're taking.

TRIP-CANCELLATION INSURANCE Trip-cancellation insurance helps you get your money back if you have to back out of a trip, if you have to go home early, or if your travel supplier goes bankrupt. Allowed reasons for cancellation can range from sickness to natural disasters to the State Department declaring your destination unsafe for travel. (Insurers usually won't cover vague fears, though, as many travelers discovered when they tried to cancel their trips in October 2001 because they were wary of flying.) In this unstable world, trip-cancellation insurance is a good buy if you're getting tickets well in advance—who knows what the state of the world, or of your airline, will be in 9 months? Insurance policy details vary, so read the fine print—and especially make sure that your airline or cruise line is on the list of carriers covered in case of bankruptcy. For information, contact one of the following insurers: **Access America** (ℂ 866/807-3982; www.accessamerica.com); **Travel Guard International** (ℂ 800/826-4919; www.travelguard.com); **Travel Insured International** (ℂ 800/243-3174; www.travelinsured.com); and **Travelex Insurance Services** (ℂ 888/457-4602; www.travelex-insurance.com).

MEDICAL INSURANCE Most health insurance policies cover you if you get sick away from home—but check, particularly if you're insured by an HMO. If you require additional medical insurance, try **MEDEX International** (ℂ 800/527-0218 or 410/453-6300; www.medexassist.com) or **Travel Assistance International** (ℂ 800/821-2828; www.travelassistance.com; for general information on services, call the company's Worldwide Assistance Services, Inc., at ℂ 800/777-8710).

LOST-LUGGAGE INSURANCE On domestic flights, checked baggage is covered up to $2,500 per ticketed passenger. On international flights (including U.S. portions of international trips), baggage is limited to approximately $9.07 per pound, up to approximately $635 per checked bag. If you plan to check items more valuable than the standard liability, see if your valuables are covered by your homeowner's policy, get baggage insurance as part of your comprehensive travel-insurance package, or buy Travel Guard's "BagTrak" product (www.travelguard.com). Don't buy insurance at the airport, as it's usually overpriced. Be sure to take any valuables or irreplaceable items with you in your carry-on luggage, as many valuables (including books, money, and electronics) aren't covered by airline policies.

If your luggage is lost, immediately file a lost-luggage claim at the airport, detailing the luggage contents. For most airlines, you must report delayed, damaged, or lost baggage within 4 hours of arrival. The airlines are required to deliver luggage, once found, directly to your house or destination free of charge.

6 Health & Safety

STAYING HEALTHY

Utah's extremes of climate—from burning desert to snow-covered mountains—can cause health problems if you're not prepared. If you haven't been to the desert before, the heat, dryness, and intensity of the sun can be difficult to comprehend. Bring a high-SPF sunblock, a hat, sunglasses with full ultraviolet protection, and moisturizing lotion for dry skin. Hikers and others planning to be outdoors should carry water—at least a gallon per person, per day.

The other potential problem is elevation. Utah's mountains rise to over 13,500 feet—there's less oxygen and lower humidity when you're up that high. This creates a unique set of problems for short-term visitors. If you have heart or respiratory problems, consult your doctor before planning a trip to the mountains. If you're in generally good health, you don't need to take any special precautions, but you may want to ease into high elevations by changing altitude gradually. Don't fly in from sea level in the morning and plan to be hiking at 10,000-foot Cedar Breaks National Monument that afternoon. Spend a day or two at 4,000- or 5,000-feet elevation to let your body adjust. Also, get lots of rest, avoid large meals, and drink plenty of nonalcoholic fluids, especially water.

State health officials have lately been warning outdoor enthusiasts to take precautions against the Hantavirus, a rare but often fatal respiratory disease first recognized in 1993. About half of the country's 200-plus confirmed cases have been reported in the Four Corners states of Colorado, New Mexico, Arizona, and Utah, and about 45% of the cases have been fatal. The disease is usually spread by the urine, feces, and saliva of deer mice and other rodents, and health officials recommend that campers avoid areas with signs of rodent droppings and thoroughly air out tents or cabins before use, especially if they've been unused for a period of time. Symptoms of Hantavirus are similar to flu, and lead to breathing difficulties and shock.

WHAT TO DO IF YOU GET SICK AWAY FROM HOME

In most cases, your existing health plan will provide the coverage you need. But double-check; you may want to buy **travel medical insurance** instead. (See the section on insurance, above.) Bring your insurance ID card with you when you travel.

If you suffer from a chronic illness, consult your doctor before your departure. For conditions like epilepsy, diabetes, or heart problems, wear a **Medic Alert Identification**

Tag (© **800/825-3785**; www.medic alert.org), which will immediately alert doctors to your condition and give them access to your records through Medic Alert's 24-hour hotline.

Pack **prescription medications** in your carry-on luggage, and carry prescription medications in their original containers, with pharmacy labels—otherwise they won't make it through airport security. Also bring along copies of your prescriptions in case you lose your pills or run out. Don't forget an extra pair of contact lenses or prescription glasses.

If you get sick, consider asking your hotel concierge to recommend a local doctor—even his or her own. You can also try the emergency room at a local hospital; many have walk-in clinics for emergency cases that are not life-threatening. You may not get immediate attention, but you won't pay the high price of an emergency room visit.

STAYING SAFE

While there are many reasons to visit Utah, the two cited most often are visiting historic sites and exploring the magnificent outdoors—especially the five national parks. However, visiting historic sites and participating in outdoor activities can lead to accidents.

When visiting such historic sites as ghost towns, gold mines, and railroads, keep in mind that they were probably built more than 100 years ago, at a time when safety standards were extremely lax, if they existed at all. Never enter abandoned buildings, mines, or railroad equipment on your own. When you're visiting commercially operated historic tourist attractions, use common sense and don't be afraid to ask questions.

Walkways in mines are often uneven and poorly lit, and are sometimes slippery due to seeping groundwater that can also stain your clothing with its high iron content. In old buildings, be prepared for steep, narrow stairways, creaky floors, and low ceilings and doorways. Steam trains are a wonderful experience as long as you remember that steam is very hot, oil and grease can ruin your clothing, and at the very least, soot will make you very dirty.

As you head into the great outdoors, keep in mind that injuries often occur when people fail to follow instructions. Pay attention when the experts tell you to stay on established ski trails, hike only in designated areas and carry rain gear, and wear a life jacket when rafting. Mountain weather can be fickle, and many of the most beautiful spots are in remote areas. Be prepared for extreme changes in temperature at any time of year, and watch out for those sudden summer afternoon thunderstorms that can leave you drenched and shivering in minutes.

7 Specialized Travel Resources

TRAVELERS WITH DISABILITIES

Travelers with disabilities should find Utah a generally easy place to get around. Many state and national parks have at least one wheelchair-accessible trail. Some historic buildings, however, are not wheelchair accessible—check before going.

The **National Park Service** issues free **Golden Access Passports** to U.S. citizens or permanent residents who are medically certified as permanently disabled or blind, regardless of age. This lifetime pass, issued at all parks, permits free entry (but doesn't cover user fees) and gives a 50% discount on park-service campgrounds and activities (but not on those offered by private concessionaires). For more information, go to www.nps.gov/fees_passes.htm or call © **888/467-2757**.

The Utah information and referral line for people with disabilities is ©️ **800/333-8824.**

Amtrak will, with 24 hours notice, provide porter service, special seating, and a discount (©️ **800/USA-RAIL**). If you're traveling with a companion, **Greyhound** will carry you both for a single fare (©️ **800/231-2222**).

Many travel agencies offer customized tours and itineraries for travelers with disabilities. **Flying Wheels Travel** (©️ **507/451-5005;** www. flyingwheelstravel.com) offers escorted tours and cruises that emphasize sports and private tours in minivans with lifts. **Accessible Journeys** (©️ **800/846-4537** or 610/521-0339; www.disabilitytravel.com) caters specifically to slow walkers and wheelchair travelers and their families and friends.

Organizations that offer assistance to disabled travelers include **MossRehab** (www.mossresourcenet.org), which provides a library of accessible-travel resources online; the **Society for Accessible Travel and Hospitality** (©️ **212/447-7284;** www.sath.org; annual membership fees: $45 adults, $30 seniors and students), which offers a wealth of travel resources for people with all types of disabilities and informed recommendations on destinations, access guides, travel agents, tour operators, vehicle rentals, and companion services; and the **American Foundation for the Blind** (©️ **800/232-5463;** www.afb.org), which provides information on traveling with Seeing Eye dogs.

For more information specifically targeted to travelers with disabilities, the community website **iCan** (www. icanonline.net/channels/travel/index.c fm) has destination guides and several regular columns on accessible travel. Also check out the quarterly magazine *Emerging Horizons* ($14.95 per year, $19.95 outside the U.S.; www. emerginghorizons.com); **Twin Peaks**

Press (©️ **360/694-2462;** http:// disabilitybookshop.virtualave.net/blist 84.htm), offering travel-related books for travelers with special needs; and *Open World Magazine,* published by the Society for Accessible Travel and Hospitality (see above; subscription: $18 per year, $35 outside the U.S.).

GAY & LESBIAN TRAVELERS

Utah is a conservative state, and residents generally don't approve of homosexuality; in fact many members of the Church of Jesus Christ of Latter-day Saints believe that it's a sin. However, Utah residents also have a firm belief in personal freedom, and will generally grant gay and lesbian travelers the same treatment as any other travelers in Utah.

The **Gay & Lesbian Community Center of Utah,** 361 N. 300 West, in Salt Lake City (©️ **888/874-2743** or 801/539-8800; www.glccu.com), is a community center, coffeehouse, and information distribution point for gays and lesbians.

The **International Gay & Lesbian Travel Association (IGLTA)** (©️ **800/ 448-8550** or 954/776-2626; www. iglta.org) is the trade association for the gay and lesbian travel industry, and offers an online directory of gay- and lesbian-friendly travel businesses; go to their website and click on "Members."

Many agencies offer tours and travel itineraries specifically for gay and lesbian travelers. **Above and Beyond Tours** (©️ **800/397-2681;** www.abovebeyondtours.com) is the exclusive gay and lesbian tour operator for United Airlines. **Now, Voyager** (©️ **800/255-6951;** www.nowvoyager. com) is a well-known San Francisco–based gay-owned and operated travel service.

SENIOR TRAVEL

Many Utah hotels and motels offer senior discounts, and more and more restaurants, attractions, and public transportation systems are now offering special rates as well. Mention the fact that you're a senior citizen when you make your travel reservations.

Members of **AARP** (formerly known as the American Association of Retired Persons), 601 E St. NW, Washington, DC 20049 (© **800/424-3410** or 202/434-2277; www.aarp.org), get discounts on hotels, airfares, and car rentals. AARP offers members a wide range of benefits, including *AARP: The Magazine* and a monthly newsletter. Anyone over 50 can join.

The **U.S. National Park Service** offers a **Golden Age Passport** that gives seniors 62 years or older lifetime entrance to all properties administered by the National Park Service—national parks, monuments, historic sites, recreation areas, and national wildlife refuges—for a one-time processing fee of $10, which must be purchased in person at any NPS facility that charges an entrance fee. Besides free entry, a Golden Age Passport also offers a 50% discount on federal-use fees charged for such facilities as camping, swimming, parking, boat launching, and tours. For more information, go to www.nps.gov/fees_passes.htm or call © **888/467-2757.**

Many reliable agencies and organizations target the 50-plus market. **Elderhostel** (© **877/426-8056;** www.elderhostel.org) arranges study programs for those aged 55 and over (and a spouse or companion of any age) in the U.S. and in more than 80 countries around the world. Most courses last 5 to 7 days in the U.S. (2–4 weeks abroad), and many include airfare, accommodations in university dormitories or modest inns, meals, and tuition. **ElderTreks** (© **800/741-7956;** www.eldertreks.com) offers small-group tours to off-the-beaten-path or adventure-travel locations, restricted to travelers 50 and older.

Recommended publications offering travel resources and discounts for seniors include: the quarterly magazine *Travel 50 & Beyond* (www.travel50andbeyond.com); *Travel Unlimited: Uncommon Adventures for the Mature Traveler* (Avalon); *101 Tips for Mature Travelers,* available from Grand Circle Travel (© **800/221-2610** or 617/350-7500; www.gct.com); *The 50+ Traveler's Guidebook* (St. Martin's Press); and *Unbelievably Good Deals and Great Adventures That You Absolutely Can't Get Unless You're Over 50* (McGraw-Hill).

FAMILY TRAVEL

The family vacation is a rite of passage for many households, one that in a split second can devolve into a *National Lampoon* farce. But as any veteran family vacationer will assure you, a family trip can be among the most pleasurable and rewarding times of your life.

Utah is a very family-friendly state, due in large part to the great influence of the Church of Jesus Christ of Latter-day Saints, which is totally family-oriented. Many tourist attractions offer family prices that are considerably lower than the per person rate, and also frequently schedule family-specific events. Throughout this book, you'll find numerous attractions, lodgings, and even restaurants that are especially well-suited to kids.

Additionally, state and national parks are great places for family vacations, and the national parks usually have excellent children's programs (be sure to ask about Junior Ranger programs). The state's many ski resorts all have special programs for kids.

Familyhostel (© **800/733-9753;** www.learn.unh.edu/familyhostel) takes the whole family, including kids ages 8 to 15, on moderately priced domestic and international learning vacations. Lectures, field trips, and sightseeing are guided by a team of academics.

You can find good family-oriented vacation advice on the Internet from sites like the **Family Travel Network** (www.familytravelnetwork.com), and **Family Travel Files** (www.thefamily-travelfiles.com), which offers an online magazine and a directory of off-the-beaten-path tours and tour operators for families.

FOR STUDENTS

You can garner savings on entrance fees and transportation with the **International Student Identity Card (ISIC)**. It also provides you with basic health and life insurance and a 24-hour help line. The card is available for $22 from **STA Travel** (© **800/781-4040,** and if you're not in North America there's probably a local number in your country; www.statravel.com), the biggest student travel agency in the world. If you're no longer a student but are still under 26, you can get an **International Youth Travel Card (IYTC)** for the same price from the same people, which entitles you to some discounts (but not on museum admissions). (*Note:* In 2002, STA Travel bought competitors **Council Travel** and **USIT Campus** after they went bankrupt. It's still operating some offices under the Council name, but they are owned by STA.)

Travel **CUTS** (© **800/667-2887** or 416/614-2887; www.travelcuts. com) offers student ID cards, discount fares on transportation, and other student-friendly services for both Canadians and US residents. Irish students should turn to **USIT** (© **01/602-1600;** www.usitnow.ie) for these services.

TRAVELING WITH PETS

Many of us wouldn't dream of going on vacation without our pets. Under the right circumstances, it can be a wonderful experience for both you and your animals. Dogs and cats are accepted at many motels around the state, but not as universally in resorts or at the more expensive hotels. Throughout this book, we've tried to consistently note those lodgings that take pets. Some properties require you to pay a fee or damage deposit in advance, and most insist they be notified at check-in that you have a pet.

An excellent resource is **www. petswelcome.com,** which dispenses medical tips, names of animal-friendly lodgings and campgrounds, and lists of kennels and veterinarians. Also check out *The Portable Petswelcome. com: The Complete Guide to Traveling with Your Pet* (Howell Book House), which features the best selection of pet travel information anywhere. Another resource is *Pets-R-Permitted Hotel, Motel & Kennel Directory: The Travel Resource for Pet Owners Who Travel* (Annenberg Communications).

Be aware that **national parks and monuments** and other federal lands administered by the National Park Service are not pet-friendly. Dogs are prohibited on all hiking trails, must always be leashed, and in some cases cannot be taken more than 100 feet from established roads. On the other hand, **U.S. Forest Service and BLM** areas, as well as practically all of Utah's **state parks,** are pro-pet, allowing dogs on trails and just about everywhere except inside buildings.

Aside from regulations, be attentive to your **pet's well-being.** Just as people need extra water in Utah's hot, dry climate, so do pets. We particularly like those clever non-spill travel water bowls sold in pet stores. And keep in mind that, particularly in southern Utah's red rock country, trails are rough, and jagged rocks can cut the pads on your dog's feet. It's a good idea to check your pet's feet frequently and to carry tweezers to remove cactus spines. Remember, too, that dogs, who usually spend most of their time sleeping, aren't used to 10-hour hikes

Tips The Peripatetic Pet

There is no punishment too severe for the human who leaves a pet inside a parked car with the windows rolled up. The car heats up faster than you'd suspect, so don't do it, even for a minute. In fact, it's a good idea never to leave a pet inside a hot car even with the windows rolled down for any length of time.

Make sure your pet is wearing a name tag with the name and phone number of a contact person who can take the call if your pet gets lost while you're away from home.

---

up mountainsides, and more than one exhausted pooch has had to be carried back to camp by its owner.

If you plan to **fly with your pet,** the FAA has compiled a list of all requirements for transporting live animals at http://airconsumer.ost.dot. gov/publications/animals.htm. You may be able to carry your pet on board a plane if it is small enough to put inside a carrier that can slip under the seat. Pets usually count as one piece of carry-on luggage. Note that summer may not be the best time to fly with

your pet: Many airlines will not check pets as baggage in the hot summer months. The ASPCA discourages travelers from checking pets as luggage at any time, as storage conditions on planes are loosely monitored, and fatal accidents are not unprecedented. Your other option is to ship your pet with a professional carrier, which can be expensive. Ask your veterinarian whether you should sedate your pet on a plane ride or give it anti-nausea medication. Never give your pet sedatives used by humans.

8 Planning Your Trip Online

SURFING FOR AIRFARES

The "big three" online travel agencies, **Expedia.com**, **Travelocity.com**, and **Orbitz.com** sell most of the air tickets bought on the Internet. (Canadian travelers should try expedia.ca and Travelocity.ca; U.K. residents can go for expedia.co.uk and opodo.co.uk.) Each has different business deals with the airlines and may offer different fares on the same flights, so it's wise to shop around. Expedia and Travelocity will also send you **e-mail notification** when a cheap fare becomes available to your favorite destination. Of the smaller travel agency websites, **Side-Step** (www.sidestep.com) has gotten the best reviews from Frommer's authors. It's a browser add-on that purports to "search 140 sites at once," but in reality only beats competitors' fares as often as other sites do.

Also remember to check **airline websites,** especially those for low-fare carriers such as Southwest, JetBlue, AirTran, WestJet, or Ryanair, whose fares are often misreported or simply missing from travel agency websites. Even with major airlines, you can often shave a few bucks from a fare by booking directly through the airline and avoiding a travel agency's transaction fee. But you'll get these discounts only by **booking online:** Most airlines now offer online-only fares that even their phone agents know nothing about. For the websites of airlines that fly to and from your destination, go to "Getting There," below.

Great **last-minute deals** are available through free weekly e-mail services provided directly by the airlines. Most of these are announced on Tuesday or Wednesday and must be purchased online. Most are only valid for travel that weekend, but some (such as Southwest's) can be booked weeks or months in advance. Sign up for weekly e-mail alerts at airline websites or check mega-sites that compile comprehensive lists of last-minute specials, such as **Smarter Living** (smarterliving.com). For last-minute trips, **site59.com** in the U.S. and **last-minute.com** in Europe often have better deals than the major-label sites.

If you're willing to give up some control over your flight details, use an **opaque fare service** like **Priceline** (www.priceline.com; www.priceline.co.uk for Europeans) or **Hotwire** (www.hotwire.com). Both offer rock-bottom prices in exchange for travel on a "mystery airline" at a mysterious time of day, often with a mysterious change of planes en route. The mystery airlines are all major, well-known carriers—and the possibility of being sent from Philadelphia to Chicago via Tampa is remote; the airlines' routing computers have gotten a lot better than they used to be. But your chances of getting a 6am or 11pm flight are pretty high. Hotwire tells you flight prices before you buy;

Priceline usually has better deals than Hotwire, but you have to play their "name our price" game. If you're new at this, the helpful folks at **Bidding-ForTravel** (www.biddingfortravel.com) do a good job of demystifying Priceline's prices. Priceline and Hotwire are great for flights within North America and between the U.S. and Europe. But for flights to other parts of the world, consolidators will almost always beat their fares.

For much more about airfares and savvy air-travel tips and advice, pick up a copy of *Frommer's Fly Safe, Fly Smart* (Wiley Publishing, Inc.).

SURFING FOR HOTELS

Shopping online for hotels is much easier in the U.S., Canada, and certain parts of Europe than it is in the rest of the world. If you try to book a Chinese hotel online, for instance, you'll probably overpay. Also, many smaller hotels and B&Bs—especially outside the U.S.—don't show up on websites at all. Of the "big three" sites, **Expedia** may be the best choice, thanks to its long list of special deals. **Travelocity** runs a close second. Hotel specialist sites **hotels.com** and **hoteldiscounts.**

Frommers.com: The Complete Travel Resource

For an excellent travel-planning resource, we highly recommend **Frommers.com** (www.frommers.com). We're a little biased, of course, but we guarantee that you'll find the travel tips, reviews, monthly vacation giveaways, and online-booking capabilities thoroughly indispensable. Among the special features are our popular **Message Boards,** where Frommer's readers post queries and share advice (sometimes even our authors show up to answer questions); **Frommers.com Newsletter,** for the latest travel bargains and insider travel secrets; and **Frommer's Destinations Section,** where you'll get expert travel tips, hotel and dining recommendations, and advice on the sights to see for more than 3,000 destinations around the globe. When your research is done, the **Online Reservations System** (www.frommers.com/book_a_trip) takes you to Frommer's preferred online partners for booking your vacation at affordable prices.

com are also reliable. An excellent free program, **TravelAxe** (www.travelaxe. net), can help you search multiple hotel sites at once, even ones you may never have heard of.

Priceline and Hotwire are even better for hotels than for airfares; with both, you're allowed to pick the neighborhood and quality level of your hotel before offering up your money. Priceline's hotel product even covers Europe and Asia, though it's much better at getting five-star lodging for three-star prices than at finding anything at the bottom of the scale.

Note: Hotwire overrates its hotels by one star—what Hotwire calls a four-star is a three-star anywhere else.

SURFING FOR RENTAL CARS

For booking rental cars online, the best deals are usually found at rental-car company websites, although all the major online travel agencies also offer rental-car reservations services. Priceline and Hotwire work well for rental cars, too; the only "mystery" is which major rental company you get, and for most travelers the difference between Hertz, Avis, and Budget is negligible.

9 The 21st-Century Traveler

Travelers have any number of ways to check their e-mail and access the Internet on the road. Of course, using your own laptop—or even a PDA (personal digital assistant) or electronic organizer with a modem—gives you the most flexibility. But even if you don't have a computer, you can still access your e-mail and even your office computer from cybercafes.

WITHOUT YOUR OWN COMPUTER

It's hard nowadays to find a city that *doesn't* have a few cybercafes. Although there's no definitive directory for cybercafes—these are independent businesses, after all—three places to start looking are at **www.cybercaptive. com**, **www.netcafeguide.com**, and **www.cybercafe.com**.

Aside from formal cybercafes, most **youth hostels** nowadays have at least one computer you can get to the Internet on. And most **public libraries** across the world offer Internet access free or for a small charge. Avoid **hotel business centers,** which often charge exorbitant rates.

Most major airports now have **Internet kiosks** scattered throughout their gates. These kiosks, which you'll also see in shopping malls, hotel lobbies, and tourist information offices

around the world, give you basic Web access for a per-minute fee that's usually higher than cybercafe prices. The kiosks' clunkiness and high price means they should be avoided whenever possible.

To retrieve your e-mail, ask your **Internet Service Provider (ISP)** if it has a Web-based interface tied to your existing e-mail account. If your ISP doesn't have such an interface, you can use the free **mail2web** service (www. mail2web.com) to view and reply to your home e-mail. For more flexibility, you may want to open a free, Web-based e-mail account with **Yahoo! Mail** (http://mail.yahoo.com). (Microsoft's Hotmail is another popular option, but Hotmail has severe spam problems.) Your home ISP may be able to forward your e-mail to the Web-based account automatically.

If you need to access files on your office computer, look into a service called **GoToMyPC** (www.gotomypc. com). The service provides a Web-based interface for you to access and manipulate a distant PC from anywhere—even a cybercafe—provided your "target" PC is on and has an always-on connection to the Internet (such as with Road Runner cable). The service offers top-quality security, but if you're worried about hackers, use your own laptop rather than a cybercafe to access the GoToMyPC system.

WITH YOUR OWN COMPUTER

Major Internet Service Providers (ISP) have **local access numbers** around the world, allowing you to go online by simply placing a local call. Check your ISP's website or call its toll-free number and ask how you can use your current account away from home, and how much it will cost.

If you're traveling outside the reach of your ISP, the **iPass** network has dial-up numbers in most of the world's countries. You'll have to sign up with an iPass provider, who will then tell you how to set up your computer for your destination(s). For a list of iPass providers, go to www.ipass. com and click on "Reseller Locator." Under "Select a Country" pick the country that you're coming from, and under "Who is this service for?" pick "Individual". One solid provider is **i2roam** (www.i2roam.com; © **866/ 811-6209** or 920/235-0475).

Wherever you go, bring a **connection kit** of the right power and phone adapters, a spare phone cord, and a spare Ethernet network cable.

Most business-class hotels throughout the world offer dataports for laptop modems, and a few thousand hotels in the U.S. and Europe now offer high-speed Internet access using an Ethernet network cable. You'll have to bring your own cables either way, so **call your hotel in advance** to find out what the options are.

Many business-class hotels in the U.S. also offer a form of computer-free Web browsing through the room TV set. We've successfully checked Yahoo! Mail and Hotmail on these systems.

If you have an 802.11b/**Wi-fi** card for your computer, several commercial companies have made wireless service available in airports, hotel lobbies, and coffee shops, primarily in the U.S. **T-Mobile Hotspot** (www.t-mobile. com/hotspot) serves up wireless connections at more than 1,000 Starbucks coffee shops nationwide. **Boingo** (www.boingo.com) and **Wayport** (www.wayport.com) have set up networks in airports and high-class hotel lobbies. IPass providers (see above) also give you access to a few hundred wireless hotel lobby setups. Best of all, you don't need to be staying at the Four Seasons to use the hotel's network; just set yourself up on a nice couch in the lobby. Unfortunately, the companies' pricing policies are byzantine, with a variety of monthly, per-connection, and per-minute plans.

Community-minded individuals have also set up **free wireless networks** in major cities around the world. These networks are spotty, but you get what you (don't) pay for. Each network has a home page explaining how to set up your computer for their particular system; start your explorations at www.personaltelco.net/ index.cgi/WirelessCommunities.

USING A CELLPHONE ACROSS THE U.S.

Just because your cellphone works at home doesn't mean it'll work elsewhere in the country (thanks to our nation's fragmented cellphone system). It's a good bet that your phone will work in major cities. But take a look at your wireless company's coverage map on its website before heading out—T-Mobile, Sprint, and Nextel are particularly weak in rural areas. If you need to stay in touch at a destination where you know your phone won't work, **rent** a phone that does from **InTouch USA** (© **800/872- 7626;** www.intouchglobal.com) or a rental car location, but beware that you'll pay $1 a minute or more for airtime.

Online Traveler's Toolbox

Veteran travelers usually carry some essential items to make their trips easier. Following is a selection of online tools to bookmark and use.

- **Visa ATM Locator** (www.visa.com), for locations of PLUS ATMs worldwide, or **MasterCard ATM Locator** (www.mastercard.com), for locations of Cirrus ATMs worldwide.
- **Intellicast** (www.intellicast.com) and **Weather.com** (www.weather. com). Both give weather forecasts for all 50 states and for cities around the world.
- **Mapquest** (www.mapquest.com). This best of the mapping sites lets you choose a specific address or destination, and in seconds, it will return a map and detailed directions.

If you're venturing deep into national parks, you may want to consider renting a **satellite phone ("satphones"),** which are different from cellphones in that they connect to satellites rather than ground-based towers. A satphone is more costly than a cellphone but works where there's no cellular signal and no towers. Unfortunately, you'll pay at least $2 per minute to use the phone, and it only works where you can see the horizon (i.e., usually not indoors). In North America, you can rent Iridium satellite phones from **RoadPost** (www.road post.com; ℂ **888/290-1606** or 905/ 272-5665). InTouch USA (see above) offers a wider range of satphones but at higher rates. As of this writing, satphones were amazingly expensive to buy, so don't even think about it.

If you're not from the U.S., you'll be appalled at the poor reach of our GSM (Global System for Mobiles) wireless network, which is used by much of the rest of the world (see below). Your phone will probably work in most major U.S. cities; it definitely won't work in many rural areas. (To see where GSM phones work in the U.S., check out www.t-mobile. com/coverage/national_popup.asp.) And you may or may not be able to send SMS (text messaging) home— something Americans tend not to do anyway, for various cultural and technological reasons. (International budget travelers like to send text messages home because it's much cheaper than making international calls.) Assume nothing—call your wireless provider and get the full scoop. In a worst-case scenario, you can always rent a phone; InTouch USA delivers to hotels.

10 Getting There

BY PLANE

Utah's only major airport is **Salt Lake City International Airport** (℃ 801/ 575-2400; www.slcairport.com); direct service is available from many cities in the United States and Canada. Airlines serving the airport include

American (℃ 800/433-7300; www. americanair.com), **America West** (℃ 800/235-9292; www.america west.com), **Continental** (℃ 800/ 525-0280; www.flycontinental.com), **Delta** (℃ 800/221-1212; www.delta. com), **Frontier** (℃ 800/432-1359;

www.flyfrontier.com), **Northwest** (© 800/225-2525; www.nwa.com), **Southwest** (© 800/435-9792; www. iflyswa.com), **SkyWest** (© 800/453-9417; www.skywest.com); and **United** (© 800/241-6522; www.ual.com). In-state flights connect Salt Lake City to several other Utah cities, including Cedar City, Moab, St. George, and Vernal. See the relevant sections in this book for additional information.

An alternative for visitors planning to go to southern Utah is to fly into **McCarran International Airport** (© 702/261-5211; www.mccarran. com) in Las Vegas, Nevada, which is only 120 miles southwest of St. George. Budget-conscious travelers should check airline and vehicle-rental prices at both airports to see which will provide the better deal for their particular circumstances.

GETTING THROUGH THE AIRPORT

With the federalization of airport security, security procedures at U.S. airports are more stable and consistent than ever. Generally, you'll be fine if you arrive at the airport **1 hour** before a domestic flight and **2 hours** before an international flight; if you show up late, tell an airline employee who will probably whisk you to the front of the line.

Bring a **current, government-issued photo ID** such as a driver's license or passport. Keep your ID at the ready to show at check-in, the security checkpoint, and sometimes even the gate. (Children under 18 do not need photo IDs for domestic flights, but the adults checking in with them should have them.)

In 2003, the TSA phased out **gate check-in** at all U.S. airports. Passengers with E-tickets can still beat the ticket-counter lines by using **electronic kiosks** or even **online check-in.** Ask your airline which alternatives are available, and if you're using a

kiosk, bring the credit card you used to book the ticket or your frequent-flier card. If you're checking bags or looking to snag an exit-row seat, you will be able to do so using most airlines' kiosks; again, call your airline for up-to-date information. **Curbside check-in** is also a good way to avoid lines, although a few airlines still ban curbside check-in; call before you go.

Security checkpoint lines are getting shorter than they were during 2001 and 2002, but some doozies remain. If you have trouble standing for long periods of time, tell an airline employee; the airline will provide a wheelchair. Speed up security by **not wearing metal objects** such as big belt buckles. If you've got metallic body parts, a note from your doctor can prevent a long chat with the security screeners. Keep in mind that only **ticketed passengers** are allowed past security, except for folks escorting disabled passengers or children.

Federalization has stabilized **what you can carry on** and **what you can't.** The general rule is that sharp things are out, nail clippers are okay, and food and beverages must be passed through the X-ray machine—but that security screeners can't make you drink from your coffee cup. Bring food in your carry-on rather than checking it, as explosive-detection machines used on checked luggage have been known to mistake food (especially chocolate, for some reason) for bombs. Travelers in the U.S. are allowed one carry-on bag, plus a "personal item" such as a purse, briefcase, or laptop bag. Carry-on hoarders can stuff all sorts of things into a laptop bag; as long as it has a laptop in it, it's still considered a personal item. The Transportation Security Administration (TSA) has issued a list of restricted items; check its website (www.tsa.gov) for details.

At press time, the TSA is also recommending that you **not lock your** checked luggage so screeners can search it by hand if necessary. The agency says to use plastic "zip ties" instead, which can be bought at hardware stores and can be easily cut off.

FLYING FOR LESS: TIPS FOR GETTING THE BEST AIRFARE

Passengers sharing the same airplane cabin rarely pay the same fare. Travelers who need to purchase tickets at the last minute, change their itinerary at a moment's notice, or fly one-way often get stuck paying the premium rate. Here are some ways to keep your airfare costs down:

- Passengers who can book their tickets **long in advance,** who can **stay over Saturday night,** or who **fly midweek** or **at less-trafficked hours** will pay a fraction of the full fare. If your schedule is flexible, say so, and ask if you can secure a cheaper fare by changing your flight plans.
- You can also save on airfares by keeping an eye out in local newspapers for **promotional specials** or **fare wars,** when airlines lower prices on their most popular routes. You rarely see fare wars offered for peak travel times, but if you can travel in the off-months, you may snag a bargain.
- Search **the Internet** for cheap fares (see "Planning Your Trip Online").
- Join **frequent-flier clubs.** Accrue enough miles, and you'll be rewarded with free flights and elite status. It's free, and you'll get the best choice of seats, faster response to phone inquiries, and prompter service if your luggage is stolen, your flight is canceled or delayed, or if you want to change your seat. You don't need to fly to build frequent-flier miles—**frequent-flier credit cards** can provide thousands of miles for doing your everyday shopping.
- For many more tips about air travel, including a rundown of the major frequent-flier credit cards, pick up a copy of *Frommer's Fly Safe, Fly Smart* (Wiley Publishing, Inc.).

BY CAR

About 80% of Utah's visitors arrive by private motor vehicle, in part because it's so easy: The state is accessed by **I-80** from the west or east, **I-70** from the east, **I-15** and **I-84** from the north, and **I-15** from the southwest. Salt Lake City is 600 miles from Albuquerque, 500 miles from Denver, 430 miles from Las Vegas, and 650 miles from Phoenix. Keep in mind that

---

Tips **Travel in the Age of Bankruptcy**

At press time, several major U.S. airlines were struggling in bankruptcy court and most of the rest weren't doing very well either. To protect yourself, **buy your tickets with a credit card,** as the Fair Credit Billing Act guarantees that you can get your money back from the credit card company if a travel supplier goes under (and if you request the refund within 60 days of the bankruptcy). **Travel insurance** can also help, but make sure it covers against "carrier default" for your specific travel provider. And be aware that if a U.S. airline goes bust mid-trip, a 2001 federal law requires other carriers to take you to your destination (albeit on a space-available basis) for a fee of no more than $25, provided you rebook within 60 days of the cancellation.

there will be long distances between services approaching Utah from any direction, as well as within the state.

Before you set out on a road trip, you might want to join the **American Automobile Association (AAA)** (© **800/222-4357;** www.csaa.com for Northern California, Nevada, and Utah information), which has hundreds of offices nationwide. The Salt Lake City office is located at 560 E. 500 South (© **800/541-9902** or 801/364-5615), and is open Monday through Friday from 8:30am to 5:30pm. AAA also has offices in Ogden (© **801/476-1666**), Orem (© **801/225-4801**), and St. George (© **435/656-3990**). Members receive excellent maps and emergency road service; AAA will even help you plan an exact itinerary.

BY TRAIN

Amtrak's *California Zephyr* stops in several Utah towns, including Salt Lake City, on its run between Chicago and San Francisco. You can get a copy of Amtrak's national timetable from any Amtrak station or your travel agent, or by contacting Amtrak (© **800/USA-RAIL;** www.amtrak. com). Also request a brochure outlining prices, and be sure to ask about any money-saving promotions Amtrak may be offering.

11 Packages for the Independent Traveler

Before you start your search for the lowest airfare, you may want to consider booking your flight as part of a travel package. Package tours are not the same thing as escorted tours. Package tours are simply a way to buy the airfare, accommodations, and other elements of your trip (such as car rentals, airport transfers, and sometimes even activities) at the same time and often at discounted prices—kind of like one-stop shopping. Packages are sold in bulk to tour operators—who resell them to the public at a cost that usually undercuts standard rates.

Gray Line Motor Tours, 3359 S. Main St., Suite 804, Salt Lake City, UT 84115 (© **800/309-2352** or 801/534-1001; www.grayline.com), offers several tours of Salt Lake City and the surrounding area.

American Orient Express, 5100 Main St., Suite 300, Downers Grove, IL 60515 (© **877/854-3545** or 630/663-4550; www.americanorient express.com), offers vintage train cars outfitted in polished mahogany and brass, plus dining cars decked out with china, silver, crystal, and linen, with cuisine to match. It offers a variety of tours, several of which include jaunts through Utah.

Well-respected national companies that offer tours to Utah's national parks and other destinations include **Maupintour** (© **800/255-4266;** www. maupintour.com) and **Tauck Tours** (© **800/788-7885;** www.tauck.com).

A number of companies also offer specialized tours for outdoor-recreation enthusiasts. See chapter 4 for details.

One good source of package deals is the airlines themselves. Most major airlines offer air/land packages, including **American Airlines Vacations** (© 800/321-2121; www.aa vacations.com), **Delta Vacations** (© 800/221-6666; www.delta vacations.com), **Continental Airlines Vacations** (© 800/301-3800; www. coolvacations.com), and **United Vacations** (© 888/854-3899; www. unitedvacations.com). Several big **online travel agencies**—Expedia, Travelocity, Orbitz, Site59, and Lastminute.com—also do a brisk business in packages. If you're unsure about the pedigree of a smaller packager, check with the Better Business Bureau in the city where the company is based, or go online at www.bbb.org. If a packager won't tell you where it's based, don't fly with them.

Travel packages are also listed in the travel section of your local Sunday newspaper. Or check ads in the national travel magazines such as *Arthur Frommer's Budget Travel Magazine, Travel & Leisure, National Geographic Traveler,* and *Condé Nast Traveler.*

Package tours can vary by leaps and bounds. Some offer a better class of hotels than others. Some offer the same hotels for lower prices. Some offer flights on scheduled airlines, while others book charters. Some limit your choice of accommodations and travel days. You are often required to make a large payment up front. On the plus side, packages can save you money, offering group prices but allowing for independent travel. Some even let you add on a few guided excursions or escorted day trips (also at prices lower than if you booked them yourself) without booking an entirely escorted tour.

Before you invest in a package tour, get some answers. Ask about the **accommodations choices** and prices for each. Then look up the hotels' reviews in a Frommer's guide and check their rates for your specific dates of travel online.

Finally, look for **hidden expenses.** Ask whether airport departure fees and taxes, for example, are included in the total cost.

12 Escorted General-Interest Tours

Escorted tours are structured group tours, with a group leader. The price usually includes everything from airfare to hotels, meals, tours, admission costs, and local transportation.

Many people derive a certain ease and security from escorted trips. Escorted tours—whether by bus, motor coach, train, or boat—let travelers sit back and enjoy their trip without having to spend lots of time behind the wheel. All the little details are taken care of; you know your costs up front; and there are few surprises. Escorted tours can take you to the maximum number of sights in the minimum amount of time with the least amount of hassle—you don't have to sweat over the plotting and planning of a vacation schedule. Escorted tours are particularly convenient for people with limited mobility.

On the downside, an escorted tour often requires a big deposit up front, and lodging and dining choices are predetermined. As part of a cloud of tourists, you'll get little opportunity for serendipitous interactions with locals. The tours can be jam-packed with activities, leaving little room for individual sightseeing, whim, or adventure—plus they also often focus only on the heavily touristed sites, so you miss out on the lesser-known gems.

Before you invest in an escorted tour, ask about the **cancellation policy:** Is a deposit required? Can they cancel the trip if they don't get enough people? Do you get a refund if they cancel? If *you* cancel? How late can you cancel if you are unable to go? When do you pay in full? *Note:* If you choose an escorted tour, think strongly about purchasing trip-cancellation insurance, especially if the tour operator asks you to pay up front. See the section on "Travel Insurance," earlier in this chapter.

You'll also want to get a complete **schedule** of the trip to find out how much sightseeing is planned each day and whether enough time has been allotted for relaxing or wandering solo.

The **size** of the group is also important to know up front. Generally, the smaller the group, the more flexible the itinerary, and the less time you'll spend waiting for people to get on and off the bus. Find out the **demographics** of the group as well. What is the age range? What is the gender breakdown? Is this mostly a trip for couples or singles?

Discuss what is included in the **price.** You may have to pay for transportation to and from the airport. A box lunch may be included in an excursion, but drinks might cost extra. Tips may not be included. Find out if you will be charged if you decide to opt out of certain activities or meals.

Before you invest in a package tour, get some answers. Ask about the **accommodations choices** and prices for each. Then look up the hotels' reviews in a Frommer's guide and check their rates for your specific dates of travel online.

Finally, if you plan to travel alone, you'll need to know if a **single supplement** will be charged and if the company can match you up with a roommate.

13 Getting Around

BY CAR

Driving yourself is the best way to get around Utah; in fact, it's the only way to get to many destinations. However, visitors who plan to drive their own cars in Utah will find that steep mountain roads can put a severe strain on their vehicles, particularly on the cooling and braking systems. Tires rated for mud and snow are needed in most regions in winter and are required on roads leading to several major ski areas from November through March. Also keep in mind that Utah is a big state; it's a 5-hour drive from Salt Lake City to St. George, and it can easily take 6 or 7 hours to get from St. George to Moab.

CAR-RENTAL AGENCIES Car rentals are available in every sizable town and city in the state, and almost always at local airports. Widely represented agencies include **Advantage** (© 800/777-5500; www.arac.com), **Alamo** (© 800/462-5266; www.goalamo.com), **Avis** (© 800/230-4898; www.avis.com; TTY/TDD 800/331-1212), **Budget** (© 800/527-0700; www.budgetrentacar.com), **Dollar** (© 800/800-4000; www.dollarcar.com), **Hertz** (© 800/654-3131; www.hertz.com), **National** (© 800/227-7368; www.nationalcar.com), and **Thrifty** (© 800/847-4389; www.thrifty.com).

INSURANCE Before you drive off in a rental car, be sure that you're insured. If you already hold a private auto insurance policy, you're most likely covered in the United States for loss of or damage to a rental car, and liability in case of injury to any other party involved in an accident. Be sure to find out whether you are covered in the area you are visiting and whether the type of car you're renting is included under your contract.

Many **major credit cards** provide some degree of coverage as well—provided they were used to pay for the rental. Call your credit-card company for exact terms.

If you are **uninsured,** your credit card may provide primary coverage as long as you decline the rental agency's insurance. This means that the credit card will cover damage or theft of a rental car for the full cost of the vehicle. (In a few states, however, theft is not covered.)

Credit cards will not cover **liability,** or the cost of injury to an outside party

Utah Driving Distances & Times

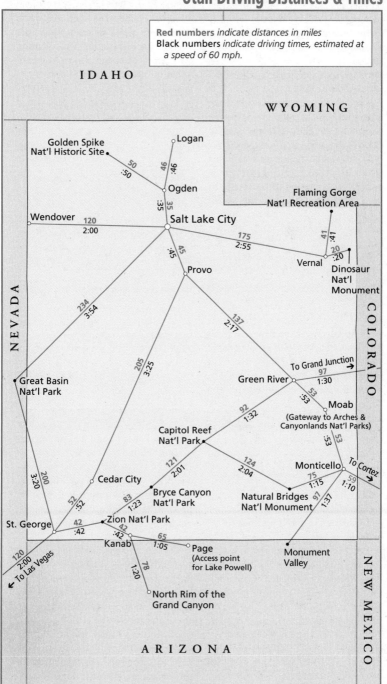

Red numbers *indicate distances in miles*
Black numbers *indicate driving times, estimated at a speed of 60 mph.*

IDAHO

WYOMING

Logan

Golden Spike
Nat'l Historic Site

50
:50

46
:46

Ogden

35
:35

Flaming Gorge
Nat'l Recreation Area

Wendover   120
2:00

Salt Lake City

175
2:55

45
:45

41
:41

20
:20

Provo

Vernal

Dinosaur
Nat'l
Monument

NEVADA

234
3:54

137
2:17

COLORADO

205
3:25

To Grand Junction →
97
1:30

Green River

Great Basin
Nat'l Park

92
1:32

53
:53

Moab
(Gateway to Arches &
Canyonlands Nat'l Parks)

Capitol Reef
Nat'l Park

124
2:04

53
:53

53
:53

200
3:20

121
2:01

Monticello

To Cortez

Cedar City

75
1:15

59
1:10

52
:52

83
1:23

Bryce Canyon
Nat'l Park

Natural Bridges
Nat'l Monument

91
1:37

St. George

42
:42

Zion Nat'l Park

42
:42

65
1:05

Kanab

Page
(Access point
for Lake Powell)

Monument
Valley

120
2:00
← To Las Vegas

78
1:20

North Rim of the
Grand Canyon

NEW MEXICO

ARIZONA

and/or damage to an outside party's vehicle. If you do not hold an insurance policy, you may want to seriously consider purchasing additional liability insurance from your rental company. Be sure to check the terms, however; some agencies only cover liability if the renter is not at fault.

The basic insurance coverage offered by most rental companies, known as the **Loss/Damage Waiver (LDW)** or **Collision Damage Waiver (CDW),** usually covers the full value of the vehicle with no deductible if an outside party causes an accident or other damage to the rental car. Liability coverage varies according to the company policy and state law, but the minimum is usually at least $15,000. If you are at fault in an accident, however, you will be covered for the full replacement value of the car but not for liability.

DRIVING RULES Utah law requires all drivers to carry proof of insurance as well as a valid driver's license. Safety belts are required for drivers and all front-seat passengers; restraints are required for all children under 10, regardless of where they are sitting. Radar detectors are permitted. Children under the age of 2 are required to be in federally approved safety seats. Helmet use is mandatory for motorcyclists and their passengers under the age of 18.

MAPS You can get an official state highway map at State Welcome Centers or by mail (see "Visitor Information," earlier in this chapter). Otherwise, maps are available at bookstores, gas stations, or from the American Automobile Association if you're a member (see "Getting There," earlier in this chapter). **State Welcome Centers** are located along I-15 near Brigham City and St. George, along I-80 near Echo Junction, along I-70 near Thompson Springs, and on U.S. 40 in Jensen (near Vernal).

ROADSIDE ASSISTANCE In case of an accident or road emergency, call 911. American Automobile Association members can get free emergency road service wherever they are, 24 hours a day, by calling AAA's emergency number (© **800/AAA-HELP**). The AAA website is www.aaa.com.

14 Tips on Accommodations

Utah offers a variety of lodging options, from typical American chain motels to luxury hotels—primarily in Salt Lake City, Park City, and Deer Valley, plus delightful bed and breakfasts, rustic cabins, and some pleasant and inexpensive mom-and-pop independent motels.

The chains here are the same ones you see everywhere else in America: Best Western, Comfort, Days Inn, Embassy Suites, Hampton Inn, Hilton, Holiday Inn, Motel 6, Quality Inn, Sheraton, Sleep Inn, Super 8, Travelodge, and so on. They look just about the same as those found elsewhere, and have the same levels of service. In most cases, their rooms are little more than boring boxes of various sizes, with beds and the appropriate plumbing and heating fixtures. If you're lucky, you'll get a decent view out the window. Since quite probably one of the main reasons you've come to Utah is to enjoy the magnificent outdoors, these chains might be just what the doctor ordered.

On the other hand, if you are exploring Temple Square and enjoying the numerous cultural offerings in Salt Lake City, our choice for lodging would be the Inn at Temple Square. At Bryce Canyon National Park, we love to stay in one of their delightful Bryce Lodge cabins. And if you really want to be pampered after a hard day on the slopes, you can't beat the upscale properties at Park City and Deer Valley.

Another option is a B&B. There are numerous bed and breakfast inns discussed in the following pages, and when you take into consideration the delicious breakfasts prepared at most of them, the rates are fairly reasonable. Why spend $90 for a boring motel room and then another $10 to $15 for breakfast when for just a bit more you can instead sleep in a handsome home, often uniquely decorated, and be served a delightful home-cooked breakfast?

Other lodging choices in Utah include cabins and a handful of small independent motels. Both are usually fairly inexpensive, although they often lack the facilities, such as pools, spas, exercise equipment, etc., that you'll find in most chains. We still prefer the cabins and independents, though, because they're often a very good value and the rooms usually have at least some personality (can anybody actually describe the decor of the last Super 8 or Days Inn they stayed at?), and cabins, although sometimes a bit primitive, are often in beautiful settings.

SAVING ON YOUR HOTEL ROOM

The **rack rate** is the maximum rate that a hotel charges for a room. Hardly anybody pays this price, however. To lower the cost of your room:

- **Ask about special rates or other discounts.** Always ask whether a room less expensive than the first one quoted is available, or whether any special rates apply to you. You may qualify for corporate, student, military, senior, or other discounts. Mention membership in AAA, AARP, frequent-flier programs, or trade unions, which may entitle you to special deals as well. Find out the hotel policy on children—do kids stay free in the room or is there a special rate?

- **Dial direct.** When booking a room in a chain hotel, you'll often get a better deal by calling the individual hotel's reservation desk than at the chain's main number.

- **Book online.** Many hotels offer Internet-only discounts, or supply rooms to Priceline, Hotwire, or Expedia at rates much lower than the ones you can get through the hotel itself.

- **Remember the law of supply and demand.** Resort hotels are most crowded and therefore most expensive on weekends, so discounts are usually available for midweek stays. Business hotels in downtown locations are busiest during the week, so you can expect big discounts over the weekend. Many hotels have high-season and low-season prices, and booking the day after "high-season" ends can mean big discounts.

- **Look into group or long-stay discounts.** If you come as part of a large group, you should be able to negotiate a bargain rate, since the hotel can then guarantee occupancy in a number of rooms. Likewise, if you're planning a long stay (at least 5 days), you might qualify for a discount. As a general rule, expect 1 night free after a 7-night stay.

- **Avoid excess charges and hidden costs.** When you book a room, ask whether the hotel charges for parking. Use your own cellphone, pay phones, or prepaid phone cards instead of dialing direct from hotel phones, which usually have exorbitant rates. And don't be tempted by the room's minibar offerings: Most hotels charge through the nose for water, soda, and snacks. Finally, ask about local taxes and service charges, which can increase the cost of a room by 15% or more. If a hotel insists upon tacking on a surprise "energy surcharge" that wasn't mentioned at check-in or a "resort fee" for amenities you didn't use, you can often make a case for getting it removed.

- **Book an efficiency.** A room with a kitchenette allows you to shop for groceries and cook your own meals. This is a big money saver, especially for families on long stays.

LANDING THE BEST ROOM

Somebody has to get the best room in the house. It might as well be you. You can start by joining the hotel's frequent-guest program, which may make you eligible for upgrades. A hotel-branded credit card usually gives it owner "silver" or "gold" status in frequent-guest programs for free.

Always ask about a corner room. They're often larger and quieter, with more windows and light, and they often cost the same as standard rooms. When you make your reservation, ask if the hotel is renovating; if it is, request a room away from the construction. Ask about nonsmoking rooms, rooms with views, and rooms with twin, queen- or king-size beds. If you're a light sleeper, request a quiet room away from vending machines, elevators, restaurants, bars, and discos. Ask for one of the rooms that have been most recently renovated or redecorated.

If you aren't happy with your room when you arrive, say so. If another room is available, most lodgings will be willing to accommodate you.

15 Suggested Itineraries

Although there are many reasons to visit Utah, two of the most popular are to explore its splendid national parks and to see the many temples and tabernacles of the Church of Jesus Christ of Latter-day Saints and related sites in the Salt Lake City and Provo areas.

UTAH'S NATIONAL PARKS

There are five delightful national parks in southern Utah, plus a national recreation area and a national monument. In addition, just over the state line in Arizona is the north rim of the awe-inspiring Grand Canyon. These can be visited in a somewhat circuitous loop of just under 1,000 miles. Allow 10 to 14 days, although 3 weeks would be even better. Also note that sections of this drive may be impassable in winter. You'll find details in chapters 10 through 16.

Start your journey in St. George, in Utah's southwest corner (the closest major airport is in Las Vegas, Nevada). From here, drive north and east to Zion National Park, known for its mammoth natural stone sculptures

and unbelievably narrow slot canyon called The Narrows. Hike a few of the trails and look for hanging gardens along the moist rock walls before continuing east and south to the town of Kanab, a good spot to spend the night before venturing southeast into Arizona and to the North Rim of Grand Canyon National Park, which offers truly awe-inspiring views.

From the Grand Canyon's north rim, head back north and then east to Page, Arizona, for a quick stop—and perhaps a boat ride—at Lake Powell, part of Glen Canyon National Recreation Area. From here, continue east and then south across the Navajo Indian Reservation to Monument Valley Navajo Tribal Park, which straddles the Arizona-Utah state line. On either a self-guided or guided tour you'll see classic western scenery made famous in movies such as 1939's *Stagecoach*, which starred a young John Wayne.

Now continue north to the town of Moab to spend a few days visiting

Arches and Canyonlands national parks, where you'll see spectacular natural arches and other rock formations and have opportunities for hiking, mountain biking, Jeeping, and rafting on and along the Colorado and Green rivers. From Moab, you face a long but mostly scenic drive north, west, south, and then west again to Capitol Reef National Park, one of our favorite parks, where you'll see beautiful, rugged country along with a historic orchard and schoolhouse and some badlands where famed outlaw Butch Cassidy is said to have hidden out between train and bank robberies.

Leaving Capitol Reef, head south on very scenic Utah 12 over Boulder Mountain and through Grand Staircase-Escalante National Monument, possibly stopping for a short hike to Calf Creek Falls before heading on to Bryce Canyon National Park, in our opinion the West's top national park. Spend the night in the park or nearby so you can be on the rim of Bryce Amphitheater at sunrise, the absolute best time to see the colorful and often whimsically-shaped rock formations known as hoodoos. From Bryce Canyon, go west through pretty Red Canyon, then south and west to Cedar Breaks National Monument—a high-altitude smaller version of Bryce Canyon—before going west to Cedar City to pick up I-15 for the drive back to St. George and possibly Las Vegas.

TOUR OF LDS CHURCH SITES

Although the Church of Jesus Christ of Latter-day Saints (LDS) has temples and tabernacles around the world, and especially in Utah, those who want to see the church's grandest structures and learn about its history and/or its beliefs will head to Salt Lake City and nearby Provo. We suggest you spend at least 4 days in Salt Lake City with an additional day for the trip to Provo. Details are in chapters 6 and 8.

Your journey begins at Temple Square, where you can take a free guided tour of the grounds, Assembly Hall, and Tabernacle, with stops at the visitor centers. After the tour, make sure to go to the Beehive House, the family home of early church leader Brigham Young, and stop at the Brigham Young Monument. Nearby, the beautiful Joseph Smith Memorial Building (built as a hotel in 1911) houses church offices and also has a big-screen theater where you can see a film about the early history of the LDS church. Schedule at least a half-day to trace your ancestors at the church's Family History Library and learn a bit about why it is so important to Mormons to know their ancestors. Take a break and wander around the incredible 4 acres of gardens on the roof of the new Conference Center of the Church of Jesus Christ of Latter-day Saints—the views are stupendous.

While in Salt Lake City, you may also want to visit the Museum of Church History and Art, which contains an interesting collection, and also see the exhibits on church leaders and others at the Pioneer Memorial Museum and Utah State Historical Society Museum. Finally, make a pilgrimage to This is the Place Heritage Park, a state park that commemorates the spot where, in 1847, church leader Brigham Young and the first group of pioneers first set eyes on the Salt Lake Valley.

From Salt Lake City, head 45 miles south to Provo to visit Brigham Young University, America's largest church-owned private university. Here you can get a guided tour of the campus, explore the university's museums, and visit another genealogical center. While in the Provo area, be sure to stop at the Crandall Historical Printing Museum. Although not a church property, this museum contains information on the church, including a replica of the printing press used to print the first Book of Mormon in 1830, as well as displays and printing press replicas dating to Gutenberg's mid-1400s press.

From Provo, you can either return to Salt Lake City, or continue south to the state's magnificent red rock country (see "Utah's National Parks," above).

16 Recommended Books & Films

Those planning vacations in Utah can turn to a number of sources for background on the state and its major cities. Western buffs should enjoy Pearl Baker's *The Wild Bunch at Robbers Roost,* about the area in southeastern Utah where Butch Cassidy hung out with the Sundance Kid, among others. A fun publication for movie nuts is *"Where God Put the West": Movie Making in the Desert,* by Bette L. Stanton. It describes Hollywood's invasion of southeastern Utah to create those great John Wayne classics we all grew up on. The photos alone make it worth the purchase price.

If you're intrigued—as we were—by the Mormon religion, look for *What do Mormons Believe?* by Rex E. Lee, an easy-to-read short book; or for a more detailed history, *Church History in the Fullness of Time,* prepared by the Church Educational System and published by the Church of Jesus Christ of Latter-day Saints.

The vast public lands in southern Utah—five glorious national parks plus several spectacular recreation areas—offer innumerable possibilities for exploration, and anyone interested in exploring their trails and backcountry should check out the Falcon Guides (© **800/582-2665;** www.falconguide.com). They have books on hiking, mountain biking, rock climbing, and scenic driving. And if you're planning to visit several of Utah's great state parks, an excellent handbook is *Utah State Parks,* by Jan Bannan, from The Mountaineers publishers.

FAST FACTS: Utah

Area Codes The area code is **801** in the Wasatch Valley, which includes Salt Lake City, Provo, and Ogden. Most of the rest of the state is in the **435** area code.

Business Hours Banks are typically open Monday through Thursday from 9am to 3pm, Friday from 9am to 6pm. Drive-up windows may be open later. In general, business hours are Monday through Friday from 9am to 5pm. Many stores are also open on Friday evening and Saturday; those in major shopping malls have Sunday afternoon hours as well. Some supermarkets are open 24 hours a day.

Car Rentals See "Getting Around," earlier in this chapter.

Emergencies In almost all parts of Utah, dial © **911** for fire, police, or ambulance. No coins are needed at pay phones for 911 calls. In a few rural areas, you need to dial "0" (zero) for an operator.

Embassies/Consulates See "Fast Facts: For the International Traveler," in chapter 3.

Holidays See "Calendar of Events," earlier in this chapter.

Hotlines See "Useful Telephone Numbers" at the end of this section.

Information See "Visitor Information," earlier in this chapter.

Liquor Laws The legal drinking age is 21. Utah's drinking laws are a bit odd, but you can buy alcoholic beverages almost everywhere in the state. You can buy 3.2% beer (read on if you're not sure what that means) and malt coolers in supermarkets and convenience stores 7 days a week; stronger beer, wine, and hard liquor are available only at state-owned liquor stores and package agencies, which are closed Sundays and state holidays.

Buying liquor, beer, or wine by the drink is a bit more complicated. Most of the better restaurants can serve alcoholic beverages with meals starting at noon. In most cases, you'll have to ask for a drink—they won't offer to serve you one. Some establishments are licensed as taverns and can sell 3.2% beer only. There are also "private clubs," which actually aren't private at all: They're essentially bars, and may or may not be attached to restaurants. You have to be a member to enter, but you can go in as a guest of a member or buy a 2-week membership, usually for $5 to $10. Private clubs can serve beginning at 10am Monday through Saturday and at noon on Sunday. Liquor by the drink cannot be sold after 1am Monday through Saturday or after midnight on Sunday.

Compared to beer available elsewhere, 3.2% beer, which is sold only in Utah, Oklahoma, Colorado, and Kansas, has less alcohol. According to the Budweiser people, 3.2% beer has about 4% alcohol by volume (which is equivalent to 3.2% alcohol by weight), whereas full-strength American beers have about 5% alcohol by volume.

Lost & Found Be sure to tell all of your credit card companies the minute you discover your wallet has been lost or stolen and file a report at the nearest police precinct. Your credit card company or insurer may require a police report number or record of the loss. Most credit card companies have an emergency toll-free number to call if your card is lost or stolen; they may be able to wire you a cash advance immediately or deliver an emergency credit card in a day or two. Visa's U.S. emergency number is © **800/847-2911** or 410/581-9994. American Express cardholders and traveler's check holders should call © **800/221-7282.** MasterCard holders should call © **800/307-7309** or 636/722-7111. For other credit cards, call the toll-free number directory at © **800/555-1212.**

If you need emergency cash over the weekend when all banks and American Express offices are closed, you can have money wired to you via **Western Union** (© **800/325-6000**; www.westernunion.com).

Identity theft or fraud are potential complications of losing your wallet, especially if you've lost your driver's license along with your cash and credit cards. Notify the major credit-reporting bureaus immediately; placing a fraud alert on your records may protect you against liability for criminal activity. The three major U.S. credit-reporting agencies are **Equifax** (© **800/766-0008**; www.equifax.com), **Experian** (© **888/397-3742**; www.experian.com), and **TransUnion** (© **800/680-7289**; www.transunion.com). Finally, if you've lost all forms of photo ID call your airline and explain the situation; they might allow you to board the plane if you have a copy of your passport or birth certificate and a copy of the police report you've filed.

Newspapers/Magazines The state's two largest daily newspapers, both published in Salt Lake City, are the *Salt Lake City Tribune* (www.sltrib. com) and the *Deseret News* (www.deseretnews.com); the latter is owned by the LDS Church. Several other towns and regions have daily newspapers, and many smaller towns publish weeklies. About a dozen Utah newspapers can be found online, with links from the Internet Public Library site, www.ipl.org. You can get national newspapers such as *USA Today* and the *Wall Street Journal* on the streets of Salt Lake City and at major hotels; newspapers from other major U.S. cities can be found at bookstores such as Barnes & Noble, which has several outlets in the Salt Lake City and Provo areas.

Police Dial ⓒ **911** almost everywhere, except in a few rural areas where you must dial "0" (zero) for an operator.

Safety See "Health & Safety," earlier in this chapter.

Smoking The Utah Indoor Clean Air Act prohibits smoking in any public building or office and in all enclosed places of public access. This includes restaurants but not private clubs, lounges, or taverns.

Taxes A combination of state and local sales taxes, from 6% to 7.5%, is added to your bill in all areas of Utah except Indian reservations. Local lodging taxes usually add an additional 3% or 4%.

Time Zone Utah is on mountain time, 1 hour ahead of the West Coast and 2 hours behind the East Coast. The state recognizes daylight saving time, which is usually in effect from the first Sunday in April to the last Sunday in October.

Useful Telephone Numbers For road conditions in Salt Lake City, call ⓒ **801/964-6000;** for the rest of the state, call ⓒ **800/492-2400.** The poison control hot line is ⓒ **800/456-7707** or 801/581-2151.

Weather Contact the **National Weather Service** (ⓒ **801/524-5133;** www. wrh.noaa.gov/saltlake).

3

For International Visitors

Whether it's your first visit or your tenth, a trip to the United States may require an additional degree of planning. This chapter provides some specifics about getting to the United States as economically and effortlessly as possible, plus some helpful information about how things are done in Utah—from receiving mail to making a local or long-distance telephone call.

1 Preparing for Your Trip

ENTRY REQUIREMENTS

Check at any U.S. embassy or consulate for current information and requirements. You can also obtain a visa application and other information online at the **U.S. State Department**'s website, at **www.travel.state.gov**.

VISAS The U.S. State Department has a **Visa Waiver Program** allowing citizens of certain countries to enter the United States without a visa for stays of up to 90 days. At press time these included Andorra, Australia, Austria, Belgium, Brunei, Denmark, Finland, France, Germany, Iceland, Ireland, Italy, Japan, Liechtenstein, Luxembourg, Monaco, the Netherlands, New Zealand, Norway, Portugal, San Marino, Singapore, Slovenia, Spain, Sweden, Switzerland, and the United Kingdom. Citizens of these countries need only a valid passport and a round-trip air or cruise ticket in their possession upon arrival. If they first enter the United States, they may also visit Mexico, Canada, Bermuda, and/or the Caribbean islands and return to the United States without a visa. Further information is available from any U.S. embassy or consulate. Canadian citizens may enter the United States without visas; they need only proof of residence.

Citizens of all other countries must have (1) a valid passport that expires at least 6 months later than the scheduled end of their visit to the United States, and (2) a tourist visa, which may be obtained without charge from any U.S. consulate.

To obtain a visa, the traveler must submit a completed application form (either in person or by mail) with a 1½-inch-square photo, and must demonstrate binding ties to a residence abroad. Usually you can obtain a visa at once or within 24 hours, but it may take longer during the summer rush from June through August. If you cannot go in person, contact the nearest U.S. embassy or consulate for directions on applying by mail. Your travel agent or airline office may also be able to provide you with visa applications and instructions. The U.S. consulate or embassy that issues your visa will determine whether you will be issued a multiple- or single-entry visa and any restrictions regarding the length of your stay.

British subjects can obtain up-to-date visa information by calling the **U.S. Embassy Visa Information Line** (② **0891/200-290**) or by visiting the "Consular Services" section of the American Embassy London's website at www.usembassy.org.uk.

Irish citizens can obtain up-to-date visa information through the **Embassy of the USA Dublin,** 42 Elgin Rd., Dublin 4, Ireland (© **353/1-668-8777**) or by checking the "Consular Services" section of the website at www.usembassy.ie.

Australian citizens can obtain up-to-date visa information by contacting the **U.S. Embassy Canberra,** Moonah Place, Yarralumla, ACT 2600 (© **02/6214-5600**) or by checking the U.S. Diplomatic Mission's website at http://usembassy-australia.state.gov/consular.

Citizens of **New Zealand** can obtain up-to-date visa information by contacting the **U.S. Embassy New Zealand,** 29 Fitzherbert Terrace, Thorndon, Wellington (© **644/472-2068**), or get the information directly from the "Services to New Zealanders" section of the website at http://usembassy.org.nz.

MEDICAL   REQUIREMENTS
Unless you're arriving from an area known to be suffering from an epidemic (particularly cholera or yellow fever), inoculations or vaccinations are not required for entry into the United States. If you have a medical condition that requires **syringe-administered medications,** carry a valid signed prescription from your physician—the Federal Aviation Administration (FAA) no longer allows airline passengers to pack syringes in their carry-on baggage without documented proof of medical need. If you have a disease that requires treatment with **narcotics,** you should also carry documented proof with you—smuggling narcotics aboard a plane is a serious offense that carries severe penalties in the U.S.

For **HIV-positive visitors,** requirements for entering the United States are somewhat vague and change frequently. According to the latest publication of *HIV and Immigrants: A Manual for AIDS Service Providers,* the Immigration and Naturalization Service (INS) doesn't require a medical exam for entry into the United States, but INS officials may stop individuals because they look sick or because they are carrying AIDS/HIV medicine.

If an HIV-positive noncitizen applies for a non-immigrant visa, the question on the application regarding communicable diseases is tricky no matter which way it's answered. If the applicant checks "no," INS may deny the visa on the grounds that the applicant committed fraud. If the applicant checks "yes" or if INS suspects the person is HIV-positive, it will deny the visa unless the applicant asks for a special waiver for visitors. This waiver is for people visiting the United States for a short time, to attend a conference, for instance, to visit close relatives, or to receive medical treatment. It can be a confusing situation. For up-to-the-minute information, contact **AIDSinfo** (© **800/448-0440** or 301/519-6616 outside the U.S.; www.aidsinfo.nih.gov) or the **Gay Men's Health Crisis** (© **212/367-1000;** www.gmhc.org).

DRIVER'S   LICENSES Foreign driver's licenses are mostly recognized in the U.S., although you may want to get an international driver's license if your home license is not written in English.

PASSPORT INFORMATION
Safeguard your passport in an inconspicuous, inaccessible place like a money belt. Make a copy of the critical pages, including the passport number, and store it in a safe place, separate from the passport itself. If you lose your passport, visit the nearest consulate of your native country as soon as possible for a replacement. Passport applications are downloadable from the websites listed below.

Note: The International Civil Aviation Organization has recommended a policy requiring that *every* individual who travels by air have a passport. In response, many countries are now requiring that children must be issued their own passport to travel internationally, where before those under 16 or so may have been allowed to travel on a parent or guardian's passport.

FOR RESIDENTS OF CANADA

You can pick up a passport application at one of 28 regional passport offices or most travel agencies. Canadian children who travel must have their own passport. However, if you hold a valid Canadian passport issued before December 11, 2001, that bears the name of your child, the passport remains valid for you and your child until it expires. Passports cost C$85 for those 16 years and older (valid 5 years), C$35 for children 3 to 15 (valid 5 years), and C$20 for children under 3 (valid 3 years). Applications, which must be accompanied by two identical passport-sized photographs and proof of Canadian citizenship, are available at travel agencies throughout Canada or from the central **Passport Office,** Department of Foreign Affairs and International Trade, Ottawa, ON K1A 0G3 (✆ **800/567-6868;** www.dfait-maeci.gc.ca/passport). Processing takes 5 to 10 days if you apply in person, or about 3 weeks by mail.

FOR RESIDENTS OF THE UNITED KINGDOM

As a member of the European Union, you need only an identity card, not a passport, to travel to other EU countries. However, you do need a passport in order to visit countries outside of the EU. To pick up an application for a standard 10-year passport (5-year passport for children under 16), visit the nearest Passport Office, major post office, or travel agency. You can also contact the **United Kingdom Passport Service** at ✆ **0870/571-0410** or

visit its website at www.passport.gov.uk. Passports are £33 for adults and £19 for children under 16, with another £30 fee if you apply in person at a Passport Office. Processing takes about 2 weeks (1 week if you apply at the Passport Office).

FOR RESIDENTS OF IRELAND

You can apply for a 10-year passport, costing €57, at the **Passport Office,** Setanta Centre, Molesworth Street, Dublin 2 (✆ **01/671-1633;** www.irlgov.ie/iveagh). Those under age 18 and over 65 must apply for a €12 3-year passport. You can also apply at 1A South Mall, Cork (✆ **021/272-525**) or over the counter at most main post offices.

FOR RESIDENTS OF AUSTRALIA

You can get an application from your local post office or any branch of Passports Australia, but you must schedule an interview at the passport office to present your application materials. Call the **Australian Passport Information Service** at ✆ **131-232,** or visit the government website at www.passports.gov.au. Passports for adults are A$144 and for those under 18 are A$72.

FOR RESIDENTS OF NEW ZEALAND

You can pick up a passport application at any New Zealand Passports Office or download it from their website. Contact the **Passports Office** at ✆ **0800/225-050** in New Zealand or 04/474-8100, or log on to www.passports.govt.nz. Passports for adults are NZ$80 and for children under 16 NZ$40.

CUSTOMS
WHAT YOU CAN BRING IN

Every visitor more than 21 years of age may bring in, free of duty, the following: (1) 1 liter of wine or hard liquor;

(2) 200 cigarettes, 100 cigars (but not from Cuba), or 3 pounds of smoking tobacco; and (3) $100 worth of gifts. These exemptions are offered to travelers who spend at least 72 hours in the United States and who have not claimed them within the preceding 6 months. It is altogether forbidden to bring into the country foodstuffs (particularly fruit, cooked meats, and canned goods) and plants (vegetables, seeds, tropical plants, and the like). Foreign tourists may bring in or take out up to $10,000 in U.S. or foreign currency with no formalities; larger sums must be declared to U.S. Customs on entering or leaving, which includes filing form CM 4790. For more specific information regarding U.S. Customs, contact your nearest U.S. embassy or consulate, or the **U.S. Customs** office (*©* **202/927-1770** or www.customs.ustreas.gov).

WHAT YOU CAN TAKE HOME

U.K. citizens returning from a non-EU country have a customs allowance of: 200 cigarettes; 50 cigars; 250g of smoking tobacco; 2 liters of still table wine; 1 liter of spirits or strong liqueurs (over 22% volume); 2 liters of fortified wine, sparkling wine or other liqueurs; 60cc (ml) of perfume; 250cc (ml) of toilet water; and £145 worth of all other goods, including gifts and souvenirs. People under 17 cannot have the tobacco or alcohol allowance. For more information, contact HM Customs & Excise at *©* **0845/010-9000** (from outside the U.K., 020/8929-0152), or consult their website at www.hmce.gov.uk.

For a clear summary of **Canadian** rules, request the booklet *I Declare,* issued by the **Canada Customs and Revenue Agency** (*©* **800/461-9999** in Canada, or 204/983-3500; www.ccra-adrc.gc.ca). Canada allows its citizens a C$750 exemption, and if you meet the age requirements set by the province or territory where you enter Canada (age 18 in some areas, age 19 in others), you're allowed to bring back duty-free one carton of cigarettes, one can of tobacco, 40 imperial ounces of liquor, and 50 cigars. In addition, you're allowed to mail gifts to Canada valued at less than C$60 a day, provided they're unsolicited and don't contain alcohol or tobacco (write on the package "Unsolicited gift, under $60 value"). All valuables should be declared on the Y-38 form before departure from Canada, including serial numbers of valuables you already own, such as expensive foreign cameras. *Note:* The $750 exemption can only be used once a year and only after an absence of 7 days.

The duty-free allowance in **Australia** is A$400 or, for those under 18, A$200. Citizens age 18 and over can bring in 250 cigarettes or 250 grams of loose tobacco, and 1,125 milliliters of alcohol. If you're returning with valuables you already own, such as foreign-made cameras, you should file the form called "Goods Exported in Passenger Baggage" before you leave Australia. A helpful brochure available from Australian consulates or Customs offices is *Know Before You Go.* For more information, call the **Australian Customs Service** at *©* **1300/363-263,** or log on to www.customs.gov.au.

The duty-free allowance for **New Zealand** is NZ$700. Citizens over 17 can bring in 200 cigarettes, 50 cigars, or 250 grams of tobacco (or a mixture of all three if their combined weight doesn't exceed 250g); plus 4.5 liters of wine and beer, or 1.125 liters of liquor. New Zealand currency does not carry import or export restrictions. Fill out a certificate of export, listing the valuables you are taking out of the country; that way, you can bring them back without paying duty. Most questions are answered in a free pamphlet available at New Zealand consulates and Customs offices: *New Zealand Customs Guide for Travellers, Notice no. 4.* For more information, contact **New Zealand Customs,** The Customhouse, 17–21 Whitmore St., Box 2218, Wellington (© **0800/428-786** or 04/473-6099; www.customs.govt.nz).

HEALTH INSURANCE

Although it's not required of travelers, health insurance is highly recommended. Unlike many European countries, the United States does not usually offer free or low-cost medical care to its citizens or visitors. Doctors and hospitals are expensive, and in most cases will require advance payment or proof of coverage before they render their services. Policies can cover everything from the loss or theft of your baggage and trip cancellation to the guarantee of bail in case you're arrested. Good policies will also cover the costs of an accident, repatriation, or death. See "Insurance" in chapter 2 for more information. Packages such as **Europ Assistance's "Worldwide Healthcare Plan"** are sold by European automobile clubs and travel agencies at attractive rates. **Worldwide Assistance Services, Inc.** (© **800/821-2828;** www.worldwideassistance.com) is the agent for Europ Assistance in the United States.

Though lack of health insurance may prevent you from being admitted to a hospital in nonemergencies, don't worry about being left on a street corner to die: The American way is to fix you now and bill the living daylights out of you later.

INSURANCE FOR BRITISH TRAVELERS   Most big travel agents offer their own insurance and will probably try to sell you their package when you book a holiday. Think before you sign. **Britain's Consumers' Association** recommends that you insist on seeing the policy and reading the fine print before buying travel insurance.

The Association of British Insurers (© **020/7600-3333;** www.abi.org.uk) gives advice by phone and publishes *Holiday Insurance,* a free guide to policy provisions and prices. You might also shop around for better deals: Try **Columbus Direct** (© **020/7375-0011;** www.columbusdirect.net).

INSURANCE FOR CANADIAN TRAVELERS   Canadians should check with their provincial health plan offices or call **Health Canada** (© **613/957-2991;** www.hc-sc.gc.ca) to find out the extent of their coverage and what documentation and receipts they must take home in case they are treated in the United States.

MONEY

CURRENCY   The U.S. monetary system is very simple: The most common **bills** are the $1 (colloquially, a "buck"), $5, $10, and $20 denominations. There are also $2 bills (seldom encountered), $50 bills, and $100 bills (the last two are usually not welcome as payment for small purchases). All the paper money was recently redesigned, making the famous faces adorning them disproportionately large. The old-style bills are still legal tender.

There are seven denominations of coins: 1¢ (1 cent, or a penny); 5¢ (5 cents, or a nickel); 10¢ (10 cents, or a dime); 25¢ (25 cents, or a quarter); 50¢ (50 cents, or a half dollar); the new gold-colored "Sacagawea" coin worth $1; and, prized by collectors, the rare, older silver dollar.

Note: The "foreign-exchange bureaus" so common in Europe are rare even at airports in the United States, and nonexistent outside major cities. It's best not to change foreign money (or traveler's checks denominated in a currency other than U.S. dollars) at a small-town bank, or even a branch in a big city; in fact, leave any currency other than U.S. dollars at home—it may prove a greater nuisance to you than it's worth.

TRAVELER'S CHECKS Though traveler's checks are widely accepted, make sure that they're denominated in U.S. dollars, as foreign-currency checks are often difficult to exchange. The three traveler's checks that are most widely recognized—and least likely to be denied—are **Visa, American Express,** and **Thomas Cook.** Be sure to record the numbers of the checks, and keep that information in a separate place in case they get lost or stolen. Most businesses are pretty good about taking traveler's checks, but you're better off cashing them in at a bank (in small amounts, of course) and paying in cash. Remember: You'll need identification, such as a driver's license or passport, to change a traveler's check.

CREDIT CARDS & ATMS Credit cards are the most widely used form of payment in the United States: **Visa** (Barclaycard in Britain), **MasterCard** (EuroCard in Europe, Access in Britain, Chargex in Canada), **American Express, Diners Club,** and **Discover.** There are, however, a handful of stores and restaurants that do not take credit cards, so be sure to ask in advance. Most businesses display a sticker near their entrance to let you know which cards they accept. (*Note:* Businesses may require a minimum purchase, usually around $10, to use a credit card.)

It is strongly recommended that you bring at least one major credit card—Visa and MasterCard are the most widely accepted in Utah, with American Express and Discover next. Hotels and airlines usually require a credit-card imprint as a deposit against expenses, and in an emergency a credit card can be priceless.

You'll find **automated teller machines (ATMs)** on just about every block—at least in almost every town—across the country. Some ATMs will allow you to draw U.S. currency against your bank and credit cards. Check with your bank before leaving home, and remember that you will need your personal identification number (PIN) to do so. Most accept Visa, MasterCard, and American Express, as well as ATM cards from other U.S. banks. Expect to be charged up to $3 per transaction, however, if you're not using your own bank's ATM.

One way around these fees is to ask for cash back at grocery stores that accept ATM cards and don't charge usage fees. Of course, you'll have to purchase something first.

ATM cards with major credit card backing, known as "debit cards," are now a commonly acceptable form of payment in most stores and restaurants. Debit cards draw money directly from your checking account. Some stores enable you to receive "cash back" on your debit-card purchases as well.

SAFETY

GENERAL SAFETY SUGGESTIONS Although tourist areas are generally safe, U.S. urban areas tend to be less safe than those in Europe or Japan. You should always stay alert. This is particularly true of large American cities. Utah is generally a very safe state, but as Salt Lake City grows, problems will increase.. If you're in doubt about which neighborhoods are safe, don't hesitate to make inquiries with the hotel front desk staff or the local tourist office.

Tips **Travel Tip**

Be sure to keep a copy of all your travel papers separate from your wallet or purse, and leave a copy with someone at home should you need it faxed in an emergency.

Avoid deserted areas, especially at night, and don't go into public parks after dark unless there's a concert or similar occasion that will attract a crowd.

Avoid carrying valuables with you on the street, and keep expensive cameras or electronic equipment bagged up or covered when not in use. If you're using a map, try to consult it inconspicuously—or better yet, study it before you leave your room. Hold onto your pocketbook, and place your billfold in an inside pocket. In theaters, restaurants, and other public places, keep your possessions in sight.

Always lock your room door—don't assume that once you're inside the hotel you are automatically safe and no longer need to be aware of your surroundings. Hotels are open to the public, and in a large hotel, security may not be able to screen everyone who enters.

DRIVING SAFETY   Driving safety is important too, and carjacking is not unprecedented. Question your rental agency about personal safety and ask for a traveler-safety brochure when you pick up your car. Obtain written directions—or a map with the route clearly marked—from the agency showing how to get to your destination.

(Many agencies now offer the option of renting a cellphone for the duration of your car rental; check with the rental agent when you pick up the car. Otherwise, contact **InTouch USA** at ℂ **800/872-7626** or www.intouchusa. com for short-term cellphone rental.) And, if possible, arrive and depart during daylight hours.

If you drive off a highway and end up in a dodgy-looking neighborhood, leave the area as quickly as possible. If you have an accident, even on the highway, stay in your car with the doors locked until you assess the situation or until the police arrive. If you're bumped from behind on the street or are involved in a minor accident with no injuries, and the situation appears to be suspicious, motion to the other driver to follow you. Never get out of your car in such situations. Go directly to the nearest police precinct, well-lit service station, or 24-hour store.

Park in well-lit and well-traveled areas whenever possible. Always keep your car doors locked, whether the vehicle is attended or unattended. Never leave any packages or valuables in sight. If someone attempts to rob you or steal your car, don't try to resist the thief/carjacker. Report the incident to the police department immediately by calling ℂ **911.**

2 Getting to the U.S.

Most people flying to Utah will use Salt Lake City International Airport. Airlines offering international flights into Salt Lake City include **American** (ℂ 800/433-7300; www.americanair. com), **Continental** (ℂ 800/525-0280; www.flycontinental.com), **Delta** (ℂ 800/221-1212; www.delta.com), **Northwest** (ℂ 800/225-2525; www. nwa.com; and **United** (ℂ 800/241-6522; www.ual.com). International travelers can also fly to O'Hare International Airport in Chicago, DIA in Denver, LAX in Los Angeles, or JFK in New York, and catch connecting flights to Salt Lake City from there.

AIRLINE DISCOUNTS   The smart traveler can find numerable ways to reduce the price of a plane ticket simply by taking time to shop around. For example, overseas visitors can take advantage of the APEX (Advance Purchase Excursion) reductions offered by all major U.S. and European carriers. For more money-saving airline advice, see "Getting There," in chapter 2. For the best rates, compare fares and be flexible with the dates and times of travel.

IMMIGRATION AND CUSTOMS CLEARANCE   Visitors arriving by air, no matter what the port of entry, should cultivate patience and resignation before setting foot on U.S. soil. Getting through immigration control can take as long as 2 hours on some days, especially on summer weekends, so be sure to carry this guidebook or something else to read. This is especially true in the aftermath of the September 11, 2001, terrorist attacks, when security clearances were considerably beefed up at U.S. airports.

People traveling by air from Canada, Bermuda, and certain countries in the Caribbean can sometimes clear Customs and Immigration at the point of departure, which is much quicker.

3 Getting Around the U.S.

BY PLANE   Some large airlines (for example, Northwest and Delta) offer travelers on their transatlantic or transpacific flights special discount tickets under the name **Visit USA,** allowing mostly one-way travel from one U.S. destination to another at very low prices. These discount tickets are not on sale in the United States and must be purchased abroad in conjunction with your international ticket. This system is the best, easiest, and fastest way to see the United States at low cost. You should obtain information well in advance from your travel agent or the office of the airline concerned, since the conditions attached to these discount tickets can be changed without advance notice.

BY TRAIN   Amtrak (© 800/USA-RAIL; www.amtrak.com) connects Salt Lake City to both the east and west coasts. International visitors (excluding Canada) can also buy a **USA Rail Pass,** good for 15 or 30 days of unlimited travel on Amtrak (© 800/USA-RAIL; www.amtrak.com). The pass is available through many overseas travel agents. Prices in 2003 for a 15-day pass were $295 off-peak, $440 peak; a 30-day pass costs $385 off-peak, $550 peak. With a foreign passport, you can also buy passes at some Amtrak offices in the United States, including locations in San Francisco, Los Angeles, Chicago, New York, Miami, Boston, and Washington, D.C. Reservations are generally required and should be made for each part of your trip as early as possible. Regional rail passes are also available.

Visitors should be aware of the limitations of long-distance rail travel in the United States. With a few notable exceptions, service is rarely up to European standards: Delays are common, routes are limited and often infrequently served, and fares are rarely significantly lower than discount airfares.

BY BUS   Although bus travel is often the most economical form of public transit for short hops between U.S. cities, it can also be slow and uncomfortable—certainly not an option for everyone (particularly when Amtrak, which is far more luxurious, offers similar rates). **Greyhound/ Trailways** (© **800/231-2222;** www. greyhound.com), the sole nationwide bus line, offers an **International Ameripass** that must be purchased before coming to the United States, or by phone through the Greyhound International Office at the Port Authority Bus Terminal in New York City (© **212/971-0492**). The pass can be obtained from foreign travel agents or through Greyhound's website (order at least 21 days before your departure to the U.S.) and costs less than the domestic version. 2003 passes cost as follows: 4 days ($160), 7 days ($219), 10 days ($269), 15 days ($329), 21 days ($379), 30 days ($439), 45 days ($489), or 60 days ($599). You can get more info on the pass at the website, or by calling ✆ **402/330-8552.** In addition, special rates are available for seniors and students.

BY CAR   Unless you plan to spend the bulk of your vacation time in a city where walking is the best and easiest way to get around (read: New York City or New Orleans), the most cost-effective, convenient, and comfortable way to travel around the United States is by car. The interstate highway system connects cities and towns all over the country; in addition to these high-speed, limited-access roadways, there's an extensive network of federal, state, and local highways and roads. Some of the national car-rental companies include **Alamo** (✆ 800/462-5266; www.alamo.com), **Avis** (✆ 800/230-4898; www.avis.com), **Budget** (✆ 800/527-0700; www.budget.com), **Dollar** (✆ 800/800-3665; www.dollar.com), **Hertz** (✆ 800/654-3131; www.hertz.com), **National** (✆ 800/227-7368; www.nationalcar.com), and **Thrifty** (✆ 800/847-4389; www.thrifty.com).

If you plan to rent a car in the United States, you probably won't need the services of an additional automobile organization. If you're planning to buy or borrow a car, automobile-association membership is recommended. **AAA, the American Automobile Association** (✆ **800/222-4357**), is the country's largest auto club and supplies its members with maps, insurance, and, most important, emergency road service. The cost of joining runs from $63 for singles to $87 for two members, but if you're a member of a foreign auto club with reciprocal arrangements, you can enjoy free AAA service in America. See "Fast Facts," below, for more information.

FAST FACTS: For the International Traveler

Automobile Organizations   Auto clubs will supply maps, suggested routes, guidebooks, accident and bail-bond insurance, and emergency road service. The **American Automobile Association (AAA)** is the major auto club in the United States. If you belong to an auto club in your home country, inquire about AAA reciprocity before you leave. You may be able to join AAA even if you're not a member of a reciprocal club; to inquire, call AAA (✆ **800/222-4357**). AAA is actually an organization of regional auto clubs; so look under "AAA Automobile Club" in the White Pages of the telephone directory. AAA has a nationwide emergency road service telephone number (✆ 800/AAA-HELP).

Business Hours   Offices are usually open weekdays from 9am to 5pm. Banks are open weekdays from 9am to 3pm or later and sometimes Saturday mornings. Stores typically open between 9 and 10am and close between 5 and 6pm from Monday through Saturday. Stores in shopping complexes or malls tend to stay open late: often until about 9pm, and many malls and larger department stores are open on Sundays. Discount stores and supermarkets are often open later than other stores, and some supermarkets are open 24 hours a day.

Currency & Currency Exchange   See "Money" under "Preparing for Your Trip," earlier in this chapter.

Drinking Laws   See "Liquor Laws" under "Fast Facts: Utah," in chapter 2.

Electricity   Like Canada, the United States uses 110 to 120 volts AC (60 cycles), compared to 220 to 240 volts AC (50 cycles) in most of Europe,

Australia, and New Zealand. If your small appliances use 220 to 240 volts, you'll need a 110-volt transformer and a plug adapter with two flat parallel pins to operate them here. Downward converters that change 220–240 volts to 110–120 volts are difficult to find in the United States, so bring one with you.

Embassies & Consulates All embassies are located in the nation's capital, Washington, D.C. Some consulates are located in major U.S. cities, and most nations have a mission to the United Nations in New York City. If your country isn't listed below, call for directory information in Washington, D.C. (© **202/555-1212**) or log on to **www.embassy.org/embassies**.

The following countries have consulates in the Salt Lake City area: **France** (no physical office; © 801/437-6647); **Italy,** 1937 W. Lawrence Circle, South Jordan (© 801/254-7500); **Mexico,** 230 W. 400 South, Suite 200, Salt Lake City (© 801/521-8502); **New Zealand,** 1379 N. Brookhurst Circle, Centerville (© 801/296-2494); **Norway,** 130 S. Redwood Rd., North Salt Lake (© 801/936-1170); **Sweden,** 28 S. 400 East, Salt Lake City (© 801/ 532-8664); **Switzerland,** 4641 S. Hunters Ridge Circle, Holladay (© 801/ 272-7102); and **Uruguay,** 8191 S. 700 East, Sandy (© 801/256-0182).

The embassy of **Australia** is at 1601 Massachusetts Ave. NW, Washington, DC 20036 (© **202/797-3000;** www.austemb.org). There are consulates in New York, Honolulu, Houston, Los Angeles, and San Francisco.

The embassy of **Canada** is at 501 Pennsylvania Ave. NW, Washington, DC 20001 (© **202/682-1740;** www.canadianembassy.org). Other Canadian consulates are in Buffalo (NY), Detroit, Los Angeles, New York, and Seattle.

The embassy of **Ireland** is at 2234 Massachusetts Ave. NW, Washington, DC 20008 (© **202/462-3939;** www.irelandemb.org). Irish consulates are in Boston, Chicago, New York, and San Francisco.

The embassy of **Japan** is at 2520 Massachusetts Ave. NW, Washington, DC 20008 (© **202/238-6700;** www.embjapan.org). Japanese consulates are located in many cities including Atlanta, Boston, Detroit, New York, San Francisco, and Seattle.

The embassy of **New Zealand** is at 37 Observatory Circle NW, Washington, DC 20008 (© **202/328-4800;** www.nzemb.org). New Zealand consulates are in Los Angeles, Salt Lake City, San Francisco, and Seattle.

The embassy of the **United Kingdom** is at 3100 Massachusetts Ave. NW, Washington, DC 20008 (© **202/462-1340;** www.britainusa.com). Other British consulates are in Atlanta, Boston, Chicago, Cleveland, Houston, Los Angeles, New York, San Francisco, and Seattle.

Emergencies Call © **911** to report a fire, call the police, or get an ambulance anywhere in the United States. This is a toll-free call. (No coins are required at public telephones.)

If you encounter serious problems, contact the **Traveler's Aid International** (© **202/546-1127;** www.travelersaid.org) to help direct you to a local branch. This nationwide, nonprofit, social-service organization geared to helping travelers in difficult straits offers services that might include reuniting families separated while traveling, providing food and/or shelter to people stranded without cash, or even emotional counseling. If you're in trouble, seek them out.

Gasoline (Petrol) Petrol is known as gasoline (or simply "gas") in the United States, and petrol stations are known as both gas stations and service stations. Gasoline costs about half as much here as it does in Europe (about $1.50 to $1.60 per gallon at press time), and taxes are already included in the printed price. One U.S. gallon equals 3.8 liters or .85 Imperial gallons.

Holidays Banks, government offices, post offices, and many stores, restaurants, and museums are closed on the following legal national holidays: January 1 (New Year's Day), the third Monday in January (Martin Luther King Jr. Day), the third Monday in February (Presidents' Day, Washington's Birthday), the last Monday in May (Memorial Day), July 4 (Independence Day), the first Monday in September (Labor Day), the second Monday in October (Columbus Day), November 11 (Veterans' Day/Armistice Day), the fourth Thursday in November (Thanksgiving Day), and December 25 (Christmas). Also, the Tuesday following the first Monday in November is Election Day and is a federal government holiday in presidential-election years (held every four years, and next in 2004).

Legal Aid If you are "pulled over" for a minor infraction (such as speeding), never attempt to pay the fine directly to a police officer; this could be construed as attempted bribery, a much more serious crime. Pay fines by mail, or directly into the hands of the clerk of the court. If accused of a more serious offense, say and do nothing before consulting a lawyer. Here the burden is on the state to prove a person's guilt beyond a reasonable doubt, and everyone has the right to remain silent, whether he or she is suspected of a crime or actually arrested. Once arrested, a person can make one telephone call to a party of his or her choice. Call your embassy or consulate.

Mail If you aren't sure what your address will be in the United States, mail can be sent to you, in your name, c/o General Delivery at the main post office of the city or region where you expect to be. (Contact the U.S. Postal Service at ℂ **800/275-8777** or www.usps.com, for information on the nearest post office.) The addressee must pick up mail in person and must produce proof of identity (driver's license, passport, etc.). Most post offices will hold your mail for up to 1 month, and are open Monday to Friday from 8am to 6pm, and Saturday from 9am to 3pm.

Generally found at intersections, mailboxes are blue with a red-and-white stripe and carry the inscription "U.S. Mail". If your mail is addressed to a U.S. destination, don't forget to add the five-digit postal code (or ZIP code), after the two-letter abbreviation of the state to which the mail is addressed (**UT** for Utah). This is essential to prompt delivery.

At press time, domestic postage rates were 23¢ for a postcard and 37¢ for a letter. For international mail, a first-class letter of up to ½ ounce costs 80¢ (60¢ to Canada and Mexico); a first-class postcard costs 70¢ (50¢ to Canada and Mexico); and a preprinted postal aerogramme costs 70¢.

Measurements See the chart on the inside front cover of this book for details on converting metric measurements to U.S. equivalents.

Newspapers & Magazines The national newspapers and magazines generally available in Utah include the *New York Times, USA Today,* the *Wall Street Journal, Newsweek, Time,* and *U.S. News & World Report.* The state's major daily newspapers are the *Salt Lake City Tribune* and the *Deseret News.*

Taxes The United States has no value-added tax (VAT) or other indirect tax at the national level. Every state, county, and city has the right to levy its own local tax on all purchases, including hotel and restaurant checks, airline tickets, and so on. Sales taxes in Utah vary, but usually total 6% to 7.5%. On top of that, a tax of 3% to 4.5% is added to your lodging bill.

Telephone, Telegraph, Telex & Fax The telephone system in the United States is run by private corporations, so rates, especially for long-distance service and operator-assisted calls, can vary widely. Generally, hotel sur- charges on long-distance and local calls are astronomical, so you're usu- ally better off using a **public pay telephone,** which you'll find clearly marked in most public buildings and private establishments as well as on the street. Convenience grocery stores and gas stations always have them. Many convenience groceries and packaging services sell **prepaid calling cards** in denominations up to $50; these can be the least expensive way to call home. Many public phones at airports now accept American Express, MasterCard, and Visa credit cards. **Local calls** made from public pay phones in most locales cost either 25¢ or 35¢. Pay phones do not accept pennies, and few will take anything larger than a quarter.

You may want to look into leasing a cellphone for the duration of your trip (p. 32).

Most long-distance and international calls can be dialed directly from any phone. **For calls within the United States and to Canada,** dial 1 fol- lowed by the area code and the seven-digit number. **For other interna- tional calls,** dial 011 followed by the country code, city code, and the telephone number of the person you are calling.

Calls to area codes **800, 888, 877,** and **866** are toll-free. However, calls to numbers in area codes **700** and **900** (chat lines, bulletin boards, "dat- ing" services, and so on) can be very expensive—usually a charge of 95¢ to $3 or more per minute, and they sometimes have minimum charges that can run as high as $15 or more.

For **reversed-charge or collect calls,** and for person-to-person calls, dial 0 (zero, not the letter O) followed by the area code and number you want; an operator will then come on the line, and you should specify that you are calling collect, or person-to-person, or both. If your operator- assisted call is international, ask for the overseas operator.

For **local directory assistance** ("information"), dial 411; for long-distance information, dial 1, then the appropriate area code and 555-1212.

Telegraph and telex services are provided primarily by Western Union. You can bring your telegram into the nearest Western Union office (there are hundreds across the country) or dictate it over the phone (✆ **800/ 325-6000**). You can also telegraph money, or have it telegraphed to you, very quickly over the Western Union system, but this service can cost as much as 15% to 20% of the amount sent.

Most hotels have **fax machines** available for guest use (be sure to ask about the charge to use it). Many hotel rooms are even wired for guests' fax machines. A less expensive way to send and receive faxes may be at stores such as **The UPS Store** (formerly Mail Boxes Etc.), a national chain of retail packing service shops. (Look in the Yellow Pages directory under "Packing Services.")

There are two kinds of telephone directories in the United States. The so-called **White Pages** list private households and business subscribers in alphabetical order. The inside front cover lists emergency numbers for police, fire, ambulance, the Coast Guard, poison-control center, crime-victims hotline, and so on. The first few pages will tell you how to make long-distance and international calls, complete with country codes and area codes. Government numbers are usually printed on blue paper within the White Pages. Printed on yellow paper, the so-called **Yellow Pages** list all local services, businesses, industries, and houses of worship according to activity with an index at the front or back. (Drugstores/pharmacies and restaurants are also listed by geographic location.) The Yellow Pages also include city plans or detailed area maps, postal ZIP codes, and public transportation routes.

Time The continental United States is divided into **four time zones:** eastern standard time (EST), central standard time (CST), mountain standard time (MST) which includes all of Utah, and Pacific standard time (PST). Alaska and Hawaii have their own zones. For example, noon in New York City (EST) is 11am in Chicago (CST), 10am in Salt Lake City (MST), 9am in Los Angeles (PST), 8am in Anchorage (AST), and 7am in Honolulu (HST).

Daylight saving time is in effect in Utah and most of the country from 1am on the first Sunday in April through 1am on the last Sunday in October. Daylight saving time moves the clock 1 hour ahead of standard time.

Tipping Tips are a very important part of certain workers' income, and gratuities are the standard way of showing appreciation for services provided. (Tipping is certainly not compulsory if the service is poor!) In hotels, tip **bellhops** at least $1 per bag ($2–$3 if you have a lot of luggage) and tip the **chamber staff** $1 to $2 per day (more if you've left a disaster area for him or her to clean up). Tip the **doorman** or **concierge** only if he or she has provided you with some specific service (for example, calling a cab for you or obtaining difficult-to-get theater tickets). Tip the **valet-parking attendant** $1 every time you get your car.

In restaurants, bars, and nightclubs, tip **service staff** 15% to 20% of the check, tip **bartenders** 10% to 15%, tip **checkroom attendants** $1 per garment, and tip **valet-parking attendants** $1 per vehicle.

As for other service personnel, tip **cab drivers** 15% of the fare; tip **skycaps** at airports at least $1 per bag ($2–$3 if you have a lot of luggage); and tip **hairdressers** and **barbers** 15% to 20%.

Toilets You won't find public toilets or "restrooms" on the streets in most U.S. cities, but they can be found in hotel lobbies, bars, restaurants, museums, department stores, railway and bus stations, and service stations. Large hotels and fast-food restaurants are probably the best bet for good, clean facilities. If possible, avoid the toilets at parks and beaches, which tend to be dirty; some may be unsafe. Restaurants and bars in resorts or heavily visited areas may reserve their restrooms for patrons. Some establishments display a notice indicating this. You can ignore this sign or, better yet, avoid arguments by paying for a cup of coffee or a soft drink, which will qualify you as a patron.

4

The Active Vacation Planner

Utah is one big outdoor adventure, with millions of acres of public lands where you can cast for trout or herd cattle, go rock climbing or four-wheeling, sail or ski. The state boasts five spectacular national parks, seven national monuments, two national recreation areas, one national historic site, seven national forests, some 22 million acres administered by the federal Bureau of Land Management (BLM), and 45 state parks. But who's counting? It's enough to say that almost 80% of Utah's 85,000 square miles are yours to enjoy.

If you're a seasoned active traveler, you might want to skip section 1; it should be a good primer, though, for those who are new to this kind of travel or who haven't been to Utah before. Section 2 provides some up-to-date information on visiting Utah's national parks. Following that are descriptions of activities you can pursue in Utah, from A to Z. We'll point you to the best places in the state to pursue your interests, and give you the general information you'll need to get started. You'll find more details in the appropriate regional chapters. Have fun!

1 Preparing for Your Active Vacation

WHAT TO PACK & WHAT TO RENT

Planning for a trip into the great outdoors immediately brings to mind those cartoons of vacationers loaded down with equipment and surrounded by golf clubs, skis, cameras, tents, canoes, and bikes. If a car or light truck is your mode of transportation, try to keep the heaviest items between the axles and as close to the floor of your vehicle as possible; this helps improve handling. If you have a bike rack on the rear bumper, make sure the bike tires are far from the exhaust pipe; an owner of one bike shop told us he does a good business replacing exhaust-cooked mountain-bike tires. Those with roof racks will want to measure the total height of their packed cars before leaving home. Underground parking garages often have less than 7 feet of clearance.

One alternative to carrying all that stuff is renting it. Many sporting-goods shops in Utah rent camping equipment; virtually all ski areas and popular mountain-bike areas offer rentals; and major boating centers such as Lake Powell and Lake Flaming Gorge rent boats. You'll find many rental sources listed throughout this book.

In packing for your trip, you'll want to be prepared for all your favorite activities, of course, but you'll also want to be prepared for a land of extremes that often has an unforgiving climate and terrain. Those planning to hike or bike should take more drinking water than they think they'll need—experts recommend at least 1 gallon of water per person per day on the trail—as well as high-SPF sunblock, hats and other protective clothing, and sunglasses with ultraviolet protection. Summer visitors should carry rain gear for the typical afternoon thunderstorms, plus jackets or sweaters for cool evenings. Winter visitors will need not only warm parkas and hats, but also lighter clothing—the bright sun at midday, even in the mountains, can make it feel like June.

STAYING SAFE & HEALTHY IN THE OUTDOORS

The wide-open spaces and rugged landscape that make Utah such a beautiful place to explore can also be hazardous to your health, especially if you're not accustomed to the extreme climate; see "Health & Safety," in chapter 2, for details on dealing with desert climes and high altitudes. The isolation of many of the areas that you'll seek out means there may be no one around to help in an emergency, so you must be prepared, like any good Boy Scout. See "What to Pack & What to Rent," above, for tips on what to bring. Also, be sure to carry a basic first-aid kit that includes a pair of tweezers—very handy for removing tiny cactus spines from tender flesh. Most important of all, check with park offices, park rangers, and other local outdoor specialists about current conditions before heading out.

OUTDOOR ETIQUETTE

Many of the wonderful outdoor areas you'll be exploring in Utah are quite isolated; although you're probably not the first human being to set foot here, you may feel like you are. Not too long ago, the rule of thumb was to "leave only footprints;" these days, we're trying to not even leave footprints. It's relatively easy to be a good outdoor citizen—it's mostly common sense. Pack out all trash, stay on established trails, be especially careful not to pollute water, and, in general, do your best to have as little impact on the environment as possible. The best among us go even further, carrying a small trash bag to pick up what others have left behind.

2 Adventure Travel

There are plenty of opportunities for adventure in Utah—and some terrific outfitters to help you plan and execute the trip you've been dreaming of. You can take part in a cattle drive; thrill to the excitement of white-water rafting on the Green or Colorado rivers; scale a sheer rock wall in Zion National Park; or head out into some of the most spectacular scenery in the country on foot or on bicycle, or in a four-wheel-drive vehicle. The variety of tours available seems almost endless, but the tour operators can help you find the one for you. And in some cases, you can work with an operator to plan your own customized trip—all it takes is money.

Below are some of the most respected national companies operating in Utah. Most specialize in small groups and have trips geared to various levels of ability and physical condition. They also offer trips in a range of price categories, from basic to luxurious, and of varying length. Numerous local outfitters, guides, and adventure travel companies are discussed throughout this book. For a complete list of outfitters in Utah, as well as a lot of other useful information and web links, contact the **Utah Travel Council,** 300 N. State St., Council Hall, Salt Lake City, UT 84114 (© **800/200-1160** or 801/538-1030; fax 801/538-1399; www.utah.com).

- **Austin-Lehman Adventures,** P.O. Box 81025, Billings, MT 59108 (© **800/575-1540** or 406/655-4591; www.austinlehman.com), a merger of Backcountry and Adventures Plus, offers guided multi-day mountain biking, hiking, and combination tours in the Bryce Canyon and Zion national parks areas.

- **Backroads,** 801 Cedar St., Berkeley, CA 94710-1800 (© **800/462-2848** or 510/527-1555; fax 510/527-1444; www.backroads.com), offers a variety of guided multi-day road biking, mountain biking, and hiking tours in the national parks in southern Utah, including trips that feature jet boat rides.
- **Bicycling Adventures,** P.O. Box 11219, Olympia, WA 98508 (© **800/ 443-6060** or 360/786-0989; www.bicycleadventures.com), offers guided multiday hiking and biking excursions in Zion and Bryce Canyon national parks.
- **GORPtravel,** P.O. Box 1486, Boulder, CO 80306 (© **877/532-4677;** www.gorptravel.com), formerly American Wilderness Experience, offers mountain biking, hiking, four-wheeling, horseback riding, rafting excursions, and cattle drives throughout the West, including numerous multi-day trips in Utah.
- **Moguls Ski & Snowboard Tours,** 6707 Winchester Circle, Boulder, CO 80301 (© **800/666-4857;** www.skimoguls.com), provides customized skiing and snowboarding packages at all of Utah's major resorts, plus golf, fishing, and other summer vacation packages.
- **The World Outdoors,** 2840 Wilderness Place, Suite F, Boulder, CO 80301 (© **800/488-8483** or 303/413-0938; www.theworldoutdoors.org), formerly Roads Less Traveled, offers a variety of trips, including multi-sport adventures that include hiking, mountain biking, horseback riding, and rafting in the Canyonlands area, plus hiking/biking trips in Bryce Canyon and Zion National parks, and the north rim of Grand Canyon National Park.

3 Visiting Utah's National Parks

For many people, including us, the best part of a Utah vacation is exploring the state's five national parks (www.nps.gov). Unfortunately, these beautiful national treasures have become so popular that they're being overrun by visitors at a time when the federal government is cutting budgets, making it difficult for the parks to cope with their own success.

> **Impression**
> *Surely the United States of America is not so poor we cannot afford to have these places, nor so rich we can do without them.*
> —Newton Drury, National Park Service Director, 1940–1951

To get the most out of your national park visit, try to go in the off-season. The parks are busiest in summer, when most children are out of school, so try to visit at almost any other time. Fall is usually best. Spring is okay, but it can be windy and there may be snow at higher elevations. Winter can be delightful if you don't mind snow and cold. If you have to travel in summer, be patient. Allow extra time for traffic jams and lines, and try to hike some of the longer and lesser-used trails. Rangers will be able to tell you which trails are best for getting away from the crowds.

If you plan to visit a number of national parks and monuments within the time frame of a year, **National Parks Passes,** which cost $50 each, will save you money. The passes are good at all properties under the jurisdiction of the National Park Service, but not at sites administered by the Bureau of Land Management, National Forest Service, or other federal or state agencies. The National Parks Passes provide free entrance for the pass-holder and all vehicle occupants to National Park Service properties that charge vehicle entrance fees, and the pass-holder, spouse, parents, and children for sites that charge per person fees. The passes can be purchased at park entrance stations and visitor centers, by phone (☏ **888/GO-PARKS**) or online (www.nationalparks.org).

Also available at park service properties, as well as at other federal recreation sites that charge entrance fees, are **Golden Age Passports,** for those 62 and older, which have a one-time fee of $10 and provide free admission to all national parks and monuments, plus a 50% discount on other park fees such as camping. **Golden Access Passports,** free for blind or permanently disabled U.S. citizens, have the same benefits as the Golden Age Passports described above, and are available at all federal recreation sites that charge entrance fees.

Golden Eagle Passes are available from U.S. Forest Service, Bureau of Land Management, and Fish and Wildlife areas. At a cost of $65 for one year from the date of purchase, these passes allow the bearer, plus everyone traveling with him or her in the same vehicle, free admission to all National Park Service properties plus other federal recreation sites that charge fees. The National Parks Passes discussed above can be upgraded to Golden Eagle status for $15.

4 Outdoor Activities A to Z

Utah offers a surprisingly wide range of outdoor activities, from desert hiking and four-wheeling to fishing and, of course, skiing. The **GORP** (Great Outdoor Recreation Page) website, at **www.gorp.com**, offers detailed information on these and many other activities, with links to related sites. Another excellent website is **www.outdoorutah.com**, where you can order a free copy of the annual *Outdoor Utah Vacation Guide,* and connect to their other websites (www.bicycleutah.com, www.backcountryutah.com, and whitewaterutah.com). You can also reach them at **Bicycle Utah,** P.O. Box 711069, Salt Lake City, UT 84171-1069 (☏ **801/278-6294**). You'll also find a variety of visitor information and planning resources in chapter 2.

This is truly a do-it-yourself kind of state, and you'll have no trouble finding detailed topographic maps—essential for wilderness trips—plus whatever equipment and supplies you need. And despite the well-publicized cuts in budgets and work forces in national parks, recreation areas, and forests, every single ranger we encountered was happy to take time to help visitors plan their backcountry trips. In addition, many sporting-goods shops are staffed by area residents who know local activities and areas well, and are happy to help the would-be adventurer. In almost all cases, if you ask, there will be someone willing and able to help you make the most of your trip.

BOATING   For a state that's largely desert, Utah certainly has a lot of lakes and reservoirs, from huge Lake Powell in the south to Lake Flaming Gorge in the north, with numerous reservoirs in between. We highly recommend both of the above-mentioned lakes, which are administered as national recreation areas and have complete marinas with boat rentals. Don't forget the state parks, such as Jordanelle, which is near Park City, and Quail Creek—with the state's warmest water—near St. George. One of our favorites is picturesque but chilly Strawberry Reservoir, southeast of Park City in the Uinta National Forest. For information on boating in state parks, contact **Utah State Parks and Recreation** (p. 64).

CAMPING   Utah is the perfect place to camp; in fact, at some destinations, such as Canyonlands National Park, it's practically mandatory. Just about every community of any size has at least one commercial campground, and campsites are available at all the national parks and national recreation areas, though these campsites are often crowded in summer. Those who can stand being without hot showers for a day or so can often find free or very reasonable campsites just outside the national parks, in national forests, and on Bureau of Land Management lands. Other good bets are found at Utah's state parks; among those with the best campgrounds are Kodachrome, just outside Bryce Canyon National Park; Coral Pink Sand Dunes, just west of Kanab; and Snow Canyon, near St. George.

A growing number of state and federal campgrounds allow visitors to reserve sites, although often only in the busy summer months. At press time, Zion was the only one of Utah's five national parks to accept reservations, but that could change. However, throughout Utah there are more than 100 national forest campgrounds and numerous state parks that will reserve sites. To check on campground reservation possibilities for National Park Service properties, contact the **National Park Reservation Service** (© **800/365-2267;** TDD 888/ 530-9796; http://reservations.nps.gov) or use the link from the individual park's website. U.S. Forest Service campground reservations are available through the **National Recreation Reservation Service** (© **877/444-6777** or 518/885- 3639; TDD 877/833-6777; www.reserveusa.com); and reservations for state parks can be made with **Utah State Parks and Recreation** (© **800/322-3770** or 801/322-3770; www.stateparks.utah.gov).

CATTLE DRIVES   Opportunities abound for you to play cowboy on cattle drives that last from a single day to a week or longer. You can actually take part in the riding and roping, just like Billy Crystal did in *City Slickers.* You'll certainly get a feel for what it was like to be on a cattle drive 100 years ago, though the conditions are generally much more comfortable than what real cowboys experienced. Each cattle drive is different, so you'll want to ask very specific questions about food, sleeping arrangements, and other conditions before plunking down your money. It's also a good idea to book your trip as early as possible. A good company is **Rockin' R Ranch,** 10274 S. Eastdell Dr., Sandy, UT 84092 (© **801/733-9538;** fax 801/942-2680; www.rocknrranch.com).

FISHING   Utah has more than 1,000 lakes, plus countless streams and rivers, with species that include rainbow, cutthroat, Mackinaw, and brown trout, plus striped bass, crappie, bluegill, walleye, and whitefish. Lake Flaming Gorge and Lake Powell are both great fishing lakes, but Strawberry Reservoir is Utah's premier trout fishery—in fact, it's one of the best in the West. Fly-fishing is especially popular in the Park City area and in the streams of the Wasatch-Cache National Forest above Ogden. Contact the **Utah Division of Wildlife Resources,** 1594 W. North Temple (P.O. Box 146301), Salt Lake City, UT 84114 (© **877/592-5169** or 801/538-4700; fax 801/538-4745; www.wildlife. utah.gov), for the weekly statewide fishing report.

Fishing licenses are available from state wildlife offices and sporting-goods stores, and can also be purchased at the Division of Wildlife Resources website (www.wildlife.utah.gov). Keep in mind that several fishing locations, such as Lake Powell and Lake Flaming Gorge, cross state lines, and you'll need licenses from both states.

FOUR-WHEELING   The Moab area, and Canyonlands National Park in particular, are probably the best-known four-wheeling destinations in Utah, but there are also plenty of old mining and logging roads throughout the national forests and on BLM land. Those with dune buggies like to head for Coral Pink

Sand Dunes State Park, west of Kanab. For information on four-wheeling, contact **Utah State Parks and Recreation,** the **U.S. Forest Service,** and the **Bureau of Land Management** (p. 67).

GOLF   Utah's golf courses are known for their beautiful scenery and variety of challenging terrain. They range from mountain courses set among the beautiful forests of the Wasatch to desert courses with scenic views of red rock country. The warm climate of St. George, in Utah's southwest corner, makes this area a perfect location for year-round golf, and St. George has become the premier destination for visiting golfers—the area's Sunbrook Golf Course is probably Utah's best. In northern Utah, the course at the Homestead Resort near Park City is well worth the trip. A free directory of the state's 80-plus courses is available from the **Utah Travel Council** (p. 61); or check out www.uga.org.

HIKING   Hiking is the best—and sometimes only—way to see many of Utah's most beautiful and exciting areas, and the state is interlaced with hiking trails. Particularly recommended destinations include all five of Utah's national parks. You'll find splendid forest trails and more of a wilderness experience at Flaming Gorge National Recreation Area and in the Wasatch Mountains around Ogden and Logan. Those looking for spectacular views won't do better than the trails on BLM land around Moab. In Grand Staircase-

> **Impression**
> *You can't see anything from your car. You've got to get out of the damn thing and walk!"*
> —author Edward Abbey

Escalante National Monument, east of Bryce Canyon, you'll discover numerous undeveloped, unmarked hiking routes that explore some of the nation's most rugged country. State parks with especially good trails include Kodachrome, near Bryce Canyon National Park; Jordanelle, near Park City; Dead Horse Point, just outside the Island in the Sky District of Canyonlands National Park; and Escalante, in the town of Escalante.

Keep weather conditions in mind when hiking, such as the brutal summer heat around St. George and the likelihood of ice and snow on high mountain trails from fall through spring. Because of loose rock and gravel on trails in the southern part of the state, wear good hiking boots with aggressive soles and firm ankle support.

HORSEBACK RIDING   It's fun to see the Old West the way the pioneers did—from the back of a horse. Although you won't find many dude ranches in Utah, you can find plenty of stables and outfitters who lead rides lasting from an hour to several days. We particularly recommend the rides at Bryce and Zion national parks—it's hard to beat the scenery—although you're likely to be surrounded by a lot of other riders and hikers. If you'd like a bit more solitude, head north to the mountains around Logan in the Wasatch Front or to Flaming Gorge National Recreation Area.

HOUSEBOATING   Among the best ways to experience either Lake Powell or Flaming Gorge Lake is from the comfort of a houseboat. Marinas at each lake rent them, although you'll find the best selection at Lake Powell. Houseboats provide all the comforts of home—toilets, showers, sleeping quarters, and full kitchens—but in somewhat tighter quarters. Some of the larger ones have facilities for up to a dozen people. You don't have to be an accomplished boater to drive one: Houseboats are easy to maneuver, and can't go very fast. No boating

Life on the Open Road: Planning an RV or Tenting Vacation

One of the best ways to explore Utah, especially in the warm months, is in an RV—a motor home, truck camper, or camper trailer—or a tent, if you don't mind roughing it a bit more. If you own an RV, we advise you to have the mechanical systems checked out thoroughly, keeping in mind that there are some extremely steep grades in Utah. After that's done, pack up and go. If you don't have an RV or a tent, why not rent one for your Utah trip?

Why Camp?   One advantage to this type of travel is that many of the places you'll want to go, such as Canyonlands National Park, don't offer any lodging. If you can't accommodate yourself, you'll end up sleeping 30 or 40 miles away and missing those spectacular sunrises and sunsets and that inexplicable feeling of satisfaction that comes from living the experience rather than merely visiting it. If you have special dietary requirements, you won't have to worry about trying to find a restaurant that can meet your needs; you'll be able to cook for yourself, either in your motor home or trailer or on a camp stove.

There are disadvantages, of course. Tents, small trailers, and truck campers are cramped, and even the most luxurious motor homes and trailers provide somewhat close quarters. Facilities in most commercial campgrounds are less than what you'd get in moderately priced motels, and if you cook your own meals, you miss the opportunity to experience the local cuisine. But, all this aside, camping is just plain fun—especially in a setting as spectacular as this one.

Renting an RV   Camping to save money is possible if you limit your equipment to a tent, a pop-up tent trailer, or a small pickup-truck camper, but renting a motor home will probably end up costing as

license is required, but you'll need to reserve your houseboat in advance, especially in summer, and send in a sizable deposit.

MOUNTAIN BIKING   Although there are a few areas where road biking is popular (we heartily recommend using a road bike at Zion National Park), Utah really belongs to mountain bikers. With some of the grades you'll find, be sure you have plenty of gears. Moab claims to be Utah's mountain biking capital, but there's no dearth of opportunities in other parts of the state, either. Be aware that mountain bikes must remain on designated motor-vehicle roads in most national parks, but are welcome almost everywhere in areas administered by the U.S. Forest Service and Bureau of Land Management. In addition to the exciting and often challenging slickrock trails of Moab, you'll find excellent trail systems just outside of Zion and Bryce Canyon national parks. We also like the warm-weather biking at Brian Head Ski Resort near St. George.

RIVER RAFTING, KAYAKING & CANOEING   The Green and Colorado rivers are among the top destinations in the United States for both serious white-water as well as flat-water rafting; they're also popular with kayakers and canoeists. A favorite river trip, with plenty of white water, is down the Green much as driving a compact car, staying in moderately priced motels, and eating in family-style restaurants. That's because motor homes go only a third (or less) as far on a gallon of gas as compact cars, and they're expensive to rent—generally between $1,000 and $1,200 per week in mid-summer, when rates are highest.

If you're flying into the area and renting an RV upon arrival, choose your starting point carefully. Because most of Utah's national parks are closer to Las Vegas than Salt Lake City, you could save by starting and ending your trip in Vegas. The nation's largest rental company, with outlets in both Salt Lake City and Las Vegas, is **Cruise America** (📞 **800/ RV4-RENT;** www.cruiseamerica.com). Information on additional rental agencies, as well as tips on renting, can be obtained from the **Recreation Vehicle Rental Association,** 3930 University Dr., Fairfax, VA 22030 (📞 **703/591-7130;** fax 703/591-0734; www.rvra.org).

Choosing a Campground   After you get a rig or a tent, you'll need a place to put it. Camping in the national parks, other federal lands, state parks, and many communities is discussed in the relevant sections of this book. For a brochure on the excellent campgrounds in Utah's state parks, contact **Utah State Parks and Recreation** (p. ###). Members of the **American Automobile Association (AAA)** can request the club's free *Southwestern CampBook,* which includes campgrounds and RV parks in Utah, Arizona, Colorado, and New Mexico. Major bookstores carry several massive campground directories, including *The Unofficial Guide to the Best RV and Tent Campgrounds in the Southwest & South Central Plains* (Wiley Publishing); *Trailer Life Campgrounds, RV Parks & Services* (www. rv.net); and *Woodall's Campground Directory* (www.woodalls.com).

River through Dinosaur National Monument. Trips on the Green also start in the town of Green River, north of Moab. The Colorado River sees more boaters than the Green, and has a greater range of conditions, from flat, glassy waters to rapids so rough they can't be run at all. Most Colorado River trips start in Moab. Several companies rent rafts, canoes, or kayaks, and give you some instruction. They'll also help you decide which stretches of river are suitable for your abilities and thrill-seeking level, and can arrange for a pick-up at the take-out point. See chapter 15 for details on contacting these outfitters.

Although river trips through Arizona's Grand Canyon, which we discuss as a side trip from Utah in chapter 10, are very popular, they're actually too popular for us, especially in mid-summer, when rafts are bumper-to-bumper. A worthwhile and lesser-known river trip is along the San Juan River in Bluff. This relaxing excursion will take you to relatively unknown archaeological sites and striking rock formations.

A recorded report on statewide river flows and reservoir information is available from the **Colorado Basin River Forecast Center** (📞 **801/539-1311;** www.cbrfc.gov). For additional information, contact the **Bureau of Land Management,** 324 S. State St., Suite 301 (P.O. Box 45155), Salt Lake City, UT

84145-0155 (© **801/539-4001; fax 801/539-4013;** www.ut.blm.gov) and the **Utah Travel Council,** Council Hall, 300 N. State Street, Salt Lake City, UT 84114 (© **800/200-1160** or 801/538-1030; fax 801/538-1399; www.utah.com).

ROCK CLIMBING   This dizzying sport is growing in popularity in Utah. It's growing so much, in fact, that several popular areas have imposed moratoriums on bolting, and allow climbers to use existing bolt holes only. Among the more dramatic rock-climbing spots is Zion National Park, where climbing is as much a spectator sport as a participatory activity. You'll also find some inviting walls of stone in Snow Canyon State Park near St. George, in Logan Canyon, and throughout the Wasatch Mountains in the Salt Lake City area.

For additional information, contact the **Utah Travel Council** or the government agency that controls the land you're interested in (p. 61).

SKIING & OTHER WINTER SPORTS   Utah residents like to brag that the state has "the greatest snow on earth"—and one winter trip just might convince you they're right. Utah's ski resorts are characterized by absolutely splendid powder, runs as scary or mellow as you'd like, and a next-door-neighbor friendliness many of us thought was extinct. With a few notable exceptions—particularly Park City, Deer Valley, and Snowbird—you won't find the poshness and amenities that dominate many of the ski resorts next door in Colorado, but you won't find the high prices, either. What you will discover are top-notch ski areas that are surprisingly easy to reach—half are within an hour's drive of Salt Lake City Airport. And they're relatively uncrowded, too: Utah generally receives about a third of the skiers that Colorado gets, so you'll see fewer lift lines and plenty of wide-open spaces.

Cross-country skiers can break trail to their heart's content in Utah's national forests, or explore one of the developed cross-country areas. Particularly good are the mountains above Ogden and the old logging and mining roads southeast of Moab. Several downhill resorts, including Brian Head, Sundance, and Solitude, offer groomed cross-country trails, and some of the hiking trails at Bryce Canyon National Park are open to cross-country skiers in winter. Snowmobilers can generally use the same national forest roads as cross-country skiers, and both cross-country skiers and snowmobilers head to Cedar Breaks National Monument in winter, when those are the only ways to get into the monument.

Growing in popularity is snowshoeing, which is not only easy but cheap. Among our favorite destinations is Bryce Canyon National Park.

Winter outdoor recreationists can call © **801/364-1581** for the daily avalanche and mountain weather report from the U.S. Forest Service (www.wrh.noaa.gov/saltlake), © **800/492-2400** for statewide road conditions, and © **801/524-5133** for a statewide weather forecast. Contact **Ski Utah,** 150 W. 500 South, Salt Lake City, UT 84101 (© **800/SKI-UTAH** or 801/534-1779; fax 801/521-3722; www.skiutah.com), for a free copy of the *Ski Utah Vacation Planner,* which contains information on downhill and cross-country ski areas, as well as other winter recreation possibilities; and call © **801/521-8102** for the daily ski report.

WILDLIFE VIEWING & BIRDING   The great expanses of undeveloped land in Utah make it an ideal habitat for wildlife, and in most cases it isn't even necessary to hike very far into the backcountry to spot creatures. There's plenty for you to see—waterbirds at many lakes and reservoirs, elk and antelope in the Wasatch Mountains, lizards and snakes in the red rock country of the south, and deer and small mammals practically everywhere. All of the national parks and many state parks have excellent wildlife-viewing possibilities: Coral Pink Sand Dunes near Kanab is known for its luminescent scorpions, and Escalante State Park boasts the best wetland bird habitat in southern Utah. Hikers on Boulder Mountain, near Escalante, are likely to see deer, elk, and wild turkey, and birders will enjoy the wide variety of songbirds found here.

The mountains above Ogden and Logan are especially good places to spot elk, deer, and even moose. The relatively remote Flaming Gorge National Recreation Area is one of the best areas in the state to find wildlife, so don't be surprised if a pronghorn (an antelope-like creature) joins you at your campsite. Birders have a good chance of seeing osprey, peregrine falcons, swifts, and swallows along the cliffs; and hikers on the Little Hole National Recreation Trail just below Flaming Gorge Dam should watch for a variety of birds, including bald eagles in winter. Antelope Island State Park in the Great Salt Lake is another good destination for bird-watchers.

5

An Introduction to the Wasatch Front

From Logan in the north to Provo in the south, the strip known as the Wasatch Front—the Wasatch Mountains and Salt Lake Valley, including Salt Lake City—holds some 80% of Utah's population and practically all of its industry. But this isn't your typical urban center; in fact, one of the things we find particularly attractive about this area is its casual atmosphere. There's no urban feel and little high-energy tension here, and residents don't see themselves as city dwellers. These Wasatch Front communities, even Salt Lake City, Ogden, and Provo—the state's largest cities—are just overgrown towns. We like that.

Although this certainly feels like small-town America, calling these cities unsophisticated is unfair. Attending a performance by the Utah Symphony or Mormon Tabernacle Choir, both world-class performing arts organizations, will silence any big-city naysayer. But what really matters, and what is the big draw for many people who come to work and live here, as well as those who come to play, is what lies beyond the cities' boundaries. This isn't the barren rock and desert that often come to mind when you think of Utah; this is mountain Utah, with lush canyons, rushing streams, stately pines, and some of the best skiing in America. In fact, winter sports conditions are so good here that the Wasatch Front was chosen as the site for the 2002 Winter Olympics.

Tucked away in delightful little canyons are easily accessible ski and snowboard resorts that boast awesome scenery and usually more than 500 inches of powder snow each winter. But there is also an abundance of warm weather activities here. Lakes and reservoirs offer boating, fishing, and swimming; the best known are the Great Salt and Utah lakes, but we'll also tell you about our favorites—two undiscovered jewels. The forests are terrific for hiking, mountain biking, and horseback riding.

This is also a wonderful place to relive frontier history. You can visit the spot where the final spike was driven to complete the first transcontinental railroad, the oldest continuously operating saloon in Utah, and the fort where 19th-century mountain men gathered to exchange news and swap furs for supplies. You can also trace the history of the Church of Jesus Christ of Latter-day Saints, which has its world headquarters in Salt Lake City, and explore a terrific collection of airplanes chronicling the history of flight.

1 How We've Covered This Area

Because this is such a large region—175 miles from top to bottom—you probably won't be touring the entire Wasatch Front; you're more likely to set your sights on specific destinations and explore those particular areas. To make our coverage of the region more manageable, we've divided it into three chapters.

The Wasatch Front

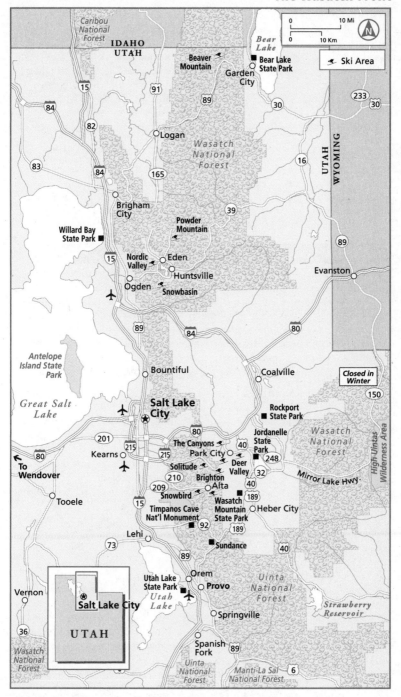

Caribou National Forest

IDAHO
UTAH

Beaver Mountain

Bear Lake

Bear Lake State Park

Garden City

Logan

Wasatch National Forest

UTAH
WYOMING

Brigham City

Willard Bay State Park

Powder Mountain

Nordic Valley
Eden
Huntsville
Ogden
Snowbasin

Evanston

Antelope Island State Park

Great Salt Lake

Bountiful

Coalville

Closed in Winter

Salt Lake City

Rockport State Park

Wasatch National Forest

High-Uintas Wilderness Area

To Wendover

Kearns

The Canyons
Park City
Solitude
Brighton
Alta
Snowbird
Deer Valley

Jordanelle State Park

Mirror Lake Hwy

Tooele

Timpanos Cave Nat'l Monument

Wasatch Mountain State Park

Heber City

Lehi

Sundance

Vernon

Salt Lake City

UTAH

Utah Lake State Park
Utah Lake

Orem
Provo

Uinta National Forest

Strawberry Reservoir

Springville

Spanish Fork

Wasatch National Forest

Uinta National Forest

Manti-La Sal National Forest

Ski Area

0   10 Mi
0   10 Km

Chapter 6 covers Salt Lake City, Utah's capital and major population center, which is the home of the world headquarters of the Church of Jesus Christ of Latter-day Saints (Mormons); the Great Salt Lake, one of the country's most remarkable natural wonders; and Antelope Island State Park.

Chapter 7 explores the northern section of the Wasatch Front, including Ogden, an excellent starting point for discovering Utah's Old West; the pretty town of Logan; and Golden Spike National Historic Site, a must-see for railroad buffs. This area is a great base for outdoor recreation, with four ski resorts as well as rugged mountains that provide numerous recreation opportunities year-round.

Chapter 8 covers the southern half of the Wasatch Front, from Park City, home of several of the state's best ski resorts, to Provo, site of Brigham Young University. This area also includes the splendid cave formations of Timpanogos Cave National Monument, plus a handful of lakes and state parks—real hidden gems that make this a terrific warm-weather playground as well. Provo makes a good base for skiing, hiking, or horseback riding at Sundance Resort in Provo Canyon.

2 Outdoor Pursuits Along the Wasatch Front

The Wasatch Front is mountain Utah, with lofty pines, rushing streams, and, in winter, an abundance of light, powdery snow. The rugged mountains and steep canyons that surround the Great Salt Lake Valley are home to lush forests, cool lakes and reservoirs, and plenty of sunshine—just right for an hour-long nature walk, an early-morning birding excursion, an exciting day of downhill skiing or mountain biking, a relaxing weekend fishing trip, or any of a number of other adventures.

WINTER SPORTS

Nowhere else in the American West will you find so many excellent ski resorts in one place. Just fly into Salt Lake City, rent a car or hop a shuttle, and you can be on the slopes of your choice in about an hour. It doesn't get any easier. Solitude and Brighton—which welcome snowboarders as well as downhill skiers—are in Big Cottonwood Canyon. At the top of Little Cottonwood Canyon is graceful, sylvan Alta, with clouds of light snow; down the canyon is the more developed Snowbird. If you crave the lap of luxury, head for the Park City resorts—Park City, The Canyons, and elegant Deer Valley—where you'll find "champagne" snow and European-style lodges. Nordic Valley, Powder Mountain, and Snowbasin, near Ogden, plus Beaver Mountain, almost in Idaho, are all at the other end of the scale, simply offering good skiing on long, uncrowded runs—no pretensions here. Rustic, comfortably posh Sundance is nestled in the pines on the eastern slope of Mt. Timpanogos, north of Provo.

Those who prefer other winter recreation have plenty of options. The old logging and mining roads throughout the national forests are great for cross-country skiing. Sundance Nordic Center, near Provo, offers groomed trails and lots of spectacular mountain scenery. Park City also has a Nordic center, called White Pine, that offers splendid cross-country skiing for everyone from beginner to expert. Solitude Nordic Center, Utah's oldest cross-country ski center, even has a children's trail.

WARM-WEATHER FUN

After the winter snows melt into fields of wildflowers, hiking boots, mountain bikes, and horses replace snowboards, skis, and snowmobiles. Hikers and mountain bikers share most of the trails here, including the well-maintained downtown riverside trails in both Provo and Ogden. Favorites are the 30-mile Historic Union Pacific Rail Trail, from Park City to Echo Reservoir, and the 5-mile Indian Trail, which leads through a dense forest in Ogden Canyon. The national forests are popular for horseback riding; some of the best opportunities are in the rugged country outside Logan and at Park City.

There's boating at Utah Lake State Park, but it gets crowded, especially on weekends. The Great Salt Lake is popular with both powerboaters and sail-boaters. For our money, it's well worth the drive to go boating in Strawberry Reservoir, a beautiful lake set in a quiet national forest that offers great hiking. Or head to the lake at Jordanelle State Park, one of Utah's newest parks. Both lakes provide launching ramps and boat rentals. Ogden's Fort Buenaventura is essentially a historical park, so finding several delightful ponds here, with canoe rentals, was a nice surprise.

Strawberry Reservoir also offers some of the best fishing in the state. The lakes and streams in the Wasatch-Cache National Forest above Ogden are good trout habitat. The streams above Park City are also a good bet for fly-fishing.

The Wasatch Front is dotted with golf courses. Our favorites, for both the challenge and scenic beauty they offer, include Park Meadows Golf Club, in Park City; the course at Wasatch Mountain State Park; and Wolf Creek Golf Resort, near Ogden.

WILDLIFE VIEWING & BIRDING

Because the Wasatch Front (like most of Utah) is largely undeveloped, you'll find plenty of opportunities for wildlife viewing and birding. Practically any-where in the mountains, you have a chance of spotting deer, elk, and maybe even a moose, plus smaller animals such as badgers, chipmunks, and rabbits. Willard Bay State Park near Ogden is a good place to see deer, smaller creatures, and waterbirds; the Great Salt Lake is home to a variety of saltwater birds. At Antelope Island State Park, you're virtually guaranteed to see buffalo—relatively domesticated ones, not actual "wildlife," per se—as well as pronghorn and a multitude of birds.

6

Salt Lake City

Nestled between the Wasatch Mountains on the east and the Great Salt Lake on the west, at an elevation of 4,330 feet, lies Salt Lake City. Utah's capital and major population center is small as modern American cities go, with a population of just over 180,000. But travelers come from around the world to visit magnificent Temple Square, world headquarters of the Church of Jesus Christ of Latter-day Saints (LDS), and to hear the inspired voices of the unequaled Mormon Tabernacle Choir.

Although Salt Lake City may be best known for its religious affiliations, and has an undeserved reputation as a stodgy, uptight town where you can't get a drink, the city is growing in popularity as a home base for skiers and other outdoor enthusiasts. Exhilarating outdoor recreation possibilities are only about an hour's drive from the city, and include some of the country's best ski resorts; miles of terrific mountain trails for hiking, biking, and horseback riding; and the intriguing Great Salt Lake. With its rising prominence as a home base for skiing and other outdoor activities, Salt Lake City is beginning to shed its image as "that boring Mormon town with the choir."

Incidentally, one of the first things visitors notice upon arrival is how sensibly organized and pleasantly wide the streets are. Early church leader Brigham Young laid out the city streets in a grid pattern, with the Temple at the center, and decreed that the streets should be 132 feet wide so that a team of four oxen and a wagon could make a U-turn. A more tantalizing tale has it that the streets were made wide enough for polygamist Young and all his wives to walk comfortably down the street arm-in-arm, with no one forced into the gutter.

1 Orientation

ARRIVING

BY PLANE   Direct flights connect Salt Lake City to almost 70 cities in the United States and Canada. **Salt Lake City International Airport** (© **800/595-2442** or 801/575-2400; www.slcairport.com) is located just north of I-80 at exit 115, on the west side of the city. Airlines serving the airport include American (© 800/433-7300; www.aa.com), America West (© 800/235-9292; www.americawest.com), Continental (© 800/523-3273; www.continental.com), Delta/SkyWest (© 800/221-1212; www.delta.com), Frontier (© 800/432-1359; www.frontierairlines.com), Northwest (© 800/225-2525; www.nwa.com), Southwest (© 800/435-9792; www.iflyswa.com), and United (© 800/864-8331; www.united.com).

BY CAR   Salt Lake City is 303 miles north of St. George, 238 miles northwest of Moab, 45 miles north of Provo, and 35 miles south of Ogden. You can reach it from the east or west via I-80 and from the north or south via I-15.

BY TRAIN   **Amtrak** has several trains arriving daily from both coasts. The station is at 340 S. 600 West (© **800/872-7245;** www.amtrak.com).

VISITOR INFORMATION

The **Salt Lake Convention and Visitors Bureau** has an information center downtown in the Salt Palace, 90 S. West Temple (© **800/541-4955** or 801/521-2822; www.visitsaltlake.com). It's open Monday through Friday from 8:30am to 5pm (until 6pm from Memorial Day to Labor Day), Saturday and Sunday from 9am to 5pm. Additional information centers, staffed 9am to 9pm daily, can be found in the baggage areas in Salt Lake City International Airport Terminals I and II. There is another information center just off I-80 at 7200 West, open Wednesday through Sunday from 9:30am to 5pm.

CITY LAYOUT

Salt Lake City is laid out in a simple grid system centered on Temple Square. The roads bounding the Square are North Temple, South Temple, West Temple, and Main Street, with the center of town at the southeast corner (the intersection of Main and South Temple), which is the site of the Brigham Young Monument. The numbers in the road names increase from here by 100s in the four cardinal directions, with West Temple taking the place of 100 West, 100 North called North Temple, and 100 East known as State Street.

Addresses may seem confusing at first, but are really quite clear once you get accustomed to them. For instance, 1292 S. 400 West lies almost 13 blocks south of Temple Square and 4 blocks west, and 243 N. 600 East is about 2 blocks north and 6 blocks east.

A variety of detailed city maps can be purchased at most bookstores. The *Salt Lake Visitor's Guide,* available free at the visitor center, includes maps showing the approximate location of many restaurants, motels, and attractions.

NEIGHBORHOODS IN BRIEF

Downtown   The downtown area, centered on Temple Square, is both a business district and the administrative center for the LDS Church. Church offices, the Family History Library, the Museum of Church History and Art, and other church buildings surround the Square. This is most likely where you'll spend the bulk of your time. Within a few blocks south, west, and east are hotels, restaurants, stores, and two major shopping centers. Within a couple of blocks are the Salt Palace Convention Center, the Maurice Abravanel Concert Hall, and the Capitol Theatre.

Capitol Hill   The Capitol Hill district lies north of the Square and encompasses the 40 acres around the Utah State Capitol Building and Council Hall. Some lovely old homes are located in the blocks surrounding the Capitol.

Marmalade District   The blocks west of the Capitol to Quince Street are known as the Marmalade District. The streets in this small area were named for the nut and fruit trees brought in by early settlers, and the houses represent a variety of the city's early architectural styles.

Avenues District   The Avenues District lies east of the Capitol and north of South Temple. Most of the larger homes here date from the silver boom in Little Cottonwood Canyon, when they were built by successful miners and merchants. Today, the tenants are mostly college students and young professionals.

Salt Lake City Neighborhoods

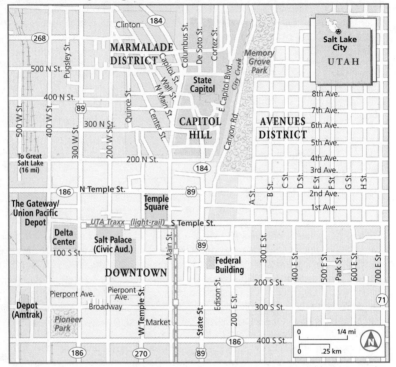

2 Getting Around

BY CAR   This is an easy city to explore by car, in large part because of the wide streets and abundant parking. National car-rental companies here include **Advantage** (© 800/777-5500 or 801/531-1199), **Alamo** (© 800/327-9633 or 801/575-2211), **Avis** (© 800/331-1212 or 801/575-2847), **Budget** (© 800/527-0700 or 801/575-2500), **Dollar** (© 800/800-4000 or 801/575-2580), **Enterprise** (© 800/325-8007 or 801/537-7433), **Hertz** (© 800/654-3131 or 801/575-2683), and **National** (© 800/227-7368 or 801/575-2277). All of these companies either have offices at the airport or will deliver a car to the airport for you.

You'll find many public parking lots in the downtown area, costing from $1 to $7 per day. Some lots are free with validation from participating merchants or restaurants. Street parking downtown is metered, costing 25¢ per half-hour, and usually limited to 1 or 2 hours. Parking for larger RVs and motor homes is limited; there's one large lot—the entire block between North and South Temple and 200 and 300 West—where you can park for $2 to $6 per hour. You might also try the lot behind the Capitol, where there are some designated large-vehicle spaces; East Capitol Street, which is not metered, is a possibility as well.

BY PUBLIC TRANSPORTATION   The **Utah Transit Authority** (© 801/743-3882; www.utabus.com) provides **bus service** throughout the city, with a free fare zone in the downtown area, roughly from 400 South to North Temple, continuing up Main Street to 500 North to include the State Capitol, and between 200 East and West Temple. You can ride free within this zone, getting on and off as many times as you'd like. The fee for traveling in the other zones is $1.25 per person; 60¢ for seniors and those with disabilities. Some buses are wheelchair accessible, and all have bicycle carriers. **Traxx,** a light-rail system also operated by the Utah Transit Authority, with the same contact information and same rates as the Utah Transit Authority's bus service, runs 15 miles from the Sandy Civic Center in the Salt Lake City suburb of Sandy north to Delta Center in downtown Salt Lake City. The trains are wheelchair accessible and bicycles are permitted. Route schedules and maps for both the buses and light rail are available at malls, libraries, and visitor centers.

BY TAXI   For a taxi, contact the **City Cab** (② **801/363-5550**), **Yellow Cab** (② **801/521-2100**), or **Ute Cab** (② **801/359-7788**), all available 24 hours a day.

FAST FACTS: Salt Lake City

American Express   The American Express office is located at 215 S. State St. (② **801/596-0083**). It's open Monday through Friday from 9am to 5pm.

Business Hours   Banks are usually open Monday through Friday from 9am to 5pm, often until 6pm on Friday; some have hours on Saturday. Small stores are usually open Monday through Saturday, with some also open on Sunday afternoon. A growing number of department stores, and most chain discount stores and supermarkets, are open daily and until 9pm at least one or two evenings a week. Some supermarkets are open 24 hours a day.

Doctors   For physician referrals, contact the **Utah Medical Association** (② **801/355-7477**). In an emergency, dial ② **911**.

Emergencies   Dial ② **911** for police, fire, or ambulance.

Hospitals   **LDS Hospital,** 8th Avenue and C Street (② **801/408-1100**), and **Salt Lake Regional Medical Center,** 1050 E. South Temple (② **801/350-4111**), both have 24-hour emergency rooms.

Newspapers/Magazines   The two major daily newspapers are the *Salt Lake Tribune* (www.sltrib.com) and the *Deseret News* (www.deseretnews.com). The *Salt Lake City Magazine* is a slick publication with a section on current events.

Police   For emergencies, call ② **911**. The non-emergency police phone number is ② **801/799-3000**.

Post Office   The main post office is at 1760 W. 2100 South; the branch closest to downtown is at 230 W. 200 South (② **800/275-8777**; www.usps.com for hours and locations of other post offices).

Road & Traffic Conditions   For statewide road and traffic conditions, call ② **800/492-2400**.

Taxes   Sales tax in Salt Lake City is 6.6%; restaurant tax totals 7.6%; lodging taxes total 11.2% within the city limits, 10.1 to 11.1% in Salt Lake County outside the municipal boundaries.

Weather   Call ② **801/575-7669** for weather reports.

3 Where to Stay

You'll have no trouble finding comfortable, conveniently located accommodations in Salt Lake City, usually at relatively reasonable rates. In fact, a building boom of new rooms for the 2002 Olympics resulted in a surplus of lodging, so if you check around, you're likely to find rates that are significantly lower than the rates listed here.

Among the more affordable major chains and franchises (usually charging under $75 for two persons), we recommend the **Days Inn,** 315 W. 3300 South (© 800/329-7466 or 801/486-8780); **Econo Lodge,** 715 W. North Temple (© 877/233-2666 or 801/363-0062); **Super 8,** 616 S. 200 West (© 800/800-8000 or 801/534-0808); and **Travelodge,** 144 W. North Temple (© 800/578-7878 or 801/533-8200).

Slightly more expensive are the **Comfort Suites Airport,** 172 N. 2100 West (© **800/424-6423** or 801/715-8688); **Hampton Inn Downtown,** 425 S. 300 West (© **800/426-7866** or 801/741-1110); and **Radisson Hotel Salt Lake City Airport,** 2177 W. North Temple (© **800/333-3333** or 801/364-5800).

Prices listed here are the rack rates, which virtually no one actually pays; the actual price that you will pay will most likely be significantly lower. Make a point of asking for discounts, which are often given to seniors, members of the military, business travelers, and members of travel clubs such as AAA. **Salt Lake Reservations** (© **800/847-5810**), operated by the Salt Lake Convention & Visitors Bureau, often offers the lowest rates available.

VERY EXPENSIVE

The Grand America Hotel 🌟🌟🌟   This premier downtown hotel, opened in March of 2001, is the place to stay for those who want the utmost in service and accommodations, and are willing to pay for it. Occupying an entire city block in downtown Salt Lake City, the Grand America is reminiscent of majestic European hotels, with more than 450,000 square feet of hand-tooled marble and granite. The exquisitely designed rooms include deluxe executive suites boasting 880 square feet of comfort and elegance, and beautifully appointed deluxe rooms with patios and balconies overlooking pool and garden areas. The concierge floor has a lounge. All rooms are equipped with large screen TVs, three telephones, dataports, and the finest quality furnishings.

555 S. Main St., Salt Lake City, UT 84111. © 800/621-4505 or 801/258-6000. Fax 801/258-6911. www. grandamerica.com. 775 units, including 395 suites. $225–$280 double; $275–$4,500 suite. AE, DC, DISC, MC, V. **Amenities:** 2 restaurants; 2 indoor and 1 outdoor heated pools; fitness center; Jacuzzi; sauna; business center; shopping arcade; 24-hr. room service; in-room massage; laundry service; dry cleaning. *In room:* A/C, TV, dataport, iron.

EXPENSIVE

The Armstrong Mansion Bed & Breakfast 🌟🌟   This stately red-brick mansion exudes an atmosphere of splendor and luxury. The B&B is an opulent Queen Anne–style Victorian home decorated with antiques and reproductions. It features such architectural delights as stained-glass windows and an intricately carved oak staircase. The four-story mansion, built in 1893 and listed on the National Register of Historic Places, was renovated in 1994 and now has an elevator. The stencils on the walls are reproductions of the mansion's original decorative patterns, discovered during renovation. A variety of rooms are available; most have queen-size beds though a few have kings. Most units have whirlpool tubs. The full all-you-can-eat breakfast buffet—served between 7:30 and 10am—consists of a hot dish, breads, and a variety of fruits.

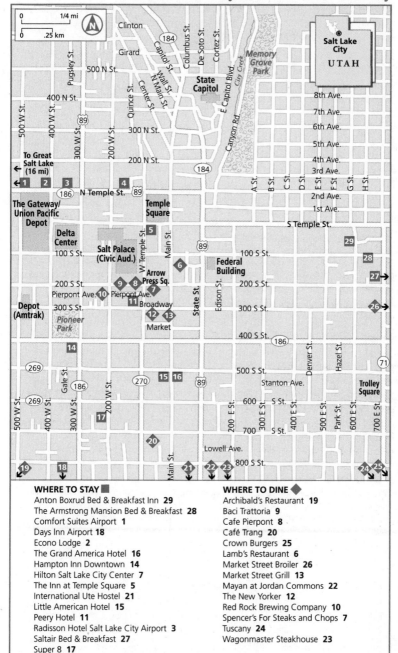

WHERE TO STAY

Anton Boxrud Bed & Breakfast Inn **29**
The Armstrong Mansion Bed & Breakfast **28**
Comfort Suites Airport **1**
Days Inn Airport **18**
Econo Lodge **2**
The Grand America Hotel **16**
Hampton Inn Downtown **14**
Hilton Salt Lake City Center **7**
The Inn at Temple Square **5**
International Ute Hostel **21**
Little America Hotel **15**
Peery Hotel **11**
Radisson Hotel Salt Lake City Airport **3**
Saltair Bed & Breakfast **27**
Super 8 **17**
Travelodge **4**

WHERE TO DINE

Archibald's Restaurant **19**
Baci Trattoria **9**
Cafe Pierpont **8**
Café Trang **20**
Crown Burgers **25**
Lamb's Restaurant **6**
Market Street Broiler **26**
Market Street Grill **13**
Mayan at Jordan Commons **22**
The New Yorker **12**
Red Rock Brewing Company **10**
Spencer's For Steaks and Chops **7**
Tuscany **24**
Wagonmaster Steakhouse **23**

667 E. 100 South, Salt Lake City, UT 84102. © **800/708-1333** or 801/531-1333. Fax 801/531-0282. www. armstrongmansion.com. 13 units. $99–$229 double. Children stay free in family units. Rates include full breakfast. AE, DISC, MC, V. **Amenities:** Spa; massage. *In room:* A/C, TV.

Hilton Salt Lake City Center   This handsome, modern hotel has spacious, well-appointed rooms, an excellent restaurant, and a good location just 2 blocks from Temple Square and across the street from the convention center. Each pleasantly decorated unit contains either one king or two queen beds, a large working desk, a safe, an armoire with TV, two phones with dataports, and a combination shower/tub. Standard extras include voice mail, and two suites have whirlpool tubs. Guest rooms have good views of the city and surrounding mountains, especially dramatic near the top of the 18-story building.

On site are a bar and two restaurants—Spencer's For Steaks and Chops (p. 84), specializing in steaks and chops, and the more casual Trofi Restaurant. There is a sundeck, conference facilities, an ATM, and a souvenir shop, and the hotel offers free newspaper delivery.

255 S. West Temple, Salt Lake City, UT 84101. © **800/HILTONS** or 801/328-2000. Fax 801/532-1953. www. saltlakecenter.hilton.com. 499 units. $79–$229 double; from $195 suite. AE, DC, DISC, MC, V. Covered parking (6 ft. 6 in. height limit) $7, or $10 valet. Pets accepted. **Amenities:** 2 restaurants; bar; indoor lap-size pool; hydrotherapy pool; exercise room; sauna; concierge; car-rental desk; airport shuttle; business center; limited room service (6am–11pm daily); in-room massage (for a fee); dry cleaning. *In room:* A/C, TV, dataport, coffeemaker, hair dryer, iron.

The Inn at Temple Square ★★   A beautiful hotel brimming with 18th-century European elegance and style, The Inn at Temple Square is an exquisite little gem, offering wonderful service, food, and facilities. Built in 1930, the hotel has been restored and then some—it offers an experience reminiscent of the grand hotels of old, but with a warm, homey touch. The lobby is like a living room, with fine artwork, couches, and chairs you can sink into. On the mezzanine level, you'll find a baby grand piano, a library with inviting reading areas, and a fireplace. Spacious guest rooms have a comfortable, old-world feel.

The Inn is centrally located, just across from Temple Square and within easy walking distance of downtown theaters, restaurants, spectator sports, historic sites, and shopping. Passages Restaurant serves three meals Monday through Saturday in a casual setting. Amenities include valet parking. The entire facility is smoke-free.

71 W. South Temple, Salt Lake City, UT 84101. © **800/843-4668** or 801/531-1000. Fax 801/536-7272. www. theinn.com. 95 units. $135–$155 double; $170–$270 suite. Rates include full breakfast. AE, DC, DISC, MC, V. **Amenities:** Restaurant (American); free passes to a nearby health club; airport shuttle; limited room service (6:30–9:30am, 11am–2pm and 5–10pm Mon–Sat; hours are shorter on Sun); same-day dry cleaning. *In room:* A/C, TV, dataport, hair dryer, iron.

ⓚ Kids   Family-Friendly Hotels

Little America Hotel (p. 81)   This upscale hotel is popular with the whole family in part because of its sun deck with an indoor/outdoor pool and its separate outdoor pool.

Saltair Bed & Breakfast (p. 81)   The spacious cottages and the bungalow offer great spots for kids to relax and play without having to worry about disturbing other guests.

Little America Hotel ★★ *Kids* Little America is among Salt Lake City's finest hotels, offering a wide variety of rooms, all individually decorated. Choices range from standard courtside units to extra-large deluxe tower suites in the 17-story high-rise. All are gracefully yet comfortably appointed in French provincial style, and come complete with 31-inch color TVs and pay-per-view movies. The locally popular coffee shop opens at 5am; there's also a steakhouse and lounge. The hotel offers valet parking, and has a second-floor sun deck with an indoor/outdoor pool plus a separate, beautifully landscaped outdoor pool. There are banquet and conference facilities here.

500 S. Main St., Salt Lake City, UT 84101. © 800/453-9450 or 801/363-6781. Fax 801/596-5911. www. littleamerica.com/slc. 850 units, including 22 suites. $82–$169 double; $975 suite. AE, DC, DISC, MC, V. **Amenities:** 2 restaurants; lounge; 2 pools (outdoor heated, indoor/outdoor heated); state-of-the-art health club; Jacuzzi; sauna; concierge; shopping arcade; salon; limited room service (6am–midnight); in-room massage; laundry service; dry cleaning. *In room:* A/C, TV w/ pay movies.

Peery Hotel ★★ *Finds* Among our top choices for those who appreciate the ambiance of a historic hotel, the Peery is one of the few truly historic hotels in Salt Lake City. Completed in 1910, it has been fully renovated and restored to its former understated European elegance, offering comfortable, tastefully decorated accommodations. The lobby is delightful, with old-style pigeonholes for letters and a grand staircase to the upper floors. Each unique, handsomely appointed room contains period furnishings, pedestal sinks with antique brass fixtures, a queen or king bed, and desk. Some units have refrigerators, and several suites have whirlpool tubs. The entire hotel is nonsmoking.

110 W. 300 South (Broadway), Salt Lake City, UT 84101. © 800/331-0073 or 801/521-4300. Fax 801/364-3295. www.peeryhotel.com. 73 units. $129–$159 double; $189 and up suite (suite rates include breakfast for two). AE, DC, DISC, MC, V. Parking fee $7.50 per day self, $10 per day valet. **Amenities:** 2 restaurants; lounge; exercise room; concierge; business center; limited room service (4 to 9pm); same-day laundry service and dry cleaning. *In room:* A/C, TV, dataport, coffeemaker, hair dryer, iron.

MODERATE

Anton Boxrud Bed & Breakfast Inn ★★ This beautiful three-story red-brick structure, built in 1901, is listed on the Salt Lake City Historical Register as "Victorian Eclectic." A boardinghouse from 1938 to 1968, it's now a lovely, comfortable bed-and-breakfast inn. Each room is individually decorated with a mix of antiques and reproductions; all have queen beds with down comforters. Pocket doors and stained-glass windows grace the sitting room, where guests gather to enjoy evening refreshments. An outdoor Jacuzzi is available year-round, and a private business office for guest use is furnished with a fax, copier, phone, and modem. The homemade full breakfast includes a hot dish, and a continental breakfast is available for early risers. Special diets can be accommodated. The entire property is nonsmoking.

57 S. 600 East, Salt Lake City, UT 84102. © 800/524-5511 or 801/363-8035. Fax 801/596-1316. www. antonboxrud.com. 7 units, 2 single rooms with shared bathroom. $78–$140 double. Rates include full breakfast. AE, DC, DISC, MC, V. **Amenities:** Outdoor Jacuzzi. *In room:* A/C, no phone.

Saltair Bed & Breakfast ★ *Kids* Established in 1980, the Saltair is one of the oldest continuously operating B&Bs in Utah, although the building itself is quite a bit older. Now listed on the National Historic Register, it was constructed in 1903 and housed Salt Lake City's Italian Consulate in the early part of the century. Named for a resort built on the Great Salt Lake in the late 1800s, this inn boasts an enormous collection of Saltair memorabilia, from humorous postcards to knickknacks of all kinds. Units vary in size and specifics, from standard rooms to suites to cottages to a fully equipped bungalow. The cottages and bungalow are especially good for those traveling with children. All units are comfortably furnished with an eclectic variety of antiques, and goose-down comforters grace each bed. Some bathrooms have showers only, others have shower/tub combos, and one has a whirlpool tub for two. Several units have fully equipped kitchens.

164 S. 900 East, Salt Lake City, UT 84102. ℭ **800/733-8184** or 801/533-8184. Fax 801/595-0332. www.salt-lakebandb.com. 13 units, 3 with shared bathroom. $55–$109 double; $99–$185 suites, cottages, and bungalow. Rates include full/continental breakfast (except in kitchen units). AE, DC, DISC, MC, V. **Amenities:** Outdoor Jacuzzi. *In room:* A/C, TV, kitchen in some units, no phone.

INEXPENSIVE

International Ute Hostel   Located in a safe residential neighborhood, this hostel offers bunk beds in three dorm rooms, plus two private rooms (each with one queen bed). It's just a short walk to the Traxx light-rail line, which provides easy access to downtown attractions. As you would expect, everyone shares bathrooms and showers. Facilities include a fully equipped kitchen with free beverages, and lounges with cable TV. Particularly popular with international students, the hostel is unusually clean and provides free linen, tea and coffee, and safe deposit boxes. Complimentary pick-up at the airport, train and bus depots, or information center is available, as is free off-street parking. Inexpensive bike, ski, skate, and golf rentals can be arranged. Smoking is not permitted.

21 E. Kelsey Ave., Salt Lake City, UT 84111. ℭ **801/595-1645.** Fax 801/539-0291. www.infobytes.com/ute-hostel. 14 beds in 3 dorm units, 2 private units. $15 dorm bed; $35 private unit. No credit cards. **Amenities:** Jacuzzi. *In room:* A/C, no phone.

CAMPGROUNDS

Salt Lake KOA/VIP   This huge, well-maintained campground is the closest camping and RV facility to downtown Salt Lake City. Facilities include two pools, a hot tub, two playgrounds, a video arcade, two coin-operated laundries, several bathhouses, a convenience store with RV supplies, propane, an RV and car wash, well-maintained grassy areas for tents, and large shade trees. It offers 14 instant phone hookups, 200 sites with 50-amp power, and a jogging/pet-walk/bicycle trail behind the campground. RVers who plan to hook up to the campground's water supply will need regulators to control the erratic water pressure. Bus route 50 heads east on North Temple to downtown sights.

1400 W. North Temple, Salt Lake City, UT 84116. ℭ **800/226-7752** or 801/328-0224. Fax 801/355-1055. www.campvip.com. 396 sites. $22–$36; camping cabins $45. MC, V. Advance reservations recommended May–Sept. Pets accepted. **Amenities:** 2 outdoor pools; Jacuzzi; coin-op washers and dryers.

4 Where to Dine

Salt Lake City restaurants are more casual than those in most major American cities. The service is generally excellent and very friendly. Alcoholic drinks are not offered when diners are seated, so except in private clubs, you'll have to ask for a drink.

EXPENSIVE

Market Street Broiler   *Value*   SEAFOOD/STEAK/PASTA   Market Street Broiler combines the atmosphere of the San Francisco wharf with the Southwest's famed mesquite grilling wood to produce—drum roll, please—mesquite-grilled fresh seafood. The Broiler's lobby is actually a fresh-fish market (open daily 9am to 9pm); you could take some fish home to prepare yourself, but it's a lot more fun to sit at the counter around the glass-enclosed kitchen and watch the chef-artisans do their thing with some mesquite, a match, and fish that's flown in fresh daily. Those not interested in a show can eat in the upstairs dining room or on the patio in summer.

More casual than the Market Street Grill, the Broiler offers the same excellent food at lower prices. Our favorites here include the scallops, shrimp, and halibut plate, prepared on a skewer with bell peppers and onion. We also like the fish and chips—your choice of salmon or halibut. Although seafood is definitely the specialty here, those not interested in fish won't leave hungry—other entrees include hickory-smoked barbecued baby back ribs, barbecued chicken, and certified black Angus steaks. Full liquor service is available.

260 S. 1300 East. ⒸⒸ 801/583-8808. www.gastronomyinc.com. Reservations not accepted. Main courses lunch $6–$40; main courses dinner $7–$42. AE, DC, DISC, MC, V. Mon–Thurs 11am–10pm; Fri–Sat 11am–10:30pm; Sun 4–9pm (from 11am in summer).

Market Street Grill ★★★ SEAFOOD/STEAK   A fancier version of Market Street Broiler (reviewed above and owned by the same company), the Market Street Grill is quite possibly Utah's best seafood restaurant. Expect a wait before you're led into the noisy, somewhat cramped dining room. The place is packed for good reason: Fresh fish is flown in daily from around the world, and the Grill knows how to do it up right.

We recommend the Pacific red snapper Monterey, served with fresh tomato sauce, mushrooms, garlic, white wine, and Gulf shrimp; and the cioppino, a seafood stew of lobster tail, shrimp, crab, cockles, snapper, and scallops—or choose one of about two dozen other seafood offerings. You'll also find a good choice of dinner salads, pastas, and excellent black Angus steaks. From 3 to 7pm the restaurant offers a fixed-price early bird dinner special: a choice of slow-roasted prime rib, Alaskan halibut, or Atlantic salmon for $15.99. Look for all the standard breakfast choices, plus a seafood omelet, of course; lunch includes salads, sandwiches, pasta, steaks, and a variety of seafood dishes; and there's also a good Sunday brunch. Full liquor service is available.

A similar lunch, dinner, and Sunday brunch menu is served at the **Market Street Grill–Cottonwood,** 2985 E. 6580 South (Ⓒ **801/942-8860**).

48 Market St. Ⓒ **801/322-4668.** www.gastronomyinc.com. Reservations not accepted. Lunch $7–$29; dinner $11–$45. AE, DC, DISC, MC, V. Mon–Thurs 6:30am–10pm; Fri 6:30am–11pm; Sat 7am–3pm and 4–11pm, Sun 9am–3pm and 4–9pm.

The New Yorker ★★★ AMERICAN   Among Utah's finest restaurants, the New Yorker oozes quiet sophistication, with rich woods, understated elegance, excellent food, and impeccable service. Technically a private club, you'll have to buy a membership to enter ($4), but trust us—it's worth it. The New Yorker offers complete liquor service—unlike many Utah restaurants, you can buy a drink here without ordering any food.

From the dining room dinner menu, you might choose the Maryland crab cakes, which aficionados say are as good as—or better than—those you'll find anywhere; the certified Angus beef filet mignon with cabernet sauce and blue cheese; or the roasted rack of American lamb. Lunch brings dishes such as deep-fried Gulf white shrimp, served with fries, coleslaw, and cocktail sauce; veal schnitzel with green peppercorns and lemon butter sauce; sandwiches; and salads. In the less formal cafe you'll find somewhat lighter fare, such as a bacon-and-avocado burger, fried camembert and pear with red pepper jelly, and an excellent cobb salad.

60 W. Market St. ℭ **801/363-0166.** www.gastronomyinc.com. Reservations recommended. Dining room main courses $6–$20 lunch, $20–$39 dinner; cafe main courses $7–$20. AE, DC, DISC, MC, V. Dining room Mon–Thurs 11:30am–2:30pm and 5:30–10pm; Fri 11:30am–2:30pm and 5:30–10:30pm; Sat 5:30–10:30pm. Cafe Mon–Thurs 11:30am–10:30pm; Fri 11:30am–11pm; Sat 5:30–11pm.

Spencer's For Steaks and Chops ★★★ STEAK/CHOPS   This sophisti-cated chophouse is the perfect spot to celebrate a special occasion, or to just sit back and enjoy one of the best steaks you've ever tasted. The handsomely appointed dining room reminds us of a library in the country home of a British lord, with dark wood, tapestry-like fabrics and wall coverings, historic photos, soft lighting, and intimate and comfortable booths. Service is attentive and efficient.

Beef is king here—aged, well-marbled USDA prime beef that is simply and (to our thinking) perfectly prepared. We heartily recommend the New York strip, or the super-tender filet mignon. Other choices include prime rib, grilled vegetable pasta, double cut lamb chops, and a broiled chicken chop. Seafood lovers can choose among the fresh fish of the day (flown in daily), grilled salmon, Alaskan king crab, or grilled prawns on linguini. Main courses include a house salad and hot, crusty bread. Accompaniments, such as the garlic skin-on smashed potatoes or Burgundy mushrooms, are extra. The lunch menu includes a half-pound burger, a chicken-breast sandwich on sourdough bread, grilled salmon, any of the dinner steaks, and entree salads such as Caesar with salmon.

Spencer's is technically a private club, so you'll need to pay about $4 to join. It has an extensive wine list and an excellent selection of single malt Scotches, along with what is probably the best selection of cigars in the area.

Hilton Salt Lake City Center, 255 S. West Temple. ℭ **801/238-4748.** www.spencersforsteaksandchops. com/slc. Reservations recommended. Lunch items $6.95–$13; dinner main courses $15–$35. AE, DC, DISC, MC, V. Mon–Thurs 11:30am–2:30pm and 5–10pm; Fri 11:30am–2:30pm and 5–11pm; Sat 5–11pm; Sun 5–10pm.

Tuscany ★★ NORTHERN ITALIAN   Come to the Tuscany for top-notch food and wine in a quaintly elegant setting on a wooded lot at the foot of the Wasatch Mountains. The restaurant is fittingly built to resemble an Italian mountain lodge, with massive beams, cathedral ceilings, an extensive use of rock, Old World murals, stained glass, and three enormous fireplaces. The northern Italian cuisine has been tempered with western influences, resulting in delicious dishes such as hardwood-grilled, double-cut pork chop with scallion mashed potatoes, balsamic roasted onions and pan juices; gnocchi Bolognese, which are potato gnocchi with traditional creamy meat sauce and smoked buf-falo mozzarella; and our favorite: oven roasted fillet of salmon with pesto-smoked bacon crust served with toasted vegetable couscous. And be sure to save room for one of their house-made desserts such as bread pudding with pears and dried cranberries, or vanilla bean crème brûlée with fresh berries. In summer you can dine alfresco in a lovely garden. Full liquor service is available.

2832 E. 6200 South. ℭ **801/277-9919.** www.tuscanyslc.com. Main courses lunch $8.75–$15; main courses dinner $14–$23. AE, DC, DISC, MC, V. Tues–Fri 11:30am–2pm; Mon–Sat 5–10pm; Sun 10am–1:30pm brunch and 5–9pm.

MODERATE

Archibald's Restaurant AMERICAN   Located in a restored 1877 flour mill that's listed on the National Historic Register, Archibald's is a comfortable step back in time. In each booth, you'll find a picture and brief discussion of one of Archibald Gardner's 11 wives. Menu items here range from American standards—burgers, top sirloin steak, or salmon—to more creative fare, such as the chicken jubilee—strips of breaded chicken breast sautéed with fresh ginger, garlic, tomatoes, cilantro, onions, pepper flakes, and coconut. We heartily recommend the halibut and chips, or the ginger chicken salad—grilled chicken and almonds over shredded lettuce, with olives, green onions, mushrooms, snow peas, and a sesame-ginger dressing. Full liquor service is available.

1100 W. 7800 South, West Jordan (in Gardner Village; see "Nearby Attractions," later in the chapter, for directions). ✆ **801/566-6940.** www.gardnervillage.com. Reservations accepted only for parties of 8 or more. Main courses lunch $5–$8; main courses dinner $8–$18. AE, DISC, MC, V. Mon–Thurs 11am–9pm; Fri–Sat 11am–10pm.

Baci Trattoria 🌟 NORTHERN ITALIAN This handsome and popular restaurant serves excellent Italian cuisine, and plenty of it. The dining room is decidedly modern, with bright yellow walls, a high ceiling, colorful contemporary art, and a long, curved, stainless-steel bar. Patio dining is available in warm weather. The menu includes a wide selection of innovative pizzas, baked in a wood-burning oven, plus pastas, chicken, veal, steaks, and seafood. Try the lasagna—either meat or vegetarian—or the *Pappardelle al Telefono,* pasta ribbons with creamy tomato sauce and mozzarella. The staff is friendly and efficient. Full liquor service is available.

134 W. Pierpont Ave. ✆ **801/328-1500.** www.gastronomyinc.com. Main courses lunch and dinner $5.50–$33.50. AE, DC, DISC, MC, V. Mon–Thurs 11:30am–3pm and 5–10pm; Fri 11:30am–3pm and 5–11pm; Sat 5–11pm.

Cafe Pierpont (Kids) MEXICAN A lively Americanized version of a Mexican cantina, Cafe Pierpont is decorated with red, green, and white streamers (the colors of the Mexican flag) and other festive touches that give the restaurant an every-day-is-a-fiesta atmosphere. Portions are generous, to say the least, and the quality is excellent, although those accustomed to the fiery chile of New Mexico may find some of the dishes here a bit tame. All of the standard tacos, enchiladas, and burritos are available, along with more exotic Mexican specialties and a good selection of fresh seafood. But the fajitas are the real attraction—choose from mesquite-grilled chicken or beef, delivered to your table sizzling hot along with onions, guacamole, black beans, and hot tortillas. We also recommended the coconut-dipped jumbo Mexican white shrimp, an appetizer served with jalapeño jelly. Finish up with the flan, a traditional Mexican custard covered with caramel sauce. Full liquor service is available.

122 W. Pierpont Ave. ✆ **801/364-1222.** www.gastronomyinc.com. Main courses $7–$18. AE, DC, DISC, MC, V. Mon–Thurs 11:30am–10pm; Fri 11:30am–11pm; Sat 4–11pm; Sun 5–9pm.

Lamb's Restaurant 🌟🌟 (Finds) AMERICAN/CONTINENTAL Opened in 1919 in the northern Utah town of Logan, by Greek immigrant George Lamb, this restaurant moved to Salt Lake City's Herald Building in 1939 and has been serving the Who's Who of Utah here ever since. But this isn't one of those fancy places that you go to just to be seen; Lamb's is successful because it consistently serves very good food at reasonable prices, with friendly, efficient service.

Decorated with antiques and pieces from the 1920s and 1930s, Lamb's is comfortable and unpretentious. The extensive menu offers mostly basic American and continental fare, although the restaurant's Greek origins are also evident. In a tip of the hat to the restaurant's moniker, several lamb dishes appear on the menu, including broiled French-style lamb chops and barbecued lamb shank.

Other popular dinner selections—all available after 11:30am and cooked to order—are broiled black Angus New York steak topped with bleu cheese, grilled baby beef liver with sautéed onions, steamed finnan haddie (smoked haddock), Greek-style broiled chicken breasts with oregano, and grilled fresh rainbow trout. You'll also find a good selection of sandwiches and salads, daily pasta and salad specials, and a variety of desserts, including an extra-special rice pudding. There's live background music in varying styles Thursday, Friday, and Saturday evenings. Full liquor service is available.

169 S. Main St. ✆ **801/364-7166.** Main courses $5–$21. AE, DC, DISC, MC, V. Mon–Fri 7am–9pm; Sat 8am–9pm.

Mayan at Jordan Commons *Kids* MEXICAN   This huge restaurant (it seats 1,000) puts on a show as you chow down on variations of Mexican standards. The restaurant is spread over three floors and resembles an ancient Mayan temple in a tropical rainforest, complete with foliage, bird sounds, and even some talking animals. The walls are molded concrete, the floor looks like granite, and there's a lovely waterfall cascading 35 feet into a pool—watch for the divers. The menu offers a wide selection of Mexican choices, from salads to tacos and burritos. Especially good are the shrimp tacos, served in a soft corn tortilla, with coleslaw, guacamole, and pico de gallo sauce; and the Mayan Two-Fisted Burrito, a huge burrito that's stuffed with shredded cheese, black beans, Mexican rice, lettuce, pico de gallo, and your choice of fajita-style steak or chicken, and smothered with enchilada sauce and melted cheese. Full liquor service is available.

9400 S. State, Sandy. ✆ **801/304-4600.** www.jordancommons.com. Main courses $8–$13. AE, DISC, MC, V. Mon–Thurs 11am–10pm; Fri–Sat 11am–11pm; Sun 11:30am–9pm.

Red Rock Brewing Company ⚜ AMERICAN   This busy, somewhat noisy brewpub is an excellent choice for a lunch or dinner accompanied by local beer. It has a warehouse-like atmosphere, with a high ceiling, brick walls, wood tables and chairs, and a long wooden bar that faces a wood-burning oven. Popular with local businesspeople, the restaurant offers a good variety of dishes, from nine types of wood-fired pizza to sandwiches such as the Italian sausage grinder and the French-onion steak sandwich. Entrees include chicken Parmesan, beef or vegetarian lasagna, chicken schnitzel, a fried seafood platter, and that brewpub standard: fish and chips. They offer terrific home-brewed root beer, plus cream and orange sodas, and a different homemade ice cream each day. Eight or nine styles of beer are available at any given time. Full liquor service is also available.

254 S. 200 West. ✆ **801/521-7446.** Main courses $6–$16. AE, DISC, MC, V. Sun–Thurs 11am–11pm; Fri–Sat 11am–midnight; bar open 1 hr. later than the dining room each night.

Wagonmaster Steakhouse ⚜⚜ *Kids* AMERICAN   For a taste of the wild West of the 1800s, come to the Wagonmaster—you'll dine inside a covered wagon at a table covered with a red-and-white-checked cloth, while outside a gas-fueled bonfire roars. There's even a staged shootout between the Marshal and a bad 'un. The menu ranges from steak—aged USDA choice and grilled to order—to chicken and dumplings to barbecued pork ribs to deep-fried shrimp. There's a prime rib special, a children's menu, and full liquor service.

5485 S. Vine St., Murray. ✆ **801/479-6901.** www.wagonmastersteakco.com. Main courses $8–$25. AE, DISC, MC, V. Tues–Thurs 5:30–10pm; Fri–Sat 5–10pm. From I-15, take exit 303 and head east on 5300 South to Vine St. and turn right; the restaurant will be ahead on your left.

INEXPENSIVE

Café Trang ⚜⚜ *Value* VIETNAMESE/CHINESE   This family-owned and -operated restaurant has been known for serving the best Vietnamese food in the state practically since it opened in 1987. The restaurant now also offers Chinese

---

Kids Family-Friendly Restaurants

Cafe Pierpont (p. 85)   A noisy, festive atmosphere and lots of finger food make the Cafe Pierpont a favorite with kids.

Crown Burgers (see below)   All kids like fast-food joints; this is one even parents will like. The char-broiled burgers are fresh and good, and the hunting lodge–like setting is much more pleasant than your average McDonald's.

Mayan at Jordan Commons (p. 86)   Children love the atmosphere— a Mayan temple in a tropical rainforest, with a waterfall, divers, and talking animals—plus the yummy Mexican finger foods.

Wagonmaster Steakhouse (p. 86)   Staged shootouts, a roaring fire, and seating inside a covered wagon make this a favorite with kids.

---

dishes—mostly Cantonese with some Vietnamese influences. The entire restaurant has been recently remodeled. The new Oriental-style orange and black lacquer chairs glow warmly against the rich hunter green carpet and dark orange walls; Vietnamese paintings grace the walls; and two large aquariums further enhance the decor. Menu items are listed by number—from 1 to 197—with brief English descriptions of each. A popular vegetarian specialty is the fried bean curd with grilled onions and crushed peanuts, served with rice papers, a vegetable platter, and peanut sauce. We enjoyed the spicy *Bun Ga Xao,* rice vermicelli noodles with sautéed chicken and lemongrass, served with grilled onions and peanuts. Beer and wine are available with meals upon request.

There's a second location in the Cottonwood Mall, 4835 S. Highland Dr., Holladay (✆ **801/278-8889**).

818 S. Main St. ✆ **801/539-1638.** Reservations recommended in winter. Main courses $5–$12. AE, DISC, MC, V. Mon–Thurs 11am–10pm; Fri–Sat 11am–10:30pm; Sun noon–10pm.

Crown Burgers ✪ *Kids* FAST FOOD   In-the-know locals say this place serves the best fast-food burger—they're all char-broiled—in Salt Lake City. But this isn't your average hamburger joint. Decorated like a European hunting lodge, with wall sconces, chandeliers, and a stone fireplace, Crown is something of an upscale fast foodery—but you still order at the counter, wait for your number to be called, and pick up your paper-wrapped food yourself. The mini-chain's signature burger is a cheeseburger piled with pastrami; the menu also offers a variety of other burgers, beef burritos, hot pastrami sandwiches, steak sandwiches, gyros, fishburgers, fries, onion rings, and more. The food is good, hot, and fast. No alcohol is served.

Additional Salt Lake City locations include 377 E. 200 South (✆ **801/532-1155**) and 118 N. 300 West (✆ **801/532-5300**).

3190 S. Highland Dr. ✆ **801/467-6633.** Main courses $2.15–$6.60. AE, DISC, MC, V. Mon–Sat 10am–10pm. From downtown, follow State St. south to 2100 South and turn left (east); go about 1½ miles and turn right (south) onto Highland Dr.; Crown is about 2 miles down on your right.

5 Exploring Temple Square

This is the sacred ground for the members of the Church of Jesus Christ of Latter-day Saints, also known as Mormons. (See Appendix A, "Utah in Depth," to learn about the history of the church and modern Mormonism.) The 10-acre **Temple Square** ★★★ is enclosed by 15-foot walls, with a gate in the center of each. In addition to the church buildings, the square houses lovely gardens and statuary, and the North and South Visitor Centers, which have exhibits on the church's history and beliefs, interactive videos, and films. Also in the North Center is an 11-foot-tall replica of the awe-inspiring sculpture *Christus,* a statue of Christ by Danish artist Bertel Thorvaldsen.

The majestic **Temple** is used only for the LDS church's most sacred ceremonies and is not open to the public. Brigham Young chose the site within 4 days of entering the valley, and work began on the six-spired granite structure in 1853. It took 40 years to complete.

The oval **Tabernacle** seats 6,500 people and has one of the West's largest unsupported domed roofs. The Tabernacle has fantastic acoustics and has served as the city's cultural center for over a century.

On Thursday evenings at 8pm, you can listen to the **Mormon Tabernacle Choir** ★★★ rehearse (except when they're on tour; call ℂ **801/240-3221** to check), and on Sunday mornings you can attend their broadcast from 9:30 to 10am (you must be seated by 9:15am). The choir, composed entirely of volunteers, was formed shortly after the first pioneers arrived; many husband and wife members and families participate, sometimes over several generations. The Tabernacle organ has been rebuilt several times, and has grown from the original 1,600 pipes and two manuals to 11,623 pipes and five manuals. The organ is said to have an instantly recognizable signature sound. Half-hour organ recitals take place year-round, Monday through Saturday at noon, Sunday at 2pm. In summer, an additional 2pm recital is scheduled Monday through Saturday. Admission to these performances is free.

The Gothic-style **Assembly Hall** was constructed in 1880 from leftover granite from the Temple and has lovely soaring white spires and stained-glass windows. Free concerts are offered here most weekends; inquire at a visitor center for schedules. Two monuments stand in front of the Assembly Hall: One depicts a pioneer family arriving with a handcart filled with their belongings, and the second commemorates the salvaging of the first crops from a plague of crickets (seagulls swooped down and ate the insects).

Guided tours of the square, lasting approximately 45 minutes and available in 30 languages, leave every few minutes from the flagpole in front of the Tabernacle; personnel in the visitor center can direct you. Tour guides provide a general history of the church (touching upon the church's doctrine) and take you around the square, briefly explaining what you are seeing. Our favorite part of the tour is in the Tabernacle: To demonstrate the incredible acoustics, the group is ushered to the back of the seats while someone stands at the podium and drops three pins—the sound is as clear as a bell! The tour ends at the North Visitor Center with a short film on Mormon beliefs. You are then asked to fill out a card with your name and address, indicating whether you'd like to receive a visit from Mormon missionaries.

The square is bounded by Main Street on the east and North, South, and West Temple streets. The LDS Church recently purchased the stretch of Main Street on the square's east side, closed it to traffic, and transformed it into a lovely park with trees, flowers, walking paths, and benches; a large reflecting pool dominates the area, displaying a mirror image of the magnificent Temple.

Across North Temple Street from the Square is the **Conference Center of the Church of Jesus Christ of Latter-day Saints** (ℂ **801/240-0075**). This huge complex has a **main auditorium** for worship services and meetings, and conference rooms that could easily hold a Boeing 747, plus a magnificent **proscenium theater** that seats 900, and a four-level underground parking facility with 1,300 spaces.

When the church leaders realized there would be four acres of **roof** over the conference center, they decided to do something special. And boy did they—the designers have created a wild landscape resembling a Utah mountain on the outside of the roof. There are bristlecone pines, aspens, Serbian spruces, 21 native meadow grasses, and 300 varieties of Utah wildflowers. An immense fountain flows in four directions and eventually into the Conference Center spire, from which it streams south to cascade 67 feet down the south face of the building. The roof is a serene oasis in the middle of a busy bustling city—people sit or stroll and enjoy the views of the city set against the Wasatch Mountains.

The Conference Center is open Monday through Saturday from 9am to 9pm; free guided tours of the complex are offered approximately every 15 minutes.

The enclosed Temple Square is open daily from 6am to 10pm. Visitor centers are open daily from 9am to 9pm; tours are given between 9am and 8:10pm. Hours are reduced on Christmas. Call © **800/537-9703** or 801/240-2534 for more information. Buses 3, 4, 5, 23, or 50 will get you here. Allow 1 to 3 hours.

6 More Attractions

Family History Library ★★   This incredible facility contains what is probably the world's largest collection of genealogical records under one roof. The growing collection is composed of a substantial number of records from around the United States, fairly comprehensive data from Scotland and England, and information from many other countries. Most of the records, which date from about 1550 to 1920, are from governments, various churches and other organizations, and individuals.

The Mormons created such a huge genealogical library because they believe that families are united for eternity through marriage and other sacred ordinances given in the temples. These ordinances, such as baptism ceremonies, can be done on behalf of ancestors—hence the interest in tracing all deceased family members.

When you enter the library, help is available to assist with your research. There are forms you can fill out with any and all data you already know (so come prepared with copies of whatever you have), and you will be directed from there. An orientation is given to newcomers and includes a handout and a map of the library. Volunteers are stationed around the library to help with anything you need.

Some of the records are in books, and many have been converted to microfilm, microfiche, and computer files. The volunteers will show you how to use any unfamiliar machines. One of the easiest ways to begin a search is to start

---

Tips **Info on the Church of Jesus Christ of Latter-day Saints**

An excellent source for information on places to visit for those interested in the history and beliefs of the Church of Jesus Christ of Latter-day Saints is www.lds.org/placestovisit.

with the place where your ancestors lived, because records are organized first by the geographical origin. From there, you can spend hours immersed in discovering the whos, whats, wheres, and whys of your family history—we know, we did it!

35 N. West Temple. ℂ 801/240-2331. www.familysearch.org. Free admission. Mon 7:30am–5pm; Tues–Sat 7:30am–10pm. Closed major holidays and July 24. Bus: 3, 4, 5, 23, or 50 to Temple Sq.

HISTORIC BUILDINGS & MONUMENTS

Beehive House ⭐   This house was built in 1854 as Brigham Young's family home. Young also kept an office here and entertained church and government leaders on the premises. Young, a lover of New England architecture, utilized much of that style in his house, including a widow's walk for keeping an eye on the surrounding desert. Today, visitors can get a glimpse of the lifestyle of this famous Mormon leader by taking a guided tour of the house. It has been decorated with period furniture (many pieces original to the home) to resemble the way it appeared when Young lived here, as described in a journal kept by his daughter Clarissa. Young's bedroom is to the left of the entrance hall. The Long Hall, where formal entertaining took place, is on the second floor; it was also used as a dormitory to house visitors. Young's children gathered in the sewing room, where they helped with chores, bathed by the cozy stove, and studied Christian principles. Only one of Young's 27 wives lived in the Beehive House at a time; the rest, with some of the children, lived next door in the **Lion House** (not open for tours) or in other houses. Built of stuccoed adobe in 1855 through 1856, the Lion House was named for the stone lion guarding its entrance.

Before you leave, stop at **Eagle Gate,** a 76-foot gateway that marked the entrance to the Brigham Young homestead, located at the corner of State Street and South Temple. It's been altered several times over the years, and the original wooden eagle has been replaced by a 4,000-pound metal version with a 20-foot wingspan. Allow about an hour.

67 E. South Temple. ℂ 801/240-2671. Free admission. Mon–Sat 9:30am–4:30pm (until 6:30pm in summer); Sun 10am–1pm; closes at 1pm on all holidays. Bus: 3, 4, 5, 23, or 50 to Temple Sq.; walk a half block east.

Brigham Young Monument   This marker, near the southeast corner of Temple Square, was placed here to honor Young, the other pioneers who accompanied him here in 1847, and the American Indians and fur trappers who preceded them. Allow 15 minutes.

At Main and S. Temple sts.

Capitol Building ⭐   Built between 1912 and 1915 of unpolished Utah granite and Georgia marble, the capitol, considered one of the finest examples of Renaissance Revival style in the West, rests on a hill in a beautifully landscaped 40-acre park. The state symbol, the beehive (representing industry and cooperation), is a recurring motif both inside and out. Those who don't want to take the free tour can walk through on their own.

The **Rotunda,** which stretches upward 165 feet, is decorated with murals painted during the WPA years (the four largest depict important scenes in the state's early history) and houses several busts of prominent historical figures, including Brigham Young and Philo T. Farnsworth, the man whom we can all thank for bringing us television. The chandelier is astounding—weighing 6,000 pounds and hanging from a 7,000-pound chain.

Other rooms include the State Reception Room, known as the Gold Room because the walls are made from locally mined gold-traverse marble; the offices

Downtown Salt Lake City Attractions

Beehive House **11**
Brigham Young Monument **9**
Capitol Building **1**
Clark Planetarium **12**
Classic Cars International Antique
    Auto Museum of Utah **16**
Conference Center of the Church of
    Jesus Christ of Latter-day Saints **4**
Council Hall **2**
Family History Library **7**

Gallivan Center **14**
Governor's Mansion **13**
Joseph Smith Memorial Building **10**
Liberty Park **17**
Museum of Church History and Art **6**
Pioneer Memorial Museum **3**
Salt Lake Art Center **8**
Temple Square **5**
Utah State Historical Society Museum **15**

Greater Salt Lake Valley Attractions

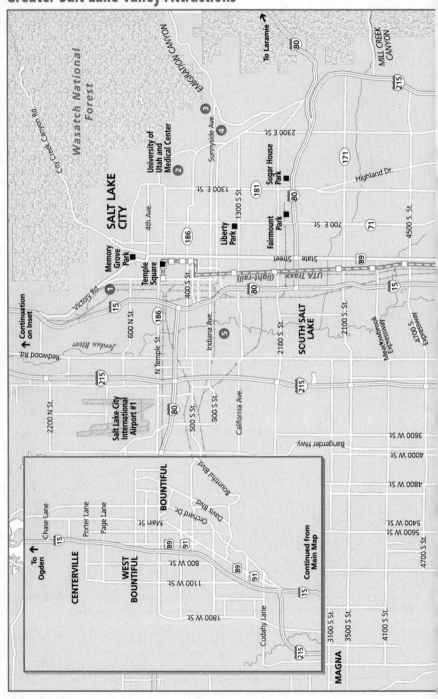

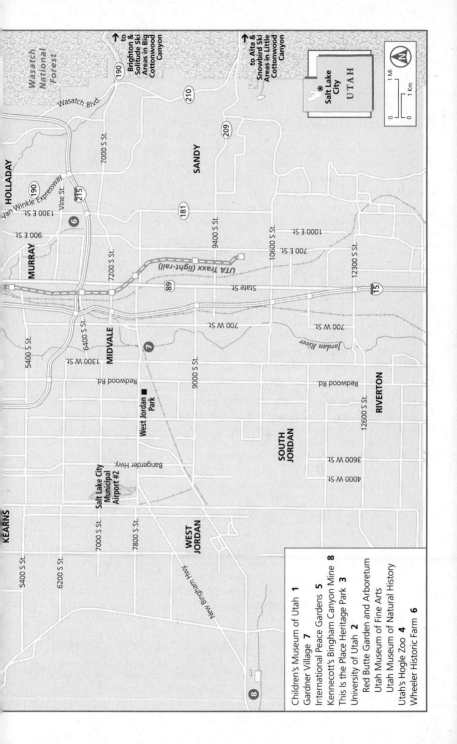

Children's Museum of Utah **1**
Gardner Village **7**
International Peace Gardens **5**
Kennecott's Bingham Canyon Mine **8**
This Is the Place Heritage Park **3**
University of Utah **2**
Red Butte Garden and Arboretum
Utah Museum of Fine Arts
Utah Museum of Natural History
Utah's Hogle Zoo **4**
Wheeler Historic Farm **6**

of the governor and lieutenant governor at the west end; the Hall of Governors, a portrait gallery that honors all those who have served as governor of Utah since statehood in 1896; and at the east end, the offices of Utah's attorney general. Downstairs, you'll find a small souvenir shop and some exhibits, including a large topographical map of Utah.

The third floor houses the Senate, House of Representatives, and Supreme Court of Utah. You can either climb one of the two marble staircases or take the elevator. The state legislature meets for 45 days in January and February; visitors are welcome to sit in the galleries on the fourth floor, which overlook the chambers. In front of the House of Representatives, you'll see a replica of the Liberty Bell, one of 53 bronzed and cast in France in 1950. Allow at least an hour to explore here.

Capitol Hill, at the north end of State St. ℂ 801/538-3000, or 801/538-1563 for tour information. Free admission and tours. Building open daily 8am–8pm; guided tours every half hour Mon–Fri 9am–4pm. Bus: 23 up Main St.

Council Hall   Completed in 1866, Council Hall is a fine example of Federal-Greek Revival architecture. Originally located downtown, it first served as City Hall and the meeting place for the Territorial Legislature; in the early 1960s it was dismantled, coded, and reassembled—block by sandstone block, 325 of them—in its present location. Today, it houses the Utah Travel Council (www.utah.com) upstairs; the ground floor contains a bookstore and gift shop. Allow about ¾ of an hour.

Capitol Hill, 300 N. State St. ℂ 800/Utah-Fun, 800/200-1160, or 801/538-1900. Free admission. Mon–Fri 8am–6pm; Sat 9am–5pm. Bus: 23 to the Capitol.

Governor's Mansion   Silver magnate Thomas Kearns built this palatial home in 1898, sparing no expense to make it as lavish as possible. African and Italian marble and exotic woods from around the world were used extensively throughout. Kearns' widow deeded it to the state in 1937, and the 36-room mansion is now the governor's residence. It suffered a devastating fire just before Christmas 1993, but has been fully restored to its 1902 appearance (1902 was the year that Kearns and his family first moved in). The best time to see the mansion is in December, when it's elaborately decorated for Christmas. Allow about half an hour.

603 E. South Temple. ℂ 801/538-1005. Free admission. Apr–Sept Tues–Thurs 2–4pm; call for hours at other times. Bus: 11.

Joseph Smith Memorial Building   Formerly the historic Hotel Utah, this magnificent building has been renovated and converted into offices, meeting spaces, restaurants, and reception areas (it's very popular for wedding receptions). Between 1911 and 1987, this was a world-renowned hotel; the lobby retains its art-glass ceiling and massive marble pillars, and the architectural details have been lovingly restored throughout. It's worth a stop for a peek inside.

There are 200 computers in the **FamilySearch Center** (ℂ **801/240-4383**), and a staff to help with your genealogical research. A big-screen 500-seat theater offers free (but ticket required, call ℂ **801/240-4383** for schedule and to reserve a ticket) showings of an hour-long movie about the life of Christ. Allow half an hour to an hour and a half.

15 E. South Temple. ℂ 800/537-9703 or 801/240-1266. Free admission. Mon–Sat 9am–9pm. Bus: 3, 4, 5, or 50 to Temple Sq.

MUSEUMS

Clark Planetarium ★ *Kids*   This state-of-the-art planetarium presents star shows depicting the wonders of the universe, light shows, and big screen movies in Utah's only 3-D IMAX theater. It also contains a variety of interactive exhibits ranging from a display about the names of the planets to a Foucault pendulum, plus a rotating relief globe. Allow 1 to 3 hours.

110 S. 400 West. ℂ 801/456-7827. www.clarkplanetarium.org. Free admission to museum; shows $6–$7 adults, $3–$4 children 12 and under. Mon–Thur 11am–9pm; Fri–Sat 9am–midnight; Sun 11am–6pm. Bus: 18.

Classic Cars International Antique Auto Museum of Utah   More than 200 antique and classic cars are packed into several showrooms here, and many are for sale. Although the collection is constantly changing, among the vehicles we admired were a 1903 Steven Duryea, a beautiful bright yellow 1926 Stutz Bearcat, an elegant 1929 dual cowl Duesenberg, a 1936 Packard V-12 two-door convertible, several 1959 big-finned Cadillac convertibles, and a 1925 Packard Phaeton convertible owned by gangster Al Capone. There are usually a number of muscle cars from the 1960s as well. All cars in the collection, whether original or restored, are fully operational. You'll also see antique slot machines, gas pumps, and a jukebox. Allow at least 45 minutes to an hour.

355 W. 700 South. ℂ 801/322-5509. www.classiccarmuseumsales.com. Admission $6 adults, $4 seniors 55 and over and children 12 and under. Mon–Sat 9am–4pm and by appointment. From Temple Sq., head south on Main St. to 700 South; turn right (west) and go 3½ blocks.

Gallivan Center   Some call this Salt Lake City's outdoor living room. You'll find intimate spaces, performances, food, all kinds of characters and activities, and good vantage points for watching the goings-on. Wander through the large art exhibit and the gigantic outdoor chessboard with waist-high pieces, and enjoy the pond, amphitheater, outdoor ice skating rink (call for hours and rates), and aviary. Allow 30 minutes.

239 S. Main St. (the entire block between Main and State sts., and 200 and 300 South). ℂ **801/535-6110.** Free admission. Daily 7am–10pm. Bus: 23 along Main St.

Museum of Church History and Art   This collection of church art and artifacts, started in 1869, includes Utah's earliest Mormon log home, rare 1849 Mormon gold coins, and a scale model of Salt Lake City in 1870. The history of the LDS Church is related in the exhibits that describe each of the church presidents, from Joseph Smith to the present; activities include multimedia programs, films, and puppet shows. There's also a museum shop (closed Sundays). Allow 1 hour.

45 N. West Temple. ℂ 801/240-3310. Free admission. Mon–Fri 9am–9pm; Sat–Sun and most holidays 10am–7pm. Bus: 3, 4, 5, or 50 to Temple Sq.

Pioneer Memorial Museum   Operated by the Daughters of Utah Pioneers, this museum, housed in a Grecian-style building, contains an immense collection of pioneer portraits and memorabilia. The main floor contains paintings, photos, and the personal effects of church leaders Brigham Young and Heber C. Kimball. The collection also includes a manuscript room, household displays, and exhibits on spinning, weaving, railroading, mining, and guns. The restored 1902 steam fire engine is our favorite exhibit. All four stories are packed with relics of Utah's history. You can walk through on your own or with the aid of a guide sheet; tours are also available. A 12-minute film is shown throughout the day. Allow 1 hour.

300 N. Main St. ℭ 801/538-1050. www.pioneermemorialmuseum.org. Free admission; contributions welcome. Mon–Sat 9am–5pm; closed major holidays. Bus: 23.

Salt Lake Art Center   Changing exhibits feature contemporary works by local, regional, and national artists. There are generally several simultaneous exhibitions in a variety of media, including paintings, photographs, sculptures, and ceramics. Allow at least 1 hour, and check the schedule for lectures, poetry readings, concerts, and workshops.

20 S. West Temple. ℭ 801/328-4201. www.slartcenter.org. Free admission; donations welcome. Tues–Thurs and Sat 10am–5pm; Fri 10am–9pm; Sun 1–5pm. Bus: 23 along South Temple.

University of Utah   Members of the Church of Jesus Christ of Latter-day Saints opened the University of Deseret in 1850, just 2½ years after they arrived in the Salt Lake Valley. It closed 2 years later, due to lack of funds and the greater need for primary education, but reopened in 1867 as a business academy. The name changed in 1892, and the growing school moved to its present location in 1900. The university now sprawls over 1,500 acres on the east side of the city.

The university's **Red Butte Garden and Arboretum** ★★ (ℭ 801/581-4747; www.redbuttegarden.org) features 50 acres of display gardens and another 100 acres in their natural state, with 4 miles of nature trails. Located in the foothills of the Wasatch Mountains, this is a terrific spot to take a break from hectic city sightseeing. The gardens are open May through September, Monday through Saturday from 9am to 8pm, Sunday from 9am to 5pm; October through April, Tuesday through Sunday from 10am to 5pm. Admission is $5 for adults, and $3 for children 4 to 17 and seniors 60 and over. From downtown, drive east on 400 South, past the university entrance, continuing until 400 South becomes Foothill Drive; turn east on Wakara Way and continue to the entry drive. Allow 2 hours.

The University is also home to the **Utah Museum of Fine Arts** and the **Utah Museum of Natural History** (both below).

University of Utah. General information line ℭ 801/581-7200. www.utah.edu.

Utah Museum of Fine Arts ★★★   This is among the very best art museums in the state, boasting a permanent collection of more than 17,000 objects. Displays might include Greek and Egyptian antiquities, Italian Renaissance works, art by European masters, early American art, 20th century lithographic prints and photography, and art objects from Southeast Asia, China, Japan, and African and pre-Columbian cultures. Changing exhibits highlight shows from other institutions and private collections. The 74,000-square-foot museum has over 20 galleries, a bookstore, a cafe, a community education center, and a sculpture garden. Allow 2 to 4 hours.

At the University of Utah, 410 Campus Center Dr. ℭ 801/581-7332 or 801/581-7049. www.umfa.utah.edu. Admission is free. Mon–Fri 10am–5pm; Sat and Sun noon–5pm. Closed major holidays. Bus: 4.

Utah Museum of Natural History *Kids*   Located in the old university library building, this museum covers more than 200 million years. Some 200 exhibits—including some intriguing dinosaur exhibits—take you on a journey through time, describing the geologic and natural history of Utah right up to the present. Allow 1 hour.

At the University of Utah, 1390 E. 220 South. ℭ 801/581-4303. www.umnh.utah.edu. Admission $6 for adults, $3 for seniors 62 and older and children 3–12. Mon–Sat 9:30am–5:30pm; Sun and holidays noon–5pm. Bus: 4.

Utah State Historical Society Museum   Housed in the waiting room of the 1909 Denver and Rio Grande Railroad Depot, this museum exhibits historic artifacts, photos, and paintings. You'll see full-size replicas of a Conestoga wagon and a Mormon handcart, as well as one of the artificial hearts developed in 1976 by the University of Utah's Dr. Robert Jarvik. The large gift shop offers a variety of Western gifts and toys, plus an excellent selection of books. Allow a half hour.

300 S. 450 West. © 801/533-3500. www.history.utah.org. Free admission. Mon–Fri 8am–5pm. Bus: 81 along 200 South; walk a block south on Rio Grande.

PARKS & GARDENS

International Peace Gardens ★   Begun in 1939 by the Salt Lake Council of Women, the Peace Gardens have expanded over the years and now belong to the city. Take a stroll along the Jordan River, through the many gardens and past statuary and displays representing different countries; benches are scattered about for moments of rest and contemplation. Allow about 1 hour.

Jordan Park, 1060 S. 900 West. © 801/974-2411 or 801/972-7800. Free admission. May–Sept. 8am–dusk. Bus: 16.

Liberty Park ★★ *Kids*   This delightful city park has trails for walking and jogging, tennis courts, a small lake with ducks and paddleboat rentals, picnic facilities, a playground, a children's garden, a children's amusement park, a museum, and an excellent aviary. Covering 100 acres, this is a favorite gathering spot for locals, as well as one of the best dog-walking areas in the city (dogs must be leashed and owners must clean up after them). In the park, the **Chase Home Museum of Utah Folk Arts** (© 801/533-5760; www.folkartsmuseum.org), located in the historic Brigham Young/Chase home, contains exhibits of pioneer art, American Indian art, and other folk art. Allow a half hour. **Tracy Aviary** (© 801/322-2473 for recorded information, or 801/596-8500; www.tracy aviary.org), in the southwest section of the park, has more than 400 birds, including a number of endangered species. There's a special exhibit of Australian parrots called lories ($1 extra per person), and free-flying bird shows are presented during the summer (call for schedule). Allow at least 1 hour.

Between 500 and 700 East, and 900 and 1300 South. Entrances from 900 and 1300 South. © 801/972-7800 for the city parks department. Park and museum admission free; Tracy Aviary admission $4 adults, $2 seniors 65 and older, $2.50 children 4–12. Park daily 6am–11pm (dawn–dusk in winter). Museum open Mon–Thur noon–5pm and Fri–Sun 2–7pm from Memorial Day–Labor Day; Sat–Sun noon–5pm Apr–Memorial Day and Labor Day–Oct; closed Nov–Mar. Tracy Aviary daily 9am–6pm (closes 4:30pm Nov–Mar). Bus: 6, 10, 27, 32, or 44.

This Is the Place Heritage Park   Brigham Young and the first wave of Mormon pioneers got their first glimpse of the Salt Lake Valley at the site of this historic park. A tall granite and bronze sculpture was erected in 1947 to commemorate the centennial of their arrival. The park, which covers more than 1,600 acres, offers hiking along part of the trail used by the pioneers, with opportunities for cross-country skiing in winter. This is a good place for wildlife viewing and birding in winter and spring, with additional songbirds and raptors present in summer and fall. There's a picnic area, but no camping, and a visitor center contains exhibits depicting the Mormon pioneers' trek from Illinois to the Great Salt Lake Valley in 1847. Allow 30 minutes.

Also here, **Old Deseret** is a pioneer village comprised of original buildings from across the state along with some reproductions. In summer and during special events it becomes a living-history museum of the period from 1847 to 1869, with costumed villagers and a variety of demonstrations and activities, including wagon rides. Allow 1 to 2 hours. For a week each December the village becomes the setting of a pioneer Christmas celebration.

2601 E. Sunnyside Ave. ℭ 801/582-1847. www.thisistheplace.org. Admission free to park and visitor center. Admission to Old Deseret in summer and during special events $7 adults, $5 children 3–11 and seniors 62 and over. Self-guided tours of Old Deseret in off-season $2 per person. Park open daily dawn–dusk; visitor center open Mon–Sat 9am–6pm; Old Deseret open Mon–Sat 10am–6pm in summer; call for off-season hours. Bus: 4.

Utah's Hogle Zoo ★ *Kids*   This small, modern zoo near the entrance to Emigration Canyon is home to 1,100 animals representing over 250 species. You'll find a solarium with exotic plants and birds, tropical gardens, rare Grevy's zebras, and a giraffe house with a balcony so you can look eye-to-eye with the tall-necked creatures. Among the newer residents of the zoo are a pair of Amur tiger cubs and a baby Colobus monkey, all born at the zoo in 2003. In summer, rides on a small replica of an 1869 steam train are offered for the bargain-basement price of $1. As with any zoo, it's best to visit in one of the cooler seasons, or at least the coolest part of the day, when more animals are out and about. Allow 1 to 2 hours. The Discovery Theatre presents three children's programs daily.

2600 E. Sunnyside Ave. ℭ 801/582-1631. www.hoglezoo.org. Admission $7 adults, $5 children 3–12 and seniors 65 and older. Daily 9am–5pm (grounds close 6:30pm). Closed Christmas and New Year's Day. Bus: 4.

ESPECIALLY FOR KIDS

In addition to what's listed below, the **Clark Planetarium** (p. 95), **Utah's Hogle Zoo** (see above), **Liberty Park** (p. 97), and the **Utah Museum of Natural History** (p. 96) are great places for kids.

Children's Museum of Utah ★★ *Kids*   With more than 140 permanent exhibits, this is the place for kids of all ages to explore: Children can get their faces painted, pilot a jet, or excavate a woolly mammoth on an archaeological dig. The museum also features a child-size grocery store where kids can be both shoppers and checkers, and a room where shadows "stick" to a wall. A "color factory" helps children discover music, dance, and theater through colors—they actually create color in the Chromolator and use the Bubbelator to play a tune. Children must be accompanied by an adult. Allow 1 to 3 hours. *Note:* As we went to press, plans and a major fund-raising campaign were underway to relocate the museum to larger quarters; call or check the website for the current location.

840 N. 300 West. ℭ 801/322-5268 or 801/328-3383. www.childmuseum.org. Admission $4, free for children under 1. Mon–Thurs and Sat 10am–5pm; Fri 10am–8pm. Closed Mon mid–Sept through Dec. Bus: 70.

Wheeler Historic Farm *Kids*   This living-history dairy farm, where you can see demonstrations of farming and other activities from the late 19th century, contains hundred-year-old farm buildings, a small petting zoo, and a nature preserve. Activities include experiencing various farm chores, such as egg gathering and cow milking, farm house tours, and tractor-driven wagon rides. Allow 1 to 2 hours. A variety of annual events are also offered, including a scarecrow masquerade, a holiday lights festival, breakfast with Santa, and a summer camp week.

In Cottonwood Regional Park, 6351 S. 900 East (just north of I-215 exit 9). ℭ 801/264-2241. www.wheeler farm.com. Free admission to farm; $1–$2 fees for tours and other activities. Daily dawn–dusk. Bus: 9 or 27.

NEARBY ATTRACTIONS

Gardner Village   This quaint village is a cluster of restored historic homes and buildings surrounding Gardner Mill, a flour mill built by Scottish immigrant Archibald Gardner in 1877. Brass plaques tell the stories of each of the historic structures. The mill, which is on the National Historic Register, now houses a large store specializing in country furniture and gift items, as well as Archibald's Restaurant (p. 84). Close to two dozen shops in the other historic buildings, connected by red brick paths, sell a wide range of items, including art, crafts, clothing, candy, quilts, dolls, and home furnishings. There's also a spa, a bakery, and a picturesque duck pond. Plan to spend at least an hour here.

1100 W. 7800 South, West Jordan. © 801/566-8903. www.gardnervillage.com. Free admission. Shops open Mon–Sat 10am–8pm Apr–Dec; 10am–6pm Jan–Mar. The village is 12 miles south of downtown. From I-15 take exit 301 and head west on 7200 South, turn left (south) onto Redwood Rd. and left again on 7800 South, they are on the left (north) side of the road. From I-215, take exit 13 for Redwood Rd. and follow directions above.

Kennecott's Bingham Canyon Mine ★ *Kids*   The world's largest open-pit copper mine, at 2½ miles wide and three-quarters of a mile deep, is quite a sight to see, and almost as fascinating are the huge—and we do mean huge—trucks that transport the ore. The visitor center, 2,000 feet above the floor of the open-pit mine, offers a spectacular view, and you might even see an explosion, as rock is blasted away to expose more copper ore. In addition to the observation area, the visitor center has interactive exhibits—including 3-D microscopes for examining minerals—and offers a 14-minute video presentation that relates the mine's history and geology and describes its operations. Proceeds from admission fees are donated to local charities. Allow about 1 hour.

Utah 48 (7200 South), about 25 miles southwest of Salt Lake City outside Copperton. © 801/252-3234. Admission $4 per car, $2 per motorcycle. Apr–Oct daily 8am–8pm. Closed Nov–Mar. Take I-15 south to exit 301 for Midvale; head west on Utah 48 to the mine.

7 Organized Tours

Gray Line–Innsbruck Tours, 3359 S. Main St., Suite 804 (© **801/534-1001;** www.grayline.com), offers several tours of the city and surrounding areas, including the Bingham Copper Mine and Great Salt Lake. A 4- to 5-hour tour of the city and Mormon Trail costs $27, and a 4½-hour tour to the mine, which includes a stop at the beach on the Great Salt Lake, is $35. A 6-hour tour of the city and the Great Salt Lake costs $37, and a 5-hour tour to Park City and through the nearby mountains costs $39.

8 Outdoor Pursuits & Spectator Sports

OUTDOOR PURSUITS

Salt Lake City is an excellent base for skiing and snowboarding (see chapters 7 and 8), and there are also plenty of opportunities for hiking and other warm-weather activities just outside the city in the 1.3-million acres of the Wasatch-Cache National Forest. For maps and detailed trail information, contact the **Wasatch-Cache National Forest,** 125 S. State St. (© **801/524-3900;** www.fs.fed.us/r4/wcnf). Another good source of information is the nonprofit **Public Lands Information Center** (© **801/466-6411**) located in the REI building (see below).

Gart Sports outlets (www.gartsports.com) can meet most of your recreational equipment needs. There are several locations in the Salt Lake City area, including 5550 S. 900 East, Murray (© 801/263-3633), and 10200 S. State St., Sandy (© 801/566-7404). **Recreational Equipment, Inc. (REI),** 3285 E. 3300 South (© 801/486-2100; www.rei.com), offers a wide range of sporting goods, both sales and rentals. A good source for sales and rentals of ski and golf equipment, bikes, and in-line skates is **Utah Ski & Golf,** 134 W. 600 South, in downtown Salt Lake City (© 801/355-9088; www.utahskigolf.com), and at several other locations.

BIKING   You'll find a number of bikeways along city streets, some separate from but running parallel to the road, some a defined part of the road with a line designating the bike lane, and others sharing the driving lane with motor vehicles. From mid-May through September, City Creek Canyon, east of Capitol Hill, is closed to motor vehicles. It's open to hikers and in-line skaters at any time, and bicyclists can use the road on odd-numbered days. For information on the best places to bike, as well as rentals and repairs, stop at **Canyon Sports,** 1844 E. Fort Union Blvd. (© 800/736-8754 or 801/942-3100; www.canyon sports.com); or **Guthrie Bicycle,** downtown at 156 E. 200 South (© 801/363-3727), and at 731 E. 2100 South (© 801/484-0404).

BOATING   The Great Salt Lake, at the city's front door, has marinas on the south shore and on Antelope Island (see below).

FISHING   Trout can be found in the rivers feeding into the Great Salt Lake, although no fish can live in the lake itself. Popular spots include Big and Little Cottonwood creeks and Mill Creek. Fishing licenses are required; you can get one, along with maps and suggestions, at most sporting-goods stores.

GOLF   There are nine city courses with one central contact for general information and reservations: © 801/485-7730 or 801/484-3333 for the automated tee-time reservation system; www.slc-golf.com. Rates range from $5.50 to $12.50 for 9 holes and $20 to $25 for 18 holes, and all courses require reservations. The 18-hole, par-72 **Bonneville,** 954 Connor St. (© 801/583-9513), has hills, a large ravine, and a creek. The 9-hole, par-36 **Forest Dale,** 2375 S. 900 East (© 801/483-5420), is a redesigned historic course with huge trees and challenging water hazards. The 18-hole, par-72 **Glendale,** 1630 W. 2100 South (© 801/974-2403), features fine bent grass greens and splendid mountain views. The **Jordan River** course, 1200 N. Redwood Rd. (© 801/533-4527), is a challenging executive par 3, 9-hole course that meanders along the banks of the Jordan River. There are two 18-hole courses at **Mountain Dell** (© 801/582-3812), in Parley's Canyon east on I-80: the par-71 lake course and the par-72 canyon course, with breathtaking views and a strong likelihood of seeing deer, elk, moose, and other wildlife. The 9-hole, par-34 **Nibley Park,** 2730 S. 700 East (© 801/483-5418), is a good beginner course. The 18-hole, par-72 **Rose Park,** 1386 N. Redwood Rd. (© 801/596-5030), is flat but challenging. The city's top course is the 18-hole, par-72 **Wingpointe,** 3602 W. 100 North, near the airport (© 801/575-2345), a very challenging links-style course designed by Arthur Hills.

JOGGING   Memory Grove Park and City Creek Canyon are both terrific places for walking and jogging. The park is on the east side of the Capitol, and the canyon follows City Creek to the northeast. In town, you can stop at one of the city parks, such as Liberty Park (p. 97).

SPECTATOR SPORTS

The National Basketball Association's **Utah Jazz** (© 801/325-7328; www.utah jazz.com) usually packs the house, so get your tickets early. They play at the Delta Center, 301 W. South Temple. The **Utah Grizzlies** (© 801/988-8000; www.utahgrizz.com), of the International Hockey League, play in the "E" Center, 3200 S. Decker Lake Dr., West Valley City (off I-215 exit 20). The **Utah Blitzz** (© 801/401-8000; www.utahblitzz.com), the city's professional soccer team, plays at the University of Utah's Rice Eccles Stadium, 451 S. 1400 East.

If you want to take in a minor league baseball game, the Pacific Coast League's **Salt Lake Stingers** (© 801/485-3800; www.stingersbaseball.com), a Triple-A affiliate of the Anaheim Angels, plays at Franklin Covey Field, at the intersection of 1300 South and West Temple. The **University of Utah's Runnin' Utes** and **Lady Utes** (© 801/581-8849; www.utahutes.com) compete in 10 women's and 9 men's Division I sports (the women's gymnastics team is phenomenal). Tickets are usually available on fairly short notice, although it's best to call far in advance for football games.

9 Shopping

Salt Lake City, although not as interesting a shopping destination as places like Park City, does offer plenty of spending opportunities. Many Salt Lake City stores are closed on Sundays (the influence of the LDS Church); typical store hours are Monday through Saturday from 9am to 6pm. Shopping malls (with the exception of the ZCMI Center) are often open Sunday afternoons from noon to 5 or 6pm, and also stay open a few hours later on weeknights.

The **Temple Square** area is the city's top shopping destination. The best place to start is **Crossroads Plaza,** 50 S. Main St. (© 801/531-1799; www.crossroads plaza.com), right across the street from the square. This enclosed mall houses well over 100 shops, services, and eateries, and can satisfy almost all of your wants and needs, from books and clothing to music boxes and original art.

Nearby, **Mormon Handicraft,** 15 W. South Temple (© 800/843-1480 or 801/355-2141; www.mormonhandicraft.com) was opened during the Depression to encourage home industry and preserve pioneer arts. It carries a large inventory of quilting fabrics and supplies, as well as handmade quilts. It also carries a wide variety of other crafts, plus religious books and videos.

Another popular shopping spot is **Historic Trolley Square,** 600 South at 700 East (© 801/521-9877), where you'll find modern shops, galleries, and restaurants in an old-fashioned setting. You'll also see two of the city's original trolley cars, a historic water tower, and two of the city's first street lamps.

The newest shopping phenomenon in the city is **The Gateway,** 90 S. 400 West (© 801/456-0000; www.shopthegateway.com), which opened in late 2001. The Gateway is a large open-air shopping mall, as well as an entertainment and dining center. It covers two city blocks near the Delta Center, and contains numerous retail businesses, plus movie theaters, museums and other attractions, and restaurants. The historic Union Pacific Railroad Depot serves as the main entrance.

Although we can't yet call Salt Lake City an arts center, it does have a growing arts community, along with a dozen or so galleries. One of the oldest galleries in Salt Lake City, the **Phillips Gallery,** 444 E. 200 South (© 801/364-8284; www.phillips-gallery.com), represents about 80 artists, 90% of who are Utahns, displaying everything from traditional to contemporary paintings,

---

Moments   **Jordan Commons—An Uncommon Experience**

The Jordan Commons complex encompasses 2 city blocks at 9400 South State St., south of downtown Salt Lake City in Sandy. The complex boasts sixteen 35mm movie theaters plus one 70mm large-format super-screen theater—all with digital sound. The theaters surround a food court with a stupendous variety of edibles: cuisines from Australian to Chinese to Italian to Mexican (see Mayan at Jordan Commons on p. 86), plus a deli, coffee shop, and of course popcorn. The theaters are equipped with chairs large enough to accommodate food trays, so you can bring your dinner in with you! Call ⓒ **801/304-4636** or check the Web at www.jordancommons. com for movie information and tickets.

---

sculptures, and ceramics. **Tivoli Gallery,** 255 S. State St. (ⓒ **801/521-6288**), carries works by 19th- and 20th-century American and European artists, including Utah artists. The cooperative **Leftbank Gallery,** 242 S. 200 West (ⓒ **801/ 539-0343**), shows works by newer and lesser-known artists.

10 Salt Lake City After Dark

There's always something going on in Salt Lake City, which is working hard to lose its image as a dull place where the sidewalks get rolled up every night. Check the Friday editions of the *Salt Lake Tribune* or *Deseret News* for listings of upcoming events. For additional entertainment news and listings, pick up one of the city's free papers, including *The Event* and *Salt Lake City Weekly,* which also offers alternative news articles. The Salt Lake City Convention and Visitors Bureau (p. 75) also publishes calendars of events.

Among the top entertainment venues in Salt Lake City is **The "E" Center,** 3200 S. Decker Lake Dr., West Valley City (ⓒ **800/888-8400** or 801/988-8888 for the box office; www.theecenter.com), an arena-style venue that hosts numerous sports events (see "Spectator Sports," above) plus big name touring entertainers in its 3,700-seat theater.

THE PERFORMING ARTS

Tickets for performances at a variety of venues can be obtained from **Art-Tix** (ⓒ **888/451-2787** or 801/355-2787; www.arttix.org).

The highly acclaimed **Utah Symphony & Opera** ★★★ (ⓒ **801/533-6683;** www.utahsymphonyopera.org), combines one of the country's top symphony orchestras and the well-respected Utah Opera Company. They present four operas a year plus a year-round symphony season at Abravanel Hall, 123 W. South Temple, an elegant 2,800-seat venue known for its excellent acoustics.

The nationally acclaimed **Ballet West** ★★ (ⓒ **801/323-6900;** www. balletwest.org) performs at the historic Capitol Theatre, 50 W. 200 South. The September to March season usually brings four productions, ranging from classical to contemporary. Modern dance is presented by the **Repertory Dance Theatre** (ⓒ **801/534-1000;** www.rdtutah.org) and the **Ririe-Woodbury Dance Company** (ⓒ **801/297-4241;** www.ririewoodbury.com), with performances at the historic Capitol Theatre, located at 50 W. 200 South; the Rose Wagner Performing Arts Center, located at 138 W. 300 South; and other venues.

The **Pioneer Theatre Company,** 300 S. 1400 East, Room 325 (ⓒ **801/581-6961;** www.ptc.utah.edu), is Utah's resident professional theater. Located on the university campus, its repertoire ranges from classical to contemporary plays and musicals. Recent productions have included *Man of La Mancha, The Diary of Anne Frank, The Miracle Worker,* and *South Pacific.*

The **Hale Centre Theatre,** 3333 S. Decker Lake Dr., West Valley City (© 801/984-9000; www.halecentretheatre.org), just down the road from the "E" Center, features locally produced and performed plays and musical comedies.

THE CLUB & MUSIC SCENE

As Salt Lake City grows, it's shedding its strait-laced image and is actually beginning to hold its own with other western cities in catering to the hard-drinking, hard-dancing crowd. Some of the following establishments are so-called private clubs, so you'll have to buy a short-term membership (see "Liquor Laws," on p. 45).

One of the city's more with-it and cosmopolitan nightspots is **Club Axis,** 108 S. 500 West (© 801/519-2947; www.clubaxis.com), an upscale bar with a loud DJ and live music. This place attracts Salt Lake City's dot-com millionaire types. The **Dead Goat Saloon,** 119 S. West Temple, in Arrow Press Square (© 801/ 328-4628; www.deadgoat.com), is a fun, funky bar featuring live blues bands. Monday is the time to go for big name acts. For country dancing to live music or a DJ, head out to the Salt Lake City suburb of Sandy and **New Sandy's Station,** 8925 S. 255 West (© 801/255-2078; www.sandysstation.com).

Quite likely Utah's largest sports bar, **Port O' Call Social Club,** 400 S. West Temple (© 801/521-0589; www.portocall.com), boasts 40 TV screens, a game room with pool tables and pinball machines, and a patio. Walls are covered with sports memorabilia.

If you're seeing a performance at the Capitol Theatre, stop by **Club Baci,** 140 W. Pierpont Ave. (© 801/328-1333), afterwards; it's only about a half block northeast. Another good before- or after-theater choice is the **New Yorker,** 60 W. Market St. (© 801/363-0166). For one of the best martinis around, stop at **Kristauf's Private Club,** 16 W. Market St. (© 801/366-9490), a favorite of business types and other well-dressed tipplers.

11 The Great Salt Lake & Antelope Island State Park

You wouldn't expect to come across what is essentially a small ocean in the middle of the desert, but here it is: the Great Salt Lake. The lake is all that's left of ancient Lake Bonneville, which once covered most of western Utah and parts of Idaho and Nevada. Unlike its mother lake, the Great Salt Lake has no outlet, so everything that flows into it—some two million tons of minerals annually— stays here until someone or something—usually brine flies, brine shrimp, birds, or humans—removes it. Minerals, including salt, potassium, and magnesium, are mined here; don't be surprised to see front-end loaders moving huge piles of salt to the Morton Company along I-80, on the lake's south shore.

This natural wonder might be worth checking out, but don't expect much. Although Salt Lake City residents enjoy spending weekends at the lake, it isn't really a major tourist destination, and facilities are limited. Boaters should bring their own boats, as no rentals are available. Despite its salinity, this is a relatively flat lake—kind of like a big puddle—so don't pack your surfboard.

ANTELOPE ISLAND STATE PARK 🏕

The largest of 10 islands in the Great Salt Lake, measuring about 5 miles wide and 15 miles long, Antelope Island was named by Kit Carson and John Frémont in 1843 for the many pronghorns they found here. Hunting wiped out the herd by the 1870s, but buffalo were introduced in 1893—there are now some 600 of them—and pronghorn have recently been reintroduced. The beaches of Antelope Island don't have the fine-grained sand and shells of an ocean beach; rather, they're a mixture of dirt and gravel. But the water is a great place to relax; because of its high salinity, you don't have to work very hard to stay afloat.

ESSENTIALS

GETTING THERE   Antelope Island is about 30 miles northwest of Salt Lake City and about 16 miles southwest of Ogden. Take I-15 to exit 335, go 6½ miles west to the park entrance, and cross the 7½-mile causeway to the island.

VISITOR INFORMATION   Contact **Antelope Island State Park,** 4528 W. 1700 South, Syracuse, UT 84075-6868. The visitor center (© **801/773-2941;** www.stateparks.utah.gov), open daily in summer from 10am to 5pm and in winter daily from 10am to 3pm, has exhibits and information on the Great Salt Lake and the island's wildlife and migratory birds.

FEES & REGULATIONS   Day-use fees are $8 per vehicle and $4 for walkins and those on bicycles or in-line skates. The marina offers dock rental overnight. Pets are welcome in the park but must be leashed.

OUTDOOR PURSUITS

BIKING, HIKING & HORSEBACK RIDING   You'll find more than 30 miles of hiking trails and bike and horse paths on the island, most of which are closed to vehicular traffic. Although generally unmarked, trails follow old ranch roads. Check at the visitor center or talk with a ranger before heading out; they can fill you in on current conditions and tell you where you're most likely to spot wildlife.

The 3-mile **Lake Side Trail** leaves the Bridger Bay Campground and follows the beach around the northwestern tip of the island to the group camping area on White Rock Bay. The walk is magnificent at sunset. Other trails take you away from the crowds, where you might catch a glimpse of buffalo or other wildlife.

BOATING   Those who brought boats with them will find a marina with restrooms, docks, and fresh water for cleaning boats, but little else.

SWIMMING   The largest beach is at Bridger Bay, where you'll find picnic tables and modern restrooms with outdoor showers to wash off the salt.

WILDLIFE WATCHING   You can drive to the buffalo corral and see these great shaggy creatures fairly close up. If you head into the less-traveled areas, you might spot pronghorn, deer, buffalo, bobcats, elk, coyote, and bighorn sheep.

The annual bison roundup takes place in late November and early December. You can usually see wranglers herding the bison into corrals on the last weekend of November (binoculars are helpful), and get a close-up view the next weekend as the bison receive their annual checkups. Call to find out exactly when the roundup will take place.

CAMPING

There are two camping areas in the park: **Bridger Bay Campground** offers primitive camping, or you can use the parking area at **Bridger Bay Beach.** Although neither offers hookups, each area does have modern restrooms with showers; Bridger Bay Beach has picnic tables as well. The cost is $12 per night. Reservations, for a $7 fee, are available at © **800/322-3770.**

MORE TO SEE & DO

Ten miles south of the visitor center, down a paved road, is the **Fielding Garr Ranch House.** The original three-room adobe house, built in 1848, was inhabited until the state acquired it in 1981. In addition to the ranch house, there's a small building that served as a schoolroom by day and sleeping quarters for the farmhands at night, plus a spring house, the only freshwater source.

There's a snack bar at the ranch (open only when the ranch is open), as well as a large, shady picnic area. Half-hour wagon rides are available. Check with the visitor center for current ranch hours as well as schedules and rates for wagon rides.

GREAT SALT LAKE STATE PARK

This is a good spot to launch your boat (assuming you thought to bring one, since there are no rentals), but not what we would call a great vacation destination. A less-than-exciting stretch of muddy/sandy beach greets you, but the expanse of water and distant islands can be lovely, especially at dusk or early in the morning. Prickly pear cactus blooms along the shore of the Great Salt Lake in the late spring. And for those susceptible to the lure of the sea, this huge inland ocean is mysteriously irresistible any time of year. Sailing and water sports are the main attractions here—or you can simply laze on the beach. Facilities include picnic tables, open showers for washing off salt and sand, and modern restrooms.

Be forewarned, though. The air can be heavy with the stench of rotting algae at times, making even a brief stroll on the beach quite unpleasant. At other times, when the wind is right or the lake is high enough, trekking out to the water's edge is downright enjoyable. As we mentioned before, if you bring your own boat, this is a perfect spot for getting out onto the Great Salt Lake.

ESSENTIALS

Great Salt Lake State Park is 16 miles west of Salt Lake City. Take I-80 west to exit 104; head east on the frontage road about 2 miles to the park entrance. The marina is open year-round, and the beach is open daily from dawn to dusk, with free admission. Boat slips and a launching ramp are available, but there are no boat rentals. Contact **Great Salt Lake State Park,** P.O. Box 16658, Salt Lake City, UT 84116-0658 (© **801/250-1898;** www.stateparks.utah.gov). Park headquarters are located at the marina.

7

The Northern Wasatch Front: Utah's Old West

In the mountains to the north of Salt Lake City lies another world. Here you'll discover Ogden, which owes its prosperity to the transcontinental railroad. The city is a good starting point for discovering northern Utah's Old West heritage. Ogden is also a great home base for outdoor recreation: There's skiing at three nearby resorts in the winter, plus hiking and horseback riding in the rugged mountains in the summer. Considered mandatory for all railroad buffs is a pilgrimage to Golden Spike National Historic Site, the point at which the east and west coasts of the United States were joined by rail in 1869. North of Ogden is the pretty little town of Logan, which offers good hiking, horseback riding, and biking opportunities.

1 Ogden: Utah's West at Its Wildest

35 miles N of Salt Lake City

Located in the deltas of the Ogden and Weber rivers, Ogden has always been a bit different, a city apart from the rest of Utah. Although founded by Mormon pioneers and called home by a sizable Mormon population, Ogden really began life as a popular rendezvous site for mountain men and fur trappers in the 1820s, and became—much to the chagrin of the church—a seriously rowdy railroad town in the 1870s. It retains some of that devil-may-care attitude today.

But Ogden's current popularity has little to do with such sinful beginnings. Like other Wasatch Front communities, the bustling city of more than 60,000 has fine little museums and historic sites, as well as good restaurants and hotels. More important, though, is its location: At an elevation of 4,300 feet, Ogden serves as a perfect base for enjoying the surrounding mountains, whatever your preference—skiing, snowmobiling, hiking, mountain biking, horseback riding, or boating. Mt. Ben Lomond Peak, which lies to the north of the city, may look familiar—it's said to have inspired the famous Paramount Pictures logo.

ESSENTIALS

GETTING THERE   Ogden is easily accessible from the north and south via I-15, and from the east and northwest on I-84. Shuttle service to and from Salt Lake International Airport ranges from $35 to $45 one-way; try **Express Shuttle** (© 800/397-0773) or **Arrow Transportation** (© 888/277-6976). For best service, call at least 24 hours in advance.

VISITOR INFORMATION   The **Ogden/Weber Convention and Visitor's Bureau** maintains an information center at Union Station, 2501 Wall Ave., Suite 201, Ogden, UT 84401 (© 866/867-8824 or 801/627-8288; www. ogdencvb.org). From I-15 north/I-84 west, take exit 344A and head east to Wall Avenue; turn north (left) to the station. The bureau is open in summer Monday

Where to Stay & Dine in Downtown Ogden

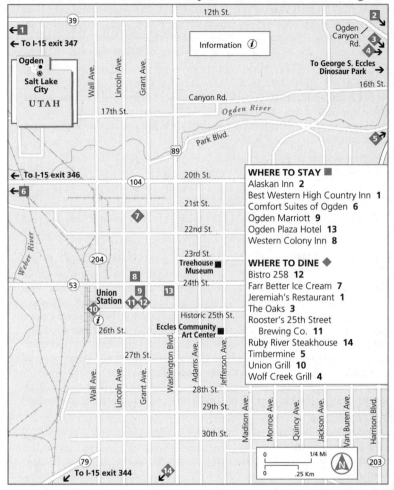

WHERE TO STAY ■
Alaskan Inn **2**
Best Western High Country Inn **1**
Comfort Suites of Ogden **6**
Ogden Marriott **9**
Ogden Plaza Hotel **13**
Western Colony Inn **8**

WHERE TO DINE ◆
Bistro 258 **12**
Farr Better Ice Cream **7**
Jeremiah's Restaurant **1**
The Oaks **3**
Rooster's 25th Street
  Brewing Co. **11**
Ruby River Steakhouse **14**
Timbermine **5**
Union Grill **10**
Wolf Creek Grill **4**

through Friday 8am to 6pm, Saturday 10am to 4pm; the rest of the year Monday through Friday 8am to 5pm.

For information on the national forests in the area, contact the **Ogden Ranger District,** Wasatch-Cache National Forest, 507 25th St., Suite 103, Ogden, UT 84401 (© **801/625-5112;** www.fs.fed.us/r4/wcnf). You can also inquire at the visitor center at Union Station.

GETTING AROUND Driving is the easiest way to explore Ogden. The streets are laid out in typically neat Mormon-pioneer fashion, but with a slightly different nomenclature. Those running east to west are numbered from 1st Street in the north to 47th in the south, and north-south streets are named for U.S. presidents and other historical figures. Most people define the city center as the intersection of 25th Street and Washington Boulevard.

Car-rental agencies include **Avis** (© 800/831-2847 or 801/394-5984), **Enterprise** (© 800/736-8222 or 801/399-5555), and **Hertz** (© 800/654-3131 or 801/621-6500).

The **Utah Transit Authority** (© 888/RIDE-UTA; www.rideuta.com) provides regular bus transportation throughout the greater Ogden area, daily with
limited service on Sundays. Exact fares are required; schedules are available at
the information center. For 24-hour taxi service, call **Yellow Cab Co.** (© 801/
394-9411).

FAST FACTS   The **IHC McKay-Dee Hospital Center** is at 4401 Harrison
Blvd. (© 801/627-2800, or 801/398-2020 in emergencies). The **main post
office** is at 3680 Pacific Ave. (© 800/275-8777; www.usps.com for additional
locations and hours). The local **newspaper** is the *Standard Examiner.* **Sales tax**
is just over 6%.

WHAT TO SEE & DO

Eccles Community Art Center   Built in 1893, this two-and-a-half-story tur-
reted, castlelike mansion was the home of David and Bertha Eccles. Throughout her life, Bertha welcomed community groups into her home and made it
known to her family that she wished the house to be used for education and cultural enrichment. It became the home of the Ogden Community Arts Council
in 1959.

Changing art exhibits in the Main House feature works by local, regional, and
national artists in a variety of media. The Carriage House sales gallery offers
local arts and crafts, including paintings, pottery, fabric art, and jewelry. The
new Renaissance Complex offers ongoing educational programs and houses the
ticket office for the Ogden Symphony and Ballet West. Two state-of-the-art
dance studios were recently added. Outside is a sculpture and flower garden
complete with a fountain and benches so you can rest your weary feet and enjoy
the view. Allow an hour and a half, and call ahead for a schedule of events and
information on classes in the visual arts and dance.

2580 Jefferson Ave. © 801/392-6935. www.ogden4arts.org. Free admission. Mon–Fri 9am–5pm; Sat
9am–3pm. Closed major holidays. From I-15, take exit 345 and head east on 24th St. to Jefferson Ave.; turn
right (south) and go 2 blocks.

Fort Buenaventura ✪   With a replica of an 1846 fort and trading post, and
exhibits depicting the mountain men and fur trade of the area back to the
1820s, this county-run park shows what life was like in this rugged land before
"civilization" arrived. Built in 1846 by fur trapper and horse trader Miles
Goodyear, Fort Buenaventura was the first permanent Anglo settlement in the
Great Basin. The Mormons bought the fort when they arrived in 1847, and the
city of Ogden grew up around it.

Today, the reconstructed fort helps explain the area's transition from stomp-
ing grounds of Anglo trappers and nomadic American Indian tribes to a permanent settlement (a good illustration of the so-called "taming of the American
West"). Rangers lead tours of the fort (included in the admission fee), and the
park has ponds, canoes for rent ($5 per hour), a picnic area, and a pleasant
campground ($15 tents, $20 RVs with electric and water hookups), and an RV
dump station. A 2-mile hiking trail meanders around the park, and fishing in
the Weber River is permitted with a current license. The park also has a kids'
fishing pond, open only to children 12 and younger, who do not need a license.
The visitor center has exhibits of American Indian artifacts typical of the area.
Scheduled to open by summer 2004 is a replica of a Shoshone Indian camp.
Allow at least 1 hour.

Fort Buenaventura hosts several traditional mountain-man rendezvous each
year, with music, Dutch-oven food, and a variety of contests that typically

include a tomahawk throw, a canoe race, a shooting competition, and foot races, with all competitors in pre-1840s dress. The rendezvous are usually scheduled on Easter (with a nondenominational sunrise service and Easter-egg hunt) and Labor Day weekends. A Pioneer Skills Festival takes place on July 24th. Mountain-man supplies are available in a shop at the fort every Saturday.

2450 South "A" Ave. © 801/399-8099. www.co.weber.ut.us/parks/buenaventura/. Admission $3 per person. Apr–Sept open daily 8am–8pm; Oct–Mar open daily 9am–5pm. From downtown Ogden, take 24th St. west across the railroad tracks and turn south onto "A" Ave.

George S. Eccles Dinosaur Park ★★ Kids
Wander among life-size reproductions of more than 100 prehistoric creatures from the Cretaceous and Jurassic periods in this 5-acre fantasyland playground. The smallest is about the size of a turkey and the enormous tyrannosaurus rex is 30 feet high, 49 feet long, and weighs about 7 tons. There's also a 33-foot-long parasaurdophus (a duck-billed dinosaur), a triceratops with its three horns, and a winged lizard, or pteranadon. There's even a replica of a 65-million-year-old volcano. Don't be alarmed if you hear peculiar sounds emitting from the creatures—the personnel are simply attempting to make your visit as realistic as possible. New in 2003 was the Elizabeth Dee Shaw Stewart Museum, where you'll find exciting hands-on exhibits of the latest dinosaur finds from Utah and around the world. It also includes a sand pit where budding paleontologists can excavate real dinosaur bones. Don't forget to visit the park's live reptiles and stop by the cafe and gift shop before leaving. Allow 2 hours.

1544 E. Park Blvd., Ogden River Pkwy. © 801/393-3466. www.dinosaurpark.org. Admission $5 adults, $3 children 3–12, free for children 2 and younger, $4 students with IDs and seniors 62 and older. Memorial Day–Labor Day Mon–Sat 10am–8pm, Sun noon–6pm; Apr–Memorial Day and Labor Day–Oct Mon–Sat 10am–6pm, Sun noon–5pm; Nov–Mar Mon–Sat 10am–5pm, Sun noon–5pm. Closed Easter, Thanksgiving, and Christmas. From I-15 exit 347, take 12th St. east 5 miles.

Hill Aerospace Museum ★
You'll get a close-up view of more than 60 planes, plus missiles and bombs, on your self-guided walking tour through this museum. On December 7, 1999, the Lindquist–Stewart Fighter Gallery was dedicated; it houses a number of century series fighters. Aircraft on display include the rare B-17 "Flying Fortress," one of the few P-38s around, the SR-71 "Blackbird" spy plane, a Soviet MIG 21 fighter, and two aircraft that are still flyable: a JN-4 "Jenney" and a Piper L-4A "Grasshopper," painted and marked to look like one that flew in support of the Allied invasion of North Africa in November 1942. You'll also see a World War II chapel, an exhibit of historic Air Force uniforms, a fire truck, a Gatling gun, and a Norden bombsight. Displays illustrate the history of the Air Force, how aircraft fly, and what the Air Force does today. The gift shop offers a wide range of Air Force–related items. Allow 1 hour.

7961 Wardleigh Rd., Hill Air Force Base. © 801/777-6818. www.hill.af.mil/museum. Free admission; donations welcome. Daily 9am–4:30pm. Closed New Year's Day, Thanksgiving, and Christmas. From I-15, take exit 341 to the museum.

Treehouse Children's Museum Kids
Both kids and grown-ups will find this an entertaining, hands-on learning experience. You can climb into a tree house; create books, bookmarks, cards, or stationery at the Pen and Ink Studio; or step into stories from classic literature such as the tales of King Arthur and Robin Hood. Experiment with a drum or marimba to make your own music in the "Pick Up a Stick and Play" exhibit, or visit a home like those found in China. New in 2003-04, the "American Dream" exhibit boasts a giant lighted floor map

of the United States; a theater with programs on American history; a miniature Oval Office complete with a replica of the President's desk; and Independence Hall, where kids can make an American flag or print out a copy of the Bill of Rights and/or a "Kids' Bill of Rights." The agricultural history of the U.S. is highlighted in the "American Barn," with a genuine plastic cow waiting to be milked. In the museum's "Utah Heritage" area, kids explore a pioneer schoolhouse and store, and try their hands at creating American Indian pictographs. Daily events include theater programs and group craft activities based on children's books; call for information. Just like the kids it attracts, Treehouse keeps growing and changing—so who knows what you might find on your visit? Allow at least 1 hour. *Note:* Treehouse Children's Museum plans a move to new quarters in 2005 or 2006, so call before going.

455 23rd St. © 801/394-9663. www.treehousemuseum.org. Admission $2 adults, $4 children from walking age to 15. Open Mon–Thurs and Sat 10am–6pm; Fri 10am–9pm. Closed Mon afternoons when school is in session, plus New Year's Day, Thanksgiving, and Christmas. Located 1 block east of Washington Blvd. at the corner of 23rd and Adams sts.

Union Station   This stately depot faces historic 25th Street, with lovely flowers and a fountain gracing the cobbled courtyard in front. Built in 1924 to replace the original depot, which was destroyed by fire, the station now houses several museums, an art gallery, a gift shop, the Union Grill (p. 122), a visitor information center, and the Ogden/Weber Convention and Visitors Bureau. Plan to spend an hour or two here.

The station's restored **lobby** houses the information center. The immense room boasts murals at each end commemorating the building of the railroad and the linking of east and west (which you can learn more about on a visit to Golden Spike National Historic Site; see p. 123). Both 12-by-50-foot murals were done in the late 1970s by Edward Laning, based on murals he painted in 1935 for New York's Ellis Island Immigration Building.

The **Utah State Railroad Museum** displays gas turbine locomotive designs and has an extensive HO-gauge layout that depicts the construction and geography of the 1,776-mile transcontinental route. Wander around on your own, or let a railroad buff guide you through, describing the whys and wherefores of what you're seeing.

The **Browning Firearms Museum** displays Browning guns from 1878 to modern times. There's also a replica of an 1880s gun shop and a film describing the Browning legacy.

The **Browning-Kimball Car Collection** features beautiful examples of classic cars, mostly luxury models. You can see about a dozen vehicles from the early 1900s, including a 1901 curved-dash Oldsmobile, Pierce-Arrows from 1909 and 1931, and a 1932 Lincoln. There is also a display of historical license plates and early gas pumps.

The **Natural History Museum** displays dinosaurs, aquatic life forms, fossilized wood, and plant material along with exhibits depicting earth processes and the area's geologic past. Don't miss the rare dinosaur egg or the collection of Utah trilobite.

The **Gallery at the Station** exhibits a variety of art through invitational and competitive shows.

Outside, the **Eccles Rail Center** pays tribute to the Goliaths of the rails—locomotives designed to pull long trains through the steep mountains of the West. On display are the Big Blow, a gas turbine rated at more than twice the horsepower of typical modern locomotives, and the largest diesel locomotive, the Centennial.

2501 Wall Ave. ℭ **801/629-8535.** Admission to museums $4 adults, $3 seniors 65 and over, $2 children under 12. Mon–Sat 10am–5pm. Closed New Year's Day, Thanksgiving, and Christmas. Take exit 344 off I-15 and follow 31st St. east to Wall Ave.; go north 6 blocks.

WALKING TOUR:	HISTORIC DOWNTOWN OGDEN— A WALK THROUGH THE HISTORY OF THE AMERICAN WEST

Start: 2148 Grant Ave.

Finish: 2539 Washington Blvd.

Time: 1-2 hours

Best Times: Any.

Worst Times: None, although windy days in winter can be biting cold.

Begin your tour at 2148 Grant Ave., on Tabernacle Square, where you'll find:

❶ Miles Goodyear Cabin and Daughters of Utah Pioneers Museum

This cottonwood log cabin was built in 1845 on the Weber River at Fort Buenaventura, which is now a county-run park (p. 108). The cabin is believed to be the first permanent pioneer home in Utah. Next door, the 1902 Gothic-style brick Relief Society Building now houses the Daughters of Utah Pioneers Museum (ℭ **801/393-4460**), containing pioneer photographs, artifacts, and memorabilia. Both the museum and cabin are open for visitors Monday through Saturday during the summer.

Now head south on Grant Avenue for 3 blocks to 298 24th St., the:

❷ Ogden Post Office

This is one of two fine examples of Classical Revival Federal architecture in Utah (the other is the Salt Lake City post office). This building, constructed between 1905 and 1909, held a post office, a courthouse, and offices until 1974. The lobby, elevator, second-floor courtroom, and much of the beautiful woodwork have been lovingly renovated and restored. The building now houses a reception center and other offices.

Turn east on 24th Street; a block down the street, at 385 24th St., you'll reach the:

❸ Eccles Building

This steel-framed, brick-faced, boxlike 1913 building with "Chicago-style" windows combines elements of the Prairie style with classical details, evident in the terra-cotta figurines and geometric motifs along the second- and eighth-floor cornices.

Turn south onto Washington Boulevard, and continue to 2415 Washington Blvd. to see:

❹ Peery's Egyptian Theater

Built as a movie theater in the Egyptian Revival style in 1924, the cinema reopened in 1997 after extensive renovation. The facade has four fluted columns, with two sculpted Pharaohs between each, plus two sculptures of deities perched on the roof. The exotic interior is equally unusual for this area: The proscenium is decorated with paintings of Egyptian figures and colorful columns. Adjoining the theater is the David Eccles Conference Center, a two-story building designed to complement the theater and meet a wide variety of conference needs.

Cross the street now to 2510 Washington Blvd., the:

❺ Former Bigelow Hotel

This Italian Renaissance Revival hotel, built in 1927 around the remains of the 1890 Reed Hotel, is a handsome reminder of the opulent 1920s, and is listed on the National Register of Historic Places.

Cross again to 2539 Washington Blvd., to see the:

⑥ Municipal Building

One of the finest representations of the Art Deco style of architecture in Utah, this building is also an excellent example of a WPA project. Built in 1939, the building is composed of a series of rectangular brick blocks with glazed terra-cotta trim, symmetrically tapered to the tall central mass— grand and awe-inspiring.

Finally, take a few minutes to walk along Historic 25th Street. This collection of early-20th-century buildings has been undergoing a much-needed renovation over the last few years. Many of the old businesses have moved to suburban shopping centers, but antiques shops, restaurants, and pubs are now taking over.

NEARBY ATTRACTIONS
HUNTSVILLE: "THE SIN & SALVATION TOUR"

Locals jokingly refer to visiting Huntsville as taking the "Sin and Salvation Tour." The town is about 15 miles east of Ogden on Utah 39; it'll take you 20 to 25 minutes to get there, but it's well worth the drive.

First, stop at the **Shooting Star Saloon** ⚔, 7350 E. 200 South (℃ **801/745-2002**), for a draft beer and one of the best hamburgers in the state. Established in 1879, this is said to be the oldest continuously operating saloon in Utah. The decor is eclectic, to say the least—dollar bills are pinned to the ceiling, and the walls are decorated with animal-head trophies, steer skulls, and cowboy art; there's a handsome oak back bar built in 1895. A pool table and a jukebox round out the fun. Don't forget to pat the St. Bernard's (stuffed) head that's hanging above one of the booths. The Shooting Star is open Wednesday through Saturday from noon and Sunday from 2pm; it usually closes around midnight, give or take an hour. Operating under Utah's liquor laws as a tavern, the Shooting Star serves beer only, and no one under 21, even with parents, is permitted in the saloon.

Now that you've done a bit of sinning, head to the **Abbey of Our Lady of the Holy Trinity Trappist Monastery,** 1250 S. 9500 East (℃ **801/745-3784;** www.xmission.com/~hta), for a bit of saving. To get here, take Utah 39, turn southeast (right) at the Huntsville American Legion Hall, and follow the signs. This community of about two dozen monks established themselves here in 1947 to live "an austere and simple life of prayer and manual labor." They farm, raise Herefords, and sell whole-grain cereals, freshly made peanut butter, wooden bowls, and honey. The reception room and chapel are open to the public, and visitors are welcome to attend any of the scheduled services. Call for the current schedule.

A HISTORIC FAMILY-FUN CENTER IN FARMINGTON

Lagoon, 375 N. Lagoon Dr., Farmington (℃ **800/748-5246** or 801/451-8000; www.lagoonpark.com), is a delightful combination of amusement park, water park, and entertaining historical park. In the beginning, swimming was the attraction; then, in 1906, an early version of a roller coaster opened. Next came a carousel of 45 hand-carved animals (still in operation today), and so on. Now there are more than 125 rides, including The Spider, new in 2003, which is essentially a spinning roller coaster—not for the faint of heart! There's also a **Midway** with games, shops, food courts, and entertainment.

Lagoon's Pioneer Village represents the Utah of a hundred years ago, with one of America's finest collections of horse-drawn carriages, plus a gun collection and exhibits of pioneer and American Indian artifacts. But it's not just a museum: You can browse through 19th-century shops and ride the stagecoach or train.

If it's water you delight in, visit the **Lagoon A Beach,** with a 65-foot twisting, turning enclosed tube ride, three serpentine slides, and white-water rapids that you shoot in a river tube. For the less intrepid, there's a lazy river with crystal-clear waterfalls, exotic tunnels, steamy hot tubs, and sultry lagoons.

Admission costs $30.95 for adults and children 51 inches and taller, $25.95 for children 4 and older but under 51 inches tall, $16 for toddlers 3 and under, and $18.50 for seniors 65 and over. There is a parking fee of $6 for cars and pickups, and $9 for oversized vehicles and vehicles with trailers. The park is open daily, usually from 10 or 11am, between Memorial Day and Labor Day; and weekends from mid-April to May and the month of September; hours vary so call for the current schedule. The park is closed in winter, but opens for a special Halloween event for 3 or 4 weeks in October. To get here from I-15 northbound, take exit 325; southbound, take exit 327.

Lagoon has an RV park and campground with more than 200 shady sites, both pull-through with hookups and grassy tent sites. The campground has a mini-store, and campers receive Lagoon admission discounts. Rates range from $20 for tent and no-hookup RV sites up to $28 for pull-through RV sites with full hookups.

SPORTS & OUTDOOR PURSUITS

The nearby Wasatch-Cache National Forest offers plenty of opportunities for outdoor recreation (see "Visitor Information," on p. 106). For camping and other equipment and supplies, stop by **Gart Sports SuperStore,** in the Newgate Mall, 36th Street and Wall Avenue (© 801/392-5500).

BIKING   The **Ogden River Parkway** ★★ is a 3.1-mile handicapped-accessible paved path along the Ogden River, extending from the mouth of Ogden Canyon west to Washington Boulevard. It's excellent for walking, jogging, and bicycling; it also leads to Big D Sports Park, Lorin Farr Park (p. 116), and George S. Eccles Dinosaur Park (p. 109).

There are two strenuous road rides east of Ogden. The **Trappers Loop Road** winds 9 miles along Utah 167 from Mountain Green (exit 92 off I-84) north to Huntsville. This route alternates between wide-open meadows backed by high mountain peaks and tall evergreens and aspens that seem to envelop you.

The second ride, along **Snowbasin Road,** climbs more than 2,000 feet from Pineview Reservoir to the base of Snowbasin Ski Resort. Your efforts will be rewarded at the end with stunning views of the ski runs and towering peaks.

You can get additional trail information at the visitor center in Union Station (p. 110)—ask for the Ogden Trails Network brochure. For bicycle repairs and accessories, stop at **Bingham Cyclery,** 3259 Washington Blvd. (© 801/399-4981), or **Canyon Sports,** 705 W. Riverdale Rd. (© 801/621-4662). In Eden, **Diamond Peaks,** at the junction of Utah highways 158 and 162 (© 801/745-0101; www.peakstuff.com), offers rentals, repairs, and sales of bikes, boards, and skis. Bike rentals start at $12 per hour.

CLIMBING   A wide variety of indoor climbing challenges, with some 4,000 square feet of climbing surface, can be found at **Ben Lomond Climbing Center,** 2370 N. U.S. 89 (© 801/737-7274; www.geocities.com/blclimbingcenter). The center is open Monday through Friday from 2 until 10pm, Saturday from noon until 10pm, and Sunday from noon until 6pm. Day passes cost $8 for adults and $6 for youths 15 and younger. Family rates are also available.

Moments **Escape to a Wildlife Sanctuary**

For a delightful escape from civilization, visit the **Ogden Nature Center,** 966 W. 12th St. (© 801/621-7595), a 127-acre wildlife sanctuary and reha-bilitation center where injured birds are treated and released back into the wild. There are trails (including one fully accessible trail for those with disabilities) for warm-weather strolling or, when snow blankets the ground, snowshoeing and cross-country skiing. Watch for golden eagles, prairie falcons, goshawks, red-tailed hawks, great horned owls, and long-eared owls. A Learning and Visitors Center houses hawks, ravens, and other birds, plus a variety of exhibits and a gift shop. The center sponsors naturalist-led educational programs; call for a schedule. Admission is $2.50 for ages 12 through 62; $1 for children 4 through 11 and seniors over 62; and free for those 3 and under. Hours September through May are Monday through Saturday from 10am to 4pm; June through August Monday through Friday 10am to 6pm, Saturday 10am to 4pm. To get here from I-15, take exit 347 and head east on 12th Street. Allow at least 2 hours.

FISHING   Brown, rainbow, cutthroat, brook, and lake trout are abundant in the waters of the Wasatch-Cache National Forest around Ogden. You might also find perch, bass, catfish, whitefish, and crappie. Popular spots to wet your line include Pineview Reservoir, Causey Reservoir, and the Ogden and Weber rivers. For supplies and tips on where they're biting, stop at **Anglers' Inn,** 5296 S. Free-way Park Dr. near exit 341 (© 801/773-1166). For guided fishing trips in the area, check with **Red Rock Ranch and Outfitters** in Huntsville (© 801/745-6393; www.redrockranchandoutfitters.com).

GOLF   Golfers will find an abundance of opportunities in the Ogden area, which boasts challenging courses with spectacular views of the surrounding mountains. Public courses include **Wolf Creek Golf Resort,** 3900 N. Wolf Creek Dr., Eden (© 801/745-3365), a challenging 18-hole championship par-73 course that overlooks Pineview Reservoir in Ogden Valley, which has green fees of $30 to $65. There's also the **Mount Ogden Golf Course,** 1787 Consti-tution Way (© 801/629-0699), an 18-hole, par-71 championship course located on the east side of the city against the mountains, which charges $25 for 18 holes; and **El Monte Golf Course,** 1300 Valley Dr. (© 801/629-0694), a scenic 9-hole, par-35 course of rolling hills and old-style greens in Ogden Canyon, with fees of $10 for 9 holes.

The **Golf City Family Fun Center,** 1400 E. 5600 South (© 801/479-3410), in south Ogden, offers something for the entire family. There's a driving range (lit at night), a baseball and softball batting cage, miniature golf, and a 9-hole, par-27 course ($5).

For one of the finest practice areas around, try **Mulligan's Golf and Games,** 1690 W. 400 North, exit 349 off I-15 (© 801/392-4653), which features a 9-hole, par-31 course that costs $7.50 for 9 holes. It also has two 18-hole minia-ture golf courses and a driving range that's lit at night.

HIKING   The **Ogden River Parkway** (p. 113) is great for walking. Several hiking trails are accessible from the east side of downtown Ogden. **Indian Trail** takes off from the parking area at 22nd Street and Buchanan Avenue and winds about 4.2 miles along a narrow path through thick stands of oak, spruce, and fir

trees. The trail offers some of the finest views of the canyon from above—
particularly of the waterfall at the mouth of Ogden Canyon—before dropping
down to the parking area on Utah 39. This moderately difficult trail takes about
4 hours one-way.

A little over a half-mile along Indian Trail, **Hidden Valley Trail** cuts off sharply
to the south. The route is difficult, climbing steadily through the old Lake Bonneville terraces, and is surrounded by dense stands of oak, maple, and aspen. After
2 miles, you'll reach a turnaround; from here, enjoy a clear view of the rugged
face of Mt. Ogden to the southeast. The hike takes about 2 hours one-way.

An easy 1½-hour hike is the **Mt. Ogden Exercise Trail,** linking the parking lots
at 29th and 36th streets. It's mostly flat and surfaced with bark chips. The trail
follows the east edge of a golf course much of the way, encountering splashing
streams and even occasional wildlife. The views are inspiring at sunrise and sunset.

For additional trail information, ask for the Ogden Trails Network brochure
at the visitor information center in Union Station (p. 110). It describes a number of hiking trails, some of which are also open for biking and horseback riding.

HORSEBACK RIDING   There are numerous opportunities for horseback
riding in the national forest around Ogden. For custom guided trail rides, contact **Red Rock Ranch and Outfitters,** 13555 E. Utah 39 and Causey Way,
Huntsville (© **801/745-4305** or 801/745-6393; www.redrockranchandoutfitters.
com). A 30-minute children's ride costs $20; rates for adults and older children
are $30 for the first hour, $20 for the second hour, and $10 for each hour after
that. The ranch also offers Dutch-oven dinner rides, wagon rides in summer,
and horse-drawn sleigh rides in winter. **Rocking C Ranch,** 1 Ant Flat Rd.,
Huntsville (© **877/762-5462;** www.utahsnowmobile.com), offers ranch vacation packages starting at $749 for adults and $649 for children 5 to 18 for 4 days
and 3 nights at the ranch.

Ask at the visitor information center in Union Station (p. 110) for information on other area outfitters, forest and trail maps, and the Ogden Trails Network brochure, which describes three trails open to horseback riding.

ICE-SKATING & CURLING   The **Ice Sheet,** 4390 Harrison Blvd., in the
southeast part of the city (© **801/399-8750**), offers year-round ice-skating, a
learn-to-skate program, hockey and figure-skating clinics, clinics on curling (one
of the newest Olympics sports), and skate rentals. Call for current rates and
schedules.

WATER SPORTS   Willard Bay State Park and Pineview Reservoir (p. 116) are
your destinations for boating, waterskiing, and swimming. Also see the discussion on Lagoon (p. 112) and Lorin Farr Park (p. 116).

WINTER SPORTS   Deep snow turns the mountains surrounding Ogden
into a winter playground, with four delightful family-oriented ski resorts (see
section 3 of this chapter) and seemingly unlimited forest trails for cross-country
skiers, snowshoers, and snowmobilers. Among the companies offering snowmobile treks are **Red Rock Ranch and Outfitters** (see above), **Rocking C Ranch**
(see above) and **High Adventure Rentals** (© **801/782-7860**). Full-day snowmobile rentals cost from $90 to $120 for one person.

An exciting way to ski some of the most fantastic snow in the West is to stay
away from the groomed trails, lift lines, and parking lots and take to the skies with
Diamond Peak Heli-ski Adventures (© **801/745-4631;** www.diamondpeaks.
com), based in Ogden. Helicopters deliver you to the tops of several privately-
owned northern Utah mountains, where you'll find no developed trails, just

pure natural snow. One drop plus a full-day lift ticket at Powder Mountain Resort (see "Skiing Ogden Valley & the Northern Wasatch Front," later in this chapter) costs about $140; a six-run heli-ski tour, with lunch, costs $595; and for $1,800 a day and up you get your own helicopter, guides, lunch, and all the skiing you want.

PARKS & RECREATION AREAS

For boating and waterskiing, head 10 miles north to **Willard Bay State Park,** 900 W. 650 North #A, Willard, UT 84340 (© **435/734-9494;** www.stateparks. utah.gov). In addition to water sports, 9,900-acre Willard Reservoir offers birding and wildlife viewing. There are two marinas, restrooms with showers, 92 campsites (some with RV hookups), and an RV dump station. A trail leads to a wide sandy beach for swimming and sunbathing. Other footpaths branch off toward the ponds to the east, where ducks and geese often paddle. There are some open waterfront campsites, but most are along a meandering access road among the cottonwoods and willows that are abundant along Willard Creek. The day-use fee is $9 per vehicle; camping costs $14 to $20. Take I-15 exit 354 to South Marina, or exit 360 for North Marina.

Located in the Ogden Ranger District of the Wasatch-Cache National Forest (© **801/625-5112;** www.fs.fed.us/r4/wcnf), **Pineview Reservoir** is about 6 miles east of Ogden via Utah 39. Surrounded by towering mountains and forested hillsides, the 2,874-acre reservoir is a popular water sports destination. Created by the construction of an earth-and-rock dam in 1937, it has two boat ramps and two designated swimming areas. Anglers catch smallmouth and largemouth bass, black bullhead catfish, crappie, bluegill, yellow perch, and tiger muskie. The **North Arm Wildlife Viewing Trail,** accessible from Utah 162 where the North Fork of the Ogden River enters the reservoir, is an easy ⅔-mile round-trip walk through a riparian wetland, where you're likely to see northern orioles, yellow warblers, and white-crowned sparrows, plus ducks, geese, hawks, and mule deer. The best viewing times are spring and early summer.

The Forest Service's **Anderson Cove Campground,** at 5,000 feet elevation along the south edge of the reservoir, has paved roads and 69 sites, and costs $14 per night. It's usually open from May through September or October, and has vault toilets and drinking water. For reservations contact the National Recreation Reservation Service (© **877/444-6777;** www.reserveusa.com).

The day-use-only **Big D Sports Park,** 1250 Park Blvd., Ogden River Parkway (© **801/629-8284**), has a playground; soccer, baseball, and volleyball fields; a basketball court; and pavilions, shelters, and picnic grounds.

If you need to cool off, head to **Lorin Farr Park,** 700 Canyon Rd., Ogden River Parkway (© **801/629-8253,** or 801/629-8691 for pool). Facilities include water slides, a swimming pool, a playground, a skateboard park, and a picnic area with grills. The park is open year-round, but the pool is open in summer only. Admission to the park is free, but there are charges for swimming (call for current rates and schedules).

SPECTATOR SPORTS

Weber State University, southeast of downtown, belongs to the Big Sky Athletic Conference and the Mountain West Athletic Conference. Basketball and women's volleyball are played at **Stewart Stadium** at the south end of campus, while football games take place at **Dee Events Center,** 4450 Harrison Blvd. (© **801/626-8500**). Contact the school's athletic department (© **801/626-6500**) for schedules.

Ogden also has a minor league baseball team. A short season "A" team affiliate of the Milwaukee Brewers, the **Raptors** play from mid-June to early September at **Lindquist Field,** 2330 Lincoln Ave. (✆ **801/393-2400**).

SHOPPING

At one time a bawdy collection of saloons, rooming houses, brothels, and opium dens, Ogden's 25th Street has become the "in" place to shop and eat. Among its historic buildings, you'll find several antiques shops, specialty stores, restaurants, and bars. Among our favorite stops here are the **Pan Handler,** 260 25th St. (✆ **801/392-6510**), where you'll find all sorts of kitchenware. Needlepointers should make a point of visiting the **Needlepoint Joint,** 241 25th St. (✆ **801/ 394-4355**).

Those searching for their favorite chains or specialty shops will find boutiques, department stores, way too many eateries, and a 14-screen movie theater at **Newgate Mall,** 36th Street and Wall Avenue (✆ **801/621-1161;** www. newgatemall.com/html). Among the mall's more than 85 tenants are Dillard's, Mervyn's, Sears, Gart Sports SuperStore, Gap, Victoria's Secret, Bath & Body Works, Eddie Bauer, Quilted Bear, Spencer's Gifts, Radio Shack, Footlocker, Blindside, and KB Toy Express. The mall is open Monday through Saturday from 10am to 9pm and Sunday from noon to 6pm.

WHERE TO STAY

In addition to the choices described below, the Ogden area is home to several affordable chain motels. **Sleep Inn,** 1155 S. 1700 West, Ogden, UT 84401 (✆ **800/424-6423** or 801/731-6500), and **Days Inn,** 3306 Washington Blvd., Ogden, UT 84403 (✆ **800/329-7466** or 801/399-5671), charge between $60 and $90 for two people; and doubles under $50 can usually be had at **Super 8 Motel,** 1508 W. 2100 South, Ogden, UT 84401 (✆ **800/800-8000** or 801/ 731-7100).

Room tax totals about 9%. Pets are not allowed unless otherwise noted.

Alaskan Inn ✿✿✿   You'll find the wilds of Alaska in Utah at this enchanting bed-and-breakfast, where the unique rooms and cabins transport you to a land of tundra, snow-capped peaks, tall pines, polar bears, and cascading waterfalls. Guests stay in the handsome 12-room log lodge or in one of the 11 cabins. Most units come with coffeemakers, and all have complete entertainment centers with large TVs. All units also have whirlpool tubs for two; cabins contain freestanding showers as well. In the popular Northern Lights room, you can gaze at a light show of the Aurora Borealis while lounging in bed or soaking in the tub. Or perhaps you'd prefer the Bears' Den, with a cozy cavelike atmosphere and a waterfall. Cabins are more simply furnished, but continue the Alaska theme; you can dwell in a trapper's cabin or listen to the call of the bull moose along the Kenai River.

Located some 15 minutes from downtown Ogden, the inn is set among tall pines along the Ogden River, with easy access to hiking trails in the national forest. Full breakfasts are served in your room or cabin. Free tours of the inn are offered daily from 1 to 3pm. Smoking is not permitted.

435 Ogden Canyon Rd., Ogden, UT 84401. ✆ 888/707-8600 or 801/621-8600. Fax 801/394-4054. www. alaskaninn.com. 23 units. Sun–Thurs $125–$180 double; Fri, Sat, and holidays $140–$195 double. Rates include full breakfast. AE, DISC, MC, V. Not suitable for children under 18. *In room:* A/C, TV, fridge.

Best Western High Country Inn ✿   This attractive hotel offers comfortable, attractively furnished rooms with a bright, airy feel and modern Western decor.

Guests have a choice of one or two queen beds or one king. Amenities include ski lockers and ski tuning, and the very popular Jeremiah's Restaurant (p. 120).

1335 W. 12th St., Ogden, UT 84404. ℭ **800/594-8979** or 801/394-9474. Fax 801/392-6589. 111 units. $55–$75 double. AE, DC, DISC, MC, V. Just off I-15 exit 347. Pets accepted with a deposit. **Amenities:** Restaurant (American); outdoor heated pool; exercise room; indoor Jacuzzi; coin-op washers and dryers. *In room:* A/C, TV, fridge, coffeemaker, hair dryer, iron.

Ogden Plaza Hotel ★★ This handsome, seven story Art Deco-style property bills itself as Ogden's only "boutique" hotel. Standard rooms are average-size and well-appointed, with top-quality furnishings and a comfortable but refined atmosphere. The junior suites, although just one room, are much more spacious, with upgraded amenities, a sofa sleeper, and an in-room safe. And the one two-room executive suite is the top of the line, with just about every amenity you can imagine. All units have two-line telephones, full-size desks, and an array of other amenities. The hotel has secure covered parking, valet service, same-day dry cleaning, and meeting rooms.

2401 Washington Blvd., Ogden, UT 84405. ℭ **866/394-9400** or 801/394-9400. Fax 801/395-8448. www.ogdenplazahotel.com. 137 units. Sun–Thurs $69–$99 double, $129–$275 junior and full suite; Fri, Sat, and holidays $79–$109 double, $179–$350 junior and full suite. AE, DISC, MC, V. Pets accepted with deposit. **Amenities:** Fitness center; business center; coin-op laundry; laundry service; same-day dry cleaning. *In room:* A/C, TV, dataport, coffeemaker, iron.

Western Colony Inn *Value* Those seeking a clean, well-maintained room at very reasonable rates will like the small, two-story Western Colony. Each unit has two firm queen-size beds, simple decor, and a bathroom with combination tub/shower and separate vanity. Fridges and microwaves are available at no charge, and several restaurants are within walking distance. Renovation of all rooms was underway in 2003-2004.

234 24th St., Ogden, UT 84401. ℭ **801/627-1332.** Fax 801/392-0600. 14 units. Apr–Sept $35–$49 double; Oct–Mar $30–$35 double. AE, DISC, MC, V. Small pets accepted. *In room:* A/C, TV.

IN HUNTSVILLE

Jackson Fork Inn ★★ *Finds* A delightful alternative to standard hotels, this unique little inn was formerly an old family barn, believed to have been constructed in the 1930s. It's now in its third location. Each unit has two stories, with a spiral staircase leading to an upstairs bedroom loft. Accommodations are brightly painted and cheery, with one or two queen-size beds and a full bathroom; four rooms have whirlpool tubs. The charming Jackson Fork Inn restaurant (p. 122) serves dinner only. A "Jackson fork," incidentally, is a type of hay fork used to load hay into the loft area of a barn. Smoking is not permitted here.

7345 E. 900 South (Utah Hwy. 39), Huntsville, UT 84317. ℭ **800/255-0672** or 801/745-0051. www.jackson forkinn.com. 7 units. Sun–Thurs $70–$110 double; Fri, Sat, and holidays $80–$120 double. Rates include breakfast. AE, DC, DISC, MC, V. Pets accepted for an additional fee. **Amenities:** Restaurant (continental). *In room:* A/C, no phone.

IN EDEN

Moose Hollow Luxury Condominiums ★★ This condo project, situated on 2,600 acres, is ideal for those who are coming to this area for outdoor recreation, and is especially perfect for large families or several families traveling together. The complex consists of 14 buildings containing 12 condo units each, plus eight buildings containing six townhouses each. The exteriors are of stone, peeled log, and cedar siding. Each unit is individually but similarly decorated, with slate floor entryways and lots of wood furniture, such as knotty pine armoires. All units have gas fireplaces and vaulted lofts. Each townhouse also has

Booked aisle seat.

Reserved room with a view.

With a queen – no, make that a king-size bed.

With Travelocity, you can book your flights and hotels together, so
you can get even better deals than if you booked them separately.
You'll save time and money without compromising the quality of
your trip. Choose your airline seat, search for alternate airports, pick your
hotel room type, even choose the neighborhood you'd like to stay in

Travelocity

**Visit www.travelocity.com
or call 1-888-TRAVELOCITY**

a two-car garage. The landscape is rife with aspen, maple, birch, and pine trees; waterfalls and streams; and an abundance of shrubbery and wildflowers. The complex has a sand volleyball court and paved foot trails. Next door is Wolf Creek golf course, an 18-hole championship par-73 course, and nearby are opportunities for horseback riding, mountain biking, hiking, fishing, water-skiing, cross-country skiing, and snowmobiling.

5088 E. Moose Hollow Dr. (P.O. Box 660), Eden, UT 84310. (C) **800/958-1311** or 801/745-9653. Fax 801/745-0224. www.moosehollowcondos.com. 216 2–4 bedroom units. Winter $225–$375; summer $200–$350; spring and fall $150–$250; rates considerably higher during Christmas holiday season. AE, MC, V. **Amenities:** Outdoor pool; oversize Jacuzzi; sauna. *In room:* A/C, TV, kitchen.

Snowberry Inn Bed & Breakfast ★★   The Snowberry, built in 1992, is a large, comfortable log cabin–style inn within 15 minutes of three ski areas and convenient to all the outdoor activities available in the surrounding national forest. Each room is individually decorated with antiques and collectibles that relate to its theme (Indian, Pioneer, and so on). The Pioneer room is handicapped-accessible. Each room has its own bathroom, some with shower only; the Alaskan has a clawfoot tub but no shower.

Amenities include a game room with pool table and darts; and babysitting can be arranged. The inn has an open, friendly atmosphere; guests are welcome to gather around the tall kitchen counter for coffee while the morning meal is being prepared. A full gourmet breakfast is served each morning, and during the 2-hour daily social "hour" wine, nonalcoholic beverages, and appetizers are served. Smoking is permitted outside only.

1315 N. Utah Hwy. 158 (P.O. Box 795), Eden, UT 84310. (C) **888/334-3466** or 801/745-2634. Fax 801/745-3140. www.snowberryinn.com. 7 units. $85–$115 double. Rates include breakfast. AE, DISC, MC, V. From Ogden, follow Utah 39 east about 8 miles and turn north on Utah 158; the inn is about 2½ miles up on the west side of the road. Pets accepted with prior approval. **Amenities:** Outdoor Jacuzzi; game room with pool table and darts; in-room massage; babysitting can be arranged. *In room:* No phone.

CAMPING

In addition to the following options, the national forest offers camping in the Pineview Recreation Area, discussed earlier in the chapter in "Parks & Recreation Areas," which also covers camping at Willard Bay State Park. There is also camping at Fort Buenaventura (p. 108) and at Lagoon (p. 112).

Century RV & Mobile Home Park   This campground, conveniently located just off the interstate and close to downtown, has shade trees, grass, and pull-through and back-in gravel sites. There's also a large tent area, the usual bathhouse with hot showers, a dump station, a convenience store, a coin-operated laundry, a playground, a game room, and a heated outdoor pool. Cable TV hookups are available.

1399 W. 2100 South (1 block west of I-15 exit 346), Ogden, UT 84401. (C) **801/731-3800**. Fax 801/731-0010. cp1399@aol.com. 166 sites. $20–$26. AE, DISC, MC, V.

Cherry Hill Camping Resort ★   This immaculately maintained campground is part of a large complex that contains a water park, a miniature golf course, and batting cages. You'll find manicured lawns, shade trees, and paved interior roads, along with a heated pool, recreation hall, and game room. The campground offers complete RV hookups, a dump station, a convenience store, and loads of sites for tent camping. Services are limited from November to March.

1325 S. Main St. (2 blocks south of I-15 exit 331), Kaysville, UT 84037. (C) **888/446-2267** for reservations, or 801/451-5379. Fax 801/451-2267. www.cherry-hill.com. 240 sites. Apr–Oct $26–$32; lower Nov–Mar. MC, V.

WHERE TO DINE

ABC Mandarin SZECHUAN/MANDARIN/CANTONESE   With its large windows and booths along three walls, this looks like an American cafe or coffee shop with a few Asian accents: about a half dozen faux marble-top tables, Chinese dragons on one wall, and a large tank of tropical fish. But the food is thoroughly Chinese—the menu is even written in both Chinese and English. All the standards are here for lunch, from chicken chow mein and several kinds of fried rice to Mongolian beef and sweet-and-sour shrimp. The dinner menu is expanded to include three-course family dinners and a variety of other dishes. Imported and domestic beers are available.

5260 S. 1900 West, Roy. ℂ 801/776-6361. Main courses $4.25–$5.75 lunch, $7–$11 dinner. AE, DISC, MC, V. Mon–Thurs 11am–10pm; Fri–Sat 11am–11pm. From I-15, take exit 342 for Riverdale Rd. west; follow it to 1900 West, and turn right.

Bistro 258 AMERICAN/EUROPEAN   This casual, airy restaurant is located in one of the oldest buildings in this part of Ogden, built in 1888 and restored in 1984. There's a narrow front dining room and a magnificent old wooden bar complete with mirrors behind the glassware, a large atrium dining room in back, and a flower- and shrub-filled outdoor patio for warm weather dining. Chef-owners Michael Attento and Todd Ferrario blend American and European cuisines for their changing menu, with selections such as Gorgonzola and balsamic topped New York steak or saffron cream seafood linguine. There's a children's menu and full liquor service.

258 Historic 25th St. ℂ 801/394-1595. Main courses lunch $2–$10, dinner $8–$20. AE, MC, V. Mon–Thurs 11am–10pm; Fri–Sat 11am–11pm.

Jeremiah's Restaurant ★★ *Finds* AMERICAN   For some of the best burgers in northern Utah, as well as a wide variety of basic American dishes and great breakfasts, head to Jeremiah's. A favorite of locals—at least in part because it serves large portions at very reasonable prices—the restaurant has consistently been voted "Best Breakfast in Northern Utah" in *Salt Lake City Weekly*'s readers poll. In addition to about a dozen styles of burgers—including a buffalo burger and a meatless burger—you'll find sirloin steak, smoked pork chops, a variety of salads and sandwiches, and several chicken dishes. We recommend the halibut fish and chips, served with coleslaw. The extensive breakfast menu ranges from about a dozen omelets to various meat and egg options to pancakes. There is a break-of-dawn breakfast special between 6 and 9am. The huge, popular scones and cinnamon rolls are served all day. Full liquor service is available.

Best Western High Country Inn, 1307 W. 1200 South. ℂ 801/394-3273. Main courses $4–$14. AE, DISC, MC, V. Mon–Sat 6am–10pm; Sun 7am–9pm.

The Oaks ★★ AMERICAN   This restaurant's delightful location—nestled among the pines in Ogden Canyon, with patio dining over the bubbling and

---

Moments Farr Better Ice Cream

Choose from over 50 flavors of ice cream and a wide range of malts, shakes, sundaes, frozen yogurt, and sherbets at **Farr Better Ice Cream— Utah's Original Ice Cream Shoppe**, 286 21st St. (ℂ **801/393-8629**), in business since 1929. Cones start at $1.31. Hours are Monday through Saturday from 9am to 10pm (until 11pm in summer).

crashing Ogden River—simply can't be beat. The Oaks began as a resort about a hundred years ago, in a location a mile down the canyon, but moved to its present spot in 1933, when it evolved into a hamburger and hot dog joint—the kind that passed food to its customers through a window. Purchased by Keith and Belinda Rounkles in 1981, it evolved further, into a full-service sit-down eatery. Today, the rugged Western decor, accented by historic photos, maps, and post cards, provides the perfect venue for a family-friendly, home-style eatery. Food is good, solid, American fare, made mostly from scratch. Breakfast, served until noon, features all the usuals, along with huevos rancheros and some exotic omelets. The lunch and dinner menus bring a variety of burgers and sandwiches, including the house specialty: sliced sirloin smothered with mushrooms, onions, and green peppers and topped with mozzarella and American cheese, served on a French bun. Evening dinner specials, such as charbroiled steak, halibut, or salmon, are also offered, and there's a pasta of the day at both lunch and dinner. Utah microbrews and other beers are served with meals.

750 Ogden Canyon (Utah Hwy. 39). © 801/394-2421. Main courses $4–$20. AE, DISC, MC, V. Memorial Day–Labor Day 8am–10:30pm; rest of year 8am–8pm. Closed Thanksgiving and Christmas.

Roosters 25th Street Brewing Co AMERICAN

This two-story, red-brick brew pub, with its prominently displayed brewing vats and intriguing metal and wood tables, is locally popular for both its food and its beers. Pizzas come in several varieties, including a vegetarian version with mushrooms, peppers, asparagus, spinach, mozzarella, and sun-dried tomatoes. Beer-battered fish-and-chips, that old pub standard, is light and crisp. For an appetizer, try the crunchy Onion Loops, onion slices hand-dipped in a homemade beer batter. Also on the menu are several fish dishes, fresh seafood, chicken, pasta, beef, and some excellent specialty sandwiches. Patio seating is available in good weather. As you might expect, freshly brewed beer is served.

253 Historic 25th St. © 801/627-6171. www.roostersbrewingco.com. Reservations not accepted. Main courses $6.95–$22, sandwiches and salads $5.95–$7.95. AE, DC, DISC, MC, V. Mon–Thurs 11:30am–10pm; Fri–Sat 11:30am–11pm; Sun 10am–9pm. Parking $2.

Ruby River Steakhouse ✮ STEAK

If steak, beer, and country music are what you seek, look no further than Ruby River. This large restaurant is about as Western as you can get, with stone fireplaces, log walls, and two huge trees to support the roof. Cowboy hats and fascinating hand-painted cowboy boots round out the decor, with country music in the background. Beef here is 21-day-aged USDA Choice, hand-cut, seasoned, and double broiled. Try the 16-ounce rib-eye or New York (12- or 16-ounce), or a thick slice of the slow-roasted prime rib, served with fresh horseradish. Those not in the mood for beef can choose from among several chicken, pork, and fish dishes, such as the barbecued chicken and baby back ribs combo or the broiled salmon fillet served on a bed of barbecue sauce and topped with ground red, green, and black pepper. Ruby River brews its own beer—try the light, spicy red ale or the dark, malty porter—and also offers wine and full liquor service, including a number of exotic specialty drinks.

4286 Riverdale Rd. © 801/622-2320. Reservations not accepted for parties of fewer than 10, but you can call to be put on a call-ahead list, which will decrease your wait. Lunch $6–$14, dinner $12–$25. AE, DISC, MC, V. Mon–Thurs 11am–10pm; Fri–Sat 11am–11pm; Sun 3–9pm.

Timbermine ✮ Kids STEAK/SEAFOOD

Utah's mining days are the theme here—the rough-timbered rooms resemble mine shafts, and collectibles and antiques from the mining era are scattered about. Arrive early for our choice—the prime rib, which often sells out. The menu also offers a variety of steaks, fish, and seafood; barbecue is featured on Monday, Tuesday, and Wednesday nights. For dessert, try the Timber pie, a chocolate chip cookie concoction topped with vanilla ice cream and chocolate sauce. Full liquor service is available.

1701 Park Blvd. © 801/393-2155. www.timbermine.com. Reservations accepted for parties of 10 or more. Main courses $13.95–$33. AE, DC, DISC, MC, V. Mon–Thurs 5–10pm; Fri–Sat 5–11pm; Sun 5–9pm. Follow 12th St. (which becomes Canyon Rd.) east to the mouth of Ogden Canyon, turn right on Valley Dr., and then right again onto Park Blvd.

Union Grill AMERICAN   Set in historic Union Station, the Union Grill has a lively decor of Art Deco–style stained glass and bright colors. The windows look out on a view of trains rumbling by. The menu includes fresh fish, pasta, homemade soups, salads, and sandwiches, along with daily specials. Spicy Cajun dishes are especially tasty, as is the fresh flame-broiled salmon. Three choices of pasta sauces are always available. Full liquor service is available.

Union Station, 2501 Wall Ave. © 801/621-2830. Main courses $4.95–$18. AE, DC, DISC, MC, V. Mon–Thurs 11am–10pm; Fri–Sat 11am–10:30pm.

Wolf Creek Grill ★ AMERICAN   This upscale golf club restaurant is a good place to stop for lunch and dinner whether you're a golfer or not. The dining room, with a tall cathedral ceiling, offers spectacular views of the surrounding mountains, a sparkling lake, and the golf course's rolling greens. The dinner menu includes innovative variations on basic American favorites, such as baby back ribs with chipotle barbecue sauce, slow baked and then finished on the grill; and oven-roasted chicken breast with braised vegetables and a Gruyère cheese crust. There are also pizzas, burgers, pastas, and salads. Full liquor service is available.

Wolf Creek Golf Resort, 3900 N. Wolf Creek Dr. © 801/745-3737. www.wolfcreekresort.com. Main courses $6.25–$19. AE, DISC, MC, V. Memorial Day–Labor Day daily 11:30am–10pm; rest of year daily 4–9pm. Follow Utah 39 east from Ogden about 10 miles, turn north onto Utah 158 for about 4 miles, and turn north on Powder Mountain Rd. to Wolf Creek Golf Resort.

IN HUNTSVILLE

Jackson Fork Inn CONTINENTAL   A charming country atmosphere pervades the Jackson Fork Inn, housed in an old converted barn (p. 118). The menu includes excellent beef, such as filet mignon, T-bone steak, and slow-roasted prime rib; chicken teriyaki; seafood selections such as salmon, halibut, shrimp, and calamari; and a changing vegetarian entree. Full liquor service is available.

7345 E. 900 South (Utah Hwy. 39), Huntsville. © 801/745-0051. Reservations recommended. Main courses $9.50–$27. AE, DISC, MC, V. Mon–Sat 5–9:30pm; Sun brunch 10am–2pm.

OGDEN AFTER DARK

During the school year, Weber State University's Department of Performing Arts (© **801/626-6800**) presents live entertainment at **Dee Events Center,** 4450 Harrison Blvd. (© **801/626-8500**); call for a schedule.

For classical offerings, contact the **Ogden Symphony and Ballet,** 638 E. 26th St. (© **801/399-9214;** www.symphonyballet.org), which presents a variety of performances, ranging from solo violin recitals to pops concerts to ballets such as *The Nutcracker,* at various venues.

The **Utah Musical Theatre** (© **800/978-8457** in Utah, or 801/626-7775) offers three Broadway musicals each summer at Peery's Egyptian Theater (p. 111). Recent productions have included classics such as *The King and I, South Pacific, Annie Get Your Gun,* and *Fiddler on the Roof,* as well as newer musicals like *City of Angels.*

The **Golden Spike Events Center,** 1000 N. 1200 West (© **800/442-7362** or 801/399-8798), has surround seating for more than 6,000 people and hosts concerts, rodeos, horse races, monster truck rallies, circuses, auctions, and other special events. Call for current events. If you're lucky, you might get to see a chariot race—remember Ben Hur?—or a cutter race, which is a race for chariots outfitted for snow!

For after-hours entertainment, the **City Club,** 264 25th St. (© **801/392-4447**), offers good food and nonstop Beatles music; while **Beatniks,** 240 25th St. (© **801/395-2859**), features jazz and blues. You can hear live music starting most nights at 9pm at **Brewski's,** 244 25th St. (© **801/394-1713**), a popular bar with great pizza and more neon lights than you've ever seen. The **Outlaw,** 1204 W. 21st St. (© **801/334-9260**), offers country music and dancing, plus pool tables and darts.

2 Where East Met West: Golden Spike National Historic Site

50 miles NW of Ogden, 90 miles NW of Salt Lake City

If you love steam trains, as we do, you won't want to miss a visit to **Golden Spike National Historic Site** ★★. On May 10, 1869, the Central Pacific met the Union Pacific at Promontory Summit, and America's east and west coasts were finally joined by rail. The nation's second transcontinental telegraph had been strung along the track as it was laid, and as the final spike was driven home, the signal "Done" flashed across the country—and jubilation erupted from coast to coast. A ragged town of tents quickly sprang up along the track at Promontory Summit, but within 8 months the railroads moved their terminal operations to Ogden. In 1904, the Lucin Cutoff bypassed Promontory altogether, and in 1942 the rails were torn up for use in military depots.

Today there are less than 2 miles of track here, re-laid on the original roadbed, where you can see fully functional replicas of the two engines, the Central Pacific's "Jupiter" and Union Pacific's "119," that met here in 1869. From mid- to late spring into early October, the magnificent machines are on display and make short runs (inquire at the visitor center for a schedule). Presentations are given track-side.

ESSENTIALS

Admission for up to a week costs $7 per vehicle from May through mid-September and $5 per vehicle the rest of the year. There are no camping facilities. Outside attractions are open daily during daylight hours.

GETTING THERE   From Ogden, head north on I-15 to exit 368, turn west on Utah 83 for 29 miles to a sign for Golden Spike, turn south, and continue for 7½ miles.

INFORMATION/VISITOR CENTER   Contact **Golden Spike National Historic Site,** P.O. Box 897, Brigham City, UT 84302-0897 (© **435/471-2209;** www.nps.gov/gosp). The park's visitor center is open daily Memorial Day to Labor Day from 8am to 6pm, and the rest of the year from 9am to 5:30pm. From late October through April it's closed Monday and Tuesday, and is also closed Thanksgiving, Christmas, and New Year's Day. Restrooms, picnic areas, and a bookstore are located at the visitor center, which also offers slide programs, films, and museum exhibits detailing the linking of the nation. Ranger programs take place daily; check at the visitor center for the current schedule.

SPECIAL EVENTS   The park has several special events throughout the year, with free admission. On May 10, there's a reenactment of the original **Golden Spike Ceremony,** with food, souvenirs, and handicrafts. Reenactments are also held periodically throughout the summer. On the second Saturday in August, the **Annual Railroader's Festival** features reenactments of the Golden Spike ceremony, a spike-driving contest, and handcar races and rides. Hot food, crafts booths, and live music add to the festivities. Although not free (regular entrance fees apply), the **Annual Railroader's Film Festival and Winter Steam Demonstration,** held during the Christmas season, is a lot of fun, with classic Hollywood railroad films and a special appearance by one of the two resident steam locomotives.

EXPLORING THE HISTORIC SITE
BY CAR
Die-hard railroad buffs can drive the self-guided **Promontory Trail Auto Tour** along 7 miles of the historic railroad grades. A booklet explaining the markers along the tour is available at the visitor center. You'll see the two parallel grades laid by the competing companies (see box below), clearings for sidings, original rock culverts, and many cuts and fills. Allow about 1¼ hours.

ON FOOT
The **Big Fill Trail** is a 1½-mile loop along part of the original rail beds to the Big Trestle site and the Big Fill. The Big Fill was created when some 250 dump-cart teams and more than 500 workers—mostly Chinese immigrants—dumped load after load of rock and dirt into a ravine to create the 170-foot-deep, 500-foot span of fill required to lay the Central Pacific's track. The Union Pacific built their trestle just 150 feet away. It was never intended to be a permanent structure; speed was the goal, rather than strength. Constructed by hand by Irish and Mormon crews in 1869, the last spike went into the 85-foot-high, 400-foot-long trestle on May 5, just 36 days after it was begun.

(*Fun Fact* **The Great Train Race**

A transcontinental railroad had been a dream for Americans since railroads first appeared on the scene in the 1830s, but the problems involved with building such a system were tremendous. By the time the Civil War began there were numerous rail lines in the East, but few in the West, and none that linked the coasts. Finally the government acted and selected two companies, with each to receive loans and land for each mile of track laid. One company would start in Omaha, Nebraska and head west, while the other would start in Sacramento, California and head east.

Because the companies received loans and land for each mile of track laid, each wanted to put down as much track as possible. With trains carrying supplies following the workers as they laid down track, the race became ridiculous—opposing crews actually passed each other, furiously building parallel road beds, in sight of each other, in opposite directions! An end to this silliness finally came when Congress named Promontory, Utah as the meeting spot. Two symbolic golden spikes were driven in with a silver-plated hammer to mark the occasion, and the country was finally united by rail.

You can hike on either the Central Pacific or Union Pacific rail bed, although the Central Pacific rail bed is an easier walk. Markers along both grades point out cuts and fills, quarries, vistas, and caves.

This is the desert, so bring water, wear a hat, and be prepared for mosquitoes and ticks. Remember that rattlesnakes, though rare on the trail, have the right-of-way. And be glad that you weren't one of the workers in that backbreaking effort of 1869.

3 Skiing Ogden Valley & the Northern Wasatch Front

You'll find splendid powder skiing, low prices, few lift lines, and friendly people in abundance at the relatively undeveloped ski areas of northern Utah. Don't expect fancy lodges (at least not yet), but do be prepared for breathtaking scenery, a wide variety of fine terrain, and a relaxed family atmosphere.

THE OGDEN VALLEY RESORTS

These resorts are just northwest of Ogden; to reach any of them, take I-15 exit 347 onto 12th Street and follow Utah 39 east. **Nordic Valley** and **Powder Mountain** are just off Utah 158, and **Snowbasin** is off Utah 226.

NORDIC VALLEY SKIING & TUBING

Family-oriented **Nordic Valley Ski Area,** 3567 Nordic Valley Way, Eden, UT 84310 (© **801/745-3511;** fax 801/392-1293), Utah's smallest and least expensive ski area, has among the best night-lighting systems in the state. Refreshingly informal and casual, Nordic Valley is a favorite of Ogden-area families because it's a good place to learn to ski, with enough variety to keep everyone satisfied. The terrain is rated 30% beginner, 50% intermediate, and 20% advanced. Annual snowfall averages 300 inches. Several runs have been designed specifically for snowboarders.

Nordic Valley has two double chairlifts serving 18 runs on 85 acres, and snow-making on 50 acres. The vertical drop is 1,200 feet from the top elevation of 6,400 feet. The ski area is generally open mid-November to mid-March, with lifts operating Monday through Saturday from 9:30am to 10pm and Sunday from 9:30am to 5pm.

To get here from I-15, follow Utah 39 east about 11 miles, turn north (left) onto Utah 158 for about 3 miles, then turn west (left), following signs to the ski area.

LIFT TICKETS   Day passes (9:30am to 6pm) for adults and children 6 and older cost $20; seniors 65 and older pay $10; and children 5 and younger pay $5. Night skiing (3:30 to 10pm) costs $15 for adults and children 6 and older. Seniors 65 and older pay $10, and children 5 and younger pay $5.

LESSONS & PROGRAMS   The **ski school** offers private and group lessons lasting 1½ hours at rates of $30 for one person, $38 for two people, and $46 for three people. Two-hour group classes are $15 per person, with a minimum of four people. The ski shop has equipment for rent and accessories for sale. No child-care facilities are available.

WHERE TO STAY & DINE   There's no overnight lodging on the mountain; see "Where to Stay," in the Ogden section of this chapter, for nearby accommodations. **Nordic Valley Lodge** serves hot sandwiches, homemade soups, pizza, and hot and cold beverages. You can relax around the fireplace or pot-bellied stove on a cold day or outside on the deck when it's sunny and warm.

POWDER MOUNTAIN RESORT

This is a family ski area in two respects: It was begun in 1972 by the Cobabe family, who still own and run it, and it's aimed at providing a variety of skiing opportunities to suit everyone in your family. There are plenty of beginner runs, which seem to grade upwards in difficulty as you move from the Sundown area to the Timberline area and then the Hidden Lake area, so that by the time you're skiing Three Miles, you can consider yourself an intermediate and try cruising over the big, swooping blue fields. There's no dearth of expert and powder skiing in the wilds, either. Powder Mountain uses snow cats and shuttle buses to transport skiers to more than 2,400 acres of spectacular powder that are not served by its lifts—it's an out-of-bounds, backcountry skier's dream come true. A bonus is the view: On a clear day, you can see across the Great Salt Lake and sometimes all the way to Park City.

Powder Mountain is also a favorite among snowboarders; boarding is allowed everywhere.

Powder Mountain Resort, P.O. Box 450, Eden, UT 84310 (© **801/745-3772,** or 801/745-3771 for snow conditions; www.powdermountain.com), has one quad, one triple and two double chairs, two surface lifts, and one platter lift, servicing 2,800 acres of packed runs and powder skiing. 700 acres of backcountry powder skiing is accessible by snow cat, plus another 1,200 acres on the back side of the mountain, with return to the lift via shuttle bus. The terrain is rated 10% beginner, 50% intermediate, and 40% advanced. With over 500 inches of snowfall annually, Powder Mountain doesn't have—or need—any snow-making. The elevation at the summit is 8,900 feet; the vertical drop is 2,000 feet. The season is generally mid-November to mid-April, with day skiing from 9:30am to 4:30pm and night skiing until 10pm.

From I-15, follow Utah 39 east about 11 miles, turn north (left) onto Utah 158, and drive about 8 miles to the ski area.

LIFT TICKETS An all-day adult lift ticket is $41, a half-day ticket is $34, a children's (ages 6–12) all-day ticket is $24, and a children's half-day ticket is $20; night-skiing passes are $18 for adults and $13 for children. Seniors 65 and over pay $34. Kids 5 and under ride the lift free.

LESSONS & PROGRAMS The **ski school** offers a full range of ski and snowboarding lessons and other activities, both group and private, from half-day to multi-day. These include children's lessons, a program designed especially for and taught by women, and guided Alpine tours. Private lessons start at $55; group lessons cost $25 per person. Powder Mountain Lodge and Sundown Lodge both have ski shops where skis and snowboards are available for rent and accessories are for sale. No child-care facilities are available.

WHERE TO STAY & DINE Most skiers stay in Ogden (see "Where to Stay," in the Ogden section of this chapter), but for those who want to sleep slope-side, the **Columbine Inn** (© **801/745-3772;** fax 801/745-3619), has five rooms and two suites with a pleasant ski-chalet atmosphere. The lodging is located at the main parking lot next to the lodge, and plans for expansion are underway. Doubles cost $85 to $110, with suites going for $190 to $255. Room tax is 9.25%. No smoking is permitted.

Powder Mountain Lodge serves homemade soups and sandwiches. **Hidden Lake** provides food at the summit. The **Powder Keg** serves sandwiches and draft beer around a cozy fireplace.

SNOWBASIN ★★

Among America's oldest ski areas (it opened in 1939), Snowbasin remained a locals' secret until it hosted the downhill and Super G competition at the 2002 Olympics. Word of the area's great terrain got out, and skiers have been flocking to the resort ever since. Particularly popular for its top-to-bottom intermediate runs, Snowbasin offers plenty of untracked powder; long, well-groomed trails; and Utah's third-largest vertical drop. Beginners have plenty of terrain on which to develop their ski-legs, and some great transitional runs off the Wildcat lift will help them graduate from novice to intermediate status. With its wide-open powder bowls and new Olympic downhill courses, expert skiing at Snowbasin has been growing by leaps and bounds.

Snowbasin Resort, P.O. Box 460, Huntsville, UT 84317 (© **801/620-1000,** or 801/620-1100 for snow conditions; fax 801/620-1314; www.snowbasin.com), has 53 runs, rated 20% beginner, 50% intermediate, and 30% advanced. Included in its 2,650 acres are beautiful powder bowls and glade skiing. Snowbasin has one high-speed quad, one double, and four triple chairlifts, plus two high-speed eight-passenger gondolas and a tram that serves the starting point for the downhill race courses. Lift-served vertical drop is 2,950 feet from the 9,350-foot summit. All lifts are open to snowboarders, with retaining devices required. With about 400 inches of annual snowfall, Snowbasin has not really needed snowmaking equipment, although snow-making has been added to assure an early season opening. The ski season generally runs from Thanksgiving to mid-April, with lifts operating daily from 9am to 4pm.

To reach Snowbasin from Salt Lake City, take I-15 to exit 326, then go north on U.S. 89 for about 10 miles. At the mouth of Weber Canyon, merge onto I-84 eastbound, which you take several miles to exit 92 for Mountain Green. Head east about 2 miles and turn north (left) onto Utah 167 (Trapper's Loop). Go about 5 miles to Utah 226, where you turn left and drive 3 miles to the resort.

LIFT TICKETS   All-day adult lift tickets cost $54, half-day tickets are $44, a children's (ages 7–12) all-day ticket is $33, a children's half-day ticket is $26, and seniors over 65 pay $44 for a full day and $29 for a half-day. Kids 6 and under can ride the lift free.

LESSONS & PROGRAMS   The **ski school** (© **801/399-4611**) offers both private and group skiing and snowboarding lessons for all ages and abilities, with rates starting at $35 for a 2-hour group lesson and $135 for a 2-hour private lesson (or $349 for an all-day private lesson). Learn-to-ski packages and half- or full-day children's programs—the Littlecat Kittens for ages 4 to 6, and Youth for ages 7 to 11—are also available. The Grizzly Center at the base offers ski and snowboard equipment rental and repair, plus clothing and accessories for sale. No nursery or child-care facilities are available.

WHERE TO STAY & DINE   No lodging is available at the ski area itself; most skiers stay in the Ogden area (see "Where to Stay," in the Ogden section). In preparation for the Olympics, Snowbasin built three handsome restaurants—one at the base and two on the mountain. All serve American fare in a mountain lodge atmosphere; we prefer either of the on-mountain restaurants for their wondrous views.

NORTHERN WASATCH FRONT (NEAR THE IDAHO BORDER)
BEAVER MOUNTAIN SKI AREA ☆

Skiing at **Beaver Mountain Ski Area** is like going home to see the folks. Located at the top of beautiful Logan Canyon in the Wasatch-Cache National Forest, this small resort has been operated by the Seeholzer family since 1939. The emphasis is on friendliness, personal attention, and, as Ted Seeholzer puts it, "helping skiers find the right runs for them." You'll find plenty of snow, a good mix of terrain, well-maintained slopes, and a northeast exposure that makes morning runs a warm, sunny experience. Snowboarders are welcome. Both bump skiers and snowboarders like the steep Lue's Run (named for Ted's mother, Luella), while hotdoggers are directed to Harry's Hollow (named for Ted's father), which has plenty of bumps—and is located right under a lift so everyone can see you showing off.

Beaver Mountain Ski Area, 1351 E. 700 North (P.O. Box 3455), Logan, UT 84321 (© **435/753-0921,** or 435/753-4822 for ski reports; fax 435/753-0975; www.skithebeav.com), receives an average of 400 inches of snow annually and has a top elevation of 8,800 feet and a vertical drop of 1,600 feet. A new triple chairlift has opened an additional 200 acres of terrain, bringing the total skiable acres to 664. There are also three double chairlifts. The terrain is mostly intermediate and there are 22 runs. The season runs from early December through March, with the lifts operating daily from 9am to 4pm. The mountain is closed on Christmas Day.

Take I-15 to exit 364, then go east on U.S. 89 about 50 miles through Logan and Logan Canyon, and take the turnoff to the ski area.

LIFT TICKETS All-day adult lift tickets cost $28; cost for children 11 and under and seniors 65 to 69 is $22; and for those 70 and over it's $14.

LESSONS & PROGRAMS The **ski school** offers group and private lessons. Private lessons start at $40 per hour. Group lessons are offered in packages, such as the learn-to-turn package for beginners that includes a group lesson, equipment rental, and beginner hill ski pass for $45 per person. In the lodge, you'll find ski rentals, lockers, and a small shop that sells clothing and accessories. No child-care facilities are available.

WHERE TO STAY & DINE Most lodging and restaurants can be found 27 miles west in Logan (see section 4 of this chapter). A cafeteria at the day lodge sells hamburgers, sandwiches, and soft drinks.

Nearby places to stay include **Beaver Creek Lodge,** P.O. 139, Millville, UT 84326 (© **800/946-4485** or 435/946-3400; fax 435/946-3620; www.beaver creeklodge.com), a half-mile east of the ski area along U.S. 89. Open year-round, this 11-room log lodge offers all the modern conveniences you could hope for, in a spectacular mountain setting surrounded by the national forest. Spacious guest rooms contain log furnishings, handmade bed quilts, TVs and VCRs, and whirlpool tubs with showers. A large common room offers a stone fireplace and big-screen TV with VCR, and the decks offer panoramic views. There's hiking, mountain biking, horseback riding, and snowmobiling on the property and in the surrounding national forest (see "Sports & Outdoor Pursuits," in section 4 of this chapter). Rates are $99 to $129 in winter and $79 to $89 in summer, with Friday and Saturday night rates the highest; breakfast and dinner are available at an additional charge. Room tax is 9%. No smoking is permitted.

A small **RV park,** with 15 sites for RVs and tents, is open at Beaver Mountain Ski Area in summer, with showers and lots of trees. RV sites with hookups cost $15; tent sites go for $10. A large tent and a yurt are available from April through November (call for details).

4 Logan

46 miles N of Ogden, 81 miles NE of Salt Lake City

Nestled in the fertile Cache Valley, at an elevation of 4,525 feet, Logan is flanked by the rugged Wasatch and Bear River mountains. Once part of prehistoric Lake Bonneville, then home to the Blackfoot, Paiute, Shoshone, and Ute Indians, the valley is now a rich farming area famous for its cheeses and high-tech businesses. Mountain men arrived in the 1820s to trap beaver in the Logan River, caching (hence the valley's and county's name) the pelts in holes they dug throughout the area. Then, in 1856, Mormon pioneers established several villages in the valley.

Today, with a population of about 49,000, Logan is a small city, but with many of the attractions of its larger neighbors to the west. Particularly worthwhile are visits to the LDS Church's Tabernacle and Temple, both handsome 19th-century structures; and a drive out to the American West Heritage Center for a trip through 100 years of Western history: 1820 to 1920. Thanks in part to Utah State University, Logan suffers from no lack of art exhibits, live music, or theater.

But nobody who comes to Logan really wants to spend much time indoors. Beautiful Logan Canyon and the nearby mountains are a delightful escape for hikers, mountain bikers, equestrians, anglers, and rock climbers.

ESSENTIALS

GETTING THERE   From Salt Lake City and Ogden, take I-15 north to exit 364, then follow U.S. 89/91 northeast about 24 miles to downtown Logan. Those flying to Salt Lake City can arrange transportation with the **Cache Valley Limo's Airport Shuttle** (© **800/658-8526** or 435/563-6400); or **Airport Shuttle** (© **435/755-5008**). Two-days notice is recommended for both companies; round-trip fares for both companies are about $75.

VISITOR INFORMATION   The Cache Valley Tourist Council's **Visitor Information Center** is located at 160 N. Main St., Logan, UT 84321 (© **800/ 882-4433** or 435/752-2161; fax 435/753-5825; www.tourcachevalley.com). It's open Monday through Friday from 9am to 5pm.

GETTING AROUND   As with most Utah cities, Logan is laid out on a grid, with the center at the intersection of Main (north to south) and Center (east to west). Tabernacle Square is the block to the northeast of the intersection. U.S. 89/91 enters town on a diagonal from the southwest, along the golf course at the south end of town. Utah State University is located on the northeast side of town, north of U.S. 89 between 700 and 1400 East.

The **Logan Transit District Transportation System,** or LTD (© **435/752-2877;** www.ltdbus.org) is a **free** citywide bus service. Buses run Monday through Friday 6:30am to 9:30pm and Saturday 9:30am to 6:30pm, except major holidays. A route map is available at the visitor information center on Main Street (described in the previous section). For a cab, call **Logan Taxi** (© **435/753-3663**).

Car-rental agencies with offices in Logan include **Enterprise,** 1155 N. Main
(✆ 800/325-8007 or 435/755-6111); **Hertz,** 447 N. Main (✆ 800/654-3131
or 435/752-9141); and **Palmers Freedom Car Rental,** 1220 N. Main (✆ 435/
752-2075).

FAST FACTS The **Logan Regional Hospital,** 1400 N. 500 East (✆ **435/
716-1000**), has a 24-hour emergency room. The **main post office** is at 75 W.
200 North (✆ **800/275-8777;** www.usps.com, for hours and additional
locations).

WHAT TO SEE & DO

Although not open to the public, you can still view the outside of the handsome
LDS Temple, 200 N. 200 East (✆ **435/752-3611**). The site of the temple was
known to the Shoshone as "a most sacred place" and was where they held their
healing ceremonies. It's on a slight rise and can be seen from just about anywhere
in the valley. The temple was completed in 1884, and its octagonal towers give
the four-story limestone structure the appearance of a medieval castle.

American West Heritage Center This living history museum, covering
160 acres, tells the story of the Old West from 1820 to 1920. It includes the
Jensen Historical Farm, an authentic 1917 farm where visitors can learn about
farming in the early 20th century; and the **Pioneer Era Area** (1845 to 1870),
which describes homesteading and life in a dugout or log cabin. There are also
areas depicting life in American Indian villages and the military. Allow 2 hours.
The **Festival of the American West** (special fees; see below), held in late July or
early August, features arts and crafts demonstrations, American Indian villages,
military encampments, Western art exhibits, Western music and food, and a
pageant that tells the story of the founding of the American West.

4025 South U.S. 89/91 (6 miles south of Logan), Wellsville. ✆ 800/225-3378 or 435/245-6050. www.
americanwestcenter.org. Admission $6 adults, $4 children under 12, $5 students with ID and seniors 55 and
older, $20 family (parents and up to 4 dependent children under 21); Festival admission $15 adults, $8 children
under 12, $10 students with ID, $13 seniors 55 and older, $65 family (parents and up to 4 dependent chil-
dren under 21). Memorial Day–Labor Day Mon–Sat 10am–5pm. Welcome Center open Memorial Day–Labor
Day Mon–Sat 8am–5pm; rest of year Mon–Fri 8am–5pm. Closed New Year's Day, Thanksgiving, and Christmas.

Cache Museum—Daughters of the Utah Pioneers Housed in the same
building as the information center, this small museum displays pioneer artifacts
from 1859 to 1899—basically the first 40 years of Mormon settlement in the
area. You can see guns, musical instruments (including the first organ used in
the LDS Tabernacle), handmade pioneer furniture, clothing, and kitchen items.
On exhibit are several pieces of furniture made by Brigham Young for his daughter Luna Young Thatcher, who lived in Logan. Allow 30 minutes.

160 N. Main St. ✆ 435/752-5139. Free admission. June–Labor Day Tues–Fri 10am–4pm.

LDS Tabernacle The Tabernacle was built from locally quarried stone in a
style that's an amalgam of Greek, Roman, Gothic, and Byzantine. The main
stone, quartzite, is from Green Canyon, 8 miles northeast of Logan; the white
limestone used for the corners and trimmings came from Idaho. Construction
started in 1864 but took 27 years to complete. The main hall and balcony can
accommodate about 1,800 people, and the pipe organ is a work of art. The pillars are made of wood that has been expertly painted to simulate marble, a tech-
nique widely used throughout pioneer Utah. Allow 30 minutes. There's also an
extensive genealogical library, open to the public.

100 N. Main St. ✆ 435/755-5555. Free admission. June–Aug daily 9am–5pm.

Utah State University   Founded in 1888, Utah State University (USU) is situated on a bench that was once the shore of the great Lake Bonneville. Established through the Federal Land Grant Program as the Agricultural College of Utah, USU has about 20,000 students and an international reputation for research and teaching.

Old Main was the first USU building, begun just a year after the college was established, and is the oldest building in continuous use on any Utah college campus. At various times, it has housed nearly every office and department of the school. Its tall bell tower is a campus landmark.

The **Museum of Anthropology,** Room 252, Old Main (𝒞 **435/797-1230** or 435/797-0219) has exhibits on the early inhabitants of the Great Basin as well as on the peoples of Polynesia and other areas around the world. It's open Monday through Friday from 8am to 5pm; admission is free. Allow 45 minutes.

The **Nora Eccles Harrison Museum of Art,** 650 N. 1100 East (𝒞 **435/797-0163**), displays a fine collection of ceramics and offers changing exhibits in a variety of media. It's open Tuesday through Friday from 10:30am to 4:30pm (Wednesday until 8pm), Saturday noon to 5pm. Allow 1 hour. Admission is free. Pick up an **Art Walk** guide at the museum, which will direct you on a tour of the outdoor art on campus.

102 Old Main. 𝒞 **435/797-1000.** www.usu.edu. The 400-acre campus lies north of U.S. 89 and mostly east of 800 East. To get to the campus, drive north on I-15 and take Exit 364. Drive east through Brigham City and the Canyon. The highway turns into Main St. Turn right on 500 North. When you get to the hill, turn left up the slope. Parking is just past the traffic light on the right.

Willow Park Zoo *Kids*   This small but intriguing zoo is home to a variety of animals, from lemurs to elk to bobcats, including one of the best collections of waterfowl in the region, with more than 100 species. Children are invited to feed the ducks, geese, and trout. The attractive grounds have a lovely, grassy play and picnic area shaded by tall trees. Some of the animal enclosures are on the small side, and not as animal-friendly as those in many modern big-city zoos, but the personnel are making improvements when and where they can, money and space permitting. Allow 1½ hours.

419 W. 700 South. 𝒞 **435/750-9893.** 25¢ per person suggested donation, children under 5 free. Daily 9am–dusk. Closed New Year's Day, Thanksgiving, and Christmas. From Main St., head west on 600 South for 3 blocks, turn south (left) onto 300 West for 1 block, then west (right) onto 700 South.

SPORTS & OUTDOOR PURSUITS

Many of the outdoor recreation opportunities in this area are in the Wasatch-Cache National Forest, which covers almost 2 million acres of northern Utah. For maps and other information, contact the **Logan Ranger District** office, 1500 E. U.S. 89, Logan, UT 84321-4373 (𝒞 **435/755-3620;** www.fs.fed.us/r4/wcnf). For outdoor equipment and supplies, as well as knowledgeable staff to help you find the best spot for your particular activity, stop by **Gart Sports,** 1050 N. Main (𝒞 **435/752-4287**), or **Al's Sporting Goods,** 1617 N. Main (𝒞 **435/752-5151**).

You'll find excellent watersports, fishing, and wildlife viewing at **Bear Lake State Park** (𝒞 **435/946-3343;** www.stateparks.utah.gov), along the Utah-Idaho border about 40 miles northeast of Logan via U.S. 89. The state's second-largest freshwater lake (20 miles long and 8 miles wide), Bear Lake is known for the azure blue of its water, caused by the suspension of calcium carbonate (limestone) particles in the lake. Facilities include boat ramps and rentals, a marina, picnic areas, campgrounds, and a 4.2-mile paved walking/biking trail. Deer are often seen in the park, and bird-watchers may spot ducks, geese, white pelicans, herons, and sandhill cranes, among other species. Anglers catch lake trout and huge cutthroat trout. Elevation is 5,900 feet. The day-use fee is $7 per vehicle; camping costs $7 to $20.

BIKING Cache Valley's patchwork of farms and villages offer excellent road biking through the countryside on well-maintained roads, and mountain bikers have plenty of opportunities in the Wasatch-Cache National Forest. For tips on the best biking spots, contact the visitor center or the ranger district office (p. 129). Each June the Utah Multiple Sclerosis Society (© **800/527-8116** or 801/493-0113; www.fightmsutah.org) sponsors **Utah's Best Dam MS 150 Bike Tour,** in which more than 500 participants pedal 75 miles each day along Cache Valley's back roads. The funds raised are donated to help in the battle against multiple sclerosis.

BIRDING Northern Utah has great birding, especially from spring through early fall in the area's wetlands. Two particularly good spots are along the Bear River west of Logan, and Cutler Marsh (get directions at the visitor center). These spots offer opportunities to see great blue herons, snowy egrets, white pelicans, western grebes, and a variety of other wetlands species. Information is available on the website for the local chapter of the **National Audubon Society,** http://bridgerlandaudubon.org, where you'll find information on local birding events and a checklist of species seen in the area.

FISHING Logan River and Bear River offer wonderful fly-fishing, and streams throughout the area are popular for rainbow, albino, cutthroat, and brook trout. Bear Lake (p. 131) offers great lake fishing (including ice-fishing in winter) for trophy cutthroat and lake trout. For tips on where they're biting, stop at **Rivers Wild,** 516 S. Main St. (© **435/752-0714**), a full-service fly shop.

HIKING There are numerous hiking possibilities in the Wasatch-Cache National Forest east of Logan, and Logan Canyon in particular offers spectacular scenery. Among the easy hikes is the **Spring Hollow Trail,** located about 6.5 miles up Logan Canyon, which leads a half mile to one of the area's most photographed rivers. Stop at the visitor center or the forest service office (p. 129) for a free brochure and other information.

HORSEBACK RIDING The **Beaver Creek Lodge,** in Logan Canyon (© **800/946-4485** or 435/946-3400), is about 25 miles northeast of Logan on U.S. 89 just east of Beaver Mountain Ski Resort. One-, 1½-, and 3-hour guided rides are available for beginner through expert levels, costing from $20 to $55. Trails include a wide range of terrain, from rolling hills covered with aspens, pine trees, and wildflowers, to mountaintops. The challenging rides to the top of a mountain reward you with panoramic views of the forest. Reservations are recommended. See p. 128 for more information on Beaver Creek Lodge.

ROCK CLIMBING The sheer rock walls of Logan Canyon make this one of the most challenging climbing areas in the West. There's an abundance of vertical and overhanging limestone and quartzite faces, and more than 275 routes have been developed—most are bolt-protected sport climbs. For detailed information and climbing site recommendations, stop at the visitor center or **Bitter Sweet Climbing Wall,** 51 S. Main St. (© **435/752-8152**), which sells and rents climbing equipment, and also has an indoor climbing gym.

SNOWMOBILING & OTHER WINTER FUN Snowmobiling opportunities can be found throughout the Wasatch-Cache National Forest. Rentals are available at **Beaver Creek Lodge** (p. 128), which offers access to more than 300 miles of groomed snowmobile trails. Full-day rental rates are $129 to $159. Information on snowmobiling, snowshoeing, and cross-country skiing can be obtained from the Wasatch-Cache National Forest's **Logan Ranger District Office.** Rentals of cross-country skis and snowshoes are available at **Gart Sports** (p. 131). Downhill skiing is at **Beaver Mountain Ski Area** (p. 128).

SPECTATOR SPORTS

A member of the Big West Athletic Conference, **Utah State University** competes in all major sports, winning conference championships in football, men's basketball, and women's outdoor track in recent years. Contact the school's ticket office (© **888/878-2831** or 435/797-0305; www.usu.edu) for information.

WHERE TO STAY

Among the reliable chains in Logan that usually charge under $80 for two people are **Best Western Baugh Motel,** 153 S. Main St. (© **800/462-4154** or 435/752-5220), and **Best Western Weston Inn,** 250 N. Main St. (© **800/532-5055** or 435/752-5700). In the $45 to $65 range are **Days Inn,** 364 S. Main St. (© **800/329-7466** or 435/753-5623), **Comfort Inn,** 447 N. Main St. (© **800/ 424-6423** or 435/752-9141), and **Super 8,** 865 U.S. 89/91 (© **800/800-8000** or 435/753-8883). All addresses are Logan, UT 84321.

Rates are highest in summer, and lowest usually during the first 3 or 4 months of the year. Lodging tax totals 9.25%.

Alta Manor Suites This modern lodging, built in 1994 in the Old English Tudor style, has spacious suites that are elegantly furnished with Queen Anne reproductions. All units have whirlpool baths and separate showers, natural-gas fireplaces, TVs with several premium movie channels, and queen beds. There's one wheelchair-accessible room. The property is entirely smoke-free and pets are not allowed.

45 E. 500 North, Logan, UT 84321. © **435/752-0808.** Fax 435/752-2445. 8 units. $99–$109 double. AE, DC, DISC, MC, V. *In room:* A/C, TV, kitchen.

WHERE TO DINE

The Bluebird AMERICAN   The Bluebird opened in 1914 as a candy shop and soda fountain, and soon expanded to include a few lunch items on its menu. In 1921, it moved to its present location, expanding its menu again to include dinner. Today, the Bluebird continues to offer good food along with fountain treats. The decor, reminiscent of the 1920s, features the original marble behind the soda fountain and a mural depicting Logan from 1856 to modern times.

The menu offers the old-fashioned luncheon fare you'd expect, including a Monte Cristo and a minced ham sandwich. English-style chips can be ordered with any sandwich. There are also several full meal offerings for lunch, including a 6-ounce sirloin steak, chicken teriyaki, and a 5-ounce halibut steak. In addition to a few sandwiches, the dinner menu brings such options as vegetarian pasta primavera, chicken-fried steak, and the popular slow-roasted prime rib. No alcohol is served.

19 N. Main St. © **435/752-3155.** Main courses $5–$6.50 lunch, $5.50–$13 dinner. AE, DISC, MC, V. Mon–Thurs 11am–9:30pm; Fri–Sat 11am–10pm. Just north of Center St.

Kate's Kitchen ★★ AMERICAN   Kate was born in 1992, so it's her dad who is presently running the restaurant. Family-style home cooking is served in the large, informal dining room, and everything here is homemade—even the ice cream. Menu choices include Kate's pot roast, rotisserie or teriyaki chicken, country-style barbecued ribs, or roasted pork tenderloin. Dinners are served family-style, with platters of your entree and bowls of sides that are passed around your table. They come with plenty of homemade muffins and honey butter, fresh garden salad with house dressing, homemade mashed potatoes (baby red potatoes, whole milk, and real butter) with gravy or seasoned rice, and corn on the cob or the veggie of the day. If you need more, just flag down a server; you can't miss them—they're the ones wearing hats. Once a month, Kate's offers an all-you-can-eat prime-rib dinner by reservation only; call to see when it's on. An early-bird supper for $9.95 is available Tuesday through Thursday from 4 to 6pm. No alcohol is served.

71½ E. 1200 South. (℃ **435/753-5733,** or 435/753-1223 for takeout. www.kateskitchen.net. Reservations accepted for parties of 8 or more. Main course prices for those over 12 $10–$12; children 12 and younger pay 50¢ for each birthday. MC, V. Tues–Sat 4–10pm. Closed Christmas, New Year's Day, and July 4. Follow Main St. south and take Utah 165 towards Hyrum (the left fork when U.S. 89/91 heads right to Wellsville); turn east (left) onto 1200 South.

LOGAN AFTER DARK

The **Utah Festival Opera Company,** 59 S. 100 West (℃ **800/262-0074** or 435/750-0300, ext. 106), presents a summer series of grand operas, light operettas, and musicals at the historic Ellen Eccles Theatre, 43 S. Main St. Recent productions have included Offenbach's opera *The Tales of Hoffman,* Sigmund Romberg's operetta *The Student Prince,* and musicals such as *Fiddler on the Roof* and *Carousel.* A number of other productions, ranging from modern dance performances to big band concerts, are staged at the **Ellen Eccles Theatre** (℃ **435/752-0026;** www.elleneccclestheatre.org). Contact the theater for the current schedule.

The **Old Lyric Repertory Company,** 28 W. Center St. (℃ **435/797-1500** or 435/797-0305; www.usu.edu/lyric), founded at Utah State University in 1967, presents a variety of comedies, dramas, and musicals, with equity actors, during its 8-week summer season. USU's **Performing Arts Department** (℃ **435/797-0305**) also presents plays and concerts featuring both students and faculty, plus a performing arts series showcasing national and international artists, during the school year.

The Southern Wasatch Front: World-Class Skiing & More

In this chapter, we head to the mountains south and east of Salt Lake City. The following sections are arranged geographically from north to south, from the Cottonwood Canyon and Park City resorts to Provo and nearby Timpanogos Cave National Monument, with a few stops in between, including pristine Strawberry Reservoir, Robert Redford's Sundance Resort and Institute, and a fun old train.

1 The Cottonwood Canyon Resorts: Brighton, Solitude, Alta & Snowbird

You say you want snow? Here it is, some 500 inches of it piling up every year, just waiting for you powder-hungry skiers to make that short drive from Salt Lake City. You'll find Brighton and Solitude ski resorts in Big Cottonwood Canyon, and Alta and Snowbird ski resorts in its sister canyon, Little Cottonwood.

If you're skiing on a budget, stay at the more affordable Salt Lake City lodgings rather than at the resorts themselves. The resorts are so close—less than an hour's drive—that city dwellers sometimes hit the slopes after a hard day at the office!

But this area is more than just a winter playground. Big Cottonwood Canyon, cut by ancient rivers over more centuries than we can imagine, is a spectacular setting for warm-weather picnicking, camping, mountain biking, and hiking. Rugged, glacier-carved Little Cottonwood Canyon is filled with lush fields of summer wildflowers, the brilliant hues of autumn, and then a winter blanket of champagne powder snow.

GETTING THERE

BY CAR From Salt Lake City, take I-215 south to exit 7; follow Utah 210 south. Turn east onto Utah 190 to reach Solitude and Brighton in Big Cottonwood Canyon; continue on Utah 210 south and east to Snowbird and Alta in Little Cottonwood Canyon. From Salt Lake City International Airport, it'll take about an hour to reach any of the four ski areas.

BY BUS The **Utah Transit Authority** (© 801/287-4636, or 801/287-4657 TDD; www.utabus.com) provides bus service from downtown Salt Lake City hotels and various park-and-ride lots throughout the city into Big and Little Cottonwood Canyons during ski season. Cost is $5 round-trip.

BY SHUTTLE Lewis Bros. Stages (© 877/491-8111 or 801/359-8677; www.lewisbros.com) offers shuttles from the airport ($56 round-trip) and major Salt Lake City hotels (call your hotel for rates).

BIG COTTONWOOD CANYON

Utah 190 will take you through Big Cottonwood Canyon to Brighton and Solitude. Each turn along your drive to the summit of this 15-mile-long canyon brings you to yet another grand, dizzying vista. Rock climbers love these steep, rugged canyon walls—watch for them as you drive.

BRIGHTON SKI RESORT ☞

In operation since 1936, the low-key, family-friendly **Brighton Ski Resort,** 12601 Big Cottonwood Canyon Rd., Brighton, UT 84121 (© **800/873-5512** or 801/532-4731; www.brightonresort.com), is where many Utahns learn to ski and snowboard—the ski and snowboard school is highly regarded. Children 10 and under stay and ski free with their parents, and teens particularly enjoy the bumps of Lost Maid Trail as it winds through the woods. But don't let its reputation as a beginner's mountain fool you: Brighton's slopes are graced with a full range of terrain, all the powder you can imagine, and virtually no crowds. You'll find more Utahns than out-of-staters on the slopes here—Brighton is located just 35 miles from downtown Salt Lake City at the top of Big Cottonwood Canyon, and visitors tend to stay away because of the paucity of area lodgings. So there's always plenty of elbow room on the intermediate and advanced slopes on the weekends, and you'll probably have them all to yourself on weekdays. You can explore the slopes until late in the day: Brighton lights up 200 acres for night skiing.

Brighton is also one of the best snowboarding destinations in the state.

Brighton has three high-speed quad lifts, one triple, three double chairs, and a rope tow serving over 850 acres in the Wasatch-Cache National Forest. The lift-served vertical drop is 1,745 feet, with a vertical drop of almost 2,000 feet accessible by hiking. Base elevation is 8,755 feet. Of the 66 runs, 21% are rated beginner, 40% intermediate, and 39% advanced. Lifts are open daily from 9am to 4pm, early November to late April, with night skiing and snowboarding Monday through Saturday from 4 to 9pm. The resort can make snow on 200 acres, but with 500 inches of average snowfall per year, the man-made stuff isn't usually necessary.

Brighton has a beautiful 20,000-square-foot day lodge, with ticket windows, restrooms, a common area, a ski rental and repair facility, and a convenient depot for those using the bus.

See p. 135 for information on getting to the ski area.

LIFT TICKETS   All-day passes cost $41; night skiing, $24. Children 10 and under pay half price or ski free with an adult (limit two children per adult). Seniors 70 and over ski for $10.

LESSONS & PROGRAMS   **Brighton Ski & Snowboard School,** located in the Alpine Rose building, offers both private and group lessons. Group lessons cost $55 including equipment and lift ticket, or $28 for the lesson only. Private lessons start at $60 for 1 hour. Night skiing lessons cost $26, including a lift ticket. The ski and snowboard school also offers a variety of workshops and clinics, including a telemark series as well as adult parallel, senior, children's, and women's workshops.

WHERE TO STAY & DINE   **Brighton Lodge,** at the ski resort (© **800/873-5512** or 801/532-4731; www.brightonresort.com), has 20 units, ranging from dorm-style rooms (which sleep up to four) to luxurious suites, with rates of $90 to $155 double. The lodge's heated swimming pool and large outdoor Jacuzzi will help loosen those sore muscles before your next day of skiing. Room tax is about 9½%. You'll find cafeteria-style dining for all three meals and a bar that opens for lunch and stays open through après-ski and dinner.

WARM-WEATHER FUN Mountain biking and hiking are popular activities, but note that lifts are not open in summer.

SOLITUDE MOUNTAIN RESORT

Solitude, 12000 Big Cottonwood Canyon, Solitude, UT 84121 (© **800/748-4754** or 801/534-1400; www.skisolitude.com), is a friendly, family-oriented resort that hasn't been "discovered" yet, so lift lines are virtually nonexistent. The snow is terrific, and it's easy to reach—just 28 miles from downtown Salt Lake City in Big Cottonwood Canyon. Like its next-door neighbor, Brighton—which is connected to Solitude via the Solbright Trail—Solitude enjoys excellent powder and few crowds. Its 1,200-plus acres of skiable terrain range from well-groomed, sunny beginner and intermediate trails to gently pitched bowls and glades. The mountain is well designed, with runs laid out so beginners won't suddenly find themselves in more difficult terrain. Intermediates have wide-open bowls in which to cruise and practice their powder skiing, several excellent forest runs, and some great bumpy stretches on which to hone their mogul skills. Advanced skiers have many long fall lines, open powder areas, and steeply graded chutes.

Solitude is the state's only downhill ski area with a world-class Nordic center out its back door: The University of Utah and U.S. Olympic teams train here. The resort also has an ice skating rink.

Solitude operates one high-speed quad lift, one fixed-grip quad, two triples, and four doubles to service 64 runs and three bowls. Runs are rated 20% beginner, 50% intermediate, and 30% advanced/expert. The resort is open from early November to late April, daily from 9am to 4pm. With a summit elevation of 10,035 feet and a vertical drop of 2,047 feet, Solitude receives an average snowfall of more than 500 inches.

See p. 135 for information on getting to the ski area.

LIFT TICKETS All-day passes cost $45 for adults, $10 for seniors 70 and older; those 6 and under ski free. Afternoon half-day adult lift tickets are $39.

LESSONS & PROGRAMS Solitude's **ski school** offers group and private lessons. Adult group classes are $40 for a half day, $60 for all day; call for rates for customized private lessons. The **Moonbeam Learning Center,** for kids 4 through 12, offers an all-day program, including lunch, for $75; the afternoon-only program is $50.

Tips Great Cross-Country Skiing

Solitude Nordic Center ⭐⭐ is Utah's oldest cross-country ski area. It has 20 kilometers (12 miles) of groomed trails, including a children's trail. The center is located between Solitude and Brighton at 8,700 feet and connects the two downhill resorts. Trails pass through alpine forests and meadows and around frozen Silver Lake. The **Silver Lake Day Lodge** offers rentals, equipment for sale, lessons, and light snacks. Trail passes for ages 11 to 69 cost $10 for a full day, $7 for a half day. Those 10 and under or 70 and over ski free.

WHERE TO STAY & DINE   The **Inn at Solitude** is a full-service luxury hotel, with 46 rooms and nightly rates from $145 to $350. Its restaurant, **St. Bernard's,** offers fine dining with a menu from Europe's Alpine regions. Only dinner is served.

The 36-unit **Creekside at Solitude** is centrally located in the resort village, close to three of the lifts and the day lodge. One- to three-bedroom condo units go for $160 to $690. The restaurant serves regional and Italian cuisine for lunch and dinner. The resort also manages more than **160 additional condo units** in six buildings, including units with three bedrooms plus den, with prices ranging from $145 to $720.

Adjacent to the Apex Chairlift and with terrific views of the mountain, the day lodge **Last Chance Mining Camp** offers hearty breakfast and lunch fare, and aprés-ski refreshments. The **Sunshine Grill** is partway up the mountain at 9,000 feet elevation. It has a sunny deck and terrific views of the slopes, and serves lunch, plus snacks on weekends and holidays.

For an unusual experience, reserve dinner at the **Yurt** (© **800/748-4754,** ext. 5709), in the forest above the main lodge. You can either cross-country ski or snowshoe through the evergreens to get to your elegant five-course gourmet meal, served at a table set with linen, silver, and crystal. Dress is casual, but the meal isn't.

Room tax in this area is 9½%.

WARM-WEATHER FUN   Solitude remains open in summer, offering chair-lift rides, mountain bike rentals, 18-hole mountainside disc golf, and a place to hike or just kick back and watch the wildflowers grow.

LITTLE COTTONWOOD CANYON

With towering peaks rising 11,000 feet above the road on both sides, Utah 210 takes you on a lovely scenic drive through the canyon. Located at the junction of Utah 209 and Utah 210, the mouth of Little Cottonwood Canyon is where pioneers quarried the granite used to build the LDS Church's Salt Lake Temple.

ALTA SKI AREA ✦✦✦

Alta, P.O. Box 8007, Alta, UT 84092-8007 (© **801/359-1078;** www.alta.com), is famous for its snow—over 500 inches of some of the lightest powder in the world—and at $42 for an all-day lift ticket, it's an excellent value. Located about 45 minutes southeast of Salt Lake City, at the top of Little Cottonwood Canyon, Alta is an excellent choice for serious skiers of all levels. Beginners have their share of runs, and there's even a bit of easy-going tree skiing through the woods for the more adventurous novices. Intermediates will find plenty of open cruis-ing ground, forested areas, and long, arcing chutes to glide through, plus oppor-tunities to work on their bumps technique (try Challenger for a moderately pitched set) or practice their turns in the powder. Experts will find an abundance of the Cottonwood Canyons' famous powder and spectacular runs, like steep, long Alf's High Rustler. Alta offers much for the expert and the extreme skier— far too much to cover here—but hard-core skiers should know that you'll have to step out of the bindings and do a bit of hiking to get to some of the longest drops and best powder-laden runs.

Alta's fans are many and loyal. That's because the emphasis here is on quality skiing, and to protect that quality, Alta has chosen to limit its uphill capacity. This is a classic ski resort, with both European-style terrain *and* sensibilities. This means that people are turned away on those occasions when the ski gods determine there are already enough skiers on the mountain. An announcement is made on 530 AM radio about a half hour before the closure.

Alta is one of the few western ski areas left that forbids snowboarding.

More than 50 runs are served by one detachable quad, one detachable triple, two triples, four doubles, and five surface tows. Alta has 2,200 skiable acres, with snow-making on 50 acres. Although it's famous for its expert runs, Alta also has fine beginner and intermediate trails. The breakdown is 25% beginner, 40% intermediate, and 35% advanced, with a base elevation of 8,530 feet rising to 10,550 feet at the top, yielding a vertical drop of 2,020 feet. Alta is generally open from mid-November to mid-April, with lifts operating daily from 9:15am to 4:30pm.

Alta Ski Lifts Company owns and operates only the ski area; all other businesses and services are privately run. At the base of Albion and Sunnyside lifts, you'll find a day lodge with cafeteria, lift-ticket sales, day care, the ski school, and rentals. Two more cafeterias are located on the mountain. A transfer tow connects the Albion and Wildcat lift areas; in this base area, there are four lodges with dining facilities, ski rentals, and kids' programs.

See p. 135 for information on getting to the ski area.

LIFT TICKETS   All-day all-lift tickets cost $42, with half-day tickets at $33. Beginner lifts only are $33, and children 12 and younger ski for $33. There are also combination lift tickets for both Alta and Snowbird.

LESSONS & PROGRAMS   Founded in 1948 by Alf Engen, the highly regarded **ski school** (✆ **801/359-1078**) is recognized for its contribution to the development of professional ski instruction. Morning and afternoon (half-day) group lessons cost $35 to $45; private instruction starts at $65 for a 1-hour lesson. The **Children's Ski Adventures** program, for ages 4 to 12, offers fun skill development, and lessons in ski etiquette. Choose either a 2-hour or all-day program.

Alta's **day-care program** (✆ **801/742-3042**) is open to children ages 2 months to 10 years old; reservations are encouraged. Call for current rates.

WHERE TO STAY & DINE   Our favorite places to stay in Alta are slope-side. The following accommodations add a 15% service charge to your bill in lieu of tipping; room tax adds about 11%.

Alta Lodge (✆ **800/707-2582** or 801/742-3500; www.altalodge.com) is perhaps the quintessential mountain ski lodge—simple and rustic, with a touch of class. The lodge has Jacuzzis, saunas, a general store, a kids' program, a bar, and a restaurant with superb food. The comfortable units range from small and basic dormitory rooms to handsome corner rooms with fireplaces and a balcony. Rates, including breakfast and dinner, range from $243 to $479 for two, or $103 to $128 per bed in a small dorm room.

Rustler Lodge (✆ **888/532-2582** for reservations, or 801/742-2200; fax 801/742-3832; www.rustlerlodge.com) is elegant yet relaxed, with a great mountain-lodge ambience, a spa, and rooms that range from basic to deluxe (several two-room suites are available). Rates, including full breakfast and dinner, range from $279 to $705 for two; a bed for one in a dorm room, with breakfast and dinner, costs $112 to $162.

SNOWBIRD SKI & SUMMER RESORT ★★

The combination of super skiing and snowboarding plus super facilities lures both hard-core enthusiasts seeking spectacular powder, and those who enjoy the pampering that accompanies a stay at a full-service resort. Consistently rated among America's top-ten ski resorts, **Snowbird,** P.O. Box 929000, Snowbird, UT 84092-9000 (© **800/453-3000** or 801/742-2222, or 801/933-2100 for snow conditions; www.snowbird.com), is Alta's "younger, slicker sister." You'll find the same wonderful snow here, but with a wider range of amenities, including Snowbird's extremely popular spa and salon—worth the trip even if you don't ski. Some, however, find Snowbird's dense, modern village and resort atmosphere cold compared to Alta's historic, European-style lodges and classic, ruggedly Western atmosphere and attitude.

Expert skiers love Snowbird, which has plunging cliff runs like Great Scott, one of the steepest runs in the country. Mogul-meisters will want to take the Peruvian or Gad II lifts to a great variety of fall lines on some steep and sinuous runs.

But beginners and intermediates haven't been forgotten, and their runs are also top-notch. There are even some "family-only" ski zones. Novices might want to head over to explore West Second South, set in a woodsy glade, or the less crowded Baby Thunder area. Intermediates will enjoy the excellent runs coming off the Gad II lift; if you decide to take the tram, wait around a bit at the top while your fellow riders take off so that you'll have these blue runs all to yourself—the next tramload won't get dumped off for another 5 minutes.

The entire mountain is open to snowboarders, and the resort also provides snowmobile adventures and cat skiing and snowboarding.

Snowbird has 85 runs on 2,500 acres, rated 27% beginner, 38% intermediate, and 35% advanced/expert. The ski season generally runs from mid-November to mid-May, although the record-breaking 600 inches—that's 50 feet—of snow that fell in 1994–1995 allowed Snowbird to keep the lifts running through the Fourth of July—the latest lift-served skiing ever in Utah. From a base elevation of 7,760 feet, the vertical rise of 3,240 feet reaches Hidden Peak at 11,000 feet.

An aerial tram transports 125 skiers and boarders at a time up 2,900 vertical feet to Hidden Peak in about 8 minutes. It's quick, but can feel like a crowded New York City subway. Snowbird also has three high-speed detachable quads, seven doubles, and two rope tows, giving it a total uphill capacity of 16,800 skiers per hour. The tram and lifts operate between 9am and 4:30pm daily, except for one that operates until 8:30pm for night skiing Wednesdays and Fridays, and luge on Tuesdays, Thursdays, and Saturdays.

LIFT TICKETS   Adult lift tickets cost $48 for a full day and $41 for a half day; for both lifts and tram, the cost is $57 and $49, respectively. Children 12 and under ski free with parents (limit of two kids per parent). Seniors 65 and over are charged $37, or $45 including tram. There are also combination lift tickets for both Snowbird and Alta.

LESSONS & PROGRAMS   The **ski and snowboarding school** offers an all-day class (which includes lunch); a package for first-timers; and specialized workshops for racers, women, snowboarders, half-pipe riders, or seniors. Full-day classes start at about $80; a 1-hour private ski lesson starts at about $100.

Established in 1977, Snowbird's **Disabled Skier Program** is among the best in the country. Using state-of-the-art adaptive ski devices and a team of specially trained instructors, the program is available to both children and adults. Sit-skis, mono-skis, and outriggers are available at no extra cost.

HELI-SKIING   Between December 15 and April 15, helicopter skiing is available on more than 40,000 acres from **Wasatch Powderbird Guides**

Tips   Off the Slopes at Snowbird

Don't miss the popular **Cliff Spa and Salon** (© 801/933-2225), which offers a lap pool and huge whirlpool, aerobic and weight-training rooms, and individual treatment rooms for massages, body wraps, mud baths, and hydrotherapy. The **Snowbird Canyon Racquet Club** (© 801/947-8200), 15 minutes from the slopes, features 23 tennis courts (10 indoor), racquetball, and aerobic and cardiovascular facilities. Snowbird provides a variety of facilities for children, including a state-licensed day-care center and a youth camp; call for details.

(© 800/974-4354 or 801/742-2800; www.powderbird.com). Daily rates (seven runs, a continental breakfast, and lunch) are $770 per person from mid-January through the third week of March, and $630 per person at other times.

WHERE TO STAY & DINE   The approximately 900 rooms at Snowbird range from standard lodge units to luxurious condominiums with kitchens and fireplaces. **Snowbird Central Reservations** (© 800/453-3000) books all lodging for the resort and can also arrange air and ground transportation. Room tax adds about 11%.

The **Cliff Lodge, Spa, and Conference Center** is located in a ski-in, ski-out pedestrian mall. Practically all of the 532 rooms, with mission-style furnishings, have splendid views of the mountain or canyon. Choose a standard or extra-large room, or a one- or two-bedroom suite. You'll find a splendid spa, restaurants, shops, and practically anything else you might want. Rooms are $170 to $229 double, and suites start at $380.

The Lodge at Snowbird, The Inn, and **Iron Blosam Lodge** are condominium properties, offering rooms, efficiencies, studios, and one-bedroom and one-bedroom-with-loft units. Many have Western decor and Murphy beds and/or sofa beds. Rates range from $150 to $800.

The **Aerie Restaurant** (© 801/933-2160), on the top floor of the Cliff Lodge, features New American dining with spectacular views, and serves a skier's breakfast buffet in the winter ($14.95), and dinner year-round. Entree prices range from $18 to $27. Also in Cliff Lodge, the **Keyhole Junction** (© 801/933-2025) serves spicy Southwestern cuisine for lunch and dinner in the summer, dinner-only in winter. Dinner prices range from $7 to $24. On level B of Cliff Lodge is the **Atrium** (© 801/933-2181), with tremendous alpine views. It features a buffet lunch in winter and a light breakfast buffet in summer, with prices from $12 to $22. The Atrium Espresso Bar is open daily.

For steak and seafood, try the **Steak Pit** (© 801/933-2260), in Snowbird Center, open for dinner daily. Prices range from $14 to $36. On level 3 of the Snowbird Center is the **Forklift Restaurant** (© 801/933-2240), serving breakfast and lunch daily. Prices range from $7 to $11. The **Lodge Bistro** (© 801/933-2145) is on the pool level in the Lodge at Snowbird, offering an eclectic dinner menu in an intimate setting. Entrees range from $10 to $28.

WARM-WEATHER FUN   After the skiers go home for the season, Snowbird is still active with hikers and mountain bikers. A lift hauls mountain bikers up the slopes. In July, Snowbird's music program includes live jazz and performances by the Utah Symphony; call for details.

2 Park City: Utah's Premier Resort Town

31 miles E of Salt Lake City

Utah's most sophisticated resort community, Park City, reminds us of Aspen, Colorado, and Taos, New Mexico—other historic Western towns that have made the most of excellent ski terrain while evolving into popular year-round vacation destinations, offering a casual Western atmosphere with a touch of elegance.

A silver boom brought thousands to Park City in the 1870s, and that boom continued for 50 years, giving Park City a population of 10,000 at its height, with more than 30 saloons along Main Street and a flourishing red-light district. Then came the Depression and plummeting mineral prices, leaving Park City to doze in the summer sun and under a blanket of winter snow. In 1963, the area's first ski lift was built (rates were $2.50 for a weekend of sledding and skiing), and Park City was on the road to becoming one of the West's most popular ski towns.

Today's visitors will find three separate ski areas, lodgings that range from basic to luxurious, some of the state's most innovative restaurants and best shops, an abundance of fine performing arts events, many of Utah's liveliest nightspots, and plenty of hiking, mountain biking, fishing, and other outdoor opportunities.

As in many tourist towns, prices here can be a bit steep; if you're watching your wallet, avoid visiting during the Christmas season and other peak periods. Those who are really pinching pennies might want to stay in Salt Lake City and drive to Park City in the morning for a day of skiing, exploring, or adventuring.

ESSENTIALS

GETTING THERE   Most visitors fly into Salt Lake City International Airport and drive or take a shuttle to Park City. Driving time from the airport is about 35 minutes. At I-80 exit 145, take Utah 224 into Park City.

Lewis Bros. Stages (© 877/491-8111 or 801/359-8677; www.lewisbros.com) has been serving the Park City area since 1948 and offers frequent shuttles from the Salt Lake City airport and hotels ($56 round-trip), as well as transportation from Park City to Big and Little Cottonwood Canyons (call for prices).

Other companies offering shuttle service between Salt Lake City and Park City include **Park City Transportation** (© 800/637-3803 or 435/649-8567; www.parkcitytransportation.com) and **All Resort Express** (© 800/457-9457 or 435/649-3999; www.allresort.com).

VISITOR INFORMATION   The **Park City Chamber of Commerce/Convention and Visitors Bureau,** 1910 Prospector Ave. (P.O. Box 1630), Park City, UT 84060 (© 800/453-1360 or 435/649-6100; www.parkcityinfo.com), is open Monday through Friday from 8am to 5pm. It operates a visitor information center at 750 Kearns Blvd. (Utah 248) where it junctions with Park Avenue (Utah 224) as you enter town, open daily from 9am to 6pm; and another center in the Park City Museum, 528 Main St., open Monday through Saturday from 10am to 7pm and Sunday from noon to 6pm.

GETTING AROUND   Parking in Park City is limited, especially in the historic Main Street area, and it is just plain awful if you're driving a motor home or pulling a trailer. If you've arrived in a car, the best plan is to park it and ride the free city bus. There's metered parking (in effect from 11am to 8pm) along Main Street and in Swede Alley, which parallels Main to the east. There's a fairly large parking lot near the upper (south) end of Main Street.

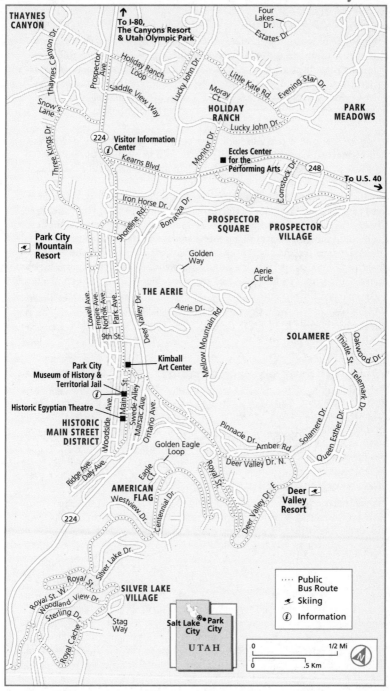

The Park City Area

THAYNES CANYON

To I-80,
The Canyons Resort
& Utah Olympic Park

Four Lakes Dr.

Estates Dr.

Thaynes Canyon Dr.

Prospector Ave.

Holiday Ranch Loop

Saddle View Way

Lucky John Dr.

Little Kate Rd.

Evening Star Dr.

Snow's Lane

Moray Ct.

HOLIDAY RANCH

Lucky John Dr.

PARK MEADOWS

Three Kings Dr.

224

Visitor Information Center

Kearns Blvd.

Monitor Dr.

Eccles Center for the Performing Arts

Comstock Dr.

248

To U.S. 40

Iron Horse Dr.

Bonanza Dr.

Shoreline Rd.

PROSPECTOR SQUARE

PROSPECTOR VILLAGE

Park City Mountain Resort

Golden Way

Aerie Circle

THE AERIE

Aerie Dr.

Mellow Mountain Rd.

SOLAMERE

Oakwood Dr.

Thistle St.

Telemark Dr.

Lowell Ave.
Empire Ave.
Norfolk Ave.
Park Ave.

Deer Valley Dr.

9th St.

Kimball Art Center

Park City Museum of History & Territorial Jail

Historic Egyptian Theatre

HISTORIC MAIN STREET DISTRICT

Main St.
Swede Alley
Marsac Ave.
Woodside Ave.
Ontario Ave.

Golden Eagle Loop

Pinnacle Dr.

Amber Rd.

Solamere Dr.

Queen Esther Dr.

Ridge Ave.
Daly Ave.

AMERICAN FLAG

Westview Dr.

Eagle Ct.

Centennial Dr.

Royal St.

Deer Valley Dr. N.

Deer Valley Dr. E.

Deer Valley Resort

224

Silver Lake Dr.

Royal St. W.
Royal St.

Woodland

View Dr.

SILVER LAKE VILLAGE

Sterling Dr.

Stag Way

Royal Cache

Salt Lake City

Park City

UTAH

..... Public Bus Route

Skiing

(i) Information

0 _____ 1/2 Mi
0 _____ .5 Km

143

Tips **Step Back in Time**

Be sure to pick up a copy of the *Park City Main Street Historic Walking Tour* brochure at one of the visitor information centers. It will lead you to 45 buildings and historic sites that have somehow managed to survive fires, hard times, and progress through the decades. The historic walk, complete with engaging anecdotes, really brings the town's lively past to life.

If you still want to rent a car and brave the parking problems, rental agencies here include **All Resort Car Rental,** 1821 Sidewinder Dr. (© **800/457-9457** or 435/649-3999) and **Enterprise,** 6560 N. Landmark Dr. (© **800/736-8222** or 435/655-7277).

Park City's very efficient free transit system offers several routes throughout Park City and the surrounding area, daily from 7am until 1am. The **Main Street Trolley** links Main Street and Park City Mountain Resort, and **public buses** travel to the outlying areas. Pick up the *Transit System Guide* brochure for a good route map and specific schedules. The weekly booklet *This Week in Park City* contains helpful info plus several area maps, including one of Main Street. Both are available at the visitor centers and many lodgings.

FAST FACTS To take care of injury or illness, go to **Park City Healthcare,** 1665 Bonanza Dr. (© **435/649-7640;** www.parkcityclinic.com) or **Snow Creek Emergency & Medical Center,** 1600 Snow Creek Dr. (© **435/655-0055**). The main **post office** is at 450 Main St. (© **800/275-8777**). The local newspaper is the *Park Record,* published every Wednesday and Saturday.

SKIING THE PARK CITY AREA RESORTS

The three area ski resorts, all within a few minutes' drive of each other, are vastly different. There's something for everyone here: Posh **Deer Valley** is Utah's version of very upscale Beaver Creek, Colorado, and big and lively **Park City** is the party resort. **The Canyons** is casual and friendly. Snowboarders are welcome at Park City Mountain Resort and The Canyons, but not Deer Valley.

Many skiers try all three resorts, and if you're going to do so, it will pay to do a bit of advance planning. The three resorts offer what they call a **Silver Passport,** which is a discounted multi-day package for use at all three resorts. There are various restrictions, though, including that it MUST be purchased before your arrival in Park City, and that it must be purchased in conjunction with lodging. Contact the resorts or area lodging properties for details.

DEER VALLEY RESORT ★★★

If you're looking for a first-class experience in every way, this is the spot for you. Unquestionably Utah's most elegant and sophisticated resort, **Deer Valley,** P.O. Box 1525, Park City, UT 84060 (© **800/424-3337** or 435/649-1000, or 435/649-2000 for snow conditions; www.deervalley.com), offers perfectly manicured slopes, guest service attendants, heated sidewalks, and some of the state's finest dining and lodging. Along with all this, you get fantastic skiing—especially if you crave long, smooth, perfectly groomed cruising runs that let you enjoy the spectacular mountain scenery around you. Although half of the terrain is rated intermediate, beginners love Success, a long run that gives them the feeling they're actually getting somewhere. In addition, much of the intermediate terrain is fit for advancing novices, as the entire mountain is kept very skiable.

Experts will find some steep, scary-enough trails on top, through majestic aspen and evergreen glades, plus plenty of woodsy terrain to weave through. Deer Valley is primarily a pampering resort experience, meant for cruising the wide lanes of impeccably groomed snow all day, then hobnobbing all evening with the rich—and often famous—over gourmet meals in the plush lodges.

Six bowls and 88 runs are spread over Empire Canyon, Deer Crest, Flagstaff, Bald, and Bald Eagle Mountains, served by a total of 19 chairlifts—seven high-speed quad lifts, a high-speed gondola, two fixed-grip quads, seven triples, and two double chairs. The base is at 6,570 feet with the summit at 9,570 feet, yielding a 3,000-foot vertical drop. The ski season generally runs from early December to mid-April, with lifts operating daily from 9am to 4:15pm. The 1,750 skiable acres are rated 15% beginner, 50% intermediate, and 35% advanced. Deer Valley has snow-making over 600 acres.

From Utah 224, head southeast on Deer Valley Drive to the resort.

LIFT TICKETS   All-day lift tickets cost $69 for adults ($71 during holidays), $38 for children 4 to 12, $18 for children 3 and under, and $48 for seniors 65 and older.

LESSONS & PROGRAMS   There are several **ski school** options at Deer Valley, including private and group lessons, workshops, and clinics. Group lessons for 3 hours cost $105 for adults (not including lift ticket); private lessons start at $95 per hour.

The licensed **child-care center,** open daily from 8:30am to 4:30pm, costs $85 per day for kids ages 2 months to 12 years, and includes lunch.

WHERE TO DINE ON THE MOUNTAIN   Snow Park Lodge (© 435/ 645-6632), at the base, houses a bakery, two restaurants, and a lounge. **Snow Park Restaurant,** serving breakfast and lunch daily, features a natural-foods buffet as well as standard soup-and-sandwich fare. The **Seafood Buffet,** open Monday through Saturday evenings, offers hearty hot dishes, a salad and seafood buffet, and fancy desserts. The **Snow Park Lounge** serves hors d'oeuvres after 3:30pm.

Silver Lake Lodge (© 435/645-6715), midway up the mountain, serves a variety of quick-and-easy food all day, including continental breakfasts (with fresh-baked pastries), salads, grilled fare, and pizzas. There's also a fine continental dining room, the **Mariposa** (© 435/645-6715), open evenings only.

PARK CITY MOUNTAIN RESORT 😊😊
Park City Mountain Resort, P.O. Box 39, Park City, UT 84060 (© **800/222-7275** or 435/649-8111, or 435/647-5449 for snow reports; www.parkcity mountain.com), one of Utah's largest and liveliest resorts, is where the U.S. Ski and Snowboard Olympic team comes to train. It's an official training site of the U.S. Ski and Snowboard Association as well. What brings them here? Plenty of dependable, powdery snow and a variety of terrain and runs that offer something for everyone. Surveys continually rank Park City among the country's top resorts for both its terrain and its challenging runs. And, because it's located right in the heart of Park City, what more could you ask for in terms of amenities?

Beginners will find plenty of great training ground, blessedly free of that frequent mountain problem—hordes of advanced skiers whizzing their way right through the green runs on their way to the bottom. After they have a good handle on the sport, beginners and novices can head up the lift to Summit House and then glide down their own scenic 3½-mile green run. Intermediates will find good cruising ground and powder runs; experts can delight in some 1,000 acres of wide-open bowls and hair-raising narrow chutes. After a good storm, the locals know to rise early, race to the top of the Jupiter Bowl, and carve their way back down through fresh powder.

The resort has four six-passenger high-speed lifts, one high-speed quad, five triples, and four double chairs servicing 100 runs on 3,300 acres; plus one Magic Carpet people mover in the Kids Mountain Adventure area. There's even a triple-chair access lift directly from Park City's Old Town onto the mountain, as well as two runs (Quit 'n' Time and Creole) that lead back into town, so those staying in Park City proper don't have to ride back and forth to the base resort every day. Trails are rated 18% beginner, 44% intermediate, and 38% expert. With a base elevation of 6,900 feet and summit of 10,000 feet, the vertical drop is 3,100 feet. The season generally runs from late November to mid-April, with lifts operating daily between 9am and 4pm. Night operations usually run from Christmas through March from 4 to 9pm, and include a snowboard park. Park City has snow-making capabilities on 500 acres.

The **Resort Center,** at the base of the mountain, houses the ski school, equipment sales and rentals, a restaurant and bar, lockers, and a ticket office.

The resort is off of Main Street.

LIFT TICKETS   All-day lift ticket fees vary throughout the season, but average about $60 for adults, $32 for children 7 to 12, and $28 for seniors 65 to 69. Children 6 and under and seniors 70 and older ski free.

LESSONS & PROGRAMS   The **Park City Mountain Resort Ski and Snowboard School** (© 800/227-2754) offers a wide variety of choices for every level, including group and private lessons for adults and children 7 to 13, plus a **Kids Mountain Adventure** for ages 3 to 6 that includes equipment rental, a snack, lunch, and lessons. Group lessons start at about $45 for 2 hours; a 1-hour private lesson costs $80 to $120; and Kids Mountain Adventure starts at $110. Customized packages are available.

WHERE TO DINE ON THE MOUNTAIN   In addition to the wide variety of options in Park City (see "Where to Dine"), you'll find the following slopeside facilities. None require reservations.

The **Food Court,** at the Legacy Lodge, offers homemade breakfast and dinner buffets. For lunch it offers soups and stews, sandwiches, pizza, a salad bar, and fresh roasted meats. A bar on the third floor offers après-ski live entertainment.

Mid-Mountain Lodge is at the base of Pioneer Lift on the Mid-Mountain Ski Run, at 8,700 feet. Built around 1898, the lodge may be the oldest original mine building in Park City. Completely renovated in recent years, it's open daily for lunch, serving vegetarian dishes, homemade soups and stews, salads, burgers, sandwiches, and pizza.

Summit Smoke House & Grill, at the top of the Bonanza chairlift, serves lunch and boasts an outdoor deck with magnificent panoramic views and a cozy fireplace inside. The **Snow Hut,** at the bottom of the Silverlode six-passenger lift, serves breakfast and lunch daily.

THE CANYONS

The Canyons Resort, 4000 The Canyons Resort Dr., Park City, UT 84098 (© 888/CANYONS or 435/649-5400; www.thecanyons.com), America's fifth largest ski area, offers a wide variety of terrain on eight distinct mountains, with an excellent people-moving system to get you to the runs that you want to ski quickly and efficiently. In the past few years, intermediate and expert terrains have been greatly expanded. The large beginners' area offers gentle slopes and grand views.

The resort has 146 runs on more than 3,500 skiable acres, serviced by one high-speed gondola, five high-speed quad chairs, four fixed-grip quad chairs, two triple chairs, one double chair, one eight-person Cabriolet, and two surface lifts. It receives an average of 355 inches of snow a year, and has snow-making on 400 acres. The vertical drop serviced by lifts is 3,190 feet, from a base elevation of 6,800 feet. The summit elevation is 9,990 feet. Runs are rated 14% beginner, 44% intermediate, and 42% advanced. The season usually runs from late November to mid-April, with lifts operating daily from 9am to 4pm.

The Red Pine and lower-lot day lodges offer ski and snowboard rentals, and the base lodge houses a day-care center.

The Canyons is on the west side of Utah 224 a few miles south of I-80.

LIFT TICKETS   Adult lift tickets cost $64 for a full day ($69 during holidays); children 7 to 12 and seniors pay $38. Kids 6 and under ride the lifts free.

LESSONS & PROGRAMS   The **ski school** offers lessons for both skiing and snowboarding, starting at $64 for a 2-hour group clinic. Private lessons start at $110 for 1 hour.

WHERE TO DINE ON THE MOUNTAIN   Among the ski area's restaurants are the **Red Pine Lodge,** featuring lunches of pizza, fresh grilled entrees, hearty soups, and a salad bar; **Smokies Smokehouse,** which offers barbecue and Cajun fare in an informal setting for lunch and dinner; and **The Cabin,** an upscale restaurant offering regional dishes with Southwestern ingredients for breakfast, lunch, and dinner.

OTHER WINTER FUN

CROSS-COUNTRY SKIING   **White Pine Touring Center** (© 435/649-8701 or 435/615-5858), is Park City's cross-country ski center, with 11 miles of groomed trails on the Park City Golf Course on Utah 224, on the north side of town. The center offers rentals, instruction (including skating and telemark lessons), guided tours, and sales and service. The terrain is rated 60% beginner,

---

◖Moments The Olympics Live On!

Park City's $100-million **Utah Olympic Park,** 3000 Bear Hollow Dr. (© **435/658-4200;** www.utaholympicpark.com), constructed for the 2002 Olympics, has six state-of-the-art ski jumps, a 1,335-meter bobsled/luge track, a freestyle aerials training and competition hill, a day lodge, a ski museum, and an exhibit on the 2002 games. The U.S. Ski Team uses the facility regularly, and it's open year-round for both guided and self-guided tours. On summer Saturdays, there are demonstrations of freestyle aerials and ski jumping. The Olympic Park also offers bobsled runs and schedules workshops on freestyle aerials and ski jumping, even for amateurs (call for schedules and rates). Tickets for guided tours, which includes admission to the ski museum and 2002 Olympics games exhibit, cost $10 for adults, $9 for youths 13 to 17 and seniors 65 and older, and $6 for children from 3 to 12. Tickets for a self-guided tour and admission to the museum and 2002 games exhibit cost $8, $6, and $4, respectively; and tickets for a self-guided tour only cost $5, $3, and $2, respectively. Call for current hours.

20% intermediate, and 20% advanced. Full-day trail passes cost $10 for adults, $5 for kids 7 to 12; children 6 and younger and seniors over 65 ski free. White Pine is open daily from 9am to 6pm, usually from mid-November through March.

SNOWMOBILE & SLEIGH RIDES   Guided snowmobiling tours and sleigh rides are available at the scenic Rockin' R Ranch, east of Park City in Weber Canyon, from **Rocky Mountain Recreation** (© **800/303-7256** or 435/645-7256; www.rockymtnrec.com). A sleigh ride, with dinner, costs $59 for adults, $39 for children 12 and under. Snowmobile trips range from $60 to $145 for the driver ($20 to $45 for a passenger), depending on length. Also offering a variety of snowmobile tours and sleigh rides, at similar rates, is **SnowWest Snowmobiles** (© **888/896-7669** or 435/645-7669; www.utahsnowmobiling.com).

WARM-WEATHER FUN IN & AROUND PARK CITY

ALPINE SLIDE   Individual sleds speed down a plastic bobsled-like track that's over a half-mile long at **Park City Mountain Resort** (see p. 145; © **800/ 222-7275** or 435/649-8111; www.parkcitymountain.com). Riders control the speed of their sleds. Cost is $9 for adults and $3 for children 6 and younger.

FLY-FISHING   Anglers have plenty of opportunities for fishing in the streams in the mountains around Park City, either on their own or with local guides. For tips on where they're biting, as well as equipment and information on guided trips, check with **Jans Mountain Outfitters,** 1600 Park Ave. (© **800/745-1020** or 435/649-4949; www.jans.com), or **Park City Fly Shop,** 2065 Sidewinder Dr., Prospector Square (© **800/324-6778** or 435/645-8382; www.pcflyshop.com).

HIKING & MOUNTAIN BIKING   The mountains around Park City offer numerous trails for hiking and mountain biking. For a short hike with a variety of terrain and good views of both mountains and town, try the 1½-mile **Sweeny Switchbacks Trail,** on the west side of town above the Wasatch Brew Pub.

The 30-mile **Historic Union Pacific Rail Trail State Park** hiking and biking path follows the old Union Pacific railroad bed from Park City to Echo Reservoir. It offers wonderful views of meadows, the volcanic crags of Silver Creek Canyon, the Weber River, Echo Reservoir, and the steep walls of Echo Canyon. You might spot deer, elk, moose, and bald eagles along the trail. An end-of-the-trail pick-up service is available from **Daytrips** (© **888/654-8294** or 435/654-8294; www.daytrips.com).

More than 30 miles of dirt roads and single-track trails at **Park City Mountain Resort** (see p. 145; © **800/222-7275** or 435/649-8111; www.parkcitymountain. com) are open to hikers and mountain bikers, who can ride the PayDay chairlift up and then bike or hike down. Tickets cost $9 for a single ride, or $16 for an all-day pass. **Deer Valley Resort** (see p. 144; © **800/424-3337** or 435/649-1000; www.deervalley.com) offers more than 50 miles of panoramic trails for both hikers and bikers, with chairlift access in summer (call for rates). As you might expect, the terrain is steep and beautiful.

For a good description of several other area trails, pick up a copy of the free *Park City Hiking & Biking Trail Map* at either visitor center and at sporting goods shops.

HORSEBACK RIDING   Guided trail rides are available from several outfitters in the area. **Rocky Mountain Recreation** (p. 148) operates stables at Park City Mountain Resort, at Deer Valley Resort, and at 2,300-acre Rockin' R Ranch. It operates daily from late May to late October. Rates start at $37 for adults and $34 for children 6 to 11 for a 1-hour ride. Rides up to 6 hours and rides with meals are also offered so call for details.

MORE TO SEE & DO IN PARK CITY

Kimball Art Center This highly respected center for visual arts, housed in a historic 1929 building, has three galleries, with changing exhibits, both classic and contemporary, that include national and international traveling shows, as well as works by local artists. This nonprofit community art center also sponsors classes, workshops, and seminars throughout the year. Each summer on the first weekend in August, it produces the Park City Arts Festival, an outdoor exhibit featuring works by about 200 fine artists. Allow about ¾ hour.

638 Park Ave., at the bottom of Main St. ⓒ 435/649-8882. www.kimball-art.org. Free admission; suggested donation $3 adults, $1 children. Wed–Fri and Mon 10am–5pm; Sat–Sun noon–5pm. All bus loops stop here.

Park City Museum of History & Territorial Jail The original territorial jail downstairs is a must-see—the dark, tiny cells were state-of-the-art in 1886! The upstairs is a bit more civilized, displaying a stagecoach, 19th-century mining equipment, historic photographs, and early ski gear. You'll also see an exhibit describing the destruction that fires wrought on the town over the years. The museum also houses a visitor center. Allow about 1½ hours.

528 Main St. ⓒ 435/649-6104. www.parkcityhistory.org. Free admission. Mon–Sat 10am–7pm; Sun noon–6pm. Main St. Trolley.

SHOPPING

Historic Main Street is lined with galleries, boutiques, and a wide variety of shops, with transportation conveniently provided by the Main Street Trolley. You won't find many bargains here, but prices aren't too far out of line for a tourist and ski town, and are downright reasonable when compared to places like Aspen and Santa Fe.

Animal lovers will likely be captivated by renowned photographer Thomas Mangelsen's stunning photographs at **Images of Nature,** 364 Main St. (ⓒ 888/ 238-0233 or 435/649-7598; www.mangelsen.com). No zoo photos here—these images were all taken in the wild, and range from the playful to the serene, in a variety of sizes, framed or unframed. **Flat Rabbet Gallery,** 421 Main St. (ⓒ 435/ 649-2155), specializes in antique posters, many from Europe, plus all the official Olympic posters since 1924. They also carry a variety of antique winter prints, both European and local.

It's Christmas year-round at nearby **Christmas on Main Street,** 442 Main St. (ⓒ 435/645-8115), with a good selection of ornaments and candles, a variety of Santas, and numerous other goodies.

No Place Like Home, Park City Plaza at Bonanza Drive and Prospector Avenue (ⓒ 435/649-9700), is the place to go for kitchen and home accessories. Choose from glassware, gadgets, gourmet coffee beans, bed and bath items, and lots more.

Bargain hunters will want to head to the **Factory Stores at Park City,** 6699 N. Landmark Dr. (ⓒ 435/645-7078; www.shopparkcity.com). From downtown Park City, take Utah 224 north to I-80, but don't get on; instead, go west on the south frontage road to the mall. Among the best outlet malls we've seen, this place houses more than 60 stores, including Banana Republic, Bass, Bose, Brooks Brothers, Carter's Childrenswear, Eddie Bauer, Gap, KB Toys, Levi's, Liz Claiborne, Nike, Old Navy, Samsonite, and Tommy Hilfiger. There's plenty of parking, including room for RVs.

Tips **A Helping Hand for Room Reservations**

Although it's possible to book reservations directly with individual lodges, many people find it more convenient to go the one-stop shopping route, making all their arrangements directly with one of the resorts (see contact information above under "Skiing the Park City Area Resorts").

WHERE TO STAY

The Park City area offers a wide variety of places to stay, and it's probably home to the largest portion of the state's deluxe accommodations. Even some of the most luxurious properties, however, lack air-conditioning; at this elevation— 6,900 feet in Park City and higher in the mountains—it's seldom needed.

Among the franchise properties in Park City are the **Best Western Landmark Inn,** 6560 N. Landmark Dr., Park City, UT 84098 (© **800/548-8824** or 435/649-7300), with rates for two from $49 to $189; **Hampton Inn and Suites,** 6609 N. Landmark Dr., Park City, UT 84098 (© **800/426-7866** or 435/645-0900), with rates of $79 to $239 for two; **Holiday Inn Express Hotel & Suites,** 1501 W. Ute Blvd., Park City, UT 84098 (© **800/465-4392** or 435/658-1600), with rates of $79 to $189 for two; and **Radisson Inn,** 2121 Park Ave., Park City, UT 84098 (© **800/649-5012** or 435/649-5000), with rates of $79 to $339 for two.

Rates are almost always higher—sometimes dramatically so—during ski season, and rates during Christmas week can be absurd. You'll find the best bargains in spring and fall. Sales and lodging taxes in Park City total just over 10%. Pets are not allowed, unless otherwise noted.

IN DEER VALLEY

Goldener Hirsch Inn ★★   This chateau-style inn combines warm hospitality with European charm reminiscent of the inn's sister hotel in Salzburg, the Hotel Goldener Hirsch. Austrian antiques dot the common areas and decorate the walls. Guest rooms are elegantly furnished with hand-painted and -carved Austrian furniture, king beds with down comforters, and minibars stocked with snacks and nonalcoholic beverages. Suites boast wood-burning fireplaces and small private balconies. The excellent restaurant is Austrian in decor, and features international cuisine. In summer, you can dine outdoors on the flower-filled deck.

7570 Royal St. East, Silver Lake Village, Deer Valley (P.O. Box 859), Park City, UT 84060. © **800/252-3373** or 435/649-7770. Fax 435/649-7901. www.goldenerhirschinn.com. 20 units. Winter (including continental breakfast) $250–$925 double; summer $100–$250 double. AE, MC, V. Closed mid-Apr to mid-June and Oct–Nov. **Amenities:** Restaurant (American); activities desk. *In room:* A/C, TV, dataport, minibar, hair dryer, iron.

Stein Eriksen Lodge ★★★   This luxurious, full-service lodge offers a warm and friendly atmosphere. Opened in 1982 under the direction of Stein Eriksen, the Norwegian 1952 Olympic gold medalist, the hotel retains the Scandinavian decor and charm of his original plan. The lobby is most impressive, with a magnificent three-story stone fireplace fronted by an elegant seating area. There are 13 rooms in the main lodge, with the remaining units in nearby buildings. The connecting sidewalks are heated, and the grounds are beautifully landscaped, with aspen trees, manicured lawns, and flowers cascading over rock gardens and retaining walls. The spacious deluxe rooms, each individually decorated, contain a king or queen bed, plenty of closet space, a whirlpool tub, vaulted ceiling, and tasteful, solid wood furniture. The one- to five-bedroom suites come with all sorts of amenities. The three large mountain chalet-style townhouse suites each have a stone fireplace, full kitchen with service for eight, and private deck. Rooms receive newspaper delivery, turndown service, and twice-daily maid service in winter, and VCR/DVD players are available to rent. There are nature trails, a conference center, a ballroom, secretarial service and valet parking.

The lodge offers two dining venues. The **Glitretind Restaurant** (see p. 153) serves three meals daily (New American). **Troll Hallen Lounge,** open from 11:30am to midnight, offers an extensive beverage service and light meals, with hors d'oeuvres or fresh shellfish from the oyster bar available for aprés-ski.

Deer Valley Resort (P.O. Box 3177), Park City, UT 84060. ☎ **800/453-1302** or 435/649-3700. Fax 435/649-5825. www.steinlodge.com. 170 units. Winter (including buffet breakfast) $670–$910 double, from $1100 suite; mid-Apr to late Nov $175–$215 double, from $255 suite. AE, DC, DISC, MC, V. **Amenities:** 2 restaurants (New American); outdoor heated pool; exercise room; full-service spa; Jacuzzi; sauna; concierge; business center with secretarial services and conference room; 24-hr. room service; in-room massage; babysitting; dry cleaning. *In room:* TV, dataport, coffeemaker, hair dryer, iron.

IN PARK CITY

Chateau Aprés Lodge *Value*   For those on a budget, this lodge is a good option close to the slopes. It looks like a Swiss Alps–style lodge from the outside—simple but attractive. Rooms are basic and clean, each with a queen bed or a double and a single, plus a small hide-a-bed and a private shower-only bathroom. The separate men's and women's dorms each have a shared bathroom. The entire facility is nonsmoking.

1299 Norfolk Ave. (P.O. Box 579), Park City, UT 84060. ☎ **800/357-3556** or 435/649-9372. Fax 435/649-5963. www.chateauapres.com. 32 units. Winter $85 double; summer $50 double; dorm rooms $30 per bed. Rates include continental breakfast. AE, DISC, MC, V. *In room:* TV.

The Old Miners' Lodge—A Bed & Breakfast Inn *✿*   Established in 1889 as a boardinghouse for local miners, this lodge still exudes the spirited warmth and hospitality of that time. Rooms are comfortably decorated with antiques, country pieces, and some historic photos. Each is named for a historic figure of Park City and is outfitted with touches suiting the individual's persona. The spacious suites come with mini-refrigerators; two have hide-a-beds and king beds. Some units boast terrific views of the valley and surrounding mountains.

The lodge is virtually ski-in/ski-out. Evening refreshments are served in the large living room, where guests occasionally gather around the fireplace. There's no TV, but plenty of reading material and games will keep you occupied, and the outdoor Jacuzzi will soothe your muscles after a day of skiing. The full breakfast is a hearty meal that often includes a variety of egg dishes, waffles, French toast, or pancakes, plus cereal and granola. Smoking is not permitted inside.

615 Woodside Ave. (P.O. Box 2639), Park City, UT 84060. ☎ **800/648-8068** or 435/645-8068. Fax 435/645-7420. www.oldminerslodge.com. 12 units. Winter $110–$270 double; summer $70–$130 double. Rates include breakfast. AE, DC, DISC, MC, V. **Amenities:** Outdoor Jacuzzi. *In room:* No phone.

Old Town Guest House *✿* *Finds*   This cozy little B&B is perfect for outdoor enthusiasts—the innkeeper is a backcountry ski guide in winter and avid hiker and biker in summer. The inn is within easy walking distance of both the Park City Mountain Resort and Main Street. The delightfully homey living room retains its original 1910 fireplace. The decor is country, with lodgepole pine furniture and hardwood floors throughout, but as with most historic bed-and-breakfasts, each guest room is unique. Treasure Hollow has its own entrance, queen bed, TV/VCR, phone, and private bathroom with shower. Two small rooms in back have private toilets and sinks, but share a shower. Each has a queen bed and a small table with chairs. McConky's Suite, upstairs, contains a queen bed in one room and bunk beds in another, a whirlpool tub and shower, TV/VCR, and phone.

Guests are welcome to use the outdoor deck and Jacuzzi. The hearty breakfasts served here will sustain your energy throughout a day of hiking, biking, or skiing.

1011 Empire Ave. (P.O. Box 162), Park City, UT 84060. © 800/290-6423, ext. 3710, or 435/649-2642. Fax 435/649-3320. www.oldtownguesthouse.com. 4 units. Winter (including breakfast) $95–$199 double; summer $75–$99 double. AE, MC, V. **Amenities:** Jacuzzi. *In room:* TV/VCR in most rooms, some no phone.

Washington School Inn ✮ Housed in an 1889 limestone schoolhouse that's nestled against the Wasatch Mountains, this lovely country inn has managed to preserve its original charm even though it's now completely modernized. The exterior has been faithfully restored to its late-19th-century appearance, and the interior has been reorganized to better meet the requirements of an inn while remaining true to its historical roots. Rooms are individually decorated, many in country style, with antiques and reproductions from different periods. All units have air-conditioning and shower/tub combos. Two suites have wood-burning fireplaces.

Facilities include a Jacuzzi and lounge area, a sauna, and a bicycle storage area and ski lockers with outside access. There's also high-speed wireless Internet service. A lovely summer garden and patio area have recently been added. The inn provides a full breakfast buffet each morning, afternoon tea in summer, and hearty aprés-ski refreshments in winter.

543 Park Ave. (P.O. Box 536), Park City, UT 84060. © 800/824-1672 or 435/649-3808. Fax 435/649-3802. www.washingtonschoolinn.com. 15 units. Winter $145–$265 double, $245–$410 suite; summer $95–$150 double, $150–$175 suite. Rates include breakfast. AE, DISC, MC, V. **Amenities:** Jacuzzi; sauna; activities desk. *In room:* A/C, TV.

WHERE TO DINE

For a smallish town, Park City has a wonderful selection of very good restaurants. Several menu guides are available free at the visitor centers. **Albertson's Food & Drug,** 1800 Park Ave. (© **435/649-6134**) has an excellent salad bar, deli, and bakery, and is a good choice for stocking up on groceries before heading to a condo or into the mountains.

Cafe Terigo ✮✮ EUROPEAN/CONTINENTAL This upscale eatery is a good choice when you want innovative cuisine in a classy atmosphere. In fine weather, you can dine outdoors under a large umbrella; otherwise, sit in the simple yet elegant European-style cafe, which is outfitted with brocade upholstered booths, white tablecloths, fresh flowers, and wrought-iron chandeliers. The lunch menu offers burgers and a variety of sandwiches, such as a grilled vegetable sandwich, composed of sweet onions, zucchini, mushrooms, roasted red peppers, and provolone cheese on homemade focaccia. Dinner brings such main courses as honey- and ginger-glazed duck breast served with jasmine rice; grilled flank steak with garlic mashed potatoes and a wild mushroom sauce; and baked halibut with a corn pancake, served on a bed of artichoke hearts and asparagus. There's also a variety of pastas and unusual pizzas with toppings such as shrimp and artichoke hearts. The cafe serves a mean lemonade and offers espresso and full liquor service.

424 Main St. © 435/645-9555. www.terigo.citysearch.com. Main courses $9.95–$15lunch, $12–$28 dinner. AE, MC, V. Daily 11:30am–2:30pm and 5:30–10pm. Main St. Trolley.

The Claim Jumper Steak House ✦ STEAK/RIBS/SEAFOOD   This three-story brick-and-masonry building opened in 1913 as the New Park Hotel, where all meals, including Sunday dinner, were 50¢. Prices are a bit higher now, but red meat eaters will find that dinner at this locally popular Western-style restaurant is well worth the cost. Decor here is elegant Old West saloon, with Victorian-style wallpaper, dark wood trim, and high ceilings. All steaks are char-broiled over an open flame. We especially recommend the prime rib (11 or 16 oz.) and the baseball steak—a super-thick center cut sirloin steak. The Claim Jumper is also the place to come for thick buffalo steaks. Other options include Utah trout, king crab, a full rack of baby back ribs, and the daily pasta special. All dinners come with a huge salad, hot bread, and your choice of potato. There are also similar Claim Jumper restaurants in St. George and Heber City, Utah, but the three Utah Claim Jumpers are not affiliated with the Claim Jumper chain found in other states. Full liquor service is available.

573 Main St. ✆ **435/649-8051.** www.claimjumperutah.com. Main courses $9.95–$30. AE, DC, DISC, MC, V. Sun–Wed 5–9pm; Thurs–Sat 5–10pm. Main St. Trolley.

The Eating Establishment ✦ (Kids) AMERICAN   The Eating Establishment, probably the oldest continuously operating restaurant on Park City's historic Main Street (since 1972), is casual and comfortable, a great choice for families or anyone who wants a heaping serving of comfort food at very reasonable prices. The dining room is accented with brick and light wood, fireplaces, and scenic photos of Utah. The enclosed patio was recently remodeled in an airy Southwest style. The extensive menu features breakfast until 4pm (a variety of omelets, skillet dishes, eggs, Belgian waffles, fruit-filled crepes, and lox and bagels). Lunch choices, served from 11am until closing, include wonderful charbroiled burgers, fish-and-chips, salads, a variety of sandwiches, and barbe-cued pork, beef, or chicken. Dinners are served from 5pm, with choices includ-ing salads, excellent barbecued baby back ribs, a certified black Angus strip steak, several pasta selections, and fresh seafood specials. Desserts, such as the raspberry chocolate torte, mud pie, and New York–style cheesecake are made in-house. Full liquor service is available.

The cafeteria-style **Eating Establishment Express,** at Park City Mountain Resort at the bottom of the PayDay lift (✆ **435/649-7289**), offers a similar menu for breakfast and lunch.

317 Main St. ✆ **435/649-8284.** Main courses $5.25–$8.95 breakfast and lunch, $7.50–$20 dinner. AE, DISC, MC, V. Daily 8am–10pm. Main St. Trolley.

Glitretind Restaurant ✦✦✦ NEW AMERICAN   Located in the elegant Stein Eriksen Lodge (p. 150), this equally stylish restaurant is our pick for the very best dining in the Park City area, and possibly the entire state. The Glitretind serves innovative, impeccably prepared meals in a modern, airy din-ing room with views of the spectacular Wasatch Mountains. The menu changes with the seasons, and reflects the New American style of executive chef Zane Holmquist. Breakfast offerings include French toast, pancakes, a fruit plate, and omelets; for lunch choose a soup, salad, sandwich, or full meal. At dinner, we suggest that (if available) you start with the grilled vegetable and lentil strudel or the seared buffalo carpaccio, then choose for your main course the Tea and Szechuan Pepper Crusted Duck Breast—Muscovy duck breast crusted with a floral spiced mixture of ground jasmine tea and Szechuan peppercorns, then pan seared and briefly roasted. The restaurant has an excellent wine list and also offers full liquor service.

Stein Eriksen Lodge, Deer Valley. ☏ **435/649-3700.** www.steinlodge.com. Reservations requested. Main courses $4–$15 breakfast, $7–$13 lunch, $21–$36 dinner. AE, DC, DISC, MC, V. Mon–Sat 7–10am and 11:30am–2:30pm; Sunday brunch 10:30am–2:30pm; daily 6–9pm. Bus: Deer Valley Loop.

Grappa Italian Restaurant 🐾🐾 ITALIAN

At this elegant, award-winning restaurant, everything is made from scratch, using the freshest herbs and vegetables available—preparing the tomato sauce alone requires cases of roma tomatoes each day. Located in a century-old building at the top of Main Street, Grappa's feels like a Tuscan farmhouse. The restaurant has three floors, with a small patio on the ground floor and a larger second-floor deck with a delightful view of historic Main Street and the surrounding mountains. Baskets of fresh fruits and vegetables decorate the dining areas.

The menu changes frequently, but popular dishes often include spaghetti with Italian sausage and red and yellow peppers; lemon-baked spring chicken served with green olives, cherry tomatoes, baby potatoes, and a zucchini tartlet; and pan-seared king salmon with fennel, spinach, tomatoes, and a creamy portobello risotto. The meats, such as the filet mignon with wild mushrooms, are seasoned in the style of southern French and Italian cooking, then grilled or rotisseried over a wood-burning flame. There's an excellent wine list, as well as full liquor service.

151 Main St. ☏ **435/645-0636.** www.grapparestaurant.com. Reservations required. Main courses $22–$34. AE, DISC, MC, V. Winter daily 5–10pm; summer Wed–Mon 5:30–10pm; may close several weeks in Nov and Apr. Main St. Trolley.

Purple Sage 🐾🐾 AMERICAN

Serving what they call "American Western cuisine," this upscale dinner restaurant, which opened in 2003, is owned and operated by the same people who do such a great job at nearby Cafe Terigo (reviewed at the beginning of this section). The atmosphere is what we might describe as "refined casual western," and the menu offers innovative and sometimes fascinating variations on American favorites. Beef eaters will especially enjoy the New York steak, which has a spicy rub and is served with bacon-wrapped asparagus and sweet corn relish. We also recommend the grilled shrimp in chipotle-and-leek sauce, served on golden polenta cakes; and the sautéed chicken and sweet peppers in tequila lime cream sauce on a bed of fettuccine. The restaurant offers full liquor service.

434 Main St. ☏ **435/655-9505.** Main courses $15–$24 dinner. AE, MC, V. Daily 5:30–10pm; closed Sundays in summer. Main St. Trolley.

Wahso—An Asian Grill 🐾 ASIAN

This distinctively elegant restaurant boasts an Art Deco and Victorian interior furnished with authentic Asian screens, an ebony fireplace, and carvings and pictures from around the world. The food is equally unique, an amalgamation of traditional Asian ingredients with French cooking style, which gives rise to deliciously light and healthy offerings. Entrees change frequently, but might include specialties such as Szechuan-style grilled filet mignon, soy- and ginger-glazed sea bass, and spicy Balinese stir-fry of shrimp. Be sure to save room for the dessert specialty—crème brûlée in a coconut shell. Premium sake, imported beer, and an extensive wine list are available.

577 Main St. ☏ **435/615-0300.** www.wahso.com. Main courses $19–$28. AE, DISC, MC, V. Daily 5–10pm. Main St. Trolley.

Wasatch Brew Pub AMERICAN

Views of the brewing area and Main Street dominate the scene in this popular, noisy brewpub. You can get well-prepared typical pub grub for lunch, including fish-and-chips, burgers, beer-battered shrimp, various pizzas, and cheese steaks. The dinner menu offers many of the same lunch items but adds some more adventurous selections, such as fresh Utah trout with roasted garlic herb butter, pine nut–crusted salmon with fresh basil sauce, and rack of New Zealand lamb with fresh mint sauce. You'll find a sports bar upstairs and an outside patio for warm-weather dining. In addition to the brewery's own award-winning beers, full liquor service is available.

250 Main St. © 435/649-0900. www.wasatchbeers.com. Reservations not accepted. Main courses $6.50–$8.95 lunch, $7.50–$18 dinner. AE, MC, V. Daily 11am–10pm (bar until midnight). Main St. Trolley.

MUSIC & MORE IN THE MOUNTAINS: THE PERFORMING ARTS

Summer in Park City resounds with music and theater, with free concerts, major festivals, and a variety of other events on the docket. For details on the entertainment mentioned in this section, as well as information about other performing arts events, contact the **Park City Chamber of Commerce/Convention and Visitors Bureau** (p. 142).

Throughout the summer, **free concerts** are presented each Wednesday from 6 to 8pm at City Park. One week you might hear bluegrass, the next, classical, and yet another it might be rock or jazz.

The **Utah Symphony Summer Series at Deer Valley Resort** (© 801/533-6683; www.utahsymphony.org) takes place in July and August. The program includes classical masterpieces like Tchaikovsky's *1812 Overture,* plus jazz and popular works by composers such as Rodgers and Hammerstein and John Philip Sousa. The stage faces the mountainside; bring a chair or blanket and relax under the stars. Call the box office for schedule and ticket information.

The **Park City International Music Festival at The Canyons Resort** (© 435/649-5309; www.pcmusicfestival.com) presents classical performances year-round, and goes all out for its summer concert series from early July to early August. Classical musicians from around the world attend, and programs feature soloists, chamber music, and full orchestras.

The 1,300-seat **Eccles Center for the Performing Arts,** 1750 Kearns Blvd. (© 435/655-3114; 888/451-2787 to buy tickets from Artix; www.ecclescenter. org), presents a wide variety of top national performing arts companies. Recent productions have ranged from the Royal Shakespeare Company's *Hamlet* to singer Kathy Mattea to the Missoula Children's Theater's *The Pied Piper.*

The **Historic Egyptian Theatre,** 328 Main St. (© 888/243-5779 or 435/649-9371; fax 435/649-0446; www.egyptiantheatrecompany.org), was built in 1926 in the popular Egyptian Revival style. Originally used for vaudeville and silent films, this was the first theater in Park City to offer the "new talking pictures." Today, the Egyptian is the home of the Egyptian Theatre Company, which presents a variety of dramas, comedies, musicals, and other productions throughout the year.

PARK CITY AFTER DARK: THE CLUB SCENE

Known as Utah's Party Town, Park City probably has the best nightlife in the state. If you're looking for drinking and dancing, join a private club (memberships are available on a short-term basis, usually for $5, and membership entitles you to bring several guests). The following are busiest during ski season, and generally have fewer nights of live music at other times.

Adolph's, 1500 Kearns Blvd. (© 435/649-7177), is mainly a social bar with piano music on some nights. **Cisero's,** downstairs at 306 Main St. (© 435/649-6800), with a large dance floor, hosts good bands. **J.B. Mulligan's Club & Pub,**

804 Main St. (© **435/658-0717**), also has live music, including a variety of jazz, reggae, bluegrass, and funk; and you can get food—try their peppercorn burger— between 5 and 10pm. Another nightspot for live jazz, funk, or acoustic is **Mother Urban's Ratskeller,** 625 Main St. (© **435/615-7200**).

You'll find two bars at **The Club,** 449 Main St. (© **435/649-6693**): The downstairs one serves food and drinks; upstairs, there's dancing to a DJ. **Harry O's,** 427 Main St. (© **435/647-9494;** www.clubharryos.com), is very popular, with a huge dance floor and live band or DJ nightly. Friendly, sociable **Bistro Bar,** 412 Main St. (© **435/649-8230**), is the oldest private club on Main Street. Popular sports bars are the **Broken Thumb,** 1299 Little Kate Rd. (© **435/647-3932**), and the **Upper Deck,** 570 Main St. (© **435/649-0011**).

3 Side Trips from Park City: Heber Valley Historic Railroad, Strawberry Reservoir & Some Great State Parks

The southern Wasatch Front isn't just about skiing. The wonderful lakes and parks near Park City are some of Utah's best-kept secrets. To the northeast is Rockport State Park, a man-made lake that attracts watersports enthusiasts, from swimmers to ice-fishermen, year-round. Not far from Park City is Jordanelle State Park, which is a great boating lake, and Wasatch Mountain State Park, which is Utah's second-largest state park and a major golf destination. Heading southeast from Park City, you'll reach Heber City, whose main claim to fame is its historic steam train. A bit farther afield along U.S. 40 is pristine Strawberry Reservoir, one of our favorite water playgrounds.

HEBER VALLEY HISTORIC RAILROAD

For those who love old trains, who want to see first-hand some of the history of the American West, or who simply enjoy beautiful scenery, we heartily recommend a ride on the **Heber Valley Historic Railroad** ★★. This 100-year-old excursion train provides an exciting step back into the past, while also offering a fun ride through a delightful diversity of landscapes. Excursions ranging from 1½ to 3½ hours are offered on both steam and vintage diesel trains, and a number of special event trips are scheduled, including murder mysteries, sunset excursions, and the "Polar Express" Christmas trip. Train cars have restrooms, snack bars, and souvenir shops.

The views along the shores of Deer Creek Lake and through beautiful Provo Canyon are wonderful at any time, but fall is one of the prettiest seasons to ride the train, as the mountainsides are decorated with the rich hues of changing leaves—the reds of oak and maple, and the golds of cottonwood and aspen stand out against the ever-present greens of piñon, juniper, spruce, and pine.

The train depot is in Heber City, 20 miles south of Park City via Utah 248 and U.S. 40. Round-trip tickets cost $16 to $24 for adults, $10 to $14 for children 3 to 12, and $13 to $21 for seniors 60 and older. Rates are higher for special events, and one-way tickets are also available (call for rates). There are four daily runs in summer, with a reduced schedule the rest of year. The ticket office is open daily from 9am to 5pm. For information contact **Heber Valley Historic Railroad,** 450 S. 600 West, Heber City, UT 84032 (© **435/654-5601,** or 801/ 581-9980 from Salt Lake City; fax 435/654-3709; www.hebervalleyrr.org).

ROCKPORT STATE PARK

Rockport, one of the Utah State Park system's man-made lakes, is a fun destination offering a full range of outdoor activities, from windsurfing to wildlife watching. In the winter, add ice-fishing and cross-country skiing. Facilities at the half-mile-wide, 3-mile-long lake include a marina, a boat ramp and courtesy docks, a picnic area, and camping spots in a variety of settings. The Wanship Dam, at the north end of the lake, is an important water-storage and flood-control dam on the Weber River, which has its headwaters high in the Uinta Mountains.

ESSENTIALS
GETTING THERE   From Park City, head east on I-80 for about 10½ miles to exit 156, then go 5 miles south on Utah 32 along the western bank of Rockport Lake to the access road. The park entrance is at the lake's southern tip. Turn east to the park entrance, and then follow the road around to the north along the eastern bank.

INFORMATION, FEES & REGULATIONS   Contact **Rockport State Park,** 9040 N. Utah 302, Peoa, UT 84061-9702 (✆ **435/336-2241;** www.stateparks. utah.gov). Open year-round, the park has a day-use fee of $7 per vehicle. Pets are allowed, but must be confined or leashed.

OUTDOOR PURSUITS
CROSS-COUNTRY SKIING   Groomed cross-country ski trails run through the open sagebrush, and these offer a better chance of seeing wildlife than the more forested areas in the surrounding national forest.

HIKING & WILDLIFE WATCHING   A 4-mile round-trip hike takes off from Juniper Campground. This easy, relatively flat walk among juniper and sagebrush offers an opportunity to glimpse mule deer, yellow-belly marmots, badgers, raccoons, weasels, skunks, and ground squirrels. Less visible are elk, moose, coyote, bobcat, and cougar. Birds abound, and sometimes you can spot Western grebes, Canada geese, whistling swans, great blue herons, and golden and bald eagles. More frequently seen are ducks, red-tailed hawks, magpies, scrub jays, and hummingbirds.

WATER ACTIVITIES   The day-use area, located about 3½ miles north of the park entrance, offers the best swimming. The lake is also popular for boating, windsurfing, water-skiing, sailing, kayaking, and fishing. Both the lake and river are home to rainbow and brown trout, yellow perch, and small-mouth bass. Unfortunately, there are no equipment outfitters nearby.

CAMPING
Eighty-six RV and tent campsites are located in six areas around the lake. The first campground is to the right of the access road, along the Weber River rather than the lake. Sites are shady and provide easy access to a trail along the river, handy for fishermen. The remainder of the sites lie between the road and the lake, along its eastern bank, and most have vault toilets only. One campground, Juniper, has 36 sites with water and electric hookups, a dump station, and modern restrooms. Sites cost $8 to $17. The park generally fills on weekends, but reservations (with a $7 nonrefundable fee) can be made by calling ✆ **800/322-3770** or through the state parks website.

JORDANELLE STATE PARK ⭐⭐
Two recreation areas provide access to **Jordanelle Reservoir** in the beautiful Wasatch Mountains. Both areas are great for boating, fishing, picnicking, and camping. The reservoir is shaped rather like a boomerang, with the dam at the elbow. The Perimeter Trail connects the highly developed **Hailstone Recreation**

Site to the more primitive **Rock Cliff Recreation Site.** Hailstone is on the terraced peninsula poking into the upper arm just above the dam; Rock Cliff is at the southeastern tip of the lower arm of the reservoir. Hailstone's camping and picnicking areas face the widest part of the reservoir, which is perfect for speedboats, water-skiing, and personal watercraft. The narrow arm reaching down to Rock Cliff is designated for low-speed water use. Trails—27 miles of them—circle the reservoir and connect to other area trails. They're open to hikers, mountain bikers, horseback riders, and cross-country skiers.

ESSENTIALS
GETTING THERE   From Park City, head east on Kearns Boulevard (Utah 248) for about 3¾ miles; at U.S. 40, go southeast 4 miles to exit 8 and follow the entrance road east into Hailstone. From Heber City, take U.S. 40 northwest about 6 miles. For Rock Cliff, follow U.S. 40 northwest from Heber City for about 4 miles, then head east onto Utah 32 for about 6 miles to the entrance. From Park City, continue southeast on U.S. 40 past Hailstone for about 2 miles to Utah 32, then east about 6 miles to the entrance.

INFORMATION, FEES & REGULATIONS   Contact **Jordanelle State Park,** Utah 319 no. 515 Box 4, Heber City, UT 84032 (© **435/649-9540;** www. stateparks.utah.gov). Stop at the **visitor center** at Hailstone or the **Nature Center** at Rock Cliff, a nature-oriented visitor center, for information and trail maps. The exhibit room in the visitor center at Hailstone presents an overview of human history in the area.

The park is open year-round at Hailstone, and May through September at Rock Cliff. Day-use hours in summer are 6am to 10pm; October through March, 8am to 5pm. The visitor centers are open April through September from 9am to 6pm. The day-use fee is $9 per vehicle.

In order to protect the abundance of wildlife, particularly birds, pets are not allowed at Rock Cliff. They're welcome at Hailstone, but must be confined or leashed. Bicycling is permitted on established public roads, in parking areas, and on the Perimeter Trail.

HAILSTONE RECREATION SITE
At Hailstone, you'll find three camping areas and a group pavilion, along with a swimming beach and a picnic area that's available for day use. The 76-slip marina offers camping, picnicking supplies, boat rentals, a small restaurant, an amphitheater, boat ramps, a wheelchair-accessible fishing deck, and a fish-cleaning station.

OUTDOOR PURSUITS   A concessionaire offers ski boats (about $225 for a half day) and fishing boats (about $475 for a half day).

CAMPING   Hailstone's three camping areas have walk-in tent sites, RV/tent sites without hookups, and RV sites with water and electric hookups. Facilities include modern restrooms, showers, a small coin-op laundry, and a playground. Cost is $14 to $17. For reservations (with a $7 fee), call © **800/322-3770.**

ROCK CLIFF RECREATION SITE
Rock Cliff contains three walk-in camping areas; picnic tables; the **Nature Center,** which offers maps, environmental programs, and exhibits on the various habitats of the area and how man's activities impact them; and the **Jordanelle Discovery Trail,** a boardwalk interpretive trail that winds through the Provo River riparian terrain.

BIRDING **Rock Cliff** offers great opportunities for birding 🖈, with more than 160 species either living here or passing through, and eagles and other raptors nesting in the area. Situated as it is among numerous riparian wetlands, Rock Cliff is designed to protect these sensitive habitats. Trails and boardwalks traverse the area, and bridges cross the waterways at four points, enabling you to get quite close to a variety of wetland life without inadvertently doing any harm to their habitats.

CAMPING You'll find three walk-in campgrounds with 50 sites and two modern restrooms with showers. These sites are more nature-oriented than those at Hailstone and are scattered over 100 acres, providing great privacy. Cost is $14 to $17. The site doesn't have any areas for RVs.

WASATCH MOUNTAIN STATE PARK

The second-largest of Utah's state parks (after Antelope Island), at 21,592 acres, Wasatch Mountain State Park is also the state's most developed state park, and among its most popular. This year-round destination is well maintained, well serviced, and easy to enjoy, and it just keeps getting better. This is a terrific golf and camping destination, and trails are continually being expanded to meet the demands of hikers and mountain bikers. In winter, a network of groomed cross-country skiing and snowmobiling trails lead from the park into the surrounding forest, and both cross-country ski and snowmobile rentals are available. Wasatch Mountain's rangers offer a variety of instructive and interpretive programs. Fall is the best time to visit: The incomparable juxtaposition of rich reds, ochers, and deep evergreens will exceed your wildest imaginings.

ESSENTIALS

GETTING THERE It's about 5½ miles from Heber City to the park: From downtown, turn west on Utah 113 (100 South) to Midway; following signs for the state park, jog north on 200 West, then west on 200 North, and finally north again on Homestead Drive. The visitor center is located on Homestead Drive (where it becomes Snake Creek Road), in the park.

INFORMATION/VISITOR CENTER For advance information, contact **Wasatch Mountain State Park,** P.O. Box 10, Midway, UT 84049-0010 (© **435/ 654-1791;** www.stateparks.utah.gov). The visitor center, on Homestead Drive (where it becomes Snake Creek Road), also serves as a lounge for golfers. Its open daily from 8am to 5pm and includes a large mountain lodge–style room with comfortable seating. Rangers are on hand to discuss park activities and provide trail maps and other information.

FEES & REGULATIONS The day-use fee is $5 per vehicle. Pets are welcome in the park, but must be confined or leashed.

RANGER PROGRAMS Interpretive programs take place most Friday and Saturday summer nights at the amphitheater, and a junior ranger program is offered Saturday mornings. The stocked pond adjacent to the visitor center provides fishing fun for children under 16 in summer; call for details.

OUTDOOR PURSUITS

CROSS-COUNTRY SKIING A 7.4-mile Nordic ski track, with both diagonal stride and skating lanes, is laid out on the golf course. Neither dogs nor snowmobiles are allowed on the track, which is open from 8am to 5pm. Another area at the southern end of the park, which was the 2002 Olympics site for biathlon and cross-country skiing competitions, is available for cross-country skiing, snowshoeing, tubing, and other nonmotorized winter sports. Cross-country skis are available for rent at the golf course pro shop; cost is $10 for a full day and $7 for a half day for everyone 9 and older, and $7 and $5 respectively for those 8 and younger.

GOLF   With a USGA-sanctioned 36-hole, par-72 course, golfing is the most popular pastime here. Ten lakes are scattered throughout the tree-lined fairways, and the views of the lovely Heber Valley are grand. Facilities include a full-service pro shop, driving range, practice greens, and a cafe. The course is open daily during daylight hours. Another 36 holes, at the Soldier Hollow Golf Course at the southern end of the park, are expected to be completed by summer 2004.

Fees on weekdays are $10 for 9 holes, $20 for 18 holes. Weekends and holidays, the fees are $11 and $22, respectively. Pull carts and riding carts are available. Tee times should be reserved (© **435/654-0532**) the preceding Monday (starting at 7am) for weekends, and the preceding Thursday for weekdays.

HIKING & WILDLIFE WATCHING   The **Pine Creek Nature Trail** is just over a mile in length and encompasses three smaller loops. Many songbirds make their homes in the trees along the trail, so watch for Steller's jays, chickadees, wrens, robins, and Western tanagers. You might also see the tracks of mule deer along the creek, where they come to forage. From the large parking area in Pine Creek campground, follow the half-mile trail to the Pine Creek trailhead, which lies just north of the Oak Hollow loop. The trail begins at an elevation of 6,100 feet and climbs 220 feet, crossing Pine Creek four times and traversing several boulder ridges. The trail guide describes some of the plants you'll see on this hike. Don't attempt the trail after a rain, as it becomes quite muddy and slick. No bikes or motorized vehicles are allowed. Be sure to take water, a sun hat, and binoculars.

Literature describing the plant and animal life of the park is available at the camp manager's office near the entrance to the campground and at the visitor center.

MOUNTAIN BIKING   An 18-mile loop affords great fun for mountain bikes. The road leaves the visitor center and heads west, winding through magnificent wooded country and offering occasional breathtaking views of the valley.

SNOWMOBILING   The park's 90 miles of groomed trails, very popular among snowmobilers, take you into Pine Creek, Snake Creek, and American Fork Canyons. Warming stations are located at the clubhouse and visitor center.

CAMPING

Four camping loops in the **Pine Creek Campground** provide a total of 139 sites, including about 80 that are off-limits to tenters. All have modern restrooms, and all except Little Deer Creek, the smallest loop, have showers. Some sites are nestled among trees and are quite shady; others are more open. All except Little Deer Creek have paved parking pads, water, electricity, picnic tables, and barbecue grills; some also have sewer hookups. A dump station is located near the entrance to the campground. Camping fees are $11 at Little Deer Creek and $17 to $20 in the other three loops. Reservations (with a $7 nonrefundable reservation fee) are advised and can be made by calling © **800/ 322-3770** or through the state parks website.

STRAWBERRY RESERVOIR ⭑⭑

Located along U.S. 40 in the eastern portion of the Uinta National Forest, the jewel-like Strawberry Reservoir is a terrific water playground offering amazing fishing, as well as boating, hiking, and mountain biking. It's also great for cross-country skiing, ice-fishing, and snowmobiling in winter.

Utah's premier trout fishery—indeed, one of the premier trout fisheries in the West—Strawberry Reservoir is home to huge cutthroat and rainbow trout and kokanee salmon, so it's no surprise that fishing is the number-one draw. Fishing boats with outboard motors are available at **Strawberry Bay Marina** (© 435/548-2261); call for current rates.

Strawberry Reservoir has four marinas, with the largest at Strawberry Bay. This is the only one that provides year-round services, including a restaurant and lodging at **Strawberry Bay Lodge** (© 435/548-2500); the others offer limited services.

Campgrounds are located at each of the four marinas on the reservoir. Sites in the Strawberry Bay and Soldier Creek campgrounds have hookups; Aspen Grove and Renegade do not. The fee is $12 to $24. Boat ramps and fish-cleaning facilities are located adjacent to each campground. Reservations can be made for a limited number of designated campsites by contacting the National Recreation Reservation Service (© 877/444-6777; www.reserveusa.com).

To get to Strawberry Reservoir from Heber City, drive 21½ miles southeast on U.S. 40 and turn south onto the access road. After about a half mile, you'll come to the USFS visitor center for Strawberry Reservoir.

For information, contact the **Heber Ranger District,** P.O. Box 190, Heber City, UT 84032 (© 435/654-0470; www.fs.fed.us/r4/uinta), or stop by the **Strawberry Visitor Center** (© 435/548-2321). Day use is free in some parts of the complex, but there's a $4 fee for boat-ramp parking and there are day-use parking fees in other areas.

4 Sundance Resort

14 miles NE of Provo, 50 miles SE of Salt Lake City

Situated in beautiful Provo Canyon, at the base of 12,000-foot Mt. Timpanogos, Sundance is a year-round resort that emphasizes its arts programs as much as its skiing and other outdoor activities. That should come as no surprise—it's owned by actor/director Robert Redford, who bought the property in 1969 and named it after his character in the classic film *Butch Cassidy and the Sundance Kid.* You might recognize the area: Redford and director Sydney Pollack set their 1972 film *Jeremiah Johnson* here.

The goal for Sundance was to create a place where the outdoors and the arts could come together in a truly unique mountain community, and it seems to be a success. The rustic yet elegant, environmentally friendly retreat is a full-service ski resort in winter. During the summer, you'll find great hiking trails and other outdoor activities, as well as the Sundance Institute, which Redford founded in 1980 to support and encourage independent American filmmaking and playwriting.

ESSENTIALS

GETTING THERE   Sundance is less than an hour's drive from Salt Lake City via I-15. From Park City, take U.S. 189 south to Sundance. From Provo, take I-15 to exit 275, go east on Utah 52 for 5½ miles, turn north on U.S. 189 up Provo Canyon for 7 miles, and turn north on Utah 92 for about 2 miles to Sundance. In winter, the road beyond Sundance is often closed by snow.

A van shuttle service connects Sundance with both Salt Lake International Airport and Provo Airport. Call **Sundance Resort** (see below) for information and to arrange for pick-up.

So You Wanna Be in Pictures: The Sundance Institute

Forget Cannes; forget Hollywood. If you want to be (or at least be up on) the next art-house cinema sensation, go to Utah.

Tired of waiting for the next Great American Novel, many people have traded their reading glasses for tubs of popcorn, and are packing the movie houses to catch the latest work of the new creative hero: the American independent filmmaker. These next Tarantinos have to start somewhere—and that somewhere is, more often than not, the Sundance Film Festival.

For more than 20 years, the hottest independent films have been discovered at this week-long January event, hosted by Robert Redford's Sundance Institute. (The festival doesn't actually take place at Sundance, however; it's held 30 miles away, in Park City, covered earlier in this chapter.) The festival has seen the rise to glory of many pictures, including *sex, lies, and videotape; Reservoir Dogs; Slacker; Gas Food Lodging; The Good Girl; Like Water for Chocolate; Hoop Dreams;* and *The Station Agent* —and that's just the short list.

Hosting the nation's premier annual film festival is only part of the Sundance Institute's role in the world of American cinema. Think you might have what it takes? Then it might be a good idea to plan a summer trip to Sundance to participate in the Institute's Filmmakers Lab.

Since Robert Redford founded the Institute, it has brought some of the finest and most well-respected directors, actors, and producers to Utah each June to serve as advisors while students rehearse, shoot, and edit scenes from their works. Denzel Washington and Glenn Close have lent their services; so have directors Terry Gilliam and Sydney Pollack, producer James L. Brooks, and actor Morgan Freeman. Redford himself even stops by occasionally to lend a hand. Sundance also runs workshops to help writers polish their scripts, directors polish their actors, and producers polish their negotiating skills.

Admission to the festival—as a filmmaker or as an audience member—is nonexclusive; that means you and I can rub shoulders with the rich and famous and up-and-coming. To receive a free guide, or to reserve tickets, contact the **Sundance Institute** (✆ 801/328-3456 or 877/733-8497 for tickets; www.sundance.org).

VISITOR INFORMATION   For information on all facilities and activities, plus lodging reservations, contact **Sundance Resort,** R.R. 3 Box A-1, Sundance, UT 84604 (✆ **800/892-1600** or 801/225-4100; www.sundanceresort.com).

SKIING SUNDANCE

Sundance is known for its quiet, intimate setting and lack of lift lines. It offers runs for all levels—some quite challenging—including several delightfully long cruising trails for novices. The area is gaining a reputation as a good place to learn to ski or snowboard. The two levels of skiing are pretty well separated from each other: The beginner and some of the intermediate terrain are on the front mountain, whereas the prime blue runs and all of the expert slopes are on the back mountain. The expert crowd will be pleased with the steep glades, precipitous bump runs (due to the general lack of traffic, the mountain never really bumps up too high, though), and untracked snow on the back mountain, where you'll have to work at it to run into another skier.

The terrain is rated 20% beginner, 40% intermediate, and 40% advanced, with a total of 45 runs over 450 skiable acres. One quad and two triple chairlifts, plus a handle tow, serve the mountain, which has a vertical drop of 2,150 feet, from a base elevation of 6,100 feet to the top at 8,250 feet. Sundance is usually open from mid-December to early April, and has state-of-the-art snowmaking equipment on the entire front mountain. Lifts operate daily from 9am to 4:30pm.

Bearclaw's Cabin, the only mountaintop day lodge in Utah, offers snacks and hot drinks, as well as stupendous views. **Creekside** day lodge, at the base of the ski area, serves excellent quick lunches during ski season. Equipment rental and sales are available.

LIFT TICKETS   Adult all-day lift tickets cost $30 on weekdays, and $40 on weekends and holidays; lift tickets for children 6 to 12 are $18, under 6 ski free; seniors over 65 pay $10. If you're staying at the resort, the lift ticket is included in your room rate.

LESSONS & PROGRAMS   The **ski school** at Sundance offers private and group lessons daily, as well as specialized workshops. Two-hour private lessons start at $105; group lessons start at $35 for 2 hours. Learn-to-ski or -snowboard packages, which include a half-day group lesson and an all-day pass, cost $50.

Sundance Kids ski school offers several programs, including group lessons and all-day programs that include supervision, lunch, and instruction. There is no day-care facility.

CROSS-COUNTRY SKIING & SNOWSHOEING   Sundance's excellent **Nordic Center** ★★★ is 1½ miles north of the main Sundance entrance. It has about 21 miles of groomed Nordic and snowshoe trails. Classic, skating, and telemark rentals and lessons are available. Trail passes for adults cost $11 for a full day, or $8 after 2pm. Children 12 and under and seniors over 65 ski free.

WARM-WEATHER FUN

An abundance of warm-weather activities and spectacular scenery make Sundance just as popular a destination in the summer as during the winter. A quad ski lift operates in warm weather (usually from late May through late October), carrying hikers and bikers to upper trails, and offering scenic rides to anyone. Lift rides cost $7, $4 for seniors 65 and older, and free for children 5 and younger (who musts be accompanied by an adult).

FLY-FISHING   The **Provo River** provides great fly-fishing just 10 minutes away for rainbow, cutthroat, and German brown trout. Licenses and information are available at the Sundance General Store (p. 164). Sundance offers guided fishing trips, including equipment rentals. Rates start at $135 for group, $175 for private, half-day fly-fishing trips.

HIKING & MOUNTAIN BIKING   Sundance is home to a terrific network of close to a dozen trails, some of which connect to trails farther afield in the Uinta National Forest, 88 W. 100 North, Provo, UT 84601 (© **801/342-5780;** www.fs.fed.us/r4/uinta). The resort's trails range from hour-long nature walks to all-day affairs, and include three summit trails to the top of Mt. Timpanogos.

The **Sundance Nature Trail,** a 1- to 1½-hour round-trip hike, winds through groves of spruce, oak, and maple, and across alpine meadows, before reaching a cascading waterfall. The **Great Western Trail,** one of the Wasatch Front's most spectacular trails, climbs nearly 4,000 feet to some amazing scenic vistas. It starts at the base of Aspen Grove, winds to the crest of North Fork and American Fork canyons, and ends at the top of Alta ski area. This is an 8- to 10-hour round-trip hike.

Mountain bikers will find the mountain trails at Sundance fun and challenging. Bikers can minimize some of the work by taking their bikes up the lift and pedaling down. The mountain biker's trail-use fee is $9, which includes one lift ride; a full-day pass, including unlimited use of the lift, costs $16.

Contact the resort for a comprehensive trail guide.

HORSEBACK RIDING The **Sundance Stables** offer guided mountain rides of 1 hour and up, starting at about $40 per person. Call the main number at Sundance for information.

SHOPPING

The **General Store** at Sundance was the inspiration for the Sundance Catalog; it may have come to you in the mail at some time or another. If so, you'll recognize the American Indian art and jewelry, local crafts, and high-end Southwest-style clothing and outdoor wear that line the shelves. Sundance's eco-sensitive bath-product line, Sundance Farms, is available here as well. You'll also find hiking and fishing apparel and gear (including licenses and rentals) in warm weather, ski accessories in winter, and fresh-baked goodies year-round. The store is open daily from 9am to 9pm.

WHERE TO STAY

Sundance offers standard rooms, studios, and cottage suites that range from $205 to $350 per night, as well as larger mountain suites and several luxury mountain homes that cost from $315 to $1,000 per night. Each suite is outfitted with well-crafted handmade furnishings that match the rustic luxury of the entire resort, as well as American Indian crafts, stone fireplaces, and outdoor decks; most have fully equipped kitchens. All accommodations come complete with Sundance's own natural bath products—such as eco-sensitive oatmeal soap. Contact the **Sundance Resort,** R.R. 3 Box A-1, Sundance, UT 84604 (© **800/892-1600** or 801/225-4100; www.sundanceresort.com) for information and reservations.

WHERE TO DINE

The Sundance restaurants' unique culinary approach stresses the use of natural, seasonal ingredients, and dishes are often prepared with such locally raised products as corn-fed lamb, fresh trout, fresh chicken, and lots of fresh fruits and vegetables. Dinner reservations are recommended, particularly in peak seasons. Full liquor service is available.

The **Tree Room** ★★ (© **801/223-4200** for reservations), the resort's most elegant dining room for over 25 years, is the place for relaxing, romantic dinners with wine and candlelight. Decorated with American Indian art and artifacts from Redford's private collection, the rustic room seats diners in cozy booths and at intimate tables. Seasonal menus might include appetizers such as truffled brie tart, spice-roasted duck breast with lentil puree, and grilled pear with balsamic syrup. Entree choices might be herb-crusted rack of lamb or pan-roasted striped bass with a ragout, topped with a mussel sauce. It's open daily from 5pm, with dinner entree prices from $24 to $36, or a four-course tasting menu for $60.

The **Foundry Grill,** a less formal eatery serving seasonal ranch-style cuisine, serves three meals daily. Wood is the predominant feature in both the decor and the preparation of food—a wood oven and wood-fired grill and rotisserie are the main cooking equipment here. Offerings include soups, salads, sandwiches, and pizzas, with most items in the $8 to $15 range.

The **Owl Bar** is just next door. This is the same 1890s bar frequented by Butch Cassidy's Hole-in-the-Wall Gang, moved here from Wyoming—but now locals and resort guests belly up to the Victorian rosewood bar to order their favorite tipple. A limited grill menu is available; it's open from 3pm weekdays and noon weekends.

5 Provo & Environs

45 miles S of Salt Lake City, 258 miles NE of St. George

The second-largest metropolitan area in Utah, **Provo** (elevation 4,500 feet) and its adjacent communities have a population of over 300,000. The main draw here is Brigham Young University, with its attendant museums, cultural events, and spectator sports. Provo also makes a good base for exploring the nearby mountains, Timpanogos Cave National Monument, and the quite spectacular gardens and other attractions at Thanksgiving Point in nearby Lehi. The Ute Indian tribe reigned here until Mormon leader Brigham Young sent 30 families south from Salt Lake City in March 1849 to colonize the area. Today, the city remains primarily Mormon; many restaurants, stores, and attractions are closed Sundays.

South of Provo lies **Springville,** a town of about 14,000 that likes to refer to itself as "Utah's Art City." Although not primarily a tourist destination, it boasts one of the state's finest art museums. **Orem,** which abuts Provo on the northwest, is the home of various high-tech businesses. Utah Lake State Park, just west of downtown Provo, is great for boating, and the surrounding Wasatch Mountains abound with natural beauty and recreational opportunities.

ESSENTIALS

GETTING THERE Provo and Orem are easily accessible from the north or south by I-15. If you're driving in from the east on I-70, take exit 156 at Green River and follow U.S. 6 northwest to I-15 north.

Amtrak (© 800/872-7245; www.amtrak.com) offers passenger service to Provo. The train station is located at 600 South and 300 West.

VISITOR INFORMATION The **Utah County Convention and Visitors Bureau** runs a visitor center in the magnificent Historic Utah County Courthouse, 51 S. University Ave., Suite 111, Provo, UT 84601 (© 800/222-8824 or 801/370-8393; www.utahvalley.org/cvb). To get to the visitor center, take I-15 exit 268, follow Center Street east to University, turn south past the courthouse, and then turn east, where you'll find a small parking lot behind the courthouse. There's also a parking garage, with a 6-foot 8-inch height limit. Drivers of motor homes and vehicles with trailers should try to park along the street. The visitor center is open 8am to 5pm Monday through Friday; call for open hours on the weekend as they change.

For information on the surrounding national forest, contact the **Uinta National Forest,** Supervisor's Office, 88 W. 100 North, Provo, UT 84601 (© 801/342-5780; www.fs.fed.us/r4/uinta).

GETTING AROUND The easiest way to get around is by car. The streets are organized in a numbered grid pattern, beginning at the intersection of Center

Street and University Avenue in Provo. From here, the blocks increase by 100 in all four directions, such as 100 South, 200 West, 700 North, and so forth. University Parkway cuts diagonally northwest across the grid from Brigham Young University to connect with 1300 South (I-15 exit 272) in Orem. The center of Orem is the intersection of Center Street (I-15 exit 274) and Main Street. State Street (U.S. 89) crosses the city diagonally, right through the center.

Major car-rental agencies include **Budget** (© 800/237-7251), **Enterprise** (© 800/325-8007 or 801/375-7755), **Hertz** (© 800/654-3131 or 801/373-5667), and **Payless** (© 800/729-5377 or 801/374-9000).

The **Utah Transit Authority** runs about a dozen routes in and around the Provo area, with connections to Salt Lake City, Lehi, and Springville. For schedule information, call © **801/375-4636** or check the web, www.utabus.com. Route maps and schedules are also available at the visitor center in the county courthouse.

FAST FACTS The main hospital in Provo is **Utah Valley Regional Medical Center,** 1034 N. 500 West (© **801/357-7850**). The main **post office** is at 95 W. 100 South (© **800/275-8777;** www.usps.com). The local newspaper is the *Daily Herald.* The **sales tax** totals about 6.25%.

EXPLORING BRIGHAM YOUNG UNIVERSITY

Founded in 1875 by Brigham Young, Brigham Young University is the nation's largest church-owned private university, sponsored by the Church of Jesus Christ of Latter-day Saints. Home to more than 30,000 students, the beautiful 638-acre campus is located on the east side of Provo at the base of the Wasatch Mountains.

For information, contact Brigham Young University, Public Affairs and Guest Relations, Provo, UT 84602 (© **801/422-4678;** www.byu.edu). To get to the university from I-15 north, take exit 272, University Parkway, and travel east through Orem into Provo to the northwest entrance of the campus.

Free 45-minute **tours** of the campus, beginning at the visitor center, are offered Monday through Friday on the hour from 9am to 4pm. Allow at least 1 hour. Admission to campus museums is free unless otherwise noted; allow 1 to 2 hours for each of the BYU museums.

The 112-foot-tall **Centennial Carillon Tower,** a campus landmark, houses 52 bells that toll at intervals throughout the day.

The **Monte L. Bean Life Science Museum,** 1430 North, just east of the Marriott Center (© **801/378-5051**), houses extensive collections of insects, plants, reptiles, fish, shells, mammals, and birds from around the world, with an emphasis on Utah's wildlife. It's open Monday through Friday from 10am to 9pm and Saturday from 10am to 5pm.

The **Earth Science Museum,** 1683 N. Provo Canyon Rd., west of Cougar Stadium (© **801/378-3680**), offers one of Utah's largest collections of dinosaur bones from the Jurassic period. Guided tours are available by appointment. Hours are Monday from 9am to 9pm, Tuesday through Friday from 9am to 5pm, and Saturday from noon to 4pm.

The **Harris Fine Arts Center,** Campus Drive (© **801/378-2881**), houses galleries featuring American and European artists. The B. F. Larsen Gallery and Gallery 303 feature student and faculty exhibitions. The center also hosts theatrical and musical performances in its five theaters; call for the schedule and ticket prices. Hours for the center and B. F. Larsen Gallery are Monday through Friday from 8am to 9pm (later for performing arts events); Gallery 303 is open Monday through Friday from 9am to 5pm.

Where to Stay & Dine in Downtown Provo

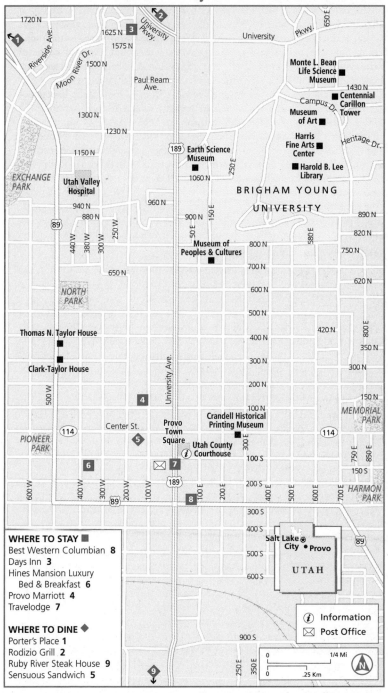

1720 N

1625 N **3**
1575 N

University Pkwy.

2

University Pkwy.

650 E

Riverside Ave.

Moon River Dr.

1500 N

Paul Ream Ave.

1300 N

1230 N

1150 N

189 **Earth Science Museum**

1060 N

250 E

Monte L. Bean Life Science Museum

1430 N

Centennial Carillon Tower

Campus Dr.

Museum of Art ■

Harris Fine Arts ■ **Center**

Heritage Dr.

■ **Harold B. Lee Library**

EXCHANGE PARK

Utah Valley Hospital

940 N
880 N
89

250 W
440 W
380 W
300 W

960 N

900 N
50 E
150 E

B R I G H A M   Y O U N G
U N I V E R S I T Y

890 N
820 N
750 N

580 E

620 N

Museum of Peoples & Cultures
■

800 N

700 N

650 N

600 N

NORTH PARK

500 N

400 N

420 N

800 E

350 N

Thomas N. Taylor House
■

300 N

300 N

Clark-Taylor House

200 N

500 W

University Ave.

4

150 N

MEMORIAL PARK

114 Center St.

Provo Town Square

5

Crandell Historical Printing Museum

100 N

114

PIONEER PARK

6

✉ **7**

Utah County *i* **Courthouse**

300 E

100 S

150 N

750 E
850 E

150 S

600 W
400 W
300 W
200 W
100 W

89

189

8

100 E
200 E

400 E
500 E
600 E
700 E

HARMON PARK

300 S

400 S

Salt Lake ⊛ City • Provo

89

WHERE TO STAY ■
Best Western Columbian **8**
Days Inn **3**
Hines Mansion Luxury
  Bed & Breakfast **6**
Provo Marriott **4**
Travelodge **7**

WHERE TO DINE ◆
Porter's Place **1**
Rodizio Grill **2**
Ruby River Steak House **9**
Sensuous Sandwich **5**

500 S

600 S

U T A H

900 S

250 E
350 E

i Information
✉ Post Office

0 ———— 1/4 Mi
0 ———— .25 Km

9

N

The state-of-the-art **Museum of Art** 🖈🖈, north of the Fine Arts Center at 492 E. Campus Dr. (© **801/378-2787**), is one of the largest museums in the West. Its 14,000-piece collection includes something for everyone, from ceramics to sculpture, paintings to pottery. You'll see everything from etchings by Rembrandt and Monet to jade and ivory from Asia. The museum also contains a gift shop and a cafe that serves lunch. Hours are Tuesday, Wednesday, and Friday from 10am to 6pm; Monday and Thursday from 10am to 9pm; and Saturday from noon to 5pm. Admission is charged for special exhibitions only.

The **Museum of Peoples and Cultures,** in Allen Hall, 700 N. 100 East (© **801/422-0020**), focuses on the cultures of the Western Hemisphere, but also looks at Colombian, Egyptian, Israeli, Polynesian, and Syrian societies. It's open Monday through Friday from 8am to noon and 1 to 5pm.

The **Harold B. Lee Library** (© **801/378-2926**) is the largest library in Utah, with more than three million bound volumes. Library hours are Monday through Saturday from 7am to midnight. The fourth floor houses the second-largest **genealogical library** (© **801/378-6200**) in the world, with free services to everyone. It's open Monday through Saturday from 8am to 9:30pm.

MORE TO SEE & DO IN THE PROVO AREA

Here in Provo, home of Brigham Young University, it should be no surprise that you'll see a number of stately homes that once belonged to well-to-do church officials, as well as commercial buildings constructed to serve the growing community. Stop at the **visitor center** in the Utah County Courthouse (p. 165) for a booklet describing the city's dozens of historic buildings. Actually, the **Utah County Courthouse** itself is well worth a visit. This magnificent structure was built of Manti limestone in the 1920s. Notice the marble floors and detailing, the fine collection of artwork displayed on the walls, and the overall feeling of grandeur emanating from the classical balance of the design.

The **Provo Town Square,** at the intersection of University Avenue and Center Street, contains the core of Provo's business community, which developed beginning in the 1890s. Here you'll see the 1900 **Knight Block,** a big red building with a large clock; the **Gates & Snow Furniture Co.,** to the east of the Knight Block, with one of Utah's best pressed-tin fronts; and the **Zion Bank,** at the northwest corner, situated in what was originally the Bank of Commerce building. West along Center Street sits a row of period storefronts, with the newer businesses now occupying them.

An interesting historic home is the **Thomas N. Taylor House,** 342 N. 500 West. "T.N.T.," as he was known, was manager of the Taylor Brothers Store and served as mayor of Provo and president of the Utah Stake of the LDS Church. His home, built in the first decade of the 20th century, exemplifies the kind of house most second-generation Utahns aspired to have. Nearby is the **Clark-Taylor House,** 310 N. 500 West, thought to be the oldest home in Utah Valley still standing on its original site. The adobe structure was built in 1854, with later additions of the two-story front, the trim around the windows, and the gables. Neither of these houses are open for tours.

Heading out of town, a turnout on U.S. 189, about 4 miles north and east of Provo, affords awe-inspiring views of **Bridal Veil Falls,** a double cataract waterfall that drops 607 feet to the Provo River. This is also a good spot to begin hikes into Provo Canyon.

Crandall Historical Printing Museum   The greatest invention of all time, according to museum founder Louis Crandall, was that of moveable type and the printing press by Johannes Gutenberg in Germany in the mid-1400s. Prior to that time, all printing was painstakingly done by hand. The printing press was the first step toward a literate society, enabling the eventual mass production of books, and their accessibility for more and more people.

This growing museum starts with that press—believed to be the only working replica in the United States—and takes visitors on a tour of printing through the centuries. You'll see a working replica of the English common press, used by Benjamin Franklin to print *Poor Richard's Almanac;* a working replica of the press used to print the first Book of Mormon in 1830; and numerous other replicas and antique presses, up to a relatively modern Linotype machine. Of special interest is a rare original—and quite beautiful—page from one of Gutenberg's Bibles. Allow 1 hour.

275 E. Center St. ℂ **801/377-7777.** Admission $3 per person. Mon–Fri 9am–2pm; other hours by appointment. Closed major holidays. Downtown Provo, about 3 blocks east of University Ave.

John Hutchings Museum of Natural History   Born in 1889, John Hutchings had an insatiable curiosity about the world around him. He collected and studied numerous objects, discussing his observations with friends and family. His collections are the core of this museum, which houses mineral displays and rare specimens of varacite and crystal aluminum, and describes their links to mining districts of the region. There are also dinosaur bones; flamingo tracks from Spanish Fork Canyon; a piece of tusk from a woolly mammoth; tools and pottery from early man; and artifacts from Utah's early residents, including a shotgun owned by famed outlaw Butch Cassidy. Allow 45 minutes.

55 N. Center St., Lehi. ℂ **801/768-7180.** Admission free but donations appreciated. Tues–Sat 11am–5pm. Bus: 10 from Provo. From I-15 exit 282, follow Main St. west to Center St. and turn right.

Springville Museum of Art ★★   The art of Utah is the cornerstone of this fine museum, housed in part in a 1937 Spanish colonial revival–style building. The museum contains one of the finest displays of Utah art available, arranged in chronological order to illustrate the development of art in the state. Of its nine galleries, four are reserved for changing exhibits of historical and contemporary art of Utah. The museum also has an excellent (and little-known) collection of Russian working-class Impressionism. The museum contains a research library and bookstore, and offers a series of lectures. Allow about one hour for your visit.

126 E. 400 South, Springville. ℂ **801/489-2727.** www.sma.nebo.edu. Free admission; donations accepted. Mon–Tues and Thur–Sat 10am–5pm; Wed 10am–9pm; Sun 3–6pm. Closed legal holidays. From I-15 exit 263, go east to Springville, entering town on 400 South.

Thanksgiving Point ★★ *Kids*   This huge complex, developed by the cofounders of WordPerfect software as an expression of gratitude to their community, includes a splendid dinosaur museum—the **North American Museum of Ancient Life.** Billed as the largest dinosaur museum in the world, this is where you'll see some of the longest and tallest dinosaur replicas ever put on display, plus fossils and related exhibits on paleontology. The museum contains a children's discovery room, a fossil lab where you can see paleontologists at work, a wide screen theater, and a museum store selling practically everything dinosaur related. Allow 2 hours. Elsewhere at Thanksgiving Point are the delightful **Thanksgiving Gardens**—55 acres of themed gardens, including topiary, butterfly, fragrance, herb, and English rose gardens, plus an unusual waterfall garden, all connected by some 2 miles of landscaped brick pathways. The Children's

Discovery Garden, designed to encourage children's imaginations, contains a large Noah's Ark, an underground exhibit area, and a hedge maze. Allow 2 hours. There's also **Farm Country,** with an animal park and exhibits on the farming life (allow 1 to 2 hours), plus an amphitheater, a golf course (see below), numerous shops, and several restaurants. Wagon and carriage rides are also offered. You will find various educational programs here.

3003 N. Thanksgiving Way, Lehi. © **888/672-6040** or 801/768-2300. www.thanksgivingpoint.com. Admission to museum: $14 adults, $11 children 3–12 and seniors 65 and older, under 3 free. Call for fees for gardens and other sites and activities. Grounds open Mon–Sat; call for hours for specific venues. Closed New Year's Day, Thanksgiving, and Christmas. From I-15 exit 287, go west to Thanksgiving Way.

SPORTS & OUTDOOR PURSUITS

One of the top spots for fishing, boating, and swimming in this area is **Utah Lake State Park** ★★, 4400 W. Center St. (© **801/375-0731;** www.stateparks. utah.gov), Utah's largest freshwater lake. The 96,600-acre lake is especially popular with owners of speedboats, personal watercraft, and sailboats, although you will see the occasional canoe or kayak. Mountains dominate the view in all directions, and at night, the lights of the city illuminate the panorama to the east. Anglers catch channel catfish, walleye, white bass, black bass, and several species of panfish. There are boat-launching ramps, but there are no boat rentals. Although there are no hiking or biking trails in the park itself, the **Provo River Parkway Trail** leads from the edge of the park into Provo Canyon (see below).

The park's 54-site campground is open April through October only; the park is open for day use year-round. The campground has no RV hookups, but you will find a dump station as well as modern restrooms with showers. Day-use hours are 6am to 10pm in summer, 8am to 5pm in winter. Day use costs $9 per vehicle. Camping costs $17; reservations (with a $7 nonrefundable fee) can be made by calling © **800/322-3770** or through the state parks website. Take I-15 exit 268B, Center Street west; it's about 3 miles to the park.

Outdoor recreation enthusiasts also head into the **Uinta National Forest,** which practically surrounds Provo and offers hundreds of miles of hiking, mountain biking, and horseback riding trails. Check with the **Forest Supervisor's office,** 88 W. 100 North (© **801/377-5780;** www.fs.fed.us/r4/uinta), for maps and tips on where to go.

Right in town, the 9-mile **Provo River Parkway Trail** winds from Utah Lake to Provo Canyon, following the Provo River part of the way. This slag trail (slag is the rock that's left over from mining when the desired metal is removed) is open to both bikers and hikers.

Among the public golf courses in the area are **Thanksgiving Point Golf Club** in Lehi (© **801/768-7400**), an 18-hole, par-72 championship course designed by golf pro Johnny Miller; **Cascade Fairways Golf Course,** 1313 E. 800 North, Orem (© **801/225-6677**), which has a driving range and 9 holes and is par-35; **East Bay Golf Course,** 1860 S. East Bay Blvd. (© **801/373-6262**), on the south side of the city, which is an 18-hole, par-71 course with a driving range, lodging, and RV facilities; and the **Seven Peaks Resort Golf Course,** 1450 East 300 North (© **801/375-5155**), a short but challenging mountainside 18-hole, par-59 course with spectacular views of the city.

WATER & ICE FUN

Seven Peaks Water Park   This is the place for a wide variety of water fun—you'll encounter dozens of heated water attractions on 26 acres abutting the mountains. The facilities include a large wave pool, winding slides, children's pools, an activity pool, large pavilions and shaded cabanas, plenty of grass, a gift shop, and food vendors. Tubes are available for rent.

The adjacent **Peaks Ice Arena** (© 801/377-8777), built especially for the 2002 Olympics, contains two Olympic-size ice-skating rinks that are open to the public. Skate rental is available. The arena is open year-round; call for the current rates and schedule.

1330 E. 300 North. © 801/373-8777. www.sevenpeaks.com. All-day admission to the Water Park $17.95 adults, $13.95 children 4–11, free for seniors 60 and older and toddlers 3 and under; half-day (after 4pm) $10.50 ages 4–59. The Water Park is open late May to early Sept Mon–Sat 11am–8pm. From I-15 exit 268, head east on Center St. Bus: 3.

SPECTATOR SPORTS

Brigham Young University is part of the Mountain West Conference. The **Cougars football** team plays at the 65,000-seat Cougar Stadium; tickets are hard to come by, so call as far in advance as possible. The **basketball** team plays in the 23,000-seat Marriott Center; you usually won't have too much trouble getting tickets. For general information on all BYU sports teams, call © **801/ 378-4911** or check the athletic department's website at www.byucougars.com. For tickets, call © **800/322-2981** or 801/378-2981, or buy online at www. byutickets.com.

WHERE TO STAY

In addition to the following listings, affordable chain and franchise motels in Provo, with rates usually between $45 and $80 for two people, include **Best Western Columbian,** 70 E. 300 South, Provo, UT 84606 (© 800/321-0055 or 801/373-8973); **Best Western Cotton Tree Inn,** 2230 N. University Pkwy., Provo, UT 84604 (© 800/662-6886 or 801/373-7044); **Days Inn,** 1675 N. 200 West, Provo, UT 84604 (© 800/329-7466 or 801/375-8600); **Econo Lodge,** 1625 W. Center St., Provo, UT 84601 (© 800/553-2666 or 801/373-0099); **Sleep Inn,** 1505 S. 40 East, Provo, UT 84601 (© 800/424-6423 or 801/377-6597); **Super 8 Motel,** 1288 S. University Ave., Provo, UT 84601 (© 800/800-8000 or 801/375-8766); and **Travelodge,** 124 S. University Ave., Provo, UT 84601 (© 800/578-7878 or 801/373-1974).

Rates are highest in summer, lowest in late winter and early spring. Rates are often significantly higher during Brigham Young University special events, and rooms can be very scarce at graduation time. Tax added to lodging bills is just under 11%. Pets are not allowed unless otherwise noted.

Hines Mansion Luxury Bed & Breakfast ★★ Built in 1895 for mining and real-estate magnate Russell Spencer Hines, this Victorian-style mansion is a true gem, and makes a wonderful spot to celebrate a special occasion or to simply relax and soak up some historic charm. Innkeepers Sandy and John Rowe have retained the mansion's historical ambience and integrity, while adding all the modern touches you'd expect and more. Every guest room is unique, but each has 1890s decor, a queen or king bed, antique and reproduction furnishings, a TV with VCR, robes, and a two-person whirlpool tub plus a separate private bathroom. The Penthouse, which occupies the entire top floor of the mansion, boasts a queen-size pillow-top bed, a 46-inch TV with VCR, and spectacular views of the city and nearby mountains through huge oval windows from the two-person whirlpool tub.

Fresh-baked cookies and fresh fruit are served each evening, and complimentary sparkling cider is placed in each room. The delightful breakfasts feature fruit, yogurt, and a hot gourmet dish such as baked egg puffs or pecan pancakes. Smoking is not permitted.

383 W. 100 South, Provo, UT 84601. © **800/428-5636** or 801/374-8400. Fax 801/374-0823. www. hinesmansion.com. 9 units. $109–$199. Rates include full breakfast. MC, V. Not recommended for children. *In room:* A/C, TV/VCR.

Provo Marriott   This well-regarded high-rise hotel in downtown Provo provides comfortable—even luxurious—accommodations with splendid views (especially from the upper floors) and all the amenities you could want, including coffeemakers, irons and ironing boards, hair dryers, and dataports with high-speed Internet access. Public areas and bedrooms are handsomely appointed, decorated primarily in light earth tones. Some in-room fridges and VCRs are available, and some units have whirlpool tubs. Allie's American Grille serves three meals daily.

101 W. 100 North, Provo, UT 84601. © **888/825-3162** or 801/377-4700. Fax 801/377-4708. www.marriott hotels.com/slcvo. 331 units. $99–$179 double. AE, DC, DISC, MC, V. Free covered parking (height limit 6 ft. 9in.). **Amenities:** Restaurant (American); 2 heated pools (indoor and outdoor); fitness center; Jacuzzi; sauna; limited room service (6:30am–11pm); coin-op laundry; same-day dry cleaning. *In room:* A/C, TV, dataport, coffeemaker, hair dryer, iron.

CAMPGROUNDS

Lakeside RV Campground   Situated along the Provo River, this campground offers the best of both worlds—it's close to the attractions and restaurants of Provo, and it offers a quiet camping experience with trees, flowers, grassy areas, ducks, and geese. In addition to the usual bathhouse, dump station, and RV hookups, the campground has a self-serve laundry, a heated pool, a nature walk, horseshoe pits, a volleyball area, a playground, and a game room. A store sells groceries, and propane is available. You can fish in the Provo River, or head to Utah Lake, just a quarter-mile away.

4000 W. Center St., Provo, UT 84601. © **800/906-5267** for reservations, or 801/373-5267. www.lakesiderv campground.com. 148 sites (all RV sites, 112 with full hookups, 32 with water & electric). $16–$24 for 1 or 2 people. MC, V. From I-15 exit 268, go west 2 miles. Pets are not permitted in the tent area.

WHERE TO DINE

Provo is a conservative, family-oriented city; many restaurants do not serve alcohol, and a number are closed on Sundays. In addition to the restaurants discussed below, we heartily recommend the Tree Room, at the nearby Sundance Resort (see p. 161).

Porter's Place ★★ *Kids* STEAK/AMERICAN   One of Utah's more colorful and controversial characters, Porter Rockwell served as a bodyguard for LDS church leaders Joseph Smith and Brigham Young, was accused but acquitted of attempting to assassinate the lieutenant governor of Missouri, and was blamed for, but not charged with, other murders. Named in Rockwell's "honor," Porter's Place is an Old West–style restaurant with a large regional following. Housed in a 1915 building, the restaurant has the look of an old saloon, with red-brick walls, heavy wood tables, and historic photos. There's also a counter (actually a bar from an 1883 Montana saloon) with tractor seats for stools.

Porter's specializes in thick steaks and fresh fish. The lunch menu features a variety of burgers, including a buffalo burger and a huge 1-pound beef burger, plus sandwiches. Especially popular at dinner are the top sirloin steaks, ranging from 5 to 24 ounces, and the buffalo steaks. Portions are generally large, but the dinner menu also offers 10 "lite dinners" with smaller portions. A local bakery provides the breads and pastries; fountain treats such as old-fashioned sodas, malts, and banana splits are available as well. Despite the saloon-like appearance and handsome old bar, no alcohol is served.

24 W. Main St., Lehi ℂ 801/768-8348. Main courses $4.75–$12 lunch, $5.95–$28 dinner. AE, DC, DISC, MC, V. Mon–Thurs 10am–10pm; Fri–Sat 10am–11pm. From I-15 exit 282, go west on Main St.

Rodizio Grill BRAZILIAN STEAKHOUSE A unique dining experience awaits you at Rodizio's. The salad bar—with more than 35 ultra-fresh hot and cold selections—could make up a meal in itself. Choose from crab salad, tuna salad, roasted pork salad, chicken salad, artichoke salad, fruit salad, and Caesar salad, to name a few. When you're ready for your main course, the servers will roll up to your table with carts laden with numerous succulent meat dishes for you to choose from. Choices include top sirloin in garlic and cheese, Brazilian pot roast, chicken wings in a special hot sauce, marinated pork loin, and a mild and flavorful Brazilian sausage. Or you can just have a sandwich, which is anything but simple here: the Ipanema Chicken Salad is tender chicken in a creamy dressing mixed with oranges and walnuts; and the Rodizio Turkey BLT combines bacon-wrapped turkey with lettuce, tomato, mozzarella cheese, and a special dressing. There's live Brazilian music on weekends, and full liquor service is available.

575 E. University Pkwy., University Mall, Orem. ℂ 801/224-4745. Fixed-price lunch $7.95–$10.95, dinner $11–$16. AE, DC, MC, V. Sun–Thurs 11am–10pm; Fri–Sat 11am–11pm.

Ruby River Steakhouse ⚡ STEAK If a thick, juicy, sizzling steak is your idea of the perfect meal, then Ruby River is for you. And if you also happen to like country western music, cowboy boots, and cold beer, you'll be even happier. Decor is strictly Western, with a large painting of galloping wild horses, a rock fireplace, and a bar with tall tables and buckets of peanuts. Beef is USDA Choice, aged 21 days, hand-cut, seasoned, and double-broiled at 1,600°F. Choices range from the New York cut (voted Utah's best steak in various polls) to tender filet mignon, rib-eye, T-bone, and porterhouse. There's also the very tasty slow-roasted prime rib, served with fresh-grated horseradish and sour cream. Although steak is really the reason to come here, the restaurant also does an admirable job with its slow-roasted baby back ribs with Louisiana-style barbecue sauce, and its several chicken dishes, including chicken breast in a sweet raspberry wheat beer marinade. Also offered are a fresh fish of the day and a broiled salmon fillet with barbecue sauce. Side dishes include a tasty potato that's baked and then dipped in a garlic batter and deep-fried, and a yam that's baked, then dipped in a cinnamon batter and deep-fried. Do you sense a theme? Several microbrews from the company's Ogden restaurant (p. 121) are served, along with a number of other beers, wine by the glass and bottle, and a complete liquor bar.

1454 S. University Ave. (in the Holiday Inn). ℂ 801/371-0648. Reservations not accepted. Main courses $5.95–$14 lunch, $12–$25dinner. AE, DISC, MC, V. Mon–Thurs 11am–10pm; Fri–Sat 11am–11pm; Sun 11am–9pm. Just north of I-15 exit 266.

Sensuous Sandwich *Value* SANDWICHES You can eat at one of the few tables at this speedy sandwich shop or you can take your selection with you. All sandwiches come with the usual condiments, including spicy brown mustard and lettuce, as well as extras such as horseradish, olives, avocado, green pepper, lettuce, and cheese. Top-of-the-line is, of course, the Sensuous Sandwich, with ham, turkey, roast beef, and jack cheese. Also available are pastrami, crab, chicken breast, and tuna. No alcohol is served.

There's a second location at 378 E. University Parkway, Orem (✆ **801/225-9475**).

163 W. Center St. ✆ **801/377-9244**. Sandwiches by the inch $2 (4 in.)–$9.60 (24 in.). MC, V. Mon–Sat 10:30am–8pm. From I-15 exit 268, follow Center St. east.

PROVO AFTER DARK

The **Brigham Young University Theatre,** on the BYU campus (✆ **801/378-4322**), presents more than a dozen theatrical productions each year. A variety of musicals, comedies, and dramatic productions are staged by the Theatre Arts Program at **Utah Valley State College,** 800 West 1200 South, Orem (✆ **801/222-8982**).

From summer through early fall, you can see live musicals and concerts under the stars at the **SCERA Shell Theatre,** 699 S. State St., in SCERA Park, Orem (✆ **801/225-2569;** www.scera.org). The season usually includes several locally produced Broadway musicals, plus a variety of concerts, ranging from pop to country to classical.

Johnny B's Comedy Club, 177 W. 300 South (✆ **801/377-6910**), is a popular place for stand-up. Shows usually start at 9pm on Thursday, 8pm and 10pm on Friday and Saturday. No alcohol is served. At **Atchafalaya,** 210 W. Center St. (✆ **801/373-9014**), the bar area offers live bands, DJs, and karaoke in a Bourbon Street atmosphere. The adjacent cafe serves Louisiana Cajun cuisine.

6 Timpanogos Cave National Monument

20 miles N of Provo, 35 miles S of Salt Lake City

This national monument is actually composed of three caves—Hansen, Middle, and Timpanogos—that are linked together by man-made tunnels. Martin Hansen discovered the first cavern in 1887 while tracking a mountain lion. The other two were reported in the early 1910s, and the connecting tunnels were constructed in the 1930s. The caves are filled with 47 kinds of cave formations, from stalactites and stalagmites to draperies and helictites. The caves aren't easy to reach, but their beauty and variety make them worth the rough 1½-hour trek to the mouth.

ESSENTIALS

The caves are accessible only from early May to late October, daily from 7am to 5:30pm (8am to 5pm after September 7). The caves close in winter because snow and ice make the access trail too hazardous.

GETTING THERE/ACCESS POINTS   From Provo, head north on I-15 to exit 287, then east on Utah 92 to the visitor center, which is on the south side of the road. For a beautiful but slow drive, when you leave the caves, continue east and then south on Utah 92 through American Fork Canyon, which is narrow and winding, and turn west on U.S. 189 back to Provo. From Salt Lake City, take I-15 south to exit 287, and proceed as above.

INFORMATION/VISITOR CENTER   Contact **Timpanogos Cave National Monument** at R.R. 3, Box 200, American Fork, UT 84003-9803 (✆ **801/756-5238;** www.nps.gov/tica). The visitor center is on the south side of Utah 92. It is open May to September 6 daily from 7am to 5:30pm, and September 7 to late October daily 8am to 5pm.

Note that parking at the visitor center is limited for large vehicles, such as motor homes over 20 feet. Although small, the visitor center offers a short film about the caves, a few explanatory displays and booklets, and postcards for sale. You'll find a snack bar and gift shop next to the center, as well as two picnic areas located along the shady banks of the American Fork River. One is across from the visitor center; a larger one, with fire grills and restrooms, is about a quarter mile west.

FEES & REGULATIONS   One-hour cave tours cost $6 for adults, $5 for children 6 to 15, $3 for children 3 to 5, and free for children under 3; 90-minute "Introduction to Caving" tours, available only to those 14 and older, cost $15 per person. The U.S. Forest Service also charges a $3 per vehicle fee to enter American Fork Canyon, where the national monument is located. Pets are not allowed on the trail or in the caves.

EXPLORING THE MONUMENT

The only way to see the caves is on a ranger-guided tour. Allow about 3 hours total for the basic cave tour—1½ hours hiking up to the cave, an hour in the caves, and 30 to 45 minutes hiking back down. The tours are limited to 20 persons and often fill up early in the morning, so it's best to call ahead and reserve your space with a credit card. The "Introduction to Caving" tours are about a half-hour longer and are limited to five people. Reservations are required. The temperature inside the caves is around 45°F (7°C) (about the same as a refrigerator), with humidity of 100%, so take a jacket or sweatshirt.

THE HIKE TO THE CAVES   The change in elevation between the visitor center (at about 5,600 feet) and the cave entrance is 1,065 feet, and the steep trail is 1½ miles long; it's a physically demanding walk, but quite rewarding. The trail is not navigable by either wheelchairs or strollers and should not be attempted by anyone with breathing, heart, or walking difficulties. Wear good walking shoes and carry water and perhaps a snack.

This is a self-guided hike, so you can travel at your own pace, stopping at the benches along the way to rest and enjoy the views of the canyon, the Wasatch Range, and Utah Valley. A trail guide, available at the visitor center, will help you identify the wildflowers growing amid the Douglas fir, white fir, maple, and oak trees. You'll also spot chipmunks, ground squirrels, lizards, and a myriad of birds along the way. Restrooms are available at the cave entrance, but not inside the cave or along the trail.

TOURING THE CAVES   The basic ranger-guided cave tour is along a surfaced, well-lit, and fairly level route. You'll enter at the natural entrance to Hansen Cave and continue through Hansen, Middle, and Timpanogos Caves. Nature decorated the limestone chambers with delicately colored stalactites, stalagmites, draperies, graceful flowstone, and helictites (curvy formations for which the caves are famous), all in soft greens, reds, yellows, and white. The huge cave formation of linked stalactites at the Great Heart of Timpanogos is quite impressive, and the profusion of bizarre, brilliant white helictites in the Chimes Chamber of Timpanogos is stunning. Mirror-like cave pools reflect the formations. The "Introduction to Caving" tours take you to less developed sections, and require some crawling through tight places.

You'll need high-speed film or a flash if you're taking photos; tripods are not allowed. Remember that the formations are fragile and easily damaged, even by a light touch of your hand—the oils from your skin will change the formations' chemical makeup.

Dinosaurs & Natural Wonders in Utah's Northeast Corner

Utah has more than its share of natural treasures, with Zion and Bryce Canyon national parks and the other wonderful red rock areas of southern Utah springing to mind first. But tucked away in the state's far northeastern corner, more rugged and less accessible, lies a playground of great scenic beauty, filled with fascinating historic (and prehistoric) sites. And you won't have to fight throngs of tourists here: This land where the dinosaurs once roamed is still relatively undiscovered and unspoiled.

1 Vernal: Gateway to the Region's Top Recreational Areas

175 miles E of Salt Lake City

A perfect base for exploring Dinosaur National Monument (just 20 miles from town) and Ashley National Forest, Vernal, at 5,280 feet in elevation, is the largest community in the region. You'll find all the services you might need, as well as a few attractions that serve as a good introduction to the compelling geologic and natural history of the area.

ESSENTIALS

GETTING THERE   From Heber City, U.S. 40 leads east, past Strawberry Reservoir (there's world-class fishing here if you have time to stop; see p. 160) and through Duchesne and Roosevelt, each of which have a few motels, restaurants, and services, before reaching Vernal (158 miles from Heber City).

From I-70, take exit 156 west of Green River and follow U.S. 6/191 north 68 miles through Price and Helper, branching northeast above Helper to follow U.S. 191 for 44 beautiful mountainous miles to Duchesne. Then take U.S. 40 east for 58 miles to Vernal.

The **Uintah County Airport** (© 435/789-3400) is located about 1½ miles southeast of the center of town, providing twice-daily flights to and from Denver year-round on **Great Lakes Airlines** (© 800/554-5111; www.greatlakes av.com).

VISITOR INFORMATION   Information on area lodging, dining, and recreational facilities can be obtained from the **Dinosaurland Travel Board,** 55 E. Main St., Vernal, UT 84078 (© 800/477-5558 or 435/789-6932; www. dinoland.com), open Monday through Friday from 8am to 5pm. You can also get information at the **Utah Welcome Center** in Jensen, about 13 miles southeast of Vernal on U.S. 40, which is open in summer daily from 8am to 8pm and in winter daily from 9am to 5pm.

GETTING AROUND   Car rentals are available at the airport from **Avis** (© 800/331-1212 or 435/789-7264), or in town from **Utah Motor Co.**

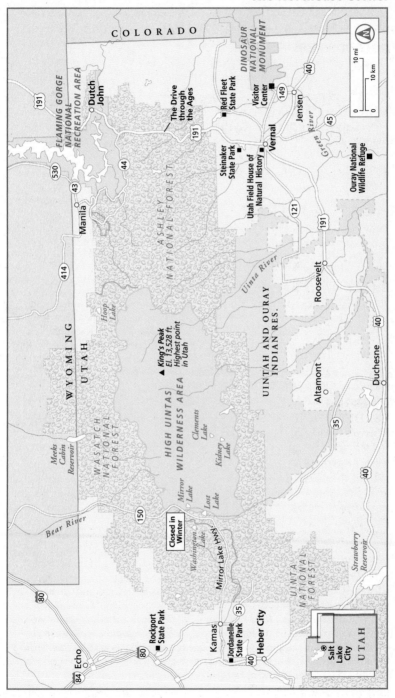

(© 435/789-0454). Local transportation is available from **T Taxi** (© 435/789-6120) and **Vernal City Cab** (© 435/790-1212).

OUTDOOR PURSUITS

In addition to the outdoor recreation areas discussed here, see the sections "Dinosaur National Monument" and "Flaming Gorge National Recreation Area," later in the chapter.

ASHLEY NATIONAL FOREST

This vast forest encompasses more than a million acres of beautiful mountain country, including Flaming Gorge National Recreation Area (p. 185) and the High Uintas Wilderness. **Kings Peak,** in the High Uintas Wilderness Area, is Utah's tallest mountain, at 13,528 feet. Throughout the national forest, you'll find numerous opportunities for hiking, backpacking, fishing, camping, cross-country skiing, and other activities. The Forest Service also rents out its guard stations and yurts, which make an excellent base for exploring the mountains north of Vernal (see "Where to Stay," later in this chapter).

Information is available from the **Vernal Ranger District office,** 355 N. Vernal Ave., Vernal, UT 84078 (© **435/789-1181;** www.fs.fed.us/r4/ashley), open Monday through Friday from 8am to 5pm.

OURAY NATIONAL WILDLIFE REFUGE

Hundreds of species of migratory birds and waterfowl make their home in this 11,987-acre wetlands refuge, which lies south of Vernal along the Green River. A 9-mile car tour route begins at the visitor contact station; you'll also find hiking trails and an observation tower. In addition to a variety of birds, you're likely to see mule deer.

To get here from Vernal, take U.S. 40 west about 14 miles and turn left (south) onto Utah 88 for about 14 miles to the refuge entrance. The visitor contact station is about a mile from the entrance. Entry is free. The refuge is open daily year-round, from an hour before sunrise to an hour after sunset. Contact the refuge office, HC 69, Box 232, Randlett, UT 84063-2042 (© **435/545-2522;** http://refuges.fws.gov) for more information.

RED FLEET STATE PARK

Located 10 miles north of Vernal, at 4335 North U.S. 191, this scenic park—it looks like a junior version of Lake Powell—offers fishing, boating, swimming, and camping, plus about 200 well-preserved dinosaur tracks. The 750-acre Red Fleet Reservoir was named for three large deep-red sandstone rock formations that resemble the hulls of ships. You'll encounter sandy beaches, rock cliffs, and plenty of open water; good fishing for rainbow and brown trout, bluegill, and bass; and wildlife such as rabbits, ground squirrels, mule deer, and the occasional bobcat. On chilly mornings, golden eagles are sometimes spotted sunning themselves on rock outcroppings; other birds that frequent the park include hawks, vultures, owls, and bluebirds.

The **dinosaur tracks,** which are about 200 million years old, are found on a large slab of rock that slants down into the water and is located across the reservoir from the park's boat ramp. The greatest number of tracks can be seen when the water level is low, from late summer through winter. You can reach the tracks by boat or by swimming (wear a life jacket so you can return easily), or via a 1½-mile hike (one-way) from a Bureau of Land Management road. To reach the BLM road, continue north along U.S. 191 1 mile past the turnoff to Red Fleet.

> **Tips**   **The Drive Through the Ages**
>
> One of the most scenic drives in the state is the Flaming Gorge–Uintas Scenic Byway—U.S. 191 from Vernal up to Manila and Flaming Gorge National Recreation Area—one of the first designated national scenic byways in the United States. The 67-mile route climbs through foothills covered with pine and juniper trees into the Uinta Mountains; signs along the way explain the evolution of the intriguing geologic formations you'll see. Near Flaming Gorge, you'll pass the billion-year-old rock core of the Uinta Mountains. Stop at some of the many turnouts for scenic views, short walks, and wildlife viewing—watch for bighorn sheep, elk, mule deer, and moose, especially in spring.

Turn right (east) just past mile marker 212, cross a cattle guard, and drive 2.3 miles on the paved road to the trailhead. This is just a small turnout with a sign at the trail; a stock tank sits across the road, partly hidden by bushes and trees. Allow about 2 hours for the moderate hike over low, sandy hills. In winter, when the reservoir is frozen, it's a quick walk from the boat ramp across the ice to the tracks (provided it's thick enough to cross—please use caution).

Park facilities include the boat ramp, fish-cleaning stations, an RV dump station, and a 38-site campground. Although the campground is essentially a parking lot, it does offer splendid panoramic views across the lake. There are also grassy areas for tents, plus tables and fire pits. You'll find modern restrooms but no showers or RV hookups. Camping costs $11; the day-use fee is $5 per vehicle. Gates are open daily from 6am to 10pm in summer, 8am to 5pm in winter. Call © **435/789-4432** for information; 800/322-3770 for campsite reservations. The Utah State Parks website is www.stateparks.utah.gov.

STEINAKER STATE PARK

Steinaker offers a sandy swimming beach, good fishing for rainbow trout and largemouth bass, and an attractive campground, just 7 miles north of Vernal at 4335 N. U.S. 191. This reservoir, which covers 780 acres when full, is also popular with water-skiers and boaters. Unfortunately, there are no rental facilities nearby.

Wildlife here includes mule deer, jackrabbits, cottontails, ground squirrels, porcupines, and an occasional elk or bobcat. Migratory waterfowl are often seen in spring and fall, and the park also attracts American robins, pheasants, and golden eagles. The landscape is composed primarily of juniper and sagebrush, with cottonwoods and aspen trees near the lake. Spring usually brings out an abundance of wildflowers, such as Indian paintbrush, larkspur, and sego lily. There are several unmarked hiking trails—ask a ranger for directions—and additional hiking opportunities nearby on property managed by the Bureau of Land Management.

Facilities include a boat ramp, fish-cleaning station, and RV dump station. The tree-shaded campground contains 31 sites and modern restrooms, but no showers or RV hookups. Picnic tables, barbecue grills, and fire pits are available. Camping costs $11; the day-use fee is $5. Gates are open daily from 7am to 10pm in summer, from 8am to 5pm in winter. Call © **435/789-4432** for information; 800/322-3770 for campsite reservations. The Utah State Parks website is www.stateparks.utah.gov.

SEEING THE SIGHTS IN TOWN

Daughters of Utah Pioneers Museum   This small museum offers a fine display of pioneer relics and photos, and a history of the settling of the area from the mid-1800s. Allow half an hour.

500 W. 200 South St. Donations requested. June–Labor Day Mon–Sat 10am–6pm. Closed rest of year.

Utah Field House of Natural History State Park Museum   This park gets a new, larger building with more exhibit space and a theater by the summer of 2004, where visitors will get a close-up look at a huge dinosaur skeleton and will encounter exhibits on paleontology, geology, and the Fremont and Ute cultures. Kids will love the **Dinosaur Garden** 🎯🎯, with 18 life-size models of dinosaurs and other prehistoric creatures in a delightful garden that simulates the dinosaurs' actual habitat. You should start your visit at the theater for a look at paleontologists at work in the field. There's a gift shop with dinosaur-related souvenirs and books. Allow at least 1 hour.

495 E. Main St. ✆ **435/789-3799.** www.stateparks.utah.gov. Call for current admission prices. Memorial Day–Labor Day daily 8am–7pm; rest of year 9am–5pm. Closed Thanksgiving, Christmas, and New Year's Day.

Western Heritage Museum 🎯   This well-organized and attractive museum is a good stop for those interested in the prehistoric Fremont Indians—in fact, it contains one of the country's best collections of Fremont Indian objects. It also has 1880s Ute artifacts and displays of historic rifles, fossils, and rocks. Pioneer life is depicted in a country store, a blacksmith shop with tack and saddles, a one-room schoolhouse, a barber shop, and a bedroom, kitchen, and parlor. Clothing fashions from 1880 to 1930 are also on display. The museum features changing art exhibits, and early horse-drawn wagons and farm equipment are on display outside. Allow an hour.

Western Park, 328 E. 200 South. ✆ **435/789-7399.** Free admission. Memorial Day–Labor Day Mon–Sat 9am–6pm; rest of year Mon–Fri 9am–5pm, Sat 10am–2pm.

WHERE TO STAY

There are more than a dozen motels in the town of Vernal, including chain and franchise properties such as **Best Western Antlers,** 423 W. Main St. (✆ **888/ 791-2929** or 435/789-1202); **Best Western Dinosaur Inn,** 251 E. Main St. (✆ **800/528-1234** or 435/789-2660); **Days Inn,** 260 W. Main St. (✆ **800/ 382-1011** or 435/789-1011); **Econo Lodge,** 311 E. Main St. (✆ **800/553-2666** or 435/789-2000); and **Super 8,** 1624 W. Main St. (✆ **800/800-8000** or 435/ 789-4326). Rates for two people range from about $50 to $100, with the highest rates in summer. Room tax adds about 9%.

Another lodging option in this area is to stay at one of the **U.S. Forest Service's guard stations or yurts** 🎯, located in spectacular forest settings some 25 to 35 miles north of Vernal in the Ashley National Forest. Rates range from $25 to $40 per night, and the facilities offer a range of amenities and sleeping capacities and are available year-round. For details, contact the Vernal Ranger District office, 355 N. Vernal Ave., Vernal, UT 84078 (✆ **435/789-1181;** www.fs.fed. us/r4/ashley).

Split Mountain Motel   This small mom-and-pop operation is comfortable, attractively furnished, and exceptionally well maintained. Rooms are decorated in light tones, with wood-grain furnishings, and many display photos of the area. Most units have combination shower/tubs, although some have showers only; all have fridges and microwaves. Amenities include free morning coffee.

There's no swimming pool, but you'll find a pool and water slide just a half block away.

1015 E. U.S. 40, Vernal, UT 84078. ℂ **435/789-9020.** Fax 435/789-9023. 40 units. $48–$54 double. AE, DC, DISC, MC, V. Small pets allowed with prior approval. *In room:* A/C, TV, fridge.

CAMPING

Among the area campgrounds with full RV hookups and hot showers is **Dinosaurland KOA,** 930 N. Vernal Ave., Vernal, UT 84078 (ℂ **800/562-7574** or 435/789-2148; www.dinokoa.com), which is open from April through October. It has 65 RV sites and 30 grassy tent sites, with rates from $19 to $22 for tent sites and $24 to $28 for RV sites. This KOA also has five one-room cabins at $35 to $39 for two people. Both **Red Fleet State Park** (p. 178) and **Steinaker State Park** (p. 179) have camping but no RV hookups.

WHERE TO DINE

Bakeries and delicatessens can be found at **IGA,** 575 W. Main St. (ℂ **435/789-2001**), and **Smith's,** 1080 W. Main St. (ℂ **435/789-7135**).

Betty's Cafe 🄰 *Value* AMERICAN   This simple, down-home cafe is a local favorite, and we can see why. It serves well-prepared homemade food at reasonable prices. Breakfast, which includes all the usual offerings, is served all day. Lunch brings sandwiches, half- and quarter-pound burgers, plus such choices as chicken-fried steak, liver and onions, roast beef, and hamburger steak. No alcoholic beverages are served.

416 W. Main St. ℂ **435/781-2728.** Main courses $3.95–$11. No credit cards. Mon–Sat 6am–4pm; Sun 6am–noon.

7-11 Ranch Restaurant 🄰 AMERICAN   A good family restaurant offering home-style food in a comfortable, Western-style setting, the 7-11 Ranch Restaurant had its beginnings in 1933, when Warren "Fat" Belcher sold a cow and bought a hot dog stand. Now owned by Belcher's daughter Connie and her husband Jerry Pope, the restaurant has changed a bit—you won't even find hot dogs on the menu—but you can count on friendly service and a wide range of American favorites. There's a variety of burgers—including a huge 1-pound killer—plus hot and cold sandwiches, deep-fried halibut and other seafood, excellent chef's salads, homemade chili, pork chops, and chicken in a variety of forms. There are also steaks, barbecued beef or pork ribs, and prime ribs on Fridays. Breakfasts consist of the usual American favorites.

77 E. Main St. ℂ **435/789-1170.** Main courses $4.50–$15. AE, DISC, MC, V. Mon–Sat 6am–10pm.

2 Dinosaur National Monument

20 miles E of Vernal, 195 miles E of Salt Lake City

In some ways, this park is two separate experiences: a look at the lost world of dinosaurs on one side, and a scenic wonderland of colorful rock, deep river canyons, and a forest of Douglas fir on the other.

About 150 million years ago, the region was a warm land of ferns, conifers, grasses, ponds, and rivers. This made it a suitable habitat for dinosaurs, including vegetarians such as Diplodocus, Apatosaurus, and Stegosaurus; and sharp-toothed carnivores, such as Allosaurus, that hunted their vegetarian cousins. When these huge creatures died, most of their skeletons decayed and disappeared, but in at least one spot, floodwaters washed dinosaur carcasses into the bottom of a river. Here they were preserved in sand and covered with sediment, creating the largest quarry of Jurassic-period dinosaur bones ever discovered.

But visitors who limit their trip to the Dinosaur Quarry, fascinating as it is, miss quite a bit. Encompassing 325 square miles of stark canyons at the confluence of two rivers, the monument also offers hiking trails, pioneer homesteads, thousand-year-old rock art, spectacular panoramic vistas, wildlife-watching opportunities, and the thrills of white-water rafting.

The Yampa, Green, and smaller rivers bring life-giving water into the area, creating microclimates that support hanging gardens of mosses and ferns, cottonwoods, and even an occasional Douglas fir—all just yards from the predominant landscape of sagebrush, cactus, and dwarfed piñon and juniper trees. Wildlife includes species that can survive the harsh extremes of the high desert climate—bighorn sheep, coyote, rabbits, and snakes—but you'll also find mule deer, beaver, and porcupine along the river banks. Birds that are occasionally spotted include peregrine falcons, sage grouse, and Canada geese.

ESSENTIALS

GETTING THERE/ACCESS POINTS/VISITOR CENTERS   Straddling the Utah–Colorado state line, Dinosaur National Monument is accessible via two main roads—one from each state—that don't connect inside the monument.

The **main visitor center** and the Dinosaur Quarry are 20 miles east of Vernal. To get here, take U.S. 40 to Jensen and head north on Utah 149 for 7 miles. At the visitor center's shop, you can buy books, hiking and driving guides, maps, and, of course, model dinosaurs. The main visitor center is open daily, Memorial Day to Labor Day from 8am to 7pm, and in winter from 8am to 4:30pm. It is closed New Year's Day, Thanksgiving, and Christmas.

Administrative offices and a small **visitor center** are located about 2 miles east of the town of Dinosaur, Colorado, at the intersection of U.S. 40 and Harpers Corner Drive. This visitor center offers a short slide program; hours are daily 8am to 6pm in summer and Monday through Friday from 8am to 4:30pm at other times. The center is closed for federal holidays.

Several other monument entrances exist, all without visitor centers: At the far eastern edge of the monument off U.S. 40, an entry road leads to Deerlodge Park (open in summer only); at the northern tip, off Colo. 318, a road goes to the Gates of Lodore; just inside the Utah border at Jones Hole Fish Hatchery, a road leads into the park via the Jones Hole Road from Vernal; and at the Rainbow Park section, you'll find a park entry road off Island Park Road (impassable when wet) from the monument's western edge.

INFORMATION   Contact **Dinosaur National Monument,** 4545 E. U.S. 40, Dinosaur, CO 81610-9724 (© **435/781-7700** or 970/374-3000; fax 970/374-3003; www.nps.gov/dino). In addition, the nonprofit **Intermountain Natural History Association,** 1291 E. U.S. 40, Vernal, UT 84078 (© **800/845-3466;** www.dinosaurnature.com), offers numerous publications, maps, posters, and videos on the park and its geology, wildlife, history, and dinosaurs. Information on area lodging, dining, and recreational facilities can be obtained from the **Dinosaurland Travel Board** (p. 176).

FEES, BACKCOUNTRY PERMITS, REGULATIONS & SAFETY   The entry fee, charged only at the main Utah entrance, is $10 per vehicle or $5 per person for those on foot, on motorcycles, or on bicycles, for up to 1 week. Camping fees are additional (see www.nps.gov/dino/camp.htm for the various camping fees); backcountry overnight camping permits, although free, are required and available from park rangers.

Regulations forbid damaging or taking anything, particularly fossils and other natural, historical, and archaeological items. Off-road driving is not permitted. Dogs must be leashed at all times. Pets are not allowed in buildings, on trails, more than 100 feet from developed roads, or on river trips.

Rangers warn that the rivers are not safe for swimming or wading; the water is cold and the current is stronger than it appears.

SEASONS/AVOIDING THE CROWDS   Summer is the busiest and hottest time of the year at Dinosaur National Monument, with daytime temperatures often soaring into the upper 90s. Winters are a lot quieter but can be cold, with fog, snow, and temperatures below zero. The best times to visit are spring (although you should be prepared for rain showers) and fall (perhaps the very best time, when the cottonwood trees turn a brilliant gold).

RANGER PROGRAMS   Rangers present a variety of activities in summer, including evening campfire programs; check the schedules posted at either visitor center.

SEEING THE HIGHLIGHTS

Those with only a short amount of time should make their first stop the **Dinosaur Quarry.** It's accessible only from the Utah side and is the only place in the monument where you can see dinosaur bones. It contains the remains of many long-vanished species, including fossils of sea creatures two to three times older than any land dinosaurs. This area is believed to be one of the world's most concentrated and accessible deposits of the fossilized remains of dinosaurs, crocodiles, turtles, and clams. The quarry—which looks like a long slab of frozen pudding with bones sticking out of it—is enclosed in the visitor center, along with exhibits that help make sense of this prehistoric zoo. There's one section of bones that you can actually reach out and touch, and models show what paleontologists believe these dinosaurs looked like when they still had their skin.

After spending about an hour in the quarry, drive the **Tour of the Tilted Rocks,** which takes an hour or two. Then, if time remains, or if you're heading east into Colorado anyway, take another few hours to drive the scenic **Harpers Corner Drive** (see the next section for descriptions of both drives).

EXPLORING DINOSAUR NATIONAL MONUMENT BY CAR

Drives in both the Utah and Colorado sections of the park allow motorists to see spectacular scenery in relative solitude. Brochures for each of the following drives are available at the visitor centers.

From the Quarry visitor center on the Utah side of the park, the **Tour of the Tilted Rocks** along Cub Creek Road is a 24-mile round-trip drive that's suitable for most passenger cars. This route takes you to 1,000-year-old rock art left by the Fremont people, a pioneer homestead, and views of nearby mountains and the Green River. Watch for prairie dogs both alongside and on the road. Although mostly paved, the last 2 miles of the road are dirt and narrow, and may be dusty or muddy. Allow 1 to 2 hours.

For the best scenic views, drive to Colorado and take the **Harpers Corner Drive.** This paved, 62-mile round-trip has several overlooks offering panoramic views into the gorges carved by the Yampa and Green rivers, a look at the derby-shaped Plug Hat Butte, and close-ups of a variety of other colorful rock formations. The drive also provides access to the easy quarter-mile round-trip Plug

Hat Nature Trail and the moderately difficult 2-mile round-trip Harpers Corner Trail (see below). Allow about 2 hours for the drive, more if you plan to do some hiking.

OUTDOOR PURSUITS

BOATING To many people, the best way to see this beautiful, rugged country is from the river, where you can admire the scenery while crashing through thrilling white water and floating over smooth, silent stretches. About a dozen outfitters are authorized to **run the Yampa and Green rivers** through the monument, offering trips ranging from 1 to 5 days, usually from mid-May to mid-September. Among companies providing river trips are **Hatch River Expeditions** (② **800/342-8243** or 435/789-4316; fax 435/789-8513; www.hatchriver.com); and **Dinosaur River Expeditions** (② **800/345-7238** or 435/781-0717; www. dinoadv.com). Prices start at about $75 for a 1-day trip. A complete list of authorized river-running companies is available from monument headquarters (see "Information," under "Essentials," above).

FISHING You'll catch mostly catfish in the Green and Yampa rivers, although there are also some trout. Several endangered species of fish—including the razorback sucker and humpback chub—must be returned unharmed to the water if caught. You'll need either a Utah or Colorado fishing license (or both), depending on where you plan to fish.

HIKING Because most visitors spend their time at the quarry and along the scenic drives, hikers willing to exert a bit of effort can discover spectacular and dramatic views of the colorful canyons while enjoying an isolated and quiet wilderness experience. The best times for hiking are spring and fall, but even then, hikers should carry at least a gallon of water per person, per day.

In addition to several developed trails, experienced backcountry hikers with the appropriate maps can explore miles of unspoiled canyons and rock benches. Ask rangers about the numerous possibilities.

In the Utah section of the park, you'll find extreme solitude along the **Sound of Silence Trail,** a difficult 3-mile hike that leaves Cub Creek Road about 2 miles east of the Dinosaur Quarry. This trail is designed to help you learn how to find your own way in the desert, and is not always easy to follow.

The **Desert Voices Nature Trail,** a self-guided nature trail near the quarry, offers sweeping panoramic views and a section with signs created by kids. This 1½-mile (round-trip) hike is moderately difficult.

Visitors to the Colorado side of the park enjoy the **Cold Desert Trail,** which begins at the headquarters' visitor center. This easy quarter-mile round-trip trail offers a good introduction to the natural history of this arid environment.

Panoramic vistas await visitors on the **Plug Hat Nature Trail,** an easy quarter-mile round-trip hike that introduces you to the interactions between plants and animals in the piñon juniper forest. It's located along the Harpers Corner Scenic Drive.

The very popular **Harpers Corner Trail** 🐾 begins at the end of the Harpers Corner Scenic Drive. This 2-mile round-trip hike is moderately difficult and highly recommended for a magnificent view of the deep river canyons.

CAMPING

The **Green River Campground,** 5 miles east of the Dinosaur Quarry within park boundaries, has 88 RV and tent sites, modern restrooms, drinking water, tables, and fireplaces, but no showers or RV hookups. Park rangers often give campfire talks. Cost is $12 per night; it's open mid-April through September.

Several smaller campgrounds with limited facilities are also available in the park, with fees ranging from nothing to $6; check with the visitor centers.

3 Flaming Gorge National Recreation Area ★/★

41 miles N of Vernal, 210 miles E of Salt Lake City

Tucked away in the far northeast corner of Utah and stretching up into Wyoming is **Flaming Gorge National Recreation Area,** one of the region's most scenic areas and a wonderful place for outdoor recreation. A dam was built on the Green River for flood control, water storage, and the generation of electricity, but a wonderful side effect was the creation of a huge and gorgeous lake—some 91 miles long, with more than 300 miles of shoreline—that has become one of the prime fishing and boating destinations of the region.

Here you'll find some of the best fishing in the West, well over 100 miles of hiking and mountain-biking trails, and hundreds of camp and picnic sites. It's a boater's paradise where you'll see everything from kayaks and canoes to ski and fishing boats to pontoons to gigantic houseboats with everything on board (including the kitchen sink).

Named by Major John Wesley Powell during his exploration of the Green and Colorado rivers in 1869, Flaming Gorge has a rugged, wild beauty that comes alive when the rising or setting sun paints the red rocks surrounding the lake with a fiery, brilliant palette. It's a land of clear blue water, colorful rocks, tall cliffs, dark forests, hot summer sun, and cold winter wind. It'll take more than a dam to tame Flaming Gorge.

ESSENTIALS

Flaming Gorge National Recreation Area lies in the northeast corner of Utah, crossing into the southwest corner of Wyoming. The dam and main visitor center, in the southeast section of the national recreation area, are 41 miles north of Vernal (210 miles east of Salt Lake City via U.S. 40).

GETTING THERE   From Vernal and other points south, take U.S. 191 north to its intersection with Utah 44 at the southern edge of the reservoir. U.S. 191 goes up the east side of the reservoir, leading to the dam and the community of Dutch John; Utah 44 goes around the reservoir on the west side, eventually ending at the village of Manila. Both of these towns offer accommodations, restaurants, fuel, and other services.

From I-80 in Wyoming, follow U.S. 191 south around the reservoir's east side to the dam; or Wyo. 530 and Utah highways 43 and 44 to Manila and the west and south sides of the reservoir.

INFORMATION/VISITOR CENTER   The recreation area is administered by the Ashley National Forest. For information, contact the **District Ranger,** Flaming Gorge National Recreation Area, USDA Forest Service, Box 279, Manila, UT 84046 (© **435/784-3445;** fax 435/781-5295; www.fs.fed.us/r4/ashley). The **Intermountain Natural History Association,** 1291 E. U.S. 40, Vernal, UT 84078 (© **800/845-3466;** www.dinosaurnature.com), sells maps, books, and other publications.

The **Flaming Gorge Dam Visitor Center** (© **435/885-3135**), along U.S. 191 on the east side of the recreation area, is open daily year-round (8am to 6pm in summer, 10am to 4pm in winter), except New Year's Day, Thanksgiving, and

Christmas. Here you'll find information on the geology, history, flora, and fauna of the area; the construction of the dam; and facilities and recreation possibilities.

FEES & REGULATIONS   Entry to the recreation area is $2 for 1 day or $5 for up to 16 days. Administered by the U.S. Forest Service, regulations here are based mostly on common sense, and are aimed at preserving water quality and protecting the forest and historic sites. Utah and Wyoming fishing and boating regulations apply in those states' sections of the recreation area, and the appropriate fishing licenses are required. Dogs are allowed on hiking trails but are not permitted in buildings and should be leashed at all times.

SEASONS/AVOIDING THE CROWDS   As one would expect, summer is the busy season at this major boating destination, when both the air and water are at their warmest. This is the best time to come for watersports, and with elevations from 5,600 feet to over 8,000 feet, it never gets as hot here as it does in many other parts of Utah. Although summer is the busiest time of year, this remains a relatively undiscovered destination, and you will likely have no trouble finding campsites, lodging, or boat rentals. Hikers will enjoy the area in fall. During the cold, snowy winter, this is a popular snowshoeing, cross-country skiing, and ice-fishing destination.

EXPLORING FLAMING GORGE BY CAR

Numerous viewpoints are situated along U.S. 191 and Utah 44 in the Utah section of Flaming Gorge; especially dramatic is the **Red Canyon Overlook** on the southern edge, where a rainbow of colors adorns 1,000-foot-tall cliffs. Another great overlook is **Dowd Mountain.** In Wyoming, highways are further from the lake, offering few opportunities to see the river and its canyons.

 Sheep Creek Canyon, south of Manila on the western side, has been designated a special geological area by the Forest Service because of its dramatically twisted and upturned rocks. A mostly paved 11-mile loop road cuts off from Utah 44, offering a half-hour tour of this beautiful, narrow canyon, with its lavish display of rocks that have eroded into intricate patterns, a process that began with the uplifting of the Uinta Mountains millions of years ago. This loop may be closed in winter; check at the visitor center before heading out.

OUTDOOR PURSUITS

BIKING   A number of mountain-biking trails provide splendid views of the recreation area's scenery, especially in the Utah section. Bikes are permitted in most of Flaming Gorge and adjacent Ashley National Forest, except in the High Uintas Wilderness, where all wheeled vehicles are prohibited. Bikes are also restricted, from Memorial Day to Labor Day, on a section of the Little Hole National Recreation Trail along the Green River below the dam, due to very heavy use by anglers and hikers. Keep in mind that mountain bikers here often share trails with hikers, horses, and four-wheelers. A free mountain-biking brochure is available at visitor centers.

 For a scenic and fairly easy ride, try the 5-mile one-way **Red Canyon Rim Trail.** This single track follows the south rim of the canyon, providing terrific views of the lake 1,700 feet below. Deer and elk are frequently seen in the forested areas. Watch also for interpretive signs on area wildlife and the ecosystem. Trailheads and parking are located at Red Canyon Visitor Center, Red Canyon Lodge, and Greendale Overlook.

 Death Valley Trail, a moderately difficult 15-mile round-trip ride, offers good views of the Uinta Mountains and ends with a fine view of the lake from the top of Sheep Creek Hill. The trailhead is located along Utah 44, south of Manila, at milepost 16.5.

Rentals of full-suspension mountain bikes are available at **Red Canyon Lodge** (© 435/889-3759) at rates of $10 for 1 hour, $20 for a half day, and $35 for a full day. The lodge also sponsors a mountain-bike festival each year in early August.

BOATING & HOUSEBOATING   Boaters get to enjoy a unique perspective of some memorable scenery, with magnificent fiery red canyons surrounding the lake in the Utah section, and the wide-open Wyoming badlands farther north.

Three marinas on **Lake Flaming Gorge** provide boat rentals, fuel, launching ramps, and boating and fishing supplies. **Cedar Springs Marina** (© 435/889-3795; www.cedarspringsmarina.com) is located 2 miles west of Flaming Gorge Dam; **Lucerne Valley Marina** (© 435/784-3483; www.flaminggorge.com) is on the west side of the lake, 7 miles east of Manila; and **Buckboard Marina** (© 307/875-6927) is also on the west side of the lake, off Wyo. 530, 22 miles north of Manila.

Nine boat ramps serve those who bring their own craft; boat and water-ski rentals are available at all three marinas. Although types of boats and

> **Impressions**
> The river enters the range by a flaring, brilliant red gorge, that may be seen from the north a score of miles away . . . We name it Flaming Gorge.
> —Explorer Major John Wesley Powell, May 26, 1869

costs vary, a 14-foot fishing boat with a small outboard motor usually costs about $90 per day, an 18-foot ski boat with a powerful outboard motor costs about $220 per day, and a 24-foot pontoon boat with a 50-horsepower outboard motor will cost about $200 per day. Partial day rentals are also available. At Lucerne Valley Marina, a 36-foot houseboat costs about $650 for 3 nights during the summer, with discounts in spring and fall. For all boat rentals, life jackets are included but fuel is extra.

Nonmotorized boating is permitted on a 20-acre private lake at Red Canyon Lodge (p. 190), where you can rent canoes, rowboats, and paddleboats. Rates are $8 for 1 hour, $15 for a half day, and $25 for a full day.

FISHING   You might want to bring along a muscular friend if you plan to fish Lake Flaming Gorge, which is becoming famous as a place to catch record-breaking trout, such as the 51-pound, 8-ounce lake (Mackinaw) trout caught in 1988; the 26-pound, 2-ounce rainbow caught in 1979; and the 33-pound, 10-ounce German brown caught in 1977. You'll see other cold-water species such as smallmouth bass and kokanee salmon. Fishing is popular year-round, although ice-fishermen are warned to make sure the ice is strong enough to hold them.

Cedar Springs and Lucerne Valley marinas (see "Boating & Houseboating," above) offer a variety of fishing guide services. Typical rates for one or two people in a guided trip aboard a 24-foot sport-fishing boat are $250 for 4 hours, including fishing gear but not fishing licenses. Also providing guided fishing trips on the lake, in a 28-foot sport-fishing boat, with state-of-the-art fish-finding and GPS equipment, is Bruce Parker of **Conquest Expeditions** ★★, P.O. Box 487, Manila, UT 84046 (© 435/784-3370; www.conquestexpeditions.com). His rates for a 4-hour fishing trip, with all equipment (but not fishing licenses), are $225 for one or two people and $325 for three or four people. Rates for an 8-hour fishing trip are $400 for one or two people, $500 for three or four.

Moments   Wildlife in Abundance

Flaming Gorge is one of the best places in Utah to see a wide variety of wildlife. Boaters should watch for osprey, peregrine falcons, swifts, and swallows along the cliffs. Bighorn sheep are sometimes spotted clambering on the rocky cliffs on the north side of the lake in spring and early summer. On land, be on the lookout for pronghorn antelope year-round along the west side of the lake, particularly in Lucerne Valley and in the campground. Hikers on the Little Hole National Recreation Trail should keep their eyes peeled for a variety of birds, including bald eagles in winter.

Trout fishing on the Green River below the dam is also outstanding. **Flaming Gorge Recreation Services,** based in Dutch John (© 435/885-3191; www. fglodge.com), offers guided fishing trips for one or two people, with rates of about $210 for a half-day float trip; $340 for a full day. A complete list of guides is available at the Flaming Gorge Dam Visitor Center.

You'll also find two private stocked lakes at **Red Canyon Lodge** (p. 190), one with a fully accessible fishing pier, and both open to catch and release fishing only. No state fishing license is needed, but a Red Canyon Lodge permit is required (check at the lodge office). There is also a free kids' fishing pond in front of the lodge's restaurant. Red Canyon Lodge offers on-site fly-fishing instruction (private lessons from $25), as well as a multi-day fly-fishing school (call for details).

HIKING   Many of the trails here offer spectacular, scenic views of the reservoir and its colorful canyons. Remember, though, that in most cases you'll be sharing the trail with mountain bikers, and in some cases horses and four-wheel-drive vehicles as well.

The **Red Canyon Rim Trail** runs 5 miles (one-way) from the Red Canyon Visitor Center to the Greendale Rest Area, accessible from either of those points or at Green's Lake or Canyon Rim campgrounds. The trail wanders through a forest of Douglas fir and pine, with stops along the canyon rim providing outstanding views of the lake far below (see also "Biking," above).

For an easy 3-mile round-trip hike to an overlook offering a fine view of the lake, try the **Bootleg Trail,** which starts just off U.S. 191 opposite Firefighters Memorial Campground, 3 miles south of the dam.

One trail popular with hikers is the **Little Hole National Recreation Trail,** which runs about 7 miles from the dam spillway downstream to Little Hole, where you'll find fishing platforms and picnic areas. The trail is easy to moderate and offers splendid vistas of the Green River, which appears to be a mere ribbon of emerald when seen from the cliffs above. This is a good trail for birders, who may spot osprey in summer and bald eagles in winter.

Hikers can also use the mountain-biking trails listed above. A free hiking-trails brochure is available at the visitor centers.

HORSEBACK RIDING   Many of the more than 100 miles of trails in Flaming Gorge are open to riders. Guided rides are available from **Red Canyon Stables** at Red Canyon Lodge (p. 190), with prices starting at $12 for a 1-hour ride and $45 for a half day. Rates for children under 12 are about 15% less; children must be at least 6 years old to go on rides of one or more hours. Children of any age can take stable rides for $7.95, which includes a souvenir photo. Overnight backcountry trips are also offered, starting at $150 per person per day.

SWIMMING   Sometimes you've just got to dive right in, even though the water is pretty cold. Lake Flaming Gorge has two designated swimming areas: Sunny Cove, just north of the dam, and Lucerne Beach, a mile west of Lucerne Campground. Neither has a lifeguard.

WINTER SPORTS   Ice-fishing is popular, but check with rangers first for ice conditions. Also popular from mid-January until the snow melts are cross-country skiing, snowshoeing (an excellent way to see wildlife), and snowmobiling. At Red Canyon Lodge, you can rent snowshoes for $5 per hour, $10 per half day, or $15 per day. Flaming Gorge Lodge rents complete cross-country ski packages for $10 per day and snowmobiles starting at $120 per day. See p. 190 for the lodges' contact information.

MAN-MADE ATTRACTIONS
FLAMING GORGE DAM & POWER PLANT
Completed in 1963 at a cost of $50 million for the dam and another $65 million for the power plant, Flaming Gorge is part of the Colorado River Storage Project, which also includes Glen Canyon Dam on the Colorado River along the Arizona–Utah border, Navajo Dam on the San Juan River in New Mexico, and a series of three dams on the Gunnison River in Colorado. At full capacity, the lake is 91 miles long and holds almost 4 million acre-feet of water. The dam, constructed in an arch shape for strength, is 1,285 feet long and stands some 450 feet tall; its three turbine generators can produce 152,000 kilowatts of electricity, enough to take care of the needs of 210,000 people.

The dam and power plant are open for free guided tours daily year-round (except Thanksgiving, Christmas, and New Year's Day). The total round-trip walking distance is just under half a mile. Check at the visitor center for the hours and times of the hour-long guided tours. You'll walk along the crest of the dam, then take an elevator ride to the power plant below, where you'll see the inner workings of the hydroelectric plant, with its huge transformers, generators, and turbines.

SWETT RANCH HISTORIC SITE
This homestead, listed on the National Register of Historic Places, was constructed by Oscar Swett starting in 1909, and contains two cabins, a five-room house, a meat house, a root cellar, sheds, a granary, and a barn, built and improved upon over a period of 58 years. Swett and his wife, Emma, raised nine children here, running the 397-acre ranch using only horse and human muscle power, before selling the property in 1968. From Utah 44, take U.S. 191 north for a half mile and turn west (left) onto Forest Road 158, which you follow 1½ miles to the ranch. The unpaved Forest Road is muddy when wet, and not recommended for large RVs or trailers at any time. The ranch is open for guided tours only, Thursday through Monday from Memorial Day to Labor Day only (check with the visitor center for hours). Admission is free. Allow about an hour.

CAMPING
U.S. Forest Service campgrounds are located throughout Flaming Gorge Recreation Area, and they range from primitive sites to modern facilities with showers (open in summer only) and flush toilets, but no RV hookups. Some are open year-round, others in summer only. Most sites cost $13 to $16. The more developed (and expensive) sites, including our favorite campground here, Deer Run, include use of the showers (those camping in the cheap spots get to pay $3 for a shower). Campsite reservations are available through the **National Recreation**

Reservation Service (✆ **877/444-6777** or 518/885-3639; TDD 877/833-6777; www.reserveusa.com). Dispersed forest camping (with no facilities) is free; check with forest service personnel for suggested locations. RV dump stations are located in several locations in the recreation area (check at the visitor center).

Commercial campgrounds with full RV hookups are located in Vernal (see section 2, earlier in this chapter). In Manila, you'll find a **KOA campground** (✆ **800/562-3254** or 435/784-3184), open from mid-April through mid-October, that charges from $19 to $25 for tent sites and $25 to $31 for RV sites. It also has cabins at $35 to $45 per night.

WHERE TO STAY

In addition to the lodging suggestions below, see the "Where to Stay" section in Vernal, earlier in the chapter.

Flaming Gorge Lodge   A location close to everything you'll want to do makes this well-maintained property a good choice for those seeking a modern motel room or a one-bedroom condominium. Motel rooms come with two double beds and an optional roll-away; condo units contain one queen-size bed, a single, and a hide-a-bed, plus a fully equipped kitchen. Facilities include a restaurant that serves three meals daily, a gas station, raft and mountain-bike rentals, a liquor and convenience store, and a fly and tackle shop. Guided fishing trips on the Green River are available, and the lodge offers personal watercraft rentals in the summer and snowmobile rentals in the winter (p. 189).

155 Greendale, U.S. 191 (4 miles south of Flaming Gorge Dam), Dutch John, UT 84023-9702. ✆ **435/889-3773.** Fax 435/889-3788. www.fglodge.com. 45 units. Mar–Oct $73–$117 double; Nov–Feb $67–$97 double. AE, DISC, MC, V. **Amenities:** Activities desk. *In room:* A/C, TV/VCR, kitchen in larger units.

Red Canyon Lodge 🌟🌟   A variety of delightful cabins, including some handsome new ones built in 2003, offer a range of possibilities. All have private bathrooms, two queen-size beds, a separate living room, mini fridges, limited cooking facilities, vaulted ceilings, and covered porches. Some also have free-standing wood stoves (free firewood provided), kitchenettes, and custom wood furniture. Lower-priced units have showers only; the more expensive rooms have shower/tub combos. The lodge offers two private lakes plus a kids' fishing pond, tackle shop, and fly-fishing instruction; mountain-bike rentals; hiking and mountain-biking trails; horseback rides (p. 188); a restaurant (see below); and a convenience store.

790 Red Canyon Rd. (turn off Utah 44 at milepost 3.5), Dutch John, UT 84023. ✆ **435/889-3759.** Fax 435/889-5106. www.redcanyonlodge.com. 28 units. $95–$120 double. AE, DISC, MC, V. Dogs allowed with prior approval. **Amenities:** Activities desk.

DINING

Red Canyon Lodge Dining Room AMERICAN   You'll find a classic mountain-lodge atmosphere here, along with views of tall pines and a small lake. This place is popular among locals as well as visitors. Our top choices here include the wild boar spare ribs and the elk medallions with béarnaise sauce. The menu also features steaks, chicken (try the mildly spicy Szechuan chicken pasta), fish, and slow-roasted prime rib. There are also nightly fine dining specials, such as the broiled salmon fillet with a hollandaise sauce. You'll also find standard American breakfasts, and burgers and sandwiches at lunch. Full liquor service is available.

In Red Canyon Lodge. ✆ **435/889-3759.** Reservations accepted for large parties only. Main courses $4–$10 breakfast and lunch, $8–$20 dinner. AE, DISC, MC, V. Apr to mid-Oct daily 7am–10pm; mid-Oct to Mar Fri 4–9pm, Sat 8am–9pm, Sun 8am–4pm.

10

Utah's Dixie & the Colorful Southwest Corner

Small lakes and big rocks, golf courses and ski areas, Shakespeare and the latest special effects—you'll find it all in the southwest corner of Utah, dubbed "Color Country" by the locals for its numerous and colorful rock formations. In addition to all the attractions, another reason to visit is the warm winter weather: The region's largest city, St. George, and its immediate surroundings are known as "Utah's Dixie" for the area's mild climate as well as its previous life as a Civil War–era cotton growing region. Color Country is a terrific winter playground; there's no need to ever put away the golf clubs or swimsuits in this neighborhood.

You'll find plenty to see and do in this colorful corner of Utah. Step back more than a hundred years at Mormon leader Brigham Young's winter home or cheer on the Dixie State College Rebels football team. Our favorite stops are outdoors: the rugged red rock cliffs at Snow Canyon State Park, the ruddy sands of Coral Pink Sand Dunes State Park, and the panoramic views from Cedar Breaks National Monument. This area is also a good base for those visiting the area's national parks, including Grand Canyon (pick up a *Frommer's Grand Canyon* guide), Great Basin, and Zion (see chapter 11).

This region isn't only a warm-weather destination, though. Its range of elevations means you can often lounge around the pool in the morning and build a snowman that same afternoon. From the scorching desert at St. George, it's only 74 miles—and almost 7,500 feet up—to the cool mountain forest at Cedar Breaks National Monument. Home to a variety of scenic and recreation areas (you'll even find ski resorts here), a surprising number of historic attractions, and some excellent performing arts events (such as the Utah Shakespearean Festival in Cedar City), this area also serves as the gateway to several of the area's spectacular national parks.

Despite the number of attractions, don't expect a lot of super-fancy facilities. Many of the motels and restaurants are somewhat basic—adequate, but not exciting. Keep in mind that distances are long—"nearby" can mean 100 miles away—and services may be far apart. But this is a starkly beautiful part of the American West, still very much like it was more than 100 years ago, and is well worth a visit.

1 Getting Outdoors in Utah's Color Country

This is Utah's playground, a year-round mecca for hikers, mountain bikers, golfers, boaters, anglers, and anybody else who just wants to get outdoors. Among the top spots for experiencing nature at its best are Cedar Breaks National Monument, a high-mountain oasis of towering pines and firs, with wildflowers galore; and state parks such as Snow Canyon, Coral Pink Sand Dunes, and Quail Creek.

The best seasons for outdoor activities here are based on elevation. In St. George and other lowlands, spring and fall are best, winter's okay, and summer is awful, because temperatures soar well over 100°F (38°C). However, not everyone says no to St. George in summer: Its desert climate makes it the **golfing** capital of Utah. The Sunbrook is considered the state's best course, with a challenging layout and spectacular views of the White Hills, but you can also stay a week in St. George and play a different course each day. On the other side of the seasonal coin, don't try to drive up the mountains to Cedar Breaks until June at the earliest or mid-October at the latest; the roads will be closed by snow.

A good way to see this part of Utah is on foot. **Hiking** trails abound throughout the Dixie and Fishlake national forests north of St. George. But you'll discover several of the best trails in state parks, particularly Snow Canyon State Park near St. George, and in the nearby national parks.

Biking here generally means **mountain biking.** This is true even for those who confine most of their riding to city streets, because you never know when you're going to discover that great little trail turning off into the red rock desert or up into alpine meadows. The best mountain biking is at Brian Head Resort. Both road and mountain bikes can take you to beautiful areas in and around Snow Canyon State Park near St. George.

For an area with so much desert, there's a lot of **boating** here: Utahns have created reservoirs to provide the desert and its residents with drinking and irrigation water. The best boating is at Quail Creek State Park near St. George; but for a bit more solitude try the relatively undeveloped Gunlock State Park, near Quail Creek State Park, or Minersville State Park, west of Beaver. The top **fishing** hole in these parts is at Quail Creek State Park, but plenty of smaller lakes and hidden streams are located in the national forests.

Off-road vehicles can simply be a means to get to an isolated fishing stream or hiking trail, or part of the adventure itself. The old mining and logging roads in the national forests are great for four-wheel exploring. Visitors with dune buggies will want to challenge the shifting dunes at Coral Pink Sand Dunes State Park, just outside Kanab.

An abundance of **wildlife** makes its home in this part of the state. Sure, you'll see deer, squirrels, chipmunks, and other furry creatures at Cedar Breaks National Monument and the area's national parks, but there's also animal life in the desert, including our favorites: the luminescent scorpions at Coral Pink Sand Dunes State Park and the Gila monster at Snow Canyon State Park, also home to numerous songbirds.

It may be hot down in the desert, but there's plenty of snow up on those mountaintops, and the **skiing** is great at Brian Head Resort. In winter, cross-country skiers and snowshoers will want to head to nearby Cedar Breaks National Monument after the snow closes the roads to cars.

2 St. George: Gateway to Southern Utah's Natural Wonders

120 miles NE of Las Vegas, Nevada, 305 miles SW of Salt Lake City

In the fall of 1861, Brigham Young sent 309 families to establish a cotton-growing community in the semi-arid Virgin River Valley; today, St. George has almost 50,000 inhabitants. Life in St. George, known as one of Utah's more conservative communities, is still strongly influenced by the Mormon church. At an

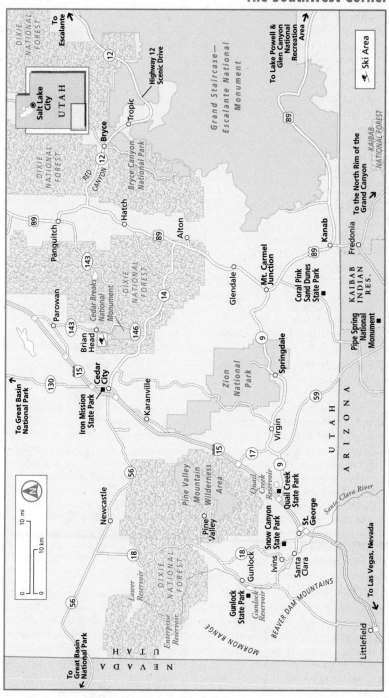

elevation of 2,800 feet, the town is also a winter home to many snowbirds—not the feathered variety, but humans who annually flee the snow and cold of more northern climes for this region's mild winters. Despite the climate, this desert city appears quite green, with tree-lined streets and lovely grassy areas. You'll find more than a half-dozen golf courses, along with recreational and cultural facilities to suit every taste.

St. George is also the gateway to some of the most spectacular scenery in the West. Zion, Bryce, and Grand Canyon national parks are within relatively easy driving distance, as are Cedar Breaks and Pipe Springs national monuments and Snow Canyon, Gunlock, and Quail Creek state parks. Depending on your itinerary, St. George may be the largest town that you stop in en route to Lake Powell and Glen Canyon National Recreation Area, Capitol Reef National Park, and the prehistoric Indian sites in the Four Corners area.

ESSENTIALS

GETTING THERE   The closest major airport is **McCarran International Airport,** in Las Vegas (© **702/261-5211;** www.mccarran.com). Most major airlines fly into McCarran, where you can rent a car and drive the 120 miles northeast on I-15 to St. George. The **St. George Shuttle** (© **800/933-8320** or 435/628-8320; www.stgshuttle.com) provides daily van service to and from the Las Vegas airport ($25 each way), and also offers transportation between St. George and Salt Lake City ($55 one-way, $105 round-trip); reservations are required.

St. George Airport, located on a bluff on the west side of the city, is served by **Skywest Airlines** (© **800/453-9417** or 435/634-3000; www.skywest.com).

St. George is on I-15. Take exit 6 (Bluff St.) or 8 (St. George Blvd.).

VISITOR INFORMATION   Before your trip, contact **Utah's Southwest Color Country,** P.O. Box 1550, St. George, UT 84771-1550 (© **800/233-8824** or 435/628-4171). A good website is www.utahsdixie.com. When you get into town, you'll find an information center operated by the **St. George Area Chamber of Commerce** in the historic Pioneer Courthouse, 97 E. St. George Blvd. (© **435/628-1658**). It's open Monday through Friday from 9am to 5pm, and Saturday from 10am to 2pm.

For information on the state and national parks in the area, as well as Dixie National Forest and land administered by the Bureau of Land Management, stop by the **Interagency Office and Visitor Center,** 345 E. Riverside Dr. (© **435/688-3246;** www.fs.fed.us/r4; www.ut.blm.gov). This is a good place to ask questions about the area's public lands, get trail recommendations, and pick up backcountry permits for the Grand Canyon. A variety of free brochures are available; and maps, books, posters, and videos are for sale. To get there, take I-15 exit 6 and turn east. The center is open Monday through Friday 7:45am to 5pm and Saturday 9am to 5pm; closed Sundays.

GETTING AROUND   The street grid system is centered on the point at which Tabernacle Street (running east-west) crosses Main Street (running north-south), with numbered streets increasing in each direction by hundreds. St. George Boulevard takes the place of 100 North, Bluff Street runs along a bluff at the western edge of the city, I-15 cuts through in a northeast direction (from exit 6 at the south end of Bluff Street to exit 8 at the east end of St. George Boulevard), and River Road lies at the eastern edge, becoming Red Cliffs Road north of St. George Boulevard. Other than that, the system stays true to the grid.

Car-rental agencies with offices in St. George include **ABC,** 33 N. 400 East St. (© **435/628-7355**); **Avis,** St. George Municipal Airport (© **435/627-2002;**

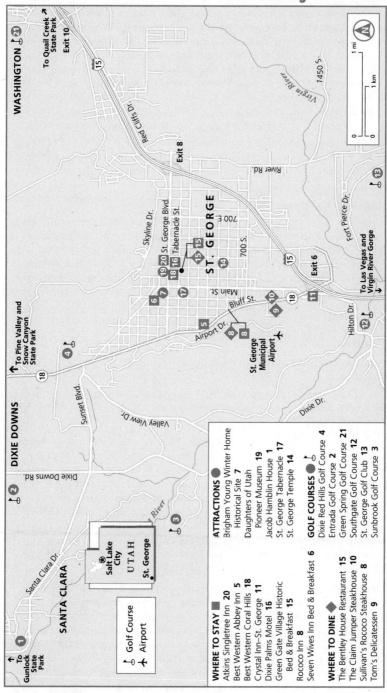

St. George & Environs

WASHINGTON

To Quail Creek State Park
Exit 10

To Pine Valley and Snow Canyon State Park

DIXIE DOWNS

Dixie Downs Rd.

SANTA CLARA

Santa Clara Dr.

Sunset Blvd.

Valley View Dr.

Dixie Dr.

Red Cliffs Dr.

Skyline Dr.

St. George Blvd.

Tabernacle St.

ST. GEORGE

700 E.

700 S.

Main St.

Bluff St.

Airport Dr.

St. George Municipal Airport

River Rd.

Fort Pierce Dr.

Hilton Dr.

Virgin River

1450 S.

Exit 8

Exit 6

Exit 18

To Las Vegas and Virgin River Gorge

To Gunlock State Park

Salt Lake City
UTAH
St. George

Golf Course
Airport

1 mi
1 km

ATTRACTIONS
Brigham Young Winter Home
  Historical Site **7**
Daughters of Utah
  Pioneer Museum **19**
Jacob Hamblin House **1**
St. George Tabernacle **17**
St. George Temple **14**

GOLF COURSES
Dixie Red Hills Golf Course **4**
Entrada Golf Course **2**
Green Spring Golf Course **21**
Southgate Golf Course **12**
St. George Golf Club **13**
Sunbrook Golf Course **3**

WHERE TO STAY
Atkins Singletree Inn **20**
Best Western Abbey Inn **5**
Best Western Coral Hills **18**
Crystal Inn–St. George **11**
Dixie Palms Motel **16**
Green Gate Village Historic
  Bed & Breakfast **15**
Rococo Inn **8**
Seven Wives Inn Bed & Breakfast **6**

WHERE TO DINE
The Bentley House Restaurant **15**
The Claim Jumper Steakhouse **10**
Sullivan's Rococo Steakhouse **8**
Tom's Delicatessen **9**

195

www.avis.com); **Budget,** St. George Municipal Airport (© **435/673-6825;** www.
budgetrentacar.com); **Enterprise,** 652 E. St. George Blvd. (© **435/634-1556**);
and **Hertz,** at St. George Municipal Airport (© **435/652-9941**) and at 166 W.
1700 South St. (© **435/674-4789;** www.hertz.com).

For a taxi, call **Quality Cab** (© **435/656-5222**).

Free on-street parking is available in much of the city, and many of the streets
are tree-lined and shady.

FAST FACTS   One of the larger hospitals in this part of the state is **Dixie
Regional Medical Center,** 544 S. 400 East (© **435/634-4000**), which provides
24-hour emergency care. The **post office** is located at 180 N. Main St. (© **800/
275-8777** for hours and other information). The regional **newspaper** is the
Daily Spectrum.

DISCOVERING MORMON HISTORY IN & AROUND ST. GEORGE

Because the Church of Jesus Christ of Latter-day Saints was the primary driving
force in the settlement of St. George, it should come as no surprise that most of
the sightseeing in town is church-related. At the town's historic buildings, staffed
by knowledgeable church members, you'll learn about the church as well as the
specific sites; expect a little sales pitch on the benefits of Christianity in general
and the Mormon faith in particular.

Brigham Young Winter Home Historical Site   Church leader Brigham
Young was one of St. George's first snowbirds. He escaped the Salt Lake City
cold during the last few winters of his life by coming south to this house. In
addition to its obvious religious importance, this home is a handsome example
of how the well-to-do of the late 19th century lived. Allow about a half hour for
the guided tour.

67 W. 200 North. © 435/673-5181. Free guided tours. Memorial Day–Labor Day daily 9am–6pm; rest of
year daily 9am–5pm. From I-15 exit 8, head west on St. George Blvd., turn right (north) onto Main St., and
turn left (west) onto 200 North.

Daughters of Utah Pioneer Museum   This museum contains an eclectic
collection of items that belonged to the pioneers who settled this area more than
100 years ago. There's some furniture—including a bed used by Brigham Young,
plus spinning wheels, an 1894 loom, guns, tools, musical instruments, and other
relics from bygone days. Historic photos, mostly of pioneer families, are on display, and copies are available for purchase. Guided tours are given by volunteers
from the Daughters of Utah Pioneers. Allow at least a half hour.

145 N. 100 East. © 435/628-7274. Free admission; donations accepted. Mon–Sat 10am–5pm. Closed second Mon of Dec to second week of Jan. From I-15 exit 8, head west on St. George Blvd. and turn right (north)
at 100 East.

Jacob Hamblin Home ⭐   This stone-and-pine house, built in 1862, is closer
to what you'd think of as a pioneer home than most of the refined houses of St.
George, and it's typical of pioneer homes throughout the West—except for one
aspect that is definitively Mormon: It has two identical bedrooms, one for each of
Hamblin's wives. You'll also notice that the dining table is set in typical Mormon
fashion, with plates upside down and chairs facing away from the table to facil-
itate kneeling for before-meal prayers. The guided tour lasts about a half hour.

Santa Clara Blvd. and Hamblin Dr., Santa Clara. © 435/673-5181. Free guided tours. Memorial Day–Labor
Day daily 9am–6pm; rest of year daily 9am–5pm. From St. George, go 3 miles west on U.S. 91 to the community of Santa Clara; watch for sign.

Pine Valley Chapel   This handsome white chapel, still used by worshippers today, was built in 1868 by Ebenezer Bryce (for whom Bryce Canyon National Park was named) and Lorenzo and Erastus Snow (for whom Snow Canyon State Park was named). The settlers of the Pine Valley logging and saw-milling community wanted to build a church that would also function as a school and community building. Bryce was approached to design it, and because of his experience as a shipbuilder, he laid out the structure as an upside-down boat. Each of the walls was constructed flat on the ground, then lifted up and tied at the corners with strips of rawhide. The chapel was constructed of local pine and ponderosa, and set on a foundation of granite and red limestone.

Pine Valley, about 40 min. from St. George (no street address; see directions at the end of this listing to locate the chapel). ✆ **435/673-5181** for information. Free guided tours. Memorial Day–Labor Day Mon–Sat 11am–5pm; Sun 1–5pm. Closed rest of year. From St. George, go north on Utah 18 to Central and head east on Forest Road 035.

St. George Tabernacle ⚐   This is the most beautiful building in St. George— an excellent example of fine old-world craftsmanship, from the hand-quarried red stone walls to the intricate interior woodwork. Its craftsmen finished pine, which was all they had, to look like exotic hardwoods and even marble. Completed in 1876 after 13 years of work, the Tabernacle served as a house of worship and town meeting hall. During the 1880s, when a nearby silver strike brought many Catholics to the area, the Tabernacle was used for a Roman Catholic high mass led by a Roman Catholic priest, but with music from the liturgy sung by the local Mormon choir—in Latin. Today, the Tabernacle functions as a community center, presenting free weekly concerts and other cultural events (see "St. George After Dark," later in the chapter). The guided tour takes about half an hour.

18 S. Main St. at Tabernacle St. ✆ **435/673-5181**. Free guided tours. Summer daily 9am–6pm; winter daily 9am–5pm. From I-15 exit 8, head west on St. George Blvd. and turn left at Main St.

St. George Temple   Completed in 1877, St. George Temple was the first Mormon temple in Utah, and is the world's oldest still in use today. The majestic white temple is not open to the general public, but you can walk among the beautiful gardens and stop at the visitor center south of the temple for a tour of the center's exhibits and a multimedia program on the beliefs of the Church of Jesus Christ of Latter-day Saints.

440 S. 300 East. ✆ **435/673-5181**. Temple not open to the public; free guided tours of visitor center exhibits. Daily 9am–9pm. From I-15 exit 8, head west on St. George Blvd. to 200 East, turn left (south) and go about 6 blocks.

SNOW CANYON STATE PARK

Among Utah's most scenic state parks, **Snow Canyon** ⚐⚐⚐ offers an abundance of opportunities for photography and hiking. The park is surrounded by rock cliffs and walls of Navajo sandstone in shades of red, layered with white and black from ancient lava flows. Hike the trails and discover shifting sand dunes, mysterious lava caves, colorful desert plants, and a variety of rock formations. You'll also encounter an attractive cactus garden and several ancient petroglyphs (ask park rangers for directions).

Because the summers here are hot—well over 100°F (38°C)—the best time to visit is any other time. Winters are mild, but nights can be chilly. Spring and fall are usually perfect weather-wise, and therefore the busiest. By the way, don't come looking for snow—Snow Canyon was named for pioneers Lorenzo and Erastus Snow, who discovered the canyon.

ESSENTIALS

GETTING THERE   The park is located 11 miles northwest of St. George, off Utah 18.

INFORMATION, FEES & REGULATIONS   For a copy of the park's brochure, contact **Snow Canyon State Park,** 1002 Snow Canyon Drive, Ivins, UT 84738 (© **435/628-2255**). Day-use fee is $5. As in most state parks, dogs are welcome, even on trails, but must be leashed. There is no visitor center here.

OUTDOOR PURSUITS

HIKING   The best way to see Snow Canyon is on foot. Several short trails make for easy full- or half-day hikes. The **Hidden Piñon Trail** ⊛ is a 1½-mile round-trip self-guided nature trail that wanders among lava rocks, through several canyons, and onto rocky flatlands, offering panoramic views of the surrounding mountains. The trail begins across the highway from the park's campground; you can pick up a brochure at the park office/entrance station. The walk is fairly easy, but allow at least an hour, especially if you're planning to keep an eye out for local vegetation such as Mormon tea, cliffrose, prickly pear cactus, and banana yucca.

An easy three-quarter-mile one-way trail leads to **Johnson Arch.** It begins just south of the campground, passes by the popular rock-climbing wall (see below) and some low sand dunes, and then leads into a small canyon with a view of Johnson Arch (named after pioneer wife Maude Johnson) high above.

Also popular is the **Lava Caves Trail,** a 1½-mile round-trip that starts just north of the campground. The caves are about a half mile along the trail, but watch carefully—it's easy to miss them. The caves were formed from liquid lava, and American Indian tribes have at times occupied the large rooms. Another quarter mile past the caves is the **West Canyon Overlook,** with a breathtaking view into West Canyon.

Several longer and steeper trails lead to spectacular views of the canyons and distant vistas; check with park rangers for details.

MOUNTAIN BIKING   Although bicycling is not allowed on park trails, West Canyon Road is open to mountain biking. The 7-mile round-trip road lies just west of the park; ask park rangers for directions. You can rent bikes at Bicycles Unlimited (p. 199).

ROCK CLIMBING   Climbers love the tall wall of rock on the east side of the road just south of the campground, but it has become so popular that the park has issued a moratorium on bolting. Check with the park office for information.

WILDLIFE WATCHING   You're likely to see cottontail rabbits, ground squirrels, and songbirds; luckier visitors may also spot desert mule deer, bobcats, coyote, kit foxes, eagles, and owls. Although it's unlikely, you may see a desert tortoise (a federally listed threatened species) or Gila monster. Snow Canyon is also home to some rattlesnakes.

CAMPING

The 36-site campground is one of the best in the state. One section has rather closely spaced sites with electric hookups; those not needing electricity can set up camp in delightful little side canyons, surrounded by colorful red rocks and Utah juniper. The views are spectacular no matter where you choose to set up. Facilities include hot showers, modern restrooms, and an RV dump station. Campsites with electricity cost $17, while those without are $14. Reservations (with a $7 nonrefundable reservation fee) are recommended from February through May and September through November; call © **800/322-3770.**

MORE OUTDOOR FUN IN THE ST. GEORGE AREA

In addition to the outdoor opportunities that Snow Canyon State Park offers, there's great hiking, biking, and fishing in the Dixie National Forest and on nearby lands administered by the Bureau of Land Management. For information, contact the Interagency Office (p. 194).

FISHING   Quail Creek and Gunlock state parks (described later in this chapter) are the local fishing holes. For equipment, licenses, and tips on where they're biting, visit **Hurst Ace Hardware & Sports Center,** 160 N. 500 West (© **435/ 673-6141;** www.hurststores.com).

GOLF   Utah's golf capital attracts golfers from around the country to more than a half-dozen public courses, known for their challenging designs, well-maintained fairways and greens, and spectacularly scenic settings. Rates given below are for winter; summer rates are usually lower. The area's best course, in our opinion, is the 18-hole, par-72 **Sunbrook Golf Course,** 2366 W. Sunbrook Dr. (© **435/634-5866**), tops in both design and magnificent scenery. Greens fees are $23.50 for 9 holes and $43 for 18 holes, carts run $5.50 and $11, respectively. Also highly rated, and considered by many to be the area's second-best course, is **Green Spring Golf Course,** 588 N. Green Spring Dr., Washington (© **435/673-7888;** www.greenspringgolfcourse.com), several miles northeast of St. George. Challenging Green Spring is an 18-hole, par-71 course, with fees of $19 for 9 holes and $37 for 18 holes; cart rentals cost $6 and $12, respectively.

Other 18-hole courses include the par-73 **St. George Golf Club,** 2190 S. 1400 East (© **435/634-5854**) and the par-70 **Southgate Golf Course,** 1975 S. Tonaquint Dr. (© **435/628-0000**). Fees at these city-owned courses are $16 for 9 holes and $27 for 18 holes, with an additional $5.50 and $11, respectively, for a cart. The par-72 **Entrada,** 2511 W. Entrada Trail (© **435/674-7500**), is an 18-hole course; greens fees, including cart, are $85. Nine-hole courses in St. George include the par-34 **Dixie Red Hills Golf Course,** 1250 N. 645 West (© **435/634-5852**), charging $16 for 9 holes.

Golfers can often save money by checking with local motels on various lodging/ golf packages (see "Where to Stay," later in this chapter). Several free guides to area golf courses are available at the **St. George Area Chamber of Commerce** (p. 194).

HIKING   Some of the best hiking in the area is at Snow Canyon State Park (p. 198) and in the Dixie National Forest to the north, which has some 200 miles of trails. Check with forest rangers for current trail conditions and be sure to carry detailed maps on any long hikes, especially if you're venturing into the Pine Valley Wilderness Area. Stop at the **Interagency Office and Visitor Center** (p. 194) for maps and details.

MOUNTAIN BIKING & ROAD BIKING   With hundreds of miles of trails in the St. George area, mountain biking has been rapidly gaining in popularity. For information on the best mountain-biking areas, plus maps, mountain-biking trail guides, bike repairs, bike accessories, and rentals, stop at **Bicycles Unlimited,** 90 S. 100 East (© **888/673-4492** or 435/673-4492; www.bicycle sunlimited.com); open Monday through Saturday 8am to 7pm. Top quality mountain bikes rent for $22 for a half day, $32 for a full day; ask about multi-day rates.

A popular road-biking trip is the scenic **24-mile loop** from St. George through Santa Clara, Ivins, and Snow Canyon State Park. The route follows paved roads with narrow shoulders but generally little traffic. Allow 2 to 3 hours.

Head north out of St. George on Bluff Street (Utah 18) and follow it to its intersection with U.S. 91. Turn west (left) and go about 6 miles to the village of Santa Clara, where you can visit the Jacob Hamblin Home (p. 196). From Santa Clara, continue west about a mile before turning north (right); follow the signs to Ivins and the Tuacahn Amphitheater. At Ivins, turn east (right) onto the Snow Canyon Road, following signs for Snow Canyon State Park, where you can easily spend from several hours to several days exploring the red rock formations, lava pools, and sand dunes. From the park, continue east to Utah 18, turn south (right), and pedal back into St. George.

SPECTATOR SPORTS

The Dixie State College Rebels are the ones to root for in St. George. The football, women's volleyball, women's soccer, men's and women's basketball, men's baseball, men's golf, and women's softball teams at this community college are often nationally ranked. You're not likely to have any trouble getting tickets to join the school's 5,500 students in Hansen Stadium or Burns Arena. Tickets cost from $5 to $10 and are available at the Athletic Department offices (© **435/ 652-7525**).

WHERE TO STAY

You'll find a good selection of lodgings in St. George, with a range of facilities and prices. Most are on St. George Boulevard and Bluff Street, within easy walking distance of restaurants and attractions. Summer is the slow season here—people tend to head to the mountains when the temperature hits 115°F (46°C)—so prices are lowest then. High seasons are spring and fall. Golfers should ask about special golf packages.

Reliable chain properties in the area include **Comfort Inn,** 999 E. Skyline Dr. (© **877/577-6740** or 435/628-4271); **Days Inn,** 150 N. 1000 East (© **800/ 527-6543** or 435/673-6123); **Hampton Inn,** 53 N. River Rd. (© **800/ HAMPTON** or 435/652-1200); **Motel 6,** 205 N. 1000 East (© **800/466- 8356** or 435/628-7979); **Quality Inn,** 1165 S. Bluff St. (© **800/231-4488** or 435/628-4481); **Ramada Inn,** 1440 E. St. George Blvd. (© **800/713-9435** or 435/628-2828); **Super 8,** 915 S. Bluff St. (© **800/800-8000** or 435/688- 8383); and **Travelodge,** 175 N. 1000 East (© **800/578-7878** or 435/673-4621).

Room tax adds just under 10% to your lodging bill. Pets are generally not accepted unless otherwise noted.

MODERATE

Atkins Singletree Inn   A few personal touches, such as dried-flower wall decorations and prints depicting area attractions, give this motel a homey feel. There's no restaurant, although several are close by, but rooms have a microwave and refrigerator. Ask about the golf package, which is better than most other deals in the area.

260 E. St. George Blvd., St. George, UT 84770. © **888/224-2254** or 435/673-6161. Fax 435/674-2406. www.singletreeinn.com. 48 units. $50–$62 double; $60–$75 family suite. Rates include deluxe continental breakfast. AE, DC, DISC, MC, V. Small pets accepted, $15 fee. **Amenities:** Outdoor heated pool; Jacuzzi; coin-op laundry. *In room:* A/C, TV, fridge, coffeemaker.

Best Western Abbey Inn   This lovely property has an elegant lobby and spacious, attractively furnished guest rooms. The pool is set in an attractive courtyard. Ten restaurants are located within a block.

1129 S. Bluff St., St. George, UT 84770. © **888/222-3946** or 435/652-1234. Fax 435/652-5950. www. bwabbeyinn.com. 130 units. $75–$95 double. Rates include full breakfast. AE, DC, DISC, MC, V. **Amenities:**

Outdoor heated pool; exercise room; large indoor Jacuzzi; game room; coin-op laundry. *In room:* A/C, TV, fridge, coffeemaker.

Best Western Coral Hills

The well-equipped rooms at the Coral Hills have a king-size bed or one or two queen-size beds, and microwaves. You'll find a putting green, and, if you're here to work, fax and photocopy services.

125 E. St. George Blvd., St. George, UT 84770. ℂ 800/542-7733 or 435/673-4844. Fax 435/673-5352. www.coralhills.com. 98 units. $62–$83 double. Rates include full breakfast buffet. AE, DC, DISC, MC, V. **Amenities:** Large indoor and outdoor heated pools, both with jetted tubs; kid's pool; exercise room. *In room:* A/C, TV, fridge, hair dryer, iron.

Crystal Inn-St. George

This handsome, full-service hotel offers comfortable, contemporary rooms for both business travelers and vacationers. Rooms come complete with computer dataport and voice mail, and some have desks. The outdoor heated pool is set in a tropical garden; the restaurant serves three meals daily, and offers complete liquor service.

1450 S. Hilton Dr., St. George, UT 84770. ℂ 800/662-2525 in Utah, or 435/628-0463. Fax 435/628-1501. www.crystalinns.com. 98 units. $59–$99 double. Rates include full breakfast. AE, DC, DISC, MC, V. Small pets accepted for a $25 fee. **Amenities:** Restaurant (American); outdoor heated pool; 4 tennis courts (lit for night play); Jacuzzi; 2 saunas; small business center. *In room:* A/C, TV, coffeemaker, iron.

Green Gate Village Historic Bed & Breakfast

One of the most delightful lodgings in St. George, this bed-and-breakfast inn is actually 10 separate buildings—all restored pioneer homes from the late 1800s, sitting in their own flower-filled little "village." You'll find genuine antiques plus modern "necessities" such as TVs and VCRs. Most rooms have shower/tub combos, though some have showers only. The Bentley House Restaurant (p. 202) serves generous breakfasts, plus dinner Thursday through Saturday. Children and babies are welcome. Tobacco use of any kind is prohibited.

76 W. Tabernacle St., St. George, UT 84770. ℂ 800/350-6999 or 435/628-6999. Fax 435/628-6989. www.greenegate.com. 15 units. $79–$189 double. Rates include full breakfast. AE, DISC, MC, V. From I-15 exit 8, head west to Main St., turn left (south) 1 block to Tabernacle St., and turn right (west) to Greene Gate Village. **Amenities:** Restaurant (American); small outdoor heated pool; Jacuzzi. *In room:* A/C, TV/VCR.

Seven Wives Inn Bed & Breakfast

There are no polygamists hiding in the attic of Seven Wives Inn anymore—as there were in the 1880s after polygamy was outlawed—but it's fascinating to imagine what things must have been like in those days. Decorated with antiques, mostly Victorian and Eastlake, the inn consists of two historic mansions: the main house, built in 1873, where the polygamists hid; and the President's house next door, a four-square Victorian built 10 years later that played host to many of the LDS Church's early presidents. Each room has a deck or balcony, and private bathroom; most units have VCRs, four have a functioning fireplace, and five have two-person whirlpool tubs—one is installed in a Model T Ford! There's a separate handicapped-accessible cottage furnished with replica pioneer furniture, an extra-large shower, a two-person whirlpool, a queen bed, and a gas fireplace. Bicycles are available for guest use; and smoking is not permitted.

The inn hosts music events and murder mysteries; and offers lunch, dessert, and high English-style tea ($8 to $15), plus romantic dinners ($30 to $50). All are by reservation only and are available to guests and nonguests alike.

217 N. 100 West, St. George, UT 84770. ℂ 800/600-3737 or 435/628-3737. Fax 435/628-5646. www.sevenwivesinn.com. 13 units. $60–$250. Rates include full breakfast. AE, DC, DISC, MC, V. **Amenities:** Restaurant (Regional); outdoor pool; in-room massage. *In room:* A/C, TV.

INEXPENSIVE

Dixie Palms Motel   Travelers on tight budgets should head to the Dixie Palms for basic lodging at bargain-basement rates. Located right in the center of town, within walking distance of several restaurants and attractions, this motel doesn't have a pool, but the rooms are clean and well maintained—and the price is right.

185 E. St. George Blvd., St. George, UT 84770. ☏ **435/673-3531**. 15 units. $26–$35 double. MC, V. **Amenities:** Restaurant. *In room:* A/C, TV, fridge, microwave.

Rococo Inn   Perched on a bluff on the west side of St. George, this white stucco motel affords great views of the city below. The basic motel rooms are clean, simply decorated, and quite attractive; each contains one king or two queen beds, a small refrigerator, and a combination shower/tub. There is an excellent restaurant, Sullivan's Rococo Steakhouse (p. 203).

511 S. Airport Rd., St. George, UT 84770. ☏ **888/628-3671** or 435/628-3671. Fax 435/673-6370. 30 units. $45–$60 double. AE, DISC, MC, V. **Amenities:** Restaurant (Steak/seafood); outdoor pool; indoor Jacuzzi. *In room:* A/C, TV, fridge.

RV PARKS

In addition to the commercial RV grounds discussed below, there is camping at Snow Canyon, Quail Creek, and Gunlock state parks.

Redlands RV Park   This large RV park has two or three trees at every site— it almost looks like a bunch of campers hiding in a forest. In addition to the usual restrooms and showers, facilities include a coin-operated laundry, a convenience store, and propane, as well as a large sauna, a heated pool, a playground, a game room, horseshoes, a shuffleboard court, and a volleyball court. Discount tickets for the golf course across the street are available.

650 W. Telegraph St., Washington, UT 84770. ☏ **800/553-8269** or 435/673-9700. www.redlandsrvpark.com. 204 sites. $16–$26. AE, MC, V. 2 miles north of St. George on Frontage Rd., at I-15 exit 10.

Settler's RV Park   Situated below a bluff just off I-15, this RV park is convenient to the area's attractions and within walking distance of shops and restaurants; golf courses are just 1½ miles away. The paved sites are fairly well spaced; once the trees grow a bit, they'll be at least partly shaded. In addition to the large, well-kept bathhouse, facilities include a coin-operated laundry, a heated pool and Jacuzzi, a playground, a game room, barbecues, a shuffleboard court, and horseshoes.

1333 E. 100 South, St. George, UT 84770. ☏ **800/628-1624** or 435/628-1624. www.settlersrvpark.com. 155 sites. $18–$26. MC, V. From I-15 exit 8, head east 1 block, turn right onto River Rd., and turn left onto 100 South.

WHERE TO DINE

In addition to the restaurants discussed below, **Seven Wives Inn Bed & Breakfast** offers unique English-style teas as well as gourmet dinners (p. 201).

The Bentley House Restaurant AMERICAN   Come to this handsome Victorian home for a romantic, elegant evening. A pianist plays quietly in the background, while antiques from the 1870s surround you. Although the menu varies, choices might include broiled filet mignon with sautéed mushrooms, chicken cordon bleu, or salmon poached in white wine. Desserts, made in-house, include a variety of pies and cheesecakes. No alcoholic beverages are served. The restaurant only serves prix-fixe dinners.

Green Gate Village Bed & Breakfast, 76 W. Tabernacle St. ☏ **435/628-7676**. Reservations required. 5-course prix-fixe dinner $24. AE, DC, DISC, MC, V. Thurs–Sat 5–9pm. Closed major holidays.

The Claim Jumper Steak House ★ *Kids* STEAK/RIBS/SEAFOOD   This handsome ranch house–style building houses some of the best red meat in town. All steaks are charbroiled over an open flame. We especially recommend the prime rib (11 or 16 oz.) and the baseball steak—a super-thick center cut sirloin. The Claim Jumper is also the place to come for thick buffalo steaks. Other options include Utah trout, king crab, a full rack of baby back ribs, and the daily pasta special. All dinners come with a huge salad, hot bread, and your choice of potato. Full liquor service is available.

1110 S. Bluff St. © 435/674-7800. www.claimjumperutah.com. Main courses $9.95–$30. AE, DC, DISC, MC, V. Sun–Wed 5–9pm; Thurs–Sat 5–10pm.

Sullivan's Rococo Steakhouse ★ STEAK/SEAFOOD   Excellent beef and the best views from any restaurant in the area make this a great spot for special occasions. Perched on a bluff overlooking St. George, Sullivan's large glass windows take full advantage of a spectacular panorama of the city and its surrounding red rock formations, especially as the sun begins to set and the city lights twinkle below. Generous portions of prime rib and a variety of steaks are king here; the Rococo is also considered to be one of the best spots in southwest Utah for lobster. All baking is done in-house, so save room for a piece of pie— the shredded apple with caramel sauce and ice cream is spectacular. Those dropping by for lunch can choose from several sandwiches, including an extra-special prime-rib sandwich, plus burgers and salads. The restaurant offers full liquor service.

511 S. Airport Rd. © 435/628-3671. Main courses $3.95–$6.95 lunch, $8.95–$33 dinner. AE, DISC, MC, V. Mon–Fri 11am–3pm; daily 5–10pm. From I-15 exit 8, head west to Bluff St. and cross over onto Airport Rd., which immediately turns left and climbs the bluff.

Tom's Delicatessen DELI   Tucked away behind a narrow storefront in a small shopping center beside the Holiday Inn, Tom's quietly goes about its business of creating tasty, filling sandwiches. A St. George institution since 1978, Tom's offers 14 hot and 21 cold selections that include just about all the basics— roast beef, turkey, pastrami and so on. You can eat in or carry your order. No alcohol is served.

175 West 900 S. Bluff, in Holiday Square. © 435/628-1822. Sandwiches $4.35–$6.05. No credit cards. Tues–Sat 11am–6pm.

ST. GEORGE AFTER DARK

St. George, with its large nondrinking Mormon population, isn't one of the West's hot spots as far as bar scenes go. Locals going out on the town will often attend a performing arts event, and perhaps stop in for a nightcap at one of the local restaurants that serve alcohol, such as Sullivan's Rococo Steakhouse (see the review earlier) or one of the hotel restaurants. Keep in mind that these are not private clubs, so you'll need to buy something to eat in order to purchase a drink.

Dixie State College's **Avenna Center,** 425 S. 700 East (ticket office © **435/ 652-7800**), is St. George's primary performing arts venue. The four-building complex hosts a wide range of performances, from country and rock concerts to symphony, ballet, and opera performances—and even sports games.

Dixie State College, 225 S. 700 East (© **435/652-7994;** www.dixie.edu), offers a variety of events throughout the school year. The Celebrity Concert Series, running from October through April, has developed a strong following for its programs of music, ballet, modern dance, and performing arts presented by national and international performers. Tickets run from $10 to $18. Recent offerings have ranged from Broadway musicals to a concert pianist to the Utah Symphony Orchestra.

Not to be outdone, the college's music and drama departments offer numerous performances, including student recitals; band, chamber singer, and jazz ensemble concerts; and theater that runs the gamut from musicals to dramas—and maybe even a Greek tragedy. Admission usually costs between $8 and $12 per person; most performances are presented at **Cox Auditorium.** Call the box office (© **435/652-7900**) to find out what's scheduled during your visit.

Music lovers will enjoy St. George's own **Southwest Symphonic Chorale and Southwest Symphony,** the only full symphony orchestra between Provo and Las Vegas. Its repertoire includes classical, opera, and popular music. Get tickets early for the annual Christmas production of Handel's *Messiah,* performed with the Dixie State College Concert Choir—it usually sells out. Concerts are scheduled from October to early June; tickets cost $5 to $12 (box office © **435/652-7800**).

Broadway musicals and plays are presented in a September through April season by **St. George Musical Theater,** 735 E. Tabernacle (© **435/628-8755;** www.sgmt.org). Recent productions have included *Fiddler on the Roof, Cheaper By the Dozen, Scrooge: the Musical,* and *Hello! Dolly;* tickets cost $10 to $13.

The **St. George Tabernacle** (p. 197) presents free concerts (including half-hour organ recitals), Monday through Friday at 12:15pm, and has a program that includes historical lectures with music by college or high school choirs, Wednesdays at 7pm. For information on these and other programs, call © **435/ 673-5181.**

Not far from St. George, at 1100 Tuacahn Drive in Ivins, is the **Tuacahn Amphitheatre and Center for the Arts,** P.O. Box 1996, St. George, UT 84771 (© **800/746-9882** or 435/652-3300; fax 435/652-3227; www.tuacahn.org). Surrounded by towering red rock cliffs, this 2,000-seat state-of-the-art outdoor theater presents original and Broadway productions during its Summer Festival of Theatre from June through September, and at other times is the venue for big name music acts, such as Kenny Rogers. It also hosts the annual Christmas Festival of Lights, during which Christmas lights illuminate the buildings and grounds at Tuacahn. Reservations are recommended. Tickets for the musicals vary, but are generally in the range of $25 to $35 for adults and $10 to $25 for children under 12. Dutch-oven dinners are served before the productions ($11 for adults and $8 for children).

3 Cedar Breaks National Monument & Brian Head Resort

Cedar City: 53 miles NE of St. George, 251 miles SW of Salt Lake City; Cedar Breaks National Monument: 21 miles E of Cedar City

This great little area is home to some unheralded—and uncrowded—natural gems. Cedar Breaks National Monument is like a miniature Bryce Canyon—a stunning multicolored amphitheater of stone, with hiking trails, camping, and a plateau ablaze with wildflowers in summer. Brian Head is Utah's southernmost ski resort, but because it has the highest base elevation of any of the state's ski areas, it gets about 450 inches of powder each winter. Where else but southern Utah can you be on the links in the morning and on the slopes by the afternoon? And because Brian Head Resort is off the average skier's beaten track, lift lines are usually nonexistent.

But this area is more than an outdoor playland—with Iron Mission State Park Museum and the nationally renowned Utah Shakespearean Festival, Cedar City happens to be a great place to step back in time and to experience some great theater. Even if neither of these attractions appeals to you, you'll probably end up in Cedar City anyway—it's where you'll find almost all of the area's accommodations and restaurants.

BASING YOURSELF IN CEDAR CITY

The community of Cedar City (elevation 5,800 feet) is a good base for those exploring this area, especially because Cedar Breaks National Monument has no lodging or dining facilities. If you're here to ski and you'd like to save money on accommodations, Cedar City also offers an economical alternative to Brian Head's more expensive condos, and it's only 28 miles from here to Brian Head's slopes (but beware: it can be a mean 28 miles when the weather's bad). In addition to the facilities that we've mentioned below, you'll find a good selection of motels, restaurants, campgrounds, gas stations, grocery stores, and other services on I-15 at exits 57, 59, and 62.

ESSENTIALS

GETTING THERE Cedar City is just off I-15, 53 miles northeast of St. George. **Skywest Airlines** (© **800/453-9417** or 435/586-3033; www.skywest. com) flies into Cedar City Regional Airport; car-rental agencies include **Enterprise**, 987 N. Main St., Suite 1 (© **435/865-7636**); **National**, located at the airport (© **435/586-4004**); and **Avis**, located at the airport and at 330 W 200 North (© **435/867-9898**).

VISITOR INFORMATION Contact the **Iron County Tourism and Convention Bureau,** 581 N. Main St. (P.O. Box 1007), Cedar City, UT 84720 (© **800/354-4849** or 435/586-5124). The visitor center is open Monday through Friday, 8am to 5pm.

FAST FACTS This area is served by Cedar City's **Valley View Medical Center,** 595 S. 75 East (© **435/586-6587**). The **post office** is located at 333 N. Main St. (© **800/275-8777** for hours and other information).

WHERE TO STAY & DINE

Lodging possibilities in Cedar City include the **Abbey Inn,** 940 W. 200 North (© **800/325-5411** or 435/586-9966); **Best Western El Rey Inn,** 80 S. Main St. (© **800/688-6518** or 435/586-6518); **Best Western Town & Country,** 200 N. Main St. (© **800/493-4089** or 435/586-9900); **Comfort Inn,** 250 N. 1100 West (© **800/424-6423** or 435/586-2082); **Days Inn,** 1204 S. Main St. (© **800/329-7466** or 435/867-8877); **Motel 6,** 1620 W. 200 North (© **800/ 466-8356** or 435/586-9200); **Ramada Inn,** 281 S. Main St. (© **800/272-6232** or 435/586-9916); **Super 8,** 145 N. 1550 West (© **800/800-8000** or 435/586-8880); and **Travelodge,** 2555 N. Freeway Dr. (© **800/578-7878** or 435/586-7435). All of the above charge less than $100 for doubles in winter; rates are slightly higher in summer. Room tax adds about 9% to lodging bills.

The **Cedar City KOA Campground,** 1121 N. Main St., Cedar City (© **800/562-9873** or 435/586-9872; or www.koa.com), is open year-round and charges $22 to $35 per site.

Heartland Cafe, 155 N. Main St. (© **435/865-9191**), is an attractive, bistro-style cafe offering a good variety of sandwiches, burgers, and homemade desserts, plus gourmet specials at dinner ($9 to $14). **Sullivan's Cafe,** 301 S. Main St. (© **435/586-6761**), offers basic American fare for all three meals daily; dinners go for $6.95 to $16. **Adriana's,** 161 S. 100 West (© **435/865-1234**), serves home-style meals for lunch (about $6) and dinner ($10 to $20). The locally recommended **Milt's Stage Stop,** 5 miles east of town on Utah 14 (© 435/586-9344), offers steak and seafood for dinner only, from $12 to $30, with complete liquor service.

Those planning trips into the nearby mountains—perhaps for a few days at Cedar Breaks National Monument, described below—can pick up supplies in Cedar City at **Albertson's Food & Drug,** 905 S. Main St. (© 435/586-9931), or **Smith's Food & Drug Center,** 633 S. Main St. (© 435/586-1203). Both have good deli departments and are open around the clock.

A BRIEF LOOK AT CEDAR CITY'S PIONEER PAST

Iron Mission State Park Museum   Horse-drawn wagons are the main focus at Iron Mission, with several dozen on display. In addition to the usual buckboards; a bullet-scarred Old West stagecoach; and some elaborate, for-the-very-very-rich-only coaches; you'll see an original Studebaker White Top Wagon (predecessor of the present-day station wagon) and several hearses.

Also on exhibit are American Indian and pioneer artifacts from the region, as well as a diorama depicting the 1850s iron furnace and equipment for which the park is named. Demonstrations of pioneer crafts, such as weaving, spinning, candle making, cooking, and toy making, are held periodically. And there are changing exhibits by local artists. Allow about an hour.

Iron Mission also manages an 1860s–70s iron foundry west of Cedar City. Ask at the desk for information and directions.

635 N. Main St., downtown Cedar City. © 435/586-9290. www.stateparks.utah.gov. Admission $2 adults, $1 children 6 to 16, free for children under 6; family rate $5. Memorial Day–Labor Day daily 9am–7pm; rest of year daily 9am–5pm. Closed Thanksgiving, Christmas, and New Year's Day.

CEDAR BREAKS NATIONAL MONUMENT ⋒

A delightful little park, Cedar Breaks is a wonderful place to spend a few hours or even several days, gazing down from the rim into the spectacular natural amphitheater, hiking the trails, and camping among the spruce, fir, and wildflowers that blanket the plateau in summer.

This natural coliseum, which reminds us of Bryce Canyon, is more than 2,000 feet deep and over 3 miles across; it's filled with stone spires, arches, and columns shaped by the forces of erosion and painted in ever-changing reds, purples, oranges, and ochers. But why "Cedar Breaks?" Well, the pioneers who came here called such badlands "breaks," and they mistook the juniper trees along the cliff bases for cedars.

ESSENTIALS

At over 10,000 feet elevation, it's always pleasantly cool at Cedar Breaks. It actually gets downright cold at night, so bring a jacket or sweater, even if the temperature is scorching just down the road in St. George. The monument opens for its short summer season only after the snow melts, usually in late May, and closes in mid-October—unless you happen to have a snowmobile or a pair of cross-country skis or snowshoes, in which case you can visit year-round.

GETTING THERE   Cedar Breaks National Monument is 21 miles east of Cedar City, 56 miles west of Bryce Canyon National Park, and 247 miles south of Salt Lake City.

From I-15, drive east of Cedar City on Utah 14 to Utah 148, turn north (left), and follow Utah 148 into the monument. If you're coming from Bryce Canyon or other points east, the park is accessible from the town of Panguitch via Utah 143. From the north, take the Parowan exit off I-15 and head south on

Moments Renaissance Delights on the Colorado Plateau: The Utah Shakespearean Festival

Southern Utah may not be a hotbed of cultural activity, but each year humble Cedar City becomes home to Utah's premier theater event, the **Utah Shakespearean Festival** ⚐. The Bard's plays have been professionally staged in this unlikely setting since 1962, and the festival has been going strong and getting better ever since, winning the prestigious Tony Award for Outstanding Regional Theatre in 2000.

The summer season, which runs from mid-June through August, includes six plays—usually three by Shakespeare and three others—in which top actors perform in true Elizabethan style in an open-air replica of the original Globe Theatre, with musicians trained in the music of the Renaissance. (If it rains, productions are moved into the adjacent enclosed theater.) In 2004 you can enjoy Shakespeare's *The Taming of the Shrew, Macbeth, As You Like It,* and *Henry IV, Part One;* plus Lerner and Loewe's *My Fair Lady; Forever Plaid,* by Stuart Ross; and *Morning's at Seven,* an enchanting, merry, and slightly mad, Tony Award–winning play by Paul Osborn. The 2004 fall season, which runs from mid-September through late October, will offer Shakespeare's *Macbeth,* Noel Coward's *Blithe Spirit,* and *The Spitfire Grill,* a warm-hearted musical based on the film by Lee David Zlotoff.

Backstage tours are offered Monday through Saturday for $7. A variety of other programs, including free literary and music seminars and special workshops, are also held during the summer season.

The festival is held on the Southern Utah University campus, 351 W. Center St., Cedar City, UT 84720. Ticket prices range from $18 to $32, with some matinees starting at $11. For tickets and information, call ☎ **800/PLAYTIX** or 435/586-7878. Tickets can also be ordered (using a credit card) on the Web (www.bard.org).

Utah 143. It's a steep climb from whichever direction you choose, and vehicles prone to vapor lock or loss of power on hills (such as motor homes) may have some problems.

INFORMATION/VISITOR CENTER   For advance information, contact the Superintendent, Cedar Breaks National Monument, 2390 West Utah 56, Suite 11, Cedar City, UT 84720-4151 (☎ **435/586-9451;** www.nps.gov/cebr).

A mile from the south entrance gate, you'll find the **visitor center,** open daily from early June to mid-October, with exhibits on the geology, flora, and fauna of Cedar Breaks. You can purchase books and maps here, and rangers can help plan your visit.

FEES & REGULATIONS   Admission costs $3 per person for those 17 and older. Regulations are similar to those at most national parks: Leave everything as you find it. Mountain bikes are not allowed on hiking trails. Dogs, which must be leashed at all times, are prohibited on all trails, in the backcountry, and in public buildings.

HEALTH & SAFETY The high elevation—10,350 feet at the visitor center—is likely to cause shortness of breath and tiredness, and those with heart or respiratory conditions should consult their doctors before going. Avoid overlooks and other high, exposed areas during thunderstorms; they're often targets for lightning.

RANGER PROGRAMS During the monument's short summer season, rangers offer nightly campfire talks at the campground; talks on the area's geology at Point Supreme, a viewpoint near the visitor center, daily on the hour from 10am to 5pm; and guided hikes on Saturday and Sunday mornings. A complete schedule is posted at the visitor center and the campground.

EXPLORING CEDAR BREAKS BY CAR

The 5-mile road through Cedar Breaks National Monument offers easy access to the monument's scenic overlooks and trailheads. Allow 30 to 45 minutes to make the drive. Start at the visitor center and nearby **Point Supreme** for a panoramic view of the amphitheater. Then drive north, past the campground and picnic ground turnoff, to **Sunset View** for a closer view of the amphitheater and its colorful canyons. From each of these overlooks, you'll be able to see out across Cedar Valley, over the Antelope and Black Mountains, into the Escalante Desert.

Continue north to **Chessman Ridge Overlook,** so named because the hoodoos directly below look like massive stone chess pieces. Watch for swallows and swifts soaring among the rock formations. Then head north to **Alpine Pond,** a trailhead for a self-guided nature trail (see "Hiking," below) with an abundance of wildflowers. Finally, you'll reach **North View,** which offers the best look into the amphitheater. The view here is reminiscent of Bryce Canyon's Queen's Garden, with its stately statues frozen in time.

OUTDOOR PURSUITS

HIKING There are no trails from the rim to the bottom of the amphitheater, but the monument does have two high-country trails. The fairly easy 2-mile **Alpine Pond Trail** loop leads through woodlands of bristlecone pines to a picturesque forest glade and pond surrounded by wildflowers, offering panoramic views of the amphitheater along the way. A printed trail guide is available at the trailhead.

A somewhat more challenging hike, the 4-mile one-way **Spectra Point Trail** (also called the Ramparts Trail) follows the rim more closely than the Alpine Pond Trail, offering changing views of the colorful rock formations. It also takes you through fields of wildflowers and by bristlecone pines that are more than 1,500 years old. You'll need to be especially careful of your footing along the exposed cliff edges, and allow yourself some time to rest—there are lots of ups and downs along the way.

Moments **A Late Summer Bonanza: The Wildflowers of Cedar Breaks**

During its brief summer season, Cedar Breaks makes the most of the warmth and moisture in the air with a spectacular wildflower show. The rim comes alive in a blaze of color—truly a sight to behold. The dazzling display begins practically as soon as the snow melts in May and reaches its peak during late July and August.

WILDLIFE WATCHING   Because of its relative remoteness, Cedar Breaks is a good place for spotting wildlife. You're likely to see mule deer grazing in the meadows along the road early and late in the day. Marmots make their dens near the rim and are often seen along the Spectra Point Trail. You'll spot ground squirrels, red squirrels, and chipmunks everywhere. Pikas, which are related to rabbits, are here too, but it's unlikely you'll see one. They're small, with short ears and stubby tails, and prefer the high, rocky slopes.

In the campground, birders should have no trouble spotting the Clark's nutcracker, with its gray torso and black-and-white wings and tail. The monument is also home to swallows, swifts, blue grouse, and golden eagles.

WINTER FUN   The monument's facilities are shut down from mid-October to late May due to the thick blanket of snow that covers the area. The snow-blocked roads keep cars out, but they're perfect for snowmobilers, snowshoers, and cross-country skiers, who usually come over from nearby Brian Head ski area (see below). Snowshoers and cross-country skiers have a variety of options, but snowmobiles are restricted to the main 5-mile road through the monument, which is groomed and marked.

CAMPING

The 30-site campground, **Point Supreme,** just north of the visitor center, is open from June to mid-September, with sites available on a first-come, first-served basis. It's a beautiful high-mountain setting, among tall spruce and fir. Facilities include restrooms, drinking water, picnic tables, grills, and an amphitheater for the ranger's evening campfire programs. No showers or RV hookups are available. Camping fee is $12 per night. Keep in mind that even in midsummer, temperatures can drop into the 30s (single digits Celsius) at night at this elevation, so bring cool-weather gear.

BRIAN HEAD RESORT

Like the ski areas in the Ogden and Logan areas, the reasons to visit Brian Head Resort are terrain and snow; the wide range of amenities you'll find in Park City, Deer Valley, and Snowbird just don't exist here. In summer, mountain bikers and hikers converge on Brian Head.

Brian Head has the distinction of being Utah's southernmost ski resort, just a short drive from the year-round shirtsleeve warmth of St. George. But with the highest base elevation of any of the state's ski areas (9,600 feet), it receives over 400 inches of powdery snow each winter. Its location makes it particularly popular with skiers from the Las Vegas area and Southern California. Another plus is the scenery: The only ski resort in Utah's famed red rock country, Brian Head Resort offers stunning views.

The resort is known for its variety of terrain, especially with snow-cat service to the top of Brian Head Peak (elevation 11,307 feet), offering spectacular advanced terrain for the adventurous. Intermediates will enjoy fine cruising runs a little farther down the mountain, and beginners can ski Navajo Mountain, an entire mountain dedicated to children and beginning skiers and snowboarders. Terrain is rated 40% beginner, 40% intermediate, and 20% advanced. One double and five triple chairs service 53 trails on 540 skiable acres. The vertical drop is 1,707 feet, from a top elevation of 11,307 feet. There are snow-making capabilities on 170 acres. The ski season generally runs from mid-November to mid-April, with lifts operating daily from 9:30am to 4:30pm. On weekends and holidays, night skiing is available from 3:30 to 9pm.

Tips   Serious Mountain Biking & Other Summer Fun

After the snow melts, bikers and hikers claim the mountain. With elevations ranging from 9,600 to 11,307 feet, Brian Head is stunningly beautiful and always cool and crisp. For those who want to see the mountains without the sweat, chairlift rides are offered in summer on Friday, Saturday, and Sunday ($8 adults, $4 children 3–12, free for kids under 3). Evenings are busy, too, with live musical entertainment ranging from jazz and country to bluegrass and classical.

Brian Head is fast becoming a major destination for serious—and we do mean serious—mountain bikers. This is a wonderful place for **mountain biking** 𝄞, with endless trails, superb scenery, and about the freshest air you're going to find. What's more, mountain biking here can be oh-so-very easy: a chairlift hauls you and your bike up the mountain ($16 for a full-day pass), or you can take a shuttle to and from several locations ($13)—leaving only the fun parts to pedal. Bike rentals start at $23 per day for adults, $20 for kids 11 and under. Contact the **Brian Head Resort Mountain Bike Park** (© 435/677-3101), **Brian Head** Sports (© 435/677-2014), or **Georg's Bike Shop** (© 435/677-2013) for details.

Snowboarders are welcome, with four terrain parks of varying ability levels, plenty of free riding terrain, and a half pipe, conditions permitting. There's a snow tubing park here as well.

For information, contact **Brian Head Resort,** P.O. Box 190008, Brian Head, UT 84719 (© **435/677-2035;** fax 435/677-3883; www.brianhead.com), or **Brian Head Chamber of Commerce & Visitor Services,** P.O. Box 190325, Brian Head, UT 84719 (© **888/677-2810** or 435/677-2810; fax 435/677-2154; www.brianheadutah.com).

From Cedar City, it's 28 miles to Brian Head; take I-15 to exit 75 and head south on the very steep Utah 143 about 12 miles.

LIFT TICKETS   An adult all-day lift ticket is $39 regular season and $46 during major holiday periods; an all-day child's (ages 6 to 12) or senior's (ages 65 and over) ticket is $26 regular season and $31 during major holiday periods. Kids 5 and under ski free with a paying adult. Transport on the Peak Express Snowcat costs an additional $5, with purchase of a lift ticket. Night skiing or snowboarding costs $8. Snow tubing is $8 for 2 hours, including tube rental.

LESSONS & PROGRAMS   The **ski school** offers private and group lessons, as well as clinics, snowboard classes, and children's ski instruction. Day care is available for children and infants; also available are packages combining day care and ski lessons. Call © **435/677-2047** for current rates.

CROSS-COUNTRY SKIING   Brian Head has 26 miles of cross-country trails—6.2 miles of them groomed—rated 50% beginner, 30% intermediate, and 20% advanced. Lessons and rentals are available at **Brian Head Sports** (© 435/677-2014); there's no charge for trail use.

WHERE TO STAY & DINE   The Brian Head area offers a variety of lodging possibilities, with winter rates ranging from about $100 to over $400 per night (higher at Christmas; lower in summer). Contact **Brian Head Chamber of Commerce & Visitor Services** (© **888/677-2810** or 435/677-2810; fax

435/677-2154; www.brianheadutah.com), **Brian Head Reservation Center** (© **800/845-9781** or 435/677-2042; fax 435/677-2827; www.brianheadtown. com/bhrc), or **Brian Head Central Reservations** (© **800/272-7426**). Room tax is about 10%. You can also stay in Cedar City, 28 miles away (see "Basing Yourself in Cedar City," earlier in this chapter).

Cedar Breaks Lodge & Spa ✦, 2223 Hunter Ridge Rd. (P.O. Box 190248), Brian Head, UT 84719 (© **888/282-3327** or 435/677-3000; www.cedarbreaks lodge.com), near the base of Navajo Peak, recently underwent an extensive multi-million-dollar renovation. It offers 120 studio, parlor, and master suites ranging from $140 to $400 in winter, $70 to $290 in summer. All rooms have whirlpool tubs, wet bars, refrigerators, microwaves, coffeemakers, and hair dryers; some also have fireplaces. Facilities include a 24-hour front desk, two restaurants, a lounge, an indoor pool, a fireside Jacuzzi, a fitness center, a sauna, and a steam room. Boasting one of Utah's top spas, the lodge has several massage therapists available, offering Swedish full body massage, deep tissue massage, sports massage, reflexology, aromatherapy baths, hydrating facials, salt glows, and herbal wraps. In short, they offer a variety of services and luxurious spa treatments. Contact the spa for more information (© **435/677-4225**).

Quick breakfasts and lunches are served at several places at Brian Head, including the **Base Lodge Grilles,** with meals from $5 to $8. The **Double Black Diamond Steak House** at Cedar Breaks Lodge & Spa (see above) offers fine dining Friday and Saturday nights only, with steaks, prime rib, and several seafood and pasta dishes in the $18 to $30 range. Reservations are recommended (© **435/677-4242**). Also at Cedar Breaks Lodge & Spa, the **Cedar Breaks Café** serves a breakfast buffet plus a la carte menu each morning, and offers casual dinners each evening. Prices range from $7 to $16. The **Cedar Breaks Private Membership Club** (memberships available) is a local gathering place, with a great selection of appetizers and the option of ordering from the Cedar Breaks Café menu.

4 Kanab: Movies, Sand Dunes & Gateway to the Grand Canyon

82 miles E of St. George, 303 miles S of Salt Lake City, 79 miles N of the Grand Canyon

Another southern Utah town founded by Mormon pioneers sent by Brigham Young in the 1870s, Kanab is best known for its starring role in the movies and on TV. This is the Wild West many of us grew up with, on TV shows like *Gunsmoke, The Lone Ranger, Death Valley Days,* and *F Troop;* and on the big screen in *Buffalo Bill, Sergeants Three, Bandolero,* and *The Outlaw Josey Wales.*

But Kanab (4,925 feet elevation) lives on more than just memories of the Old West: It also serves as a stopping point for travelers on their way to southern Utah's major sights. Visitors coming from Arizona are likely to pass through on their way to Zion and Bryce Canyon national parks. And the Grand Canyon is directly to the south, so if you're heading to the north rim, Kanab is a good choice for a home base. None of these natural wonders are all that close to Kanab, but in Utah terms, they're "just around the corner."

ESSENTIALS

GETTING THERE   Kanab is 82 miles east of St. George, 80 miles south of Bryce Canyon National Park, 42 miles east of Zion National Park, 68 miles west of Lake Powell and Glen Canyon Recreation Area, 79 miles north of the Grand

Canyon, and 303 miles south of Salt Lake City. The town is located on U.S. 89 at the junction of U.S. 89A, which crosses into Arizona just 7 miles south of town.

VISITOR INFORMATION   Contact the **Kane County Visitors Center,** 78 S. 100 East (U.S. 89), Kanab, UT 84741 (© **800/733-5263** or 435/644-5033; fax 435/644-5923; www.kaneutah.com), which is open April through November Monday to Friday 8am to 8pm and weekends 9am to 5pm and December through March Monday through Friday 9am to 5pm; closed on weekends. Another useful website is www.kanabguide.com.

GETTING AROUND   Kanab is laid out on a grid, with the center of town at the intersection of Center and Main streets. U.S. 89 comes in from the north on 300 West Street, turns east onto Center Street, south again on 100 East Street, and finally east again on 300 South. U.S. 89A follows 100 East Street south to the airport and into Arizona.

FAST FACTS   The **Kane County Hospital and Skilled Nursing Facility** is at 335 N. Main St. (© **435/644-5811**). The **post office** is at 39 S. Main St. (© **800/275-8777** for hours and other information). In an **emergency,** call © **911,** or outside of the town limits call the sheriff's office © **435/644-2667.**

CORAL PINK SAND DUNES STATE PARK

Long a favorite of dune-buggy enthusiasts (off-road vehicle users lobbied hard to have this designated a state park), Coral Pink Sand Dunes has recently been attracting an increasing number of campers, hikers, photographers, and all-around nature lovers as well. While big boys—and occasionally big girls—play with their expensive motorized toys, others hike; hunt for wildflowers, scorpions, and lizards; or just sit and wiggle their toes in the smooth, cool sand. The colors are especially rich at sunrise and sunset. Early-morning visitors will find the tracks of yesterday's dune buggies gone, replaced by the tracks of lizards, kangaroo rats, snakes, and the rest of the park's animal kingdom, who venture out in the coolness of night, after all the people have departed.

ESSENTIALS

GETTING THERE   From downtown Kanab, go about 8 miles north on U.S. 89, then southwest (left) on Hancock Road for about 12 miles to the park.

INFORMATION/VISITOR CENTER   For copies of the park brochure and off-highway-vehicle regulations, contact the **park office** at P.O. Box 95, Kanab, UT 84741-0095 (© **435/648-2800**). Information is also available online at www.stateparks.utah.gov. At the **park entry station,** you'll see a small display area with sand from around the world, fossils of the area, and live scorpions, lizards, and tadpoles.

FEES & REGULATIONS   The day-use fee is $5 per vehicle. The standard state park regulations apply, with the addition of a few extra rules due to the park's popularity with off-road-vehicle users: Quiet hours last from 10pm to 9am, a bit later in the morning than in most parks. Dunes are open to motor vehicles between 9am and 10pm and to hikers at any time. Vehicles going onto the dunes must have safety flags, available at the entry station; while on the dunes, they must stay at least 10 feet from vegetation and at least 100 feet from hikers. Dogs are permitted on the dunes but must be leashed.

RANGER PROGRAMS   Regularly scheduled ranger talks explain the geology, plants, and animals of the dunes. For a real thrill, take a guided evening

Scorpion Walk ★★, using a black light to find luminescent scorpions that make the park their home. You'll definitely want to wear shoes for this activity! Call to find out if there's one scheduled during your visit.

OUTDOOR PURSUITS

FOUR-WHEELING   This giant 1,000-acre sandbox offers plenty of space for **off-road-vehicle enthusiasts,** who race up and down the dunes, stopping to perch on a crest to watch the setting sun. Because the sand here is quite fine, extra-wide flotation tires are needed, and lightweight dune buggies are usually the vehicle of choice. Adjacent to the park on Bureau of Land Management property, you'll find hundreds of miles of trails and roads for off-highway vehicles. Unfortunately, no rentals are available.

HIKING   The best time for hiking the dunes is early morning. It's cooler then, the lighting at and just after sunrise produces beautiful shadows and colors, and there are no noisy dune buggies until after 9am. Sunset is also very pretty, but you'll be sharing the dunes with off-road vehicles. Keep in mind that hiking through fine sand can be very tiring, especially for those who go barefoot. A self-guided half-mile loop nature trail has numbered signs through some of the dunes; allow a half hour.

Several other hikes of various lengths are possible within and just outside the park, but because there are few signs—and because landmarks change with the shifting sands—it's best to check with park rangers before setting out. Those spending more than a few hours in the dunes will discover that even their own tracks disappear in the wind, leaving few clues to the route back to park headquarters.

CAMPING

The spacious and mostly shady 22-site campground, open year-round, offers hot showers, modern restrooms, and an RV dump station, but no hookups. Camping costs $14. Call ℂ **800/322-3770** for reservations, with a $7 nonrefundable fee.

MORE TO SEE & DO IN THE KANAB AREA

Frontier Movie Town   Hollywood's vision of the Wild West lives on here, with a jail, bunkhouse, bank, ranch house, and numerous other buildings created for movies filmed in the Kanab area over the years. You'll see buildings from the sets of Disney's 1973 comedy-drama *One Little Indian,* starring James Garner and Vera Miles; the 1948 classic Western *Black Bart,* with Yvonne De Carlo and Dan Duryea; the 1997 crime action flick *Truth or Consequences, N.M.,* with Kiefer Sutherland, Vincent Gallo, and Kim Dickens; and Clint Eastwood's 1976 hit *The Outlaw Josey Wales,* among others. At the Hollywood-style costume shop, you can rent Old West costumes ($7) for your own photos, or have yourself shot by the on-site professional photographer.

On the grounds is a large gift/souvenir shop, offering a wide variety of American Indian arts and crafts, cowboy hats, coonskin caps, and the like. Dinner theater programs (dinner and a Western show) are scheduled periodically for groups, but anyone can attend ($18 to $25); call to see if there's one planned during your visit. See p. 215 for a review of the C Bar C Ranch House Cafe. Allow about an hour and a half.

297 W. Center St. ℂ **800/551-1714** or 435/644-5337. www.onlinepages.net/frontier_movie_town. Free admission. Summer daily 9am–10pm; rest of year daily 10am–6pm.

Heritage House Although there are 16 historic houses in the downtown area of Kanab, this is the only one open to the public. Built in 1893, this handsome Victorian was purchased by Thomas H. Chamberlain in 1895; and by the city in 1975. The house has been restored to its original appearance, and contains household items from the late 1800s, some belonging to the original owners. Allow about ¾ hour.

At 100 South and Main sts. ℂ **435/644-2843**. Admission by donation. Apr–Sept Mon–Fri afternoons, call for details. A block south of the intersection of Center and Main sts.

Moqui Cave American Indians known as the Moqui are believed to have spent time in this cave 800 to 900 years ago. Times have changed since then, and so has the cave—the Moqui would be amazed by what they'd find here today. The Chamberlain family, descendants of Thomas and Mary Chamberlain (see Heritage House, above), bought the cave in 1951, and the following year opened a tavern and dance hall in it. Although you can't order a drink today, the unique bar is still here, along with a huge collection of objects and artifacts that ranges from authentic dinosaur tracks (more than 140 million years old) to a beautiful fluorescent mineral display. You'll also see American Indian pottery, spear points, and other art and artifacts. A large gift shop specializes in American Indian arts and crafts.

1508 S. Kanab Creek Dr., on the east side of U.S. 89, about 5½ miles north of Kanab. ℂ **435/644-8525**. www.moquicave.com. Admission $4 adults, $3.50 seniors over 60, $2.50 ages 13–17, $2 children 6–12. Memorial Day–Labor Day Mon–Sat 9am–7pm; winter 10am–4pm, but check on possible closures.

Pahreah Townsite & Movie Set Established in 1870, the community of Pahreah takes its name from a Paiute Indian word meaning "muddy water." It was a prosperous farming center until severe flooding washed away much of the farmland. But the town held on—until the last residents gave up and moved away in the 1930s. Today, visitors can see the town cemetery and a few ruins.

The Paria movie set (apparently the spelling of Pahreah was too complicated for Hollywood) has seen many of the big names of the film industry over the years. This beautiful painted desert–type section of the valley has been used for films since the 1940s

41 miles east of Kanab. For a map and to check road conditions, contact the Bureau of Land Management office, 318 N. 100 East St., Kanab, UT 84741. ℂ **435/644-4600**. Or contact Kane County Visitors Center, 78 S. 100 East, Kanab ℂ 800/733-5263 or 435/644-5033. Free admission.

WHERE TO STAY

In addition to the properties described below, you might consider the moderately priced **Best Western Red Hills,** 125 W. Center St. (ℂ **800/830-2675** or 435/644-2675); the **Holiday Inn Express,** 815 E. U.S. 89 (ℂ **800/574-4061** or 435/644-8888), adjacent to the 9-hole Coral Cliffs Golf Course; or the **Super 8 Motel,** 70 S. 200 West (ℂ **800/800-8000** or 435/644-5500).

Room tax adds 10.75% to lodging bills. Pets are not accepted unless otherwise noted.

Parry Lodge This is where the stars stayed—Frank Sinatra, Dean Martin, John Wayne, Roddy McDowell, James Garner, and Ronald Reagan, to name just a few—while filming in Kanab. In 1931, Chauncey Parry decided to open a motel for the film people who were regularly coming to town. Two chandeliers from Paris hang in the lobby, while photos of movie stars are scattered about the public areas of the colonial-feel lodge. Doors to the original bedrooms, which make up about a third of the total number, are each adorned with the name of an actor who stayed here. We particularly enjoyed the very dated Barbara Stanwyck room—small, with one double bed, a 19-inch TV, solid wood furnishings, flower-print wallpaper, and Norman Rockwell prints.

The newer rooms, which date from the 1970s, are larger; a few units come with shower only, and one room has a kitchenette. Room service is available during restaurant hours (see Parry Lodge in "Where to Dine," below).

89 E. Center St. (U.S. 89), Kanab, UT 84741. (✆) **800/748-4104** or 435/644-2601. Fax 435/644-2605. www.infowest.com/parry. 89 units. Summer $68–$73 double, $86 family unit; winter $30–$35 double (family unit closed). Rates include continental breakfast. AE, DISC, MC, V. Pets accepted with $5 fee. **Amenities:** Restaurant (American); heated outdoor pool; Jacuzzi; coin-op laundry. *In room:* A/C, TV.

Viola's Garden B&B   Comfort, a touch of elegance, and a lot of historic charm make this bed-and-breakfast inn a good choice for those seeking an upscale option. The house, which was a 1912 kit house from the Sears Roebuck catalog, has been carefully restored and enlarged by Nileen and Von Whitlock— Nileen is the granddaughter of the home's original owners, James and Harriet Swapp. Like most historic B&Bs, all the rooms are different. For instance, the Rose Garden is decorated with hand-painted fairies, an antique queen-size bed, and full bath with a clawfoot tub and separate shower. The other four rooms have private baths with tiled showers only. All rooms are on the second floor (no elevator). Rooms are decorated with period antiques and reproductions—mostly mahogany and cherry woods. Room phones and TVs are available by request. Two rooms have private balconies. There is a shared outdoor hot tub and an entertainment room with a big screen TV. Homemade breakfasts, which might include stuffed French toast or a breakfast casserole, are served in the formal dining room. Special diets can be accommodated with advance notice.

250 N. 100 West, Kanab, UT 84741. (✆) **435/644-5683.** www.violas-garden.com. $85–$115 double; lower in winter. MC, V. **Amenities:** Restaurant. *In room:* A/C, dataport, no phone.

CAMPING
Kanab RV Corral   Open year-round, this recently remodeled RV park makes a good base camp for exploring the region. The sites—half back-in and half pull-through—are a bit close together, and you do get some highway noise; however, the bathhouses are exceptionally nice (with extra-large shower stalls), the coin-operated laundry is kept spotless, and the small kidney-shaped pool is pleasant. In addition, modem hookups are available and the Kanab RV Corral offers golf packages.

483 S. 100 East, U.S. 89A, Kanab, UT 84741. (✆) **435/644-5330.** www.xpressweb.com/~rvcorral. 40 sites. $17 $20. MC, V.

WHERE TO DINE
C Bar C Ranch House Cafe AMERICAN/CAFE   This Wild West–style cafe, part of the Frontier Movie Town complex (see "More to See & Do in the Kanab Area," above), offers buffalo wings, nachos, burgers, hot dogs, fish, chicken, salads, soups, and several cuts of steak. The good selection of beverages—including beer—is very welcome after a hot, dusty trail ride. In fact, this is the only place in town where you can legally order a beer without buying some sort of food.

Frontier Movie Town, 297 W. Center St. (✆) **800/551-1714** or 435/644-5337. Main courses $2.50–$13. DISC, MC, V. Summer daily noon–10pm; call for hours the rest of the year.

Nedra's Too SOUTHWESTERN/MEXICAN   Southwest home-style cooking in a friendly, casual atmosphere is what you'll find at Nedra's. There are tables in the dining room, decorated in Southwestern style, and booths in the adjacent coffee shop. The original Nedra's ((C) **928/643-7591**), which opened in 1957 in Fredonia, Arizona (7 miles south of Kanab), and this second restaurant, opened in 1990, both use the same family recipes now being prepared by the third generation.

The delightful breakfasts, served all day, include the usual ham and eggs, omelets, and pancakes, but there's also an eye-opening chorizo and eggs, which is made with Mexican sausage, and a delicious huevos rancheros. Lunch and dinner menus offer a variety of charbroiled burgers, such as the Philly (with Swiss cheese, grilled red and green peppers, and Bermuda onions), and several sandwiches. Other options include steaks and seafood, fried chicken, and a wide choice of Mexican dishes, from burritos to enchiladas to fajitas. Beer and malt coolers are available with meals.

300 S. 100 East St. (C) **435/644-2030.** Main courses $3.50–$16; breakfast $3.75–$5.75. AE, DISC, MC, V. Summer daily 7am–11pm; rest of year daily 8am–10pm.

Parry Lodge AMERICAN   The elegant main dining room at the Parry Lodge (p. 214) is Victorian in style, with photos of the many movie stars who have stayed and dined here adorning the walls. We highly recommend the boneless chicken with gravy, cranberry sauce, and fresh, homemade, soft dumplings. Beef eaters should thoroughly enjoy the slow-roasted prime rib. Other options include poached salmon and several broiled steaks. Portions are large, but half portions of some items are available. All desserts are made daily in-house. Full liquor service is available.

89 E. Center St. (C) **435/644-2601.** Main courses $7–$20. AE, DISC, MC, V. Daily 6–10pm. Closed Nov–Easter.

The Wok Inn HUNAN/SZECHUAN/CHINESE   The decor here is Western steakhouse mixed with Chinese—you'll find Chinese lanterns, parasols, screens, and artwork, plus a Chinese garden and pagoda. The food, however, is strictly Chinese, prepared by Chinese chefs. We particularly enjoyed the moo goo gai pan and Szechuan pork. Several items on the menu are marked hot, and reliable locals informed us they are to be believed! In all, the menu includes some 50 items, including a dozen vegetarian options. Full liquor service is available.

86 S. 200 West. (C) **435/644-5400.** Main courses $4.50–$5 lunch, $6.95–$16 dinner. AE, DISC, MC, V. Mon– Fri 11:30am–10pm; Sat 1–10pm; Sun 5–10pm. From the intersection of Center and Main sts., head west on Center for 2 blocks and turn left (south) onto 200 West.

11

Zion National Park

Early Mormon settler Isaac Behunin is credited with naming his homestead "Little Zion" because it seemed to be a bit of heaven on earth. Today, 150 years later, Zion National Park ★★ will cast a spell over you as you gaze upon its sheer multicolored walls of sandstone, explore its narrow canyons, hunt for hanging gardens of wildflowers, and listen to the roar of the churning, tumbling Virgin River.

It's easy to conjure up a single defining image of the Grand Canyon or the delicately sculpted rock hoodoos of Bryce, but pinning Zion down is more difficult. It's not simply the towering Great White Throne, deep Narrows Canyon, or cascading waterfalls and emerald green pools. You'll discover an entire smorgasbord of experiences, sights, sounds, and even smells here, as you explore everything from the massive stone sculptures and monuments to the lush forests and rushing rivers. Take time to discover Zion's trails, visiting viewpoints at different times of the day to see the changing light, and let the park work its magic.

Because of its extreme range of elevations (from 3,666 to almost 9,000 feet) and weather (with temperatures soaring over 100°F/38°C in summer and a landscape carpeted by snow in winter), Zion harbors a vast array of plants and animals. About 800 native species of plants have been found: cactus, yucca, and mesquite in the hot, dry desert areas; ponderosa pines on the high plateaus; and cottonwoods and box elders along the rivers and streams. Of the 14 varieties of cactus that grow in the park, you should

especially keep an eye out for the red claret cup, which has spectacular blooms in spring. Wildflowers common in the park include manzanita, with tiny pink blossoms; buttercups; and the bright red hummingbird trumpet. You'll also see the sacred datura—dubbed the "Zion Lily" because of its abundance in the park—with its large funnel-shaped white flowers that open in the cool of night and often close by noon.

While exploring Zion, be sure to watch for "spring lines," which are areas where water seeps out of rock, and for the "hanging gardens" that accompany them. Because sandstone is porous, water can percolate down through the rock until it's stopped by a layer of harder rock. Then the water simply changes direction, moving horizontally to the rock face, where it oozes out, forming the "spring line" that provides life-giving nutrients to whatever seeds the wind delivers, which sprout into "hanging gardens"—plants and flowers that you'll see clinging to the sides of cliffs.

Speaking of living things, Zion National Park is a veritable zoo, with mammals ranging from pocket gophers to mountain lions, hundreds of birds (including golden eagles), lizards of all shapes and sizes, and a dozen species of snakes (only the Great Basin rattlesnake is poisonous, and it usually slithers away from you faster than you can run from it). Mule deer are common, and although they're seldom seen, there are also a few shy elk and bighorn sheep, plus foxes, coyote, ringtail cats, beaver, porcupines, skunks,

Zion National Park

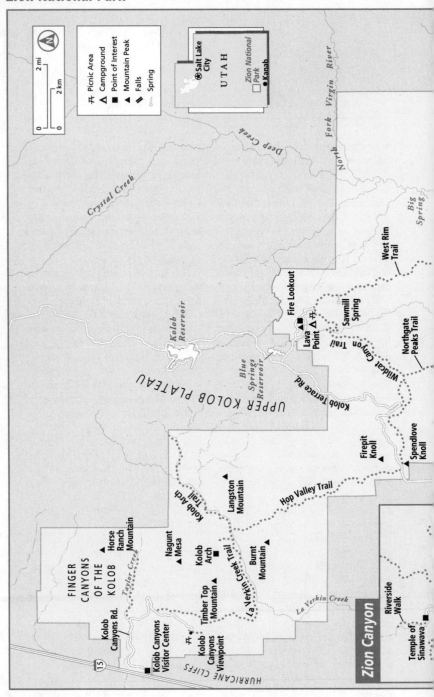

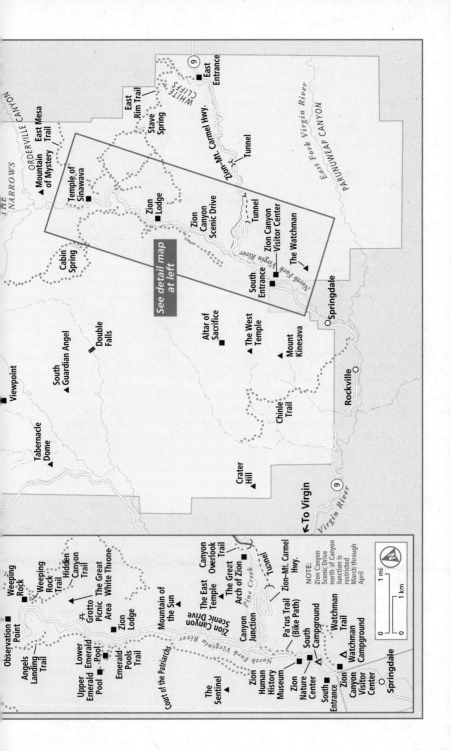

See detail map at left

NOTE: Zion Canyon Scenic Drive north of Canyon Junction is restricted March through April

← To Virgin

219

How Nature Painted Zion's Landscape

Zion National Park is many things to many people: a day hike down a narrow canyon, a rough climb up the face of a massive stone monument, a moment of quiet appreciation as the sun sets with a red glow over majestic peaks. At least to some degree, each of these experiences is possible only because of rocks—their formation, uplifting, shifting, breaking, and eroding. Of Zion's nine rock layers, the most important in creating the park's colorful formations is Navajo sandstone—at up to 2,200 feet, the thickest rock layer in the park. This formation was created some 200 million years ago during the Jurassic period, when North America was hot and dry. Movements in the earth's crust caused a shallow sea to cover windblown sand dunes, and minerals, including lime from the shells of sea creatures, glued sand particles together to form sandstone. Later crust movements caused the land to uplift, draining away the sea but leaving rivers that gradually carved the relatively soft sandstone into the spectacular shapes we see today.

So where do the colors come from? Essentially, from plain old rust. Most of the rocks at Zion are colored by iron or hematite (iron oxide), either contained in the original stone or carried into the rocks by groundwater. Although iron often creates red and pink hues, seen on many of Zion's sandstone faces, it can also result in shades of brown, yellow, black, and even green. Sometimes the iron seeps into the rock, coloring it through, but it can also stain just the surface, often in vertical streaks. Deposits of salt left by evaporating water frequently cause white streaks, and rocks are also colored by bacteria that live on their surfaces. These bacteria ingest dust and expel iron, manganese, and other minerals, which stick to the rock and produce a shiny black, brown, or reddish surface called desert varnish.

and plenty of squirrels and bats. Practically every summer visitor sees lizards of some sort, often the colorful collared and whiptail varieties, and it's easy to hear the song of the canyon wren and the call of the piñon jay.

1 Just the Facts

Located in southwest Utah, at elevations ranging from 3,666 feet to 8,726 feet, Zion National Park has several sections: **Zion Canyon,** the main part of the park, where everyone goes, and the less-visited **Kolob Terrace** and **Kolob Canyons** areas.

GETTING THERE/ACCESS POINTS   St. George and Cedar City (see chapter 10) are the closest towns with airport service. From either airport, it's easy to rent a car and drive to Zion. Utah 9 crosses Zion National Park, giving the main section of the park two entry gates—south and east. The drive into Zion Canyon (the main part of the park) from I-15 on the park's western side—following Utah 9 or Utah 17 and Utah 9 to the south entrance at Springdale, is by far the more popular, with two-thirds of park visitors arriving there. Most area lodgings and restaurants are found in Springdale, and the park's two campgrounds and the Zion Canyon Visitor Center are located just inside the south entrance. This approach has the added advantage of avoiding possible delays at the Zion–Mt. Carmel Tunnel. However, this approach is much less scenic than the eastern approach.

From the east, it's a spectacularly scenic 24-mile drive from Mt. Carmel on Utah 9, reached from either the north or south via U.S. 89. However, be aware that this route into the park drops over 2,500 feet in elevation, passes through the mile-long Zion–Mt. Carmel Tunnel, and winds down six steep switchbacks. The tunnel is too small for two-way traffic that includes vehicles larger than standard passenger cars and pickup trucks. Buses, trucks, and most recreational vehicles must be driven down the center of the tunnel, and therefore, all oncoming traffic must be stopped. This applies to all vehicles over 7 feet 10 inches wide (including mirrors) or 11 feet 4 inches tall (including luggage racks, and so on). From March through October, large vehicles are permitted in the tunnel only from 8am to 8pm daily; during other months, arrangements can be made at park entrances or by calling park headquarters (© 435/772-3256). Affected vehicles must pay a $10 fee, good for two trips through the tunnel during a 7-day period. All vehicles over 13 feet 1 inch tall and certain other particularly large vehicles are prohibited from driving anywhere on the park road between the east entrance and Zion Canyon.

You'll find Kolob Terrace Road, with additional viewpoints and trailheads, heading north off Utah 9 from the village of Virgin, about 15 miles west of the park's southern entrance. This road is closed in the winter.

The Kolob Canyons section, in the park's northwest corner, can be reached via the short Kolob Canyons Road off I-15 exit 40.

Some helpful distances: the park is 83 miles southwest of Bryce Canyon National Park; 120 miles northwest of the north rim of Grand Canyon National Park, in northern Arizona; 309 miles south of Salt Lake City; and 158 miles northeast of Las Vegas, Nevada.

INFORMATION/VISITOR CENTERS Contact Superintendent, Zion National Park, Springdale, UT 84767-1099 (© **435/772-3256;** www.nps.gov/ zion). It's best to write at least a month before your planned visit and to specify what type of information you need. Officials request that those seeking trip-planning information write rather than call, leaving the phone lines open for those needing current and changeable information such as hiking trail conditions and closures.

You can order books, maps, and videos from the nonprofit **Zion Natural History Association,** Zion National Park, Springdale, UT 84767 (© **800/635-3959** or 435/772-3264; www.zionpark.org). Some publications are available in foreign languages, and several videos can be purchased in either VHS or PAL formats. Those interested in supporting the nonprofit association can join ($35 single, $50 family) and get a 20% discount on purchases, a 10% discount on Zion Canyon Field Institute classes, and discounts at most other nonprofit bookstores at national parks, monuments, historic sites, and recreation areas.

The park has two visitor centers. The **Zion Canyon Visitor Center & Transportation Hub** (© **435/772-3256**), near the south entrance, has outdoor exhibits on the many resources available in the park and provides information on the shuttle operation. You can ask rangers questions, get backcountry permits, pick up free brochures, and purchase books, maps, videos, postcards, and posters. The smaller **Kolob Canyons Visitor Center** (© **435/586-9548**), in the northwest corner of the park off I-15, provides information, permits, books, and maps. Both visitor centers are open from 8am to 7pm in summer, with shorter varying hours the rest of the year (call to find out when).

The *Zion Map & Guide,* a free newspaper-format guide available at both visitor centers, is packed with extremely helpful information about the park.

The new **Zion Human History Museum,** located about 1 mile inside the south entrance, offers museum exhibits, park information, and an orientation program, plus a bookstore.

FEES, BACKCOUNTRY PERMITS & REGULATIONS   Entry into the park (for up to 7 days), including unlimited use of the shuttle bus (operating early April through October), costs $20 per private vehicle, or $10 per individual on foot, bicycle, or motorcycle.

Oversize vehicles are charged $10 for use of the Zion–Mt. Carmel Tunnel on the east side of the park (see "Getting There/Access Points," earlier in the chapter).

Backcountry permits, available at either visitor center, are required for all overnight hikes in the park as well as all slot canyon hikes. Permits cost $10 for one or two people, $15 for three to six, and $20 for 7 to 12 people. Camping costs $16 per night for basic campsites and $18 to $20 per night for sites with electric hookups (located in Watchman Campground).

Bicycles are prohibited in the Zion–Mt. Carmel Tunnel, in the backcountry, and on all trails except the Pa'rus Trail. Feeding or otherwise disturbing wildlife is forbidden, as is vandalizing or upsetting any natural feature of the park. Pets, which must be leashed at all times, are prohibited on all trails, in the backcountry, and in public buildings.

SEASONS/AVOIDING THE CROWDS   The park is open year-round (though visitor centers are closed Christmas Day), 24 hours a day, although weather conditions may limit some activities at certain times. For instance, you'll want to avoid long hikes in midsummer, when the park bakes under temperatures that can exceed an unbearable 110°F (43°C), or during and immediately after winter storms, when ice and snow at higher elevations can make trails dangerous.

If possible, try to avoid the peak months of June, July, and August, when Zion receives almost half of its annual visitors. The quietest months are December, January, and February, but of course it's cold then, and you may have to contend with some snow and ice. A good compromise, if your schedule permits, is to visit in April, May, September, or October, when the weather is usually good but the park is less crowded than in summer.

The best way to avoid crowds is to simply walk away from them, either taking the longer and more strenuous hiking trails or hiking into the backcountry. It's sad but true—most visitors never bother to venture far from the road, and their loss can be your gain. If you're willing to expend a little energy, you can enjoy a wonderful solitary experience. You can also avoid hordes of tourists by spending time in spectacular Kolob Canyons, in the far northwest section of the park; it receives surprisingly little use, at least compared to Zion Canyon.

RANGER PROGRAMS   Rangers present a variety of free programs and activities. Evening programs, which sometimes include a slide show, take place most nights at campground amphitheaters and Zion Lodge. Topics vary, but could include the animals or plants of the park, geology of the park, humanity's role in the park, or perhaps some unique feature such as Zion's slot canyons. Rangers also give short talks on similar subjects several times daily at the Zion Canyon Visitor Center and at other locations. Ranger-guided hikes and walks, some of which require reservations, might take you to little-visited areas of the park, on a trek to see wildflowers, or out at night for a hike under a full moon. Schedules of the various activities are posted on bulletin boards at the visitor centers, campgrounds, and other locations.

Children ages 6 to 12 can join the **Junior Rangers/Explorers** ✦ in order to participate in a variety of programs, and earn certificates, badges, and patches. Morning and afternoon sessions, each lasting 2½ hours, are scheduled daily from Memorial Day to Labor Day, with kids meeting at the Nature Center in the South Campground. There's a one-time fee of $2 per child, and the age range is strictly enforced.

2 Seeing the Highlights

The best way to see Zion is to spend a week here, starting by exploring the visitor center displays and programs, and then riding the shuttle bus to the various viewpoints (or driving in the off-season). Gradually work up from short hikes and walks to full-day and overnight treks into the backcountry. That's the ideal, but for most visitors, time and finances dictate a shorter visit.

If you have only a day or two at the park, we recommend first heading to the **Zion Canyon Visitor Center** for the orientation video and exhibits, and then talking with a ranger about the amount of time you have, your abilities, and interests. A brief visit to the new **Zion Human History Museum** (about 1 mile inside the south entrance) will give you a little more insight into humanity's role—historically and currently—in Zion. Because Zion offers such a variety of landscapes and activities, you can easily create your own itinerary. If your goal is to see as much of the park as possible in 1 full day, we suggest the following:

After a quick stop at the visitor center, hop on the free **shuttle bus,** which takes you to the major roadside viewpoints. You'll be able to get off, look at the formations, take a short walk if you like, and then catch the next shuttle for a ride to the next stop.

We particularly recommend getting off the shuttle at the **Temple of Sinawava** and taking the easy 2-mile round-trip **Riverside Walk,** which follows the Virgin River through a narrow canyon past hanging gardens. Then take the shuttle back to the lodge (total time: 2 to 4 hours). At the lodge, stop by the gift shop and perhaps have lunch in the excellent restaurant.

Near the lodge, you'll find the trailhead for the **Emerald Pools.** Especially pleasant on hot days, this easy walk through a forest of oak, maple, fir, and cottonwood trees leads to a waterfall, hanging garden, and the shimmering lower pool. This part of the walk should take about an hour round-trip, but those with a bit more time may want to add another hour and another mile to the loop by taking the moderately strenuous hike on a rocky, steeper trail to the upper pool. If you still have time and energy, head back to the south park entrance and stop at **Watchman** (east of Watchman Campground), for the 2-mile, 2-hour round-trip, moderately strenuous hike to a plateau with beautiful views of several rock formations and the town of Springdale. In the evening, try to take in a campground amphitheater program.

3 Exploring Zion by Shuttle or Car

If you enter Zion from the east, along the steep **Zion–Mt. Carmel Highway,** you'll travel 13 miles through the park to the **Zion Canyon Visitor Center,** passing **Checkerboard Mesa,** a massive sandstone rock formation covered with horizontal and vertical lines that make it look like a huge fishing net. Continuing on, you'll view a fairyland of fantastically shaped rocks of red, orange, tan, and white, as well as the **Great Arch of Zion,** carved high in a stone cliff.

A shuttle-bus system has been implemented in the main section of the park to reduce traffic congestion and the resultant problems of pollution, noise, and

Impressions

Nothing can exceed the wondrous beauty of Zion . . . in the nobility and beauty of the sculptures there is no comparison.

—Geologist Clarence Dutton, 1880

damage to park resources. The shuttle system consists of two loops: one in the town of Springdale and the other along Zion Canyon Scenic Drive, with the loops connecting at the new transit/visitor center just inside the south park entrance (p. 220). From April through October, access to Zion Canyon Scenic Drive (above Utah 9) is limited to shuttle buses, hikers, and bikers. The only exception is overnight Zion Lodge guests and tour buses connected with the lodge, which have access as far as the lodge. Shuttles run frequently—about every 6 minutes at peak times—and have room for packs, coolers, strollers, and two bicycles. In winter, when the fewest number of visitors are here, you are permitted to drive the full length of Zion Canyon Scenic Drive in your own vehicle.

Those driving into the park at the northwest corner will find a short scenic drive open year-round. The **Kolob Canyons Road** (about 45 minutes from Zion Canyon Visitor Center at I-15 exit 40) runs 5 miles among spectacular red and orange rocks, ending at a high vista. Allow about 45 minutes round-trip, with time for stopping at the numbered viewpoints. Be sure to get a copy of the *Kolob Canyons Road Guide* at the Kolob Visitor Center. Here's what you'll pass along the way:

Leaving **Kolob Canyons Visitor Center,** drive along the Hurricane Fault to **Hurricane Cliffs,** a series of tall, gray cliffs composed of limestone, and onward to **Taylor Creek,** where a piñon-juniper forest clings to life on the rocky hillside, providing a home to the bright blue scrub jay. Your next stop is **Horse Ranch Mountain,** which, at 8,726 feet, is the national park's highest point. Passing a series of colorful rock layers, where you might be lucky enough to spot a golden eagle, your next stop is **Box Canyon,** along the south fork of Taylor Creek, with sheer rock walls soaring over 1,500 feet high. Next you'll see a multicolored layer of rock, pushed upward by tremendous forces from within the earth.

Continue until you reach a canyon, which exposes a rock wall that likely began as a sand dune before being covered by an early sea and cemented into stone. Next stop is a side canyon, with large, arched alcoves boasting delicate curved ceilings. Head on to a view of **Timber Top Mountain,** which has a sagebrush-blanketed desert at its base, but is covered with stately fir and Ponderosa pine at its peak. Watch for mule deer on the brushy hillsides, especially between October and March, when they might be spotted just after sunrise or before sunset.

From here, continue to **Rockfall Overlook;** a large scar on the mountainside marks the spot where a 1,000-foot chunk of stone crashed to the earth in July 1983, the victim of erosion. And finally, stop to see the canyon walls themselves, colored orange-red by iron oxide and striped black by mineral-laden water running down the cliff faces.

4 Outdoor Pursuits

Guided hiking, rock climbing, and biking trips in the area outside the park are offered by several local companies, including **Zion Adventure Company,** 36 Lion Blvd. (P.O. Box 523), Springdale, UT 84767 (© **435/772-1001;** www. zionadventures.com); **Zion Rock and Mountain Guides,** 1458 Zion Park Blvd.

(P.O. Box 623), Springdale, UT 84767 (© **435/772-3303;** www.zionrock
guides.com); and in the same building, **Springdale Cycle Tours,** 1458 Zion
Park Blvd. (P.O. Box 501), Springdale, UT 84767 (© **800/776-2099** or 435/
772-0575; www.springdalecycles.com). Shuttle service for backcountry hikers
and bikers is available throughout the area from **Zion Canyon Transportation**
(© **877/635-5993** or 435/635-5993), and **Springdale Narrows Shuttle** (© **800/
776-2099**). Those who want to try to arrange rides with fellow hikers can make
use of a bulletin board at the visitor center.

BIKING & MOUNTAIN BIKING

Although bikes are prohibited on all trails and forbidden to travel cross-country
within the national park boundaries, two developments have helped Zion
become one of America's few bike-friendly national parks.

The **Pa'rus Trail,** open since late 1994, runs 2 miles along the Virgin River
from the South Campground entrance to Zion Canyon Scenic Drive near its
intersection with the Zion–Mt. Carmel Highway. Along the way, the trail
crosses the North Fork of the Virgin River and several creeks, and provides good
views of Watchman, West Temple, the Sentinel, and other lower canyon formations. The paved trail is open to bicyclists, pedestrians, and those with strollers
or wheelchairs, but is closed to motor vehicles.

Bikes are permitted on the park's established roads at any time, except in the
Zion–Mt. Carmel tunnel, where they are always prohibited. From April through
October, **Zion Canyon Scenic Drive** north of the Zion–Mt. Carmel Highway
is open only to shuttle buses, bicyclists, and hikers, plus tour buses and motorists
going to Zion Lodge. The rest of the year, the road is open to private motor vehicles, and the shuttle buses don't run. Bicyclists should stay to the right to allow
shuttle buses to pass.

On Bureau of Land Management and state-owned property just outside the
park, mountain bikers will find numerous rugged jeep trails that are great for
mountain biking, plus more than 70 miles of slickrock cross-country trails and
single-track trails. **Gooseberry Mesa,** above the community of Springdale, is
generally considered the best mountain-biking destination in the area, but you'll
also find good trails on nearby Wire and Grafton mesas.

Talk with the knowledgeable staff at **Springdale Cycle Tours** (see above)
about the best trails for your interests and abilities. This full-service bike shop
also offers maps, a full range of bikes and accessories, repairs, and rentals ($35
to $55 for a full day, $25 to $45 for a half day). The company also offers full-
day guided mountain bike trips outside the park, starting at $85 per person (for
a group of six), plus a variety of multi-day excursions.

HIKING

Zion offers a wide variety of hiking trails, ranging from easy half-hour walks on
paved paths to grueling overnight hikes over rocky terrain. Hikers with a fear of
heights should be especially careful when choosing trails; many include steep,
dizzying drop-offs. What follows are our top hiking suggestions.

The **Weeping Rock Trail,** among the park's shortest trails, is a half-mile
round-trip walk from the Zion Canyon Scenic Drive to a rock alcove with a
spring and hanging gardens of ferns and wildflowers. Although paved, the trail
is steep and not suitable for wheelchairs.

Another short hike is the **Lower Emerald Pools Trail** ⭐⭐, which is an easy
1-hour walk. If you want to extend your trip to a moderately strenuous 2-hour
hike you can continue along the loop. A 0.6-mile paved path from the Emerald

Pools parking area through a forest of oak, maple, fir, and cottonwood leads to a waterfall, a hanging garden, and the Lower Emerald Pool, and is suitable for those in wheelchairs, with assistance. From here, a steeper, rocky trail (not appropriate for wheelchairs) continues past cactus, yucca, and juniper another half mile to Upper Emerald Pool, with another waterfall. A third pool, just above Lower Emerald Pool, offers impressive reflections of the cliffs. The pools are named for the green color of the water, which is caused by algae.

A particularly scenic hike is the **Hidden Canyon Trail,** a 2-mile moderately strenuous hike that takes about 3 hours. Starting at the Weeping Rock parking area, the trail climbs 800 feet through a narrow water-carved canyon, ending at the canyon's mouth. Those wanting to extend the hike can go another 0.6 mile to a small natural arch. Hidden Canyon Trail includes long drop-offs and is not recommended to anyone with a fear of heights.

Another moderately strenuous but relatively short hike is the **Watchman Trail,** which starts near the transit/visitor center. This 3-mile round-trip hike gets surprisingly little use, possibly because it can be very hot in midday. Climbing to a plateau near the base of the formation called the Watchman, it offers splendid views of lower Zion Canyon, the Towers of the Virgin, and West Temple formations.

For a strenuous 4-hour, 5-mile hike—one that's definitely not for anyone with even a mild fear of heights—take the **Angel's Landing Trail** to a summit that offers spectacular views into Zion Canyon. But be prepared: The final half mile follows a narrow, knife-edge trail along a steep ridge, where footing can be slippery even under the best of circumstances. Support chains have been set along parts of the trail.

Hiking **the Narrows** 🎦🎦 is actually not really hiking a trail at all, but involves walking or wading along the bottom of the Virgin River, through a spectacular 1,000-foot-deep chasm that, at a mere 20 feet wide, definitely lives up to its name. Passing fancifully sculptured sandstone arches, hanging gardens, and waterfalls, this moderately strenuous 16-mile one-way hike can be completed in less than a day or in several days, depending on how quickly you want to go. The Narrows are subject to flash flooding and can be very treacherous. Park service officials remind hikers that they are responsible for their own safety and should check on current water conditions and weather forecasts. This hike is *not* recommended when rain is forecast. Permits are required for full-day and overnight hikes (check with rangers for details), but are not needed for easy, short day hikes, which you can access from just beyond the end of the **Riverside Walk,** a 2-mile trail that starts at the Temple of Sinawava parking area.

HORSEBACK RIDING

Guided rides in the park are available March through October from **Canyon Trail Rides,** P.O. Box 128, Tropic (✆ **435/679-8665;** www.canyonrides.com), which is based right near Zion Lodge. A 1-hour ride along the Virgin River costs $20 and a half-day ride on the Sand Beach Trail costs $45. Riders must weigh no more than 220 pounds, and children must be at least 7 years old for the 1-hour ride and 8 years old for the half-day ride. Reservations are advised.

ROCK CLIMBING

Technical rock climbers like the sandstone cliffs in Zion Canyon, although rangers warn that much of the rock is loose, or "rotten," and climbing equipment and techniques suitable for granite are often less effective on sandstone. Permits ($5) are required for overnight climbs, and because some routes may be closed at times, climbers should check at the Zion Canyon Visitor Center before setting out.

WILDLIFE VIEWING & BIRD-WATCHING

It's a rare visitor to Zion who doesn't spot a critter of some sort, from mule deer—often seen along roadways and in campgrounds—to the numerous varieties of lizards, including the park's largest, the chuckwalla, which can grow to 20 inches. The ringtail cat, a relative of the raccoon, prowls Zion Canyon at night and is not above helping itself to your camping supplies. Along the Virgin River, you'll see bank beaver, so named because they live in burrows dug into river banks instead of building dams. The park is also home to several types of squirrels, gophers, and pack rats.

If you're interested in spotting birds, you're in luck here. The rare peregrine falcon, among the world's fastest birds, sometimes nests in the Weeping Rock area, where you're also likely to see the dipper, winter wren, and white-throated swift. Also in the park are golden eagles, several species of hummingbirds, ravens, piñon jays, and possibly a roadrunner or two.

Snakes include the poisonous Great Basin rattler, found below 8,000 feet elevation, as well as nonpoisonous kingsnakes and gopher snakes. Tarantulas—those large, hairy, usually slow-moving spiders—are often seen in the late summer and fall. Contrary to popular belief, the tarantula's bite is not deadly, although it may be somewhat painful.

Remember, it's illegal to feed the wildlife. No matter how much you may want to befriend an animal by offering food, please remember that it's not healthy for the wildlife to eat human food or to get accustomed to being fed this way.

5 Camping

The absolute best places to camp are at one of the **national park campgrounds** ★★★ just inside the park's south entrance. Both of Zion's main campgrounds have paved roads, well-spaced sites, and lots of trees. Facilities include restrooms with flush toilets but no showers, a dump station, a public telephone, and sites for those with disabilities. The fee is $16 per night for basic sites, or $20 per night for sites with electric hookups.

South Campground has 126 sites (no hookups) and is usually open from April through September only. Reservations are not accepted for South Campground, which often fills by noon in summer, so get here early in the day to claim a site. Some campers stay at nearby commercial campgrounds their first night in the area, then hurry into the park the next morning, circling like vultures until a site becomes available.

Watchman Campground (© 800/365-2267 or http://reservations.nps.gov for reservations) has 168 sites, with electric hookups on two loops, and is open year-round (reservations available spring through early fall only).

Lava Point, with only six sites, is located on the Kolob Terrace. It has fire grates, tables, and toilets, but no water, and there's no fee. Vehicles are limited to 19 feet, and it's usually open from May through October.

If you can't get a site in the park, or if you prefer hot showers or complete RV hookups, there are several campgrounds in the surrounding area. The closest, **Zion Canyon Campground,** on Zion Park Boulevard a half mile south of the park entrance (© 435/772-3237; fax 435/772-3844; www.zioncamp.com), is open year-round and offers 220 sites, many of which are shaded. Although it gets quite crowded in summer, the campground is clean and well maintained; in addition to the usual showers and RV hookups, you'll find a self-service laundry, dump station, convenience store, and restaurant. Tenters are welcome; rates range from $20 to $30 for two people.

6 Accommodations

The only lodging actually in Zion National Park is Zion Lodge. The other properties listed here are all in Springdale, a village of some 350 people at the park's south entrance that has become the park's bedroom. Room tax adds 11.5% to all lodging bills. Pets are not accepted unless otherwise noted.

You can also base yourself in St. George, which is 42 miles away; Kanab, 40 miles away; or Cedar City, 56 miles away (see chapter 10 for information).

IN THE PARK

Zion Lodge ★★★ The recently refurbished motel units and cabins are nice enough, but then again, you don't come to Zion to stay indoors—you come for the scenery, and there are pretty incredible views of the majesty and glory that is Zion from the lobby's large picture windows and from the motel rooms, cabins, and suites. Each charming cabin has a private porch, stone (gas-burning) fireplace, two double beds, pine-board walls, and log beams. The comfortable motel rooms have two queen-size beds, a private porch or balcony, and all the usual amenities except TVs. Suites have one king bed, a separate sitting room, and a wet bar. Ranger programs are offered in the lodge auditorium; the gift shop sells everything from postcards to expensive silver and turquoise American Indian jewelry. The lodge fills quickly during the summer, so make reservations as far in advance as possible.

Zion National Park, UT. © **435/772-3213.** Fax 435/772-2001. Information and reservations: Xanterra Parks & Resorts, 14001 E. Iliff Ave., Suite 600, Aurora, CO 80014. © **888/297-2757** or 303/297-2757. Fax 303/297-3175. www.zionlodge.com. 121 units. Mid-Mar to Nov motel rooms $120–$125 double; cabins $128–$133 double; suites $143–$148 double. Discounts and packages available in winter. AE, DISC, MC, V. **Amenities:** Restaurant (see the Red Rock Grill, p. 230). *In room:* A/C.

NEARBY

For additional information on lodging, dining, and area attractions contact the **Zion Canyon Chamber of Commerce,** P.O. Box 331, Springdale, UT 84767 (© **888/518-7070;** www.zionpark.com).

Canyon Ranch Motel Consisting of a series of two- and four-unit cottages set back from the highway, this motel has the look of an old-fashioned auto camp on the outside but provides modern motel rooms on the interior—either new or newly remodeled. Some units have showers only, while others have shower/tub combos. Room no. 13, with two queen-size beds, offers spectacular views of the Zion National Park rock formations through its several large picture windows; views from most other rooms are almost as good. There's a nice lawn area with trees and picnic tables.

668 Zion Park Blvd. (P.O. Box 175), Springdale, UT 84767. © **435/772-3357.** Fax 435/772-3057. www.canyonranchmotel.com. 21 units. Rates per room for up to 5 people: Apr–Oct $68–$88; Nov–Mar $48–$68. AE, DISC, MC, V. Pets accepted at management discretion ($10 per pet). **Amenities:** Outdoor pool; Jacuzzi. *In room:* A/C, TV, kitchenettes available in some units.

Cliffrose Lodge & Gardens ★ With river frontage and 5 acres of lawns, shade trees, and flower gardens, the Cliffrose offers a beautiful setting just outside the entrance to Zion National Park. The architecture is Southwestern adobe style, with redwood balconies, and the outdoor rock waterfall Jacuzzi is a delight, especially in the evening. The modern, well-kept rooms and suites have all the standard motel appointments, plus unusually large bathrooms with combination shower/tubs. On the lawns, you'll find comfortable seating, including a lawn swing.

281 Zion Park Blvd. (P.O. Box 510), Springdale, UT 84767. ℂ **800/243-8824** or 435/772-3234. Fax 435/772-3900. www.cliffroselodge.com. 40 units. Summer $119–$189 per unit. Rates 20% to 40% lower in winter, except holidays. AE, DISC, MC, V. **Amenities:** Large outdoor heated pool; Jacuzzi; coin-op laundry. *In room:* A/C, TV.

Desert Pearl Inn ⭑   This imposing property offers luxurious and comfortable accommodations with beautiful views of the area's scenery from private terraces or balconies. Spacious rooms are decorated in modern Southwest style, with either two queens or a king bed. The grounds are nicely landscaped. Plans call for construction of a restaurant and additional units.

707 Zion Park Blvd., Springdale, UT 84767. ℂ **888/828-0898** or 435/772-8888. Fax 435/772-8889. www.desertpearl.com. 60 units. $78–$125 double. AE, DISC, MC, V. **Amenities:** Huge outdoor heated pool; Jacuzzi. *In room:* A/C, TV, dataport, minibar, fridge.

Flanigan's Inn ⭑⭑   Unlike most other options in the area, which serve only as good crash pads after long days spent exploring Zion, you might actually want to spend some time relaxing here. A mountain-lodge atmosphere pervades this very attractive complex of natural wood and rock, set among trees, lawns, and flowers just outside the entrance to the national park. Parts of the inn date to 1947, but all rooms were completely renovated in the early 1990s, with Southwestern decor, wood furnishings, and local art. One room has a fireplace, other units have whirlpool tubs and bidets. A nature trail leads to a hilltop vista. Summer reservations are often booked 3 to 4 months in advance.

428 Zion Park Blvd. (P.O. Box 100), Springdale, UT 84767. ℂ **800/765-7787** or 435/772-3244. Fax 435/772-3396. www.flanigans.com. 34 units. Mid-Mar to Nov and holidays $79–$199 double, $109–$209 suites; Dec to mid-Mar (except holidays) $49–$79 double, $79–$139 suite. AE, DISC, MC, V. **Amenities:** Restaurant (see the Spotted Dog Café, p. 230); outdoor heated pool; outdoor hot tub; full-service spa. *In room:* A/C, TV, units with kitchenettes available.

Harvest House Bed & Breakfast at Zion   This Utah territory–style (a style similar to Victorian) house, which was built in 1989, has a cactus garden out front and a garden sitting area in back, with a koi pond and spectacular views of the national park rock formations. Guest rooms are charming, comfortable, and quiet, with private bathrooms, an eclectic mixture of contemporary and wicker furnishings, and original art and photography dotting the walls. One upstairs room faces west and boasts grand sunset views, while the other two have private decks facing the impressive formations of Zion. The downstairs suite can accommodate up to five adults.

The gourmet breakfasts are sumptuous yet healthy, and include fresh-baked breads, fresh-squeezed orange juice, granola, fruit, yogurt, and a hot entree.

29 Canyon View Dr. (P.O. Box 125), Springdale, UT 84767. ℂ **435/772-3880.** Fax 435/772-3327. www.harvesthouse.net. 4 units. $80–$110 double. Rates include full breakfast. DISC, MC, V. Children over 6 welcome. **Amenities:** Outdoor Jacuzzi. *In room:* A/C, no phone.

Zion Park Motel   This economical motel offers comfortable, attractively furnished rooms, all recently remodeled, with either showers or combination shower/tubs. The family suite sleeps six. Adjacent are a self-service laundry, restaurant, and small but well-stocked grocery store with camping supplies and an ATM. There is also a picnic area and playground on the premises.

855 Zion Park Blvd. (P.O. Box 365), Springdale, UT 84767. ℂ 435/772-3251. www.zionparkmotel.com. 21 units. $59–$69 double; $79–$119 family suite. AE, DISC, MC, V. **Amenities:** Outdoor heated pool. *In room:* A/C, TV, full kitchens in 2 units, fridge, microwave.

7 Dining

With the exception of the Red Rock Grill, these restaurants are all located on the main road to the park through Springdale.

IN THE PARK

Red Rock Grill ⭐⭐ AMERICAN   A mountain-lodge atmosphere prevails here, complete with large windows that look out toward the park's magnificent rock formations. House specialties at dinner include an excellent slow-roasted prime rib au jus and the very popular Utah red mountain trout. Specific menu items change, but there are generally several chicken dishes, such as a skinless chicken breast basted with a spicy Caribbean sauce, and several vegetarian items, such as black bean ragout. At lunch, you'll find grilled trout, barbecued pork ribs, burgers, sandwiches, and salads; breakfasts offer all the usuals. Ask about the lodge's specialty ice creams and other exotic desserts. The restaurant will pack lunches to go, and offers full liquor service. If you are looking for something cheaper, Zion Lodge's Castle Dome Café offers an outdoor dining patio serving burgers, deli sandwiches, hot dogs, pizza, ice cream, and frozen yogurt.

Zion Lodge, Zion National Park. ℂ 435/772-3213. www.zionlodge.com. Dinner reservations required in summer. Breakfast $3.75–$6.95, lunch $4.95–$6.75, main dinner courses $9.95–$20. AE, DC, DISC, MC, V. Daily 6:30–10am, 11:30am–3pm, and 5:30–9pm.

NEARBY

Bit & Spur Restaurant & Saloon ⭐⭐ MEXICAN/SOUTHWESTERN This may look like an Old West saloon, with its rough wood-and-stone walls and exposed beam ceiling, but it's an unusually clean saloon that has a family dining room, patio seating, and walls decorated with original oil paintings. The food here is a notch or two above what we expected, a bit closer to what you'd find in a good Santa Fe restaurant. The menu includes Mexican standards such as burritos, flautas, chile rellenos, and a traditional chile stew with pork; but you'll also find more exotic creations including the *pollo relleno*—a grilled breast of chicken stuffed with cilantro pesto and goat cheese, served with pineapple salsa. Seasonal specials might include a Moroccan spiced lamb (braised lamb shank with a tamarind glaze and black-eyed pea ragout). The Bit & Spur has a full liquor license and an extensive wine list.

1212 Zion Park Blvd., Springdale. ℂ 435/772-3498. Reservations recommended. Main courses $8.50–$20. AE, DISC, MC, V. Feb–Nov daily 5–10pm (bar open until midnight); Dec–Jan Thurs–Mon 5–10pm. Closed Christmas Day.

Spotted Dog Café ⭐ AMERICAN/REGIONAL   With a greenhouse/garden atmosphere, this restaurant makes the most of the area's spectacular scenery, boasting large windows for indoor diners, plus an outdoor patio. The chef uses fresh local ingredients and herbs from the inn's garden whenever possible. Breakfast features homemade granola, fresh fruits, and juices; traditional egg dishes including trout and eggs; and wonderful omelets with fillings such as smoked salmon and brie. The dinner menu changes with the seasons, with spring seeing numerous fresh vegetable and lamb dishes; summer celebrated with innovative salads and light entrees, such as a local trout entree and mesquite roasted chicken; and fall and winter full of rich sauces, black Angus beef, pork, wild game, and scrumptious desserts. There is an excellent 2,000-bottle wine cellar; microbrewery draft beers are also available along with complete liquor service.

At Flanigan's Inn, 428 Zion Park Blvd., Springdale. ℭ 435/772-3244. Reservations recommended. Main courses $9.95–$24. AE, DISC, MC, V. Summer daily 7–11:30am and 5–10pm; reduced hours in winter.

Zion Park Gift & Deli ⭐ *Value* SANDWICHES   This is our choice for a top quality deli-style sandwich at an economical price. You can eat at one of the cafe-style tables inside or on the outdoor patio, or you can carry your sandwich off on a hike or to a national park picnic ground. All baked goods, including the excellent sandwich breads and sub rolls, are made in-house. In typical deli style, you order at the counter and wait as your meal is prepared with your choice of bread, meats, cheeses, and condiments. This is also a good breakfast stop for those who enjoy fresh-baked cinnamon rolls, muffins, banana nut bread, and similar goodies, with a cup of espresso. Locally made candy and 16 flavors of ice cream and frozen yogurt are also offered. No alcohol is served.

866 Zion Park Blvd., Springdale. ℭ 435/772-3843. $5–$10. AE, DISC, MC, V. Summer Mon–Sat 8am–9pm; reduced hours in winter.

Zion Pizza & Noodle ⭐ *Kids* PIZZA/PASTA   Located in a former LDS church with a turquoise steeple, this cafe is outfitted with small, closely spaced tables and black-and-white photos dotting the walls. Patrons order at the counter and help themselves at the beverage bar. The 12-inch pizzas, baked in a slate stone oven, are good, but New York–style pizza purists might be put off by oddly-topped specialty pies such as the Southwestern burrito pizza or the barbecued chicken pizza. But have no fear—you can also get a basic cheese pizza, or add any of some 15 extra toppings, from pepperoni to green chiles to pineapple. The noodle side of the menu offers a variety of pastas, such as penne pasta with grilled chicken, broccoli, carrots, fresh cream, and cheese; plus calzones and stromboli.

868 Zion Park Blvd., Springdale. ℭ 435/772-3815. www.zionpizzanoodle.com. Reservations not accepted. Entrees $9.95–$12. No credit cards. Summer daily from 4pm until closing; call for winter hours.

8 Two Attractions in Nearby Springdale

Just outside the south entrance to Zion National Park, in Springdale, are two worthwhile attractions.

The **Tanner Concert Series** presents multi-discipline performing arts in the stunning, 2,000-seat outdoor **O. C. Tanner Amphitheater,** just off Zion Park Boulevard. Productions range from symphony orchestra concerts and dance productions to bluegrass and cowboy poetry shows. Shows begin at 8pm every Saturday through the summer, and cost $9 for adults and $5 for youths (18 and younger). For information, contact **Dixie College,** in St. George (ℭ 435/652-7994; www.dixie.edu/tanner/index.html).

The **Zion Canyon Theatre,** 145 Zion Park Blvd. (ℭ 435/772-2400; www.zioncanyontheatre.com) boasts a huge screen—some six stories high by 80 feet wide. Here you can see the dramatic film *Zion Canyon—Treasure of the Gods,* with thrilling scenes of the Zion National Park area, including a hair-raising flash flood through Zion Canyon's Narrows and some dizzying bird's-eye views. The theater also shows a variety of other changing large format films. Admission is $8 adults, $6 seniors, $5 children 3 to 11, and is free for children under 3. The theater is open daily year-round except Christmas. Shows begin hourly April through October from 11am to 7pm (call for winter hours). The theater complex also contains a tourist information center, an ATM, a picnic area, gift and souvenir shops, a deli, an ice cream shop, a Paiute Indian exhibit, and a bookstore.

Bryce Canyon National Park

If you could visit only one national park in your lifetime, we'd send you to Bryce Canyon ★★★. Here you'll find magic, inspiration, and spectacular beauty. The main draw of the park is the thousands of intricately shaped hoodoos: those silent rock sentinels and congregations gathered in colorful cathedrals, arranged in formations that invite your imagination to run wild.

Hoodoos, geologists tell us, are simply pinnacles of rock, often oddly shaped, left standing after millions of years of water and wind have eroded the surrounding rock. But perhaps the truth really lies in a Paiute legend. These American Indians, who lived in the area for several hundred years before being forced out by Anglo pioneers, told of a "Legend People" who lived here in the old days; because of their evil ways, they were turned to stone by the powerful Coyote, and even today they remain frozen in time.

Whatever the cause, Bryce Canyon is certainly unique. Its intricate and often whimsical formations are smaller and on a more human scale than the impressive rocks seen at Zion, Capitol Reef, and Canyonlands national parks. And Bryce is far easier to explore than the huge and sometimes intimidating Grand Canyon. Bryce is comfortable and inviting in its beauty; we feel we know it simply by gazing over the rim, and we're on intimate terms after just one morning on the trail.

Although the colorful hoodoos are the first things to grab your attention, it isn't long before you notice the deep amphitheaters that enfold them, with their cliffs, windows, and arches, all colored in shades of red, brown, orange, yellow, and white that change and glow with the rising and setting sun. Beyond the rocks and light are the other faces of the park: three separate life zones due to the huge range of elevations in the park, each with its own unique vegetation; and a kingdom of animals, from the busy chipmunks and ground squirrels to the stately mule deer and their archenemy, the mountain lion.

Human exploration of the Bryce area likely began with the Paiutes, and it's possible that trappers, prospectors, and early Mormon scouts visited here in the early to mid-1800s, before Major John Wesley Powell conducted the first thorough survey of the region in the early 1870s. Shortly after Powell's exploration, Mormon pioneer Ebenezer Bryce and his wife, Mary, moved to the area and tried raising cattle. Although they stayed only a few years before moving on to Arizona, Bryce left behind his name and his oft-quoted description of the canyon as "a helluva place to lose a cow."

1 Just the Facts

GETTING THERE/ACCESS POINTS   **Bryce Canyon Airport** (✆ 435/ 834-5239), which has a 7,400-foot lighted runway, is located several miles from the park entrance on Utah 12. Charter service is provided by **Bryce Canyon**

Bryce Canyon National Park

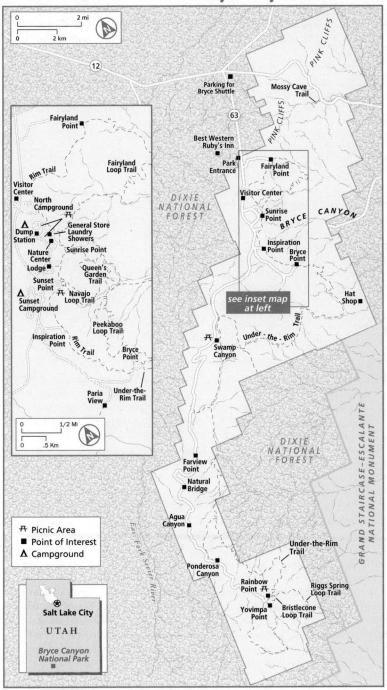

| 0 | | 2 mi |
| 0 | | 2 km |

PINK CLIFFS

12

Parking for
Bryce Shuttle

Mossy Cave
Trail

63

Best Western
Ruby's Inn

Park
Entrance

Fairyland
Point

DIXIE
NATIONAL
FOREST

Visitor Center

Sunrise
Point

BRYCE   CANYON

Inspiration
Point

Bryce
Point

see inset map
at left

Hat
Shop

Under - the - Rim   Trail

Swamp
Canyon

DIXIE
NATIONAL
FOREST

GRAND STAIRCASE-ESCALANTE
NATIONAL MONUMENT

Inset map

Fairyland
Point

Fairyland
Loop Trail

Rim Trail

Visitor
Center

North
Campground

General Store
Laundry
Showers

Dump
Station

Sunrise Point

Nature
Center

Queen's
Garden
Trail

Lodge

Sunset
Point

Navajo
Loop Trail

Sunset
Campground

Peekaboo
Loop Trail

Inspiration
Point

Rim Trail

Bryce
Point

Paria
View

Under-the-
Rim Trail

| 0 | | 1/2 Mi |
| 0 | | .5 Km |

Farview
Point

Natural
Bridge

Agua
Canyon

Eas Fork Seveer River

Picnic Area

Point of Interest

Campground

Under-the-Rim
Trail

Ponderosa
Canyon

Rainbow
Point

Riggs Spring
Loop Trail

Yovimpa
Point

Bristlecone
Loop Trail

Salt Lake City

UTAH

Bryce Canyon
National Park

Airlines (© **800/979-5050** or 435/834-5341). Car rentals are available from **Hertz,** which is located at Ruby's Inn Chevron Station, 1 mile south of Utah 12 on Utah 63 (© **800/654-3131** for national reservations, or locally at 866/866-6616 ext. 7195).

You can also fly into St. George (130 miles southwest of the park on I-15) or Cedar City (also on I-15, about 80 miles west of the park), and rent a car at either of these airports (see chapter 10).

From St. George, travel north on I-15 10 miles to exit 16, then head east on Utah 9 for 63 miles to U.S. 89, north 44 miles to Utah 12, and east 13 miles to the park entrance road. The entrance station and visitor center are just 3 miles south of Utah 12. From Cedar City (I-15 exits 57, 59, and 62), take Utah 14 west 41 miles to its intersection with U.S. 89, and follow U.S. 89 north 21 miles to Utah 12, then east 17 miles to the park entrance road.

Situated in the mountains of southern Utah, the park is traversed east to west by Utah 12, with the bulk of the park, including the visitor center, accessible via Utah 63, which branches off from Utah 12 and goes south into the main portions of the park. Utah 89 runs north to south, west of the park, and Utah 12 heads east to Tropic and eventually Escalante.

From Salt Lake City, it's approximately 240 miles to the park. Take I-15 south about 200 miles to exit 95, head east 13 miles on Utah 20, south on U.S. 89 for 17 miles to Utah 12, and east on Utah 12 for 13 miles to the park entrance road.

From Capitol Reef National Park, take Utah 24 west 10 miles to Torrey, and turn southwest onto Scenic Highway Utah 12 (through Boulder and Escalante) for about 110 miles, until you reach the park entrance road.

A couple of handy driving distances: Bryce is 83 miles east of Zion National Park and 250 miles northwest of Las Vegas, Nevada.

GETTING AROUND   In recent years, congestion has been increasing along the park's only road, making a drive through the park a less than pleasurable experience. To alleviate this, a **shuttle service** is now in effect from mid- to late May to September, between 7am and dark. Visitors can choose to park their cars at the parking and boarding area at the intersection of the entrance road and Utah 12, 3 miles from the park boundary, and ride the shuttle into the park. Those staying in the park at Bryce Canyon Lodge or one of the campgrounds can also use the shuttle, at no additional charge. The shuttle has stops at various viewpoints, as well as Ruby's Inn, Ruby's Campground, the visitor center, Sunset Campground, and Bryce Canyon Lodge. The shuttle runs every 10 to 15 minutes.

INFORMATION/VISITOR CENTER   For advance information, contact Superintendent, **Bryce Canyon National Park,** P.O. Box 170001, Bryce Canyon, UT 84717, or call weekdays between 8am and 4:30pm mountain time (© **435/ 834-5322;** www.nps.gov/brca). It's best to write at least a month before your planned visit, and specify the kind of information you require.

You can order books (in several different languages), maps, posters, and videos (in VHS and PAL formats) from the nonprofit **Bryce Canyon Natural History Association,** Box 170002, Bryce Canyon, UT 84717 (© **888/362-2642** or 435/834-4600; fax 435/834-4102; www.nps.gov/brca/nhamain.htm). The association does not offer memberships, but does give a discount to current members of other national park natural history associations.

The **visitor center,** at the north end of the park, just after you enter the park, has exhibits on the geology and history of the area and a short introductory slide show on the park. Rangers can answer questions and provide backcountry permits. Several free brochures are available, and books, maps, videos, postcards, and posters can be purchased. The visitor center is open daily year-round except Thanksgiving, Christmas, and New Year's Day. Hours are 8am to 8pm in summer, with reduced hours at other times (in the dead of the winter, the visitor center will close at 4:30pm).

FEES, BACKCOUNTRY PERMITS & REGULATIONS   Entry into the park (for up to 7 days) costs $20 per private vehicle, which includes unlimited use of the park shuttle (when it's operating). A $30 annual pass is also available. Campsites cost $10 per night.

Backcountry camping permits ($5 per trip), available at the visitor center, are required for all overnight trips into the backcountry. Backcountry camping is permitted on only two trails (see "Hiking," below).

Backcountry hikers should practice minimum-impact techniques, are prohibited from building fires, and must carry their own water. Bicycles are prohibited in the backcountry and on all trails. Feeding or otherwise disturbing wildlife is forbidden, as is vandalizing or upsetting any natural feature of the park. Dogs, which must be leashed at all times, are prohibited on all trails, in the backcountry, and in public buildings.

SEASONS/AVOIDING THE CROWDS   Although Bryce Canyon National Park receives only two-thirds the number of annual visitors that pour into Zion, the park can still be crowded, especially during its peak season from June through September, when the campgrounds are often full by 2pm. If you visit then, head for some of the lesser-used trails (ask rangers for recommendations) and start your hike as soon after sunrise as possible.

A better time to visit, if your schedule allows, is spring or fall, and if you don't mind a bit of cold and snow, the park is practically deserted from December through February—and the sight of bright red hoodoos capped with fresh white snow is something you won't soon forget.

SAFETY   While most visitors to Bryce Canyon enjoy an exciting vacation without mishap, accidents can occur, and here—possibly because of the nature of the trails—the most common injuries by far are sprained, twisted, and broken ankles. Park rangers strongly recommend that hikers—even those just out for short day hikes—wear sturdy hiking boots with good traction and ankle support.

Another concern in the park in recent years has been bubonic plague, which, contrary to popular belief, is treatable with antibiotics if caught in its early stages. The bacteria that causes bubonic plague has been found on fleas in prairie dog colonies in the park, so you should avoid contact with wild animals, particularly prairie dogs, chipmunks, ground squirrels, and other rodents. Those taking pets into the park should first dust them with flea powder.

RANGER PROGRAMS   Evening talks, which may include a slide show, take place most nights at campground amphitheaters. Topics vary, but could include such subjects as the animals and plants of the park, geology, and the role of

---

Tips Getting a Bird's-Eye View of the Park

For an unforgettable view of the canyon and its numerous formations, contact **Bryce Canyon Airlines & Helicopters** (ask for the flight desk at Ruby's Inn, ℂ **435/834-5341**). Helicopter tours last from 15 minutes to more than an hour, and the longer trips include surrounding attractions. Prices start at $60 per person, with discounts for families and groups.

humans in the park's early days. Rangers also give half-hour talks on similar subjects several times daily at various locations in the park. They also lead hikes and walks, including a moonlight hike (reservations required) and a wheelchair-accessible 1-hour canyon rim walk. Schedules are posted on bulletin boards at the visitor center, general store, campgrounds, and Bryce Canyon Lodge.

During the summer, children 12 and younger can join the **Junior Rangers** for a $1 membership fee. Junior Rangers participate in a variety of programs, and earn certificates and patches. Junior Ranger booklets are available at the visitor center. In addition, park rangers periodically conduct **special kids' activities**—usually lasting about an hour and a half—on subjects such as the park ecology. Reservations are required—contact the visitor center for information.

2 Seeing the Highlights

Because Bryce Canyon is our favorite national park, we would be happy to spend our entire vacation here. But, if you insist on being unreasonable and saving time and energy for the many other fascinating and beautiful parts of Utah, there are ways to see a good deal of Bryce in a short amount of time.

Start at the **visitor center,** of course, and watch the short slide show that explains some of the area geology. Then hop on the **Bryce Canyon Scenic Tours** van for a guided tour, complete with lively commentary (see below), or drive the 18-mile (one-way) dead-end **park road,** stopping at viewpoints to gaze down into the canyon (see "Exploring Bryce Canyon by Car," later in this chapter). An alternative is to take the **shuttle system** (discussed later in this chapter), which will take you to most of the main viewpoints.

Whichever way you choose to get around, make sure you spend at least a little time at **Inspiration Point,** which offers a splendid (and yes, inspirational) view of **Bryce Amphitheater** and its hundreds of statuesque pink, red, orange, and brown hoodoo stone sculptures.

After seeing the canyon from the top down, it's time to get some exercise, so walk at least partway down the **Queen's Garden Trail.** If you can spare 3 hours, hike down the Navajo Loop and return to the rim via Queen's Garden Trail (p. 238). Those not willing or physically able to hike into the canyon can enjoy a leisurely walk along the **Rim Trail,** which provides spectacular views into the canyon. The views are especially gorgeous about an hour before sunset. In the evening, try to take in the campground amphitheater program.

Bryce Canyon Scenic Tours & Shuttles (© **800/432-5383** or 435/834-5200; www.brycetours.com) offers 1½- to 2-hour tours year-round, leaving from Bryce Canyon Resorts next to the shuttle parking area outside the park entrance, at the intersection of the park entrance road and Utah 12, 3 miles from the park boundary. A general tour, stopping at several viewpoints, costs $26 for adults, $12 for children 5 to 15, free for children under 5. Sunrise/sunset and other specialized tours are also available.

3 Exploring Bryce Canyon by Car

The park's **18-mile scenic drive** (one-way) follows the rim of Bryce Canyon, offering easy access to a variety of views into the fanciful fairyland of stone sculptures below. Trailers are not permitted on the road, but can be left at several parking lots. All the overlooks are on your left as you begin your drive, so it's best to drive all the way to the end of the road and stop at the overlooks on your return trip. Allow 1 to 2 hours.

From the visitor center, drive 18 miles to **Yovimpa and Rainbow Point overlooks,** which offer expansive views of southern Utah, Arizona, and sometimes even New Mexico. From these pink cliffs, you can look down on a colorful platoon of stone soldiers, standing at eternal attention. A short loop trail from Rainbow Point leads to a **1,800-year-old bristlecone pine,** believed to be the oldest living thing at Bryce Canyon.

From here, drive back north to **Ponderosa Canyon Overlook,** where you can gaze down from a dense forest of spruce and fir at multicolored hoodoos, before continuing to **Agua Canyon Overlook,** which has views of some of the best color contrasts you'll find in the park. Looking almost straight down, watch for a hoodoo known as **The Hunter,** wearing a hat of green trees.

Now continue on to **Natural Bridge,** actually an arch carved by rain and wind and spanning 85 feet. From here, go on to **Farview Point,** where there's a panoramic view to the distant horizon and the Kaibab Plateau at the Grand Canyon's north rim. Passing through **Swamp Canyon,** you'll turn right off the main road to three viewpoints, the first of which is **Paria View,** with views to the south of the light-colored sandstone White Cliffs, carved by the Paria River. To the north of Paria View, you'll find **Bryce Point,** a splendid stop for seeing the awesome **Bryce Amphitheater,** the largest natural amphitheater in the park, as well as distant views of the Black Mountains to the northeast and the Navajo Mountain to the south. From here, it's just a short drive to **Inspiration Point,** offering views similar to those at Bryce Point plus the best vantage point for seeing the **Silent City,** a sleeping city cast in stone.

Return to the main road and head north to **Sunset Point,** where you can see practically all of Bryce Amphitheater, including the aptly named **Thor's Hammer** and the 200-foot-tall cliffs of **Wall Street.**

Continue north to a turnoff for your final stop at **Sunrise Point,** where there's an inspiring view into Bryce Amphitheater. This is the beginning of the **Queen's Garden Trail** 🐾🐾, an excellent choice for a walk below the canyon's rim (p. 238).

4 Outdoor Pursuits

In addition to the activities in Bryce Canyon National Park, there's plenty to do in the adjacent **Dixie National Forest.** From about early May to mid-October, you can stop at the national forest's **Red Canyon Visitor Center,** along Utah 12 about 10½ miles west of the Bryce Canyon National Park entrance road (© 435/676-2676), or contact the Powell District office of the **Dixie National Forest,** 225 E. Center St. (P.O. Box 80), Panguitch, UT 84759 (© **435/676-9300;** www.fs.fed.us/dxnf).

BIKING & MOUNTAIN BIKING

Bikes are prohibited on all trails and forbidden from traveling cross-country within the national park boundaries. This leaves the park's established scenic drive, which is open to cyclists.

Because mountain bikers are not welcome on national park hiking trails, you'll have to leave Bryce in search of trails. Fortunately, you won't have to go far. **Dave's Hollow Trail** 🐾 starts at the Bryce Canyon National Park boundary sign on Utah 63 (the park entrance road) about a mile south of Ruby's Inn. The double-track trail goes west for about a half mile before connecting with Forest Road 090, where you turn south and ride for about three-quarters of a mile before turning right onto an easy ride through Dave's Hollow to the Dave's Hollow Forest Service Station on Forest Road 087. From here, you can retrace your route for an 8-mile round-trip ride; for a 12-mile trip, turn right on Forest Road 087 to Utah 12 and then right again back to Utah 63 and the starting point. A third option is to turn left on Forest Road 087 and follow it to Tropic Reservoir (see "Fishing," below). This part of the journey does not form a loop, so you would turn around once you've reached the reservoir.

FISHING

The closest fishing hole to the park is **Tropic Reservoir,** a large lake in a ponderosa pine forest. From the intersection of Utah 63 (the park entrance road) and Utah 12, drive west about 3 miles to a gravel road, then about 7 miles south. You'll find a forest service campground open in summer, two boat ramps, and fishing for rainbow, brook, and cutthroat trout. Locals say fishing is sometimes better in streams above the lake than in the reservoir itself. For further information, contact the **Dixie National Forest** (p. 237).

HIKING

One of the things we like best about Bryce Canyon is that you don't have to be an advanced backpacker to really get to know the park. However, all trails below the rim have at least some steep grades, so wear hiking boots with a traction tread and good ankle support to avoid ankle injuries. During the hot summer months, you'll want to hike either early or late in the day, carry plenty of water, and keep in mind that the deeper you go into the canyon, the hotter it gets.

The **Rim Trail,** which does not drop into the canyon but offers splendid views from above, meanders along the rim for over 5 miles. Overlooking Bryce Amphitheater, the trail offers excellent views along the majority of its length. An easy to moderate walk, it includes a half-mile section between two overlooks—Sunrise and Sunset—that is suitable for wheelchairs. This trail is a good choice for an after-dinner stroll, when you can watch the changing evening light on the rosy rocks below.

Your best bet for getting down into the canyon and seeing the most with the least amount of sweat is to combine two popular trails—**Navajo Loop** ★★★ and **Queen's Garden.** The total distance is just under 3 miles, with a 521-foot elevation change, and it takes most hikers from 2 to 3 hours to complete the trek. It's best to start at the Navajo Loop trailhead at Sunset Point and leave the canyon on the less-steep Queen's Garden Trail, returning to the rim at Sunrise Point, half a mile to the north. The Navajo Loop section is considered fairly strenuous; Queen's Garden is rated moderate. Along the Navajo Loop section, you'll pass Thor's Hammer and wonder why it hasn't fallen, then ponder the towering skyscrapers of Wall Street. Turning onto the Queen's Garden Trail, you'll see some of the park's most fanciful formations—including majestic Queen Victoria herself, for whom the trail was named—plus the Queen's Castle and Gulliver's Castle.

Those looking for more of a challenge might consider the **Hat Shop Trail,** a strenuous 3.8-mile round-trip with a 900-foot elevation change. Leaving from the Bryce Point Overlook, you'll drop quickly to the Hat Shop, so-named because it consists of hard gray "hats" perched on narrow reddish-brown pedestals. Allow 4 hours.

For die-hard hikers who don't mind rough terrain, Bryce has two backcountry trails, usually open in summer only. The **Under-the-Rim Trail** runs for some 22.6 miles, providing an excellent opportunity to see the park's spectacular scenery on its own terms. **Riggs Spring Loop Trail,** 8.8 miles long, offers splendid views of the pink cliffs in the southern part of the park. The truly ambitious can combine the two trails for a week-long excursion. Permits, which cost $5 and are available at the visitor center, are required for all overnight trips into the backcountry.

HORSEBACK RIDING

To see Bryce Canyon the way the early pioneers did, you need to view the landscape from a horse. **Canyon Trail Rides,** P.O. Box 128, Tropic, UT 84776 (© **435/679-8665;** www.canyonrides.com), offers a close-up view of Bryce's spectacular rock formations from the relative comfort of a saddle, and welcomes first-time riders. They have a desk inside Bryce Lodge. A 2-hour ride to the canyon floor and back costs $30, including tax, per person, and a half-day trip farther into the canyon costs $45 per person. Rides are offered, weather permitting, April through November. Riders must be at least 7 years old for the 2-hour trip and at least 8 for the half-day ride, and riders can weigh no more than 220 pounds.

Guided rides are also provided by **Ruby's Scenic Rim and Outlaw Trail Rides** at Ruby's Inn (© **435/834-5341**), at similar rates; in addition, Ruby's offers a full-day ride with lunch for $79. There are age and weight limits, and reservations are recommended for both companies. Ruby's will also board your horse (call for rates).

CHUCK-WAGON DINNER RIDES   For another Old West experience, take a wagon ride through the rugged and beautiful country around Bryce to a covered-wagon camp, where the chuck wagon is all ready to serve a Dutch-oven dinner followed by Western music and dancing. Wagons leave from Old Bryce Town, across from Ruby's Inn, from late May through September, Monday through Saturday at 7pm. Cost is $30 for adults, $26 for children 9 to 15, and $18 for kids 4 to 8; tickets are available at Ruby's Inn.

WILDLIFE WATCHING

The park is home to a variety of wildlife, ranging from mule deer to the commonly seen mountain short-horned lizard, which visitors often spot while hiking down into the canyon. Occasionally you'll catch a glimpse of a mountain lion, most likely on the prowl in search of a mule-deer dinner; elk and pronghorn may also be seen at higher elevations.

The Utah prairie dog, listed as a threatened species, is actually a rodent. It inhabits park meadows, but should be avoided, as its fleas may carry disease (see "Safety," earlier in the chapter).

Of the many birds in the park, you're bound to hear the obnoxious call of the Steller's jay. Watch for swifts and swallows as they perform their exotic acrobatics along cliff faces; binoculars will come in handy.

The Great Basin rattlesnake, although pretty, should be given a wide berth. Sometimes more than 5 feet long, this rattler is the park's only poisonous reptile. However, like most rattlesnakes, it is just as anxious as you are to avoid confrontation.

WINTER FUN

Bryce is beautiful in winter, with the white snow creating a perfect frosting on the red, pink, orange, and brown statues standing proudly against the cold winds. **Snowshoes,** which are available for loan free of charge at the visitor center, may be used above the rim and in other designated areas, but not on cross-country ski tracks.

Cross-country skiers, meanwhile, will find **several marked, ungroomed trails (all above the rim)** ⚡, including the Fairyland Trail, which leads 1 mile through a pine and juniper forest to the Fairyland Point Overlook. From here, you can take the 1-mile Forest Trail back to the road, or continue north along the rim for another 1.2 miles to the park boundary. Although the entire park is open to cross-country skiers, rangers warn that it's extremely dangerous to try to ski on the steep trails leading down into the canyon. Stop at the visitor center for additional trail information, and go to Best Western Ruby's Inn, just north of the park entrance (✆ 435/834-5341), for information on cross-country ski trails and **snowmobiling** opportunities outside the park. Ruby's grooms over 31 miles of cross-country ski trails for skating and classical skiing, and also rents equipment. Use of the trails is free; ski rentals cost $7 for a half day and $10 for a full day.

5 Camping

IN THE PARK

Typical of the West's national park campgrounds, the two campgrounds at Bryce offer plenty of trees for a genuine "forest camping" experience, easy access to trails, and limited facilities. **North Campground** ⚡ has 105 sites; **Sunset Campground** has 111 sites. One loop in North Campground is open year-round; Sunset Campground is open May through September only. We prefer North Campground because it's closer to the Rim Trail—making it easier to rush over to catch those amazing sunrise and sunset colors—but we would gladly take any site in either campground. Neither has RV hookups or showers, but you will find modern restrooms with running water. North Campground accepts reservations year round through **National Recreation Reservation Service** (✆ 877/444-6777; www.reserveusa.com). Sunset Campground does not accept reservations, so get to the campground early to claim a site (usually by 2pm in summer). Cost is $10 per night at both campgrounds.

Showers ($2), a coin-operated laundry (open from 7am to 8pm), a snack bar, bundles of firewood, food and camping supplies, and souvenirs, are located at the **General Store** (for information, contact Bryce Canyon Lodge ✆ 435/834-5361), which is a healthy walk from either campground. The park service operates an RV dump station ($2 fee) in the summer. Tables on a covered porch run along one side of the building.

NEARBY

In addition to the campgrounds listed below, there is camping at Kodachrome Basin State Park; see p. 245.

King's Creek Campground　　Located above Tropic Reservoir, this forest service campground, at 8,000 feet elevation, has graded gravel roads and sites nestled among tall ponderosa pines. Facilities include flush toilets, drinking water, and an RV dump station, but no showers or RV hookups. The reservoir has two boat ramps (see "Fishing," earlier in this chapter). To get to the campground from the Bryce Canyon National Park entrance, go north 3 miles on Utah 63 to Utah 12, turn west (left), and go 2½ miles to the King's Creek Campground Road; turn south (left) and follow signs to Tropic Reservoir for about 7 miles to the campground.

Powell District, Dixie National Forest, P.O. Box 80, Panguitch, UT 84759. ✆ 435/676-9300. www.fs.fed. us/dxnf. 34 sites. $8. No credit cards. Open Mem Day–Labor Day.

Ruby's Inn RV Park & Campground   The closest campground to Bryce Canyon National Park that offers complete RV hookups, Ruby's is on the park's shuttle-bus route. Many sites are shaded, there's an attractive tent area, and adjacent to the campground are a lake and horse pasture. Campground facilities include a swimming pool, two coin-op laundries, a game room, horseshoes, barbecue grills, and a store with groceries and RV supplies. Also on the grounds are several camping cabins ($40 double), which share the campground's bathhouse and other facilities. 127 sites have RV hookups and 100 sites accommodate tents.

Utah 63 (P.O. Box 22), Bryce, UT 84764. ℂ 800/468-8660 or 435/834-5301. Nov–Mar call ℂ 435/834-5341. Fax 435/834-5481. www.rubysinn.com. 227 total sites. Full hookups $26, electric/water only $23, tent space $16. AE, DC, DISC, MC, V. Open Apr–Oct.

6 Where to Stay

Room taxes add about 9% to the total cost. Pets are not accepted unless otherwise noted.

IN THE PARK

Bryce Canyon Lodge ★★★   Location is what you're paying for here, and there's no denying that this is the perfect place to stay while visiting Bryce Canyon, allowing you to watch the play of changing light on the rock formations at various times of the day. The handsome sandstone and ponderosa pine lodge, which opened in 1924, contains a busy lobby, with information desks for horseback riding and other activities, and a gift shop that offers everything from postcards and souvenirs to Navajo rugs, top-quality silver-and-turquoise jewelry, and a good selection of fine American Indian jewelry.

The lodge suites are luxurious, with ceiling fans and separate sitting rooms. The motel rooms are simple; although the outside of the motel building looks like a hunting lodge, the guest units are pleasant, modern motel rooms, quite spacious, with two queen-size beds and either a balcony or patio. There's nothing at all wrong with them, except that the surroundings and exterior lead you to expect something more interesting. We'd choose the "rustic luxury" of one of the cabins, which are being restored to their 1920s decor. They're fairly small, although the tall ceilings give a feeling of spaciousness, with stone (gas-burning) fireplaces, two double beds, and log beams. It seems just the right place to stay in a beautiful national park setting like Bryce Canyon. Reserve 4 to 6 months in advance.

Bryce Canyon National Park, UT. ℂ 435/834-5361. Information and reservations: Xanterra Parks & Resorts, 14001 E. Iliff Ave., Suite 600, Aurora, CO 80014. ℂ 888/297-2757 or 303/297-2757. Fax 303/297-3175. www.brycecanyonlodge.com. 114 units (110 in motel rooms and cabins; 3 suites and 1 studio in lodge). $110–$115 motel double; $120–$125 cabin; $105–$135 lodge unit. AE, DISC, MC, V. Closed Nov–Mar. **Amenities:** Restaurant (p. 243); activities desk.

NEARBY

Best Western Ruby's Inn ★★ *Kids*   This large Best Western provides most of the beds used by tired hikers and canyon-rim gazers visiting Bryce Canyon National Park. The lobby, with a stone fireplace and a Western motif of animal-head trophies and Indian blankets, is among the busiest places in the area, with an ATM, small liquor store, beauty salon, 1-hour film processor, and information and activities desks where you can arrange excursions of all sorts, from horseback and all-terrain-vehicle rides to helicopter tours. Just off the lobby, you'll find a restaurant; a Western art gallery; a huge general store that carries souvenirs, cowboy hats, Western clothing, camping supplies, and groceries; and a U.S. post office. Outside are two gas stations and car rentals.

Spread among nine separate buildings, the modern motel rooms feature wood furnishings, art that depicts scenes of the area, and combination shower/tubs; some have one- or two-person whirlpool tubs. Rooms at the back of the complex will be a bit quieter, but you'll have to walk farther to all the lobby activities. Amenities include two indoor pools, one indoor and one outdoor whirlpool, a sun deck, nature and cross-country ski trails, a game room, a concierge, a business center, conference rooms, two coin-op laundries, and courtesy transportation from the Bryce Airport.

1000 S. Utah 63 (at the entrance to Bryce Canyon), Bryce, UT 84764. © 800/468-8660 or 435/834-5341. Fax 435/834-5265. www.rubysinn.com. 368 units, including 60 suites. June–Sept $96–$150 double; Apr–May and Oct $67–$120 double; Nov–Mar $46–$85 double; family suites $85–$150 year-round. AE, DC, DISC, MC, V. Pets accepted. **Amenities:** Restaurant (see Ruby's Inn Cowboy's Buffet and Steak Room, p. 243); 2 indoor pools; 1 indoor and 1 outdoor Jacuzzi; game room; concierge; multiple activities desks; car-rental desk; courtesy transportation from the Bryce Airport; business center; huge general store; small liquor store; salon; 2 coin-op laundries. *In room:* A/C, TV.

Bryce Point Bed & Breakfast ★ Each room in Lamar and Ethel LeFevre's bed-and-breakfast is named for and decorated in the style of one of the couple's children. For instance, son Les is a firefighter, so the Les and Dela room contains firefighting memorabilia and photos; and because son Lynn is in the airline industry, you'll find airplane-related mementos in Lynn and Karen's room. The decor is tasteful and not overdone, and most rooms offer beautiful views of Bryce Point through large picture windows. All units contain queen or king beds and private bathrooms (showers only). Our choice would be the delightful honeymoon cottage, beautifully furnished in country style, with a gas fireplace in the living room, full kitchen, washer/dryer, and king bed in the spacious bedroom.

Guests enjoy a large enclosed hot tub. The full breakfasts are homemade and satisfying, with selections such as bacon and eggs with pancakes and apple cider syrup. Smoking is not permitted.

61 N. 400 W. (P.O. Box 96), Tropic, UT 84776-0096. © 888/200-4211 or 435/679-8629 (voice/fax). 6 units. $70 double; $90–$120 honeymoon cottage. Rates include full breakfast. MC, V. **Amenities:** Large enclosed Jacuzzi. *In room:* TV/VCR, free use of the LeFevre's video collection, no phone.

Bryce View Lodge *Value* This basic modern American motel gets our vote for the best combination of economy and location. It consists of four two-story buildings, set back from the road and grouped around a large parking lot and attractively landscaped area. Rooms are simple but comfortable, recently refurbished, and quite quiet. Guests have access to the amenities across the street at Ruby's.

Utah 63 across from Best Western Ruby's Inn (P.O. Box 64002), Bryce, UT 84764. © 888/279-2304 or 435/834-5180. Fax 435/834-5181. www.bryceviewlodge.com. 160 units. $44–$60 double. AE, DC, DISC, MC, V. Pets accepted. **Amenities:** See Best Western Ruby's Inn, p. 244. *In room:* A/C, TV.

Foster's You'll find clean, quiet, economical lodging at Foster's. A modular unit contains small rooms, each with either one queen or two double beds, decorated with posters showing scenery of the area; bathrooms have showers only. Also on the grounds is a grocery store (open 7am–10pm, closed Oct–Feb) with a rather nice bakery.

Utah 12 (P.O. Box 21), Bryce, UT 84764. © 435/834-5227. Fax 435/834-5304. 52 units. Summer $54 double; winter $45 double. AE, DISC, MC, V. 1½ miles west of the national park access road turnoff. **Amenities:** Restaurant (see Foster's Family Steak House, p. 243). *In room:* A/C, TV.

World Host Bryce Valley Inn Located 8 miles east of the park entrance road, these simply decorated, basic motel rooms offer a clean, economical choice for park visitors. All rooms have combination shower/tubs and either one or two queen beds; one suite has two queens and a hide-a-bed, and there's one handi-capped-accessible room. Amenities include a 24-hour coin-op laundry, and a gift shop offering a large selection of American Indian arts and crafts, handmade gifts, rocks, and fossils.

199 N. Main St., Tropic, UT 84776. (*) 800/442-1890 or 435/679-8811. Fax 435/679-8846. www.brycevalley inn.com. 65 units. May–Oct $55–$60 double; Nov–Apr $36–$44 double. AE, MC, V. 8 miles east of the park entrance road. Small pets accepted (fee). **Amenities:** Restaurant (see Hungry Coyote Restaurant & Saloon, p. 243); 24-hr. coin-op washer and dryers. *In room:* A/C, TV.

7 Dining

IN THE PARK

Bryce Canyon Lodge ★★ AMERICAN   We would come here just for the mountain-lodge atmosphere, two large stone fireplaces, American Indian weav-ings and baskets, huge 45-star 1897 American flag, and large windows looking out on the park. But the food's good, too—and quite reasonably priced consid-ering this is the only real restaurant actually located in the park. House special-ties at dinner include fresh mountain trout and honey crisp chicken. The menu offers several vegetarian items, plus chicken and pasta. At lunch, you'll find grilled trout, burgers, stews, sandwiches, and salads; breakfasts offer all the usual Amer-ican standards, and there's an excellent breakfast buffet. Ask about the lodge's specialty ice creams and desserts, such as the exotic and very tasty wild "Bryce-berry" bread pudding. Service is attentive and friendly, but a bit too speedy at dinner. The restaurant will pack lunches to go and offers full liquor service.

Bryce Canyon National Park. (*) 435/834-5361. www.brycecanyonlodge.com. Reservations required for dinner. Breakfast $3.95–$7.95, lunch $5.50–$10, dinner $13–$25. AE, DC, DISC, MC, V. Daily 6:30–10am, 11:30am–3pm, and 5:30–9pm. Closed Nov–Mar.

NEARBY

Foster's Family Steak House STEAK/SEAFOOD   The simple Western decor here provides the appropriate atmosphere for a family steakhouse. This place is popular among locals for its slow-roasted prime rib and steamed Utah trout. Foster's also offers several steaks (including a 14-oz. T-bone), sandwiches, a soup of the day, and homemade Western-style chili with beans. All of the pastries, pies, and breads are baked on the premises. Bottled beer is available with meals.

Utah 12 about 1½ miles west of the park entrance road. (*) 435/834-5227. Reservations not accepted. Breakfast and lunch items $1.75–$6, main dinner courses $9–$20. AE, DISC, MC, V. Mar–Nov daily 7am–10pm; Dec–Feb daily 3–10pm.

Hungry Coyote Restaurant & Saloon AMERICAN/WESTERN   The Old West reigns supreme here, as evidenced in the rough wood walls, old ranch tools, kerosene lanterns, and warnings that patrons must "check your gun with the waitress." Red meat lovers will savor the thick 20-ounce T-bone, or a lean buf-falo burger. You can also get pork chops, grilled chicken, or local trout. The restaurant offers full liquor service.

199 N. Main St. at the World Host Bryce Valley Inn, Tropic. (*) 435/679-8822. www.brycevalleyinn.com. Breakfast $3.95–$6.95, dinner main courses $7–$21. AE, DISC, MC, V. Daily 6:30–11am and 5–10pm; reduced hours in winter.

Ruby's Inn Cowboy's Buffet and Steak Room STEAK/SEAFOOD   The busiest restaurant in the Bryce Canyon area, Ruby's moves 'em through with buf-fets at every meal, plus a well-rounded menu and friendly service. Regular menu dinner entrees include prime rib, slow-roasted baby back ribs, breaded and grilled southern Utah rainbow trout, broiled chicken breast, burgers, and salads. The breakfast buffet offers more choices than you'd expect, with scrambled eggs, fresh fruit, several breakfast meats, potatoes, pastries, and cereals. At the lunch buffet, you'll find country-style ribs, fresh fruit, salads, soups, vegetables, and breads; the dinner buffet features charbroiled thin-sliced rib-eye steak and other meats, pastas, potatoes, and salads. In addition to the large, Western-style dining room, an outdoor patio is open in good weather. Full liquor service is available.

Utah 63, the Ruby's Inn complex, Bryce. ℂ 435/834-5341. www.rubysinn.com. Reservations not accepted. Buffets: breakfast $8.50 adults and $6 children 3–12, lunch $9 and $7, dinner $14.50 and $7.50; main courses: $3.95–$14breakfast and lunch, $5.95–$20 dinner. AE, DC, DISC, MC, V. Summer daily 6:30am–10pm; winter daily 6:30am–9pm.

8 More to See & Do Just Outside Bryce Canyon

The **Best Western Ruby's Inn** (ℂ 435/834-5341), on Utah 63 just north of the Bryce Canyon National Park entrance (see "Where to Stay," earlier in this chapter), is practically a one-stop entertainment center for those looking for a bit of variety in their Bryce Canyon vacation.

Directly across Utah 63 from the motel are **Old Bryce Town Shops,** open from mid-May through September, where you'll encounter a rock shop, a Christmas store, souvenir shops, and an opportunity to buy that genuine cowboy hat you've always wanted. There's a trail especially for kids where they can look for arrowheads, fossils, and petrified wood; you can also try your hand at panning for gold.

In Ruby's vast complex, you'll find a U.S. post office, liquor store (closed Sundays and holidays), two coin-op laundries (one open 24 hours), seasonal game room, 1-hour photo lab, foreign-currency exchange (front desk), ATM, and fax and photocopy machines.

Nearby, **Bryce Canyon Country Rodeo** has bucking broncos, bull riding, calf roping, and all sorts of rodeo fun in a 1-hour program from Memorial Day weekend to mid-September, Monday through Saturday evenings at 7pm. Admission is $7 for adults and $4 for children under 12.

RED CANYON

About 9 miles west of Bryce Canyon National Park, in the Dixie National Forest, is Red Canyon, named for its vermilion-colored rock formations, which are accented by stands of rich green ponderosa pine. The canyon is a favorite of hikers and mountain bikers in summer and cross-country skiers and snowshoers in winter.

There are about a dozen trails in Red Canyon; a free map is available from the forest service (ℂ 435/826-5499). Some trails are open to hikers only, others to mountain bikers, horseback riders, and those with all-terrain vehicles. One especially scenic multi-use trail is the 5.3-mile (one-way) **Casto Canyon Trail,** which runs along the bottom of Casto Canyon. It connects with the 8.7-mile (one-way) **Cassidy Trail** and 3-mile (one-way) **Losee Canyon Trail** to produce a 17-mile loop that's ideal for a multi-day backpacking trip. Watch for elk in winter, and pronghorn and raptors year-round. The Casto Canyon and Losee Canyon Trails are considered moderate; Cassidy Trail ranges from easy to strenuous.

For maps, specific directions to trailheads, current trail conditions, and additional information, stop at the **Red Canyon Visitor Center** along Utah 12 about 10½ miles west of the Bryce Canyon National Park entrance road (ℂ 435/676-2676).

9 Kodachrome Basin: A Picture-Perfect State Park

Located about 22 miles from the entrance to Bryce Canyon National Park, Kodachrome Basin offers wonderful scenery begging to be captured on film (regardless of brand or type). Named by the National Geographic Society in 1949, the park is filled with tall stone towers—called chimneys—and pink-and-white sandstone cliffs, all set among the contrasting greens of sagebrush and piñon and juniper trees. It also abuts and makes a good base for exploring the Grand Staircase–Escalante National Monument, which is discussed later in this chapter.

Because temperatures get a bit warm here in summer—the park is at 5,800 feet elevation—the best times to visit, especially for hikers, are May, September, and October, when there are also fewer people.

ESSENTIALS

GETTING THERE   From Bryce Canyon National Park, go 3 miles north to the junction of Utah 63 and Utah 12, go east (right) on Utah 12 for about 12 miles to Cannonville, turn south onto the park's access road (there's a sign), and go about 7 miles to the park entrance.

INFORMATION, FEES & REGULATIONS   Contact the **park office** at P.O. Box 180069, Cannonville, UT 84718-0069 (✆ **435/679-8562;** www.state parks.utah.gov). Day use costs $5 per vehicle. Dogs are permitted in the park and on trails, but must be kept on leashes no more than 6 feet long. There is no visitor center here.

OUTDOOR PURSUITS

HIKING   Kodachrome Basin offers several hiking possibilities. Starting just south of the campground, the **Panorama Trail** is only moderately difficult, with no steep climbs. At first, it follows an old, relatively flat wagon route, then climbs to offer views of the park's rock formations before reaching the well-named Panorama Point. Along the way are several possible side trips, including a short walk to the **Hat Shop,** so named because the formations resemble broad-brimmed hats, and **White Buffalo Loop,** where you can try to find a formation that looks like—guess what?—a white buffalo. The optional **Big Bear Geyser Trail** is a bit more difficult, winding past Big Bear and Mama Bear before returning to Panorama Trail. Allow 2 to 3 hours for the Panorama Trail and an extra hour for Big Bear Geyser Trail.

Fans of arches will want to drive the dirt road to the trailhead for the half-mile round-trip hike to **Shakespeare Arch,** discovered by park manager Tom Shakespeare. This trail also provides views of a large chimney-rock formation.

HORSEBACK RIDING & STAGECOACH RIDES   Located in the park, **Trail Head Station** (✆ **435/679-8536** or 435/679-8787; www.brycecanyon inn.com) offers guided horseback or horse-drawn stagecoach rides. Call for rates and seasons.

WILDLIFE WATCHING   Jackrabbits and chukar partridges are probably the most commonly seen wildlife in the park, although you'll also hear the piñon jay and might see an occasional coyote or rattlesnake.

CAMPING

The park's attractive 27-site campground has flush toilets, showers, drinking water, picnic tables, barbecue grills, and an RV dump station, but no RV hookups. Camping costs $14. Reservations are available at ✆ **800/322-3770** or www.stateparks.utah.gov; a $7 nonrefundable fee will be charged.

10 Grand Staircase–Escalante National Monument & the Highway 12 Scenic Drive

Even if it didn't have a beautiful national park at each end—Bryce Canyon and Capitol Reef—the Highway 12 Scenic Byway, which passes by and through Grand Staircase–Escalante National Monument, would be well worth the drive. Here you'll find richly varied scenery: red rock spires and canyons, dense forests of tall evergreens, pastoral meadows, colorful slickrock, and plunging waterfalls. Whether you're just passing through, pausing briefly at scenic viewpoints along the way, or stopping to explore this huge national monument, you'll have plenty to see. Those driving between Bryce Canyon and Capitol Reef national parks should allow at least 4 hours for the trip, but we suggest you stop in the small community of Escalante (see "Basing Yourself in Escalante," later in this chapter), visit its fine state park, and investigate the wild areas in the Grand Staircase–Escalante National Monument and other nearby public lands.

GRAND STAIRCASE–ESCALANTE NATIONAL MONUMENT

Covering some 1.9 million acres, this vast area of red-orange canyons, mesas, plateaus, and river valleys became a national monument by presidential proclamation on September 18, 1996. Known for its stark, rugged beauty, it contains a unique combination of geological, biological, paleontological, archaeological, and historical resources.

In announcing the creation of the monument, former President Bill Clinton proclaimed, "This high, rugged, and remote region was the last place in the continental United States to be mapped; even today, this unspoiled natural area remains a frontier, a quality that greatly enhances the monument's value for scientific study." Although hailed by environmentalists, the president's action was not popular in Utah, largely because the area contains a great deal of coal and other valuable resources. Utah Senator Orrin Hatch denounced Clinton's decree, calling it "the mother of all land-grabs."

Under the jurisdiction of the Bureau of Land Management, the monument is expected to remain open for grazing and possible oil and gas drilling under existing leases (although no new leases will be issued), as well as for hunting, fishing, hiking, camping, and other forms of recreation.

Unlike most other national monuments, almost all of this vast area is undeveloped—there are few all-weather roads, only one maintained hiking trail, and two developed campgrounds. But the adventurous will find miles upon miles of dirt roads and practically unlimited opportunities for hiking, horseback riding, mountain biking on existing dirt roads, and camping.

The national monument can be divided into three distinct sections: the **Grand Staircase** of sandstone cliffs, which includes five life zones from Sonoran Desert to coniferous forests, in the southwest; the **Kaiparowits Plateau,** a vast, wild region of rugged mesas and steep canyons in the center; and the **Escalante River Canyons** section, along the northern edge of the monument, which is a delightfully scenic area containing miles of interconnecting river canyons.

ESSENTIALS

GETTING THERE   The national monument takes in a large section of southern Utah—covering an area almost as big as the states of Delaware and Rhode Island combined—with Bryce Canyon National Park to the west, Capitol Reef National Park on its northwest edge, and Glen Canyon National Recreation Area along the east and part of the south sides.

Grand Staircase–Escalante National Monument

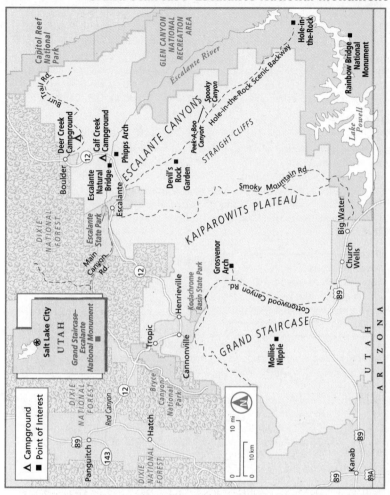

Access is via Utah 12 along the monument's northwest edge, from Kodachrome Basin State Park and the communities of Escalante and Boulder; and via U.S. 89 to the southern section of the monument, east of the town of Kanab.

INFORMATION/VISITOR CENTERS   Stop at the **Escalante Interagency Office,** on the west side of Escalante at 755 W. Main St. (Utah 12) (© **435/ 826-5499**), open daily from late March through October; or contact the Bureau of Land Management's **Kanab Visitor Center,** 745 E. U.S. 89, Kanab, UT 84741 (© **435/644-4680;** www.ut.blm.gov/monument), open daily from late March to mid-November. These offices offer maps and handouts on a variety of activities.

FEES, REGULATIONS & SAFETY   There is no charge to enter the monument; those planning overnight trips into the backcountry should obtain free permits at either of the offices listed above. Regulations are similar to those on other public lands; damaging or disturbing archaeological and historic sites in any way is particularly forbidden.

Water is the main safety concern here, whether there's too little or too much. This is generally very dry country, so those going into the monument should carry plenty of drinking water. However, thunderstorms can turn the monument's dirt roads into impassable mud bogs in minutes, stranding motorists, and potentially fatal flash floods through narrow canyons can catch hikers by surprise. Anyone planning trips into the monument should check first with one of the offices listed above for current and anticipated weather and travel conditions.

OUTDOOR PURSUITS

HIKING, MOUNTAIN BIKING & HORSEBACK RIDING   Located about 15 miles northeast of Escalante via Utah 12, the **Calf Creek Recreation Area** has a campground (p. 249), a picnic area with fire grates and tables, trees, drinking water, and flush toilets. The tree-shaded picnic and camping area lies along the creek at the bottom of a high-walled, rather narrow rock canyon. The best part of the recreation area, though, is the moderately strenuous 5½-mile round-trip hike to **Lower Calf Creek Falls.** A sandy trail leads along **Calf Creek,** past beaver ponds and wetlands, to a beautiful waterfall that cascades 126 feet down a rock wall into a tree-shaded pool. You can pick up an interpretive brochure at the trailhead.

> ## Impressions
> *On this remarkable site, God's handiwork is everywhere.*
> —Former President Bill Clinton, September 18, 1996

Although the Calf Creek Trail is the monument's only officially marked and maintained trail, numerous unmarked cross-country routes are ideal for hiking, mountain biking (on existing dirt roads only), and horseback riding. We strongly recommend that hikers stop at the Interagency Office in Escalante or the BLM office in Kanab (see p. 247) to get recommendations on hiking routes and to purchase topographic maps. Hikers need to remember that this is wild country and can be hazardous. Rangers recommend carrying at least 1 gallon of water per person per day, and say that all water from streams should be treated before drinking. The potential for flooding is high, and hikers should check with the BLM before attempting to hike through the monument's narrow slot canyons, which offer no escape during flash floods. Other hazards include poisonous snakes and scorpions and, in the wetter areas, poison ivy. Slickrock, as the name suggests, is slippery, so hikers should wear sturdy hiking boots with traction soles.

Among the popular and relatively easy-to-follow hiking routes is the footpath to **Escalante Natural Bridge;** it repeatedly crosses the river, so be prepared to get wet up to your knees. The easy 2-mile (one-way) hike begins at a parking area at the bridge that crosses the Escalante River near Calf Creek Recreation Area, 15 miles northeast of the town of Escalante. From the parking area, hike upstream to Escalante Natural Bridge, on the south side of the river. The bridge is 130 feet high and spans 100 feet.

Also starting at the Utah 12 bridge parking area is a hike downstream to **Phipps Wash.** Mostly moderate, this hike goes about 1½ miles to the mouth of Phipps Wash, which enters the river from the west. You'll find Maverick Natural Bridge in a north side drainage of Phipps Wash, and climbing up the drainage on the south side leads to Phipps Arch.

Hiking the national monument's **slot canyons** is very popular, but we can't overemphasize the importance of checking on flood potentials before starting out. A sudden rainstorm miles away can cause a flash flood through one of the monument's narrow canyons, trapping hikers.

One challenging and very strenuous slot-canyon hike is through **Peek-a-boo** and **Spooky canyons,** which are accessible from the Hole-in-the-Rock Scenic Backway (see "Sightseeing & Four-Wheeling," below). Stop at the Escalante Interagency Office for precise directions.

SIGHTSEEING & FOUR-WHEELING   Because this is one of America's least-developed large sections of public land, it offers a wonderful opportunity for exploration by the adventurous. Be aware, though, that the dirt roads inside the monument turn muddy—and impassable—when it rains.

One particularly popular road is the **Hole-in-the-Rock Scenic Backway,** which is partly in the national monument and partly in the adjacent Glen Canyon National Recreation Area. Like most roads in the monument, this should be attempted in dry weather only. Starting about 5 miles northeast of Escalante off Utah 12, this clearly marked dirt road travels 57 miles (one-way) to the Hole-in-the-Rock, where Mormon settlers, in 1880, cut a passage through solid rock to get their wagons down a 1,200-foot cliff to the canyon floor and Colorado River below.

About 12 miles in, the road passes by the sign to **Devil's Rock Garden,** an area of classic red rock formations and arches, where you'll also find a picnic area (about a mile off the main road). The road continues across a plateau of typical desert terrain, ending at a spectacular scenic overlook of Lake Powell. The first 35 miles of the scenic byway are relatively easy (in dry weather) in a standard passenger car; it then gets a bit steeper and sandier, and the last 6 miles of the road require a high-clearance 4×4 vehicle. Allow about 6 hours round-trip and make sure you have plenty of fuel and water.

Another recommended drive in the national monument is the **Cottonwood Canyon Road,** which runs from Kodachrome Basin State Park south to U.S. 89, along the monument's southern edge, a distance of about 46 miles. The road is sandy and narrow, and washboard in places, but usually passable for passenger cars in dry weather. It mostly follows Cottonwood Wash, with good views of red rock formations and distant panoramas from hilltops. About 10 miles east of Kodachrome Basin State Park, you'll find a short side road to **Grosvenor Arch.** This magnificent stone arch, with an opening 99 feet wide, was named for National Geographic Society founder and editor Gilbert H. Grosvenor, and is well worth the trip. Incidentally, a professional photographer friend of ours complained bitterly about the power lines that parallel the road, making scenic photography difficult. However, the BLM tells us that the road wouldn't exist at all if it weren't for those power lines.

WILDLIFE VIEWING & BIRDING   The isolated and rugged terrain here makes a good habitat for a number of species, including desert bighorn sheep and mountain lions. More than 200 species of birds have been seen, including bald eagles, golden eagles, Swainson's hawks, and peregrine falcons. The best areas for seeing wildlife are along the Escalante and Paria rivers and Johnson Creek.

CAMPING

Backcountry camping is permitted in most areas of the monument with a free permit, available at the Interagency Office in Escalante and BLM office in Kanab (p. 247).

There are also two designated campgrounds. **Calf Creek Campground,** in the Calf Creek Recreation Area about 15 miles northeast of the town of Escalante via Utah 12, has 13 sites and a picnic area. Open year-round, the tree-shaded campground is situated in a scenic, steep canyon along Calf Creek,

Rock or Wood—What Is This Stuff?

It looks like a weathered, multicolored tree limb, shining and sparkling in the light—but it's heavy, hard, and solid as a rock. Just what is this stuff? Why, it's petrified wood.

Back in the old days—some 135 to 155 million years ago—southern Utah was not at all like we see it today. It was closer to the equator than it is now, which made it a wet and hot land, with lots of ferns, palm trees, and conifers providing lunch for the neighborhood dinosaurs.

Occasionally, floods would uproot the trees, dumping them in flood plains and along sandbars, then burying them with mud and silt. If this happened quickly, the layers of mud and silt would cut off the oxygen supply, halting the process of decomposition—and effectively preserving the tree trunks intact.

Later, volcanic ash covered the area, and groundwater rich in silicon dioxide and other chemicals and minerals made its way down to the ancient trees. With the silicon dioxide acting as a glue, the cells of the wood mineralized. Other waterborne minerals produced the colors: Iron painted the tree trunks in reds, browns, and yellows; manganese produced purples and blues.

Sometime afterward, uplift from within the earth, along with various forms of erosion, brought the now-petrified wood to the surface in places like Utah's Escalante State Park and Grand Staircase–Escalante National Monument, breaking it into the shapes we see today in the process—one that's taken only a hundred million years or so to complete.

surrounded by high rock walls. Facilities include a volleyball court, an interpretive hiking trail (p. 248), flush toilets, and drinking water, but no showers, RV hookups, RV dump stations, or trash removal. In summer, the campground is often full by 10am. From November through March, water is turned off and only vault toilets are available. Vehicles must ford a shallow creek, and the campground is not recommended for vehicles over 25 feet long. Campsites cost $7 per night; day use is $2 per vehicle.

The national monument's other designated campground is **Deer Creek,** located 6 miles east of the town of Boulder along the scenic Burr Trail Road. Camping at the four primitive sites here costs $4; no drinking water or other facilities are available. RVs and cars can fit onto the sites here.

ESCALANTE STATE PARK

Large chunks of colorful petrified wood decorate this unique park, which offers hiking, fishing, boating, camping, and panoramic vistas of the surrounding countryside. There's wildlife to watch, trails to hike, and a 30-acre reservoir for boating, fishing, and somewhat chilly swimming. It's open all year, but spring through fall are the best times to visit. Hikers should be prepared for hot summer temperatures and carry plenty of water.

ESSENTIALS

GETTING THERE   The park is 48 miles from Bryce Canyon. It's located about 2 miles southwest of Escalante on Utah 12 at Wide Hollow Road.

INFORMATION/VISITOR CENTER   Contact **Escalante State Park,** 710 N. Reservoir Rd., Escalante, UT 84726-0350 (📞 **435/826-4466;** www.state parks.utah.gov). The **visitor center,** located near the entrance and open daily, has displays of petrified wood, dinosaur bones, and fossils, plus an exhibit explaining how petrified wood is formed.

FEES & REGULATIONS   Entry costs $5 per vehicle. As at most parks, regulations are generally based on common sense and courtesy: Don't damage anything, drive slowly on park roads, and observe quiet hours between 10pm and 7am. In addition, you're asked to resist the temptation to carry off samples of petrified wood. Pets are welcome, even on trails, but must be restrained on leashes no more than 6 feet long.

OUTDOOR PURSUITS

FISHING & BOATING   **Wide Hollow Reservoir,** located partially inside the park, has a boat ramp (sorry, no rentals are available) and is a popular fishing hole for rainbow trout and bluegill, plus ice-fishing in winter.

HIKING   The 1-mile self-guided **Petrified Forest Trail** 🐾🐾 is a moderately strenuous hike among colorful rocks, through a forest of stunted juniper and piñon pine, past a painted desert, to a field of colorful petrified wood. The hike also offers panoramic vistas of the town of Escalante and the surrounding stair-step plateaus. A free brochure is available at the visitor center. Allow about 45 minutes.

   An optional three-quarter-mile loop off the main trail leads through lots more petrified wood, but is considerably steeper than the main trail.

WILDLIFE WATCHING   This is one of the best spots in the region to see wildlife 🐾. The reservoir is home to ducks, geese, and coots. Chukar partridges wander throughout the park, and you're also likely to see eagles, hawks, lizards, ground squirrels, and both cottontails and jackrabbits. Binoculars are helpful.

CAMPING

The 22-unit **campground,** within easy walking distance of the park's hiking trails and reservoir, is open year-round. Facilities include hot showers, modern restrooms, and drinking water, but no RV hookups. Camping is $14. Reservations are available at 📞 **800/322-3770** or www.stateparks.utah.gov; a $7 nonrefundable fee will be charged.

BASING YOURSELF IN ESCALANTE

Originally called Potato Valley, this community's name was changed in the 19th century to honor Spanish explorer and missionary Father Silvestre Velez de Escalante. However, it's believed Escalante never actually visited this particular part of southern Utah on his trek from Santa Fe, New Mexico, to California a hundred years earlier. Home to nearly 100 historic buildings (a free walking-tour map is available at the information booth and at local businesses), Escalante is your best bet for lodging, food, and supplies as you travel Utah 12. At 5,868 feet elevation, it's also a good base for exploring the nearby mountains and Grand Staircase–Escalante National Monument, or for finally taking a hot shower after a week of backpacking. Be aware, though, that services in this town of 800 are limited in winter.

ESSENTIALS

GETTING THERE   Escalante is 50 miles east of Bryce Canyon National Park and 63 miles south of Capitol Reef National Park on the Highway 12 Scenic Byway. Utah 12 becomes Main Street as it goes through town.

VISITOR INFORMATION   The **National Park Service, Dixie National Forest,** and **Bureau of Land Management** operate an **Interagency Office** that provides recreation and other tourist information year-round. It's located on the west side of town at 755 W. Main St. (Utah 12), Escalante (© **435/826-5499**) and is open daily 7:30am to 5:30pm from late March through October and 8:30am to 4:30pm Monday through Friday from November to mid-March.

The **Escalante Chamber of Commerce,** P.O. Box 175, Escalante, UT 84726 (© **435/826-4810;** www.escalante-cc.com), has an information booth in summer on Main Street (Utah 12), just east of Center Street.

FAST FACT   The **post office** is at 230 W. Main St.

WHERE TO STAY

In addition to the choices listed below, three houses are available for short-term rental. **La Luz**, no street address but proprietors will give you information when you book; (reservations © **888/305-4705;** www.laluz.net), a fully furnished solar house (no TV or phone) with two baths, sleeps up to six and rents for $150 for 1 night, $100 each additional night. Next to La Luz is **Southwestern Retreat,** no street address but proprietors will give you information when you book; P.O. Box 163, Escalante, UT 84726 (© **435/826-4967;** www.southwesternretreat. com), a three-bedroom, two-bath fully furnished modular home, with TV, VCR, and phone. It sleeps up to six and costs $100 per night double, $10 per additional person.

Located 3 miles east of Escalante and back off the road, **Serenidad Retreat,** 2610 East Hwy. 12 (P.O. Box 326), Escalante, UT 84726 (© **888/826-4577;** www.escalanteretreat.com) is a nicely furnished three-bedroom, two-bath modular home with a huge—700 square feet—redwood deck, TV, VCR and videos, phone, and fireplace (wood provided); it sleeps up to 10. The cost is $95 double, $10 per additional person; weekly rates are available. Pets are welcome at all three.

Escalante's room tax is about 10%. Pets are not accepted unless otherwise noted.

Circle D Motel   You'll find clean, well-maintained basic lodging at this family-owned and -operated motel. Rooms are simply decorated and furnished, with two double beds, one or two queen beds, or a king. There's no swimming pool, but at these rates, who can complain? Smoking is not permitted.

475 W. Main St. (Utah 12), P.O. Box 305, Escalante, UT 84726. © **435/826-4297.** Fax 435/826-4402. www. utahcanyons.com/circled.htm. 30 units. $35–$45 double. AE, MC, V. Pets accepted with $5 fee. *In room:* A/C, TV.

Tips **A Fascinating Gallery/Shop**

Philip and Harriet Priska's **Serenidad Gallery,** 360 W. Main St., next to the Prospector Inn (© **888/826-4577** or 435/826-4720), offers seven rooms crammed with wild and wonderfully fun stuff. Browse among local fine art, antiques, collectibles, gift items, jewelry, and even locally handmade soaps, face creams, and lip balms. Harriet's huge collection of buttons includes her own hand-painted porcelain creations. The Priskas carry only things they particularly like, so it's especially fun to talk with them about the selection of items. The gallery/shop is open daily, from 9am to 9pm in summer and 9am to 5pm in winter.

Escalante Outfitters, Inc.   These cute little log cabins are a favorite of backpackers who want a break from sleeping on the ground. Think of this place as a cross between a motel and a campground; actually, it's closer to the auto camps of the 1930s. Built in 1994 and 1995, each cabin has either one double bed or a pair of bunk beds, a chair, a small table with a lamp, and two small windows. There's heat in cool weather and fans for warm weather. That's it. No private bathrooms are available; guests share a simple but adequate, well-maintained bathhouse. On the grounds are a duck pond, barbecue pits, picnic tables, and horseshoe pits. The former volleyball court is now a camping area for six tents. A pay phone is nearby, and there's a state liquor store on the premises.

310 W. Main St. (Utah 12), P.O. Box 570, Escalante, UT 84726. ℂ **435/826-4266.** Fax 435/826-4388. www.aros.net/~slickroc/escout. 7 units. $30 double. DISC, MC, V. Check on possible closures Nov–Feb. **Amenities:** Restaurant (see Esca-Latte Coffee Shop & Pizza Parlor, in "Where to Dine," below). *In room:* No phone.

Escalante's Grand Staircase Bed & Breakfast Inn   This beautiful B&B has spacious rooms with skylights, full private bathrooms, and beds with pillowtop mattresses. The simple modern country decor includes lodgepole pine beds, Southwestern drum tables, and pictograph designs on the walls. Four units have coffeemakers and TVs, and there's a television in the common great room as well.

The full gourmet breakfast consists of a fruit dish, juice, coffee, tea, and hot chocolate, and a main course including breakfast meats or breads. Special diets can be accommodated with advance notice. Mountain bike repairs and made-in-Utah gifts are available on-site.

280 W. Main St. (Utah 12), Escalante, UT 84726. ℂ **866/826-4890** or 435/826-4890. Fax 435/826-4889. www.escalantebnb.com. 5 units. Mar–Oct $90–$105 double; Nov–Feb $70–$100 double. DISC, MC, V. Children under 10 accepted with prior notice. **Amenities:** Jacuzzi. *In room:* A/C.

Prospector Inn   You can't miss this distinctive two-story motel, with its vertically set red-brick exterior. A notch above the usual small town motel, this is our choice for a restful night after too many days on the road. Guest rooms here are particularly quiet and spacious, furnished with two double beds and decorated with framed photos of the area's scenery. There's a small gift shop, but no swimming pool. Free morning coffee is available in the lobby.

380 W. Main St. (Utah 12), P.O. Box 296, Escalante, UT 84726. ℂ **435/826-4653.** Fax 435/826-4285. www.prospectorinn.com. 50 units. $57 double. MC, V. **Amenities:** Restaurant (see The Prospector Restaurant, in "Where to Dine," below). *In room:* A/C, TV.

WHERE TO DINE

Pizza lovers should stop at the **Esca-Latte Coffee Shop & Pizza Parlor,** located in Escalante Outfitters, 310 W. Main St. (ℂ **435/826-4266**). This is the place for true aficionados, where you can build your own 12- or 16-inch pizza by selecting up to a dozen toppings, ranging from pepperoni to pineapple. There's also a salad bar, a variety of hot and cold coffee drinks, and both draft and bottled beer. They're open Monday to Saturday from 7am to 9pm in summer, shorter hours in winter.

You'll get good regional cuisine at reasonable prices at the **Hell's Backbone Grill** (ℂ **435/335-7464**), 20 North Utah 12, on the north side of Escalante. They're open 7:30 to 10:30am, 11am to 2:30pm, and 6 to 9:30pm daily from March through October. The menu changes seasonally. For lunch you can have soup, salad, or a sandwich served on homemade sage flatbread. Dinners might include a pork chop with apple and green chile chutney, chile-rubbed filet mignon, chipotle meatloaf, or pasta with steamed veggies. Try to leave room for one of their yummy desserts: Navajo style peach crisp or maybe chocolate chile flourless torte.

The **Prospector Restaurant** (© 435/826-4653), in the Prospector Inn (see "Where to Stay", above) offers basic American and European fare in a casual atmosphere. Open hours are April through November daily from 7am to 10pm; call for winter hours.

NORTH FROM ESCALANTE ALONG SCENIC UTAH 12

Heading toward Capitol Reef National Park from the town of Escalante, you'll see rugged mountain scenery, with forests of pine and fir producing a deep green contrast to the rosy red, orange, and brown hues of the region's rock formations.

Picturesque **Posy Lake** (sometimes spelled Posey), under the jurisdiction of the **U.S. Forest Service** (© 435/826-5499), is located in a mixed conifer forest at 8,200 feet elevation, some 16 miles northwest of Escalante via Utah 12 and gravel Forest Road 153. The lake is open to nonmotorized boats only. The fishing's good—the lake is stocked with rainbow trout—and you'll also find a picnic area, two floating docks, and a boat ramp. The numerous dirt roads are popular with mountain bikers and hikers in summer, cross-country skiers and snowmobilers in winter. The **Posy Lake Campground,** open in summer only, has 22 sites, drinking water, and restrooms, but no showers, RV hookups, or trash pick-up. Camping costs $8 per night.

Visitors to **Anasazi State Park Museum,** in the village of Boulder (about 27 miles northeast of Escalante along Utah 12), step back to the 12th century A.D., when the Kayenta Anasazi (also called Ancestral Puebloans) lived here in one of the largest communities west of the Colorado River. The 6-acre park includes the ruins of the village, a full-size six-room replica of a home, a gift shop, a picnic area, a 30-seat auditorium, and a museum. From mid-May to mid-September, the park is open daily from 8am to 6pm; the rest of the year, daily from 9am to 5pm. Admission is $1 per person, maximum $5 per family. There is no campground. For more information, contact **Anasazi State Park Museum,** P.O. Box 1429, Boulder, UT 84716 (© 435/335-7308; www.stateparks.utah.gov).

Boulder Mountain 🐾🐾 offers some of the most dramatic views along Utah 12—you'll be practically in the clouds, at an elevation of 9,670 feet, atop this mountain, situated northeast of Escalante. From viewpoints such as **Point Lookout,** you'll gaze out over the colorful sandstone rock cliffs of Capitol Reef National Park to the imposing Henry Mountains, Navajo Mountain, and sights more than 100 miles away.

Those venturing into the backcountry by foot, four-wheel-drive, mountain bike, or horse will discover rugged, remote beauty; the area is also a trout fisherman's paradise, with dozens of secluded mountain lakes and streams hidden among the tall pines and firs. Don't be surprised to see mule deer, elk, and wild turkey in the open meadows.

Several beautiful and quiet campgrounds, with both RV and tent sites, are operated by the **U.S. Forest Service** (© 435/826-5499). One of them, Singletree Campground, is about 16 miles south of Torrey (see "Camping" in chapter 13). The **Wildcat Ranger Station** of the Dixie National Forest has an information center about 18 miles south of Torrey, open from Memorial Day to Labor Day.

After Boulder, it's not too much farther to Capitol Reef National Park, but first you'll reach the community of Torrey, where Utah 12 intersects with Utah 24. You can turn right here and proceed to the park. See chapter 13 for complete coverage of Capitol Reef.

13

Capitol Reef National Park

We're reluctant to write this chapter because Capitol Reef National Park ⟨★★★⟩ is one of those little-known gems, drawing far fewer visitors than its more famous neighbors, Bryce Canyon and Zion. To be honest, we'd like to be selfish and keep this jewel of a park to ourselves.

Alas, we can't. For one thing, Capitol Reef is a place you really ought to know about. For another, the secret's already getting out. Not long ago, *Outside* magazine sang the praises of Capitol Reef as one of America's eight under-visited national parks—"parks as they were meant to be."

WHAT MAKES CAPITOL REEF SO SPECIAL?

Capitol Reef National Park offers loads of that spectacular southern Utah scenery, but with a unique twist and a personality all its own. The area's geologic formations are downright peculiar; this is a place to let your imagination run wild. You'll see the appropriately named Hamburger Rocks, sitting atop a white sandstone table; the tall, rust-red Chimney Rock; the silent and eerie Temple of the Moon; and the commanding Castle. The colors of Capitol Reef's canyon walls draw from a spectacular palette, which is why some Navajos called the area "The Land of the Sleeping Rainbow."

But unlike some of southern Utah's other parks, Capitol Reef is more than just brilliant rocks and barren desert. The Fremont River has helped create a lush oasis in an otherwise unforgiving land, with cottonwoods and willows along its banks. In fact, 19th-century pioneers found the land so inviting and the soil so fertile that they established the community of Fruita, planting orchards that have been preserved by the Park Service.

Because of differences in geologic strata, elevation, and availability of water in various sections of the park, you'll find an assortment of ecosystems and terrain, as well as a variety of activities. There are hiking trails, mountain-biking trails and four-wheel-drive touring roads; a lush fruit orchard; desert wildflowers and rich, green forests; an abundance of songbirds; and a surprising amount of wildlife from lizards and snakes to the bashful ringtail cat (which isn't a cat at all, but a member of the raccoon family). You'll see thousand-year-old petroglyphs, left behind by the early Fremont and Ancestral Puebloan (also called Anasazi) peoples, and other traces of the past from the more recent Utes and Southern Paiutes, Wild West outlaws, and industrious Mormon pioneers (in the one-room Fruita Schoolhouse, their children learned the three Rs and studied the Bible and Book of Mormon).

The name Capitol Reef, which conjures up an image of a tropical shoreline, seems odd for a park composed of cliffs and canyons and situated in landlocked Utah. But many of the pioneers who settled the West were former seafaring men, and they extended the traditional meaning of the word "reef" to include these seemingly impassable rock barriers. The huge round white domes of sandstone reminded them of the domes of capitol buildings, and so this area became known as Capitol Reef.

A more accurate name for the park might be "The Big Fold." When the earth's crust uplifted some 60 million years ago, creating the Rocky Mountains and the Colorado Plateau, most of the uplifting was relatively even. But here, through one of those fascinating quirks of nature, the crust wrinkled into a huge fold. Running for 100 miles, almost all within the national park, it's known as the Waterpocket Fold.

1 Just the Facts

GETTING THERE   Capitol Reef National Park is 120 miles northeast of Bryce Canyon National Park, 204 miles northeast of Zion National Park, 224 miles south of Salt Lake City, and 366 miles northeast of Las Vegas, Nevada. The park straddles Utah 24, which connects with I-70 both to the northeast and northwest.

Those coming from Bryce Canyon National Park can follow Utah 12 northeast (see chapter 12) to its intersection with Utah 24, and follow that east into Capitol Reef. If you're approaching the park from Glen Canyon National Recreation Area and the Four Corners region, follow Utah 276 and/or Utah 95 north to the intersection with Utah 24, where you'll then go west into the park.

INFORMATION/VISITOR CENTER   For advance information, contact Superintendent, **Capitol Reef National Park,** HC 70 Box 15, Torrey, UT 84775-9602 (© **435/425-3791;** www.nps.gov.care).

The **visitor center** is located on the park access road at its intersection with Utah 24. A path alongside the access road connects the visitor center with the campground, passing the historic Fruita blacksmith shop, the orchards, and a lovely shaded picnic ground. The visitor center, open daily from 8am to 4:30pm (extended hours in summer) year-round, has exhibits on the area's geology and history as well as a 10-minute introductory slide show on the park. You can ask the rangers questions, get backcountry permits, pick up free brochures, and purchase books, maps, videos, postcards, and posters.

FEES, REGULATIONS & BACKCOUNTRY PERMITS   Entry into the park (for up to 7 days) costs $4 per vehicle or $2 per motorcycle, bicycle, or pedestrian. Free permits, available at the visitor center, are required for all overnight hiking trips into the backcountry.

Bicycles are prohibited in the backcountry and on all hiking trails. Feeding or otherwise disturbing wildlife is forbidden, as is vandalizing or upsetting any natural, cultural, or historic feature of the park. Because park wildlife refuse to follow park rules regarding wildlife diet, campers should be especially careful of where they store food, and should dispose of garbage promptly. Dogs, which must be leashed at all times, are prohibited on all trails, more than 100 feet from any road, and in public buildings.

SEASONS/AVOIDING THE CROWDS   Although Capitol Reef receives only about 600,000 visitors annually—making it among the least-visited national parks in the West—it can still be busy, especially during its peak summer season. For this reason, the best time to visit is fall, particularly October and November, when temperatures remain warm enough for comfortable hiking and camping, but are not so hot that they'll send you constantly in search of shade.

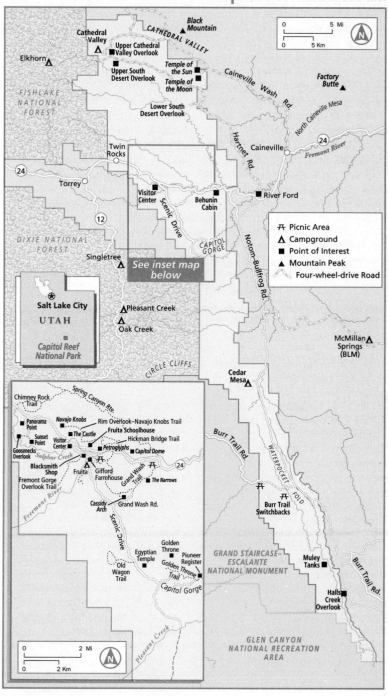

Black Mountain

CATHEDRAL VALLEY

Cathedral Valley

Upper Cathedral Valley Overlook

Elkhorn

FISHLAKE NATIONAL FOREST

Upper South Desert Overlook

Temple of the Sun

Temple of the Moon

Caineville Wash Rd.

Factory Butte

North Caineville Mesa

Lower South Desert Overlook

Hartnet Rd.

Caineville

24

Fremont River

Twin Rocks

24

Torrey

12

Visitor Center

Scenic Drive

Behunin Cabin

River Ford

Notom-Bullfrog Rd.

DIXIE NATIONAL FOREST

CAPITOL GORGE

See inset map below

Picnic Area
Campground
Point of Interest
Mountain Peak
Four-wheel-drive Road

Singletree

Salt Lake City

UTAH

Capitol Reef National Park

Pleasant Creek

Oak Creek

McMillan Springs (BLM)

CIRCLE CLIFFS

Cedar Mesa

Burr Trail Rd.

WATERPOCKET FOLD

Chimney Rock Trail

Spring Canyon Rte.

Panorama Point

Navajo Knobs

Rim Overlook–Navajo Knobs Trail

Fruita Schoolhouse

The Castle

Sunset Point

Visitor Center

Hickman Bridge Trail

Goosenecks Overlook

Petroglyphs

Capitol Dome

Sulphur Creek

Blacksmith Shop

Fruita

Fremont Gorge Overlook Trail

Gifford Farmhouse

Grand Wash Trail

24

The Narrows

Freemont River

Cassidy Arch

Grand Wash Rd.

Burr Trail Switchbacks

Scenic Drive

Egyptian Temple

Golden Throne

Pioneer Register

Old Wagon Trail

Golden Throne Trail

GRAND STAIRCASE–ESCALANTE NATIONAL MONUMENT

Muley Tanks

Burr Trail Rd.

Capitol Gorge

Halls Creek Overlook

Pleasant Creek

GLEN CANYON NATIONAL RECREATION AREA

0   5 Mi
0   5 Km

0   2 Mi
0   2 Km

You also don't have to be as cautious about flash floods through the narrow canyons as you do during the July through September thunderstorm season.

SAFETY   Although most visitors to the park enjoy a wonderful vacation without mishaps, problems can occur. Hikers should carry plenty of water, especially in summer, and watch out for rattlesnakes. Although not abundant, the Western rattlesnake has been seen in the rocks of the Grand Wash and around Fruita. Snakes prefer to avoid people, but will strike if cornered.

Afternoon thunderstorms in July, August, and September can bring flash floods, which fill narrow canyons without warning. Steep-walled Grand Wash can be particularly hazardous—avoid it whenever storms are threatening.

RANGER PROGRAMS   Rangers present a variety of free programs and activities from spring through fall. Campfire programs take place most evenings at the outdoor amphitheater next to Fruita Campground. Topics vary, but could include animals and plants, geology, and human history of the area. Rangers also lead hikes and walks and give short talks on history at the pioneer Fruita Schoolhouse and the Mormon homestead. Schedules are posted on bulletin boards at the visitor center and campground.

Kids can become Junior Rangers or Junior Geologists—they'll learn to map ancient earthquakes, inspect water bugs, and so on. The entire family can join in, too: Just pick up a Family Fun Pack at the visitor center.

2 Seeing the Highlights by Car

As with most national parks, it would be easy to spend a week or more here, hiking the trails, admiring the views, and loafing about the campground. However, those with a limited amount of time, and those who prefer the comfort of a car to the demands of the hiking trail, will still find Capitol Reef relatively easy to explore.

Start at the **visitor center,** where you can watch the short slide show explaining the park's geology and early history. From the center, the paved 25-mile round-trip **Scenic Drive** leads south into the park, offering good views of the dramatic canyons and rock formations that comprise Capitol Reef. Pick up a copy of the free Scenic Drive brochure at the entrance station and set out, stopping at viewpoints to gaze up and out at the array of colorful cliffs, monoliths, and commanding rock formations.

If the weather's dry, drive down the gravel **Capitol Gorge Road** (5 miles round-trip) at the end of the paved Scenic Drive for a look at what many consider the best backcountry scenery in the park. If you're up for a short walk, the relatively flat 2-mile (round-trip) **Capitol Gorge Trail,** which starts at the end of Capitol Gorge Road, takes you to the historic **Pioneer Register,** a rock wall where traveling pioneers "signed in" (p. 261).

Another dry-weather driving option is the **Grand Wash Road,** a maintained dirt road that's subject to flash floods, but in good weather offers an easy route into spectacular backcountry. Along the 2-mile round-trip, you'll see **Cassidy Arch;** famed outlaw Butch Cassidy is said to have hidden out nearby.

Utah 24, which crosses Capitol Reef from east to west, also has several viewpoints offering a good look at the park's features, such as monumental **Capitol Dome,** which resembles the dome of a capitol building; the aptly named **Castle** formation; the historic **Fruita Schoolhouse;** and some roadside **petroglyphs** left by the prehistoric Fremont people (see p. 260).

Butch Cassidy: Utah's Most Infamous Son

Robert LeRoy Parker wasn't a bad kid. He was born into a hard-working Mormon family in a little southwestern Utah town called Beaver on April 13, 1866. Robert was the oldest of 13 children, and was said to be a great help to his mother, working on the small ranch his parents bought in nearby Circleville.

But Circleville was where the problems began. Teenaged Robert fell in with some rather unsavory characters, including one Mike Cassidy, the ne'er-do-well role model who gave the youth his first gun, and presumably from whom young Robert took the alias Cassidy. The boy made his way to Telluride, Colorado, worked for one of the mines there for a while, and then wandered up to Wyoming. A little more wandering took him back to Telluride—and, strangely enough, the Telluride bank was robbed. Butch Cassidy had officially begun his life of crime.

In the following years, Butch—who gained the nickname after a short stint working in a butcher shop—became an expert at rustling cattle, robbing banks, and, his ultimate glory, robbing trains. Butch wanted to call his gang the Train Robbers Syndicate, but they raised such hell in celebration of their economic successes that saloonkeepers in Vernal and other Utah towns began calling them "that wild bunch," and the name stuck. The Wild Bunch would travel through Utah, hiding out in the desolate badlands that were to become Bryce Canyon, Capitol Reef, and Canyonlands national parks. Capitol Reef's Cassidy Arch was named after Butch; this area was supposedly one of his favorite hiding places.

If you've seen the 1969 movie *Butch Cassidy and the Sundance Kid,* with Paul Newman as Butch and Robert Redford as his partner-in-crime Sundance, you can't forget that spectacular scene in which Butch and his cohorts blow the door off a railroad car. Then they use way too much dynamite to open the safe, sending bills flying into the air. Apparently, the story is basically true, having taken place on June 2, 1899, near Wilcox, Wyoming. According to reports of the day, they got away with $30,000.

The Union Pacific Railroad took exception to Butch's antics. When the posses started getting a bit too close, Butch, Sundance, and Sundance's lady friend, Etta Place (Katharine Ross in the film), took off for South America, where it's said they continued a life of crime for a half dozen or so years. There are also some stories—unconfirmed—that it was in South America that Butch first killed anyone, that up until that time he had avoided bloodshed whenever possible.

According to some historians (as well as the movie version of Butch's life), Butch and Sundance were shot dead in a gun battle with army troops in Bolivia. But others say it's not so—that Butch returned to the United States, visited friends and family in Utah and Wyoming, and eventually settled in Spokane, Washington, where he lived a peaceful and respectable life under the name William T. Phillips, until he died of natural causes in 1937.

3 From Petroglyphs to a Pioneer Schoolhouse: Capitol Reef's Historic Sites

In the park, you'll find evidence of man's presence here through the centuries. The **Fremont** people lived along the river as early as A.D. 700, staying until about A.D. 1300. Primarily hunters and gatherers, the Fremont also grew corn, beans, and squash to supplement their diet, and when they abandoned the area, they left little behind. They lived in pit houses, so called because they were dug into the ground—the remains of one can be seen from the **Hickman Bridge Trail.** Many of the Fremont people's petroglyphs (images carved into rock) and some pictographs (images painted on rock) are still visible on the canyon walls. If we could read them, they might even tell us why these early Americans left the area—a puzzle that continues to baffle historians and archaeologists.

Fast-forwarding to the 19th century, prospectors and other travelers passed through the **Capitol Gorge** section of the park in the late 1800s, leaving their names on a wall of rock that came to be known as the **Pioneer Register.** You can reach it via a 2-mile loop; see p. 261.

Mormon pioneers established the appropriately named community of **Fruita** when it was discovered that this was a good locale for growing fruit. The tiny 1896 **Fruita Schoolhouse** served as a church, social hall, and community-meeting hall, in addition to functioning as a one-room schoolhouse. The school closed in 1941, but it was carefully restored by the National Park Service in 1984 and is authentically furnished with old wood-and-wrought-iron desks, a wood stove, a chalkboard, and textbooks. The hand bell used to call students to class still rests on the corner of the teacher's desk. Nearby, the **orchards** planted by the Mormon settlers continue to flourish, tended by park workers who invite you to sample the "fruits" of their labors.

The historic **Gifford Farmhouse,** built in 1908, is a typical early-20th-century Utah farmhouse. Located about a mile south of the visitor center, the authentically renovated and furnished farmhouse is open daily from mid-April through September. In addition to displays of period objects, there are often demonstrations of early homemaking skills and crafts, such as quilting and rug making. Park across the road at the picnic area; a short path leads to the farmhouse.

4 Outdoor Pursuits

Among the last areas in the continental United States to be explored, many parts of Capitol Reef National Park are still practically unknown, perfect for those who want to see this rugged country in its natural state. Several local companies offer guide and shuttle services, including **Hondoo Rivers and Trails,** P.O. Box 98, Torrey, UT 84775 (℗ **800/332-2696** or 435/425-3519; fax 435/425-3548; www.hondoo.com). Founded in 1975 by Pat and Gary George, Hondoo seeks to provide comfortable and informative backcountry experiences for small groups. **Wild Hare Expeditions,** P.O. Box 750194, Torrey, UT 84775 (℗ **888/304-HARE** or 435/425-3999; www.color-country.net/~thehare) also offers a variety of guide services, plus trailhead shuttles. Their office and shop, **The Hare Lair,** are located at 116 W. Main St., Torrey, where you'll find supplies, regional information and recommendations, maps, and guide books, plus unique gift items.

FOUR-WHEEL TOURING & MOUNTAIN BIKING

As in most national parks, bikes and four-wheel-drive vehicles are restricted to established roads, but Capitol Reef has several so-called roads—actually little more than dirt trails—that provide exciting opportunities for those using 4×4s or pedal-power. Use of ATVs is not permitted in the park.

The only route appropriate for road bikes is the 25-mile round-trip Scenic Drive, described earlier. However, both the Grand Wash and Capitol Gorge roads (see p. 258 for descriptions of these roads), plus three much longer dirt roads, are open to mountain bikes as well as four-wheel-drive vehicles. Note that rain can make the roads impassable, so check on current conditions with park rangers before setting out.

We recommend the **Cathedral Valley Loop** for mountain bikers and four-wheel-drivers. This road covers 60 miles on a variety of surfaces, including dirt, sand, and rock, and requires the fording of the Fremont River, where water is usually 1 to 1½ feet deep. You'll be rewarded with beautiful, unspoiled scenery, including bizarre sandstone monoliths and majestic cliffs, in one of the park's most remote areas. A small, primitive campground is located in Cathedral Valley (p. 262). Access to the loop is from Utah 24, just outside the park, 11.7 miles east of the visitor center at the river ford; or 18.6 miles east of the visitor center on the Caineville Wash Road, though it's best to begin at the river ford to be sure you can make the crossing.

Four-wheel-drive **tours** are provided by **Hondoo Rivers and Trails** (see the introduction to this section), costing $40 for a half day, and $75 to $90 for a full day. Multi-day tours to a variety of places in the area are also available. Mountain-bike and four-wheel-drive tours into the national park and surrounding areas are provided by **Wild Hare Expeditions** (see the introduction to this section). Full-day tours, including lunch, start at $70; a variety of other guided trips, including multi-day excursions, are offered as well. Rentals of four-wheel-drive vehicles ($75 per day) are available from **Thousand Lakes RV Park & Campground** (p. 263).

HIKING

Trails through the national park offer sweeping panoramas of colorful cliffs and soaring spires, eerie journeys through desolate steep-walled canyons, and cool oases along the tree-shaded Fremont River. Watch carefully for petroglyphs and other reminders of this area's first inhabitants. This is also the real Wild West; little has changed from the way cowboys, bank robbers, settlers, and gold miners found it in the late 1800s. In fact, one of the best things about hiking here is the unique combination of scenic beauty, American Indian art, and Western history that you'll discover.

Park rangers can help you choose trails best suited to the time of year, weather conditions, and your personal physical condition; those planning serious back-packing treks will want to buy topographic maps, available at the visitor center. The summer sun is wicked, so hats and sunscreen are mandatory, and a gallon of water per person is recommended.

Among our favorite short hikes at Capitol Reef is the 2-mile round-trip **Capitol Gorge Trail.** It's easy, mostly level walking along the bottom of a narrow canyon, but looking up at the tall, smooth walls of rock conveys a strong sense of what the pioneers must have seen and felt 100 years ago, when they moved rocks and debris to haul their wagons up this canyon. Starting at the end of the dirt Capitol Gorge Road, the hiking trail leads past the **Pioneer Register,** where prospectors and other early travelers carved their names. The earliest legible signatures were made in 1871 by J. A. Call and "Wal" Bateman.

Another short hike, but quite a bit more strenuous, is the 3½-mile round-trip **Cassidy Arch Trail.** This route offers spectacular views as it climbs steeply from the floor of Grand Wash to high cliffs overlooking the park. From the trail, you'll get several perspectives of Cassidy Arch, a natural stone arch named for outlaw Butch Cassidy, who is believed to have occasionally used the Grand Wash as a hideout. The trail is off the Grand Wash dirt road, which branches off the east side of the highway about halfway down the park's Scenic Drive.

Guided hikes and backpacking trips into the national park and surrounding areas are offered by **Hondoo Rivers and Trails** (p. 260). Day hikes cost from $75 to $90, and overnight hiking safaris have a wide range of prices, depending on the size of the party, the itinerary, the number of days, etc. Most groups are small, although large groups can be accommodated. **Wild Hare Expeditions** (p. 260) also offers guided hikes, from 2-hour treks to multi-day backpacking trips.

HORSEBACK RIDING

Horses are welcome on some park trails but prohibited on others; check at the visitor center. **Hondoo Rivers and Trails** (p. 260) offers a wide variety of riding trips. Options include 1- to 5-day trips into the backcountry of Capitol Reef National Park, nearby Boulder Mountain, and the canyons of Grand Staircase–Escalante National Monument. Some trail rides are aimed at wildflower or wildlife viewing or fall colors. Day trips start at $75; multi-day trips range from $875 to $1,575; custom tours can be arranged.

WILDLIFE WATCHING

Although summer temperatures are hot and there's always the threat of a thunderstorm, this is a good season for wildlife viewing. Many species of lizards reside in the park; you'll probably catch a glimpse of one warming itself on a rock. The western whiptail, eastern fence, and side-blotched lizards are the most common, but the loveliest is the collared lizard, dark in color but with light speckles that allow it to blend easily with lava rocks and become almost invisible to its foes. Watch for deer throughout the park, especially along the path between the visitor center and Fruita Campground. This area is also where you're likely to see chipmunks and antelope ground squirrels.

If you keep your eyes to the sky, you may spot a golden eagle, and numerous songbirds pass through each year. Although they're somewhat shy and only emerge from their dens at night, the ringtail cat, a member of the raccoon family, also makes the park his home, as do the seldom-seen bobcat, cougar, fox, marmot, and coyote.

5 Camping

IN THE PARK

The 70-site **Fruita Campground,** open year-round, offers modern restrooms, drinking water, picnic tables, fire grills, and an RV dump station, but no showers or RV hookups. It's located along the main park road, 1 mile south of the visitor center. Water may be turned off in winter, leaving only pit toilets. Camping costs $10; reservations are not accepted.

The park also has two primitive campgrounds, free and open year-round on a first-come, first-served basis. Both have tables, fire grills, and pit toilets, but no water. Check road conditions before going, as unpaved roads may be impassable in wet weather. **Cedar Mesa Campground,** with five sites, is located in the southern part of the park, about 22½ miles down Notom-Bullfrog Road (paved for only the first 10 miles), which heads south off Utah 24 just outside the eastern entrance to the park. **Cathedral Valley Campground,** with six sites, is located in the northern part of the park. From the visitor center, head east on

Impressions

The colors are such as no pigments can portray. They are deep, rich, and variegated; and so luminous are they, that light seems to flow or shine out of the rock.

—Geologist C. E. Dutton, 1880

Utah 24 about 12 miles to the Fremont River ford, ford the river, and turn north on unpaved Hartnet Road for about 25 miles. A high-clearance or four-wheel-drive vehicle is necessary.

Backcountry camping is permitted in much of the park with a free permit, available at the visitor center. Fires are forbidden in the backcountry.

NEARBY

Sandcreek RV Park & Hostel   The open, grassy area in this pleasant park affords great views in all directions, and there are numerous small but growing trees. Facilities include a large, clean bathhouse; horseshoe pits; a gift shop; an espresso bar; a dump station; and coin-op laundry. There are 12 tent sites and 12 RV sites. There is also a hostel on the property (p. 264).

540 Utah 24, 5 miles west of the park entrance (P.O. Box 750276), Torrey, UT 84775. ℰ **877/425-3578** or 435/425-3577. www.sandcreekrv.com. 24 sites (12 tent and 12 RV). $10–$15 for 2 people; $3 extra for 50-amp electric service. MC, V. Closed mid-Oct through Mar.

Singletree Campground   Located in a forest of tall pines at an elevation of 8,200 feet, this campground features paved sites that are nicely spaced. Some sites are situated in the more open center area; others are set among trees along the edge of the campground. Most popular are those sites offering distant panoramic views of the national park. Facilities include an outdoor pool; a picnic table, grill, and fire ring at each site; restrooms with flush toilets but no sinks or showers; water hydrants scattered about; an RV dump station; and a horseshoe pit and volleyball court. There are no RV hookups.

Utah 12, about 16 miles south of Torrey. Teasdale Ranger District, Dixie National Forest, P.O. Box 90, Teasdale, UT 84773. ℰ **435/425-3702.** 26 sites plus 5 multiple-family sites and 2 group areas. $10 "regular" sites; $20 multiple-family site; $35 group areas. Closed Nov to mid-May.

Thousand Lakes RV Park & Campground   Good views of surrounding rock formations are one of the perks of staying at this campground, which also has some shade trees. RV sites are gravel; tent sites are grass. Facilities include the usual bathhouse, plus a gift and convenience store, a coin-op laundry, a dump station, a heated outdoor swimming pool, horseshoes, and barbecues. Five of the cabins share a separate bathhouse; two have their own showers and toilet; and there's a Housekeeping Unit that sleeps 5 and has a kitchen and bath. In addition, Western dinners are offered Monday through Saturday, and 4×4 rentals are available at $75 per day.

Utah 24, 6 miles west of Capitol Reef National Park (P.O. Box 750070), Torrey, UT 84775. ℰ **800/355-8995** for reservations, or 435/425-3500. Fax 435/425-3510. www.thousandlakesrvpark.com. 67 sites, 8 cabins. $12.50–$18.50; $29–$55 cabin. DISC, MC, V. Closed late Nov–Mar.

6 Where to Stay

There are no lodging or dining facilities in the park itself, but the town of Torrey, just west of the park entrance, can take care of most needs. Room tax adds about 9% to lodging bills. None of the following accept pets.

In addition to the properties discussed below, Torrey has a **Days Inn,** 675 E. Utah 24 (at Utah 12) (✆ **800/329-7466** or 435/425-3111), and a **Super 8,** 600 E. Utah 24 (near the intersection of Utah 24 and Utah 12) (✆ **800/800-8000** or 435/425-3688). Also see the information on cabins at **Thousand Lakes RV Park & Campground** under "Camping," above.

Austin's Chuck Wagon Lodge and General Store   This attractive family-owned and -operated motel offers a wide range of options. The well-maintained property includes newer, modern motel rooms, which have Southwestern decor, phones, and two queen-size beds; and older, somewhat rustic units, which have knotty-pine walls, one queen bed, and no phones. Also available is a family suite, with a large living room, fully equipped kitchen, and three bedrooms that sleep six. Our choice here, however, is one of the plush but still Western-style cabins, which were completed in 2000. Measuring 576 square feet, each cabin has two bedrooms (each with a queen-size bed), a living room with a queen-size sofabed, a complete kitchen, a full bathroom with shower/tub combo, a covered porch, and a small yard with a barbecue grill and a picnic table. The grounds are attractively landscaped, with a lawn and large trees; also on the property is a grocery store/bakery.

12 W. Main St. (P.O. Box 750180), Torrey, UT 84775. ✆ **800/863-3288** or 435/425-3335. Fax 435/425-3434. www.austinschuckwagonmotel.com. 24 units. New units $64 double; older units $42 double; cabins $110 for up to 4 plus $5 for each additional person; family suite $125. AE, DISC, MC, V. Closed Nov–Feb. **Amenities:** Outdoor pool; Jacuzzi; salon; coin-op laundry. *In room:* A/C, TV.

Best Western Capitol Reef Resort   Located a mile west of the national park entrance, this attractive Best Western is one of the closest lodgings to the park. Try to get a room on the back side of the motel, where you'll be rewarded with fantastic views of the area's red rock formations. Standard units have either one king or two queen beds; mini-suites have a king bed and a queen sofa sleeper, plus a coffeemaker, refrigerator, microwave, and wet bar; full suites add a separate sitting room for the sofa sleeper, a second TV and telephone, a jetted tub, and patio. The sun deck and pool are situated out back, away from road noise, with glass wind barriers and spectacular views.

2600 E. Utah 24 (P.O. Box 750160), Torrey, UT 84775. ✆ **888/610-9600** or 435/425-3761. Fax 435/425-3300. 100 units. June–Sept $99 double, $119–$139 suite; Oct–May $59–$79 double, $69–$119 suite. AE, DC, DISC, MC, V. **Amenities:** Restaurant; outdoor heated pool; tennis/basketball court; Jacuzzi. *In room:* A/C, TV, hair dryer.

Capitol Reef Inn & Cafe   This older, Western-style motel—small, beautifully landscaped, and adequately maintained—offers guest rooms that are both homey and comfortable. The furnishings are handmade of solid wood. Only one unit has a combination shower/tub; the others have showers only. Facilities include a playground, a lovely desert garden, and an intriguing, although not old, stone kiva. There's also a book/gift shop offering American Indian crafts, guide books, and maps.

360 W. Main St. (Utah 24), Torrey, UT 84775. ✆ **435/425-3271.** www.capitolreefinn.com. 10 units. $48 double. AE, DISC, MC, V. Closed Nov–Mar. **Amenities:** Restaurant; large Jacuzzi. *In room:* A/C, TV, fridge, coffeemaker.

Sandcreek RV Park & Hostel   This hostel, in a handsome log building, consists of one large room in which everyone—both men and women—sleeps, bunkhouse style. It offers sleeping space for eight, a TV, a microwave, high ceilings, and a porch with tables and chairs. The walls, high ceiling, and beams are of ponderosa pine, and the bunk beds are made of logs. Hostellers share the bathhouse with campers (p. 263), and linens are available. You'll also find an espresso bar, laundry, horseshoe pits, and a natural stone and petrified wood labyrinth that leads to a quiet meditation area. In addition, a gift shop features handmade deer antler jewelry, and you can often see the jeweler (who is also the hostel's owner/manager) at work.

540 Utah 24, 5 miles west of the park entrance (P.O. Box 750276), Torrey, UT 84775. (℃) **877/425-3578** or 435/425-3577. www.sandcreekrv.com. Hostel $10–$12 per person. MC, V. Closed mid-Oct through March.

SkyRidge Inn Bed & Breakfast This combination bed-and-breakfast and art gallery offers a delightful alternative to the standard motel. The three-story contemporary inn, with Territorial-style appearance, has six distinctive units, each with a CD player and a private bathroom. The comfy rooms are decorated with an eclectic mix of antiques, folk sculptures, and contemporary art; two have private decks with hot tubs; another features a two-person whirlpool tub inside and a private deck.

An impressive fireplace, decorated with over 30 pounds of roofing nails, sits in the gallery/gathering room, which also contains books, games, CDs, and movies available for guest use. There is also an outdoor hot tub. The inn is set on 75 acres, with its own hiking trails and spectacular views of the national park and Boulder Mountain. Full breakfasts include homemade granola; fresh-baked coffee-cake, muffins, or cinnamon rolls; and a hot entree such as Southwest frittata or pecan griddle-cakes. Smoking is not permitted inside.

950 E. Utah 24 (P.O. Box 750220), Torrey, UT 84775. (℃) and fax **435/425-3222**. www.skyridgeinn.com. 6 units. Apr–Oct $115–$172 double; Nov–Mar $104–$155 double; additional person $25. Rates include breakfast and evening hors d'oeuvres. AE, MC, V. **Amenities:** Outdoor pool; Jacuzzi. *In room:* A/C, TV/VCR, hair dryer.

7 Dining

In addition to the restaurants discussed below, you'll find a good restaurant, open year-round, at the Best Western Capitol Reef Resort (see "Where to Stay," above).

Brink's Burgers Drive-In BURGERS/SANDWICHES This nonfranchise fast-food restaurant serves good burgers and crunchy English-style chips in a cafe-like setting and at outdoor picnic tables. In addition to better-than-average beef burgers, choices include a garden burger, chicken and fish selections, cheese sticks, onion rings, zucchini slices, breaded mushrooms, and spicy potato wedges. A wide variety of ice-cream cones and thick milk shakes are also available; no alcohol is served.

165 E. Main St., Torrey. (℃) **435/425-3710**. Most items $2–$6. MC, V. Daily 11am–9pm. Closed in winter.

Cafe Diablo ★★ SOUTHWESTERN Looks are deceiving. What appears to be a simple small-town cafe in a converted home is in fact a very fine restaurant, offering innovative beef, pork, chicken, seafood, and vegetarian selections, many created with a Southwestern flair. The menu varies, but could include pumpkinseed-crusted local trout served with cilantro-lime sauce and wild rice pancakes; medallions of local lamb marinated with sage and rosemary and served with potato roulade, asparagus, and mint sauce; and baby back pork ribs slow roasted in a chipotle, molasses, and rum glaze. Pastries and ice creams, all made on the premises, are spectacular, and beer—both microbrewed and regular—plus wines and tequilas are available. There's also patio dining, with heaters for those chilly evenings.

599 W. Main St., Torrey. (℃) **435/425-3070**. www.cafediablo.net. Main courses $16–$29. MC, V. Daily 5–10pm. Closed mid-Oct to late Apr.

Capitol Reef Inn & Cafe ★ *Finds* AMERICAN   A local favorite, this restaurant offers fine, fresh, healthy cuisine that's among the best you'll find in Utah. Famous for its locally raised trout, the cafe is equally well known for its 10-vegetable salad served with all dinner entrees. Vegetables are grown locally, and several dishes—such as spaghetti, an excellent fettuccine primavera, and shish kabobs—can be ordered vegetarian or with various meats or fish. Steaks and chicken are also served. The atmosphere is casual, with comfortable seating, American Indian rugs and crafts, and large windows. The restaurant offers an extensive wine list, plus domestic and imported beers.

360 W. Main St. © 435/425-3271. Main courses $5–$11 breakfast, $5–$12 lunch, $9–$19 dinner. AE, DISC, MC, V. Daily 7am–9pm. Closed Nov–Mar.

14

Lake Powell & Glen Canyon National Recreation Area

This huge canyon is a spectacular wonderland of stark contrasts—parched desert, deep blue water, startlingly red rocks, rich green hanging gardens. A joint effort by man and nature, Lake Powell and Glen Canyon National Recreation Area ★★★ is a huge water park, with more shoreline than the West Coast of the continental United States. It's also a place of almost unbelievable beauty, where millions of visitors each year take to the water to explore, fish, water-ski, swim, or simply lounge in the sun.

Named for Major John Wesley Powell, a one-armed Civil War veteran who led a group of nine explorers on a scientific expedition down the Green and Colorado rivers in 1869, the lake is 186 miles long and has almost 100 major side canyons that give it 1,960 miles of shoreline. And with more than 160,000 surface acres of water, it's the second-largest man-made lake in the United States (after Lake Mead).

Glen Canyon National Recreation Area, with Lake Powell at its heart, is three parks in one: a major destination for boaters and fishermen, a treasury of scenic wonders, and an important historic site. Lake Powell is best enjoyed by boat—you can glide through the numerous side canyons among delicately sculpted sandstone forms that are intricate, sensuous, and sometimes bizarre; these shapes were formed by millions of years of erosion. One rock formation that's considered a must-see for every visitor is Rainbow Bridge National Monument, a huge natural stone bridge sacred to the Navajo and other area tribes. And there's much more to see: the 1870s stone fort and trading post at Lees Ferry, the Ancestral Puebloan (also called Anasazi) ruins of Defiance House, and the dam, which supplies water and electric power to much of the West.

1 Just the Facts

ACCESS POINTS: THE MARINAS Located in southern Utah and northern Arizona, Lake Powell and Glen Canyon National Recreation Area has four major access points: **Wahweap Lodge & Marina** (✆ 928/645-2433), on the lake's south end, is the most developed, with the largest number of facilities, plus lodging, dining, and services in nearby Page, Arizona; **Bullfrog Marina** (✆ 435/684-3000) and **Halls Crossing Marina** (✆ 435/684-7000) are mid-lake, and are also fairly well developed. **Hite Marina** (✆ 435/684-2278), the lake's northernmost access point, is the smallest and least developed, with extremely limited services off-season.

These four marinas, operated by Lake Powell Resorts and Marinas, are accessible by car, operate year-round, and provide boat rentals, docks, fuel, fishing and other supplies, and accommodations. A fifth marina, **Dangling Rope,** is accessible by boat only (it's 40 lake miles north of the dam and 55 lake miles south of Halls Crossing and Bullfrog marinas), and is mainly a fuel stop, though it does offer minor repairs, limited supplies, a free dump/pump-out station, emergency medical services, and some of the best soft-serve ice cream around. A sixth marina, **Antelope Point,** has a six-lane day-use-only launch ramp onto the original channel of the river, small courtesy docks, a large graveled parking area, restrooms, and a beach access road, but no fuel or services. This ramp may close during low water levels. **Lees Ferry** is a popular river crossing, but does not offer direct access to Lake Powell.

GETTING THERE **Wahweap Lodge and Marina** and **Glen Canyon Dam** are just off U.S. 89, 6 miles north of Page, Arizona. Wahweap is 150 miles southeast of Bryce Canyon National Park; 130 miles northeast of the north rim of Grand Canyon National Park; 65 miles east of Kanab; 267 miles east of Las Vegas, Nevada; and 381 miles south of Salt Lake City. By road, **Halls Crossing** is 220 miles northeast of Wahweap, and **Bullfrog** is 283 miles northeast (both are about 100 miles from Wahweap by boat); both are reachable via Utah 276. **Hite,** 40 miles uplake from Halls Crossing and Bullfrog, is off Utah 95.

Motorists can reach the dam and **Wahweap Marina** via U.S. 89 from Kanab or Grand Canyon National Park, and via Ariz. 98 from the east. To get to the **Lees Ferry** section, south of Wahweap, drive south on U.S. 89 and then north on U.S. 89A to Marble Canyon, where you can pick up the Lees Ferry access road.

Bullfrog and **Halls Crossing** marinas, which are connected by a toll ferry mid-lake, are accessible via Utah 276, which loops southwest from Utah 95. The cost for the 25-minute, 3-mile crossing is about $9 for cars and trucks less than 20 feet long, with higher rates for longer vehicles and those with trailers. Bicyclists and adult pedestrians are charged $3 (children $1), and motorcyclists $5. Ferries run six times daily each direction mid-May through September, less frequently at other times. The service is often shut down for maintenance for several weeks in December. **Hite Marina,** in the northernmost section of the recreation area, is just off Utah 95.

Flights between Page and Southwestern cities including Phoenix and Denver are available from **Great Lakes Airlines** (© **800/554-5111;** www.greatlakesav. com). Rental cars are available at the Page Airport from **Avis** (© **800/331-1212** or 928/645-2024).

INFORMATION/VISITOR CENTERS For advance information, contact Superintendent, **Glen Canyon National Recreation Area,** P.O. Box 1507, Page, AZ 86040 (www.nps.gov/glca), or call the **Carl Hayden Visitor Center** (© **928/608-6404**). For lodging, tour, and boat-rental information, contact the licensed park concessionaire, **Lake Powell Resorts and Marinas,** Box 56909, Phoenix, AZ 85079-6909 (© **800/528-6154;** www.lakepowell.com).

Numerous services, including lodging and dining, are available in nearby Page, Arizona. For information, contact the **Page-Lake Powell Chamber of Commerce,** 644 N. Navajo Dr., Dam Plaza (P.O. Box 727), Page, AZ 86040 (© **888/261-7243** or 928/645-2741; www.pagelakepowellchamber.org). It's open daily in summer from 9am to 6pm; Monday through Friday in winter from 9am to 5pm. The **John Wesley Powell Memorial Museum** (p. 276) also provides area lodging, dining, and attraction information. Another good website is www.canyon-country.com/lakepowell.

The **Carl Hayden Visitor Center,** at Glen Canyon Dam, 2 miles north of Page, Arizona, via U.S. 89, has exhibits on the construction of the dam and

Glen Canyon National Recreation Area

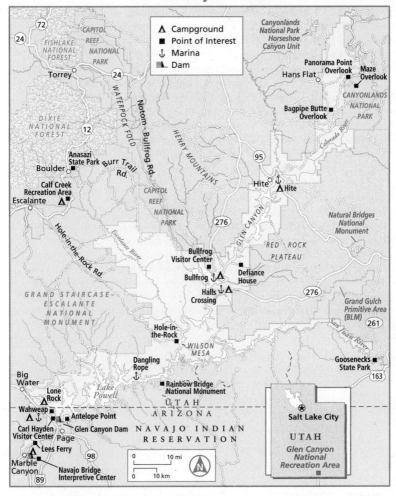

serves as the starting point for year-round guided tours of the dam, which usually take from 30 to 45 minutes. Audiovisual programs, free brochures, and books, maps, and videos are available. The visitor center is open daily 7am to 7pm from Memorial Day to Labor Day, the rest of the year 8am to 5pm.

At the **Bullfrog Visitor Center,** at mid-lake off Utah 276, you'll find a variety of exhibits and information. It's open intermittently in March, daily 8am to 5pm April through October, and closed November through February. Ranger stations at Lees Ferry, Dangling Rope, Halls Crossing, and Hite also offer park information, but these stations are only open when rangers are available.

The latest addition, the **Navajo Bridge Interpretive Center,** is located at Marble Canyon on the Colorado River, south of Page via U.S. 89A. Hours are 9am to 5pm daily, mid-April through October, and weekends 10am to 4pm in early April and November. There are outdoor exhibits, a pedestrian bridge over the river, and a bookstore.

FEES & REGULATIONS   Entry into the park costs $10 per vehicle or $3 per person for up to 7 days, or $20 for an annual pass. Boating fees are $10 for the first vessel and $4 for each thereafter, for up to 7 days; an annual pass is $20 per vessel. Backcountry permits (free) are required for overnight trips into the Escalante River section of the national recreation area.

The standard National Park Service regulations—such as not damaging anything and driving only on established roadways—apply here; additional regulations are aimed at protecting water quality of the lake by prohibiting any dumping of garbage into the water, plus requiring the containment and proper disposal of human wastes within one-fourth mile of the lake. Safe-boating requirements include mandatory use of life jackets by children 12 and under. Remember, boating regulations are slightly different in Utah and Arizona; brochures of regulations are available at the marinas.

Pets must be leashed at all times, except on houseboats, and are prohibited in public buildings. Dogs are permitted on standard, but not carpeted, houseboats.

SEASONS/AVOIDING THE CROWDS   The park is open year-round and is busiest in summer—when it's also the hottest, with temperatures sometimes topping 100°F (38°C). Spring is pleasant, but can be a bit windy. We like October, when the water's still warm enough for swimming but most of the crowds have gone home. Winter can also be beautiful, with snow only rarely dusting the rocks, and daytime temperatures usually in the 40s and 50s (single digits and teens Celsius). Another advantage to visiting in off-season: discounts on lodging and tours November through March, and on boat rentals October to May.

Where Has All The Water Gone?

Lake Powell, a huge reservoir created by the damming of the Colorado River, dominates the landscape of southern Utah with its dramatic red rock formations and beautiful deep blue water. But during the past few years we've been seeing more and more rock, and less and less water. In fact, by summer 2003, Lake Powell was at its lowest level since it was filled in 1980. We all think of Lake Powell as a vast water playground—and of course it is. But that is the by-product of it's true purpose: providing water for irrigating crops in California and providing drinking water for the residents of Phoenix, Las Vegas, and Los Angeles.

The Colorado River Compact of 1922 stipulated an allotment of water to each state within the Colorado River drainage. In 1963, the Glen Canyon Dam was built to ensure the necessary amount of water to those downstream in times of drought. As those of us who live in the Southwest are aware, we have been in increasingly serious drought conditions for several years. The law requires that a minimum specified amount of water continues to be released by the dam, but the inflow from snowmelt via the Colorado River and its tributaries has dropped drastically. By 2002, the amount of water feeding Lake Powell was only one-quarter of average, the lowest inflow amount measured since the dam was built in 1963.

Until the weather patterns change and the drought situation reverses, the water level in Lake Powell will continue to drop.

> ⸢*Tips*⸣ **A Bird's-Eye View of Lake Powell**
>
> The quickest way to see the sights is by air. **Westwind–Lake Powell Air Service** (📞 **800/245-8668** or 928/645-2494; www.westwindairtours.com) provides half-hour flights over the dam, Rainbow Bridge, and other scenic attractions (about $85 per person). Longer flights take in the Grand Canyon, Canyonlands, Monument Valley, and even Bryce Canyon, taking anywhere from 1½ to 5 hours ($175 to $250). Rates for children are about 10% less.

RANGER PROGRAMS   Amphitheater programs at Wahweap Campground take place several evenings each week in summer. Topics vary, but may include such subjects as the animals or plants of the park, geology, or the canyon's human history. Schedules are posted on bulletin boards at the campground and at the visitor center.

Kids 12 and under can become **Junior Rangers** and receive badges by completing projects in an activity book available at the Carl Hayden and Bullfrog visitor centers.

2 Exploring Lake Powell by Boat

The best way to see Lake Powell and Glen Canyon National Recreation Area is by boat, either your own or a rental, or on a boat tour. Our favorite way to explore is by **renting a houseboat** ★★ for a week and wandering among the numerous side canyons.

If your time is limited, try to spend a few hours touring the dam and seeing the exhibits in the Carl Hayden Visitor Center, particularly the excellent relief map that helps you see the big picture. Then take one of the boat tours, such as the half-day trip to Rainbow Bridge. Adventurous types might want to buy some good maps, rent a boat for the day, and explore the canyons on their own. But whatever you do, try to get to Rainbow Bridge.

BRINGING YOUR OWN BOAT   If you happened to bring your own boat, whether it's a one-person kayak or family-size cabin cruiser, you'll have a wonderful time. Boat-launching ramps are located at Wahweap, Stateline, Lees Ferry, Bullfrog, Halls Crossing, and Hite (the locations of these marinas are described earlier in the chapter). Fuel, supplies, sewage pump-out stations, drinking water, and boat repairs are available at all of the above except Lees Ferry. Services and supplies are also available at Dangling Rope Marina, about 40 miles uplake from Wahweap Marina and accessible only by boat.

As part of the Lake Powell Pure campaign, new facilities are being added for the disposal of human waste. There are eight floating restrooms/dump/pump-out stations: near the main channel at Warm Creek, at Face Canyon (near Dominguez Butte), at Rock Creek, at Oak Canyon, at the junction of the Escalante River, at the Rincon, at Hall's Creek Bay, and at Forgotten Canyon.

BOAT RENTALS   **Lake Powell Resorts and Marinas** (p. 268) rents powerboats of all sizes, from two-passenger personal watercraft to luxurious 59-foot houseboats.

Summer and early fall (through October) is the best time to be on the water, and consequently the most expensive: houseboats that sleep from 6 to 12 people range from $1,371 to $3,354 for 3 days, or $2,219 to $6,450 for 7 days. Rates for

Warning: Carbon Monoxide Danger

When you're boating in the vastness of Lake Powell, basking in the sun and breathing that clear air, it seems impossible that carbon monoxide (CO) poisoning could be a threat. Yet, at least nine people have died on Lake Powell in the last few years as a result of CO poisoning, mostly from the fumes produced by houseboat generators and boat engines. Because of its molecular configuration and the way it bonds with blood molecules, even small concentrations of carbon monoxide can cause serious illness or even death. Many houseboats vent their engine and generator exhaust at the rear of the vessel, and CO can collect under and around the rear deck. Anyone swimming or playing near this area can be overcome in a matter of minutes. Although the U.S. Coast Guard has issued a mandatory nation-wide recall for houseboats with rear exhaust vents, some experts believe this is just a temporary fix and say that extreme caution is still necessary. Don't allow anyone to swim or play near the rear deck while engines and/or generators are running, or for an hour after they've been turned off—CO can hang around that long. Sometimes CO exhaust can literally be sucked back into a boat that is underway, in what is called the "station wagon effect." Be aware of the symptoms of CO poisoning (which can include headaches, dizziness, weakness, sleepiness, nausea, and disorientation), as well as the conditions under which CO poisoning is possible.

smaller runabouts, ski boats, and personal watercraft range from $270 to $425 per day. Late fall rates are about 35% lower; spring rates are about 25% less; and in winter (January and February) you can expect rates to be about 40% lower. Ask about packages that include boat rentals plus lodging, houseboats with smaller powerboats, and powerboats with waterskiing equipment. Nonmotorized water toys are also available for rent. Most types of boats, although not necessarily all sizes, are available at Wahweap, Bullfrog, Halls Crossing, and Hite marinas. We strongly recommend making reservations well in advance (see p. 267 for the marina telephone numbers).

You can sometimes get lower rates away from the marinas. In Page, stop at **Doo Powell, Inc.,** 130 Sixth Ave. (© **800/350-1230** or 928/645-1230; www.doopowell.com), which offers a wide selection of powerboats and personal watercraft. About 12 miles northwest of Page in Big Water, Utah, is **Skylite Boat Rentals,** at U.S. 89 Mile Marker 6 (© **800/355-3795** or 435/675-3795; www.skylite.net), offering water toys—there are some great tubes that kids will love—and a range of powerboats.

Generally, anybody who can drive a car can pilot a boat. The only tricks are learning to compensate for wind and currents. Be sure to spend a few minutes practicing turning and stopping; boats don't have brakes! No lessons or licenses are required; the marinas supply all the equipment you'll need and offer some training as well.

BOAT TOURS   Year-round boat tours will take you to those hidden areas of the lake that you might never find on your own. Options range from a 1-hour trip aboard the paddle wheeler *Canyon King* ($13 adults, $10 children 11 and under) to an all-day tour to Rainbow Bridge (about $108 per adult, $71 per child; including lunch). Ask about sunset and dinner cruises, half-day trips to Rainbow Bridge, Colorado River float trips, and numerous packages that combine tours with lodging and/or RV spaces. For information and reservations, contact **Lake Powell Resorts and Marinas** (p. 268).

3 Seeing the Sights

Among the many attractions here, several deserve special mention as must-sees. We've arranged them geographically, from the south end of the lake to the north.

LEES FERRY   Downriver from Glen Canyon Dam, Lees Ferry is a historic river crossing and the site of a stone fort built by Mormon pioneers in 1874 for protection from the Navajo. It was later used as a trading post. You can see remains of the fort and a 1913 post office. Nearby at Lonely Dell, you'll find 19th- and early-20th-century ranch buildings, an orchard, and a blacksmith shop. Upriver, during low water, you can spot the remains of a steamboat, the *Charles H. Spencer,* a 92-foot-long paddle wheeler that was used briefly in the early 1900s to haul coal for a gold-dredging operation.

Lees Ferry is also the starting point for white-water river trips through the Grand Canyon, and is known for its trophy trout fishing.

GLEN CANYON DAM   Construction began on this U.S. Bureau of Reclamation project in October 1956. By the time the $155-million dam was completed in September 1963, almost 10 million tons of concrete had been poured, creating a wall 587 feet high and 3,700 feet long. It took until 1980 for the lake to reach its "full pool," covering much of the area that had been explored over 100 years earlier by Major John Wesley Powell. Today, the dam provides water storage, mostly for agriculture and hydroelectric power. Its eight generators, which cost an additional $70 million, produce more than 1 million kilowatts of electrical energy per day.

> **Impressions**
>
> *So we have a curious ensemble of wonderful features—carved walls, royal arches, glens, alcove gulches, mounds, and monuments. From which of these features shall we select a name? We decide to call it Glen Canyon.*
>
> —Explorer Major John Wesley Powell, August 3, 1869

RAINBOW BRIDGE NATIONAL MONUMENT ★★   This huge natural bridge is considered sacred by American Indians. The Navajo call it a "rainbow turned to stone," and in the summer of 1995, they briefly blocked the route to the bridge to conduct a blessing ceremony and to protest what they considered the bridge's commercialization. Located about 50 miles by boat from Wahweap, Bullfrog, and Halls Crossing marinas, the bridge is so spectacular that it was named a national monument in 1910, long before the lake was created. Believed to be the largest natural bridge in the world, Rainbow Bridge is almost perfectly symmetrical and parabolic in shape, measuring 278 feet wide and standing 290 feet above the stream bed. The top is 42 feet thick and 33 feet across.

DEFIANCE HOUSE   This archaeological site 3 miles up the middle fork of Forgotten Canyon, uplake from Halls Crossing, is believed to have been occupied by a small clan of Ancestral Puebloans between A.D. 1250 and 1275. The cliffside site includes ruins of several impressive stone rooms, food storage areas, and a kiva for religious ceremonies. The rock art panel, high along a cliff wall, includes a pictograph for which the ruin is named—an image of three warriors carrying clubs and shields. The panel also contains paintings of sheep and men.

4 Outdoor Pursuits

FISHING

Although March through November is the most popular season, the fishing is good year-round, especially for huge rainbow trout, which are often caught in the Colorado River between the dam and Lees Ferry. Lake fishermen also catch largemouth, smallmouth, and striped bass; catfish; crappie; and walleye. Because Glen Canyon National Recreation Area lies within two states, you'll need Utah and/or Arizona fishing licenses, depending on where you want to fish. The marinas sell licenses as well as fishing supplies.

HIKING, MOUNTAIN BIKING & FOUR-WHEELING

Although boating and watersports are the main activities, most of this recreation area is solid ground—actually hard rock. Lake Powell makes up only 13% of the area, so hikers and other land-based recreationists will find plenty to do. There are few marked trails, however, and changing water levels create a constantly shifting shoreline.

HIKING   Several short hikes lead to panoramic vistas of Lake Powell. For a view of the lake, Wahweap Bay, the Colorado River channel, and the sandstone cliffs of Antelope Island, drive half a mile east from the Carl Hayden Visitor Center, cross a bridge, and turn left onto an unmarked gravel road; follow it for about a mile to its end and a parking lot in an area locally known as **The Chains** (day-use area only). Heading north from the parking lot, follow the unmarked but obvious trail across sand, up slickrock, and across a level gravel section to an overlook that provides a magnificent view of the lake. This is usually a 10-minute walk (one-way). To extend the hike, you can find a way down to the water's edge, but beware: the steep sandstone can be slick.

Several hikes originate in the Lees Ferry area, including a moderate 2-mile round-trip hike through narrow **Cathedral Canyon** to the Colorado River. The trailhead is at the second turnout from U.S. 89A along Lees Ferry Road. This hike isn't along a marked trail, but rather down a wash, past intriguing rock formations. In wet weather, be alert for flash floods and deep pools. Allow 1 to 1½ hours for the round-trip hike.

Another relatively easy hike, the **River Trail,** starts just upriver from the Lees Ferry fort and follows an old wagon road to a ferry-crossing site, passing the historic submerged steamboat, the *Charles H. Spencer.* Allow about an hour for this 2-mile round-trip walk. A self-guiding booklet is available at Lees Ferry.

A heavy-duty 34-mile hike through the **Paria Canyon Primitive Area,** which departs from Lonely Dell Ranch at Lees Ferry, takes you through beautiful but narrow canyons. *Beware:* Flash flooding can be hazardous. This hike requires a permit from the Bureau of Land Management office in Kanab (© **435/644-2672;** ww.ut.blm.gov).

Although most visitors take an easy half- or full-day boat trip to see beautiful Rainbow Bridge National Monument, it is possible to hike to it, although the 14-mile one-way trail is difficult and not maintained. It crosses the Navajo Reservation and requires a permit. Contact the **Navajo Parks and Recreation Department,** P.O. Box 2520, Window Rock, AZ 86515 (© **928/871-6647;** www.navajonationparks.org).

Serious backcountry hikers should obtain current maps of the area and discuss their plans with rangers before setting out. Hikers should carry at least 1 gallon of water per person, per day.

MOUNTAIN BIKING & FOUR-WHEELING   Mountain bikers and four-wheel-drive enthusiasts must stay on established roadways within the recreation area, but quite a few challenging dirt roads can be found both in the recreation area and on adjacent federal land. Get information from the Glen Canyon National Recreation Area office (p. 268).

In the Hite area, the **Orange Cliffs** are particularly popular among mountain bikers. The 53-mile one-way **Flint Trail** connects Hite with Hans Flat in the far-northern section of the recreation area. It's rocky, with some sandy stretches and steep grades.

For a shorter ride, the **Panorama Point/Cleopatra's Chair Trail** follows recreation area routes 744, 774, and 775 for 10 miles (one-way) from Hans Flat to Cleopatra's Chair, providing a spectacular view into Canyonlands National Park. Camping in the Orange Cliffs area requires a permit, and strict regulations apply; contact the **Hans Flat Ranger Station** (© **435/259-2652**).

The Escalante River canyons of the national recreation area are accessible by four-wheel-drive vehicle via the 57-mile one-way **Hole-in-the-Rock Road,** which leaves Utah 12 5 miles east of Escalante, traversing part of the Grand Staircase–Escalante National Monument (see chapter 12). Managed by the Bureau of Land Management (© **435/644-2672;** ww.ut.blm.gov), the dirt and sometimes rocky road passes through **Devil's Rock Garden,** an area of unique rock formations, and offers a spectacular overlook of Lake Powell. Although four-wheel-drive is not always needed, the last 6 miles of the road require a high clearance vehicle. Regardless of what you're driving, you'll want to avoid the road in wet weather. Allow about 6 hours round-trip.

5 Camping

National recreation area concessionaire **Lake Powell Resorts and Marinas** (p. 268) operates year-round full-service RV parks at Wahweap, Bullfrog, and Halls Crossing, with complete RV hookups, modern restrooms, RV dump stations, drinking water, groceries, and LP gas. Wahweap and Halls Crossing have showers and coin-op laundries as well. Rates for two people are about $29 per site in summer, $20 in winter; $3 for each additional person over age 6; reservations are accepted through the concessionaire. Package deals that include RV sites and boat tours are offered.

The National Park Service operates a campground year-round at Lees Ferry, with 54 sites, flush toilets, and drinking water, but no showers or RV hookups. Reservations are not accepted; rates are $10 per site. The only camping at Hite is a primitive campground with no amenities. Cost is $6 and it's open year-round.

You'll also find several free primitive campgrounds in the recreation area's backcountry. Free dispersed camping is permitted throughout the recreation area, except within 1 mile of marinas and Lees Ferry, and at Rainbow Bridge National Monument. Those camping within one-fourth mile of Lake Powell are required to have and use self-contained or portable toilets.

6 Where to Stay & Dine

Lake Powell Resorts and Marinas (p. 268) operates all of the recreation area's lodging and dining facilities, as well as the houseboat rentals; call to make reservations and to get additional information.

Although plenty of hotels, motels, and condominium-type units are available, our choice for lodging is that wonderful floating vacation home, the **houseboat.**

Powered by two outboard motors and complete with full kitchen, bathrooms with hot showers, and sleeping areas for up to 12, houseboats serve not only as your home-away-from-home, but also as your means of exploring the fascinating red rock canyons that make Lake Powell the unique paradise it is. Hungry? There's a fridge, along with a kitchen stove with oven and a gas barbecue grill. For prices and additional information, see "Exploring Lake Powell by Boat," earlier in this chapter.

In addition to the facilities described below, a variety of motels are located in Page, Arizona. For information, contact the **Page-Lake Powell Chamber of Commerce** (p. 268).

AT WAHWEAP

If you prefer a bedroom that doesn't float, consider the **Wahweap Lodge,** the largest (350 units) and fanciest hotel in the area. Right at the Wahweap Marina, it offers good access for boat tours and rentals, has two pools and a Jacuzzi, and provides shuttle service into Page. Rooms on the west side have spectacular views of Lake Powell. Rates for two range from $89 to $155.

Restaurants at Wahweap Marina include the **Rainbow Room,** at Wahweap Lodge (*②* **928/645-2433**), providing American and Southwestern dishes along with a panoramic view of Lake Powell. All three meals are served daily; dinner main courses cost $15 to $24.

A fast-food restaurant at the marina is open from April to mid-September.

AT BULLFROG & THE OTHER MARINAS

The attractive **Defiance House Lodge,** at Bullfrog Marina, has 50 rooms with beautiful views of the lake; prices for two range from $123 to $148. The fine-dining restaurant here is open year-round; a fast-food joint is open in summer only.

Three-bedroom mobile-home family units are available at Bullfrog, Halls Crossing, and Hite marinas. Prices for up to six people are about $189 in summer, $125 at other times.

7 In Memory of John Wesley Powell: A Nearby Museum

John Wesley Powell Memorial Museum   The boat on the front lawn immediately lets you know that this small museum has something to do with water. Actually, it's dedicated to the memory of Major John Wesley Powell, who in 1869 led a small group of men on a courageous—some say foolhardy—expedition down the Green and Colorado rivers, traveling almost 1,000 miles through largely uncharted territory. The museum documents Powell's expedition with photographs, etchings, and artifacts. It also contains exhibits of American Indian arts and crafts, from ancient Ancestral Puebloan pottery to modern Navajo and Hopi weavings, pottery, and jewelry. Other highlights include fluorescent rock minerals, a stamp collection, and dinosaur tracks. Changing exhibits of works by local artists are also featured. Allow about an hour.

6 N. Lake Powell Blvd. at the corner of N. Navajo Dr., Page, AZ 86040. *②* **888/597-6873** or 928/645-9496. Fax 928/645-3412. www.powellmuseum.org. Admission $2 adults, $1 children 5–12. Mon–Fri 9am–5pm. Closed mid-Dec to mid-Feb.

15

From Moab to Arches & Canyonlands National Parks

Canyonlands country they call this— a seemingly infinite high desert of rock, with spectacular formations and rugged gorges that have been carved over the centuries by the forces of the Colorado and Green rivers. Massive sandstone spires and arches that seem to defy gravity, all colored by iron and other minerals in shades of orange, red, and brown, define the national parks of southeastern Utah. This is a land that begs to be explored—if you've come to Utah for mountain biking, hiking, four-wheeling, or rafting, this is the place to be. And the region holds a few surprises, too, from Ancestral Puebloan (also called Anasazi) dwellings and rock art to dinosaur bones.

1 Moab: Gateway to the National Parks

238 miles SE of Salt Lake City

Named for a biblical kingdom at the edge of Zion, the promised land, Moab has evolved into a popular base camp for mountain bikers, four-wheel-drive enthusiasts, hikers, kayakers, and rafters eager to explore the red rock canyon country that dominates southeastern Utah. A drive down Main Street confirms that yes, this is a tourist town, with scores of businesses catering to visitors.

Not far from the Colorado River, Moab sits in a green valley among striking red sandstone cliffs, a setting that has lured Hollywood filmmakers for hits such as John Wayne's *The Comancheros,* the biblical epic *The Greatest Story Ever Told, Indiana Jones and the Last Crusade, Thelma and Louise,* and *City Slickers II.*

It's also become a favorite location for Madison Avenue. Remember those great Chevy commercials with a car perched atop a huge red tower of stone? That's Castle Rock, one of the Moab area landmarks—and the only way to get to the top is by rock climbing or helicopter. According to Bette Stanton, local author and film historian, when the first commercial in the series was being made in 1963, Chevrolet successfully hauled a car and a negligee-clad model to the top of the 1,000-foot tower, but by the time filming was done for the day, gusty winds made it impossible for the helicopter to land to pick up the model. A crew member, carrying extra clothes, was dropped to keep her company, and after a chilly night they were both airlifted down.

Like most Utah towns, Moab was established by Mormon pioneers sent by church leader Brigham Young. But Moab was actually founded twice. The first time, in 1855, missionaries set up Elk Mountain Mission to see to the spiritual needs of the local Utes. Apparently unimpressed with the notion of abandoning their own religion for the ways of the LDS Church, the Utes killed several missionaries, sending the rest back to Salt Lake City in a hurry. It wasn't until 20 years later that the settlers tried again; this time, they successfully established a small farming and ranching community.

Today, Moab, at 4,000 feet elevation, remains a relatively small town, with only 4,000 or so permanent residents, but that still makes it the biggest community in southeastern Utah. Practically within walking distance of Arches National Park, Moab is also close to Canyonlands National Park and is surrounded by the Manti-La Sal National Forest and vast, open spaces under the jurisdiction of the Bureau of Land Management (BLM).

ESSENTIALS

GETTING THERE   Situated on U.S. 191, Moab is 30 miles south of I-70 (take exit 180 at Crescent Junction) and 53 miles north of Monticello. Moab is 399 miles northeast of the north rim of Grand Canyon National Park and 238 miles southeast of Salt Lake City. From Salt Lake City, follow I-15 south to Spanish Fork, take U.S. 6 southeast to I-70, and follow that east to Crescent Junction, where you'll pick up U.S. 191 south to Moab.

An easy way to get here from Salt Lake City is by shuttle. Contact **Airport Rapid Konnection** (© **888/655-7433** or 801/328-9920; fax 801/328-4490; www.goark.com), which charges $54 per person each way.

Canyonlands Field Airport (© **435/259-3422**; www.canyonlandsfield.com) is just 18 miles north of Moab. It offers air charter services plus some commercial flights.

The closest major airport is **Walker Field,** in Grand Junction, Colorado (© **970/244-9100;** fax 970/241-9103; www.walkerfield.com), about 125 miles east of Moab. Airlines operating at Walker Field include **America West Express/ Mesa Airlines** (© **800/235-9292** or 970/728-4868) and **SkyWest–The Delta Connection** (© **800/453-9417**). Rental cars are available from Avis, Budget, Enterprise, Hertz, National, and Thrifty.

Amtrak's (© **800/872-7245**) *California Zephyr* stops in Green River, about 52 miles north of Moab, and provides service to Salt Lake City and Grand Junction, Colorado. If you plan to go from Green River to Moab, make reservations with **Airport Rapid Konnection** (see above).

VISITOR INFORMATION   For advance information, contact the **Moab Area Travel Council,** P.O. Box 550, Moab, UT 84532 (© **800/635-6622** or 435/ 259-8825; fax 435/259-1376; www.discovermoab.com or www.canyonlands utah.com).

After you've arrived, stop by the **Moab Information Center,** in the middle of town at the corner of Main and Center streets; it's open from 8am to 9pm in summer, with slightly reduced winter hours. This multi-agency visitor center has information from the Park Service, Bureau of Land Management, U.S. Forest Service, Grand County Travel Council, and Canyonlands Natural History Association. You can get advice, watch a number of videos on Southwest attractions, pick up brochures on local businesses and outfitters, and purchase books, videos, and other materials. A board displays current weather conditions and campsite availability.

GETTING AROUND   Rentals (standard passenger cars, vans, and four-wheel-drive vehicles) are available from **Thrifty** (© **800/847-4389** or 435/259-7317) and **Budget** (© **888/806-5337** or 435/259-7494), as well as from the rental agencies at the airport (noted above). Four-wheel-drive vehicles are also available from **Slickrock 4X4 Rentals** (© **888/238-5337** or 435/259-5678).

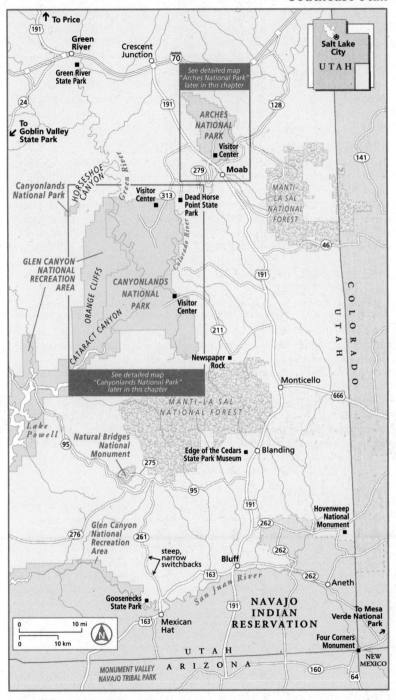

To Price

191
Green River

Crescent Junction

70

Green River State Park

24

To Goblin Valley State Park

Salt Lake City

UTAH

See detailed map "Arches National Park" later in this chapter

ARCHES NATIONAL PARK

191

128

141

Visitor Center

279

Moab

Horseshoe Canyon

Green River

Canyonlands National Park

Visitor Center

313

Dead Horse Point State Park

MANTI-LA SAL NATIONAL FOREST

46

GLEN CANYON NATIONAL RECREATION AREA

ORANGE CLIFFS

CATARACT CANYON

CANYONLANDS NATIONAL PARK

Visitor Center

Colorado River

191

211

Newspaper Rock

See detailed map "Canyonlands National Park" later in this chapter

Monticello

666

COLORADO

UTAH

MANTI-LA SAL NATIONAL FOREST

Lake Powell

Natural Bridges National Monument

95

275

Edge of the Cedars State Park Museum

Blanding

Hovenweep National Monument

Glen Canyon National Recreation Area

276

261

95

191

262

steep, narrow switchbacks

Bluff

262

163

San Juan River

262

Aneth

Goosenecks State Park

163

Mexican Hat

191

NAVAJO INDIAN RESERVATION

To Mesa Verde National Park

Four Corners Monument

NEW MEXICO

0   10 mi
0   10 km

N

UTAH
ARIZONA

160

64

MONUMENT VALLEY NAVAJO TRIBAL PARK

FAST FACTS In an emergency, dial © **911.** The full-service **Allen Memorial Hospital,** 719 W. 400 North (© **435/259-7191**), offers 24-hour emergency care. The **post office** is at 50 E. 100 North (© **800/275-8777**).

Our choice for the best grocery store in town is **City Market,** 425 S. Main St. (© **435/259-5181**), open daily from 6am to midnight. Outdoor enthusiasts can pick up sandwiches from the deli, create their own salads at the excellent salad bar, and choose fresh-baked items from the bakery before hitting the trail. The store also sells fishing licenses, money orders, and stamps; offers photo finishing and Western Union services; and contains a pharmacy.

MOUNTAIN BIKING & OTHER OUTDOOR PURSUITS

The Moab area is one of Utah's main outdoor playgrounds, an ideal spot for hiking, boating, camping, or just plain horsing around (with or without the horse). In addition to the nearby national parks, Arches and Canyonlands, which are covered in full later in this chapter, there's plenty of room to roam on land administered by the **Bureau of Land Management's Grand Resource Area** office, 82 E. Dogwood Ave., Moab, UT 84532 (© **435/259-2100;** www.ut. blm.gov), and the **Manti-La Sal National Forest's Moab Ranger District,** 2290 S. West Resource Blvd. (P.O. Box 386), Moab, UT 84532 (© **435/259-7155;** www.fs.fed.us/r4). The best source for information is the **Moab Information Center** (p. 278).

Much of the federal land surrounding Moab is isolated and remote—not somewhere you'd want to get lost. So stock up on detailed topographic and trail maps of the specific areas you plan to explore. These, along with guidebooks, compasses, and other supplies (as well as fascinating historic maps), are available, either in person or by mail order, at **T. I. Maps, Etc.,** 29 E. Center St., across from the information center (© **435/259-5529;** fax 435/259-7741; www.moab maps.com).

Because of the extreme desert heat in summer, the best time for most outdoor activities is spring or fall—even the relatively mild winters are inviting. If you end up vacationing in the middle of summer, we recommend that you do your serious hiking and mountain biking early in the day, enjoy a siesta along the river or beside a swimming pool during the heat of the afternoon, and take a short hike in the evening, just before sundown.

MOUNTAIN BIKING

With hundreds and hundreds of miles of trails, a wide variety of terrain, and spectacular scenery, Moab is easily the mountain-bike capital of Utah, and possibly of the United States (although the folks in Crested Butte, Colorado, might disagree). In addition to the mountain biking possibilities on four-wheel-drive roads in the national parks (see sections on Arches and Canyonlands national parks, later in this chapter), there are abundant trails on Bureau of Land Management and national forest lands that are much less trafficked than national park routes.

When you get into town, stop by the Moab Information Center (p. 278) for a free copy of the *Moab Area Mountain Bike Trails* pamphlet. Discuss your plans with the very knowledgeable staff here, who can help you find the trails most suitable for your interests, ability, and equipment. You can also get information, as well as rent or repair bikes, at **Slickrock Cycles,** 94 W. 415 N. Main St. (© **800/825-9791** or 435/259-1134). Bike rentals start at about $35 per day.

Bike shuttle services are available from **Acme Bike Shuttle** (© **435/260-2534**), **Coyote Shuttle** (© **435/259-8656**), **Moab Outback** (© **435/259-2667**), and

Roadrunner Shuttle (✆ 435/259-9402). Several local companies (see "Outfitters," later in this chapter) also offer guided mountain-bike tours, with group rates starting at about $80 for a half day and $95 for a full day, including bike rental. Multi-day biking/camping trips start at about $550 for a 3-day excursion.

The area's most famous trail is undoubtedly the **Slickrock Bike Trail** ⟨★★★⟩, a scenic but challenging 9.6-mile loop that crosses a mesa of heavily eroded pale orange Navajo sandstone just a few minutes from downtown Moab. Along the way, the trail offers views that take in the towering La Sal Mountains, the red rock formations of Arches National Park, a panorama of Canyonlands National Park, and the Colorado River. The trail, open to both mountain bikes and motorcycles, is physically demanding and technically difficult, and not recommended for children, novices, or those who are out of shape or have any medical problems. Allow 4 to 5 hours, and expect to have to walk your bike in some areas. If you're not sure you're ready for the Slickrock Trail, a 2.2-mile practice loop will give you an idea of what lies ahead. To get to the trailhead from the visitor information center, take Center Street east to 400 East. Turn south (right) and follow 400 East to Mill Creek Drive. Turn east (left) and follow Mill Creek Drive to Sand Flats Road, which you take 2.3 miles east to the BLM's Sand Flats Recreation Area and the trailhead.

Those looking for a somewhat less challenging experience might try the **Gemini Bridges Trail,** a 13½-mile one-way trip that shows off the area's colorful rock formations, including the trail's namesake: two natural rock bridges. Considered relatively easy, this trail follows a dirt road mostly downhill, ending at U.S. 191 just under 10 miles from the center of Moab, so it's best to arrange a shuttle. To get to the trailhead from the Moab Information Center, drive north along U.S. 191 to Utah 313, turn west (left), and go about 13 miles. Allow a full day, including getting to and from the trail, and be sure to watch for the magnificent view of Arches National Park from a hilltop as you approach U.S. 191 near the end of the ride.

Although there are dozens of fabulous trails to explore in the immediate area, mountain bikers who really want to go somewhere—perhaps all the way to Colorado—will want to check out Kokopelli's Trail and the San Juan Hut System. Winding for 142 miles across sandstone and shale canyons, deserts, and mountains, **Kokopelli's Trail** connects Moab and Grand Junction, Colorado. It combines all types of mountain biking, from demanding single track to well-maintained dirt roads, and passes primitive campsites along the way. Elevation change is about 4,200 feet. The west end of the trail is near Sand Flats Road in Moab; the east end is at the Loma Boat Launch, 15 miles west of Grand Junction. For more information contact the **Colorado Plateau Mountain-Bike Trail Association,** P.O. Box 4602, Grand Junction, CO 81502 (✆ **970/243-5602;** www.copmoba.com).

The **San Juan Hut System,** P.O. Box 773, Ridgway, CO 81432 (✆ **970/ 626-3033;** www.sanjuanhuts.com), links Moab with Telluride, Colorado, via a 206-mile-long network of backcountry dirt roads. Every 35 miles, you'll find a primitive cabin with bunks, a wood stove, a propane cooking stove, cooking gear, and groceries. The route is appropriate for intermediate-level mountain-bikers in good physical condition; more experienced cyclists will find advanced technical single tracks near the huts. The mountain biking season generally runs from June through September. The cost for riders who plan to make the whole trip is $475, which includes use of the six huts, food, sleeping bags at each hut, and maps and trail descriptions. Shorter trips and vehicle shuttles are also available.

FOUR-WHEELING

The Moab area has thousands of miles of four-wheel-drive roads, most left over from mining days. These roads offer a popular way to explore this scenic country without exerting too much energy.

A number of local companies (see "Outfitters," later in the chapter) provide guided trips, starting at about $65 per person for a half day and $100 for a full day. Photographers will enjoy the Lin Ottinger tours, designed especially for catching the right light and the best angles. You can also rent a 4×4, usually from about $100 per day, and fill it up with your kids and even the family dog (see "Getting Around," earlier in the chapter).

Those who want to hit the trail themselves, either with a rental or personal 4×4, will find a number of possibilities, from fairly easy dirt roads to "You-don't-really-expect-me-to-take-this-$40,000-SUV-up-*there*-do-you?" piles of rocks. Several four-wheel-drive trips are described in the Canyonlands section of this chapter, and a free brochure, available at the Moab Information Center (p. 278), covers several others.

Our favorite four-wheel-drive trail is **Poison Spider Mesa Trail** ★★★, which covers 16 miles of 4×4 road, providing stupendous views down to the Colorado River and Moab Valley. It's considered difficult; a short-wheelbase high-clearance vehicle is best. Allow at least 4 hours. To reach the trail from the Moab Information Center, drive north on U.S. 191 for about 6 miles and turn west (left) onto Utah 279. Continue another 6 miles to the dinosaur tracks sign, where the trail leaves the pavement to the right, passing over a cattle guard. From here, simply follow the main trail, which is usually obvious, up switchbacks, through a sandy canyon, and over some steep, rocky stretches. From a slickrock parking area on top, you can take a short walk to Little Arch, which isn't really so little.

One easy 4×4 road is the **Gemini Bridges Trail,** which four-wheelers share with mountain bikers (the trail is described earlier in the mountain-biking section). Those with 4×4s often drive the route in the opposite direction of the mountain bikers, starting at a dirt road departing from the west side of U.S. 191, about 10 miles north of the Moab Information Center. This involves more uphill driving, which is safer for motor vehicles—mountain bikers usually prefer going downhill.

The self-guided **Mill Canyon Dinosaur Trail** provides a close-up view of dinosaur bones and fossils from the Jurassic period, 150 million years ago, including a sauropod leg bone, vertebrae, ribs, and toe bones. You'll also see the fossil remains of a large tree trunk. To reach the trailhead, drive about 15 miles north of Moab on U.S. 191, then turn left at an intersection just north of highway mile marker 141. Cross the railroad tracks and follow a dirt road for about 2 miles to the trailhead. Allow about 1 hour. On the south side of the canyon, you'll see the remnants of an old copper mill that operated in the late 1800s. Also nearby are the ruins of the Halfway Stage Station, a lunch stop in the late 1800s for stagecoach travelers making the 35-mile trip between Moab and Thompson, the nearest train station at that time. From the dinosaur trailhead, go north as though you're returning to U.S. 191, but at the first intersection, turn right and drive to a dry wash, where you turn right again onto a jeep road that takes you a short distance to the stage station. The trail is managed by the **BLM's Grand Resource Area office** (p. 280).

HIKING

The Moab area offers hundreds of hiking possibilities, many of them just a few miles from town. Get information at the Moab Information Center (p. 278) and pick up the free brochure that describes seven local trails. Hikes in nearby Arches and Canyonlands national parks are described later in this chapter.

Particularly in the summer, carry at least a gallon of water per person per day; we also recommend wearing a broad-brimmed hat.

A favorite hike of the locals is the **Negro Bill Canyon Trail,** named for William Granstaff, who lived in the area in the late 1800s. Allow about 3 hours for this 4-mile round-trip hike, which is considered easy to moderate. You may get your feet wet, depending on the level of the stream you follow up the canyon. To get to the trailhead, go north from Moab on U.S. 191 to Utah 128, turn east (right), and go about 3 miles to a dirt parking area. About 2 miles up the trail, in a side canyon to the right, you'll find Morning Glory Bridge, a natural rock span of 243 feet. Watch out for the poison ivy that grows by a pool under the bridge. (In case you don't remember from your scouting manual, poison ivy has shiny leaves with serrated edges, and grows in clusters of three.)

The **Hidden Valley Trail** is a bit more challenging, taking you up a series of steep switchbacks to views of rock formations and a panorama of the Moab Valley. Allow about 4 hours for the 4-mile round-trip. To get to the trailhead, drive about 3 miles south of the Moab Information Center on U.S. 191, turn west (right) onto Angel Rock Road, and go 2 blocks to Rimrock Road. Turn north (right) and follow Rimrock Road to the parking area. The trail is named for a broad shelf, located about halfway up the Moab Rim. Many hikers turn around and head back down after reaching a low pass with great views of huge sandstone fins (the 2-mile point), but you can extend the hike by continuing all the way to the Colorado River on a four-wheel-drive road.

The highly recommended **Corona Arch Trail** offers views of three impressive arches, a colorful slickrock canyon, and the Colorado River. Allow 2 hours for this 3-mile round-trip hike, which involves a lot of fairly easy walking plus some rather steep spots with handrails and a short ladder. From Moab, go north on U.S. 191 to Utah 279, turn west (left), and go about 10 miles to a parking area on the north side of the road. You'll find a registration box and trailhead near the railroad; after crossing the tracks, follow an old roadbed onto the trail, which is marked with cairns (piles of stones).

ROCK CLIMBING

Those with the proper skills and equipment for rock climbing will find ample opportunities in the Moab area; check with the BLM (p. 280). Several companies also offer instruction and guided climbs, with rates for full-day climbs starting at $120 per person for groups of three or more. Contact **Desert Highlights,** 50 E. Center St., Moab, UT 84532 (© **800/747-1342** or 435/259-4433; www.deserthighlights.com), **Moab Desert Adventures,** 801 E. Oak St., Moab, UT 84532 (© **877/ROK-MOAB** or 435/260-2404; www.moabdesertadventures.com), or **Moab Cliffs & Canyons,** 63 E. Center St., Moab, UT 84532 (© **877/641-5271** or 435/259-3347; www.cliffsandcanyons.com). For gear or to rent climbing shoes, stop at **Pagan Mountaineering,** 88 E. Center St. (© **435/259-1117**) or **Gearheads,** 471 S. Main St. (© **435/259-4327**).

WATERSPORTS: BOATING, CANOEING, RAFTING & MORE

After spending hours in the blazing sun looking at mile upon mile of huge red sandstone rock formations, it's easy to get the idea that the Moab area is a baking, dry, rock-hard desert. Well, it is. But Moab is also the only town in Utah that sits along the **Colorado River** ★★, and it's rapidly becoming a major boating center.

You can travel down the river in a canoe, kayak, large or small rubber raft (with or without motor), or speedy, solid jet boat. Do-it-yourselfers can rent kayaks or canoes for $25 to $35 for a half day and $30 to $45 for a full day, or rafts from $50 to $85 for a half day and $65 to $115 for a full day. Half-day guided river trips cost from $35 to $45 per person; full-day trips are usually $40 to $60. Multi-day rafting expeditions, which include meals and camping equipment, start at about $150 per person for 2 days. Jet-boat trips, which cover a lot more river in a given amount of time, start at $60 for a half-day trip, with full-day trips about $85. Children's rates are usually about 20% lower. Some companies also offer sunset or dinner trips. **Sheri Griffith Expeditions** even offers a 4-day, 3-night raft trip "Expedition in Luxury," at $1,248 per person, offering fine wines and gourmet food served with white tablecloths. Your every need will be anticipated. See "Outfitters," later in the chapter.

Public boat-launching ramps are opposite Lion's Park, near the intersection of U.S. 191 and Utah 128; at Take-Out Beach, along Utah 128 about 10 miles east of its intersection with U.S. 191; and at Hittle Bottom, also along Utah 128, about 23½ miles east of its intersection with U.S. 191. For recorded information on river flows and reservoir conditions statewide, contact the **Colorado Basin River Forecast Center** (© **801/539-1311;** www.cbrfc.gov).

GOLFING

It might be hard to keep your eye on the ball at the 18-hole, par-72 **Moab Golf Club** course, 2750 S. East Bench Rd. (© **435/259-6488**). Located 5 miles south of downtown Moab in Spanish Valley (take Spanish Trail Road off U.S. 191), the challenging course, nestled among red sandstone cliffs, offers spectacular views in every direction. Open daily year-round (weather permitting), the course has a driving range, a pro shop and lessons, cart rentals, and a snack bar that's open for breakfast and lunch. Greens fees, including cart, are $37 for 18 holes, $21 for 9 holes.

HORSEBACK RIDING

Those who want to see the canyons and rock formations from the top of a horse can choose from several companies that lead guided rides (see "Outfitters," below). A 2-hour ride starts at about $30, half-day rides are $60 to $75, and full-day trips cost about $100. Sunset and dinner rides are also available, and several companies combine horseback rides with river trips.

Outfitters

Although Moab has plenty for the do-it-yourselfer, some 50 local outfitters offer guided excursions of all kinds, from lazy canoe rides to hair-raising jet-boat and four-wheel-drive adventures. The chart below lists some of the major companies that can help you fully enjoy this beautiful country. All are located right in Moab, ZIP code 84532. Advance reservations are often required. It's best to check with several outfitters before deciding on one; in addition to asking about what you'll see and do and what it costs, it doesn't hurt to make sure the company is insured and has the proper permits with the various federal agencies. Also ask about its cancellation policy, just in case.

Outfitter	4X4	Bike	Boat	Horse	Rent	Shuttle
Adrift Adventures 378 N. Main, P.O. Box 577 © 800/874-4483, 435/259-8594 www.adrift.net	•		•	•		
Canyonlands by Night & Day 1861 N. Main, P.O. Box 328 © 800/394-9978, 435/259-5261 www.canyonlandsbynight.com	•		•		•	•
Canyon Voyages Adventure Co. 211 N. Main, P.O. Box 416 © 800/733-6007, 435/259-6007 www.canyonvoyages.com	•		•		•	
Cowboy Adventures 2231 S. Main, P.O. Box 104 © 435/259-7410				•		
Dan Mick's Tours 600 Mill Creek Dr., P.O. Box 1234 © 435/259-4567 www.danmick.com	•					
Dreamride 59 E. Center, Box 1137 © 888/662-2882, 435/259-6419 www.dreamride.com		•				
Moab Cyclery 391 S. Main © 800/451-1133, 435/259-7423 www.moabcyclery.com		•			•	
Moab Rafting Co. Box 801 © 800/746-6622 or 435/259-7238 www.moab-rafting.com			•			
Navtec Expeditions 321 N. Main, P.O. Box 1267 © 800/833-1278, 435/259-7983 www.navtec.com	•		•		•	
Nichols Expeditions 497 N. Main © 800/648-8488, 435/259-3999 www.nicholsexpeditions.com		•			•	
OARS Canyonlands Tours 543 N. Main © 800/342-5938, 435/259-5865 www.oarsutah.com	•		•			
Pack Creek Ranch U.S. 191, S. of Moab P.O. Box 1270 © 435/259-5505 www.packcreekranch.com				•		
Red River Canoe Co. 702 S. Main © 800/753-8216, 435/259-7722 www.redrivercanoe.com			•			

Outfitter	4X4	Bike	Boat	Horse	Rent	Shuttle
Rim Tours 1233 South U.S. 191 ℃ 800/626-7335, 435/259-5223 www.rimtours.com		•			•	
Sheri Griffith Expeditions 2231 South U.S. 191, P.O. Box 1324 ℃ 800/332-2439, 435/259-8229 www.griffithexp.com		•	•	•	•	
Tag-A-Long Expeditions 452 N. Main ℃ 800/453-3292, 435/259-8946 www.tagalong.com	•		•		•	
Tex's Riverways 691 N. 500 West, P.O. Box 67 ℃ 435/259-5101			•		•	
Western River Expeditions 1371 North U.S. 191 ℃ 888/622-4097, 435/259-7019 www.westernriver.com			•		•	•
Xtreme Adventure Tours N. U.S. 191 ℃ 435/259-3906 www.xtremeadventuretours.com	•					

SEEING THE SIGHTS

Dan O'Laurie Museum   This small museum has numerous displays depicting the history of Moab from prehistoric times to the present. It starts with exhibits on the geology of the area and the resultant uranium and radium mining, and features an archaeology section which includes a large basket found in the Moab area. Early home medical remedies are on display, as is the first incubator, which used only a 25-watt bulb and was invented by a local doctor. You'll see primers from the early 1900s and a 1920 high-school annual called "The Whizzer," as well as the expected ranching and farming exhibits—even a handmade quilt depicting cattle brands. There's a brief display about the National Park Service, Bureau of Land Management, and U.S. Forest Service, describing their role in the area—a large one—and how they work together. Allow about an hour.

118 E. Center St. (2 blocks east of Main St.). ℃ 435/259-7985. Admission $2 for those 12 and older; $5 family. Summer Mon–Sat 1–8pm; winter Mon–Thurs 3–7pm and Fri–Sat 1–7pm.

WHERE TO STAY

Room rates are generally highest from mid-March through October, and sometimes drop by up to half in winter. Rates may also be higher during special events. Room tax of about 12¼% is added to all bills. Pets are not accepted unless otherwise noted.

Most visitors are here for the outdoors, and because they don't plan to spend much time in their rooms, many book into one of the very adequate chain and franchise motels, including **Super 8,** on the north edge of Moab at 889 N. Main St. (℃ **800/800-8000** or 435/259-8868), the town's largest lodging, with rates for two of $32 to $50 November through February, and $54 to $90 March through October; **Days Inn,** 426 N. Main St. (© **800/DAYS-INN** or 435/259-4468), with rates for two of $40 to $75 November through March, and $65 to $80 April through October; **Comfort Suites,** 800 S. Main St., Moab, UT 84532 (© **800/228-5150** or 435/259-5252), with rates for two of $70 to $120; **Motel 6,** 1089 N. Main St., Moab, UT 84532 (© **800/466-8356** or 435/259-6686), with rates for two of $35 to $76; **Sleep Inn,** 1051 S. Main St., Moab, UT 84532 (© **800/424-6423** or 435/259-4655) with rates for two of $50 to $70 November through February, and $70 to $100 March through October; **Ramada Inn,** 182 S. Main St., Moab, UT 84532 (© **888/989-1988** or 435/259-7141) with rates for two of $35 to $65 November through February, and $55 to $109 March through October; **Best Western Canyonlands Inn,** 16 S. Main St., Moab, UT 84532 (© **800/528-1234** or 435/259-2300), with rates for two of $50 to $130; and **Best Western Greenwell Inn,** 105 S. Main St., Moab, UT 84532 (© **800/528-1234** or 435/259-6151), with rates for two of $40 to $120.

Also see the **cabins** at Arch View Camp Park, Canyonlands Campground & RV Park, and Moab Valley RV & Campground under "Camping," later in the chapter.

Aarchway Inn   Just 2 miles from the entrance to Arches National Park, on the north edge of Moab, this well-maintained modern motel has large rooms with great views, decorated in Southwestern style and with photos depicting the scenic attractions of the area. The suites have whirlpool tubs. Most rooms contain two queen beds—eight family units also have queen sofabeds. There are also two apartments, with full kitchens and 46-inch TVs (call for rates). Facilities include a courtyard with barbecue grills, bike storage, conference rooms, and a gift shop. The entire property is nonsmoking.

1551 N. U.S. 191, Moab, UT 84532. © 800/341-9359 or 435/259-2599. Fax 435/259-2270. www.aarchway inn.com. 97 units. Mar–Oct $86–$108 double, $150–$170 suite; lower rates Nov–Feb. Rates include continental breakfast. AE, DC, DISC, MC, V. **Amenities:** Large outdoor heated pool; indoor Jacuzzi; exercise room; coin-op laundry. *In room:* A/C, TV.

Bowen Motel   This family-owned and -operated motel offers fairly large, comfortable, clean, basic rooms with attractive wallpaper, a king or one or two queen beds, and combination shower/tubs. Two family rooms sleep up to six persons each. The original structure was built in the 1940s, with an addition made in 1978; a major renovation was completed in 1993 and 1994. Up to two bikes may be kept in the rooms at a charge of $1 per bike per night. Several restaurants are within easy walking distance.

169 N. Main St., Moab, UT 84532. © 800/874-5439 or 435/259-7132. Fax 435/259-6641. www.bowen motel.com. 40 units. $65–$75 double; off-season 40% less. Rates include continental breakfast. AE, DC, DISC, MC, V. **Amenities:** Outdoor heated pool. *In room:* A/C, TV.

Lazy Lizard International Hostel   Located on the south side of town, behind the A-1 self-storage units, this hostel offers exceptionally clean, comfortable lodging at bargain rates for those willing to share. The main house, which is air-conditioned, has basic dorm rooms plus two private rooms. A separate building contains four additional private rooms, which look much like older motel units. The best facilities are the cabins, constructed of real logs and with beds for up to six. There's also a camping area (no hookups). Everyone shares the bathhouses, and there's a phone in the main house. Guests also have use of a fully equipped kitchen; living room with TV, VCR, and movies; gas barbecue grill; and picnic tables. Groups should inquire about the nearby houses, which can be rented by the night ($100 to $220 for 14 to 30 people).

1213 S. U.S. 191, Moab, UT 84532. (℃) **435/259-6057.** Fax 435/259-1122. www.lazylizardhostel.com. 25 dorm beds, 10 private rooms, 8 cabins; total capacity 65 persons. $9 dorm bed; $22 private room; from $27 cabin; $6 per person camping space. Showers $2 for nonguests. Hostel membership not necessary. MC, V. **Amenities:** Outdoor Jacuzzi; coin-op laundry. *In room:* A/C, no phone.

Red Stone Inn   This centrally located motel is comfortable, clean, and quiet, and decidedly welcoming to mountain bikers. The exterior gives the impression that these are cabins, and the theme continues inside as well, with attractive knotty pine walls decorated with colorful posters and maps of area attractions. Rooms are a bit on the small side, although perfectly adequate and spotlessly maintained. All rooms have kitchenettes with microwaves, coffeemakers (with coffee supplied), and refrigerators. Three handicapped-accessible rooms have combination shower/tubs—the rest have showers only. There's a covered picnic area with tables and gas barbecue grills, and a bike work stand and bike wash station. Bikes are permitted in the rooms. Guests have access to an outdoor heated pool at another motel across the street.

535 S. Main St., Moab, UT 84532. (℃) **800/772-1972** or 435/259-3500. Fax 435/259-2717. www.moabred stone.com. office@moabredstone.com. 52 units. Summer $60–$75 double; winter $30–$35 double; slightly higher in Sept and during special events. Roll-away beds $5 extra. AE, DISC, MC, V. Pets permitted with $5 fee. **Amenities:** Access to heated outdoor pool; self-serve laundry. *In room:* A/C, TV.

Sunflower Hill Bed & Breakfast Inn 🌟🌟   This country-style retreat, 3 blocks off Main Street on a quiet dead-end road, offers elegant rooms and lovely outdoor areas, and is our choice for a relaxing escape. The rooms are individually decorated—for instance, the Garden Suite boasts a colorful garden-themed mural—and have handmade quilts on the beds. Deluxe rooms have jetted tubs and private balconies. The popular French Bedroom includes a hand-carved antique bedroom set from France, stained-glass window, vaulted ceiling, white lace curtains, and large whirlpool tub and separate tiled shower. The grounds are grassy and shady, with fruit trees and flowers in abundance. Guests enjoy a swing, picnic table, and barbecue. The substantial breakfast buffet includes homemade breads and fresh-baked pastries, honey-almond granola, fresh fruits, and a hot entree such as a garden vegetable frittata, blueberry pancakes, or asparagus quiche. The inn also offers a guest laundry.

185 N. 300 East, Moab, UT 84532. (℃) **800/662-2786** or 435/259-2974. Fax 435/259-3065. www.sunflower hill.com. 12 units. Mar to mid-Nov and holidays $135–$195 double; mid-Nov to Feb $90–$140 double. Rates include full breakfast and evening refreshments. AE, DISC, MC, V. Children under 10 accepted by prior arrangement. **Amenities:** Jacuzzi; self-serve laundry. *In room:* A/C, TV, no phone.

CAMPING

In addition to the commercial campgrounds discussed here, there is also camping at Canyonlands and Arches national parks, at Dead Horse Point State Park, and at Newspaper Rock, which are discussed elsewhere in this chapter. Those camping on public lands where there are no showers can find them at the Moab Swim Center, 181 W. 400 North ((℃) **435/259-8226**).

Arch View Camp Park   This campground offers all the usual RV hookups, showers, and other amenities you'd expect in a first-class commercial RV park, plus great views into Arches National Park, especially at sunset. Located about 6 miles from the park entrance, Arch View has trees throughout the park, a grassy tent area, a convenience store, a pool, a playground, a coin-op laundry, and propane, gasoline, and diesel sales. There are also six log cabins ($30 to $35, for two people).

U.S. 191, at the junction with U.S. 313, 9 miles north of town (P.O. Box 1496), Moab, UT 84532. © **800/ 813-6622** or 435/259-7854. www.archviewresort.com. 85 sites. $20–$30 for 2 people. AE, DISC, MC, V.

Canyonlands Campground & RV Park   This campground is surprisingly shady and quiet, given its downtown location. Open year-round, it has tent sites as well as partial and full (including cable TV) RV hookups. Facilities include a dump station, self-service laundry, convenience store, playground, and outdoor heated pool. There are also six cabins ($35 for two). A City Market grocery store is within walking distance.

555 S. Main St., Moab, UT 84532. © **800/522-6848** or 435/259-6848. www.moab-utah.com/canyonlands/ rv.html. 144 sites. $21–$24 for 2 people (50-amp service $1 more). AE, DISC, MC, V.

Moab Valley RV & Campground   Situated on the north side of Moab, near the intersection of U.S. 191 and Utah 128, this campground is just 2 miles from Arches National Park. Practically any size RV can be accommodated in the extra-large pull-through sites; all sites have great views of the surrounding rock formations. Both tenters and RVers will enjoy the trees and patches of grass, and full RV hookups include cable TV connections. Facilities include an RV dump station, coin-op laundry, and convenience store, but no pool or playground. There are 12 cabins ($39 to $49 for two), which offer comfortable beds, air-conditioning, and TVs, but still require a walk to the bathhouse; plus six new cottages with private bathrooms ($60 for two). Smoking is not permitted in the cabins and cottages.

1773 N. U.S. 191, Moab, UT 84532. © **435/259-4469.** Fax 435/259-4483. www.moabvalleyrv.com. 134 sites. $24–$26 for 2 people. MC, V. Closed Nov–Feb. Dogs permitted in RV sites, but not in tent sites or cabins.

WHERE TO DINE

In addition to the restaurants discussed here, see the Bar-M Chuckwagon and Canyonlands by Night, under "Moab After Dark," below.

Buck's Grill House 🐾 AMERICAN WESTERN   This popular restaurant, among the area's best spots for steak, offers a number of choices to suit a variety of palates. The dining room's subdued Western decor is accented by exposed wood beams and Western and scenic paintings by local artist Pete Plastow. There's an attractive patio in back, away from the road, with trees and a delightful rock waterfall. The adventurous will likely enjoy our top choice here—the buffalo meat loaf, with black onion gravy and mashed potatoes. We also recommend the prime rib. Southwestern dishes include grilled chicken tacos, buffalo chorizo tacos, and the duck tamale with grilled pineapple salsa. All breads and other baked items are made in-house. Buck's offers full liquor service, a good wine list, and serves a variety of Utah microbrews.

1393 N. U.S. 191, about 1½ miles north of town. © **435/259-5201.** Main courses $5.95–$20. DC, DISC, MC, V. Daily 5:30pm–closing. Closed Dec–Jan.

Eddie McStiff's AMERICAN   This bustling, somewhat noisy brewpub is half family restaurant and half tavern, with a climate-controlled garden patio as well. You'll find Southwest decor and paintings by local artists in the dining room, while the tavern looks just as a tavern should: long bar, low light, and lots of wood. The menu changes seasonally to accommodate sports enthusiasts in spring and fall, and Europeans and families in summer. There's always a wide range of appetizers, salads, and half-pound black Angus beef burgers, plus grilled steaks and a variety of pasta dishes; lunch offers a good choice of sandwiches. Among the specialties here are grilled salmon and slow-smoked BBQ pork ribs. At least a dozen fresh-brewed beers are on tap at any given time and can also be purchased to go. Mixed drinks, wine, and beer are sold in the dining room with food only; beer can be purchased with or without food in the tavern. (You must be at least 21 to enter the tavern.)

57 S. Main St. (in McStiff's Plaza, just south of the information center). ✆ **435/259-2337.** Fax 435/259-3022. www.eddiemcstiff.com. Main courses $7–$19; pizza $4.50–$20. DISC, MC, V. Daily 11:30am–midnight. Shorter hours in winter.

Moab Brewery ECLECTIC   This open, spacious microbrewery/restaurant on the south side of town serves fresh handcrafted ales, which are brewed on-site, along with a wide variety of steaks, sandwiches, salads, soups, and vegetarian dishes. It's popular with families, who gobble down basic American fare like burgers and fresh fish. The adventuresome can choose from such items as the margarita chicken dinner, the smoked portobello mushroom pasta, and the popular St. Louis smoked ribs. The huge dining room is decorated with light woods and outdoor sports equipment, including half of a real Jeep, and a hang glider on the ceiling. Patio dining is especially delightful on a warm summer evening.

You can sample the brews—from a German-style unfiltered wheat ale to an easy-drinking American ale—at the separate bar. The brewery usually has eight of its beers available on tap at any given time. There's a gift shop plus beer-to-go in half-gallon jugs in insulated carriers. Beer is sold in the bar; in the restaurant, diners can purchase beer, wine, or mixed drinks.

686 S. Main St. ✆ **435/259-6333.** www.themoabbrewery.com. Main courses $5.95–$19. AE, DISC, MC, V. Daily 11:30am–10pm summer; 11:30am–9pm winter.

Moab Diner _(Kids)_ AMERICAN/SOUTHWESTERN   Late risers can get breakfast—among the best in town—all day here, with all the usual egg dishes, biscuits and gravy, six kinds of omelets, and a spicy breakfast burrito on offer. The decor is definitely diner, but the place does have lots of green plants (real, not plastic). Hamburgers, sandwiches, and salads are the offerings at lunch. For dinner, there's steak, shrimp, and chicken, plus liver and onions. In addition to ice cream, you can get malts and shakes, plus sundaes with seven different toppings. No alcoholic beverages are served.

189 S. Main St. (2 blocks south of Center St.). ✆ **435/259-4006.** Main courses $3.50–$13. MC, V. Daily 6am–10:30pm. Closes earlier in winter.

Poplar Place Restaurant & Pub MEXICAN/ITALIAN   This two-story corner pub has been a busy lunch and dinner stop for locals since it opened in 1972. This place serves lots of pizzas, pastas, sandwiches, soups, and Mexican dishes. We enthusiastically recommend the popular pizzas, made with homemade crust and sauces; they come with either tomato or Alfredo sauce and your choice of toppings. For the indecisive, several specialty pizzas are also listed. Also popular are chicken Parmesan and shrimp scampi, the two house specials. Mexican selections include chicken or pork burritos with green chile sauce, and what the Poplar Place calls a "Popco" a cross between a taco and a fajita, with chicken, beef, or crab. Dine inside or out on the patio. Full liquor service is available, in addition to a good selection of wine, Utah microbrews, and Guinness Stout on tap.

11 E. 100 North. ✆ **435/259-6018.** Main courses $6.75–$14; pizza $12–$19. MC, V. Daily 11:30am–10pm. Reduced hrs. in winter.

MOAB AFTER DARK

For a small town in conservative, nondrinking Utah, this is a pretty wild place. After a day on the river or in the back of a jeep, don't be surprised to see your outfitter letting his or her hair down at the **Rio Colorado Restaurant and Bar,** a block west of Main on 100 South Street (℃ **435/259-6666**). Locals just call it the Rio. There's live regional music—usually rock, reggae, or jazz—most weekend evenings in summer.

Those who want to sample the local beer should stop at **Eddie McStiff's** (p. 289), a microbrewery that's part family restaurant and part busy tavern, with several TVs and a game room with pool tables, foosball, and shuffleboard. Another good option for beer-lovers is the **Moab Brewery** (p. 290). The **Poplar Place Restaurant & Pub** (p. 290) is a long-time local watering hole.

Those looking for a foot-stompin' good time and a Western-style dinner will want to make their way to the **Bar-M Chuckwagon Live Western Show and Cowboy Supper,** 7 miles north of Moab on U.S. 191 (℃ **800/214-2085** or 435/259-2276; www.barmchuckwagon.com). Unlike most other chuck wagon suppers, the Bar-M has an indoor, climate-controlled dining room. Diners go through a supper line to pick up sliced roast beef or barbecued chicken, baked potatoes, baked beans, cinnamon applesauce, buttermilk biscuits, dessert, and nonalcoholic beverages. Vegetarian meals can be prepared with advance notice, and beer and wine coolers are available. After dinner, a stage show entertains with Western-style music, jokes, and down-home silliness from the Bar-M Wranglers. The grounds, which include a small Western village and gift shop, open at 6:30pm, with gunfights starting at 7pm, dinner at 7:30pm, and the show following supper. The Bar-M is usually open from spring to early fall, but is closed Sundays and Tuesdays; call for the current schedule. Supper and the show costs $20 for adults, $10 for children 4 to 10. Reservations are strongly recommended.

Canyonlands by Night (℃ **800/394-9978** or 435/259-5261; www. canyonlands\bynight.com) is an evening river trip, operating spring through fall, that combines a sunset boat ride with stories of outlaws, views of rock formations, and a sound-and-light show against the backdrop of the canyon walls. Before the trip, Dutch-oven dinners are served on a covered patio, with live country western entertainment. The office and dock are just north of Moab at the Colorado River Bridge. Cost for the boat trip and dinner is $40 for adults, $25 for children 6 to 12, and $9 for kids 2 to 5. Reservations are recommended.

2 Arches National Park

233 miles SE of Salt Lake City

Natural stone arches and fantastic rock formations, which look as if they were sculpted by an artist's hand, are the defining features of this park, and they exist in remarkable numbers and variety. Just as soon as you've seen the most beautiful, most colorful, most gigantic stone arch you can imagine, walk around the next bend and there's another—bigger, better, and more brilliant than the last. It would take forever to see them all, with more than 1,700 officially listed and more being discovered or "born" every day.

Exploring the park is a great family adventure. The arches seem more accessible and less forbidding than the spires and pinnacles at Canyonlands and other southern Utah parks. Just down the road from Canyonlands National Park, Arches is much more visitor-friendly, with relatively short, well-maintained trails leading to most of the park's major attractions.

Some people think of arches as bridges, but to geologists there's a big difference. Bridges are formed when a river slowly bores through solid rock. The often bizarre and beautiful contours of arches result from the erosive force of rain and snow, which freezes and thaws, dissolving the "glue" that holds the sand grains together and chipping away at the stone, until gravity finally pulls a chunk off.

Although arches usually grow slowly—*very* slowly—something dramatic happens every once in a while: like that quiet day in 1940 when a sudden crash instantly doubled the size of the opening of Skyline Arch, leaving a huge boulder lying in its shadow. Luckily, no one (at least no one we know of) was standing underneath it at the time. The same thing happened to the magnificently delicate Landscape Arch in 1991, when a slab of rock about 60 feet long, 11 feet wide, and 4½ feet thick fell from the underside of the arch. Now there's such a thin ribbon of stone that it's hard to believe it can continue standing at all.

Spend a day or a week here, exploring the terrain, watching the rainbow of colors deepen and explode with the long rays of the setting sun, and gazing at the moonlight glistening on the tall sandstone cliffs. Watch for mule deer, cottontail rabbits, and the bright green collared lizard as they go about the difficult task of desert living. And let your own imagination run wild among the Three Gossips, the Spectacles, the Eye of the Whale, the Penguins, the Tower of Babel, and the thousands of other statues, towers, arches, and bridges that await your discovery in this magical playground.

ESSENTIALS

See the Moab section of this chapter for camping options outside the park, plus lodging, restaurants, and other nearby services.

GETTING THERE   From Moab, drive 5 miles north on U.S. 191. Arches National Park is located 27 miles east of Canyonlands National Park's Island in the Sky Visitor Center, 233 miles southeast of Salt Lake City, 404 miles northeast of the north rim of Grand Canyon National Park in Arizona, and 371 miles west of Denver, Colorado.

INFORMATION/VISITOR CENTERS   For advance information, contact Superintendent, **Arches National Park,** P.O. Box 907, Moab, UT 84532-0907 (© **435/719-2299,** or 435/719-2319 TDD; www.nps.gov/arch). It's best to write early.

Books, maps, and videos on Arches as well as Canyonlands National Park and other southern Utah attractions can be purchased from the nonprofit **Canyonlands Natural History Association** (C.N.H.A.), 3031 South U.S. 191, Moab, UT 84532 (© **800/840-8978** or 435/259-6003; www.cnha.org). Some publications are available in foreign languages, and a variety of videos can be purchased in either VHS or PAL formats. Those wanting to help the nonprofit association can join and get a 20% discount on purchases.

After you arrive in the area, you can stop by the **Moab Information Center,** downtown at the corner of Main and Center streets. Hours are 8am to 9pm in summer, with slightly shorter winter hours.

The **Arches National Park Visitor Center,** located just inside the park entrance gate, provides maps, brochures, and other information. It's open 8am to 4:30pm in winter, with extended hours spring through fall.

FEES, REGULATIONS & BACKCOUNTRY PERMITS   Entry into the park (for up to 7 days) costs $10 per vehicle or $5 per motorcycle, bicycle, or pedestrian. A $25 annual pass is good for both Arches and Canyonlands

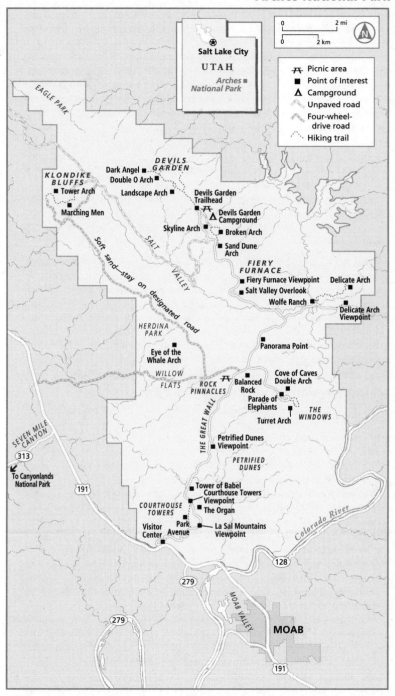

Arches National Park

Salt Lake City

UTAH

Arches National Park

0 — 2 mi
0 — 2 km

☧ Picnic area
■ Point of Interest
△ Campground
⛰ Unpaved road
⛰ Four-wheel-drive road
⋯ Hiking trail

EAGLE PARK

KLONDIKE BLUFFS

■ Tower Arch

■ Marching Men

DEVILS GARDEN

Dark Angel
Double O Arch

Landscape Arch ■

Devils Garden Trailhead

☧ Devils Garden Campground △

Skyline Arch ■ ■ Broken Arch

SALT VALLEY

■ Sand Dune Arch

FIERY FURNACE

■ Fiery Furnace Viewpoint   Delicate Arch ■

■ Salt Valley Overlook

Wolfe Ranch ■

Delicate Arch Viewpoint ■

HERDINA PARK

Soft sand—stay on designated road

■ Panorama Point

Eye of the Whale Arch

WILLOW FLATS

ROCK PINNACLES

☧ ■ Balanced Rock

Cove of Caves Double Arch ■

Parade of Elephants

Turret Arch ■

THE WINDOWS

THE GREAT WALL

■ Petrified Dunes Viewpoint

PETRIFIED DUNES

SEVEN MILE CANYON

313

To Canyonlands National Park

191

Tower of Babel ■
Courthouse Towers Viewpoint ■
The Organ ■

COURTHOUSE TOWERS

Visitor Center ■
Park Avenue ■

■ La Sal Mountains Viewpoint

Colorado River

128

279

MOAB VALLEY

MOAB

279

191

national parks, as well as Natural Bridges and Hovenweep national monuments. Free permits, available at the visitor center, are required for all overnight trips into the backcountry.

Backcountry hikers should practice minimum-impact techniques, packing out all trash. Feeding or otherwise disturbing wildlife is prohibited, as is vandalizing or disturbing any natural, cultural, or historic feature of the park. Wood fires are not permitted. Dogs, which must be leashed at all times, are prohibited in public buildings, on all trails, and in the backcountry.

SEASONS/AVOIDING THE CROWDS   Summer days here are hot, often reaching 100°F (38°C), and winters can be cool or cold, dropping below freezing at night, with snow possible. The best time to visit, especially for hikers, is in spring or fall, when daytime temperatures are usually between 60 and 80°F (16 and 27°C) and nights are cool.

Visitation to Arches is highest from March through October, with August the peak month. Parking lots are crowded and the campground is often full by late morning at those times. As with most popular parks, avoid visiting during school vacations if possible.

RANGER PROGRAMS   From March through October, rangers lead guided hikes on the Fiery Furnace Trail twice daily (see "Outdoor Pursuits," later in the chapter), as well as daily nature walks at various park locations. Evening campfire programs, from April through October, are held on topics such as rock art, geological processes, and wildlife. A schedule of events is posted at the visitor center.

Kids between the ages of 6 and 12 can pick up a **Junior Ranger** booklet at the visitor center. After completing the activities in the booklet and participating in several programs, kids pick up their badge at the visitor center.

SEEING THE PARK'S HIGHLIGHTS BY CAR

Arches is the easiest of Utah's national parks to see in a day, if that's all you can spare. An 18-mile (one-way) **scenic drive** offers splendid views of countless natural rock arches and other formations, and several easy hikes reveal additional scenery. Allow 1½ hours for the round-trip drive, adding time for optional hikes.

You can see many of the park's most famous rock formations without even getting out of your car—although we strongly urge you to venture out and explore on foot. You have the option of walking short distances to a number of viewpoints, or stretching your legs on a variety of longer hikes along the way (see "Outdoor Pursuits," later in the chapter). The main road is easy to navigate, even for RVs, but parking at some viewpoints is limited. Please be considerate and leave trailers at the visitor center parking lot or in a Moab campground.

Start out by viewing the short slide show at the **visitor center** to get a feel for what lies ahead. Then drive north past the Moab Fault to the overlook parking for **Park Avenue,** a solid rock "fin" that reminded early visitors of the New York skyline.

From here, your next stop is **La Sal Mountain Viewpoint,** where you look southeast to the La Sal Mountains, named by early Spanish explorers who thought the snow-covered mountains looked like huge piles of salt. In the overlook area is a "desert scrub" ecosystem, composed of sagebrush, saltbush, blackbrush, yucca, and prickly pear cactus. Animals that inhabit the area include the kangaroo rat, black-tailed jackrabbit, rock squirrel, several species of lizards, and the coyote.

Continuing on the scenic drive, you'll begin to see some of the park's major formations at **Courthouse Towers,** where large monoliths such as Sheep Rock, the Organ, and the Three Gossips dominate the landscape. Leaving Courthouse Towers, watch for the **Tower of Babel** on the east (right) side of the road, then proceed past the petrified sand dunes to **Balanced Rock,** a huge boulder weighing about 3,600 tons, perched on a slowly eroding pedestal.

Continuing, take a side road to the east (right) to **The Windows.** Created when erosion penetrated a sandstone fin, they can be seen after a short walk from the parking area. Also in this area are **Turret Arch** and the **Cove of Caves.** Erosion is continuing to wear away at the back of the largest cave, which means it will probably become an arch one day. A short walk from the parking lot takes you to **Double Arch,** which looks exactly like what its name implies. From the end of this trail, you can also see the delightful **Parade of Elephants.**

Return to the main park road, turn north (right) and drive to **Panorama Point,** which offers an expansive view of Salt Valley and the Fiery Furnace, which can really live up to its name at sunset.

Next, turn east (right) off the main road onto the Wolfe Ranch Road and drive to the **Wolfe Ranch** parking area. A very short walk leads to what's left of this ranch. John Wesley Wolfe and his son Fred moved here from Ohio in 1898, and in 1907 were joined by John's daughter Flora, her husband, and their two children. The cabin seen here was built for Flora's family (John's cabin was later destroyed by a flash flood). In 1910, the family decided that this was not the greatest location for a ranch, and they packed up and returned to Ohio. If you follow the trail a bit farther, you'll see some Ute petroglyphs.

More ambitious hikers can continue for a moderately difficult 3-mile round-trip excursion to **Delicate Arch,** with a spectacular view at trail's end. If you don't want to take the hike, you can still see this lovely arch, albeit from a distance, by getting back in your car, continuing down the road for 1 mile, and walking a short trail (about a 5-minute walk) to the **Delicate Arch Viewpoint.**

Returning to the park's main road, turn north (right) and go to the next stop, the **Salt Valley Overlook.** The various shades of color in this collapsed salt dome are caused by differing amounts of iron in the rock, as well as other factors.

Continue now to the viewpoint for **Fiery Furnace,** which offers a dramatic view of colorful sandstone fins. This is the starting point for 2-hour ranger-guided hikes in summer.

From here, drive to a pull-out for **Sand Dune Arch,** located down a short path from the road, where you'll find shade and sand along with the arch. This is a good place for kids to play. The trail leads across a meadow to Broken Arch (which isn't broken at all—it just looks that way from a distance).

Back on the road, continue to **Skyline Arch,** whose opening doubled in size in 1940 when a huge boulder tumbled out of it. The next and final stop is the often crowded parking area for the **Devils Garden Trailhead.** From here, you can hike to some of the most unique arches in the park, including **Landscape Arch,** which is among the longest natural rock spans in the world. It's a pretty easy 1.6-mile round-trip hike.

From the trailhead parking lot, it's 18 miles back to the visitor center.

OUTDOOR PURSUITS

BIKING   Bikes are prohibited on all trails and are not allowed to travel cross-country within the national park boundaries. This leaves the park's established scenic drive, which is open to cyclists, although you need to be aware that the

18-mile dead-end road is narrow and winding in spots and can be a bit crowded with motor vehicles in summer.

Mountain bikers also have the option of tackling one of several four-wheel-drive roads (see below). For guided mountain-bike trips outside the park, as well as rentals, repairs, and supplies, see the Moab section earlier in this chapter.

FOUR-WHEELING   Although there aren't nearly as many four-wheel-drive opportunities here as in nearby Canyonlands National Park, there are a few—but check first with rangers on possible road closures and conditions that make the routes impassable.

One possibility is the 17-mile **Klondike Bluffs to Willow Flats Road** ★★, which is best driven from north to south due to soft sand on steep grades. Turn west off the main park road 1 mile south of Devils Garden Trailhead, and follow the road up through the Salt Valley about 7.7 miles to the turnoff for Klondike Bluffs. The next 17 miles are strictly for four-wheelers, heading into high desert terrain, with panoramas of surrounding mountains and red rock formations opening out. The route also passes Eye of the Whale Arch, views of Elephant Butte (the highest point in the park at 5,653 feet), and the imposing Courthouse Towers. You'll see drifting sand dunes and the red rock Marching Men formation as well. The road brings you out at Balanced Rock parking area.

> ### Impressions
> *Ten thousand strangely carved forms in every direction, and beyond them mountains blending with clouds.*
> —Major John Wesley Powell, 1869

You can rent a four-wheel-drive vehicle or go with a jeep tour; see the Moab section, earlier in this chapter.

HIKING   Most trails here are short and relatively easy, although because of the hot summer sun and lack of shade, it's wise to carry a good amount of water on any jaunt of more than 1 hour.

One easy walk is to **Sand Dune Arch,** a good place to take kids who want to play in the sand. It's only 0.3 miles (round-trip), but you can add an extra 1.2 miles by continuing on to Broken Arch. Sand Dune Arch is hidden among and shaded by rock walls, with a naturally created giant sandbox below the arch. Resist the temptation to climb onto the arch and jump down into the sand: Not only is it dangerous, but it can also damage the arch. Those who continue to Broken Arch should watch for mule deer and kit foxes, which inhabit the grassland you'll be crossing. Allow about 30 minutes to Sand Dune Arch and back; 1 hour to Broken Arch.

From the **Devils Garden Trail,** you can see about 15 to 20 arches on a fairly long, strenuous, and difficult hike, or view some exciting scenery by following only part of the route. We suggest taking at least the easy-to-moderate 1.6-mile round-trip hike to **Landscape Arch** ★, a long, thin ribbon of stone that's one of the most beautiful arches in the park. Watch for mule deer along the way, and allow about an hour. Past Landscape Arch, the trail becomes more challenging, but offers numerous additional views, including panoramas of the curious Double O Arch and a large, dark tower known as Dark Angel. From the section of the trail where Dark Angel is visible, you are 2.5 miles from the trailhead. If you turn back at this point, the round trip will take about 3 hours.

Considered by many to be the park's best and most scenic hike, the 3-mile round-trip **Delicate Arch Trail** ★ is a moderate-to-difficult hike, with slippery slickrock, no shade, and some steep drop-offs along a narrow cliff. Hikers are rewarded with a dramatic and spectacular view of Delicate Arch. You'll see the John Wesley Wolfe ranch and have an opportunity to take a side trip to a Ute petroglyph panel that includes drawings of horses and what may represent a bighorn sheep hunt. When you get back on the main trail, watch for collared lizards—up to a foot long—which are usually bright green with stripes of yellow or rust, with a black collar. Collared lizards feed in the daytime, mostly on insects and other lizards, and can stand and run on their large hind feet in pursuit of prey. (Didn't we see this in *Jurassic Park?*)

Continuing along the trail, watch for **Frame Arch,** off to the right. Its main claim to fame is that numerous photographers have used it to "frame" a photo of Delicate Arch in the distance. Just past Frame Arch, the trail gets a little weird, having been blasted out from the cliff. Allow 2 to 3 hours.

The **Fiery Furnace Guided Hike** is a difficult and strenuous 2-mile round-trip naturalist-led hike to some of the most colorful formations in the park. Guided hikes are given into this restricted area twice daily from March through October, by reservation, and last from 2¼ to 3 hours. Cost is $6 for adults and $3 for children 6 to 12 and seniors 62 and over; reservations must be made in person, up to 7 days in advance. Permits are required to enter the Fiery Furnace on your own (the fee is unknown at press time), but special restrictions apply and there are no marked trails, so you must first speak with a ranger at the visitor center. Unless you're an experienced hiker, it's best to join a guided hike.

CAMPING IN THE PARK

Located at the north end of the park's scenic drive, **Devils Garden Campground** is Arches' only developed camping area. The 52 well-spaced sites are nestled among rocks, with plenty of piñon and juniper trees. March through October, the campground accepts reservations for some sites through **National Recreation Reservation Service** (✆ **877/444-6777;** www.reserveusa.com). In summer, the campground fills early, often by 9am, with people trying to garner the first-come first-served sites, so either make reservations or get to the campground early. Sites costs $10 per night. No showers or RV hookups are available. There's water and flush toilets in summer; chemical toilets and no water from late October to mid-March. See the Moab section earlier in this chapter for information on public showers and nearby commercial campgrounds.

3 Canyonlands National Park

34 miles W of Moab, 304 miles SE of Salt Lake City

Utah's largest national park is not for the sightseer out for a Sunday afternoon drive. Instead, it rewards those willing to spend time and energy—*lots* of energy—exploring the rugged backcountry. Sliced into districts by the Colorado and Green rivers, which are the park's primary architects, this is a land of extremes: vast panoramas, dizzyingly deep canyons, dramatically steep cliffs, broad mesas, and towering red spires.

The most accessible part of Canyonlands is the **Island in the Sky District,** in the northern section of the park, where a paved road leads to sites such as Grand View Point, which overlooks some 10,000 square miles of rugged wilderness. Island in the Sky has several easy-to-moderate trails offering sweeping vistas. A short walk provides views of Upheaval Dome, which resembles a large volcanic crater but may actually have been created by the crash of a meteorite. For the more adventurous, the 100-mile White Rim Road takes experienced mountain bikers and those with high-clearance four-wheel-drive vehicles on a winding loop tour through a vast array of scenery.

The **Needles District,** in the southeast corner, offers only a few viewpoints along the paved road, but boasts numerous possibilities for hikers, backpackers, and those with high-clearance 4×4s. Named for its tall, red-and-white-striped rock pinnacles, this diverse district is home to impressive arches, including the 150-foot-tall Angel Arch, as well as grassy meadows and the confluence of the Green and Colorado rivers. Backcountry visitors will also find ruins and rock art left by the Ancestral Puebloans (also known as Anasazi) some 800 years ago.

Most park visitors don't get a close-up view of the **Maze District,** but instead see it off in the distance from Grand View Point at Island in the Sky or Confluence Overlook in the Needles District. That's because it's inhospitable and practically inaccessible. You'll need a lot of endurance and at least several days to see even a few of its sites, such as the appropriately named Lizard Rock and Beehive Arch. Hardy hikers can visit Horseshoe Canyon in one day, where they can see the Great Gallery, an 80-foot-long rock art panel.

The park is also accessible by boat, which is how explorer Major John Wesley Powell first saw the canyons in 1869, when he made his first trip down the Green to its confluence with the Colorado, and then even farther downstream, eventually reaching the Grand Canyon. River access is from the towns of Moab and Green River; several local companies offer boat trips (see the Moab section earlier in this chapter).

Among the cottonwoods and willows along the rivers, you'll find Canyonlands' greatest variety of wildlife. Watch for deer, beaver, an occasional bobcat, and various migratory birds. Elsewhere in the park, you're apt to see red-tailed hawks in search of a tasty rodent, as well as bighorn sheep, coyotes, Colorado chipmunks, and white-tailed antelope squirrels.

ESSENTIALS

No lodging facilities, restaurants, or stores are located inside the national park. Most visitors use Moab as a base camp.

GETTING THERE/ACCESS POINTS   To reach the Island in the Sky Visitor Center, 34 miles west of Moab, take U.S. 191 north to Utah 313, which you follow south into the park. To reach the Needles Visitor Center, 75 miles southwest of Moab, take U.S. 191 south to Utah 211, which you follow west into the park. Getting to the Maze District is a bit more interesting. From I-70 west of Green River, take Utah 24 south. Watch for signs and follow two- and four-wheel-drive dirt roads east into the park.

INFORMATION/VISITOR CENTERS   For advance information, contact Superintendent, **Canyonlands National Park,** 2282 S. West Resource Blvd., Moab, UT 84532-3298 (© **435/719-2313;** www.nps.gov/cany). It's best to write at least a month before your planned visit.

Books, some very useful maps, and videos can be ordered from the nonprofit **Canyonlands Natural History Association,** 3031 South U.S. 191, Moab, UT 84532 (© **800/840-8978** or 435/259-6003; www.cnha.org). Some publications are available in foreign languages, and several videos can be purchased in either VHS or PAL formats. Those wanting to help the nonprofit association can join ($20 annually) and get a 20% discount on purchases.

After you arrive in the area, stop at the **Moab Information Center,** located in the middle of town at the corner of Main and Center streets (open 8am to 9pm in summer, with slightly shorter winter hours).

Canyonlands National Park

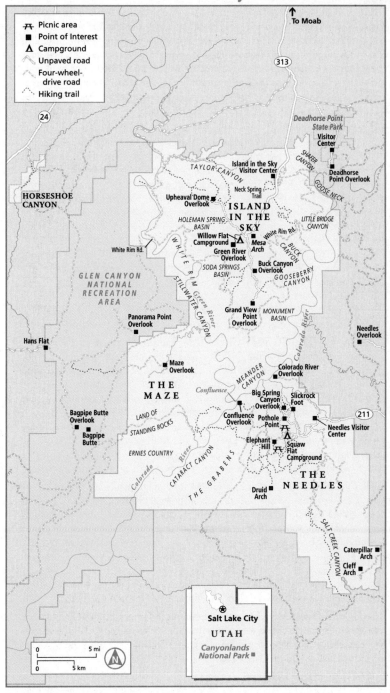

Legend:
- 🪧 Picnic area
- ■ Point of Interest
- △ Campground
- Unpaved road
- Four-wheel-drive road
- Hiking trail

To Moab

313

24

Deadhorse Point State Park
Visitor Center

TAYLOR CANYON

Island in the Sky Visitor Center

SHAFER CANYON

Deadhorse Point Overlook

GOOSE NECK

Neck Spring Trail

Upheaval Dome Overlook

ISLAND IN THE SKY

LITTLE BRIDGE CANYON

HOLEMAN SPRING BASIN

Willow Flat Campground

Mesa Arch

White Rim Rd.

White Rim Rd.

Green River Overlook

BUCK CANYON

SODA SPRINGS BASIN

Buck Canyon Overlook

GOOSEBERRY CANYON

WHITE RIM

STILLWATER CANYON

Green River

Grand View Point Overlook

MONUMENT BASIN

Colorado River

GLEN CANYON NATIONAL RECREATION AREA

Panorama Point Overlook

Needles Overlook

Hans Flat

Maze Overlook

Colorado River Overlook

THE MAZE

MEANDER CANYON

Confluence

Big Spring Canyon Overlook

Slickrock Foot

Bagpipe Butte Overlook

LAND OF STANDING ROCKS

Confluence Overlook

Pothole Point

211

Needles Visitor Center

Bagpipe Butte

ERNIES COUNTRY

Colorado River

CATARACT CANYON

Elephant Hill

Squaw Flat Campground

THE GRABENS

Druid Arch

THE NEEDLES

SALT CREEK CANYON

Caterpillar Arch

Cleff Arch

HORSESHOE CANYON

Salt Lake City

UTAH

Canyonlands National Park

0 — 5 mi
0 — 5 km

Canyonlands National Park operates two visitor centers—**Island in the Sky Visitor Center,** in the northern part of the park, and **Needles Visitor Center,** in the southern section—where you can get maps, free brochures on hiking trails, and, most important, advice from rangers. We can't overemphasize how brutal the terrain at Canyonlands can be, and it's important to know not only your own limitations, but also the limitations of your vehicle and other equipment.

FEES, REGULATIONS & BACKCOUNTRY PERMITS   Entry into the park (for up to 7 days) costs $10 per vehicle or $5 per motorcycle, bicycle, or pedestrian. A $25 annual pass is good for both Canyonlands and Arches national parks, plus Natural Bridges and Hovenweep national monuments.

Permits, available at either visitor center, are required for all overnight stays in the park except at the two established campgrounds. Permit reservations can be made in advance (© **435/259-4351**). For overnight four-wheel-drive and mountain-bike trips, permits cost $30; for overnight backpacking trips, $15.

There is also a $5 day-use fee for those visitors bringing motor vehicles, horses, or mountain bikes onto roads into Salt Creek/Horse Canyon and Lavender Canyon in the Needles District.

Backcountry hikers should practice minimum-impact techniques, packing out all trash. Feeding or otherwise disturbing wildlife is prohibited, as is vandalizing or upsetting any natural, cultural, or historic feature of the park. Wood fires are also prohibited.

Dogs, which must be leashed at all times, are prohibited in public buildings, on all trails, and in the backcountry (even in vehicles on four-wheel-drive roads).

SEASONS/AVOIDING THE CROWDS   Summers here are hot, with temperatures occasionally reaching 100°F (38°C). Winters can be cool or cold, dropping well below freezing at night, with light snow possible. The best time to visit, especially for hikers, is in spring or fall, when daytime temperatures are usually from 60 to 80°F (16 to 27°C) and nights are cool. Late-summer and early-fall visitors should be prepared for afternoon thunderstorms.

Although Canyonlands does not get nearly as crowded as most other national parks in Utah, summer is still the busiest time, and reservations for backcountry permits are recommended from spring through fall. As with most parks, if you want to escape humanity, pick the longest and most difficult trail you can handle.

SAFETY   Due to the extreme variety of terrain, the main safety problem at Canyonlands is that people underestimate the hazards. Rangers warn hikers to carry at least 1 gallon of water per person per day, be especially careful near cliff edges, avoid overexposure to the intense sun, and carry maps when going into the backcountry. During lightning storms, avoid lone trees, high ridges, and cliff edges. Four-wheel-drive vehicle operators should be aware of their vehicle's limitations and carry extra food and emergency equipment. Anyone heading out into the backcountry should let someone know where they're going and when they plan to return. Traveling alone in Canyonlands is not a good idea.

RANGER PROGRAMS   On summer evenings at Squaw Flat and Willow Flat campgrounds, rangers offer campfire programs on various aspects of the park. Short morning talks are also presented in summer at the Island in the Sky Visitor Center and at Grand View Point.

SEEING THE HIGHLIGHTS

Canyonlands is not an easy place to see in a short period of time. In fact, if your schedule permits only a day or less, we suggest skipping the Needles and Maze Districts entirely and driving directly to the **Island in the Sky Visitor Center.**

After looking at the exhibits, drive to several of the overlooks, stopping along the way for a short hike or two. Make sure you stop at the **Grand View Point Overlook,** at the south end of the paved road. Hiking the **Grand View Trail,** which is especially scenic in the late afternoon, literally gives you the "Grand View" of the park. Allow about 1½ hours for this easy 2-mile walk. We also recommend the **Upheaval Dome Overlook Trail,** which should take about half an hour and will bring you to a mile-wide crater of mysterious origins.

Perhaps a better choice for a quick visit to the park, especially for those with a bit of extra cash, is taking a guided tour—by four-wheel-drive vehicle, plane, or raft. See the Moab section of this chapter for a list of operators.

EXPLORING CANYONLANDS BY CAR

No driving tour has yet been designed to show off Canyonlands. The Island in the Sky District has about 20 miles of paved highway, some gravel roads accessible to two-wheel-drive vehicles, and several viewpoints. The Needles District has only 8 miles of paved roads and fewer viewpoints. Many (but not all) of Needles' viewpoints and trailheads are accessible only by high-clearance four-wheel-drive vehicles, mountain bikes, or plain old foot power. The Maze District has no paved roads. Essentially, both of the park's main roads lead to trailheads, and unless you plan to leave your car and hike for at least a half hour or so, it would be better to skip Canyonlands and spend your time at nearby Arches National Park, which is much more accessible by car.

Of course, if your "car" happens to be a serious 4×4, and you're equally serious about doing some hard-core four-wheeling, this is the park for you (see "Outdoor Pursuits," later in the chapter). Due to the constantly changing conditions of the dirt roads, we strongly suggest that you discuss your plans with rangers before setting out.

OUTDOOR PURSUITS

BIKING & MOUNTAIN BIKING   Bikes of any kind are prohibited on hiking trails or in the backcountry, except on designated two- and four-wheel-drive roads. Road bikes are of little use in Canyonlands, except for getting to and from trailheads, viewpoints, visitor centers, and campgrounds in the Island in the Sky and Needles Districts.

Mountain bikers will find themselves sharing four-wheel-drive roads with motor vehicles of every size, plus occasional hikers and horseback riders. Because some of the four-wheel-drive roads have deep sand in spots—which can turn into quicksand when wet—mountain biking may not be as much fun here as you'd expect, although it certainly is a challenge. It's wise to ask rangers about

---

Moments **A Bird's-Eye View of Canyonlands**

Canyonlands is beautiful, but many of its most spectacular sections are difficult to get to—to say the least. One solution is to take to the air. **Slickrock Air Guides, Inc.** (© 435/259-6216; fax 435/259-3484; www.slickrockair guides.com) offers 1-hour scenic flights over Canyonlands National Park and Dead Horse State Park (about $100) and 2½ hour flights that take in Canyonlands and Monument Valley (about $200).

If helicopters are your bag, contact **Arches & Classic Helicopter Services** (© 435/259-4637; www.moab-utah.com/archeshelicopter.html). Half-hour charter flights start at $80 per person with a five-person minimum.

current conditions on specific roads before setting out. Roads that are popular with mountain bikers include the Elephant Hill and Colorado River Overlook jeep roads, both in the Needles District. The 100-mile White Rim Road, in the Island in the Sky District, also makes a great mountain-bike trip, especially for bikers who can arrange for an accompanying 4×4 vehicle to carry water, food, and camping gear (see "Four-Wheeling," below).

FOUR-WHEELING Unlike most national parks, where all motor vehicles and mountain bikes must stay on paved roads, Canyonlands has miles of rough four-wheel-drive roads where mechanized transport is king, and jacked-up jeeps with oversize tires rule the day. Four-wheelers must stay on designated 4×4 roads, but keep in mind that the term "road" can mean anything from a graded, well-marked, two-lane gravel byway to a pile of loose rocks with a sign that says "that-a-way." Many of the park's jeep roads are impassable during heavy rains and for a day or two after.

The best four-wheel-drive adventure in the Island in the Sky District is the **White Rim Road** ★★, which winds some 100 miles through the district and affords spectacular views, from broad panoramas of rock and canyon to close-ups of red and orange towers and buttes. A high-clearance 4×4 is necessary. Expect the journey to be slow, taking 2 to 3 days, although with the appropriate vehicle, it isn't really difficult. There are primitive campgrounds along the way, but reservations and backcountry permits are needed (see "Essentials," earlier in the chapter). Mountain bikers also enjoy this trail, especially when accompanying a four-wheel-drive vehicle that can carry supplies and equipment.

Four-wheeling in the Needles District can be an end in itself, with a variety of exciting routes, or simply a means to get to some of the more interesting and remote hiking trails and camping spots. Four-wheel-drive fans will find one of their ultimate challenges on the **Elephant Hill Jeep Road,** which begins at a well-marked turnoff near Squaw Flat Campground. Although most of the 10-mile trail is only moderately difficult, the stretch over Elephant Hill itself (near the beginning of the drive) can be a nightmare, with steep, rough slickrock, drifting sand, loose rock, and treacherous ledges. Coming down the hill, you'll reach one switchback that requires you to back to the edge of a steep cliff. This road is also a favorite of mountain bikers, although bikes will have to be walked on some stretches because of the abundance of sand and rocks. The route offers views of numerous rock formations, from striped needles to balanced rocks, plus panoramas of steep cliffs and rock "stairs"; side trips can add another 30 miles. Allow from 8 hours to 3 days. Backcountry permits are needed for overnight trips.

For a spectacular view of the Colorado River, the **Colorado River Overlook Road** can't be beat. This 14-mile round-trip is popular with four-wheelers, backpackers, and mountain bikers. Considered among the park's easiest 4×4 roads, the first part is very easy indeed, accessible by high-clearance two-wheel-drives, but the second half has a few rough and rocky sections that require four-wheel-drive. Starting at the Needles Visitor Center parking lot, the road takes you past numerous panoramic vistas to a spectacular 360-degree view of the park and the Colorado River, some 1,000 feet below.

HIKING With little shade, no reliable water sources, and temperatures soaring to 100°F (38°C) in summer, rangers strongly advise that hikers carry at least a gallon of water per person per day, along with sunscreen, a hat, and all the usual hiking and emergency equipment. If you expect to do some serious hiking, try to plan your trip for the spring or fall, when conditions are much more hospitable. Because some of the trails may be confusing, hikers attempting the longer ones should carry good topographic maps, available at park visitor centers and at stores in Moab. Although the park offers dozens of hiking possibilities, we've chosen a select few of various ability requirements, listed by district.

Horseshoe Canyon   This detached section of the park was added to Canyonlands in 1971 mainly because of its **Great Gallery** ★★★, an 80-foot-long rock art panel with larger-than-life human figures, believed to be at least several thousand years old. Only one road leads into the Horseshoe Canyon Unit, and you'll have to drive some 120 miles (one-way) from Moab and then hike 6.5 miles (round-trip) to see the rock art. To get to the area by two-wheel-drive vehicle, take I-70 west from Green River about 11 miles to U.S. 24, go south about 24 miles to the Horseshoe Canyon turnoff (near the WATCH FOR SAND DRIFTS sign), turn left, and follow this maintained dirt road for about 30 miles to the canyon's west rim, where you can park. From here, it's a 1.5-mile hike down an 800-foot slope to the canyon floor, where you turn right and go 1.75 miles to the Great Gallery. There's no camping in Horseshoe Canyon, but primitive camping is available on BLM property on the rim just outside the park boundary.

Island in the Sky   The **Mesa Arch Trail** provides the casual visitor with an easy half-mile (round-trip) self-guided nature walk through an area forested with piñon and juniper trees, mountain mahogany, cactus, and a plant called Mormon tea, from which Mormon pioneers made a tea-like beverage. The loop trail's main scenic attraction is an arch, made of Navajo sandstone, that hangs precariously on the edge of a cliff, framing a spectacular view of nearby mountains. Allow about a half hour.

Another half-hour hike, although a bit steeper and moderately strenuous, leads to the **Upheaval Dome Overlook.** Upheaval Dome doesn't fit with the rest of the Canyonlands terrain—it's obviously not the result of gradual erosion like the rest of the park, but rather a dramatic deformity in which rocks have been pushed into a domelike structure. At one time, it was believed that the dome was formed by a hidden volcano, but a more recent theory suggests that a meteorite may have struck the earth here some 60 million years ago. This hike is about 1 mile round-trip; a second overlook adds about a half mile and 15 minutes.

An easy 2-mile hike, especially scenic at sunset, is the **Grand View Trail** ★, which follows the canyon rim from Grand View Point and shows off numerous canyons and rock formations, the Colorado River, and distant mountains. Allow about 1½ hours.

A bit more strenuous is the 5-mile **Neck Spring Trail,** which starts about a half mile south of the Island in the Sky Visitor Center. Allow 3 to 4 hours for this hike, which follows the paths that animals and early ranchers created to reach water at two springs. You'll see water troughs, hitching posts, rusty cans, and the ruins of an old cabin. Because of the water source, you'll encounter types of vegetation not usually seen in the park, such as maidenhair ferns and gambel oak, and wildlife such as mule deer, bighorn sheep, ground squirrels, and hummingbirds. If you climb to the top of the rim, you'll get a beautiful view of the canyons and even the Henry Mountains, some 60 miles away.

Those looking for more of a challenge can explore the **Lathrop Trail,** which meanders some 5 miles down into the canyon to the White Rim Road, affording beautiful views as you descend. Allow 5 to 7 hours for this strenuous hike over steep terrain and loose rock, remembering that it's another 5 miles back. It's possible to continue down to the Colorado River from here (another 4 miles each way), but check with rangers about the feasibility of this overnight trip before attempting it.

Needles   Trails here are generally not too tough, but keep in mind that slickrock can live up to its name, and that you'll find little shade in this area. One relatively easy hike is the **Roadside Ruin Trail,** a short (0.3 mile), self-guided nature walk that takes about a half hour round-trip and leads to a prehistoric granary, probably used by the Ancestral Puebloans some 700 to 1,000 years ago to store corn, nuts, and other foods. Although easy, this trail can be muddy when wet.

For a bit more of a challenge, try the **Slickrock Foot Trail,** a 2.4-mile loop that leads to several viewpoints and takes 2 or 3 hours. Slickrock—a general term for any bare rock surface—can be slippery, especially when wet. Viewpoints show off the stair-step topography of the area, from its colorful canyons and cliffs to its flat mesas and striped needles.

From **Elephant Hill Trailhead,** you can follow several interconnecting trails into the backcountry. The road to the trailhead is gravel, but is graded and driveable in most two-wheel-drive passenger cars; those in large vehicles such as motor homes, however, will want to avoid it. The 10.5-mile round-trip **Elephant Hill–Druid Arch hike** ✿ can be accomplished in 4 to 6 hours and is moderately difficult, with some steep drop-offs and quite a bit of slickrock. But the views are well worth it, as you hike through narrow rock canyons, past colorful spires and pinnacles, and on to the huge Druid Arch, its dark rock somewhat resembling the stone structures at Stonehenge.

The **Confluence Overlook Trail,** an 11-mile round-trip day or overnight hike, leads to a spectacular birds eye view of the confluence of the Green and Colorado rivers and the 1,000-foot-deep gorges they've carved. The hike is moderately difficult, with steep drop-offs and little shade, but it splendidly reveals the many colors of the Needles District, as well as views into the Maze District of the park. Allow 4 to 6 hours.

For those staying at Squaw Flat Campground, the **Big Spring–Squaw Canyon Loop** is a convenient, moderately difficult 7.5-mile loop over steep slickrock. This trail can be hiked in 3 to 4 hours. The trail winds through woodlands of piñon and juniper, plus nearby cliffs and mesas as well as distant mountains. Watch for wildflowers from late spring through summer.

CAMPING

There are two developed campgrounds in the park. In the Island in the Sky District, **Willow Flat Campground** (elevation 6,200 feet) has 12 sites, picnic tables, fire grates, and vault toilets; camping is $5. In the Needles District, **Squaw Flat Campground** (elevation 5,100 feet) has 26 sites, fire grates, picnic tables, flush toilets, and year-round drinking water; the fee is $10 per night. Neither campground accepts reservations. Primitive campsites are also available throughout the park for four-wheelers and backpackers (permits required; see "Essentials," earlier in the chapter).

Near Island in the Sky, the campground at **Dead Horse Point State Park** has electric hookups (see "Nearby Places of Interest," below). Additional camping facilities are available on nearby public lands administered by the Bureau of Land Management and U.S. Forest Service; commercial campgrounds and public showers are located in Moab (see the Moab section, earlier in this chapter).

NEARBY PLACES OF INTEREST
DEAD HORSE POINT STATE PARK

One of Utah's most scenic state parks, Dead Horse might be considered a junior Canyonlands. The Dead Horse Point Overlook offers a splendid view across the river to the nearby national park, as well as down past seven distinctive and colorful layers of rock to the Colorado River. A strip of land only 30 yards wide connects the point with the rest of the mesa, and in the late 1800s, this natural corral was used by cowboys who herded wild horses in, roped the ones they wanted, and left the rest to find their way out.

From Canyonlands' Island in the Sky Visitor Center, drive north out of the park for 3½ miles to the intersection with Utah 313, and turn right. The state park's visitor center is about 7½ miles down the road. From Moab, head north on U.S. 191 for 16½ miles, and turn south on Utah 313 for about 20 miles to the park (passing the access road for Canyonlands National Park).

For information, contact **Dead Horse Point State Park,** P.O. Box 609, Moab, UT 84532-0609 (© **435/259-2614;** www.stateparks.utah.gov).

The **visitor center/museum** is located near the entrance to the park, with exhibits on the park's geology, history, plants, and animals. Rangers are on hand to assign campsites and answer questions; books, posters, maps, and souvenirs are available for purchase. A video presentation on the human and geologic history of the area is shown by request; in summer, nightly campfire programs and short guided walks are scheduled.

Day-use fee is $7 per vehicle. In addition to the usual regulations requiring vehicles and bikes to stay on roads and pets to be leashed, visitors are asked to conserve water (which has to be trucked in) and to avoid stepping on cyanobacterial crusts—the fragile, bumpy, black mats composed of bacteria, algae, lichen, moss, and fungi that you'll often see along trails and roads.

CAMPING   The park's attractive campground has 21 sites, all with electric hookups and covered picnic tables, plus flush toilets and an RV dump station. However, because water must be trucked in, there are no showers, and campers are asked to conserve the small amount of water available. Because the electric outlets are hidden on the underside of picnic tables, which may be 50 or 60 feet from the site parking area, those with recreational vehicles will likely need long extension cords. Camping costs $14; reservations are accepted from mid-March to mid-October with a $7 processing fee (© **800/322-3770**). Those without reservations will find that the campground usually fills by mid-afternoon in summer.

EXPLORING THE PARK   **Dead Horse Point Overlook** is about 2 miles from the visitor center via a paved road. A short, wheelchair-accessible paved walkway leads from the parking area to a platform overlook that provides a magnificent panoramic view of the deep red canyons, the Colorado River, and distant mountains. The light is best either early or late in the day, but this is a worthwhile stop at any time.

Although you can easily drive to Dead Horse Point Overlook, it's a fun hike if you have the time. The main trail starts at the visitor center, follows the east rim of the mesa to the overlook, and returns on the west side. The fairly easy loop is 4 miles; you can add another 3 miles in side trips out to overlook points. Along the way, you'll see a variety of rock formations while scrambling over the slickrock.

Another 3.5-mile loop leads from the visitor center to a series of potholes (holes in the rock that catch rainwater and may contain tadpole shrimp and other aquatic life) and a canyon overlook.

Although it would seem at first that no animals could endure this barren, rocky terrain, you're likely to see ground squirrels, rabbits, lizards, and raptors. There are desert bighorn sheep in the area, but they're rarely seen in the park.

NEWSPAPER ROCK

This site is famous for a large sandstone panel covered with petroglyphs that date from 1,500 to 200 years ago, created by a long line of humans, from the Fremont people to the Ancestral Puebloans to the Utes and Navajo. The panel also includes initials and names left by early European-American settlers, including one J. P. Gonzales of Monticello, who herded sheep in the canyon in the early 1900s. Administered by the Bureau of Land Management's **Monticello Field Office,** P.O. Box 7, Monticello, UT 84535 (© **435/587-1500;** www.ut.blm. gov), the site is located in Indian Creek Corridor, along the road to Canyonlands' Needles District, Utah 211, about 12 miles west of U.S. 191. Camping is free at a primitive campground just across the road from Newspaper Rock, with dispersed camping for about eight tents or small RVs, but no drinking water. Vault toilets are located at Newspaper Rock.

4 North & West of the Parks

GREEN RIVER

Travelers heading north to Salt Lake City or west toward Nevada will undoubtedly pass through the village of Green River, which sits at an elevation of 4,100 feet, on I-70 along the banks of the Green River, about 54 miles northwest of Moab.

The **John Wesley Powell River History Museum,** 885 E. Main St. (P.O. Box 620), Green River, UT 84525 (© **435/564-3427**), details the phenomenal river expedition of explorer John Wesley Powell, a one-armed Civil War veteran who explored the Green and Colorado rivers in the late 1800s. Museum exhibits also discuss the geology of the region and the history of river running, with exhibits ranging from a replica of Powell's heavy wooden boat, the *Emma Dean,* to examples of boats and rafts used on the river since then. A 20-minute multimedia program on Powell's adventures is shown throughout the day. Admission is $2, $1 for those under 18, or $5 per family; it's open daily 8am to 8pm in summer and 8am to 5pm in winter.

Green River State Park, on Green River Road, P.O. Box 637, Green River, UT 84525-0637 (© **435/564-3633;** www.stateparks.utah.gov), is a lush green oasis with big old Russian olive and cottonwood trees. There's a **boat ramp** for launching your raft or canoe, but be aware that once you start heading downstream, you'll need a motor or mighty powerful arms to fight the current back to the park. The park also has a 9-hole championship **golf course** (© **435/ 564-8882**). Situated right along the river, it's open year-round (weather permitting) and has a pro shop, snacks, and carts. Fees are $9 for 9 holes and $17 for 18 if you walk the course; if you ride it's $13 and $24 respectively. Day-use park entry costs $5 per vehicle. The shady 42-site **campground,** open year-round, has modern restrooms, hot showers, and a dump station, but no RV hookups. Camping costs $14; reservations are accepted from mid-March to mid-October with a $7 nonrefundable fee (© **800/322-3770**).

Several river-running companies offer day and overnight trips on the Green. These include **Moki Mac River Expeditions, Inc.** (© **800/284-7280;** www. mokimac.com), which offers several trips on the Colorado and Green rivers. A day trip through Gray Canyon of the Green River costs $49 for adults and $39 for children 15 and under, including lunch. Multi-day trips start at $995 per person and include all gear and food. The outfitter also rents canoes at $17 per day, including life jackets and paddles for two persons.

For additional information on Green River, stop at the **Green River Information Center,** in the John Wesley Powell River History Museum (described earlier), or contact the **Emery County Travel Bureau,** 48 Farrer St. (P.O. Box 624), Green River, UT 84525 (© **888/564-3600** or 435/564-3600; www. sanrafaelcastlecountry.com).

A MAGICAL STATE PARK

Goblin Valley State Park, P.O. Box 637, Green River, UT 84525-0637 (© **435/ 564-3633;** www.stateparks.utah.gov), is filled with fantasyland rock formations, hence its name. In the light of the full moon, the little munchkins almost come alive, with shadows giving them face-like features. Bikes and motor vehicles are restricted to paved areas, but visitors are welcome to hike among the goblins, and even to climb onto them with caution. Park residents include kit foxes, rabbits, and lizards.

The 21-site **campground** is laid out in a semicircle among tall multicolored rocks of varying heights. Facilities include showers and a dump station, but no RV hookups. Day-use fee is $5 per vehicle; camping is $14.

To get here from Green River, head west on I-70 for about 10 miles to exit 147, and turn south on Utah 24 for about 25 miles to the turnoff for the park. Go about 5 miles west on a paved road, then left on a dirt road for another 7 miles—this road is very rough, resembling an unending washboard, although plans to pave it are being made.

TO THE DINOSAURS OF PRICE & BEYOND

The town of Price, founded in 1879, began as a railroad and coal-mining center. A popular midway stopover for those traveling between southern Utah's national parks and the Salt Lake City area, Price is gaining in reputation as a destination, especially for those interested in dinosaurs.

Price (elevation 5,600 feet) is 119 miles from Moab and 63 miles from the town of Green River. From I-70 exit 156, follow U.S. 191/6 northwest 57 miles. Take the business loop through the center of town and follow signs to the information center, located in the CEU Prehistoric Museum (see below), to pick up maps and brochures on the area, including a walking-tour brochure to the town's seven buildings listed on the National Register of Historic Places.

For advance information, contact **Castle Country Travel Region,** P.O. Box 1037, Price, UT 84501 (© **800/842-0789** or 435/637-3009; www.castle country.com).

Lodging possibilities in Price, both off U.S. 6 exit 240, include the **Holiday Inn,** 838 Westwood Blvd. (© **800/HOLIDAY** or 435/637-8880), and the **Super 8,** 180 N. Hospital Dr. (© **800/800-8000** or 435/637-8088).

One of the area's top attractions is the excellent **CEU Prehistoric Museum** ★★, 200 E. 100 North (© **800/817-9949** or 435/613-5060), operated by the College of Eastern Utah. Among the exhibits are the huge skeletons of an allosaurus, a Utah raptor, and a strange-looking duck-billed dinosaur known as the prosaurolophus. Watch for the large Colombian mammoth, with its long tusks, which resembles a modern elephant and roamed this area over 10,000 years ago. You'll also see exhibits on the early American Indians of Utah—describing how they lived and adapted to changing environments—and displays of rare 1,000-year-old clay figures created by the Fremont people. Children will encounter a variety of interactive exhibits designed just for them, including a sandbox where they can do their own paleontological dig. The museum is open April through September, daily from 9am to 6pm, and October through March, Monday through Saturday from 9am to 5pm. Admission is free; donations are welcome.

To see more dinosaurs, you'll have to drive about 35 miles out of town. Designated a National Natural Landmark in 1966, the **Cleveland-Lloyd Dinosaur Quarry** is a major world source of dinosaur fossils, where over 30 complete skeletons, 12,000 bones, and a dinosaur egg have been discovered. The visitor center has a complete allosaurus skeletal reconstruction and a stegosaurus wall mount on display. At the quarry itself—enclosed in two metal buildings—you can see bones in place where they were found, and sometimes watch scientists at work. There's also a 1.5-mile loop nature trail, with a descriptive brochure available at the trailhead, and a 1.25-mile round-trip hike to a scenic viewpoint. On the grounds are drinking water, restrooms, and picnic tables. The quarry is open 10am to 5pm Friday through Sunday, from early March to Memorial Day and Labor Day to the end of September, and daily from Memorial Day through Labor Day. User fees are $3 for adults and $2 for those 6 to 17; kids under 6 are admitted free. For advance information, contact the Bureau of Land Management office in Price (© **435/636-3600;** www.blm.gov/utah/price/quarry.htm). To get here from Price, take Utah 10 southwest about 15 miles to Utah 155 south, following dinosaur signs another 20 miles to the quarry. The last 13 miles are on a gravel road; allow about 1 hour from Price.

For a look at the somewhat more recent history of the area, go north of Price 11 miles on U.S. 191/6 to the town of Helper, and follow signs to the **Western Mining and Railroad Museum,** 296 S. Main St. (© **435/472-3009**). Crammed into the four stories of the old Helper Hotel, built in 1913, are thousands of objects and exhibits illustrating the area's mining and railroad days of the late 1800s and early 1900s. Highlights include a complete jail cell, a simulated coal mine, mine models, wine- and whiskey-making equipment from Prohibition days, pictures of mine disasters, railroad equipment and photos, and operating model trains. You can watch a 12-minute video on the area's history, wander the outdoor displays, and browse the gift shop. The museum is open Monday through Saturday, 10am to 6pm, in summer; Tuesday through Saturday, 11am to 4pm, in winter. Admission is free, although suggested donations are $2 per person or $5 per family.

A NEARBY STATE PARK

Scofield State Park, P.O. Box 166, Price, UT 84501-0166 (© **435/448-9449** summer only; www.stateparks.utah.gov), about 35 miles northwest of Price, is Utah's highest state park, at 7,600 feet. The park's picturesque lake, nestled among the hills, offers fishing and boating in summer; in winter, the main draws are ice-fishing, cross-country skiing, and snowmobiling. There are two developed campgrounds: One at the north end of the lake, with few trees, has modern restrooms but no showers; the other, located a few miles south on the east side of the lake and overlooking it, has aspens at almost every site, as well as showers and a boat ramp. Both have dump stations but neither have RV hookups. It's a lovely place to camp in summer—nights are always comfortably cool at this elevation. Day-use fee is $6 per vehicle; camping costs $11 to $14. Park facilities are closed December through April, but the lake is accessible. To get to Scofield State Park from Price, head northwest on U.S. 6 for 25 miles, then turn left (west) onto Utah 6 for 10 miles.

16

The Four Corners Area

The Four Corners area—where the borders of Colorado, New Mexico, Arizona, and Utah meet—is the major archaeological center of the United States. A vast complex of ancient villages that dominated this entire region a thousand years ago surrounds the Four Corners. Here, among the reddish-brown rocks, abandoned canyons, and flat mesas, you'll discover another world, once ruled by the Ancestral Puebloans (also known as Anasazi), and today largely the domain of the Navajo.

Wander among the scenic splendors of Monument Valley, where you'll see Navajo people tending their sheep and weaving rugs, and then step back in time to discover a civilization that vanished more than seven centuries ago, leaving behind more questions than answers. Those particularly interested in the ancient and modern American Indian tribes of the Four Corners region will want to continue their travels into Arizona, New Mexico, and Colorado. Frommer's guides to those states can provide additional information.

The southeast corner of Utah is sparsely populated—downright desolate and deserted, some might say— and you're not going to find your favorite chain motel, fast-food restaurant, or brand of gasoline right around every corner. That's assuming you can even *find* a corner. So, many travelers discover a place they like, rent a room or campsite for a few days, and take day trips. We've laid out this chapter using the town of Bluff as a base; from here, we'll take you on a series of excursions to areas that ring the town. First, we'll head southwest to Monument Valley and then northwest to Natural Bridges National Monument. We'll then head east, to Hovenweep National Monument and Four Corners Monument. Finally, we'll venture beyond Utah's borders into Colorado, where we'll visit Mesa Verde National Park, site of the most impressive cliff dwellings in the United States.

1 A Base Camp in Bluff

100 miles S of Moab, 338 miles SE of Salt Lake City

We particularly enjoy the tiny and very friendly village of Bluff, which sits near the intersection of U.S. 191 and U.S. 163, with roads leading off toward all the attractions of the Four Corners. With a population of about 300, Bluff (elevation 4,320 feet) is one of those comfortable little places with most basic services, but not a lot more. Founded by Mormon pioneers in 1880, the town's site had already been home to both Ancestral Puebloan and Navajo peoples. Local businesses distribute a free historic walking- and biking-tour guide that shows where ancient rock art and archaeological sites are located, as well as pointing out the locations of some of Bluff's handsome stone homes and other historic sites from the late 19th century.

For information on Bluff contact **The Business Owners of Bluff,** P.O. Box 326, Bluff, UT 84512 (www.bluff-utah.org). You can also get information on

Bluff, as well on the other southeast Utah communities of Blanding, Monticello, Mexican Hat, and Monument Valley, from **San Juan County Visitor Services,** P.O. Box 490, Monticello, UT 84535 (✆ **800/574-4386** or 435/587-3235; www.southeastutah.com). There is no visitor center in Bluff.

WHITE-WATER RAFTING & OTHER ORGANIZED TOURS

Situated along the San Juan River, Bluff is a center for river rafting. **Wild Rivers Expeditions,** Box 118, Bluff, UT 84512 (✆ **800/422-7654** or 435/672-2244; fax 435/672-2365; www.riversandruins.com) offers river trips on the San Juan that are both fun and educational. Led by archaeology and geology professionals, boaters see dozens of American Indian sites along the river, such as the spectacular Butler Wash Petroglyph Panel—a 250-yard-long wall of petroglyphs—plus spectacular rock formations. Trips, offered from March through October, range from a full day to more than a week, with rates starting at $120 per adult and $70 per child 12 or younger, including lunch.

Guided tours into Monument Valley Navajo Tribal Park and other scenic areas and archaeological sites are offered by **Far Out Expeditions,** 7th East St. and Mulberry Ave. (P.O. Box 307), Bluff, UT 84512 (✆ **435/672-2294;** www.faroutexpeditions.com). Prices start at $100 for a full-day Monument Valley tour in an air-conditioned four-wheel-drive van, including lunch. Especially popular with photographers, the Mystery Valley trip ($100 including lunch) visits a seldom-seen section of Monument Valley where you'll see Ancestral Puebloan ruins and delightful rock art. The company also offers custom day tours, plus day and overnight hikes, to Four Corners area canyons, where you'll see archaeological sites including cliff dwellings and dramatic rock art panels. Prices start at $70 per person (for three or more people) for a half day. Far Out Expeditions also offers lodging (p. 311) plus a shuttle service for backpackers and river runners (call for rates).

Note that both of the above companies also collect per person user fees charged by the Bureau of Land Management.

MORE TO SEE & DO

About 2.2 miles west of town is **Sand Island Recreation Site,** operated by the BLM. Located along the San Juan River among cottonwoods, Russian olives, and salt cedar, this area offers boating (there's a boat ramp) and fishing. Boaters must obtain river permits in advance from the Bureau of Land Management, P.O. Box 7, Monticello, UT 84535 (✆ **435/587-1544;** www.ut.blm.gov). Nestled between the river and a high rock bluff are picnic tables, vault toilets, and graveled campsites; camping is $6 per night, free for river-permit holders. Head west from the boat launch to see a number of petroglyphs, some of which can be seen easily on foot and others which require a boat to see. Unfortunately, you must have your own boat with you, as there are no nearby places to rent boats.

Goosenecks State Park, set on a rim high above the San Juan, offers spectacular views out over the twisting, turning river some 1,000 feet below. It's named for the sharp turns in the river, which meanders more than 5 miles to progress just 1 linear mile, and provides a look straight down through 300 million years of geologic history. You'll find picnic tables, trash cans, vault toilets, and an observation shelter, but no drinking water, in a gravelly open area at the end of the paved road. The park is open around the clock and admission is free; primitive camping is permitted at no charge. The park is about 23½ miles from Bluff, just off the route to Monument Valley Navajo Tribal Park. Head west on U.S. 163 for about 20 miles, turn north (right) on Utah 261 for about a mile, and then west (left) on Utah 316 for 2½ miles. For information, contact Goose-necks State Park, P.O. Box 788, Blanding, UT 84511-0788 (© **435/678-2238;** www.stateparks.utah.gov).

WHERE TO STAY

Lodging tax adds 9% to room bills in Bluff.

Among our choices for a good night's rest is the handsome **Desert Rose Inn** ★★, 701 W. Main St. (U.S. 191) (© **888/475-7673** or 435/672-2303; fax 435/672-2217; www.desertroseinn.com). Built in 1999, this imposing log lodge-style building houses 30 attractively decorated motel rooms, all with air-conditioning, TVs, phones, coffeemakers, combination shower/tubs, and queen or king beds. Decor is Southwestern, with log headboards, pottery-style lamps, solid-wood furnishings, and signed prints by a Hopi artist. There is also an attractive suite with a wraparound porch, king bed, and separate living room. In addition there are five pleasant cabins, a bit more rustic in appearance, each with a large walk-in shower (no tubs), two queen beds, refrigerators and microwaves, knotty pine walls and ceilings, porches, and cathedral ceilings with exposed beams. Rates for two people are $69 to $89 in summer, $49 to $69 November through March, and $125 year-round for the suite. Smoking is not permitted; pets are not accepted.

This property may be a bit older—actually it's a lot older—but we especially like the quiet, clean, and inexpensive rooms at the 28-unit **Recapture Lodge** ★, U.S. 191 (P.O. Box 309), Bluff, UT 84512-0309 (© **435/672-2281;** fax 435/672-2284; www.recapturelodge.com). This well-kept motel, located on the main street near the center of town, has an attractive Western decor and a nature trail that follows the San Juan River along the back of the property. Rooms contain combination shower/tubs, evaporative cooling, and TVs (but no phones); several budget units, with shower only and one double bed, are also available. Guests enjoy the heated pool and Jacuzzi. Rates for two range from $44 to $56 in summer and $34 to $48 the rest of the year. Pets are welcome.

Another good choice is the **Far Out Guest House,** 7th East St. and Mulberry Ave. (P.O. Box 307), Bluff, UT 84512 (© **435/672-2294;** www.faroutexpeditions. com). This restored historic home has two bedrooms, decorated in Southwestern style, with artwork and photos depicting scenes of the area. Each room has six bunk beds and a private bathroom (shower only). Both share a comfortable living room, screened porch, and fully equipped kitchen. Rates are $65 for a private room for one or two people, $75 for three or four people, $85 for five or six people, and $150 for the entire house. Smoking and pets are not permitted inside. The house is oper-ated by Far Out Expeditions, which offers guided tours of the region (p. 310) and provides cookouts and catering for groups of six or more (call for details).

Campgrounds include **Cadillac Ranch RV Park,** U.S. 191 (P.O. Box 157), Bluff, UT 84512 (© **800/538-6195** or 435/672-2262), a down-home sort of place on the east side of town with sites around a small fishing lake, where there's no license needed and no extra charge for fishing. There are 20 RV sites and 10 tent sites, restrooms with showers, and free firewood. The campground is open year-round, but water is turned off in winter. Cost per site is $17 for either RVs (with hookups) or tents; paddleboats can be rented at $4 per half hour.

WHERE TO DINE

The **Cottonwood Steakhouse** ★★, on U.S. 191 on the west side of town (© **435/672-2282**), is an Old West–style restaurant—lots of wood and a hand-some stone fireplace—that knows what to do with beef. The solid fare includes a 16-ounce T-bone steak, 12-ounce rib-eye steak, barbecue chicken or ribs, shrimp, and catfish, accompanied by large salads and Western-grilled potatoes or beans. Diners sit at picnic tables, both inside the restaurant and outside under cottonwood trees. Dinners are $11 to $22; a child's plate costs $7.95. The restaurant is open daily March through October, from 5pm in spring and fall and from 6pm in summer. Beer is available.

For a wide range of tasty bites throughout the day, do what the locals do and stop by the **Twin Rocks Cafe** ✸, on U.S. 191 on the east end of town (© 435/672-2341; www.twinrocks.com). In the shadow of the prominent Twin Rocks formation, the cafe has an open, airy dining room with large windows offering views of the surrounding red rock walls. The American and Southwest selections range from half-pound burgers to barbecue plates to vegetarian specialties. There's also a variety of sandwiches, New York strip steak, and grilled lemon herb chicken. But the most popular items by far are the regional dishes— the sheepherder's sandwich, Navajo taco, and beef stew with Navajo fry bread, a thick deep-fried bread. You can also mix your cultures with a Navajo pizza—a variety of toppings served on Navajo fry bread. Breakfast items include the standard pancakes and egg dishes, plus granola and a spicy breakfast burrito. Lunch and dinner entrees are $6.50 to $17. For those who insist on staring at the Internet instead of the area's beautiful red rocks, two computers are available. The cafe is open daily from 7am to 9pm in summer, with slightly reduced hours in winter. Microbrewed and other beers are available with meals.

2 Monument Valley Navajo Tribal Park

50 miles SW of Bluff, 150 miles S of Moab, 395 miles S of Salt Lake City, 160 miles W of Cortez, Colorado

You've seen Monument Valley's majestic stone towers, delicately carved arches, lonely windswept buttes, forbidding cliffs, and mesas covered in sagebrush. You may have seen the proud Navajo gazing out across his land, herding sheep, or weaving a beautiful rug. Perhaps you didn't know you were looking at Monument Valley, instead believing it to be Tombstone, Arizona; or Dodge City, Kansas; or New Mexico; or Colorado. And possibly you couldn't fully appreciate the deep reddish brown colors of the rocks or the incredible blue of the sky, which lost a bit of their brilliance in black and white.

For most of us, Monument Valley *is* the Old West. We've seen it dozens of times in movie theaters, on television, and in magazine and billboard advertisements. This all started in 1938, when Harry Goulding, who had been operating a trading post for local Navajo for about 15 years, convinced Hollywood director John Ford that Ford's current project, *Stagecoach,* should be shot in Monument Valley. Released the following year, *Stagecoach* not only put Monument Valley on the map, but also launched the career of a little-known actor by the name of John Wayne.

Ford and other Hollywood directors were attracted to Monument Valley then by the same elements that draw visitors today. This is the genuine, untamed American West, with a simple, unspoiled beauty of carved stone, blowing sand, and rich colors, all compliments of nature. The same erosional forces of wind and water carved the surrounding scenic wonders of the Grand Canyon, Glen Canyon, and the rest of the spectacular red rock country of southern Utah and northern Arizona. But here the result is different: Colors seem deeper, natural rock bridges are almost perfect circles, and the vast emptiness of the land around them gives the towering stone monoliths an unequaled sense of drama.

ESSENTIALS

Operated as a tribal park by the Navajo Nation (the country's largest tribe), Monument Valley (elevation 4,500 feet) straddles the border of southeast Utah and northeast Arizona. U.S. 163 goes through the valley from north to south, and a tribal park access road runs east to west.

GETTING THERE   From Moab, Monticello, and most points in eastern Utah, take U.S. 191 south to Bluff, turn west (right), and follow U.S. 163 to Monument Valley. An alternative is to turn off Utah 95 south onto Utah 261 just east of Natural Bridges National Monument, follow Utah 261 to U.S. 163, turn southwest, and follow U.S. 163 to Monument Valley. This latter route is quite scenic, but because of switchbacks and steep grades it is not recommended for motor homes or vehicles with trailers. Those coming from Arizona can take east-west U.S. 160 to U.S. 163, turn north, and follow it into Monument Valley.

INFORMATION/VISITOR CENTER   Contact **Monument Valley Navajo Tribal Park,** P.O. Box 360289, Monument Valley, UT 84536 (© **435/727-5874** or 435/727-3353), or the **Navajo Parks and Recreation Department,** P.O. Box 2520, Window Rock, AZ 86515 (© **928/871-6647;** www.navajonation parks.org).

The **visitor center/museum** is located about 4 miles east of U.S. 163 on the Monument Valley access road. It contains a viewing deck, exhibits on the geology and human history of the valley, restrooms, drinking water, a gift shop, and a restaurant that serves Navajo and American dishes for all three meals daily.

HOURS, FEES & REGULATIONS   The tribal park is open daily, May through September from 6am to 8:30pm and October through April from 8am to 5pm (closed Christmas plus the afternoon of Thanksgiving Day).

Admission is $5 for adults and free for children 9 and under. Because this park is operated by the Navajo Nation and NOT the U.S. government, National Park passes are not accepted.

Because the park is part of the Navajo Nation, laws here differ somewhat from those in Utah, in Arizona, or on public lands. All alcoholic beverages are prohibited within the boundaries of the Navajo reservation. Visitors must stay on the self-guided Valley Drive unless accompanied by an approved guide, and rock climbing and cross-country hiking are prohibited. Although photography for personal use is permitted, permission is required to photograph Navajo residents and their property, and you will usually need to pay them.

Both Utah and Arizona are on mountain time, and although the state of Arizona does not recognize daylight saving time, the Navajo Nation does.

EXPLORING MONUMENT VALLEY BY CAR

Driving the 17-mile self-guided loop lets you see most of the major scenic attractions of Monument Valley Navajo Tribal Park at your own pace, and at the lowest cost. The dirt road is a bit rough—not recommended for low-slung sports cars or vehicles longer than 24 feet, although it is passable for smaller motor homes. The road's first half mile is the worst, and you have to drive it both at the beginning and end of the loop. There are no restrooms, drinking water, or other facilities along the route, and motorists should watch for livestock. Allow about 2 hours.

A free brochure and a more detailed booklet ($1) provide rough maps and information on 11 numbered sites, such as The Mittens—rock formations that resemble (you guessed it) a pair of mittens—and the aptly named Elephant and Camel Buttes, Totem Pole, and The Thumb. You'll also see Yei-Bi-Chei, a rock formation that resembles a Navajo holy man; and John Ford Point, one of famed Hollywood director John Ford's favorite filming locations, where he shot scenes from *Stagecoach, The Searchers,* and *Cheyenne Autumn.* It's still popular with producers—watch for crews working on feature films, TV shows, or commercials.

GUIDED TOURS

Guided tours are the best way to see Monument Valley—without a guide, visitors are restricted to the 17-mile scenic drive, but **Navajo guides** 𝒸 can take you into lesser-visited areas of the tribal park, give you their personal perspectives on the landscape, and often arrange weaving demonstrations and other activities. Inquire at the visitor center for the types of tours currently available.

Tours are also available from **Goulding's** (see below), with rates of $32.50 for adults and $20.50 for children under 8 for a 3½-hour tour; $62.50 adults and $48 children for a full-day tour that includes lunch. These prices include the park admission fee. Tours are also available from **Far Out Expeditions** in Bluff (p. 310).

You can also see Monument Valley by horseback with Navajo-owned and operated **Ed Black's Monument Valley Trail Rides** (📞 435/739-4285), located a half mile north of the Monument Valley Visitor Center. Prices are $40 per person for a 90-minute trail ride and $100 per person for a 6- to 7-hour ride; riders also have to pay the monument entrance fee.

MORE TO SEE & DO

Goulding's Trading Post Museum, at Goulding's Lodge (see "Accommodations & Dining," below), is the original Monument Valley trading post opened by Harry and Leona (Mike) Goulding in 1924; it served as their home as well as a trading post for many years. Furnished much as it was in the 1920s and 1930s, the museum contains exhibits of Goulding family memorabilia, historic photos of the area, Navajo and Ancestral Puebloan artifacts and crafts, and posters and other items from movies that were filmed at the trading post and in Monument Valley. It's open year-round (call the lodge for hours); a $2 donation is requested, which goes toward scholarships for local children. Allow a half hour. Nearby, a more modern trading post sells souvenirs, books, videos, and top-quality American Indian arts and crafts.

The **Earth Spirit Multimedia Show,** in Harry and Mike's Theater, next to Goulding's Lodge (p. 315), is a 20-minute show describing the valley's history and the geology of the monoliths, utilizing magnificent photos of the area. It's shown several times nightly year-round and costs $2 (free for those who also take a Monument Valley tour with Goulding's).

CAMPING

Mittenview Campground, operated by the tribal park administration (p. 313), is across the access road from the tribal park's visitor center/museum, and offers good views of Monument Valley's rock formations. It has 99 sites with picnic tables and grills. From spring to early fall, it also has restrooms with coin-operated showers and an RV dump station. Campsites (for up to six people) cost $10 from spring to early fall and $5 at other times, when the bathhouse and dump station are shut down.

Goulding's Monument Valley Campground, on the Monument Valley access road about 3 miles west of its intersection with U.S. 163 (📞 435/727-3231; www.gouldings.com), also offers splendid views, plus full RV hookups including cable television, an indoor heated swimming pool, modern restrooms with showers, a playground, a self-serve laundry, and a large convenience store. The campground is open year-round, but with limited services from November to mid-March. Tent sites cost $16 and RV sites are $26, with discounts in winter.

ACCOMMODATIONS & DINING

Goulding's Lodge (© 800/874-0902 or 435/727-3231; www.gouldings.com), on the Monument Valley access road about 2 miles west of its intersection with U.S. 163, has 62 modern motel rooms, each with Southwestern decor, cable TV and VCR (John Wayne and other Western movies available for rent), air conditioning, hair dryer, iron and board, coffeemaker, and private patio or balcony. There's a small indoor heated pool and a restaurant serving three meals daily— American cuisine including traditional Navajo dishes, with dinner prices in the $9 to $22 range. Room rates for two are $160 from June to mid-October, $135 in April and May, and $68 to $108 the rest of the year. Taxes of 17% are added to your bill.

3 Natural Bridges National Monument

60 miles NW of Bluff, 360 miles south of Salt Lake City

Utah's first National Park Service area, Natural Bridges was designated primarily to show off and protect its three outstanding natural rock bridges, carved by streams and other forms of erosion beginning some 10,000 to 15,000 years ago. You can see the bridges from roadside viewpoints, take individual hikes to each one, or hike a loop trail that connects all three.

Giant **Sipapu Bridge** is considered a "mature" bridge. It's 220 feet high, with a span of 268 feet, and is the second-largest natural bridge in the world, after Rainbow Bridge in nearby Glen Canyon National Recreation Area (see chapter 14). **Owachomo Bridge,** the most advanced in age and possibly on the brink of collapse (then again, it could stand for centuries), is the smallest of the three at 106 feet high, with a span of 180 feet. The youngest, **Kachina Bridge,** is 210 feet high with a span of 204 feet. At 93 feet wide, it's also the thickest of the monument's bridges. All three bridges were given Hopi names: Sipapu means the "gateway to the spirit world" in Hopi legend; Owachomo is Hopi for "rock mound," so called for a rounded sandstone formation atop one side of the bridge; and Kachina was named as such because rock art on the bridge resembles decorations found on traditional Hopi kachina dolls.

ESSENTIALS

Natural Bridges National Monument is about 40 miles west of Blanding, 60 miles northwest of Bluff, 43 miles north of Mexican Hat, and about 50 miles east of Glen Canyon National Recreation Area's Hite or Halls Crossing marinas.

GETTING THERE   The national monument is located in southeast Utah, off scenic Utah 95 via Utah 275. From Monument Valley, follow U.S. 163 north to Utah 261 (just past Mexican Hat); at Utah 95, go west to Utah 275 and the Monument. Beware, though—Utah 261, although a very pretty drive, has 10% grades and numerous steep switchbacks. It's not recommended for motor homes, those towing trailers, or anyone who's afraid of heights. The less adventurous and RV-bound should stick to approaching from the east, via Utah 95.

Make sure you have enough fuel for the trip to Natural Bridges; the closest gas stations are at least 40 miles away in Mexican Hat or Blanding. In fact, there are no services of any kind within 40 miles of the Monument.

INFORMATION/VISITOR CENTER For a park brochure and other information, contact the Superintendent, **Natural Bridges National Monument,** HC 60 Box 1, Lake Powell, UT 84533-0101 (© **435/692-1234** or 435/719-2100; www.nps.gov/nabr).

A **visitor center** at the park entrance has exhibits and a video program on bridge formation, the human history of the area, and the monument's plants and wildlife. Rangers are available to advise you about hiking trails and scheduled activities. The visitor center is the only place in the monument where you can get drinking water.

FEES & REGULATIONS Entry to the monument is $6 per vehicle or $3 per person on foot, bicycle, or motorcycle. Regulations are similar to those in most areas administered by the National Park Service, with an emphasis on protecting the natural resources. Be especially careful not to damage any of the fragile archaeological sites in the monument; climbing on the natural bridges is prohibited. Overnight backpacking is not permitted within the monument, and vehicles may not be left unattended overnight. Because parking at the overlooks and trailheads is limited, anyone towing trailers or extra vehicles is asked to leave them at the visitor center parking lot. Pets must be leashed and are not allowed on trails or in buildings.

SEASONS/AVOIDING THE CROWDS Although the monument is open year-round, winters can be a bit harsh at this 6,500-foot elevation; the weather is best between late April and October. Because trailhead parking is limited and most people visit in June, July, and August, the best months to see the park, if your schedule permits, are May, September, and October.

RANGER PROGRAMS Guided hikes and walks, evening campground programs, and talks at the visitor center patio are presented from May through October. Schedules are posted at the visitor center.

SEEING THE HIGHLIGHTS

Natural Bridges National Monument probably won't be your major vacation destination, but you can easily spend a half or full day, or even 2 days, here. For those who want to take a quick look and get on to the other, larger national park lands in southern Utah, stop at the visitor center for a brief introduction, and then take the 9-mile (one-way) loop drive to the various natural bridge overlooks. Those with the time and the inclination might also take an easy hike down to Owachomo Bridge; it's a half-hour walk

OUTDOOR PURSUITS

Hiking is the number-one activity here. From the trailheads, you can hike separately to each of the bridges, or start at one and do a loop hike to all three. Be prepared for summer afternoon thunderstorms that can cause flash flooding.

⌜*Fun Fact* **Generating Electricity in the Middle of Nowhere**

Isolated virtually in the middle of nowhere, Natural Bridges National Monument has been forced to become self-sufficient. To provide power for the visitor center, offices, and employee housing, photovoltaic cells convert the sun's energy to electricity. You can see the photovoltaic cells, located across the main monument road from the visitor center, and read explanations of how they operate.

Although the possibility of encountering a rattlesnake is very small, you should still watch carefully. During the hot summers, all hikers should wear hats and other protective clothing, use sunscreen, and carry a gallon of water per person for all but the shortest walks.

The easiest hike—more of a walk—leads to **Owachomo Bridge** (0.4 mile round-trip). Look toward the eastern horizon to see the twin buttes named Bear's Ears. Allow a half hour.

The Sipapu and Kachina Bridge trails are both considered moderately strenuous—allocate about 1 hour for each. On the trek to **Sipapu Bridge,** you'll have a 500-foot elevation change, climbing two flights of stairs with three ladders and handrails on a 1.2-mile round-trip trail. This is the steepest trail in the park, and you'll have a splendid view of the bridge about halfway down. The hike takes about 1 hour.

The 1½-mile round-trip hike to massive **Kachina Bridge** has a 400-foot elevation change, descending steep slickrock with handrails. Under the bridge, you'll notice a pile of rocks that fell in June 1992, slightly enlarging the bridge opening. Allow about 1 hour.

Those planning to hike the **loop to all three bridges** can start at any of the trailheads, although rangers recommend starting at Owachomo. The round-trip, including your walk back across the mesa, is 8.6 miles. Although the trails from the rim to the canyon bottom can be steep, the walk along the bottom is easy.

CAMPING

A primitive 13-site campground has pit toilets, tables, tent pads, and grills, but no drinking water, showers, or other facilities. It's limited to vehicles no more than 26 feet long, and only one vehicle is allowed per site. Cost is $10; sites are allotted on a first-come, first-served basis.

There's also an overflow campground—essentially a big clearing—where you can stay at no charge. It's about 6 miles from the visitor center, just off Utah 261 near its intersection with Utah 95.

4 Hovenweep National Monument

35 miles NE of Bluff, 122 miles S of Moab, 366 miles SE of Salt Lake City, 47 miles W of Cortez, Colorado

Located along the Colorado–Utah border, Hovenweep contains six separate sites where you'll see some of the most striking (and most isolated) **archaeological sites** 🐾🐾 in the Four Corners area. These include castle-like towers, cliff dwellings, a kiva (a circular underground ceremonial chamber), stone rooms, walls, and petroglyphs. *Hovenweep* is the Ute word for "deserted valley," appropriate because its inhabitants apparently left around 1300.

ESSENTIALS

No lodging, food, gasoline, supplies, or even public phones are available in the national monument. The closest motels and restaurants are in Bluff (p. 311) or Cortez, Colorado.

GETTING THERE/ACCESS POINTS Access is via some paved and some graded dirt roads that become muddy—sometimes impassably so—during and immediately after rainstorms. You can get to Hovenweep's Square Tower Site, where a ranger station/visitor center is located (open daily 8am to 5pm), from either Colorado or Utah. From Utah, follow U.S. 191, southeastern Utah's major north-south route, to Utah 262, between the towns of Blanding and Bluff. Head east on Utah 262 to Hatch Trading Post; then, watching for signs, follow paved roads to the monument. One option is to take Utah 163 east from Bluff toward the village of Aneth, turn north (left) onto an unnamed paved road, and follow signs to the monument.

From Cortez, Colorado, follow U.S. 491 (formerly U.S. 666) north to the community of Pleasant View and turn west (left) onto dirt and gravel roads, following signs to the monument.

VISITOR INFORMATION   For advance information or questions about current road conditions, contact **Hovenweep National Monument,** McElmo Route, Cortez, CO 81321 (© **435/719-2100** or 970/562-4282; www.nps.gov/ hove). See above for information on how to reach the visitor center (open daily 8am to 5pm) at Hovenweep.

FEES, HOURS, REGULATIONS & SAFETY   Entry to the national monument is $6 per vehicle or $3 per person. The monument is open 24 hours a day, but trails are open from sunrise to sunset only; the ranger station is open daily from 8:30am to 4:30pm year-round.

Regulations are much the same here as at most National Park Service properties, with an emphasis on taking care not to damage archaeological sites. Summer temperatures can reach 100°F (38°C) and water supplies are limited; bring your own and carry a canteen, even on short walks. In late spring, gnats can be a real nuisance, so take insect repellent. Dogs are not permitted on trails.

EXPLORING THE MONUMENT

Hovenweep is noted for its mysterious and impressive 20-foot-tall sandstone towers, some of them square, others oval, circular, or D-shaped. Built by the Ancestral Puebloans (also known as Anasazi), the solid towers have small windows up and down their masonry sides. Archaeologists have suggested a myriad of possible uses for these structures—their guesses range from guard towers to celestial observatories, ceremonial structures to water towers or granaries.

In addition to the towers, you'll encounter the remains of cliff dwellings and a kiva, petroglyphs, stone rooms, walls, and a reconstructed dam. One of the most impressive ruins is stately **Hovenweep Castle,** probably built around A.D. 1200. Once home to several families, this site contains two D-shaped towers plus additional rooms.

Your walk among the 700-year-old buildings will take you through yucca, cactus, saltbush, juniper, and even some cottonwood trees. Watch for lizards, snakes, rabbits, hawks, ravens, and an occasional deer or fox.

At the **Square Tower Site** is a **ranger station** with exhibits, restrooms, and drinking water. This should be your first stop. The other five sites are difficult to find, and you'll need to get detailed driving directions and check on current road conditions before setting out.

At the Square Tower Site, the 2-mile **Square Tower self-guided trail** includes two loops, which can be hiked individually or together. They wind past the remains of ancient Puebloan buildings, such as the appropriately named Hovenweep Castle, and both square and round towers. A trail guide, available at the ranger station, discusses the ruins and identifies desert plants used for food, clothing, and medicine. The two loops are not difficult, but can be rough in spots; allow about 2 hours for the entire trail.

CAMPING

The 30-site Hovenweep Campground is open year-round. It has restrooms, drinking water, picnic tables, and fire pits, but no showers or RV hookups. Most sites will accommodate short trailers and motor homes under 25 feet in length. Cost is $10 per night; reservations are not accepted, but the campground rarely fills, even during the peak summer season.

5 Four Corners Monument

This is the only place in the United States where you can stand (or if you prefer, put your butt) in four states at once. Operated as a Navajo Tribal Park (with the Colorado section owned by the Ute Mountain Tribe), there's a flat monument marking the spot where Utah, Colorado, New Mexico, and Arizona meet, on which visitors can perch for photos. Official seals of the four states are displayed, along with the motto FOUR STATES HERE MEET IN FREEDOM UNDER GOD. Surrounding the monument are the flags of the four states, the Navajo Nation and Ute tribes, and the United States.

There are often crafts demonstrations here, and jewelry, pottery, sand paintings, and other crafts are for sale, along with tee shirts and other souvenirs. In addition, traditional Navajo food, such as fry bread, is available, and there's a small visitor center with information on visiting the Navajo Nation.

Located a half mile northwest of U.S. 160, the monument is open year-round, daily from 7am to 7pm in summer, with shorter hours in winter. Entry costs $3 per person over age 5; free for those 5 and younger. For information, contact the **Navajo Parks and Recreation Department,** P.O. Box 2520, Window Rock, AZ 86515 (© **928/871-6647;** www.navajonationparks.org). Allow a half hour.

6 East to Colorado & Mesa Verde

The Four Corners region was once a bustling metropolis, the home of the Ancestral Puebloan people (also called Anasazi). The single best place to explore this ancient culture is Mesa Verde National Park. Nearby, along the Colorado–Utah border, is one of America's newest national monuments, Canyon of the Ancients, created by presidential proclamation in June of 2000.

MESA VERDE NATIONAL PARK
125 miles E of Bluff, 390 miles SE of Salt Lake City

Mesa Verde ★★★ is the largest **archaeological preserve** in the United States, with almost 5,000 known sites dating from A.D. 500 to 1300, including the most impressive cliff dwellings in the Southwest.

The earliest-known inhabitants of Mesa Verde (Spanish for "green table") built subterranean pit houses on the mesa tops. During the 13th century, they moved into shallow alcoves and constructed complex cliff dwellings. These homes were obviously a massive construction project, yet the residents occupied them for only about a century, leaving in about 1300 for reasons as yet undetermined.

The area was little known until ranchers Charlie Mason and Richard Wetherill chanced upon it in 1888. Looting of artifacts followed their discovery until a Denver newspaper reporter's stories aroused national interest in protecting the site. The 52,000-acre site was declared a national park in 1906—it's the only U.S. national park devoted entirely to the works of humans.

Lightning-caused fires blackened about 50% of the park during the summers of 2000, 2002, and 2003, closing it for several weeks. Officials said that although the park's piñon-juniper forests were severely burned, none of the major archeological sites were damaged, and in fact the fires revealed some sites that they were not aware existed.

ESSENTIALS

The entrance to Mesa Verde National Park is about 10 miles east of Cortez, Colorado; 56 miles east of Hovenweep National Monument; and 125 miles east of Bluff. Entry to the park for up to 7 days costs $10 per vehicle.

For information, contact Superintendent, P.O. Box 8, **Mesa Verde National Park,** CO 81330 (© **970/529-4465;** www.nps.gov/meve).

The **Far View Visitor Center,** site of the lodge (described later in this chapter), restaurant, gift shop, and other facilities, is 15 miles off U.S. 160; it's open in summer only, from 8am to 5pm. **Chapin Mesa,** site of the park headquarters, a museum, and a post office, is 21 miles south of the park entrance on U.S. 160. The **Chapin Mesa Museum,** open daily year-round (from 8am to 6:30pm in summer, until 5pm the rest of the year), houses artifacts and specimens related to the history of the area, including objects from other nearby sites.

The cliff dwellings can be viewed daily, and in summer rangers give nightly campfire programs. In winter, the Mesa Top Loop Road, Spruce Tree House, and museum remain open, but many other facilities are closed. Food, gas, and lodging are available in the park from May to October only; full interpretive services are available from mid-June to Labor Day.

SEEING THE HIGHLIGHTS

Balcony House, Cliff Palace, and Long House can be seen up close only on ranger-led tours; tickets ($2.50) are available at the visitor center. The **Cliff Palace,** the park's largest and best-known site, is a four-story apartment complex with stepped-back roofs forming porches for the dwellings above. Its towers, walls, and kivas are all set back beneath the rim of a cliff. Climbing a 32-foot ladder permits exploration of **Balcony House. Long House,** on Wetherill Mesa, can be visited in summer only.

Rangers lead free tours to **Spruce Tree House,** another of the major cliff-dwelling complexes, only in winter, when other park facilities are closed. Visitors can also explore Spruce Tree House on their own at any time.

Although the draw here is ancient cliff dwellings rather than outdoor recreation, you'll find yourself hiking and climbing to reach the sites. None of the trails are strenuous, but the 7,000-foot elevation can make the treks tiring for visitors who aren't accustomed to the altitude. For those who want to avoid hiking and climbing, the 12-mile **Mesa Top Loop Road** makes a number of pit houses and cliffside overlooks easily accessible by car. However, if you'd really like to stretch your legs and get away from the crowds, take one of the longer **hikes** into scenic Spruce Canyon; you must register at the ranger's office before setting out.

CAMPING

Morefield Village, site of Mesa Verde's campground, is 4 miles south of the park entrance. Open from mid-April to mid-October, **Morefield Campground** (© **800/449-2288** or 970/533-7731; www.visitmesaverde.com/campground. htm) is operated by Aramark, which also operates the park's lodge and restaurants and offers guided tours (described later in this chapter). The campground has more than 400 sites, including 15 with full RV hookups. Facilities include modern restrooms, coin-operated showers and laundry, a grocery store, a gift shop, a gas station, picnic tables, grills, and an RV dump station. Reservations are accepted for the basic sites ($19 per night), although they are almost never necessary, but reservations are not accepted for the 15 sites with hookups ($25 per night).

WHERE TO STAY & DINE

There is only one lodging facility actually in the park, Far View Lodge (see below), which contains two restaurants and a bar. The company that runs the lodge also operates two other restaurants in the park—one near the campground and another near Chapin Mesa Museum. There are also numerous lodging and dining possibilities in nearby Cortez. Stop at the **Colorado Welcome Center at Cortez,** Cortez City Park, 928 E. Main St. (*©* **970/565-4048**); in advance, contact the **Mesa Verde Country Visitor Information Bureau,** P.O. Box HH, Cortez, CO 81321 (*©* **800/253-1616;** www.mesaverdecountry.com), or see *Frommer's Colorado* for lodging and dining choices in the Cortez area.

Far View Lodge   Located in the heart of Mesa Verde National Park, Far View Lodge (operated by Aramark) offers not only the most convenient location for visiting the park, but also the best views of any accommodations in the area. The facility lodges guests in 17 separate buildings spread across a hilltop. Rooms aren't fancy, but they are comfortable, with one queen-size bed or two doubles, and Southwestern decor including American Indian sand paintings. There are no TVs or phones, but each unit has a private balcony, and the views are magnificent in all directions.

The lodge restaurants serve three meals daily. Half-day guided tours of the park leave the lodge daily at 9am and 1pm, and full-day tours leave at 9:30am. Rates for half-day tours are $34 to $37 for adults, $23 to $26 for youths 5 to 17, and free for children under 5; full-day tours cost $56 to $61 for adults, $44 to $49 for youths 5 to 17, and free for children under 5.

Mesa Verde National Park (P.O. Box 277, Mancos, CO 81328). *©* **800/449-2288** or 970/533-1944. Fax 970/533-7831. www.visitmesaverde.com/accommodations.htm. 150 units. Open Apr–Oct. $82–$134 double. AE, DC, DISC, MC, V. Pets accepted with a deposit. **Amenities:** 2 restaurants (Southwestern American). *In room:* No phone.

Appendix:
Utah in Depth

Barren wasteland and scenic wonderland, an adventurer's paradise and picture-perfect Middle America—this is Utah, a land of extremes, where mountain peaks receive more than 500 inches of snow each winter and desert lowlands bake at well over 115°F (46°C) in summer. Utah is an extraordinarily beautiful place. It has a rugged beauty, with stark stone monoliths alternating with deep red canyons, tall forested mountains standing guard over a huge inland salt sea. Its history is equally colorful, from the prehistoric American Indians to the mountain men, miners, and Mormons. In this appendix, we'll introduce you to modern-day Utah, provide a background of the state's history and the influential Church of Jesus Christ of Latter-day Saints (the Mormons), and recommend some excellent books and films to get you started.

1 Utah Today

Some people think Utah is stuck in the 1950s—quaintly or annoyingly so, depending on your perspective. This time warp is due in large part to the strong church influence and the corollary Mormon emphasis on family values, which make Utah a notably family-oriented state. People here are friendly, the crime rate is low, and Utah is generally a very pleasant state to visit.

But don't expect to find a lot of partying or wild nightlife here. Liquor laws and attitudes toward alcohol in Utah are, simply put, archaic. Those of us who enjoy a glass of wine or beer or a mixed drink with lunch or dinner need to choose our restaurants carefully. Outside of Salt Lake City, even some nightspots are dry, like the country-and-western dance club in Provo that advertises "No cussin', no smokin', no drinkin'!" This isn't universal, of course; in terms of nightlife, Park City can hold its own with any of the top ski resorts in Colorado, and Moab is a fun, wild 'n' crazy kind of place—at least by Utah standards.

Changes are in the wind, though—along with some conflicts—as more and more outsiders move to Utah. Many escapees from California's smog, crime, crowds, and taxes have brought their mountain bikes and West Coast way of thinking to southern Utah's national park country, while others have been lured to the Wasatch Front, particularly between Salt Lake City and Provo, by computer and other high-tech industries setting up shop here. These newcomers—some 40,000 from California alone in the first half of the 1990s—have brought demands for more services, better restaurants, upscale shops, and a greater range of activities. They're also accused by some Utahns of bringing with them the very problems they sought to escape. A police chief in a small Utah town was criticized when he announced in 1995 that many of the crimes in his community were being committed by newcomers. It may not be politically correct to say so, he admitted, but statistics seem to back up his statement.

The growth of tourism is causing traffic congestion problems, mainly because there are so many of us, and because we all want to visit at the same time. Zion National Park has been affected the most. In 2000, in an attempt to deal with the problem, the park instituted a mandatory shuttle-bus service. Bryce Canyon National Park, too, has implemented a shuttle. If your schedule is at all flexible, avoid the busy school vacation months. You can also escape the crowds by seeking out the lesser-visited attractions, such as Capitol Reef National Park, Flaming Gorge National Recreation Area, and Utah's many spectacular state parks.

Even though its feet may be planted in the 1950s, Utah is actively looking toward the future. It's trying to tackle such problems as population growth and air pollution, for instance, head-on. But the future's not all grim: The Beehive State worked hard preparing for the 2002 Winter Olympic Games and their work paid off with a successful Olympic Games.

2 History 101

A walk through Utah is a walk through the American West. You can ponder the meaning of petroglyphs etched into canyon walls more than a thousand years ago, follow paths tread by Spanish padres hundreds of years ago, seek out the hiding places of famed outlaw Butch Cassidy, raft the same rapids explorer John Wesley Powell did in 1869, and see the railroads, homes, ranches, and spectacular houses of worship built by mountain men, miners, missionaries, and all the other pioneers who created the Utah we see today.

THE FIRST PEOPLES The first known inhabitants were the Desert Gatherers, who, from about 9000 B.C., wandered about the Great Basin and Colorado Plateau searching for food. However, being nomadic, they left little evidence of their time here. The Ancestral Puebloans (also called Anasazi) appeared in the Four Corners region at about the time of Christ; by A.D. 1200, their villages were scattered throughout present-day Utah. For some reason—possibly drought— by 1300 the villages had been abandoned, leaving the ruins we see standing today in Hovenweep National Monument and at other sites. The descendants of these early people—Shoshone, Ute, Goshute, and Paiute—were among the American Indians inhabiting the area when the first Europeans arrived.

Another prehistoric group, the Fremont peoples, settled in central Utah, establishing small villages of pit houses. They arrived about A.D. 1200, but had disappeared by the time the first Europeans reached Utah.

Spanish explorer Juan Maria Antonio Rivera and his European expedition arrived at the Colorado River near present-day Moab in 1765. Eleven years later, two Spanish Franciscan friars reached Utah Lake and mapped it, hoping to return to establish a Spanish colony. Spain did not pursue the idea, however, and the next Europeans to explore the area were fur traders in the early 1800s. Then, in July 1847, Brigham Young led the first Mormons (a nickname for members of the Church of Jesus Christ of Latter-day Saints) into the Salt Lake Valley, and the flood of Mormon immigrants began. These were the people who established Utah as we know it today.

MEET THE MORMONS The Church of Jesus Christ of Latter-day Saints was born in the 1820s when Joseph Smith had a revelation: After much prayer asking which Christian church he should join, Smith was told by God and Jesus that he would be the one to restore the church that Christ established when he walked the earth. An angel named Moroni then gave Smith some ancient inscribed gold tablets that, under divine inspiration, he was able to translate into the Book of Mormon. In 1830, Smith and his followers published the Book of Mormon and founded the Church of Jesus Christ of Latter-day Saints (LDS) in upstate New York. Smith's revelations and the fervor with which his followers believed and tried to spread the word bred hostility among their more skeptical neighbors; the early Mormons were soon forced to leave New York.

Smith and his followers settled in Ohio and Missouri in the early 1830s. A few years of prosperity were succeeded by strife, and the growing Mormon community was once again forced to flee. They established their church head-quarters at Nauvoo, Illinois, reclaiming a swampy area along the Mississippi river. Within a few years, Nauvoo was the second-largest city in Illinois, and the Mormons continued to grow and flourish, planning a university and laying the foundation for a temple. Also during these years, the practice of polygamy began slowly and quietly among church leaders. Both their nonconformism and their success bred fear and anger in their opponents, who considered Smith and his followers a political, economic, and religious threat. In 1844, a mob stormed the jail in Carthage, Illinois, where Joseph Smith and his brother Hyrum were being held on treason charges, and murdered them. Brigham Young and other church leaders soon decided that the Mormons had to move west, beyond the reach of the fearful communities and angry mobs.

Young, a confidant of Smith, became the second leader of the church, dis-playing a genius for organization in the evacuation of Nauvoo and the subse-quent migration westward in search of a new Zion. In 1846, the Mormons headed west from Illinois, establishing winter quarters on the far side of the Mis-souri River, near present-day Omaha, Nebraska. Young studied maps and journals of explorers, looking for a place that nobody else wanted, where Mormons could build their own community and practice their religion without interference.

FOUNDING ZION   In the spring of 1847, Brigham Young started out with the first group of emigrants—2 children, 3 women, and 143 men, handpicked for the journey based on their abilities. Future groups were similarly organized, mak-ing this the safest and most successful migration across the American West. When the first group reached the mouth of Emigration Canyon and looked out upon the empty wasteland of Salt Lake Valley, Young reportedly said, "This is the right place." Within hours of their arrival, the pioneers had begun building an irriga-tion system and establishing fields for growing food. In the next few days, Young chose the site of the temple and laid out the new city in a grid system beginning at the southeast corner of Temple Square. Having established their new Zion, most of the company headed back to Winter Quarters to bring their families west.

That first year almost ended the settlement before it had properly begun. The flat sod roofs leaked under heavy spring snow and rain; provisions ran low, forc-ing the pioneers to eat whatever they could find, including the sego lily bulb (now the state flower); a late frost damaged the wheat and vegetables; and drought damaged more. Then a plague of crickets descended on what was left of the crops. The people tried everything they could think of to battle the crickets—beating them, drowning them, setting them on fire—but nothing worked. Suddenly, seagulls appeared from the Great Salt Lake, devouring the insects by the thousands. After 2 weeks, the crickets were effectively eliminated, and enough of the crops were saved to feed the pioneers. The seagull is now Utah's state bird, and a monument stands in Temple Square commemorating the Mormons' deliverance from famine.

By the end of 1848, almost 3,000 Mormons had arrived in the Salt Lake Val-ley. It was now a part of the United States, ceded to the Union by Mexico. In 1849, the Mormons petitioned to have their territory declared the State of

Deseret, a name that comes from the Book of Mormon and means honeybee. Denied statehood, the territory of Utah—named after the Ute tribe—was created in 1850, with Brigham Young as territorial governor. Although no longer officially run by the church, the territory was assured of its continued influence, because the vast majority of voters were Mormons who elected church leaders to positions of authority in the civic domain as well.

In these years, non-Mormons—or "Gentiles," as the Mormons call them—began traveling through the valley, many on their way to or from the gold fields of California. Salt Lake City was an ideal spot for resting and resupplying before setting out again. The Mormons often bought horses, livestock, and supplies, in turn reselling what they didn't need to other travelers. The travelers who passed through to rest and trade took with them a collection of sometimes-confused ideas about the Mormons, including their fascinating practice of polygamy. The journals of these travelers gave the nation its first real knowledge—however incomplete—of Mormon faith and customs.

THE UTAH WAR   In 1857, a new governor was sent from Washington to supplant Young. Fearing he would be rejected, President Buchanan sent federal troops to escort him. The Mormons harassed the troops by driving off livestock and attacking their supply trains, forcing them to winter in western Wyoming. Although the Mormons were prepared to fight to keep the army out, neither Brigham Young nor President Buchanan wanted bloodshed. As the new governor entered Salt Lake City, Mormon families packed their belongings and awaited the order to move.

An estimated 30,000 Mormons left their homes in Salt Lake City and the northern settlements, moving south over a period of 2 months, leaving the capital virtually deserted by mid-May. The exodus drew national and international attention and placed the U.S. government in quite an unfavorable light—the government had persecuted innocent people, steamrolling over the fundamental right to religious freedom. An uneasy peace was finally established, the Mormons returned to their homes, and the two groups lived side by side until the outbreak of the Civil War, when the army was called back east.

BECOMING THE BEEHIVE STATE   After the close of the Civil War, attention was again directed toward the enforcement of antipolygamy laws, and many Mormons were imprisoned. Finally, in 1890, the church leaders issued a statement: Based on a revelation from God, the church was no longer teaching plural marriage and no person would be permitted to enter into it. With this major bar to statehood removed, Utah became the 45th state on January 4, 1896.

The Depression hit Utah hard; the unemployment rate reached 35% and per capita income was cut in half. Not until World War II was industry brought back to life. Several military bases established during the war became permanent installations, and missile plants were built along the Wasatch Front. After the war, steel companies reopened, the mining industry boomed, and high-tech businesses moved in. By the mid-1960s, the economy base had shifted from agricultural to industrial.

Dams were built—including Glen Canyon Dam, creating Lake Powell and Flaming Gorge Dam, creating Lake Flaming Gorge—to further the cause of industry and to ensure water and energy supplies, but they had an additional benefit: They provided recreational opportunities for a modern society with an increasing amount of discretionary income and free time. Ski resorts began opening in the Wasatch Mountains. In the early 1980s, after outsiders started showing interest in the new playground of Utah, Salt Lake City International Airport and the city's cultural center, the Salt Palace complex, expanded.

As the mining industries began winding down, tourism and service industries grew; today, they account for more of the state's economy than any other industry. In the 1990s the state lobbied hard to be named the host of the 2002 Winter Olympics, and then built numerous venues and even roads to assure that the games would be a success. The Mormons, who spent their first decades fleeing from outsiders, are now welcoming them with open arms, and they're coming in droves.

3 A Brief Look at Modern Mormonism—or Yes, You *Can* Get a Cup of Coffee in Utah

Utah is a Mormon state. Not officially, of course—strict state and federal laws keep church doctrine out of government—and not as much as in the past, when practically all Utahns (and definitely all the decision makers) were LDS church members. But because about three-quarters of the state's population belong to the Church of Jesus Christ of Latter-day Saints, and most of them take their religion very seriously, it's hardly surprising that the teachings and values of the church have a strong influence in the voting booth and echo throughout the halls of government.

Although some conflict is inevitable as government and community leaders try to adapt to Utah's growing cultural diversity, this discord means little to most visitors, who come to Utah to experience its scenery, recreation, and history. What you'll discover is that Utah is much like the rest of the United States, although generally not as hip as California or as multicultural as New York or New Mexico. The state is inhabited in large part by actively religious people who believe it's detrimental to one's health to use tobacco or addictive drugs, or to drink alcoholic or caffeinated beverages. In accordance with church teachings, Mormons generally strive to be hardworking and honest, with high moral standards.

WHAT MORMONS BELIEVE

Mormons are Christians, believing in Jesus Christ as the Son of God and the Bible as the Word of God, as do all the many offshoots of Christianity. But a significant difference is the role played by the **Book of Mormon,** which they believe to be God's Word as revealed to and translated by church founder Joseph Smith.

This book tells of two tribes of people who left Israel in Biblical times and made their way to the western hemisphere. Mormons believe that these people were the ancestors of today's American Indians. The Book of Mormon teaches that after his resurrection, Christ spent about 40 days among these people, preaching, healing, and establishing his church. The Mormons believe that Joseph Smith was commanded to restore the church as organized by Christ during his ministry on earth.

The first four principles of the faith are belief in Jesus Christ, repentance, baptism by immersion, and the laying on of hands to receive "the Gift of the Holy Ghost" (in which a priest places his hands on a church member for the transference of spirituality). Another important tenet of the church is respect for the supreme authority of church leaders and the belief in the revelations from God to these leaders.

The family unit is of paramount importance to Mormons, and they believe that marriage lasts literally forever, transcending death. They believe that sex outside of marriage, including homosexual behavior, is a sin. The church encourages the family to work, play, and study together, and young adults—most men and some women—generally spend 1 or 2 years as missionaries. Mormons also believe in the baptism and redemption of those already dead—hence their strong interest in genealogy.

It's practically impossible to discuss the church without discussing polygamy, which caused so much antagonism toward church members in the 19th century. But polygamy—or plural marriage, as the church dubbed it—has little to do with what the LDS church was and is. Polygamy came about as a "revelation" to church founder Joseph Smith in the 1840s, was practiced by a relatively small percentage of church members, and was outlawed by church officials in 1890. Today, polygamy is prohibited both by church doctrine and state law, although it does continue among an estimated 30,000 rebels, who have left the church to practice their own brand of Mormonism.

WHAT MORMONISM MEANS FOR VISITORS TO UTAH

This strong religious influence has brought about some strange laws regarding alcoholic beverages, although it's definitely not true that you can't get a drink here. Cigarettes and other tobacco products are also readily available, but smoking is prohibited by state law in all restaurants—legislation that is becoming more and more common across the United States. Although cola drinks contain caffeine, the church doesn't specifically prohibit their consumption. Some Mormons drink Coke or Pepsi; others refrain. You'll generally have no trouble at all purchasing whatever type of soft drink you want, with or without caffeine. Interestingly, there are exceptions: Although there are plenty of soda machines on the campus of church-owned Brigham Young University in Provo, they stock only noncaffeinated products, and this is also true of church offices.

What we found pleasantly surprising is that although the Mormons of Utah can be pretty tough on themselves regarding the above-mentioned "sins," virtually every Utahn we encountered in researching this book—and a great many were Mormons—were tolerant of others' beliefs and lifestyles. We can't guarantee that you won't run across some holier-than-thou busybody who insists on lecturing you on the evils of Demon Rum, tobacco, promiscuity, or homosexuality, but our experience has been that they generally respect each individual's right to make his or her own moral choices.

Be forewarned, though—Mormons are practically missionaries by definition, and will, with only the slightest encouragement, want to enthusiastically help you see the wisdom of their ways.

Because the church emphasizes the importance of family, you'll see lots of kids—Utah is noted for having the highest fertility rate in the nation. This makes Utah a very kid-friendly state, with lots of family-oriented activities and attractions. Overall, prices for kids and families are often very reasonable. And because many Mormon families observe Monday evening as a time to spend together, sports facilities, amusement parks, and similar venues often offer family discounts on Mondays; if you're traveling with your family, watch for them.

Although about 70% of Utah's population are LDS church members, you'll find that church membership varies greatly from community to community, so the number of Mormons you'll encounter will vary considerably. Although it's the world headquarters of the church, Salt Lake City is just under half Mormon; some of the smaller towns approach 100%. Of major cities, Provo has the strongest church influence. Although St. George was historically a major stronghold for church members, recent migration from other parts of the United States is gradually diluting that influence. You'll probably find the least church influence in Park City and Moab, which in recent years have attracted large numbers of outsiders.

Index

Fly.
Sleep.
Save.

Now you can book your flights and
hotels together, so you can get even better deals
than if you booked them separately.

Travelocity

**Visit www.travelocity.com
or call 1-888-TRAVELOCITY**

Travelocity,® Travelocity.com® and the Travelocity skyline logo are trademarks and/or service
marks of Travelocity.com LP. © 2003 Travelocity.com LP. All rights reserved.